C# 3.0

IN A NUTSHELL

Other Microsoft .NET resources from O'Reilly

<table>
<tr><td>Related titles</td><td>Learning C#</td><td>Programming WPF</td></tr>
<tr><td></td><td>Programming C#</td><td>Learning WCF</td></tr>
<tr><td></td><td>C# 3.0 Cookbook™</td><td>Learning ASP.NET</td></tr>
<tr><td></td><td>Programming WCF</td><td>Learning ASP.NET 2.0
with AJAX</td></tr>
</table>

**.NET Books
Resource Center**

dotnet.oreilly.com is a complete catalog of O'Reilly's books on .NET and related technologies, including sample chapters and code examples.

ONDotnet.com provides independent coverage of fundamental, interoperable, and emerging Microsoft .NET programming and web services technologies.

Conferences

O'Reilly brings diverse innovators together to nurture the ideas that spark revolutionary industries. We specialize in documenting the latest tools and systems, translating the innovator's knowledge into useful skills for those in the trenches. Visit *conferences.oreilly.com* for our upcoming events.

Safari Bookshelf (*safari.oreilly.com*) is the premier online reference library for programmers and IT professionals. Conduct searches across more than 1,000 books. Subscribers can zero in on answers to time-critical questions in a matter of seconds. Read the books on your Bookshelf from cover to cover or simply flip to the page you need. Try it today for free.

C# 3.0

IN A NUTSHELL

Third Edition

Joseph Albahari and Ben Albahari

O'REILLY®

Beijing • Cambridge • Farnham • Köln • Paris • Sebastopol • Taipei • Tokyo

C# 3.0 in a Nutshell, Third Edition
by Joseph Albahari and Ben Albahari

Published by O'Reilly Media, Inc., 1005 Gravenstein Highway North, Sebastopol, CA 95472.

O'Reilly books may be purchased for educational, business, or sales promotional use. Online editions are also available for most titles (*safari.oreilly.com*). For more information, contact our corporate/institutional sales department: (800) 998-9938 or *corporate@oreilly.com*.

Editor: John Osborn
Production Editor: Mary Brady
Copyeditor: Audrey Doyle
Proofreader: Mary Brady

Indexer: Ellen Troutman Zaig
Cover Designer: Karen Montgomery
Interior Designer: David Futato
Illustrator: Jessamyn Read

Printing History:

March 2002:	First Edition.
August 2003:	Second Edition.
September 2007:	Third Edition.

 This book uses RepKover™, a durable and flexible lay-flat binding.

ISBN-13: 978-0-596-52757-0
[M]   [3/08]

Table of Contents

Preface

Each release of C# and the .NET Framework brings new features and greater potential for productivity. C# 3.0 introduces the most significant enhancements to the language yet—with a unified querying syntax called *Language Integrated Query*, or LINQ. LINQ bridges the traditional divide between programs and their data sources—as well as bringing C# closer to functional languages such as LISP and Haskell.

The price of this growth is that there's now more to learn. While tools such as Microsoft's IntelliSense—and online references—are excellent in helping you on the job, they presume an *existing map of conceptual knowledge*. This book provides exactly that map of knowledge in a concise and unified style—free of clutter and long introductions.

Unlike earlier editions, *C# 3.0 in a Nutshell* is organized entirely around concepts and use cases, making it friendly both to sequential reading and random browsing. It also plumbs significantly greater depths than before while assuming less background knowledge—making it the most accessible edition yet.

This book covers C#, the CLR, and the core Framework assemblies. We've chosen this focus to allow space for difficult topics such as threading, security, and application domains—without compromising depth or readability. Features new to C# 3.0 and the associated Framework are flagged so that you can also use this book as a C# 2.0 reference.

Intended Audience

This book targets intermediate to advanced audiences. No prior knowledge of C# is required, but some general programming experience is necessary. For the beginner, this book complements, rather than replaces, a tutorial-style introduction to programming.

If you're already familiar with C# 2.0, you'll find more than a hundred pages dedicated to LINQ and other new C# 3.0 features. In addition, many other chapters are designed to lift your existing knowledge of C# and the core Framework.

This book is an ideal companion to any of the vast array of books that focus on an applied technology such as WPF, ASP.NET, or WCF. The areas of the language and .NET Framework that such books omit, *C# 3.0 in a Nutshell* covers in detail—and vice versa.

If you're looking for a book that skims every .NET Framework technology, this is not for you. This book is also unsuitable if you want a replacement for IntelliSense (i.e., the alphabetical listings of types and type members that appeared in previous editions).

How This Book Is Organized

The first three chapters after the introduction concentrate purely on C#, starting with the basics of syntax, types, and variables, and finishing with advanced topics such as unsafe code and preprocessor directives. If you're new to the language, you should read these chapters sequentially, with the exception of Chapter 4, whose sections can be read in any order.

The remaining chapters cover the core .NET Framework, including such topics as LINQ, XML, collections, I/O and networking, memory management, reflection, attributes, security, threading, application domains, and native interoperability. You can read most of these chapters randomly, except for Chapters 6, 7, and 13, which lay a foundation for subsequent topics. The three chapters on LINQ are also best read in sequence.

What You Need to Use This Book

The examples in this book require a C# 3.0 (or 2.0) compiler in conjunction with the Microsoft .NET Framework 3.5 (or 3.0/2.0). You will also require Microsoft's .NET documentation. The easiest way to get all three—along with an integrated development environment—is to install Microsoft Visual Studio. Any edition is suitable for what's taught in this book, including Visual Studio Express (currently a free download). Visual Studio also includes an express edition of SQL Server, required to run the LINQ to SQL examples, and IntelliSense, which pops up type member listings as you type.

Another option, if you don't mind using a plain-text editor and building at the command line, is to download the .NET Framework SDK. This includes the compiler, .NET documentation, and additional command-line tools.

The lightest option is to download and install just the Microsoft .NET Framework Runtime. This includes the command-line compiler; however, it doesn't include other command-line tools or any documentation.

Conventions Used in This Book

Figure P-1 is a sample diagram depicting how we illustrate types throughout this book. Abstract classes are shown as a slanted rectangle, and interfaces are shown as a circle. Inheritance is shown as a solid line from the subtype, ending with a hollow triangle that points to the supertype. We use a line with a solid diamond to annotate any kind of relationship (whether an association, aggregation or composition).

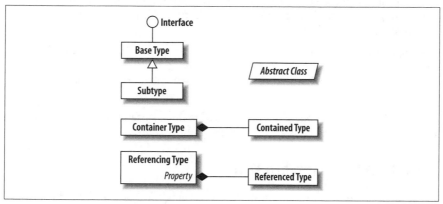

Figure P-1. Sample diagram

The following typographical conventions are used in this book:

Italic
> Indicates new terms, URIs, filenames, and directories

`Constant width`
> Indicates C# code, keywords and identifiers, and program output

`Constant width bold`
> Shows a highlighted section of code

`Constant width italic`
> Shows text that should be replaced with user-supplied values

> This icon signifies a tip, suggestion, or general note.

> This icon indicates a warning or caution.

Using Code Examples

This book is here to help you get your job done. In general, you may use the code in this book in your programs and documentation. You do not need to contact us for permission unless you're reproducing a significant portion of the code. For example, writing a program that uses several chunks of code from this book does not require permission. Selling or distributing a CD-ROM of examples from O'Reilly books *does* require permission. Answering a question by citing this book and quoting example code does not require permission. Incorporating a significant amount of example code from this book into your product's documentation *does* require permission.

We appreciate, but do not require, attribution. An attribution usually includes the title, author, publisher, and ISBN. For example: "*C# 3.0 in a Nutshell*, by Joseph Albahari and Ben Albahari. Copyright 2007 Ben Albahari and Joseph Albahari, 978-0-596-52757-0."

If you feel your use of code examples falls outside fair use or the permission given above, feel free to contact us at *permissions@oreilly.com*.

We'd Like to Hear from You

Please address comments and questions concerning this book to the publisher:

O'Reilly Media, Inc.
1005 Gravenstein Highway North
Sebastopol, CA 95472
800-998-9938 (in the United States or Canada)
707-829-0515 (international or local)
707-829-0104 (fax)

We have a web page for this book, where we list errata, examples, and any additional information. You can access this page at:

http://www.oreilly.com/catalog/9780596527570

Code listings and additional resources are provided at:

http://www.albahari.com/nutshell/

To comment or ask technical questions about this book, send email to:

bookquestions@oreilly.com

For more information about our books, conferences, Resource Centers, and the O'Reilly Network, see our web site at:

http://www.oreilly.com

Safari® Books Online

 When you see a Safari® Books Online icon on the cover of your favorite technology book, that means the book is available online through the O'Reilly Network Safari Bookshelf.

Safari offers a solution that's better than e-books. It's a virtual library that lets you easily search thousands of top tech books, cut and paste code samples, download chapters, and find quick answers when you need the most accurate, current information. Try it for free at *http://safari.oreilly.com.*

Acknowledgments

Joseph Albahari

First, I want to thank my brother and coauthor, Ben Albahari, for persuading me to take on what has become a highly successful project. Some chapters required working closely together, and this brought us closer together as brothers. I particularly enjoyed working with Ben in probing difficult topics. He shares my willingness to question conventional wisdom, and the tenacity to pull things apart until it becomes clear how they *really* work.

The technical review team was superb and I have the highest praise for the people involved, many of which are current or former Microsoft employees. Nicholas Paldino's thoroughness and breadth of knowledge contributed significantly to the quality of the book, as did Joel Pobar's knowledge of the CLR, which is second to none. I'm also most grateful to Krzysztof Cwalina, Matt Warren, Glyn Griffiths, Ion Vasilian, Brad Abrams, Sam Gentile, and Adam Nathan.

In addition, I want to thank my editor, John Osborn, for all his time and effort in coordinating the project, the copyeditor, Audrey Doyle, for providing the final polish, and members of my family, Sonia Albahari and Miri Albahari, for their support. My sister Miri, having recently had a book published herself, was able to empathize well with the loss of spare time!

My thanks also to Lutz Roeder, whose .NET Reflector tool provided one of the primary means by which to pull things apart, and the readers of my web e-book, "Threading in C#," whose feedback—as well as being useful—was a constant source of encouragement while writing *C# 3.0 in a Nutshell*.

Finally, I want to thank my company, Egton Software Services, for willingly embracing LINQ at such an early opportunity. I'm particularly grateful to James Miles for his enthusiasm and creativeness: our initial adoption team was invaluable in gaining the real-world experience necessary to write about this technology prior to its official release.

Ben Albahari

Because my brother wrote his acknowledgments first, you can infer most of what I want to say. :) We've actually both been programming since we were kids (we shared an Apple IIe; he was writing his own operating system while I was writing Hangman), so really it's about time we wrote a book together. I hope the enriching experience we had writing the book will translate into an enriching experience for you reading the book.

I'd also like to thank my former colleagues at Microsoft. There are many smart people who work there, not just in terms of intellect but in a broader emotional sense, and I miss working with them. In particular, I learned a lot from Brian Beckman, to whom I am indebted.

Introducing C# and the .NET Framework

C# is a general-purpose, type-safe, object-oriented programming language. The goal of the language is programmer productivity. To this end, the language balances simplicity, expressiveness, and performance. The chief architect of the language since its first version is Anders Hejlsberg (creator of Turbo Pascal and architect of Delphi). The C# language is platform-neutral, but it was written to work well with the Microsoft .NET Framework.

Object Orientation

C# is a rich implementation of the object-orientation paradigm, which includes *encapsulation*, *inheritance*, and *polymorphism*. Encapsulation means creating a boundary around an *object*, to separate its external (public) behavior from its internal (private) implementation details. The distinctive features of C# from an object-oriented perspective are:

Unified type system
> The fundamental building block in C# is an encapsulated unit of data and functions called a *type*. C# has a *unified type system*, where all types ultimately share a common base type. This means that all types, whether they represent business objects or are primitive types such as integrals, share the same basic set of functionality. For example, any type can be converted to a string by calling its ToString method.

Classes and interfaces
> In the pure objected-oriented paradigm, the only kind of type is a class. In C#, there are several other kinds of types, one of which is an *interface* (similar to Java interfaces). An interface is like a class except it is only a definition for a type, not an implementation. It's particularly useful in scenarios where multiple inheritance is required (unlike languages such as C++ and Eiffel, C# does not support multiple inheritance of classes).

Properties, methods, and events

In the pure object-oriented paradigm, all functions are *methods* (this is the case in Smalltalk). In C#, methods are only one kind of *function member*, which also includes *properties* and *events* (there are others too). Properties are function members that encapsulate a piece of an object's state, such as a button's color or a label's text. Events are function members that simplify acting on object state changes.

Type Safety

C# is primarily a *type-safe* language, meaning that types can interact only through protocols they define, thereby ensuring each type's internal consistency. For instance, C# prevents you from interacting with a *string* type as though it were an *integer* type.

More specifically, C# supports *static typing*, meaning that the language enforces type safety at *compile time*. This is in addition to *dynamic* type safety, which the .NET CLR enforces at *runtime*.

Static typing eliminates a large class of errors before a program is even run. It shifts the burden away from runtime unit tests onto the compiler to verify that all the types in a program fit together correctly. This makes large programs much easier to manage, more predictable, and more robust. Furthermore, static typing allows tools such as IntelliSense in Visual Studio .NET to help you write a program, since it knows for a given variable what type it is, and hence what methods you can call on that variable.

C# is called a *strongly typed language* because its type rules (whether enforced statically or dynamically) are very strict. For instance, you cannot call a function that's designed to accept an integer with a floating-point number, unless you first *explicitly* convert the floating-point number to an integer. This helps prevent mistakes.

Strong typing also plays a role in enabling C# code to run in a sandbox—an environment where every aspect of security is controlled by the host. In a sandbox, it is important that you cannot arbitrarily corrupt the state of an object by bypassing its type rules.

Memory Management

C# relies on the runtime to perform automatic memory management. The CLR has a garbage collector that executes as part of your program, reclaiming memory for objects that are no longer referenced. This frees programmers from explicitly deallocating the memory for an object, eliminating the problem of corrupt pointers, encountered in languages such as C++.

C# does not eliminate pointers: it merely makes them unnecessary for most programming tasks. For performance-critical hotspots and interoperability, pointers may be used, but they are permitted only in blocks that are explicitly marked unsafe.

Platform Support

C# is typically used for writing code that runs on Windows platforms. Although Microsoft standardized the C# language and the CLR through ECMA, the total amount of resources (both inside and outside of Microsoft) dedicated to supporting C# on non-Windows platforms is relatively small. This means that languages such as Java are sensible choices when multiplatform support is the name of the game. Having said this, C# can be used to write cross-platform code in the following scenarios:

- C# code may run on the server and dish up DHTML that can run on any platform. This is precisely the case for ASP.NET.
- C# code may run on a runtime other than the Microsoft Common Language Runtime. The most notable example is the Mono project, which has its own C# compiler and runtime, running on Linux, Solaris, Mac OS X, and Windows.
- C# code may run on a host that supports Microsoft Silverlight (supported for Windows and Mac OS X). This is a new technology that is analogous to Adobe's Flash Player.

C#'s Relationship with the CLR

C# depends on a runtime equipped with a host of features such as automatic memory management and exception handling. The design of C# closely maps to the design of the CLR, which provides these runtime features (although C# is technically independent of the CLR). Furthermore, the C# type system maps closely to the CLR type system (e.g., both share the same definitions for primitive types).

The CLR and .NET Framework

The .NET Framework consists of a runtime called the *Common Language Runtime* (CLR) and a vast set of libraries. The libraries consist of core libraries (which this book is concerned with) and applied libraries, which depend on the core libraries. Figure 1-1 is a visual overview of those libraries (and also serves as a navigational aid to the book).

The CLR is the runtime for executing *managed code*. C# is one of several *managed languages* that get compiled into managed code. Managed code is packaged into an *assembly*, in the form of either an executable file (an *.exe*) or a library (a *.dll*), along with type information, or *metadata*.

Managed code is represented in *Intermediate Language* or *IL*. When the CLR loads an assembly, it converts the IL into the native code of the machine, such as x86. This conversion is done by the CLR's JIT (Just-In-Time) compiler. An assembly retains almost all of the original source language constructs, which makes it easy to inspect and even generate code dynamically.

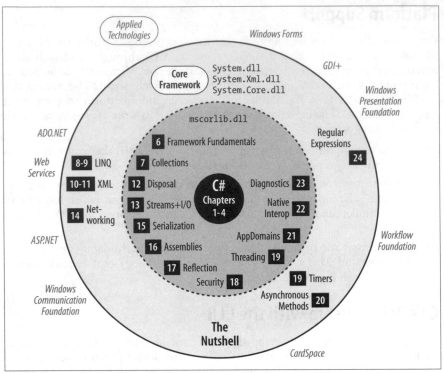

Figure 1-1. This depicts the topics covered in this book and the chapters in which they are found. The names of specialized frameworks and class libraries beyond the scope of this book are grayed out and displayed outside the boundaries of The Nutshell.

 Lutz Roeder's .NET Reflector application is an invaluable tool for examining the contents of an assembly (you can also use it as a decompiler).

The CLR performs as a host for numerous runtime services. Examples of these services include memory management, the loading of libraries, and security services.

The CLR is language-neutral, allowing developers to build applications in multiple languages (e.g., C#, Visual Basic .NET, Managed C++, Delphi.NET, Chrome .NET, and J#).

The .NET Framework consists of libraries for writing just about any Windows-based application. Chapter 5 gives an overview of the .NET Framework libraries.

What's New in C# 3.0

C# 3.0 features are centered on *Language Integrated Query* capabilities, or *LINQ* for short. LINQ was inspired by the work done on Comega (formerly known as X# and Xen). Erik Meijer was the primary architect who worked closely with Anders Hejlsberg to incorporate that work into C#.

LINQ enables SQL-like queries to be written directly within a C# program and checked *statically* for correctness. The architecture of LINQ allows queries to execute either locally or remotely. The .NET Framework provides LINQ-enabled APIs across local collections, remote databases, and XML. C# 3.0 features include:

- Lambda expressions
- Extension methods
- Implicitly typed local variables
- Query comprehensions
- Anonymous types
- Object initializers
- Implicitly typed arrays
- Automatic properties
- Partial methods
- Expression trees

Lambda expressions are like miniature functions created on the fly. They are a natural evolution of anonymous methods introduced in C# 2.0, and in fact, completely subsume the functionality of anonymous methods. For example, the following lambda expression squares an integer:

```
Func<int,int> square = x => x * x;
Console.WriteLine (square(3));        // 9
```

For people familiar with *functional programming* languages, such as Scheme and Haskell, lambda expressions will be a familiar construct. The primary use case in C# is with LINQ queries, such as the following:

```
string[] names = { "Tom", "Dick", "Harry" };
IEnumerable<string> filteredNames =            // Include only names
   Enumerable.Where (names, n => n.Length >= 4);  // of >= 4 characters.
```

Extension methods extend an existing type with new methods, without altering the type's definition. They act as syntactic sugar, making static methods feel like instance methods. Because LINQ's query operators are implemented as extension methods, we can simplify our preceding query as follows:

```
string[] names = { "Tom", "Dick", "Harry" };
IEnumerable<string> filteredNames = names.Where (n => n.Length >= 4);
```

Implicitly typed local variables let you omit the variable type in a declaration statement, allowing the compiler to infer it. Since the compiler can determine the type of filteredNames, we can further simplify our query:

```
var filteredNames = names.Where (n => n.Length == 4);
```

Query comprehension syntax provides SQL-style syntax for writing queries. Comprehension syntax can simplify certain kinds of queries substantially, as well as serving as syntactic sugar for lambda-style queries. Here's the previous example in comprehension syntax:

```
var filteredNames = from n in names where n.Length >= 4 select n;
```

Anonymous types are simple classes created on the fly that are commonly used in the final output of queries:

```
var query = from n in names where n.Length >= 4
            select new {
                         Name = n,
                         Length = n.Length
                       };
```

Here's a simpler example:

```
var dude = new { Name = "Bob", Age = 20 };
```

Implicitly typed arrays eliminate the need to state the array type, when constructing and initializing an array in one step:

```
var dudes = new[]
{
    new { Name = "Bob", Age = 20 },
    new { Name = "Rob", Age = 30 }
};
```

Object initializers simplify object construction by allowing properties to be set inline after the constructor call. Object initializers work with both anonymous and named types. The following example shows the new C# 3.0 feature and the equivalent code in C# 2.0:

```
// C# 3.0
Bunny b1 = new Bunny { Name="Bo", LikesCarrots=true, LikesHumans=false };

// C# 2.0
Bunny b2 = new Bunny();
b2.Name = "Bo";
b2.LikesHumans = false;
```

Automatic properties cut the work in writing properties that simply get/set a private backing field. In the following example, the compiler automatically generates a private backing field for X:

```
public class Stock
{
  // C# 3.0:
            public decimal X { get; set; }

    // C# 2.0:
            private decimal y;
            public decimal Y
            {
              get { return y;  }
              set { y = value; }
            }
}
```

Partial methods let an auto-generated partial class provide customizable hooks for manual authoring. LINQ to SQL makes use of partial methods for generated classes that map SQL tables. Here is an example of a pair of partial methods, one auto-generated and the other hand-authored:

```
// PaymentFormGen.cs - auto-generated
partial class PaymentForm
{
    ...
    partial void ValidatePayment (decimal amount);
}

// PaymentForm.cs - hand-authored
partial class PaymentForm
{
    ...
    partial void ValidatePayment (decimal amount)
    {
        if (amount > 100)
            ...
    }
}
```

Expression trees are miniature code DOMs that describe lambda expressions. The C# 3.0 compiler generates expression trees when a lambda expression is assigned to the special type Expression<TDelegate>:

```
Expression<Func<string,bool>> predicate = s => s.Length > 10;
```

Expression trees make it possible for LINQ queries to execute remotely (e.g., on a database server) because they can be introspected and translated at runtime (e.g., into a SQL statement).

2

C# Language Basics

In this chapter, we introduce the basics of the C# language.

A First C# Program

Here is a program that multiplies 12 by 30, and prints the result, 360, to the screen. The double-forward slash indicates that the remainder of a line is a *comment*.

```
using System;              // importing namespace

class Test                 // class declaration
{
  static void Main ()      //   method declaration
  {
    int x = 12 * 30;       //      statement 1
    Console.WriteLine (x); //      statement 2
  }                        //   end of method
}                          // end of class
```

At the heart of this program lies two *statements*. Statements in C# execute sequentially. Each statement is terminated by a semicolon:

```
int x = 12 * 30;
Console.WriteLine (x);
```

The first statement computes the *expression* 12 * 30 and stores the result in a *local variable*, named x, which is an integer type. The second statement calls the Console class's WriteLine *method*, to print the variable x to a text window on the screen.

A *method* performs an action in a series of statements, called a *statement block*—a pair of braces containing zero or more statements. We defined a single method named Main:

```
static void Main ()
{
    ...
}
```

Writing higher-level functions that call upon lower-level functions simplifies a program. We can refactor our program with a reusable method that multiplies an integer by 12 as follows:

```
using System;

class Test
{
    static void Main ()
    {
        Console.WriteLine (FeetToInches (30));      // 360
        Console.WriteLine (FeetToInches (100));     // 1200
    }

    static int FeetToInches (int feet)
    {
        int inches = feet * 12;
        return inches;
    }
}
```

A method can receive *input* data from the caller by specifying *parameters* and *output* data back to the caller by specifying a *return type*. We defined a method called FeetToInches that has a parameter for inputting feet, and a return type for outputting inches:

```
static int InchesToFeet (int feet) {...}
```

The *literals* 30 and 100 are the *arguments* passed to the FeetToInches method. The Main method in our example has empty parentheses because it has no parameters, and is void because it doesn't return any value to its caller:

```
static void Main ()
```

C# recognizes a method called Main as signaling the default entry point of execution. The Main method may optionally return an integer (rather than void) in order to return a value to the execution environment. The Main method can also optionally take an array of string arguments (that will be populated with any arguments passed to the executable). For example:

```
static int Main (string[] args) {...}
```

An array (such as string[]) represents a fixed number of elements of a particular type. Arrays are specified by placing square brackets after the element type and are described in the "Arrays" section later in this chapter.

Methods are one of several kinds of functions in C#. Another kind of function we used was the * *operator*, used to perform multiplication. There are also *constructors*, *properties*, *events*, *indexers*, and *destructors*.

In our example, the two methods are grouped into a class. A *class* groups function members and data members to form an object-oriented building block. The Console class groups members that handle command-line input/output functionality, such as the WriteLine method. Our Test class groups two methods—the Main method and the FeetToInches method. A class is a kind of *type*, which we will examine in the "Type Basics" section later in this chapter.

At the outermost level of a program, types are organized into *namespaces*. The using directive was used to make the System namespace available to our application, to use the Console class. We could define all our classes within the TestPrograms namespace, as follows:

```
using System;

namespace TestPrograms
{
  class Test  {...}
  class Test2 {...}
}
```

The .NET Framework is organized into nested namespaces. For example, this is the namespace that contains types for handling text:

```
using System.Text;
```

The using directive is there for convenience; you can also refer to a type by its fully qualified name, which is the type name prefixed with its namespace, such as System.Text.StringBuilder.

Compilation

The C# compiler compiles source code, specified as a set of files with the *.cs* extension, into an *assembly*. An assembly is the unit of packaging and deployment in .NET. An assembly can be either an *application* or a *library*. A normal console or Windows *application* has a Main method and is an *.exe*. A library is a *.dll* and is equivalent to an *.exe* without an entry point. Its purpose is to be called upon (referenced) by an application or by other libraries. The .NET Framework is a set of libraries.

The name of the C# compiler is *csc.exe*. You can either use an IDE such as Visual Studio .NET to call csc automatically, or compile manually from the command line. To compile manually, first save a program to a file such as *MyFirstProgram.cs*, and then invoke csc (located under *<windows>/Microsoft.NET/Framework*) from the command line as follows:

```
csc MyFirstProgram.cs
```

This produces an application named *MyFirstProgram.exe*.

Assemblies are explained in detail in Chapter 16.

Syntax

C# syntax is based on C and C++ syntax. In this section, we will describe C#'s elements of syntax, using the following program:

```
using System;

class Test
{
  static void Main ()
  {
    int x = 12 * 30;
    Console.WriteLine (x);
  }
}
```

Identifiers and Keywords

Identifiers are names that programmers choose for their classes, methods, variables, and so on. These are the identifiers in our example program, in the order they appear:

```
System   Test   Main   x   Console   WriteLine
```

An identifier must be a whole word, essentially made up of Unicode characters starting with a letter or underscore. C# identifiers are case-sensitive. By convention, arguments, local variables, and private fields should be in camel case (e.g., myVariable), and all other identifiers should be in Pascal case (e.g., MyMethod).

Keywords are names reserved by the compiler that you can't use as identifiers. These are the keywords in our example program:

```
using   class   static   void   int
```

Here is the full list of C# keywords:

See correction.

abstract	As	base	bool	break
byte	Case	catch	char	checked
class	Const	continue	decimal	default
delegate	Do	double	else	enum
event	Explicit	extern	false	finally
fixed	Float	for	foreach	goto
if	Implicit	in	int	interface
internal	Is	lock	long	namespace
new	Null	object	operator	out
override	Params	private	protected	public
readonly	ref	return	sbyte	sealed
short	sizeof	stackalloc	static	string
struct	switch	this	throw	true
try	typeof	uint	ulong	unchecked
unsafe	ushort	using	virtual	void
while				

Avoiding conflicts

If you really want to use an identifier that clashes with a keyword, you can do so by qualifying it with the @ prefix. For instance:

```
class class  {...}     // illegal
class @class {...}     // legal
```

The @ symbol doesn't form part of the identifier itself. So @myVariable is the same as myVariable.

Contextual keywords

The language also has *contextual keywords*, which, while recognized by the compiler, can still be used, unqualified, as identifiers. These are:

add	ascending	by	descending	equals
from	get	global	group	in
into	join	let	on	orderby
partial	remove	select	set	value
var	where	yield		

With contextual keywords, ambiguity cannot arise within the context in which they are used.

Literals, Punctuators, and Operators

Literals are primitive pieces of data statically embedded into the program. These are the literals we used in our example program:

```
12   30
```

Punctuators help demarcate the structure of the program. These are the punctuators we used in our example program:

```
;   {  }
```

The semicolon is used to terminate a statement. This means that statements can wrap multiple lines:

```
Console.WriteLine
    (1 + 2 + 3 + 4 + 5 + 6 + 7 + 8 + 9 + 10);
```

The braces are used to group multiple statements into a statement block.

An *operator* transforms and combines expressions. Most operators in C# are denoted with a symbol, such the multiplication operator, *. We will discuss operators in more detail later in the chapter. These are the operators we used in our example program:

```
.  ()   *   =
```

The period refers to a member of something. The parentheses are used when declaring or calling a method; empty parentheses are used when the method accepts no arguments. The equals sign is used for *assignment* (the double-equals sign, ==, is used for equality comparison, as we'll see later).

Comments

C# offers two different styles of source-code documentation: *single-line comments* and *multiline comments*. A single-line comment begins with a double-forward slash and continues until the end of the line. For example:

```
int x = 3;    // comment about assigning 3 to x
```

A multiline comment begins with /* and ends with */. For example:

```
int x = 3;    /* this is a comment that
                 spans two lines */
```

Comments may embed XML documentation tags, explained in the section "XML Documentation" in Chapter 4.

Type Basics

A *type* defines the blueprint for a value. A *value* is a storage location denoted by a *variable* or a *constant*. A variable represents a value that can change, whereas a constant represents an invariant (we will visit constants later in the chapter). We created a local variable named x in our first program:

```
static void Main ()
{
    int x = 12 * 30;
    Console.WriteLine (x);
}
```

All values in C# are an *instance* of a specific type. The meaning of a value, and the set of possible values a variable can have, is determined by its type. The type of x is int.

Predefined Type Examples

Predefined types are types that are specially supported by the compiler. The int type is a predefined primitive type for representing the set of integers that fit into 32 bits of memory, from -2^{31} to $2^{31}-1$. We can perform functions such as arithmetic with instances of the int type as follows:

```
int x = 12 * 30;
```

Another predefined C# type is the string type. The string type represents a sequence of characters, such as ".NET" or "http://oreilly.com". We can manipulate strings by calling functions on them as follows:

```
string message = "Hello world";
string upperMessage = message.ToUpper();
Console.WriteLine (upperMessage);          // HELLO WORLD

int x = 2007;
message = message + x.ToString();
Console.WriteLine (message);               // Hello world2007
```

The primitive bool type has exactly two possible values: true and false. The bool type is commonly used to conditionally branch execution flow based with an if statement. For example:

```
bool simpleVar = false;
if (simpleVar)
  Console.WriteLine ("This will not print");

int x = 5000;
bool lessThanAMile = x < 5280;
if (lessThanAMile)
  Console.WriteLine ("This will print");
```

 In C#, predefined types (also referred to as built-in types) are recognized with a C# keyword. The System namespace in the .NET Framework contains many important types that are not predefined by C# (e.g., DateTime).

Custom Type Examples

Just as we can build complex functions from simple functions, we can build complex types from primitive types. In this example, we will define a custom type named UnitConverter—a class that serves as a blueprint for unit conversions:

```
using System;

public class UnitConverter
{
  int ratio;                                          // field
  public UnitConverter (int unitRatio) {ratio = unitRatio; } // constructor
  public int Convert  (int unit)   {return unit * ratio; } // method
}

class Test
{
  static void Main ()
  {
    UnitConverter feetToInchesConverter = new UnitConverter(12);
    UnitConverter milesToFeetConverter  = new UnitConverter(5280);

    Console.WriteLine (feetToInchesConverter.Convert(30));    // 360
    Console.WriteLine (feetToInchesConverter.Convert(100));   // 1200
    Console.WriteLine (feetToInchesConverter.Convert(
              milesToFeetConverter.Convert(1)));   // 63360
  }
}
```

Members of a type

A type contains *data members* and *function members*. The data member of UnitConverter is the *field* called ratio. The function members of UnitConverter are the Convert method and the UnitConverter's *constructor*.

Symmetry of predefined types and custom types

A beautiful aspect of C# is that predefined types and custom types have few differences. The primitive int type serves as a blueprint for integers. It holds data—32 bits—and provides function members that use that data, such as ToString. Similarly our custom UnitConverter type acts as a blueprint for unit conversions. It holds data—the ratio—and provides function members to use that data.

Constructors and instantiation

Data is created by *instantiating* a type. Primitive types can be instantiated simply by using a literal. For example, the following line instantiates two integers (12 and 30), which are used to compute a third instance, x:

```
int x = 12 * 30;
```

The new operator is needed to create a new instance of a custom type. We created and declared an instance of the UnitConverter type with this statement:

```
UnitConverter feetToInchesConverter = new UnitConverter(12);
```

Immediately after the new operator instantiates an object, the object's *constructor* is called to perform initialization. A constructor is defined like a method, except that the method name and return type are reduced to the name of the enclosing type:

```
public class UnitConverter
{
  ...
  public UnitConverter (int r) { ratio = r; }        // constructor
  ...
}
```

Instance versus static members

The data members and function members that operate on the *instance* of the type are called instance members. The UnitConverter's Convert method and the int's ToString method are examples of instance members. By default, members are instance members.

Data members and function members that don't operate on the instance of the type, but rather on the type itself, must be marked as static. The Test.Main and Console.WriteLine methods are static methods. The Console class is actually a *static class*, where *all* its members are static. You never actually create instances of a Console—one console is shared across the whole application.

To contrast instance versus static members, the instance field Name pertains to an instance of a particular Panda, whereas Population pertains to the set of all Panda instances:

```
using System;

public class Panda
{
```

```
    public string Name;              // instance field
    public static int Population;    // static field

    public Panda (string n)          // constructor
    {
      Name = n;                      // assign the instance field
      Population = Population + 1;    // increment the static Population field
    }
  }

  class Test
  {
    static void Main()
    {
      Panda p1 = new Panda ("Pan Dee");    // create new Panda instance
      Panda p2 = new Panda ("Pan Dah");    // create new Panda instance
      Console.WriteLine (p1.Name);         // access instance field
      Console.WriteLine (p2.Name);         // access instance field
      Console.WriteLine (Panda.Population); // access static field
    }
  }

  OUTPUT:
  Pan Dee
  Pan Dah
  2
```

The public keyword

The public keyword exposes members to other classes. In this example, if the Name field in Panda was not public, the Test class could not call it. Marking a member public is how a type communicates: "Here is what I want other types to see— everything else is my own private implementation details." In object-oriented terms, we say that the public members *encapsulate* the private members of the class.

Conversions

C# can convert between instances of compatible types. A conversion always creates a new value from an existing one. Conversions can be either *implicit* or *explicit*: implicit conversions happen automatically, and explicit conversions require a *cast*. In the following example, we *implicitly* cast an int to a long type (which has twice the capacity of an int) and *explicitly* cast an int to a short type (which has half the capacity of an int):

```
int x = 123456;    // int is a 32-bit integer
long y = x;        // implicit conversion to 64-bit integer
short z = (short)x; // explicit conversion to 16-bit integer
```

Implicit conversions are allowed when both of the following are true:

• The compiler can guarantee they will always succeed.

• No information is lost in conversion.

Conversely, *explicit* conversions are required when one of the following is true:

- The compiler cannot guarantee they will always succeed.
- Information may be lost during conversion.

Most conversions are built into the language, such as the previously shown numeric conversions. Occasionally, it is useful to write *custom conversions*—we explain this in the section "Operator Overloading" in Chapter 4.

Value Types Versus Reference Types

All C# types fall into the following categories:

- Value types
- Reference types
- Pointer types

Value types comprise most built-in types (specifically, all numeric types, the char type, and the bool type) as well as custom struct and enum types.

Reference types comprise all class, array, delegate, and interface types.

The fundamental difference between value types and reference types is how they are handled in memory. Pointer types fall outside mainstream C# usage, and we cover them in the section "Unsafe Code and Pointers" in Chapter 4.

Value types

The content of a *value type* variable or constant is simply a value. For example, the content of the built-in value type int is 32 bits of data.

You can define a custom value type with the struct keyword (see Figure 2-1):

```
public struct Point { public int X, Y; }
```

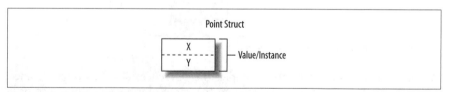

Figure 2-1. A value type instance in memory

The assignment of a value type instance always *copies* the instance. For example:

```
static void Main ()
{
  Point p1 = new Point( );
  p1.X = 7;

  Point p2 = p1;            // assignment causes copy

  Console.WriteLine (p1.X); // 7
  Console.WriteLine (p2.X); // 7
```

```
p1.X = 9;                    // change p1.X

Console.WriteLine (p1.X);  // 9
Console.WriteLine (p2.X);  // 7
}
```

Figure 2-2 shows that p1 and p2 have independent storage.

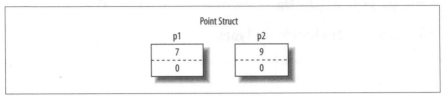

Figure 2-2. Assignment copies a value type instance

Reference types

A reference type is more complex than a value type, having two parts: an *object* and the *reference* to that object, as shown in Figure 2-3. The content of a reference type variable or constant is a reference to an object that contains the value. Here is the Point type from our previous example rewritten as a class, rather than a struct:

```
public class Point { public int X, Y; }
```

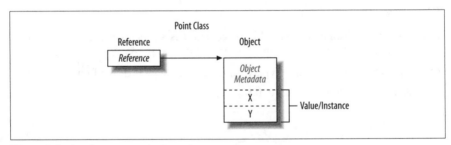

Figure 2-3. A reference type instance in memory

Assigning a reference type variable copies the reference, not the object instance. This allows multiple variables to refer to the same object—something not ordinarily possible with value types. If we repeat the previous example, but with Point now a class, an operation to X affects Y:

```
static void Main ()
{
  Point p1 = new Point();
  p1.X = 7;

  Point p2 = p1;             // copies p1 reference

  Console.WriteLine (p1.X);  // 7
  Console.WriteLine (p2.X);  // 7
```

```
        p1.X = 9;                    // change p1.X

    Console.WriteLine (p1.X);  // 9
    Console.WriteLine (p2.X);  // 9
}
```

Figure 2-4 shows that p1 and p2 are two references that point to the same object.

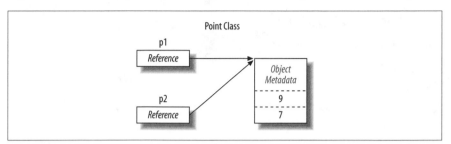

Figure 2-4. Assignment copies a reference

Null

A reference can be assigned the literal null, indicating that the reference points to no object:

```
class Point {...}
...

Point p = null;
```

In contrast, a value type cannot have a null value:

```
struct Point {...}
...

Point p = null; // compile-time error
int x = null;   // compile-time error
```

 C# also has nullable types, as we explain in the "Nullable Types" section in Chapter 4.

Storage overhead

Value type instances occupy precisely the sum of the memory occupied by their fields. In this example, Point takes 8 bytes of memory:

```
struct Point
{
  int x;  // 4 bytes
  int y;  // 4 bytes
}
```

Reference types require separate allocations of memory for the reference and object. The object consumes as many bytes as its fields, plus additional administrative overhead. The precise overhead is intrinsically private to the implementation of the .NET runtime, but at minimum the overhead is 12 bytes, used to store a key to the object's type, as well as temporary information such as its lock state for multithreading and a flag to indicate whether it has been fixed from movement by the garbage collector. Each reference to an object requires an extra four or eight bytes, depending on whether the .NET runtime is running on a 32- or 64-bit platform.

Predefined Type Taxonomy

The predefined types in C# are:

Value types

- Numeric
  - — Signed integer (sbyte, short, int, long)
  - — Unsigned integer (byte, ushort, uint, ulong)
  - — Real number (float, double, decimal)
- Logical (bool)
- Character (char)

Reference types

- String (string)
- Object (object)

Predefined types in C# alias Framework types in the System namespace. There is only a syntactic difference between these two statements:

```
int i = 5;
System.Int32 i = 5;
```

The predefined *value* types are also known as *primitive types*. Primitive types are so called because they are the atoms, or smallest possible building blocks of data, in a language, and most have a direct representation in machine code. For example, the floating-point numbers in C# are matched by the floating-point numbers in most processors:

```
                      // Underlying hexadecimal representation
int i = 7;            // 0x7
bool b = true;        // 0x1
char c = 'A';         // 0x41
float f = 0.5f;       // uses IEEE floating-point encoding
```

Numeric Types

C# has the predefined numeric types shown in Table 2-1.

Table 2-1. Predefined numeric types in C#

C# type	System type	Suffix	Category	Size	Range	Notes
sbyte	SByte		Integral	8 bits	-2^7 to 2^7-1	

Table 2-1. Predefined numeric types in C# (continued)

C# type	System type	Suffix	Category	Size	Range	Notes
short	Int16		Integral	16 bits	-2^{15} to $2^{15}-1$	
int	Int32		Integral	32 bits	-2^{31} to $2^{31}-1$	
long	Int64	L	Integral	64 bits	-2^{63} to $2^{63}-1$	
byte	Byte		Integral	8 bits	0 to 2^8-1	Unsigned
ushort	UInt16		Integral	16 bits	0 to $2^{16}-1$	Unsigned
uint	UInt32	U	Integral	32 bits	0 to $2^{32}-1$	Unsigned
ulong	UInt64	UL	Integral	64 bits	0 to $2^{64}-1$	Unsigned
float	Single	F	Real	32 bits	$\pm{\sim}10^{-45}$ to ${\sim}10^{38}$	Single-precision
double	Double	D	Real	64 bits	$\pm{\sim}10^{-324}$ to ${\sim}10^{308}$	Double-precision
decimal	Decimal	M	Real	128 bits	$\pm{\sim}10^{-28}$ to ${\sim}10^{28}$	Base 10

See Correction

C# Language Basics

Of the *integral* types, int and long are first-class citizens and are favored by both C# and the runtime. The other integral types are typically used for interoperability or when space efficiency is paramount.

Of the *real* number types, float and double are called *floating-point types* and are typically used for scientific calculations. The decimal type is typically used for financial calculations, where base-10-accurate arithmetic and high precision are required.

Numeric Literals

Integral literals can use decimal or hexadecimal notation; hexadecimal is denoted with the 0x prefix. For example:

```
int x = 127;
long y = 0x7F;
```

Real literals can use decimal and/or exponential notation. For example:

```
double d = 1.5;
double million = 1E06;
```

Numeric literal type inference

By default, the compiler *infers* a numeric literal to be either double or an integral type:

- If the literal contains a decimal point or the exponential symbol (E), it is a double.
- Otherwise, the literal's type is the first type in this list that can fit the literal's value: int, uint, ulong, and long.

For example:

```
Console.WriteLine (        1.0.GetType( )); // Double (double)
Console.WriteLine (       1E06.GetType( )); // Double (double)
Console.WriteLine (        1.GetType( ));   // Int32  (int)
Console.WriteLine ( 0xF0000000.GetType( )); // UInt32 (uint)
```

Numeric suffixes

Numeric suffixes explicitly define the type of a literal (suffixes can be either lower- or uppercase), as shown in Table 2-2.

Table 2-2. Suffixes for numeric literals

Category	C# type	Notes	Example
F	float		float f = 1.0F;
D	double		double d = 1D;
M	decimal		decimal d = 1.0M;
U	uint or ulong	Combinable with L	uint i = 1U;
L	long or ulong	Combinable with U	ulong i = 1UL;

The suffixes U and L are rarely necessary, because the uint, long, and ulong types can nearly always be either *inferred* or *implicitly converted* from int:

```
long i = 5;    // implicit lossless conversion from int literal to long
```

The D suffix is technically redundant, in that all literals with a decimal point are inferred to be double. And you can always add a decimal point to a numeric literal:

```
double x = 4.0;
```

The F and M suffixes are the most useful and should always be applied when specifying float or decimal literals. Without the F suffix, the following line would not compile, because 4.5 would be inferred to be of type double, which has no implicit conversion to float:

```
float f = 4.5F;
```

The same principle is true for a decimal literal:

```
decimal x = -1.23M;    // Will not compile without the M suffix.
```

The semantics of numeric conversions are described in detail in the following section.

Numeric Conversions

Integral to integral conversions

Integral conversions are *implicit* when the destination type can represent every possible value of the source type. Otherwise, an *explicit* conversion is required. For example:

```
int x = 123456;      // int is a 32-bit integral
long y = x;          // implicit conversion to 64-bit integral
short z = (short)x;  // explicit conversion to 16-bit integral
```

Floating-point to floating-point conversions

A float can be implicitly converted to a double, since a double can represent every possible value of a float. The reverse conversion must be explicit.

Floating-point to integral conversions

All integral types may be implicitly converted to all floating-point numbers:

```
int i = 1;
float f = i;
```

The reverse conversion must be explicit:

```
int i2 = (int)f;
```

 When you cast from a floating-point number to an integral, any fractional portion is truncated; no rounding is performed. The static class System.Convert provides methods that round while converting between various numeric types (see Chapter 6).

Implicitly converting a large integral type to a floating-point type preserves *magnitude* but may occasionally lose *precision*. This is because floating-point types always have more magnitude than integral types, but may have less precision. Rewriting our example with a larger number demonstrates the following:

```
int i1 = 100000001;
float f = i1;        // magnitude preserved, precision lost
int i2 = (int)f;     // 100000000
```

Decimal conversions

All integral types can be implicitly converted to the decimal type, since a decimal can represent every possible C# integral value. All other numeric conversions to and from a decimal type must be explicit.

Arithmetic Operators

The arithmetic operators (+, -, *, /, %) are defined for all numeric types except the 8- and 16-bit integral types:

```
+    Addition
-    Subtraction
*    Multiplication
/    Division
%    Remainder after division
```

Increment and Decrement Operators

The increment and decrement operators (++, --) increment and decrement numeric types by 1. The operator can either precede or follow the variable, depending on whether you want the variable to be updated *before* or *after* the expression is evaluated. For example:

```
int x = 0;
Console.WriteLine (x++);   // outputs 0; x is now 1
Console.WriteLine (++x);   // outputs 2; x is now 2
Console.WriteLine (--x);   // outputs 1; x is now 1
```

Specialized Integral Operations

Integral division

Division operations on integral types always truncate remainders. Dividing by a variable whose value is zero generates a runtime error (a DivisionByZeroException):

```
int a = 2 / 3;     // 0

int b = 0;
int c = 5 / b;     // throws DivisionByZeroException
```

Dividing by the *literal* 0 generates a compile-time error.

Integral overflow

At runtime, arithmetic operations on integral types can overflow. By default, this happens silently—no exception is thrown. While the C# specification is agnostic as to the result of an overflow, the CLR always causes wraparound behavior. For example, decrementing the minimum possible int value results in the maximum possible int value:

```
int a = int.MinValue;
a--;
Console.WriteLine (a == int.MaxValue); // True
```

Integral arithmetic overflow check operators

The checked operator tells the runtime to generate an OverflowException rather than failing silently when an integral expression or statement exceeds the arithmetic limits of that type. The checked operator affects expressions with the ++, --, (unary) -, +, -, *, /, and explicit conversion operators between integral types.

checked can be used around either an expression or a statement block. For example:

```
int a = 1000000;
int b = 1000000;

// Check an expression
int c = checked (a*b);

// Check every expression in a statement block
```

```
checked
{
    ...
    c = a * b;
    ...
}
```

You can make arithmetic overflow checking the default for all expressions in a program by compiling with the /checked+ command-line switch (in Visual Studio, go to Advanced Build Settings). If you then need to disable overflow checking just for specific expressions or statements, you can do so with the unchecked operator. For example, the following code will not throw exceptions—even if compiled with /checked+:

```
int x = int.MaxValue;
int y = unchecked (x + 1);
unchecked { int z = x + 1; }
```

Overflow checking for constant expressions

Regardless of the /checked compiler switch, expressions evaluated at compile time are always overflow-checked—unless you apply the unchecked operator:

```
int x = int.MaxValue + 1;              // Compile-time error
int y = unchecked (int.MaxValue + 1);  // No errors
```

Bitwise operators

C# supports standard C-style bitwise operations, as shown in Table 2-3.

Table 2-3. Bitwise operators

Operator	Meaning	Sample expression	Result
~	Complement	~0xfU	0xfffffff0U
&	And	0xf0 & 0x33	0x30
|	Or	0xf0 | 0x33	0xf3
^	Exclusive Or	0xff00 ^ 0x0ff0	0xf0f0
<<	Shift left	0x20 << 2	0x80
>>	Shift right	0x20 >> 1	0x10

Eight- and 16-Bit Integrals

The 8- and 16-bit integral types are byte, sbyte, short, and ushort. These types lack their own arithmetic operators, so C# implicitly converts them to larger types as required. This can cause a compile-time error when trying to assign the result back to a small integral type:

```
short x = 1, y = 1;
short z = x + y;              // Compile-time error
```

In this case, x and y are implicitly converted to int so that the addition can be performed. This means the result is also an int, which cannot be implicitly cast back to a short (because it could cause loss of data). To make this compile, we must add an explicit cast:

```
short z = (short) (x + y);   // ok
```

Special Float and Double Values

Unlike integral types, floating-point types have values that certain operations treat specially. These special values are NaN (Not a Number), +∞, −∞, and −0. The float and double classes have constants for NaN, +∞, and −∞, as well as other values (MaxValue, MinValue, and Epsilon). For example:

```
Console.WriteLine (double.NegativeInfinity);   // -Infinity
```

Table 2-4 shows the constants that represent special values for double and float.

Table 2-4. Special floating-point values

Special value	Double constant	Float constant
NaN	double.NaN	float.NaN
+∞	double.PositiveInfinity	float.PositiveInfinity
−∞	double.NegativeInfinity	float.NegativeInfinity
−0	−0.0	−0.0f

Dividing a nonzero number by zero results in an infinite value. For example:

```
Console.WriteLine ( 1.0 /  0.0);          //  Infinity
Console.WriteLine (-1.0 /  0.0);          // -Infinity
Console.WriteLine ( 1.0 / -0.0);          // -Infinity
Console.WriteLine (-1.0 / -0.0);          //  Infinity
```

Diving zero by zero, or subtracting infinity from infinity, results in a NaN. For example:

```
Console.WriteLine ( 0.0 /  0.0);              //  NaN
Console.WriteLine ((1.0 /  0.0) - (1.0 / 0.0));  //  NaN
```

When using ==, a NaN value is never equal to another value, even another NaN value:

```
Console.WriteLine (0.0 / 0.0 == double.NaN);   // False
```

To test whether a value is NaN, you must use the float.IsNaN or double.IsNaN method, as follows:

```
Console.WriteLine (double.IsNaN(0.0 / 0.0));   // True
```

 float and double follow the specification of the IEEE 754 format types, supported natively by almost all processors. You can find detailed information on the behavior of these types at *http://www. ieee.org*.

Note that when using object.Equals, two NaN values are equal:

```
Console.WriteLine (object.Equals(0.0 / 0.0, double.NaN));   // True
```

double Versus decimal

double is useful for scientific computations (such as computing spatial coordinates). decimal is useful for financial computations. Table 2-5 provides a summary of the differences between double and decimal.

Table 2-5. Double versus decimal

Category	double	decimal
Internal representation	Base 2	Base 10
Precision	15–16 significant figures	28–29 significant figures
Range	$\sim 10^{-324}$ to $\sim 10^{308}$	$\sim 10^{-28}$ to $\sim 10^{28}$
Special values	+0, −0, +∞, −∞, and NaN	None
Speed	Native to processor	Nonnative to processor (about 10 times slower than double)

Real Number Rounding Errors

float and double internally represent numbers in base 2. For this reason, only numbers expressible in base 2 are represented precisely. Practically, this means most literals with a fractional component (which are in base 10) will not be represented precisely. For example:

```
float tenth = 0.1f;                    // Not quite 0.1
float one   = 1f;
Console.WriteLine (one - tenth * 10f);    // -1.490116E-08
```

This is why float and double are bad for financial calculations. In contrast, decimal works in base 10 and so can precisely represent numbers expressible in base 10 (as well as its factors, base 2 and base 5). Since real literals are in base 10, decimal can precisely represent real literals such as 0.1. However, neither double nor decimal can precisely represent a fractional number whose base 10 representation is recurring:

```
decimal m = 1M / 6M;        // 0.1666666666666666666666666667M
double  d = 1.0 / 6.0;      // 0.16666666666666666
```

This leads to accumulated rounding errors:

```
decimal notQuiteWholeM = m+m+m+m+m+m;   // 1.0000000000000000000000000002M
double  notQuiteWholeD = d+d+d+d+d+d;   // 0.99999999999999989
```

which breaks equality and comparison operations:

```
Console.WriteLine (notQuiteWholeM == 1M);   // False
Console.WriteLine (notQuiteWholeD < 1.0);   // True
```

Boolean Type and Operators

C#'s bool type (aliasing the System.Boolean type) is a logical value that can·be assigned the literal true or false.

Although a boolean value requires only one bit (0 or 1) of storage, the runtime will use much more storage since this is the minimum chunk with which most lower-level parts of the system (from the runtime down to the processor) can efficiently work. For example, each element in a bool array uses two bytes of memory. The System.Collections.BitArray class can be used where the storage efficiency of one bit per boolean value is required.

Bool Conversions

No conversions can be made from the bool type to numeric types or vice versa.

Equality and Comparison Operators

== and != test for equality and inequality of any type, but always return a bool value. Value types typically have a very simple notion of equality:

```
int x = 1;
int y = 2;
int z = 1;
Console.WriteLine (x == y);    // False
Console.WriteLine (x == z);    // True
```

For reference types, equality, by default, is based on *reference*, as opposed to the actual *value* of the underlying object:

```
public class Dude
{
  public string Name;
  public Dude (string n) { Name = n; }
}

Dude d1 = new Dude ("John");
Dude d2 = new Dude ("John");
Console.WriteLine (d1 == d2);    // False
Dude d3 = d1;
Console.WriteLine (d1 == d3);    // True
```

The comparison operators, <, >, >=, and <=, work for all numeric types, but should be used with caution with real numbers (see the "Numeric Types" section earlier in this chapter). The comparison operators also work on enum type members, by comparing their underlying integral values. This is described in the "Enums" section in Chapter 3.

We explain the equality and comparison operators in greater detail in the section "Operator Overloading" in Chapter 4, and in the sections "Equality comparison" and "Order comparison" in Chapter 6.

Conditional Operators

The && and || operators test for *and* and *or* conditions. They are frequently used in conjunction with the ! operator, which expresses *not*. In this example, the UseUmbrella method returns true if it's rainy or sunny (to protect us from the rain or the sun), as long as it's not also windy (since umbrellas are useless in the wind):

```
static bool UseUmbrella (bool rainy, bool sunny, bool windy)
{
  return ! windy && (rainy || sunny);
}
```

Conditional operators *short-circuit* evaluation when possible. In the preceding example, if it is not windy, the expression (rainy || sunny) is not even evaluated.

> The & and | operators can be used in a similar manner:
>
>   return ! windy & (rainy | sunny);
>
> The difference is that they *do not short-circuit*. For this reason, they are rarely used in place of conditional operators.

The ternary conditional operator has the form q ? a : b, where if condition q is true, a is evaluated, else b is evaluated. For example:

```
static int Max (int a, int b)
{
  return (a > b) ? a : b;
}
```

Strings and Characters

C#'s char type (aliasing the System.Char type) represents a Unicode character and occupies two bytes. A char literal is specified inside single quotes:

```
char c = 'A';        // simple character
```

Escape sequences express characters that cannot be expressed or interpreted literally. An escape sequence is a backslash followed by a character with a special meaning. For example:

```
char newLine = '\n';
char backSlash = '\\';
```

Table 2-6 lists the escape sequence characters.

Table 2-6. Character and string escape sequences

Char	Meaning	Value
\'	Single quote	0x0027
\"	Double quote	0x0022
\\	Backslash	0x005C
\0	Null	0x0000
\a	Alert	0x0007
\b	Backspace	0x0008
\f	Form feed	0x000C
\n	New line	0x000A
\r	Carriage return	0x000D
\t	Horizontal tab	0x0009
\v	Vertical tab	0x000B

The \u (or \x) escape sequence lets you specify any Unicode character via its four-digit hexadecimal code.

```
char copyrightSymbol = '\u00A9';
char omegaSymbol     = '\u03A9';
char newLine         = '\u000A';
```

Char conversions

An implicit conversion from a char to a numeric type works for the numeric types that can accommodate an unsigned short. For other numeric types, an explicit conversion is required.

String Type

C#'s string type (aliasing the System.String type, covered in depth in Chapter 6) represents an immutable sequence of Unicode characters. A string literal is specified inside double quotes:

```
string a = "Heat";
```

 string is a reference type, rather than a value type. However, since a string is immutable, it takes on value-like semantics.

The escape sequences that are valid for char literals also work inside strings:

```
string a = "Blah blah.\n";
```

The cost of this is that whenever you need a literal backslash, you must write it twice:

```
string a1 = "\\\\server\\fileshare\\helloworld.cs";
```

To avoid this problem, C# allows *verbatim* string literals. A verbatim string literal is prefixed with @ and does not support escape sequences. The following verbatim string is identical to the preceding one:

```
string a2 = @"\\server\fileshare\helloworld.cs";
```

A verbatim string literal can also span multiple lines:

```
string escaped  = "First Line\r\nSecond Line";
string verbatim = @"First Line
Second Line";

Console.WriteLine (escaped == verbatim);  // True
```

You can include the double-quote character in a verbatim literal by writing it twice:

```
string xml = @"<customer id=""123""></customer>";
```

String concatenation

The + operator concatenates two strings:

```
string s = "a" + "b";
```

The righthand operand may be a nonstring value, in which case `ToString` is called on that value. For example:

```
string s = "a" + 5;   // a5
```

Since `string` is immutable, using the + operator repeatedly to build up a string can be inefficient. The `System.Text.StringBuilder` type (described in Chapter 6) should be used for efficiently building strings.

String comparisons

`string` does not support `<` and `>` operators for comparisons. You must use the string's `CompareTo` method, described in Chapter 6.

Arrays

An array represents a fixed number of elements of a particular type. The elements in an array are always stored in a contiguous block of memory, providing highly efficient access.

An array is denoted with square brackets after the element type. For example:

```
char[] vowels = new char[5];    // Declare an array of 5 characters
```

Square brackets also *index* the array, accessing a particular element by position:

```
vowels [0] = 'a';
vowels [1] = 'e';
vowels [2] = 'i';
vowels [3] = 'o';
vowels [4] = 'u';
Console.WriteLine (vowels [1]);    // e
```

This prints "e" because array indexes start at 0. We can use a `for` loop statement to iterate through each element in the array. The `for` loop in this example cycles the integer i from 0 to 4:

```
for (int i = 0; i < vowels.Length; i++)
  Console.Write (vowels [i]);          // aeiou
```

The `Length` property of an array returns the number of elements in the array. Once an array has been created, its length cannot be changed. The `System.Collection` namespace and subnamespaces provide higher-level data structures, such as dynamically sized arrays and dictionaries.

An *array initialization expression* specifies each element of an array. For example:

```
char[] vowels = new char[] {'a','e','i','o','u'};
```

All arrays inherit from the `System.Array` class, providing common services for all arrays. These members include methods to get and set elements regardless of the array type, and are described in the section "The Array Class" in Chapter 7.

Default Element Initialization

Creating an array always preinitializes the elements with default values. The default value for a type is the result of a bitwise zeroing of memory. For example, consider creating an array of integers. Since int is a value type, this allocates 1,000 integers in one contiguous block of memory. The default value for each element will be 0:

```
int[] a = new int[1000];
Console.Write (a[123]);          // 0
```

Value types versus reference types

Whether an array element type is a value type or a reference type has important performance implications. When the element type is a value type, each element value is allocated as part of the array. For example:

```
public struct Point { public int X, Y; }
...

Point[] a = new Point[1000];
int x = a[500].X;                // 0
```

Had Point been a class, creating the array would have merely allocated 1,000 null references:

```
public class Point { public int X, Y; }


...
Point[] a = new Point[1000];
int x = a[500].X;                      // runtime error, NullReferenceException
```

Before we can access point values, we need to separately instantiate 1,000 objects after instantiating the array object:

```
Point[] a = new Point[1000];
for (int i = 0; i < a.Length; i++) // iterate i from 0 to 999
   a[i] = new Point();             // set array element i with new point
```

An array *itself* is always a reference type object, regardless of element type. For instance:

```
int[] a = null;
```

Multidimensional Arrays

Multidimensional arrays come in two varieties: *rectangular* and *jagged*. Rectangular arrays represent an *n*-dimensional block of memory, and jagged arrays are arrays of arrays.

Rectangular arrays

Rectangular arrays are declared using commas to separate each dimension. Here is an example of declaring a rectangular two-dimensional array, where the dimensions are 3×3:

```
int [,] matrix = new int [3, 3];
```

The GetLength method of an array returns the length for a given dimension (starting at 0). GetLength is used to enumerate the array, as follows:

```
for (int i = 0; i < matrix.GetLength(0); i++)
  for (int j = 0; j < matrix.GetLength(1); j++)
    matrix[i, j] = i * 3 + j;
```

A rectangular array can be initialized as follows (each element in this example is
initialized to be identical to the previous example):

```
int[,] matrix = new int[,]
{
  {0,1,2},
  {3,4,5},
  {6,7,8}
};
```

Jagged arrays

Jagged arrays are declared using successive square braces to represent each dimension. Here is an example of declaring a jagged two-dimensional array, where the
outermost dimension is 3:

```
int [][] matrix = new int [3][];
```

The inner dimensions aren't specified in the declaration. Unlike a rectangular
array, each inner array can be an arbitrary length. Each inner array is implicitly
initialized to null rather than an empty array. Each inner array must be created
manually:

```
for (int i = 0; i < matrix.Length; i++)
{
  matrix[i] = new int [3];                    // create inner array
  for (int j = 0; j < matrix[i].Length; j++)
    matrix[i][j] = i * 3 + j;
}
```

A jagged array can be initialized as follows (each element in this example is initialized to be identical to the previous example):

```
int[][] matrix = new int[][]
{
  new int[] {0,1,2},
  new int[] {3,4,5},
  new int[] {6,7,8}
};
```

Simplified Array Initialization Expressions

There are two ways to shorten array initialization expressions. The first is to omit
the new operator and type qualifications:

```
char[] vowels = {'a','e','i','o','u'};

int[,]rectangularMatrix =
{
  {0,1,2},
  {3,4,5},
  {6,7,8}
```

```
};

int[][]jaggedMatrix =
{
  new int[] {0,1,2},
  new int[] {3,4,5},
  new int[] {6,7,8}
};
```

In C# 3.0, the second approach is to use the var keyword, which tells the compiler to implicitly type a local variable:

```
var i = 3;            // i is implicitly of type int
var s = "sausage";    // s is implicitly of type string

// Therefore:

var rectMatrix = new int[,]    // rectMatrix is implicitly of type int[,]
{
  {0,1,2},
  {3,4,5},
  {6,7,8}
};

var jaggedMat = new int[][]    // jaggedMat is implicitly of type int[][]
{
  new int[] {0,1,2},
  new int[] {3,4,5},
  new int[] {6,7,8}
};
```

Implicit typing can be taken one stage further with single-dimensional arrays. You can omit the type qualifier after the new keyword and have the compiler *infer* the array type:

```
var vowels = new[] {'a','e','i','o','u'};   // Compiler infers char[]
```

The elements must have identical types in order for implicit array typing to work. For example:

```
var x = new[] {1, "a"};   // error, elements are of multiple types
```

Bounds Checking

All array indexing is bounds-checked by the runtime. An IndexOutOfRange-Exception is thrown if you use an invalid index:

```
int[] arr = new int[3];
arr[3] = 1;                     // IndexOutOfRangeException thrown
```

As with Java, array bounds checking is necessary for type safety and simplifies debugging.

Generally, the performance hit from bounds checking is minor, and the JIT (Just-in-Time) compiler can perform optimizations, such as determining in advance whether all indices will be safe before entering a loop, thus avoiding a check on each iteration. In addition, C# provides "unsafe" code that can explicitly bypass bounds checking (see the section "Unsafe Code and Pointers" in Chapter 4).

Variables and Parameters

A variable represents a storage location that has a modifiable value. A variable can be a *local variable*, *parameter* (*value*, *ref*, or *out*), *field* (*instance* or *static*), or *array element*.

The Stack and the Heap

The stack and the heap are the places where variables and constants reside. Each has very different lifetime semantics.

Stack

The stack is a block of memory for storing local variables and parameters. The stack automatically grows and shrinks as a function is entered and exited. Consider the following method (to avoid distraction, input argument checking is ignored):

```
static int Factorial (int x)
{
  if (x == 0) return 1;
  return x * Factorial (x-1);
}
```

This method is recursive, meaning that it calls itself. Each time the method is entered, a new `int` is allocated on the stack, and each time the method exists, the `int` is deallocated.

Heap

The heap is a block of memory in which *objects* (i.e., reference type instances) reside. Whenever a new object is created, it is allocated on the heap, and a reference to that object is returned. During a program's execution, the heap starts filling up as new objects are created. The runtime has a garbage collector that periodically deallocates objects from the heap, so your computer does not run out of memory. An object is eligible for deallocation as soon as nothing references it.

In the following example, we create two `StringBuilder` objects, referenced by the variables `ref1` and `ref2`. The variable `ref3` is then assigned to the object referenced by `ref2`. Next, we assign both `ref1` and `ref2` to `null`. At this point, `object1` (i.e., the first `StringBuilder` object created) is eligible for garbage collection, since nothing references it. In contrast, object2 (i.e., the second StringBuilder object created) is still referenced by ref3, so it is not eligible for garbage collection. When the Main method terminates, ref3 goes out of scope, and object2 becomes eligible for garbage collection.

```
using System;
using System.Text;

class Test
{
  static void Main ()
  {
    StringBuilder ref1 = new StringBuilder("object1");
    StringBuilder ref2 = new StringBuilder("object2");
    StringBuilder ref3 = ref2;
    ref1 = ref2 = null;
    Console.WriteLine(ref3);                 // object2
  }
}
```

Value type instances (and object references) live wherever the variable was declared. If the instance was declared as a field within an object, or as an array element, that instance lives on the heap.

 You can't explicitly delete objects in C#, as you can in C++. An unreferenced object is eventually collected by the garbage collector.

The heap is also used to store static fields and constants. Unlike objects allocated on the heap (which can get garbage-collected), these will live until the application domain is torn down.

Definite Assignment

C# enforces a definite assignment policy. In practice, this means that outside of an unsafe context, it's impossible to access uninitialized memory. Definite assignment has three implications:

- Local variables must be assigned a value before they can be read.
- Function arguments must be supplied when a method is called.
- All other variables (such as fields and array elements) are automatically initialized by the runtime.

For example, the following code results in a compile-time error:

```
static void Main( )
{
  int x;
  Console.WriteLine (x);                     // compile-time error
}
```

Fields and array elements are automatically initialized with the default values for their type. The following code outputs 0, because array elements are implicitly assigned to their default values:

```
static void Main()
{
  int[] ints = new int[2];
  Console.WriteLine (ints[0]);                    // 0
}
```

The following code outputs 0, because fields are implicitly assigned to a default value:

```
class Test
{
  static int x;
  static void Main() { Console.WriteLine (x); }  // 0
}
```

Default Values

All type instances have a default value. The default value for the primitives is the result of a bitwise zeroing of memory, as shown in Table 2-7.

Table 2-7. Default values for primitive types

Type	Default value
Reference	null
Numeric type or Enum type	0
char type	'\0'
bool type	false

The default value in a custom value type (i.e., struct) is the same as the default value for each field defined by the custom type.

Parameters

A method has a sequence of parameters. Parameters define the set of arguments that must be provided for that method. In this example, the method Foo has a single parameter named p, of type int:

```
static void Foo (int p)
{
  p = p + 1;              // increment p by 1
  Console.WriteLine(p);   // write p to screen
}
static void Main() { Foo(8); }
```

Table 2-8 gives an overview of how a parameter is passed in and out of a function.

Table 2-8. Parameter modifiers

Parameter modifier	Passed by	Variable must be definitely assigned
None	Value	Going *in*
ref	Reference	Going *in*
out	Reference	Going *out*

Passing arguments by value

By default, arguments in C# are *passed by value*, which is by far the most common case. This means a copy of the value is created when passed to the method:

```
class Test
{
  static void Foo(int p)
  {
    p = p + 1;                // increment p by 1
    Console.WriteLine(p);     // write p to screen
  }

  static void Main( )
  {
    int x = 8;
    Foo(x);                   // make a copy of x
    Console.WriteLine(x);     // x will still be 8
  }
}
```

Assigning p a new value does not change the contents of x, since p and x reside in different memory locations.

Passing a reference type object by value copies the *reference*, but not the object. In the following example, Foo sees the same StringBuilder object that Main instantiated, but has an independent *reference* to it. In other words, sb and fooSB are separate variables that reference the same StringBuilder object:

```
class Test
{
  static void Foo (StringBuilder fooSB)
  {
    fooSB.Append ("test");
    fooSB = null;
  }

  static void Main( )
  {
    StringBuilder sb = new StringBuilder( );
    Foo (sb);
    Console.WriteLine (sb.ToString( ));   // test
  }
}
```

Because fooSB is a *copy* of a reference, setting it to null doesn't make sb null. (If, however, fooSB was declared and called with the ref modifier, sb *would* become null.)

The ref modifier

To *pass by reference*, C# provides the ref parameter modifier. In the following example, p and x refer to the same memory locations:

```
class Test
{
  static void Foo (ref int p)
  {
    p = p + 1;                // increment p by 1
    Console.WriteLine(p);     // write p to screen
  }

  static void Main ()
  {
    int x = 8;
    Foo (ref x);              // Ask Foo to deal directly with x
    Console.WriteLine(x);     // x is now 9
  }
}
```

Now assigning p a new value changes the contents of x. Notice how the ref modifier is required both when writing and when calling the method. This makes it very clear what's going on.

The ref modifier is essential in implementing a swap method (later, in Chapter 3 in the "Generics" section, we will show how to write a swap method that works with any type):

```
using System;

class Test
{
  static void Swap (ref string a, ref string b)
  {
    string temp = a;
    a = b;
    b = temp;
  }

  static void Main ()
  {
    string x = "Penn";
    string y = "Teller";
    Swap (ref x, ref y);
    Console.WriteLine (x);    // Teller
    Console.WriteLine (y);    // Penn
  }
}
```

A parameter can be passed by reference or by value, regardless of whether the parameter type is a reference type or a value type.

The out modifier

An out argument is like a ref argument, except it:

- Need not be assigned before going into the function
- Must be assigned before it comes *out* of the function

The out modifier is most commonly used to get multiple return values back from a method. For example:

```
using System;

class Test
{
  static void Split (string name, out string firstNames,
                     out string lastName)
  {
     int i = name.LastIndexOf(' ');
     firstNames = name.Substring (0, i);
     lastName   = name.Substring (i + 1);
  }

  static void Main( )
  {
    string a, b;
    Split ("Stevie Ray Vaughn", out a, out b);
    Console.WriteLine (a);                    // Stevie Ray
    Console.WriteLine (b);                    // Vaughn
  }
}
```

Like a ref parameter, an out parameter is passed by reference.

Implications of passing by reference

When you pass an argument by reference, you alias the storage location of an existing variable rather than create a new storage location. In the following example, the variables x and y represent the same instance:

```
using System;

class Test
{
  static int x;

  static void Main( ) { Foo(out x); }

  static void Foo(out int y)
  {
```

```
      Console.WriteLine (x);              // x is 0
      y = 1;                              // mutate y
      Console.WriteLine (x);              // x is 1
    }
  }
```

The params modifier

The params parameter modifier may be specified on the last parameter of a
method so that the method accepts any number of parameters of a particular type.
The parameter type must be declared as an array. For example:

```
using System;

class Test
{
  static int Sum (params int[] ints)
  {
    int sum = 0;
    for (int i = 0; i < ints.Length; i++)
      sum += ints[i];                     // increase sum by ints[i]
    return sum;
  }

  static void Main()
  {
    int total = Sum (1, 2, 3, 4);
    Console.WriteLine(total);             // 10
  }
}
```

You can also supply a params argument as an ordinary array. The first line in Main
is semantically equivalent to this:

```
int total = Sum (new int[] { 1, 2, 3, 4 } );
```

var—Implicitly Typed Local Variables (C# 3.0)

It is often the case that you declare and initialize a variable in one step. If the
compiler is able to infer the type from the initialization expression, you can use
the word var in place of the type declaration. For example:

```
var x = 5;
var y = "hello";
var z = new System.Text.StringBuilder();
var req = (System.Net.FtpWebRequest) System.Net.WebRequest.Create ("...");
```

This is precisely equivalent to:

```
int    x = 5;
string y = "hello";
System.Text.StringBuilder z = new System.Text.StringBuilder();
System.Net.FtpWebRequest req = (System.Net.FtpWebRequest)
                               System.Net.WebRequest.Create ("...");
```

Because of this direct equivalence, implicitly typed variables are statically typed. For example, the following generates a compile-time error:

```
var x = 5;
x = "hello";    // Compile-time error; x is of type int
```

 var can decrease code readability in the case when *you can't deduce the type purely by looking at the variable declaration*. For example:

```
Random r = new Random( );
var x = r.Next( );
```

What type is x?

In the section "Anonymous Types (C# 3.0)" in Chapter 4, we will describe a scenario where the use of var is mandatory.

Expressions and Operators

An *expression* essentially denotes a value. The simplest kinds of expressions are constants and variables. Expressions can be transformed and combined using operators. An *operator* takes one or more input *operands* to output a new expression.

Here is an example of a *constant expression*:

```
12
```

We can use the * operator to combine two operands (the literal expressions 12 and 30), as follows:

```
12 * 30
```

Complex expressions can be built because an operand may itself be an expression, such as the operand (12 * 30) in the following example:

```
1 + (12 * 30)
```

Operators in C# are classed as *unary*, *binary*, or *ternary*—depending on the number of operands they work on (one, two, or three). The binary operators always use *infix* notation, where the operator is placed *between* the two operands.

Primary Expressions

Primary expressions include expressions composed of operators that are intrinsic to the basic plumbing of the language. Here is an example:

```
Math.Log (1)
```

This expression is composed of two primary expressions. The first expression performs a member-lookup (with the . operator), and the second expression performs a method call (with the ( ) operator).

Void Expressions

A void expression is an expression that has no value. For example:

```
Console.WriteLine (1)
```

A void expression, since it has no value, cannot be used as an operand to build more complex expressions:

```
1 + Console.WriteLine(1)      // Compile-time error
```

Assignment Expressions

An assignment expression uses the = operator to assign the result of another expression to a variable. For example:

```
x = x * 5
```

An assignment expression is not a void expression. It actually carries the assignment value, and so can be incorporated into another expression. In the following example, the expression assigns 2 to x and 10 to y:

```
y = 5 * (x = 2)
```

This style of expression can be used to initialize multiple values:

```
a = b = c = d = 0
```

The *compound assignment operators* are syntactic shortcuts that combine assignment with another operator. For example:

```
x *= 2     // equivalent to x = x * 2
x <<= 1    // equivalent to x = x << 1
```

Operator Precedence and Associativity

When an expression contains multiple operators, *precedence* and *associativity* determine the order of evaluation. Operators with higher precedence execute before operators of lower precedence. If the operators have the same precedence, the operator's associativity determines the order of evaluation.

Precedence

The following expression:

```
1 + 2 * 3
```

is evaluated as follows because * has a higher precedence than +:

```
1 + (2 * 3)
```

Left-associative operators

Binary operators (except for assignment operators) are *left-associative*; in other words, they are evaluated from left to right. For example, the following expression:

```
8 / 4 / 2
```

is evaluated as follows due to left associativity:

```
( 8 / 4 ) / 2    // 1
```

You can insert parentheses to change the default order of evaluation:

```
8 / ( 4 / 2 )    // 4
```

Right-associative operators

The *assignment operators*, the unary operators, and the conditional operator are *right-associative*; in other words, they are evaluated from right to left. In this example, you can see the effect of right-to-left evaluation:

```
int x = 0;
int y = -~x;    // 1
int z = ~-x;    // -1
```

Operator Table

Table 2-9 lists C#'s operators in order of precedence. Operators in the same category have the same precedence. We explain user-overloadable operators in the section "Operator Overloading" in Chapter 4.

Table 2-9. C# operators (categories in order of precedence)

Category	Operator symbol	Operator name	Example	User-overloadable
Primary	( )	Grouping	while(x)	No
	.	Member access	x.y	No
	->	Pointer to struct (unsafe)	x->y	No
	( )	Function call	x( )	No
	[]	Array/index	a[x]	Via indexer
	++	Post-increment	x++	Yes
	--	Post-decrement	x--	Yes
	new	Create instance	new Foo( )	No
	stackalloc	Unsafe stack allocation	stackalloc(10)	No
	typeof	Get type from identifier	typeof(int)	No
	checked	Integral overflow check on	checked(x)	No
	unchecked	Integral overflow check off	unchecked(x)	No
Unary	sizeof	Get size of struct	sizeof(int)	No
	+	Positive value of	+x	Yes
	-	Negative value of	-x	Yes
	!	Not	!x	Yes
	~	Bitwise complement	~x	Yes
	++	Pre-increment	++x	Yes
	--	Post-increment	--x	Yes
	( )	Cast	(int)x	No
	*	Value at address (unsafe)	*x	No

Table 2-9. C# operators (categories in order of precedence) (continued)

Category	Operator symbol	Operator name	Example	User-overloadable
	&	Address of value (unsafe)	&x	No
Multiplicative	*	Multiply	x * y	Yes
	/	Divide	x / y	Yes
	%	Remainder	x % y	Yes
Additive	+	Add	x + y	Yes
	-	Subtract	x - y	Yes
Shift	<<	Shift left	x >> 1	Yes
	>>	Shift right	x << 1	Yes
Relational	<	Less than	x < y	Yes
	>	Greater than	x > y	Yes
	<=	Less than or equal to	x <= y	Yes
	>=	Greater than or equal to	x >= y	Yes
	is	Type is or is subclass of	x is y	No
	as	Type conversion	x as y	No
Equality	==	Equals	x == y	Yes
	!=	Not equals	x != y	Yes
Logical And	&	And	x & y	Yes
Logical Xor	^	Exclusive Or	x ^ y	Yes
Logical Or	|	Or	x | y	Yes
Conditional And	&&	Conditional And	x && y	Via &
Conditional Or	||	Conditional Or	x || y	Via |
Null Coalescing	??	Null Coalescing	x ?? y	No
Conditional	?:	Conditional	isTrue ? thenThisValue : elseThis-Value	No
Assignment	=	Assign	x = y	No
	*=	Multiply self by	x *= 2	Via *
	/=	Divide self by	x /= 2	Via /
	+=	Add to self	x += 2	Via +
	-=	Subtract from self	x -= 2	Via -
	<<=	Shift self left by	x <<= 2	Via <<
	>>=	Shift self right by	x >>= 2	Via >>
	&=	And self by	x &= 2	Via &
	^=	Exclusive-Or self by	x ^= 2	Via ^
	|=	Or self by	x |= 2	Via |
Lambda	=>	Lambda	x => x++	No

Statements

Functions comprise statements that execute sequentially in the textual order in which they appear. A *statement block* is a series of statements appearing between braces (the {} tokens).

Declaration Statements

A declaration statement declares a new variable, optionally initializing the variable with an expression. A declaration statement ends in a semicolon. You may declare multiple variables of the same type in a comma-separated list. For example:

```
string someWord = "rosebud";
int someNumber = 42;
bool rich = true, famous = false;
```

A constant declaration is like a variable declaration, except that the variable cannot be changed after it has been declared, and the initialization must occur with the declaration:

```
const double c = 2.99792458E08;
c+=10; // error
```

Local variables

The scope of a local or constant variable extends to the end of the current block. You cannot declare another local variable with the same name in the current block or in any nested blocks. For example:

```
static void Main( )
{
  int x;
  {
    int y;
    int x;            // error, x already defined
  }
  {
    int y;            // ok, y not in scope
  }
  Console.WriteLine(y); // error, y is out of scope
}
```

Expression Statements

Expression statements are expressions that are also valid statements. An expression statement must either change state or call something that might change state. Changing state essentially means changing a variable. The possible expression statements are:

- Assignment expressions (including increment and decrement expressions)
- Method call expressions (both void and nonvoid)
- Object instantiation expressions

Here are some examples:

```
// declare variables with declaration statements:
string s;
int x, y;
System.Text.StringBuilder sb;

// expression statements
x = 1 + 2;                 // assignment expression
x++;                       // increment expression
y = Math.Max(x, 5);        // assignment expression
Console.WriteLine(y);      // method call expression
sb = new StringBuilder();  // assignment expression
new StringBuilder();       // object instantiation expression
```

When you call a constructor or a method that returns a value, you're not obliged to use the result. However, unless the constructor or method changes state, the statement is completely useless:

```
new StringBuilder();    // legal, but does nothing
new string('c', 3);     // legal, but does nothing
x.Equals(y);            // legal, but does nothing
```

Selection Statements

C# has the following mechanisms to conditionally control the flow of program execution:

- Selection statements (if, switch)
- Conditional operator (? :)
- Loop statements (while, do..while, for, foreach)

This section covers the simplest two constructs: the if-else statement and the switch statement.

The if statement

An if statement executes a body of code depending on whether a bool expression is true. For example:

```
if (5 < 2 * 3)
{
  Console.WriteLine ("true");      // true
}
```

If the body of code is a single statement, you can optionally omit the braces:

```
if (5 < 2 * 3)
  Console.WriteLine ("true");      // true
```

The else clause

An if statement is optionally followed by an else clause:

```
if (2 + 2 == 5)
  Console.WriteLine ("Does not compute");
else
  Console.WriteLine ("false");          // false
```

Within an else clause, you can nest another if statement:

```
if (2 + 2 == 5)
  Console.WriteLine ("Does not compute");
else
  if (2 + 2 == 4)
    Console.WriteLine ("Computes");    // Computes
```

Changing the flow of execution with braces

An else clause always applies to the immediately preceding if statement in the statement block. For example:

```
if (true)
  if (false)
    Console.WriteLine( );
  else
    Console.WriteLine("excutes");
```

This is semantically identical to:

```
if (true)
{
  if (false)
    Console.WriteLine( );
  else
    Console.WriteLine("excutes");
}
```

We can change the execution flow by moving the braces:

```
if (true)
{
  if (false)
    Console.WriteLine( );
}
else
  Console.WriteLine("does not execute");
```

With braces, you explicitly state your intention. This can improve the readability of nested if statements—even when not required by the compiler. A notable exception is with the following pattern:

```
static void TellMeWhatICanDo (int age)
{
  if (age >= 35)
    Console.WriteLine ("You can be president!");
  else if (age >= 21)
    Console.WriteLine ("You can drink!");
  else if (age >= 18)
    Console.WriteLine ("You can vote!");
  else
    Console.WriteLine ("You can wait!");
}
```

Here, we've arranged the if and else statements to mimic the "elsif" construct of other languages (and C#'s #elif preprocessor directive). Visual Studio's auto-formatting recognizes this pattern and preserves the indentation. Semantically, though, each if statement following an else statement is functionally nested within the else statement.

The switch statement

switch statements let you branch program execution based on a selection of possible values that a variable may have. switch statements may result in cleaner code than multiple if statements, since switch statements require an expression to be evaluated only once. For instance:

```
static void ShowCard(int cardNumber)
{
  switch(cardNumber)
  {
    case 13:
      Console.WriteLine("King");
      break;
    case 12:
      Console.WriteLine("Queen");
      break;
    case 11:
      Console.WriteLine("Jack");
      break;
    case -1:                      // joker is -1
      goto case 12;               // in this game joker counts as queen
    default:                      // executes for any other cardNumber
      Console.WriteLine(cardNumber);
      break;
  }
}
```

You can only switch on an expression of a type that can be statically evaluated, which restricts it to the primitive types, string type, and enum types.

At the end of each case clause, you must say explicitly where execution is to go next, with some kind of jump statement. Here are the options:

- break (jumps to the end of the switch statement)
- goto case *x* (jumps to another case clause)
- goto default (jumps to the default clause)
- Any other jump statement—namely, return, throw, continue, or goto *label*

When more than one value should execute the same code, you can list the common cases sequentially:

```
switch (cardNumber)
{
  case 13:
  case 12:
  case 11:
    Console.WriteLine ("Face card");
    break;
  default:
```

```
    Console.WriteLine ("Plain card");
    break;
}
```

This feature of a switch statement is pivotal in terms of producing cleaner code than multiple if-else statements.

Iteration Statements

C# enables a sequence of statements to execute repeatedly with the while, do-while, and for statements.

while and do-while loops

while loops repeatedly execute a body of code while a bool expression is true. The expression is tested *before* the body of the loop is executed. For example:

```
int i = 0;
while (i < 3)
{
  Console.WriteLine (i);
  i++;
}

OUTPUT:
0
1
2
```

do-while loops differ in functionality from while loops only in that they test the expression *after* the statement block has executed. Here's the preceding example rewritten with a do-while loop:

```
int i = 0;
do
{
  Console.WriteLine(i);
  i++;
}
while (i < 3);
```

for loops

for loops are like while loops with special clauses for *initialization* and *iteration* of a loop variable. A for loop contains three clauses as follows:

```
for (initialization-clause; condition-clause; iteration-clause)
  statement-or-statement-block
```

Initialization clause
    Executed before the loop begins; used to initialize one or more variables

Condition clause
    The bool expression that, while true, will execute the body

Iteration clause
> Executed *after* each iteration of the statement block; used typically to update the loop variable

For example, the following prints the numbers 0 through 2:

```
for (int i = 0; i < 3; i++)
  Console.WriteLine (i);
```

Any of the three parts of the for statement may be omitted. One can implement an infinite loop such as the following (though while(true) may be used instead):

```
for (;;)
  Console.WriteLine("interrupt me");
```

foreach loops

The foreach statement iterates over each element in an enumerable object. Most of the types in C# and the .NET Framework that represent a set or list of elements are enumerable. For example, both an array and a string are enumerable. Here is an example of enumerating over the characters in a string, from the first character through to the last:

```
foreach (char c in "beer")
  Console.WriteLine(c);

OUTPUT:
b
e
e
r
```

We define enumerable objects in the section "Enumeration and Iterators" in Chapter 4.

Jump Statements

The C# jump statements are break, continue, goto, return, and throw. Jump statements obey the reliability rules of try statements (see the section "try Statements and Exceptions" in Chapter 4). First, a jump out of a try block always executes the try's finally block before reaching the target of the jump. Second, a jump cannot be made from the inside to the outside of a finally block.

The break statement

The break statement ends the execution of the body of a while loop, for loop, or switch statement:

```
int x = 0;
while (true)
{
  if (x++ > 5)
    break;       // break from the loop
}
// execution continues here after break
...
```

The continue statement

The continue statement forgoes the remaining statements in the loop and makes an early start on the next iteration:

```
for (int i = 0; i < 4; i++)
{
  if ((i % 2) == 0)        // true if i is even
    continue;              // continue with next iteration
  Console.WriteLine (i);
}

OUTPUT:
1
3
```

The goto statement

The goto statement transfers execution to another label within the statement block. The form is as follows:

```
goto statement-label;
```

Or, when used within a switch statement:

```
goto case case-constant;
```

A label statement is just a placeholder in a code block, denoted with a colon suffix. In this example, we write the equivalent of a basic for loop that iterates the numbers 0 through 2:

```
int i = 0;
startLoop:
if (i < 3 )
{
  Console.WriteLine(i);
  i++;
  goto startLoop;
}

// equivalent:
for (int i = 0; i < 3; i++)
  Console.WriteLine(i);
```

The goto case statement transfers execution to another case label in a switch block (see the section "The switch statement" earlier in this chapter).

The return statement

The return statement exits the method and must return an expression of the method's return type if the method is nonvoid:

```
static decimal AsPercentage(decimal d)
{
  decimal p = d * 100m;
  return p;              // return to the calling method with value
}
```

The throw statement

The throw statement throws an exception to indicate an error has occurred (see the section "try Statements and Exceptions" in Chapter 4):

```
if (w == null)
    throw new ArgumentNullException(...);
```

Miscellaneous Statements

The lock statement is a syntactic shortcut for calling the Enter and Exit methods of the Monitor class (see Chapter 19).

The using statement provides an elegant syntax for declaring a local variable that implements IDisposable (see the sections "try Statements and Exceptions" in Chapter 4 and "IDisposable, Dispose, and Close" in Chapter 12).

> Note that C# overloads the using keyword to have independent meanings in different contexts. Specifically, the using *directive* is different from the using *statement*.

Namespaces

A namespace is a domain within which type names must be unique. Types are typically organized into hierarchical namespaces—both to avoid naming conflicts and to make type names easier to find. For example, the RSA type that handles public key encryption is defined within the following namespace:

```
System.Security.Cryptography
```

A namespace forms an integral part of a type's name. The following code calls RSA's Create method:

```
System.Security.Cryptography.RSA rsa =
    System.Security.Cryptography.RSA.Create();
```

> Namespaces are independent of assemblies, which are units of deployment such as an *.exe* or *.dll* (described in Chapter 16).
>
> Namespaces also have no impact on member visibility—public, internal, private, and so on.

The namespace Keyword

Types can be declared within a namespace. For example:

```
namespace Outer.Middle.Inner
{
    class Class1 {}
    class Class2 {}
}
```

The dots in the namespace indicate a hierarchy of nested namespaces. The code that follows is semantically identical to the preceding example.

```
namespace Outer
{
  namespace Middle
  {
    namespace Inner
    {
      class Class1 {}
      class Class2 {}
    }
  }
}
```

Fully Qualified Names

You can refer to a type with is *fully qualified name*, which includes all namespaces from the outermost to the innermost. For example:

```
class Test
{
  static void Main( )
  {
    Outer.Middle.Inner.Class1 c;
  }
}
```

The using Directive

The using directive *imports* a namespace. This is a convenient way to refer to types without their fully qualified names. This example is semantically identical to our previous example:

```
using Outer.Middle.Inner;

class Test
{
  static void Main( )
  {
    Class1 c;
  }
}
```

The Global Namespace

The global namespace comprises:

- All top-level namespaces
- All types not declared in any namespace

Our previous two examples declared Test in the global namespace. In the next example, the type Class0 and the namespace Outer are both members of the global namespace:

```
class Class0 {}

namespace Outer
```

```
    {
      namespace Middle
      {
        namespace Inner
        {
          class Class1 {}
          class Class2 {}
        }
      }
    }
```

Rules Within a Namespace

Name scoping

All names present in outer namespaces are implicitly imported into inner namespaces. In this example, the names Middle and Class1 are implicitly imported into Inner:

```
namespace Outer
{
  namespace Middle
  {
    class Class1 {}

    namespace Inner
    {
      class Class2 : Class1 {}
    }
  }
}
```

If you want to refer to a type in a different branch of your namespace hierarchy, you can use a partially qualified name. In the following example, we base SalesReport on Common.ReportBase:

```
namespace MyTradingCompany
{
  namespace Common
  {
    class ReportBase {}
  }
  namespace ManagementReporting
  {
    class SalesReport : Common.ReportBase {}
  }
}
```

Name hiding

Names in inner namespaces hide names in outer namespaces. In the following example, cInner refers to Inner.Class2, and cOuter refers to Middle.Class2.

```
namespace Outer
{
```

```
namespace Middle
{
  class Class1 {}
  class Class2 {}

  namespace Inner
  {
    class Class1
    {
      Class2 cInner;
      Middle.Class2 cOuter;
    }
    class Class2 {}
  }
}
}
```

Hiding only impairs your ability to refer to something via its simple name; you can still use its fully qualified name. Hiding has no deeper runtime semantics.

 The compiler resolves all namespace rules, converting everything to fully qualified names. Compiled Intermediate Language (IL) contains no unqualified or partially qualified names.

Repeated namespaces

You can repeat a namespace declaration, as long as the type names within the namespaces don't conflict:

```
namespace Outer.Middle.Inner
{
  class Class1 {}
}

namespace Outer.Middle.Inner
{
  class Class2 {}
}
```

We can even break the example into two source files such that we could compile each class into a different assembly.

Source File #1:

```
namespace Outer.Middle.Inner
{
  class Class1 {}
}
```

Source File #2:

```
namespace Outer.Middle.Inner
{
  class Class2 {}
}
```

Nested using directive

You can nest a using directive within a namespace. This allows you to scope the using directive within a namespace declaration. In the following example, Class1 is visible in one scope, but not in another:

```
namespace N1
{
  class Class1 {}
}

namespace N2
{
  using N1;

  class Class2 : Class1 {}
}

namespace N2
{
  class Class3 : Class1 {}   // compile error
}
```

Aliasing Types and Namespaces

Importing a namespace can result in type-name collision. Rather than importing the whole namespace, you can import just the specific types you need, giving each type an alias. For example:

```
using PropertyInfo2 = System.Reflection.PropertyInfo;
class Program { PropertyInfo2 p; }
```

An entire namespace can be aliased, as follows:

```
using R = System.Reflection;
class Program { R.PropertyInfo p; }
```

Advanced Namespace Features

Extern

Extern namespaces allow your program to reference two types with the same fully qualified name (i.e., the namespace and type name are identical). This is an unusual scenario and can occur only when the two types come from different assemblies. Consider the following example.

Library 1:

```
// csc target:library /out:Widgets1.dll widgetsv1.cs

namespace Widgets
{
  public class Widget {}
}
```

Library 2:

```
// csc target:library /out:Widgets2.dll widgetsv2.cs

namespace Widgets
{
  public class Widget {}
}
```

Application:

```
// csc /r:Widgets1.dll /r:Widgets2.dll application.cs

using Widgets;

class Test
  static void Main( )
  {
    Widget w = new Widget( );
  }
}
```

The application cannot compile, because `Widget` is ambiguous. Extern namespaces can resolve the ambiguity in our application:

```
// csc /r:W1=Widgets1.dll /r:W2=Widgets2.dll application.cs

extern alias W1;
extern alias W2;

class Test
  static void Main( )
  {
    W1.Widgets.Widget w1 = new W1.Widgets.Widget( );
    W2.Widgets.Widget w2 = new W2.Widgets.Widget( );
  }
}
```

Namespace alias qualifiers

As we mentioned earlier, names in inner namespaces hide names in outer namespaces. However, sometimes even the use of a fully qualified type name does not resolve the conflict. Consider the following example:

```
namespace N
{
  class A
  {
    public class B {}                  // Nested type
    static void Main() { new A.B( ); }  // Instantiate class B
  }
}

namespace A
{
  class B {}
}
```

The Main method could be instantiating either the nested class B, or the class B within the namespace A. The compiler always gives higher precedence to identifiers in the current namespace; in this case, the nested B class.

To resolve such conflicts, a namespace name can be qualified, relative to one of the following:

- The global namespace—the root of all namespaces
- The set of extern aliases

The :: token is used for namespace alias qualification. In this example, we qualify using the global namespace:

```
namespace N
{
  class A
  {
    static void Main( )
    {
      System.Console.WriteLine(new A.B( ));
      System.Console.WriteLine(new global::A.B( ));
    }

    public class B {}
  }
}

namespace A
{
  class B {}
}
```

Here is an example of qualifying with an alias (adapted from the example in the earlier "Extern" section):

```
extern alias W1;
extern alias W2;

class Test
{
  static void Main( )
  {
    W1::Widgets.Widget w1 = new W1::Widgets.Widget( );
    W2::Widgets.Widget w2 = new W2::Widgets.Widget( );
  }
}
```

3

Creating Types in C#

In this chapter, we will delve into types and type members.

Classes

A class is the most common kind of reference type. The simplest possible class declaration is as follows:

```
class YourClassName
{
}
```

A more complex class optionally has the following:

Preceding the keyword `class`:	*Attributes* and *class modifiers*. The nonnested class modifiers are `public`, `internal`, `abstract`, `sealed`, `static`, `unsafe`, and `partial`.
Following `YourClassName`:	*Generic type parameters*, a *base class*, and *interfaces*
Within the braces:	*Class members* (these are *methods, properties, indexers, events, fields, constructors, operator functions, nested types*, and a *finalizer*)

This chapter covers all of these constructs except attributes, operator functions, and the unsafe keyword, which are instead covered in Chapter 4. The following sections will enumerate each of the class members.

Fields

A *field* is a variable that is a member of a class or struct. For example:

```
class Octopus
{
  string name;
  public int Age = 10;
}
```

Fields allow the following modifiers:

Static modifier	Static
Access modifiers	public internal private protected
Inheritance modifier	New
Unsafe code modifier	Unsafe
Read-only modifier	Readonly
Threading modifier	Volatile

The readonly modifier

The readonly modifier prevents a field from being modified after construction. A read-only field can be assigned only in its declaration or within the enclosing type's constructor.

Field initialization

Field initialization is optional. An uninitialized field has a default value (0, \0, null, false). Field initializers run before constructors:

```
string name = "anonymous";
```

Declaring multiple fields together

For convenience, you may declare multiple fields of the same type in a comma-separated list. This is a convenient way for all the fields to share the same attributes and field modifiers. For example:

```
static readonly int legs = 8,
                     eyes = 1;
```

Methods

A method performs an action in a series of statements. A method can receive *input* data from the caller by specifying *parameters*, and *output* can send data back to the caller by specifying a *return type*. A method can specify a void return type, indicating that it doesn't return any value to its caller. A method can also output data back to the caller via ref/out parameters.

A method's *signature* must be unique within the type. A method's signature comprises its name and parameter types (but not the parameter *names*, nor the return type).

Methods allow the following modifiers:

Static modifier	static
Access modifiers	public internal private protected
Inheritance modifiers	new virtual abstract override sealed
Unmanaged code modifiers	unsafe extern

Overloading methods

A type may overload methods (have multiple methods with the same name), as long as the signatures are different. For example, the following methods can all coexist in the same type:

```
void Foo (int x);
void Foo (double x);
void Foo (int x, float y);
void Foo (float x, int y);
```

However, the following pairs of methods cannot coexist in the same type, since the return type and the params modifier are not part of a method's signature:

```
void  Foo (int x);
float Foo (int x);              // compile error

void  Goo (int[] x);
void  Goo (params int[] x); // compile error
```

Pass-by-value versus pass-by-reference

Whether a parameter is pass-by-value or pass-by-reference is also part of the signature. For example, Foo(int) can coexist with either Foo(ref int) or Foo(out int). However, Foo(ref int) and Foo(out int) cannot coexist:

```
void Foo (int x);
void Foo (ref int x);     // OK so far
void Foo (out int x);     // Compile error
```

Instance Constructors

Constructors run initialization code on a class or struct. A constructor is defined like a method, except that the method name and return type are reduced to the name of the enclosing type:

```
public class Panda
{
  string name;              // define field
  public Panda (string n)   // define constructor
  {
    name = n;               // initialization code (set up field)
  }
}
...

Panda p = new Panda ("Petey");    // call constructor
```

Constructors allow the following modifiers:

Access modifiers	public internal private protected
Unmanaged code modifiers	unsafe extern

Overloading constructors

A class or struct may overload constructors. To avoid code duplication, one constructor may call another, using the this keyword:

```
using System;

public class Wine
{
  public decimal Price;
  public int Year;
  public Wine (decimal price) { Price = price; }
  public Wine (decimal price, int year) : this (price) { Year = year; }
}
```

When one constructor calls another, the *latter* executes first.

You can pass an *expression* into another constructor as follows:

```
public Wine (decimal price, DateTime year) : this (price, year.Year) { }
```

The expression itself cannot make use of the this reference, for example, to call an instance method. It can, however, call static methods.

Implicit parameterless constructors

For classes, the C# compiler automatically generates a parameterless constructor if and only if you do not define any constructors. However, as soon as you define at least one constructor, the parameterless constructor is no longer automatically generated.

For structs, a parameterless constructor is intrinsic to the struct; therefore, you cannot define your own. The role of a struct's implicit parameterless constructor is to initialize each field with default values.

Constructor and field initialization order

We saw previously that fields can be initialized with default values in their declaration:

```
class Player
{
  int shields = 50;    // initialized first
  int health = 100;    // initialized second
}
```

Field initializations occur *before* the constructor is executed, and in the declaration order of the fields.

Nonpublic constructors

Constructors do not need to be public. A common reason to have a nonpublic constructor is to control instance creation via a static method call. The static method could be used to return an object from a pool rather than necessarily creating a new object, or return various subclasses based on input arguments. The template for that pattern is shown next.

```
public class Class1
{
  Class1( ) {}                                   // private constructor
  public static Class1 Create (...)
  {
    // perform custom logic here to return an instance of Class1
    ...
  }
}
```

Object Initializers (C# 3.0)

To simplify object initialization, the accessible fields or properties of an object can be initialized in a single statement directly after construction. For example, consider the following class:

```
public class Bunny
{
  public string Name;
  public bool LikesCarrots;
  public bool LikesHumans;

  public Bunny () {}
  public Bunny (string n) { Name = n; }
}
```

Using object initializers, you can instantiate Bunny objects as follows:

```
// Note parameterless constructors can omit empty parenthesis
Bunny b1 = new Bunny { Name="Bo", LikesCarrots=true, LikesHumans=false };
Bunny b2 = new Bunny ("Bo")    { LikesCarrots=true, LikesHumans=false };
```

The code to construct b1 and b2 is precisely equivalent to:

```
Bunny b1 = new Bunny( );
b1.Name = "Bo";
b1.LikesCarrots = true;
b1.LikesHumans = false;

Bunny b2 = new Bunny ("Bo");
b2.LikesCarrots = true;
b2.LikesHumans = false;
```

The this Reference

The this reference refers to the instance itself. In the following example, the Marry method uses this to set the partner's mate field:

```
public class Panda
{
  public Panda Mate;

  public void Marry (Panda partner)
  {
    Mate = partner;
```

```
    partner.Mate = this;
  }
}
```

The this reference also disambiguates a local variable or argument from a field. For example:

```
public class Test
{
  string name;
  public Test (string name) { this.name = name; }
}
```

The this reference is valid only within nonstatic members of a class or struct.

Properties

Properties look like fields from the outside but act like methods on the inside. For example, you can't tell by looking at the following code whether CurrentPrice is a field or a property:

```
Stock msft = new Stock( );
msft.CurrentPrice = 30;
msft.CurrentPrice -= 3;
Console.WriteLine (msft.CurrentPrice);
```

A property is declared like a field, but with a { get {} set {} } block added. Here's how to implement CurrentPrice as a property:

```
public class Stock
{
  decimal currentPrice;            // The private "backing" field

  public decimal CurrentPrice      // The public property
  {
    get { return currentPrice; } set { currentPrice = value; }
  }
}
```

get and set denote property *accessors*. The get accessor runs when the property is read. It must return a value of the property's type. The set accessor is run when the property is assigned. It has an implicit parameter named value of the property's type that you typically assign to a private field (in this case, currentPrice).

Although properties are accessed in the same way as fields, they differ in that they give the implementer complete control over getting and setting its value. This control enables the implementer to choose whatever internal representation is needed, without exposing the internal details to the user of the property. In this example, the set method could throw an exception if value was outside a valid range of values.

Throughout this book, we use public fields extensively to keep the examples free of distraction. In a real application, you would typically favor public properties over public fields, in order to promote encapsulation.

Properties allow the following modifiers:

Static modifier	static
Access modifiers	public internal private protected
Inheritance modifiers	new virtual abstract override sealed
Unmanaged code modifiers	unsafe extern

Read-only and calculated properties

A property is read-only if it specifies only a get accessor, and it is write-only if it specifies only a set accessor. Write-only properties are rarely used.

A property typically has a dedicated backing field to store the underlying data. However, a property can also be computed from other data. In the next example, our Stock class has four additional read-only properties. Each has a dedicated backing field, except for Worth, which is computed on the fly:

```
public class Stock
{
  string  symbol;
  decimal purchasePrice, currentPrice;
  long    sharesOwned;

  public Stock (string symbol, decimal purchasePrice, long sharesOwned)
  {
    this.symbol = symbol;
    this.purchasePrice = currentPrice = purchasePrice;
    this.sharesOwned = sharesOwned;
  }

  public decimal CurrentPrice  { get { return currentPrice;          }
                                 set { currentPrice = value;         } }
  public string Symbol         { get { return symbol;                } }
  public decimal PurchasePrice { get { return purchasePrice;         } }
  public long    SharesOwned   { get { return sharesOwned;           } }
  public decimal Worth         { get { return CurrentPrice*SharesOwned; } }
}

class Test
{
  static void Main( )
  {
    Stock msft = new Stock ("MSFT", 20, 1000);
    Console.WriteLine (msft.Worth);           // 20000
    msft.CurrentPrice = 30;
    Console.WriteLine (msft.Worth);           // 30000
  }
}
```

Automatic properties (C# 3.0)

The most common implementation for a property is a getter and/or setter that simply reads and writes to a private field of the same type as the property. An *automatic property* declaration instructs the compiler to provide this implementation. We can redeclare the first example in this section as follows:

```
public class Stock
{
    ...
    public decimal CurrentPrice { get; set; }
}
```

The compiler automatically generates a private backing field of a compiler-generated name that cannot be referred to. The set accessor can be marked private if you want to expose the property as read-only to other types.

get and set accessibility

The get and set accessors are permitted to have different access levels. The typical use case for this is to have a public property with an internal or private access modifier on the setter:

```
public class Foo
{
    private decimal x;
    public decimal X
    {
        get        {return x;}
        internal set {x = value;}
    }
}
```

CLR property implementation

C# property accessors internally compile to methods called get_*XXX* and set_*XXX*:

```
public int  get_CurrentPrice {...}
public void set_CurrentPrice (decimal value) {...}
```

Simple nonvirtual property accessors are *inlined* by the JIT (Just-In-Time) compiler, eliminating any performance difference between accessing a property and a field. Inlining is an optimization in which a method call is replaced with the body of that method.

Indexers

Indexers provide a natural syntax for accessing elements in a class or struct that encapsulate a list or dictionary of values. Indexers are similar to properties, but are accessed via an index argument rather than a property name. The string class has an indexer that lets you access each of its char values via an int index:

```
string s = "hello";
Console.WriteLine (s[0]); // 'h'
Console.WriteLine (s[3]); // 'l'
```

The syntax for using indexers is like that of using arrays, when the index is an integer type.

 Indexers have the same modifiers as properties (see the previous section "Properties").

Implementing an indexer

In this example, we define the Portfolio class, which encapsulates a list of stocks. This indexer is identified with the this keyword and uses an int index to access a particular stock by ordinal position. The type of the indexer is a Stock (taken from our previous example).

```
public class Portfolio
{
  Stock[] stocks;
  public Portfolio (int numberOfStocks)
  {
    stocks = new Stock [numberOfStocks];
  }

  public int NumberOfStocks { get { return stocks.Length; } }

  public Stock this [int index]        // indexer
  {
    get { return stocks [index];  }
    set { stocks [index] = value; }
  }
}

class Test
{
  static void Main( )
  {
    Portfolio portfolio = new Portfolio(3);
    portfolio [0] = new Stock ("MSFT", 20, 1000);
    portfolio [1] = new Stock ("GOOG", 300, 100);
    portfolio [2] = new Stock ("EBAY", 33, 77);

    for (int i = 0; i < portfolio.NumberOfStocks; i++)
      Console.WriteLine (portfolio[i].Symbol);
  }
}
```

A type may declare multiple indexers. Our Portfolio class can be extended to also allow a stock to be returned by a symbol, with the following addition:

```
public class Portfolio
{
  ...
  public Stock this[string symbol]
  {
    get
```

```
      {
        foreach (Stock s in stocks)
          if (s.Symbol == symbol)
            return s;
        return null;
      }
    }
  }
}
...
Console.WriteLine (portfolio["GOOG"].CurrentPrice); // 300
```

Because we've not included a set clause, this particular overload is read-only.

An indexer can take any number of parameters. If both a symbol and a stock exchange were required to identify a stock, you could declare an indexer using the following syntax:

```
public Stock this [string symbol, string exchange]
{
  get { ... }  set { ... }
}
```

Here's how it would be used:

```
portfolio ["GOOG", "NASDAQ"] = new Stock ("GOOG", 300, 400, 100);
```

CLR indexer implementation

Indexers internally compile to methods called get_Item and set_Item, as follows:

```
public Stock get_Item (int index) {...}
public void set_Item (int index, Stock value) {...}
```

The name "Item" is chosen by the compiler by default—you can actually change this by decorating your indexer with the following attribute:

```
[System.Runtime.CompilerServices.IndexerName("Blah")]
```

Constants

A constant is a field whose value can never change. A constant is evaluated statically at compile time and its value is literally substituted by the compiler whenever used, rather like a macro in C++. A constant can be one of the following types: sbyte, byte, short, ushort, int, uint, long, ulong, float, double, decimal, bool, char, string, or an enum type.

A constant is declared with the const keyword and must be initialized with a value. For example:

```
public class Test
{
  public const string Message = "Hello World";
}
```

A constant is much more restrictive than a static readonly field—both in the types you can use and in field initialization semantics. A constant also differs from a static readonly field in that the evaluation of the constant occurs at compile time. For example:

```
public static double Circumference (double radius)
{
  return 2 * System.Math.PI * radius;
}
```

is compiled to:

```
public static double Circumference (double radius)
{
  return 6.2831853071795862 * radius;
}
```

It makes sense for PI to be a constant, since it can never change. In contrast, a static readonly field can have a different value per application.

A static readonly field is also advantageous when exposing to other assemblies, a value that might change in a later version. For instance, suppose assembly X exposes a constant as follows:

```
public const int MaximumThreads = 20;
```

If assembly Y references X and uses this constant, the value 20 will be baked into *assembly* Y when compiled. This means that if X is later recompiled with the constant set to 50, Y will still use the old value of 20 *until Y is recompiled*. A static readonly field avoids this problem.

Constants can also be declared local to a method. For example:

```
static void Main ( )
{
  const double twoPI  = 2 * System.Math.PI;
  ...
}
```

Constants allow the following modifiers:

Access modifiers	Public internal private protected
Inheritance modifier	new

Static Constructors

A static constructor executes once per *type*, rather than once per *instance*. A static constructor executes before any instances of the type are created and before any other static members are accessed. A type can define only one static constructor, and it must be parameterless and have the same name as the type:

```
class Test
{
  static Test( )
  {
    Console.WriteLine ("Type Initialized");
  }
}
```

Static constructors allow the following modifiers:

Unmanaged code
modifiers

`unsafe` `extern`

Static field initialization order

Static field assignments occur *before* the static constructor is called, in the declaration order in which the fields appear.

Nondeterminism of static constructors

A static constructor is always invoked indirectly by the runtime—it cannot be called explicitly. The runtime guarantees to invoke a type's static constructor *at some point* prior to the type being used; it doesn't commit, though, as to exactly *when*. For example, a subclass's static constructor can execute before or after that of its base class. The runtime may also choose to invoke static constructors *unnecessarily* early, from a programmer's perspective.

Static Classes

A class can be marked `static`, indicating that it must be comprised solely of static members and cannot be subclassed. The `System.Console` and `System.Math` classes are good examples of static classes.

Finalizers

Finalizers are class-only methods that execute just before the garbage collector reclaims the memory for an unreferenced object. The syntax for a finalizer is the name of the class prefixed with the ~ symbol:

```
class Class1
{
  ~Class1( )
  {
    ...
  }
}
```

This is actually C# syntax for overriding `Object`'s `Finalize` method, and it is expanded by the compiler into the following method declaration:

```
protected override void Finalize( )
{
  ...
  base.Finalize( );
}
```

We discuss garbage collection and finalizers fully in Chapter 12.

Finalizers allow the following modifiers:

| Unmanaged code modifier | unsafe |

Partial Classes and Methods

Partial classes allow a class definition to be split—typically across multiple files. A common scenario is for a partial class to be auto-generated from some other source (e.g., an XSD), and for that class to be augmented with additional hand-authored methods. For example:

```
// PaymentFormGen.cs - auto-generated
partial class PaymentForm { ... }

// PaymentForm.cs - hand-authored
partial class PaymentForm { ... }
```

Each participant must have the `partial` declaration; the following is illegal:

```
partial class PaymentForm {}
class PaymentForm {}
```

Participants cannot have conflicting members. A constructor with the same arguments, for instance, cannot be repeated. Partial classes are resolved entirely by the compiler, which means that each participant must be available at compile time and must reside in the same assembly.

There are two ways to specify a base class with partial classes:

- Specify the (same) base class on each participant. For example:

    ```
    partial class PaymentForm : ModalForm {}
    partial class PaymentForm : ModalForm {}
    ```

- Specify the base class on just one participant. For example:

    ```
    partial class PaymentForm : ModalForm {}
    partial class PaymentForm {}
    ```

Base classes are used for inheritance, which we describe in an upcoming section.

Partial methods (C# 3.0)

A partial class may contain *partial methods*. These let an auto-generated partial class provide customizable hooks for manual authoring. For example:

```
// PaymentFormGen.cs - auto-generated
partial class PaymentForm
{
  ...
  partial void ValidatePayment(decimal amount);
}

// PaymentForm.cs - hand-authored
partial class PaymentForm
{
  ...
  partial void ValidatePayment(decimal amount)
```

```
    {
      if (amount > 100)
        ...
    }
}
```

A partial method consists of two parts: a *definition* and an *implementation*. The definition is typically written by a code generator, and the implementation is typically manually authored. If an implementation is not provided, the definition of the partial method is compiled away. This allows auto-generated code to be liberal in providing hooks, without having to worry about code bloat. Partial methods must be void and are implicitly private.

Inheritance

A class can *inherit* from another class to extend or customize the original class. Inheriting from a class lets you reuse the functionality in that class instead of building it from scratch. A class can inherit from only a single class, but can itself be inherited by many classes, thus forming a class hierarchy. In this example, we start by defining a class called Asset:

```
public class Asset
{
  public string  Name;
  public decimal PurchasePrice, CurrentPrice;
}
```

Next, we define classes called Stock and House, which will inherit from Asset. Stock and House get everything an Asset has, plus any additional members that they define:

```
public class Stock : Asset    // inherits from Asset
{
  public long SharesOwned;
}

public class House : Asset    // inherits from Asset
{
  public decimal Mortgage;
}

class Test
{
  static void Main( )
  {
    Stock msft = new Stock( )
    { Name="MSFT", PurchasePrice=20, CurrentPrice=30, SharesOwned=1000 };

    House mansion = new House( )
    { Name="McMansion", PurchasePrice=300000, CurrentPrice=200000,
      Mortgage=250000 };

    Console.WriteLine (msft.Name);        // MSFT
    Console.WriteLine (mansion.Name);     // McMansion
```

```
      Console.WriteLine (msft.SharesOwned);    // 1000
      Console.WriteLine (mansion.Mortgage);    // 250000
    }
  }
```

The *subclasses*, Stock and House, inherit three properties from the *base class*, Asset.

 A subclass is also called a *derived class*.

A base class is also called a *superclass*.

Polymorphism

References are polymorphic. This means a reference to a base class can refer to an instance of a subclass. In the following example, there is a method to display an Asset. You can display both a Stock and a House, since they are both Assets:

```
class Test
{
  static void Main( )
  {
    Stock msft    = new Stock ... ;
    House mansion = new House ... ;
    Display (msft);
    Display (mansion);
  }

  public static void Display (Asset asset)
  {
    System.Console.WriteLine (asset.Name);
  }
}
```

Polymorphism works on the basis that subclasses (Stock and House) have all the features of their base class (Asset). The converse, however, is not true. If Display was modified to accept a House, you could not pass in an Asset:

```
static void Main() { Display (new Asset()); }    // Compile-time error

public static void Display (House house)         // Will not accept Asset
{
  System.Console.WriteLine (house.Mortgage);
}
```

Casting

An object reference can be:

- Implicitly *upcast* to a base class reference
- Explicitly *downcast* to a subclass reference

Casting affects only *references*; the object itself is not converted or altered. An upcast always succeeds; a downcast succeeds only if the object is suitably typed.

Upcasting

An upcast operation creates a base class reference from a subclass reference. For example:

```
Stock msft = new Stock(...);
Asset a = msft;                          // upcast
```

After the upcast, variable a still references the same Stock object as variable msft. The object being referenced is not itself altered or converted:

```
Console.WriteLine (a == msft);           // true
```

Although a and msft refer to the identical object, a has a more restrictive view on that object:

```
Console.WriteLine (a.Name);              // ok
Console.WriteLine (a.SharesOwned);       // error: SharesOwned undefined
```

The last line generates a compile-time error because the reference a is of type Asset, even though it refers to an object of type Stock. To get to its SharedOwned field, you must *downcast* the Asset to a Stock.

Downcasting

A downcast operation creates a subclass reference from a base class reference. For example:

```
Stock msft = new Stock( );
Asset a = msft;                          // upcast
Stock s = (Stock)a;                      // downcast
Console.WriteLine (s.SharesOwned);       // <No error>
Console.WriteLine (s == a);              // true
Console.WriteLine (s == msft);           // true
```

As with an upcast, only references are affected—not the underlying object. A downcast requires an explicit cast because it can potentially fail at runtime:

```
House h = new House( );
Asset a = h;                // Upcast always succeeds
Stock s = (Stock)a;         // Downcast fails: a is not a Stock
```

If a downcast fails, an InvalidCastException is thrown. This is an example of *dynamic type checking* (we will elaborate on this concept in the "Object Type— Static and Dynamic Type Checking" section later in the chapter).

The as operator

The as operator performs a downcast that evaluates to null if the downcast fails:

```
Asset a = new Asset( );
Stock s = a as Stock;       // s is null; no exception thrown
```

The is operator

The is operator tests whether a downcast would succeed; in other words, whether an object derives from a specified class (or implements an interface). It is often used to test before downcasting.

```
if (a is Stock)
  Console.WriteLine(((Stock)a).SharesOwned);
```

Virtual Function Members

A function marked as virtual can be *overridden* by subclasses wanting to provide
a specialized implementation. Methods, properties, indexers, and events can all be
declared virtual:

```
public class Asset
{
  ...
  public virtual decimal Liability { get { return 0; } }
}
```

A subclass overrides a virtual method by applying the override modifier:

```
public class Stock : Asset { ... }

public class House : Asset
{
  ...
  public override decimal Liability { get { return Mortgage; } }
}
```

By default, the Liability of an Asset is 0. A Stock does not need to specialize this
behavior. However, the House specializes the Liability property to return the
value of the Mortgage:

```
House mansion = new House
  { Name="McMansion", PurchasePrice=300000, CurrentPrice=200000,
    Mortgage=250000 };

Asset a = mansion;
decimal d2 = mansion.Liability;      // 250000
```

The signatures, return types, and accessibility of the virtual and overridden
methods must be identical. An overridden method can call its base class implementation via the base keyword (we will cover this shortly, in the section "The
base Keyword").

Abstract Classes and Abstract Members

A class declared as *abstract* can never be instantiated. Instead, only its concrete
subclasses can be instantiated.

Abstract classes are able to define *abstract members*. Abstract members are like
virtual members, except they don't provide a default implementation. That implementation must be provided by the subclass, unless that subclass is also declared
abstract:

```
public abstract class Asset
{
  ...
  public abstract decimal NetValue { get; }    // Note empty implementation
}
```

```
public class Stock : Asset
{
  ...                               // Override an abstract method
  public override decimal NetValue  // just like a virtual method.
  {
    get { return CurrentPrice * SharesOwned; }
  }
}

public class House : Asset     // Every nonabstract subtype must
{                              // define NetValue.
  ...
  public override decimal NetValue
  {
    get { return CurrentPrice - Mortgage; }
  }
}
```

Hiding Inherited Members

 Note that C# overloads the new keyword to have independent meanings in different contexts. Specifically, the new *operator* is different from the new *member* modifier.

A base class and a subclass may define identical members. For example:

```
public class BaseClass            { public int Counter = 1; }
public class Subclass : BaseClass { public int Counter = 2; }
```

The Counter field in the Subclass is said to *hide* the Counter field in the BaseClass. Usually, this happens by accident, when a member is added to the base type *after* an identical member was added to the subtype. For this reason, the compiler generates a warning, and then resolves the ambiguity as follows:

- References to Subclass bind to Subclass.Counter.
- References to BaseClass bind to BaseClass.Counter.

Occasionally, you want to hide a member deliberately, in which case you can apply the new modifier to the member in the subclass. The new modifier *does nothing more than suppress the compiler warning that would otherwise result*:

```
public class BaseClass            { public     int Counter = 1; }
public class Subclass : BaseClass { public new int Counter = 2; }
```

The new modifier communicates your intent to the compiler—and other programmers—that the duplicate member is not an accident.

new versus virtual

Consider the following class hierarchy:

```
public class BaseClass
{
  public virtual void Foo() { Console.WriteLine ("BaseClass.Foo"); }
```

```
    }

    public class Overrider : BaseClass
    {
      public override void Foo() { Console.WriteLine ("Overrider.Foo"); }
    }

    public class Hider : BaseClass
    {
      public new void Foo()     { Console.WriteLine ("Hider.Foo"); }
    }
```

The differences in behavior between Overrider and Hider are demonstrated in the
following code:

```
    Overrider over = new Overrider();
    BaseClass b1 = over;
    over.Foo();                        // Overrider.Foo
    b1.Foo();                          // Overrider.Foo

    Hider h = new Hider();
    BaseClass b2 = h;
    h.Foo();                           // Hider.Foo
    b2.Foo();                          // BaseClass.Foo
```

Sealing Functions and Classes

An overridden function member may *seal* its implementation so that it cannot be
overridden by further subclassing. In our earlier virtual function member example,
we could have sealed House's implementation of Liability. This prevents a class
that derives from House from overriding Liability, which provides a guarantee on
the behavior of House:

```
    public class Asset
    {
      ...
      public virtual decimal Liability { get { return 0; } }
    }

    public class House : Asset
    {
      ...
      public sealed override decimal Liability { get { return Mortgage; } }
    }
```

You can also seal the class itself (which implicitly seals all the virtual functions)
and prevent subtyping, as follows:

```
    sealed class Stock { ... }
```

Sealing a class is much more common than sealing a function member.

The base Keyword

The base keyword is similar to the this keyword. It serves two essential purposes:

- Accessing an overridden function member from the subclass
- Calling a base class constructor (see the next section)

In this example, House uses the base keyword to access Asset's implementation of Liability:

```
public class House : Asset
{
  ...
  public sealed override decimal Liability
  {
    get { return base.Liability + Mortgage; }
  }
}
```

The same approach works if Liability is *hidden* rather than *overridden*. (You can also access hidden members by casting to the base class before invoking the function.)

Constructors and Inheritance

A subclass must declare its own constructors. For example, if we define Subclass as follows:

```
public class Baseclass
{
  public int X;
  public Baseclass (int x) {this.X = x;}
}

public class Subclass : Baseclass
{
}
```

the following is illegal:

```
Subclass s = new Subclass (123);
```

Subclass must hence redeclare any constructors it wants to expose. In doing so, however, it can call any of the base class's constructors with the base keyword:

```
public class Subclass : Baseclass
{
  public Subclass (int x) : base (x) {}
}
```

The base keyword works rather like the this keyword, except that it calls a constructor in the base class.

Base class constructors always execute first; this ensures that *base* initialization occurs before *specialized* initialization.

Implicit calling of the parameterless base class constructor

If a constructor in a subclass omits the base keyword, the base type's *parameterless* constructor is implicitly called:

```
public class BaseClass
{
  public int X;
  public BaseClass () { X = 1; }
}

public class Subclass : BaseClass
{
  public Subclass() {Console.WriteLine (X);}  // 1
}
```

If the base class has no parameterless constructor, subclasses are forced to use the base keyword in their constructors.

Constructor and field initialization order

When an object is instantiated, initialization takes place in the following order:

1. From subclass to base class:
    a. Fields are initialized.
    b. Constructor arguments are evaluated.
2. From base class to subclass:
    a. Constructor bodies execute.

The following code demonstrates:

```
public class B
{
  int x = 0;         // Executes 3rd
  public B(...)      // Executes 4th
  {
     ...             // Executes 5th
  }
}

public class D : B
{
  int y = 0;         // Executes 1st
  public D(...)      // Executes 2nd
  {
     ...             // Executes 6th
  }
}
```

Overloading and Resolution

Inheritance has an interesting impact on method overloading. Consider the following two overloads:

```
static void Foo (Asset a) {}
static void Foo (House h) {}
```

When an overload is called, the most specific type has precedence:

```
House h = new House (...);
Foo(h);                         // calls Foo(House)
```

The particular overload to call is determined statically (at compile time) rather than dynamically (at runtime). The following code calls Foo(Asset), even though the runtime type of a is House:

```
Asset a = new House (...);
Foo(a);                         // calls Foo(Asset)
```

The object Type

object (System.Object) is the ultimate base class for all types. Any type can be upcast to object.

To illustrate how this is useful, consider a general-purpose *stack*. A stack is a data structure based on the principle of LIFO—"Last-In First-Out." A stack has two operations: *push* an object on the stack, and *pop* an object off the stack. Here is a simple implementation that can hold up to 10 objects:

```
public class Stack
{
  int position;
  object[] data = new object[10];
  public void Push (object obj)   { data[position++] = obj;  }
  public object Pop ()            { return data[--position]; }
}
```

Because Stack works with the object type, we can Push and Pop instances of *any type* to and from the Stack:

```
Stack stack = new Stack();
stack.Push ("sausage");
string s = (string) stack.Pop();   // Downcast, so explicit cast is needed

Console.WriteLine (s);             // sausage
```

object is a reference type, by virtue of being a class. Despite this, value types, such as int, can also be cast to and from object, and so be added to our stack. This feature of C# is called *type unification* and is demonstrated here:

```
stack.Push (3);
int three = (int) stack.Pop();
```

When you cast between a value type and object, the CLR must perform some special work to bridge the difference in semantics between value and reference types. This process is called *boxing* and *unboxing*.

Boxing and Unboxing

Boxing is the act of casting a value type instance to a reference type instance. The reference type may be either the object class or an interface (which we will visit later in the chapter). In this example, we box an int into an object:

```
int x = 9;
object obj = x;          // box the int
```

Unboxing reverses the operation, by casting the object back to the original value type:

```
int y = (int)obj;        // unbox the int
```

Unboxing requires an explicit cast. The runtime checks that the stated value type (exactly) matches the actual object type, and throws an InvalidCastException if the check fails. For instance, the following throws an exception, because long does not exactly match int:

```
object obj = 9;          // 9 is inferred to be of type int
long x = (long) obj;     // InvalidCastException
```

The following succeeds, however:

```
object obj = 9;
long x = (int) obj;
```

As does this:

```
object obj = 3.5;        // 3.5 is inferred to be of type double
int x = (int) (double) obj;    // x is now 3
```

In the last example, (int) performs a *conversion*; (double) performs an *unboxing*.

Copying semantics of boxing and unboxing

Boxing copies the value type instance into the new object, and unboxing copies the contents of the object back into a value type instance.

Static and Dynamic Type Checking

C# checks types both statically and dynamically.

Static type checking occurs at compile time. Static type checking enables the compiler to verify the correctness of your program without running it. The following code will fail because the compiler enforces static typing:

```
int x = "5";
```

Dynamic type checking occurs at *runtime*. Whenever an unboxing or downcast occurs, the runtime checks the type dynamically. For example:

```
object y = "5";
int z = (int)y;          // runtime error, downcast failed
```

Dynamic type checking is possible because each object on the heap internally stores a little type token. This token can be retrieved by calling the GetType method of object.

The GetType Method and typeof Operator

All types in C# are represented at runtime with an instance of System.Type. There are two basic ways to get a System.Type object:

- Call GetType on the instance.
- Use the typeof operator on a type name.

GetType is evaluated dynamically at runtime; typeof is evaluated statically at compile time.

System.Type has properties for such things as the type's name, assembly, base type, and so on. For example:

```
using System;

public class Point {public int X, Y;}

class Test
{
  static void Main( )
  {
    Point p = new Point( );
    Console.WriteLine (p.GetType( ).Name);           // Point
    Console.WriteLine (typeof (Point).Name);         // Point
    Console.WriteLine (p.GetType( ) == typeof(Point)); // True
    Console.WriteLine (p.X.GetType( ).Name);         // Int32
    Console.WriteLine (p.Y.GetType( ).FullName);     // System.Int32
  }
}
```

System.Type also has methods that act as a gateway to the runtime's reflection model, described in Chapter 17.

The ToString Method

The ToString method returns the default textual representation of a type instance. This method is overridden by all built-in types. Here is an example of using the int type's ToString method:

```
int x = 1;
string s = x.ToString( );      // s is "1"
```

You can override the ToString method on custom types as follows:

```
public class Panda
{
  public string Name;
  public override string ToString( ) {return Name;}
}
...

Panda p = new Panda( );
p.Name = "Petey";
Console.WriteLine(p);    // Petey
```

When you call an overridden object member such as ToString directly on a value type, boxing doesn't occur. Boxing occurs only when you cast:

```
int x = 1;
string s1 = x.ToString();    // calling on nonboxed value
object box = x;
string s2 = box.ToString();  // calling on boxed value
```

Object Member Listing

Here are all the members of object:

```
public class Object
{
  public Object();

  public extern Type GetType();

  public virtual bool Equals (object obj);
  public static bool Equals  (object objA, object objB);
  public static bool ReferenceEquals (object objA, object objB);

  public virtual int GetHashCode();

  public virtual string ToString();

  protected override void Finalize();
  protected extern object MemberwiseClone();
}
```

We describe the Equals, ReferenceEquals, and GetHashCode methods in the section "Equality comparison" in Chapter 6.

Structs

A struct is similar to a class, with the following key differences:

- A struct is a value type, whereas a class is a reference type.
- A struct does not support inheritance (other than implicitly deriving from object).

A struct can have all the members a class can, except the following:

- A parameterless constructor
- A finalizer
- Virtual members

A struct is used instead of a class when value type semantics are desirable. Good examples of structs are numeric types, where it is more natural for assignment to copy a value rather than a reference. Because a struct is a value type, each instance does not require instantiation of an object on the heap. This can be important when creating many instances of a type.

Struct Construction Semantics

The construction semantics of a struct are as follows:

- A parameterless constructor that you can't override implicitly exists. This performs a bitwise-zeroing of its fields.
- When you define a struct constructor, you must explicitly assign every field.
- You can't have field initializers in a struct.

Here is an example of declaring and calling struct constructors:

```
public struct Point
{
  int x, y;
  public Point (int x, int y) {this.x = x; this.y = y;}
}

...
Point p1 = new Point ();      // p1.x and p1.y will be 0
Point p2 = new Point (1, 1);  // p1.x and p1.y will be 1
```

The next example generates three compile-time errors:

```
public struct Point
{
  int x = 1;                      // illegal, cannot initialize field
  int y;
  public Point() {}               // illegal, cannot have
                                  // parameterless constructor

  public Point(int x) {this.x = x;}  // illegal, must assign field y
}
```

Changing struct to class makes this example legal.

Access Modifiers

To promote encapsulation, a type or type member may limit its *accessibility* to other types and other assemblies by adding one of five *access modifiers* to the declaration:

public
> Fully accessible. The implicit accessibility for members of an enum or interface.

internal
> Accessible only within containing assembly or friend assemblies. The default accessibility for nonnested types.

private
> Visible only within containing type. The default accessibility members of a class or struct.

protected
> Visible only within containing type or subclasses.

protected *internal*
> The *union* of protected and internal accessibility. (This is *less* restrictive than protected or internal alone.)

 The CLR has the concept of the *intersection* of protected and internal accessibility, but C# does not support this.

Examples

Class2 is accessible from outside its assembly; Class1 is not:

```
class Class1 {}                    // Class1 is internal (default)
public class Class2 {}             //
```

ClassB exposes field x to other types in the same assembly; ClassA does not:

```
class ClassA { int x;          } // x is private (default)
class ClassB { internal int x; }
```

Functions within Subclass can call Bar but not Foo:

```
class BaseClass
{
  void Foo()            {}        // Foo is private (default)
  protected void Bar() {}
}

class Subclass : BaseClass
{
    void Test1() { Foo(); }       // Error - cannot access Foo
    void Test2() { Bar(); }       // OK
}
```

Accessibility Capping

A type caps the accessibility of its declared members. The most common example of capping is when you have an internal type with public members. For example:

```
class C { public void Foo() {} }
```

C's (default) internal accessibility caps Foo's accessibility, effectively making Foo internal. The reason Foo would be marked public is to make for easier refactoring, should C later be changed to public.

Restrictions on Access Modifiers

When overriding a base class function, accessibility must be identical on the overridden function. For example:

```
class BaseClass            { protected virtual  void Foo() {} }
class Subclass1 : BaseClass { protected override void Foo() {} } // ok
class Subclass2 : BaseClass { public    override void Foo() {} } // error
```

The compiler prevents any inconsistent use of access modifiers. For example, a subclass itself can be less accessible than a base class, but not more:

```
internal class A {}
public class B : A {}               // error
```

Interfaces

An interface is similar to a class, but it provides a specification rather than an implementation for its members. An interface is special in the following ways:

- A class can implement *multiple* interfaces. In contrast, a class can inherit from only a *single* class.
- Interface members are *all implicitly abstract*. In contrast, a class can provide both abstract members and concrete members with implementations.
- *Structs* can implement interfaces. In contrast, a struct cannot inherit from a class.

An interface declaration is like a class declaration, but it provides no implementation for its members, since all its members are implicitly abstract. These members will be implemented by the classes and structs that implement the interface. An interface can contain only methods, properties, events, and indexers, which noncoincidentally are precisely the members of a class that can be abstract.

Here is a slightly simplified version of the IEnumerator interface, defined in System.Collections:

```
public interface IEnumerator
{
  bool MoveNext();
  object Current {get;}
}
```

Interface members have the same accessibility as the interface type and cannot declare an access modifier.

Implementing an interface means providing a public implementation for all its members:

```
internal class Countdown : IEnumerator
{
  int count = 11;
  public bool MoveNext () { return count-- > 0 ;  }
  public object Current   { get { return count; } }
}
```

You can implicitly cast an object to any interface that it implements. For example:

```
IEnumerator e = new Countdown();
while (e.MoveNext())
  Console.Write (e.Current);      // 109876543210
```

Even though `Countdown` is an internal class, its members that implement `IEnumerator` can be called publicly by casting an instance of
`Countdown` to `IEnumerator`. For instance, if a public type in the same
assembly defined a method as follows:

```
public static class Util
{
    public static object GetCountDown( ) { return new
CountDown( ); }
}
```

a caller from another assembly could do this:

```
IEnumerator e = (IEnumerator) Util.GetCountDown( );
e.MoveNext( );
```

If `IEnumerator` was itself defined as internal, this wouldn't be
possible.

Extending an Interface

Interfaces may derive from other interfaces. For instance:

```
public interface IUndoable              { void Undo( ); }
public interface IRedoable : IUndoable { void Redo( ); }
```

`IRedoable` inherits all the members of `IUndoable`.

Explicit Interface Implementation

Implementing multiple interfaces can sometimes result in a collision between
member signatures. You can resolve such collisions by *explicitly implementing* an
interface member. Consider the following example:

```
interface I1 { void Foo( ); }
interface I2 { int Foo( ); }

public class Widget : I1, I2
{
  public void Foo ( )
  {
    Console.WriteLine ("Widget's implementation of I1.Foo");
  }

  int I2.Foo ( )
  {
    Console.WriteLine ("Widget's implementation of I2.Foo");
    return 42;
  }
}
```

Because both `I1` and `I2` have conflicting `Foo` signatures, `Widget` explicitly implements `I2`'s `Foo` method. This lets the two methods coexist in one class. The only
way to call an explicitly implemented member is to cast to its interface:

```
Widget w = new Widget( );
w.Foo( );                           // Widget's implementation of I1.Foo
```

```
((I1)w).Foo( );                   // Widget's implementation of I1.Foo
((I2)w).Foo( );                   // Widget's implementation of I2.Foo
```

Another reason to explicitly implement interface members is to hide members that are highly specialized and distracting to a type's normal use case. For example, a type that implements ISerializable would typically want to avoid flaunting its ISerializable members unless explicitly cast to that interface.

Implementing Interface Members Virtually

An implicitly implemented interface member is, by default, sealed. It must be marked virtual or abstract in the base class in order to be overridden. For example:

```
public interface IUndoable { void Undo( ); }

public class TextBox : IUndoable
{
  public virtual void Undo( )
  {
     Console.WriteLine ("TextBox.Undo");
  }
}

public class RichTextBox : TextBox
{
  public override void Undo( )
  {
     Console.WriteLine ("RichTextBox.Undo");
  }
}
```

Calling the interface member through either the base class or the interface calls the subclass's implementation:

```
RichTextBox r = new RichTextBox( );
r.Undo( );                         // RichTextBox.Undo
((IUndoable)r).Undo( );            // RichTextBox.Undo
((TextBox)r).Undo( );              // RichTextBox.Undo
```

An explicitly implemented interface member cannot be marked virtual, nor can it be overridden in the usual manner. It can, however, be *reimplemented*.

Reimplementing an Interface in a Subclass

A subclass can reimplement any interface member already implemented by a base class. Reimplementation hijacks a member implementation (when called through the interface) and works whether or not the member is virtual in the base class. It also works whether a member is implemented implicitly and explicitly—although it works best in the latter case, as we will demonstrate.

In the following example, TextBox implements IUndo.Undo explicitly, and so it cannot be marked as virtual. In order to "override" it, RichTextBox must reimplement IUndo's Undo method.

```
public interface IUndoable { void Undo( ); }

public class TextBox : IUndoable
{
  void IUndoable.Undo( ) { Console.WriteLine ("TextBox.Undo"); }
}

public class RichTextBox : TextBox, IUndoable
{
  public new void Undo( ) { Console.WriteLine ("RichTextBox.Undo"); }
}
```

Calling the reimplemented member through the interface calls the subclass's implementation:

```
RichTextBox r = new RichTextBox( );
r.Undo( );                    // RichTextBox.Undo    Case 1
((IUndoable)r).Undo( );       // RichTextBox.Undo    Case 2
```

Assuming the same RichTextBox definition, suppose that TextBox implemented Undo *implicitly*:

```
public class TextBox : IUndoable
{
  public void Undo( ) { Console.WriteLine ("TextBox.Undo"); }
}
```

This would give us another way to call Undo, which would "break" the system, as shown in Case 3:

```
RichTextBox r = new RichTextBox( );
r.Undo( );                    // RichTextBox.Undo    Case 1
((IUndoable)r).Undo( );       // RichTextBox.Undo    Case 2
((TextBox)r).Undo( );         // TextBox.Undo        Case 3
```

Case 3 demonstrates that reimplementation hijacking is effective only when a member is called through the interface and not through the base class. This is usually undesirable as it can mean inconsistent semantics. This makes reimplementation most appropriate as a strategy for overriding *explicitly* implemented interface members.

Alternatives to interface reimplementation

Even with explicit member implementation, interface reimplementation is problematic for a couple of reasons:

- The subclass has no way to call the base class method.
- The base class author may not anticipate that a method be reimplemented and may not allow for the potential consequences.

Reimplementation can be a good last resort when subclassing hasn't been anticipated. A better option, however, is to design a base class such that reimplementation will never be required. There are two ways to achieve this:

- When implicitly implementing a member, mark it virtual if appropriate.

• When explicitly implementing a member, use the following pattern if you anticipate that subclasses might need to override any logic:

```
public class TextBox : IUndoable
{
  void IUndoable.Undo()         { Undo(); }   // Calls method below
  protected virtual void Undo() { Console.WriteLine ("TextBox.Undo"); }
}

public class RichTextBox : TextBox
{
  protected override void Undo() { Console.WriteLine
      ("RichTextBox.Undo"); }
}
```

If you don't anticipate any subclassing, you can mark the class as sealed to preempt interface reimplementation.

Interfaces and Boxing

Casting a struct to an interface causes boxing. Calling an implicitly implemented member on a struct does not cause boxing:

```
interface  I { void Foo();         }
struct S : I { public void Foo() {} }


...
S s = new S();
s.Foo();          // no boxing

I i = s;          // box occurs when casting to interface
i.Foo();
```

Writing a Class Versus an Interface

As a general rule:

• Use classes and subclasses for types that naturally share an implementation.
• Use interfaces for types that have independent implementations.

Consider the following classes:

```
abstract class Animal {}
abstract class Bird          : Animal {}
abstract class Insect        : Animal {}
abstract class FlyingCreature : Animal {}
abstract class Carnivore     : Animal {}

// Concrete classes:

class Ostrich : Bird {}
class Eagle   : Bird, FlyingCreature, Carnivore {}   // Illegal
class Bee     : Insect, FlyingCreature {}            // Illegal
class Flea    : Insect, Carnivore {}                 // Illegal
```

The Eagle, Bee, and Flea classes do not compile because inheriting from multiple classes is prohibited. To resolve this, we must convert some of the types to interfaces. The question then arises, which types? Following our general rule, we could say that insects share an implementation, and birds share an implementation, so they remain classes. In contrast, flying creatures have independent mechanisms for flying, and carnivores have independent strategies for eating animals, so we would convert FlyingCreature and Carnivore to interfaces:

```
interface IFlyingCreature {}
interface ICarnivore      {}
```

In a typical scenario, Bird and Insect might correspond to a Windows control and a web control; FlyingCreature and Carnivore might correspond to IPrintable and IUndoable.

Enums

An enum is a special value type that lets you specify a group of named numeric constants. For example:

```
public enum BorderSide { Left, Right, Top, Bottom }
```

We can use this enum type as follows:

```
BorderSide topSide = BorderSide.Top;
bool isTop = (topSide == BorderSide.Top);    // true
```

Each enum member has an underlying integral value. By default:

- Underlying values are of type int.
- The constants 0, 1, 2... are automatically assigned, in the declaration order of the enum members.

You may specify an alternative integral type, as follows:

```
public enum BorderSide : byte { Left, Right, Top, Bottom }
```

You may also specify an explicit underlying value for each enum member:

```
public enum BorderSide : byte { Left=1, Right=2, Top=10, Bottom=11 }
```

 The compiler also lets you explicitly assign *some* of the enum members. The unassigned enum members keep incrementing from the last explicit value. The preceding example is equivalent to the following:

```
public enum BorderSide : byte { Left=1, Right, Top=10,
Bottom }
```

Enum Conversions

You can convert an enum instance to and from its underlying integral value with an explicit cast:

```
int i = (int) BorderSide.Left;
BorderSide side = (BorderSide) i;
bool horizontal = (int) side <= 2;
```

You can also explicitly cast one enum type to another. Suppose HorizontalAlignment is defined as follows:

```
public enum HorizontalAlignment
{
  Left = BorderSide.Left,
  Right = BorderSide.Right,
  Center
}
```

A translation between the enum types uses the underlying integral values:

```
HorizontalAlignment h = (HorizontalAlignment) BorderSide.Right;
// same as:
HorizontalAlignment h = (HorizontalAlignment) (int) BorderSide.Right;
```

The numeric literal 0 is treated specially by the compiler in an enum expression and does not require an explicit cast:

```
BorderSide b = 0;     // no cast required
if (b == 0) ...
```

There are two reasons for the special treatment of 0:

- The first member of an enum is often used as the "default" value.
- For *combined enum* types, 0 means "no flags."

Flags Enumerations

You can combine enum members. To prevent ambiguities, members of a combinable enum require explicitly assigned values, typically in powers of two. For example:

```
[Flags]
public enum BorderSides { Left=1, Right=2, Top=4, Bottom=8 }
```

To work with combined enum values, you use bitwise operators, such as | and &. These operate on the underlying integral values:

```
BorderSides leftRight = BorderSides.Left | BorderSides.Right;

if ((leftRight & BorderSides.Left) != 0)
    System.Console.WriteLine ("Includes Left");    // Includes Left

string formatted = leftRight.ToString();   // "Left, Right"

BorderSides s = BorderSides.Left;
s |= BorderSides.Right;
Console.WriteLine (s == leftRight);   // True

s ^= BorderSides.Right;                   // Toggles BorderSides.Right
Console.WriteLine (s);                    // Left
```

By convention, the Flags attribute should always be applied to an enum type when its members are combinable. If you declare such an enum without the Flags attribute, you can still combine members, but calling ToString on an enum instance will emit a number rather than a series of names.

By convention, a combinable enum type is given a plural rather than singular name.

For convenience, you can include combination members within an enum declaration itself:

```
[Flags]
public enum BorderSides
{
  Left=1, Right=2, Top=4, Bottom=8,
  LeftRight = Left | Right,
  TopBottom = Top  | Bottom,
  All       = LeftRight | TopBottom
}
```

Enum Operators

The operators that work with enums are:

```
=   ==   !=   <   >   <=   >=   +   -   ^   &   |   ~
+=  -=   ++  --   sizeof
```

The bitwise, arithmetic, and comparison operators return the result of processing the underlying integral values. Addition and subtraction are permitted between an enum and an integral type, but not between two enums.

Type-Safety Issues

Consider the following enum:

```
public enum BorderSide { Left, Right, Top, Bottom }
```

Since an enum can be cast to and from its underlying integral type, the actual value it may have may fall outside the bounds of a legal enum member. For example:

```
BorderSide b = (BorderSide) 12345;
Console.WriteLine (b);              // 12345
```

The bitwise and arithmetic operators can produce similarly invalid values:

```
BorderSide b = BorderSide.Bottom;
b++;                               // No errors
```

An invalid BorderSide would break the following code:

```
void Draw (BorderSide side)
{
  if      (side == BorderSide.Left)  {...}
  else if (side == BorderSide.Right) {...}
  else if (side == BorderSide.Top)   {...}
  else                               {...} // assume BorderSide.Bottom
}
```

One solution is to add another else clause:

```
...
else if (side == BorderSide.Bottom) ...
else throw new ArgumentException ("Invalid BorderSide: " + side, "side");
```

Another workaround is to explicitly check an enum value for validity. The static `Enum.IsDefined` method does this job:

```
BorderSide side = (BorderSide) 12345;
Console.WriteLine (typeof(BorderSide), Enum.IsDefined (side));    // False
```

Unfortunately, `Enum.IsDefined` does not work for flagged enums. However, the following helper method (a trick dependent on the behavior of `Enum.ToString( )`) returns true if a given flagged enum is valid:

```
static bool IsFlagDefined (Enum e)
{
  decimal d;
  return ! decimal.TryParse(e.ToString( ), out d);
}

[Flags]
public enum BorderSides { Left=1, Right=2, Top=4, Bottom=8 }

static void Main( )
{
  for (int i = 0; i <= 16; i++)
  {
    BorderSides side = (BorderSides)i;
    Console.WriteLine (IsFlagDefined (side) + " " + side);
  }
}
```

Nested Types

A *nested type* is declared within the scope of another type. For example:

```
class TopLevel
{
  class Nested { }
}
```

A nested type has the following features:

- It can access the enclosing type's private members and everything else the enclosing type can access.
- It can be declared with the full range of access modifiers, rather than just `public` and `internal`.
- The default visibility for a nested type is `private` rather than `internal`.
- Accessing a nested type from outside the enclosing type requires qualification with the enclosing type's name (like when accessing static members).

All types can be nested; however, only classes and structs can *nest*.

Here is an example of accessing a private member of a type from a nested type:

```
public class TopLevel
{
  static int x;
```

```
class Nested
{
  static void Foo( ) {Console.WriteLine (TopLevel.x);}
}
}
```

Here is an example of applying the protected access modifier to a nested type:

```
public class TopLevel
{
  protected class Nested { }
}

public class SubTopLevel : TopLevel
{
  static void Foo() { new TopLevel.Nested( ); }
}
```

Here is an example of referring to a nested type from outside the enclosing type:

```
public class TopLevel
{
  public class Nested { }
}

class Test
{
  TopLevel.Nested n;
}
```

Nested types are used heavily by the compiler itself, when it generates private classes that capture state for constructs such as iterators and anonymous methods.

> If the sole reason for using a nested type is to avoid cluttering a namespace with too many types, use a nested namespace instead. A nested type should be used because of its stronger access control restrictions, or when the nested class must access private members of the containing class.

Generics

C# has two separate mechanisms for writing code that is reusable across different types: *inheritance* and *generics*. Whereas inheritance expresses reusability with a base type, generics express reusability with a "template" that contains "placeholder" types. Generics, when compared to inheritance, can *increase type safety* and *reduce casting and boxing*.

> C# generics and C++ templates are similar concepts, but they work differently. We explain this difference in the section "C# Generics Versus C++ Templates," later in this chapter.

Generic Types

A generic type declares *generic parameters*—placeholder types to be filled in by the consumer of the generic type, which supplies the *generic arguments*. Here is a generic type Stack<T>, designed to stack instances of type T. Stack<T> declares a single generic parameter T:

```
public class Stack<T>
{
  int position;
  T[] data = new T[100];
  public void Push (T obj)      { data[position++] = obj;  }
  public T Pop ()               { return data[--position]; }
}
```

We can use Stack<T> as follows:

```
Stack<int> stack = new Stack<int>();
stack.Push(5);
stack.Push(10);
int x = stack.Pop();
```

Stack<int> fills in the generic parameter T with the generic argument int, implicitly creating a type on the fly (the synthesis occurs at runtime). Stack<int> effectively has the following definition (substitutions appear in bold, with the class name hashed out to avoid confusion):

```
public class ###
{
  int position;
  int[] data;
  public void Push (int obj)    { data[position++] = obj;  }
  public int Pop ()             { return data[--position]; }
}
```

Technically, we say that Stack<T> is an *open type*, whereas Stack<int> is a *closed type*. You can only instantiate a closed type, because all the placeholder types must be filled in.

Why Generics Exist

Generics exist to write code that is reusable across different types. Suppose we need a stack of integers, but we don't have generic types. We would have two options. The first and most primitive solution is to copy code from an existing stack implementation, changing the name of the type and the element type to match our specific element type:

```
public class IntStack
{
  int position;
  int[] data = new int [10];
  public void Push (int obj)    { data[position++] = obj;  }
  public int Pop ()             { return data[--position]; }
}
```

Clearly, the problem with this approach is that you have to write a new implementation every time you want a different element type. We can overcome this problem with a second option. We can use inheritance, and write a stack that is generalized by using object as the element type:

```
public class ObjectStack
{
  int position;
  object[] data = new object[10];
  public void Push (object obj)   { data[position++] = obj;  }
  public object Pop ()            { return data[--position]; }
}
```

However, ObjectStack doesn't work as well as IntStack for specifically stacking integers. Despite the ugliness of having to copy and paste code, IntStack gives us *increased type safety* and *reduced casting and boxing*, when compared to ObjectStack. The following code comparison shows the use of ObjectStack versus IntStack:

```
{
  ObjectStack stack = new ObjectStack(); // creates object[], boxed storage
  stack.Push ("s");                      // no error pushing wrong type
  int i = (int)stack.Pop();              // downcast needed, runtime error
}
{
  IntStack stack = new IntStack();       // creates int[], nonboxed storage
  stack.Push ("s");                      // compile error pushing wrong type
  int i = stack.Pop();                   // downcast unnecessary, can't fail
}
```

What we need is both a general implementation of a stack that works for all element types, and a way to easily specialize that stack to a specific element type for increased type safety and reduced casting and boxing. Generics give us precisely this, by allowing us to parameterize the element type. Stack<T> has the benefits of both ObjectStack and IntStack. Like ObjectStack, Stack<T> is written once to work *generally* across all types. Like IntStack, Stack<T> is *specialized* for a particular type—the beauty is that this type is T, which we substitute on the fly.

ObjectStack is functionally equivalent to Stack<object>.

IntStack is functionally equivalent to Stack<int>.

Generic Methods

A generic method declares generic parameters within the signature of a method.

With generic methods, many fundamental algorithms can be implemented in a general-purpose way only. Here is a generic method that swaps two values of any type:

```
static void Swap<T> (ref T a, ref T b)
{
  T temp = b;
  a = b;
```

```
        b = temp;
    }
```

Swap<T> can be used as follows:

```
    int x = 5;
    int y = 10;
    Swap (ref x, ref y);
```

Generally, there is no need to supply type parameters to a generic method, because the compiler can implicitly infer the type. If there is ambiguity, generic methods can be called with the type parameters as follows:

```
    Swap<int> (ref x, ref y);
```

Within a generic *type*, a method is not classed as generic unless it *introduces* generic parameters (with the angle bracket syntax). The Pop method in our generic stack merely uses the type's existing generic parameter, T, and is not classed as a generic method.

Methods and types are the only constructs that can introduce generic parameters. Properties, indexers, events, fields, methods, operators, and so on cannot declare generic parameters, although they can partake in any generic parameters already declared by their enclosing type. In our generic stack example, for instance, we could write an indexer that returns a generic item:

```
    public T this [int index] { get { return data [position]; } }
```

Declaring Generic Parameters

Generic parameters can be introduced in the declaration of classes, structs, interfaces, delegates (covered in Chapter 4), and methods. Other constructs, such as properties, cannot *introduce* a generic parameter, but can *use* one. For example, the property Value uses T:

```
    public struct Nullable<T>
    {
        public T Value {get;}
    }
```

A generic type or method can have multiple parameters. For example:

```
    class Dictionary<TKeyType, TValueType> {...}
```

To instantiate:

```
    Dictionary<int,string> myDic = new Dictionary<int,string>( );
```

Or (in C# 3.0):

```
    var myDic = new Dictionary<int,string>( );
```

Generic type names and method names can be overloaded as long as the number of generic parameters is different. For example, the following two type names do not conflict:

```
    class A<T> {}
    class A<T1,T2> {}
```

By convention, generic types and methods with a *single* generic parameter typically name their parameter T, as long as the intent of the parameter is clear. When using *multiple* generic parameters, each parameter is prefixed with T, but has a more descriptive name.

typeof and Generics

The typeof operator requires specifying the number of parameters when asking for the type of an open type, as follows:

```
class A<T> {}
class A<T1,T2> {}
...

Type a1 = typeof(A<>);
Type a2 = typeof(A<,>);
```

Here is an example of asking for the type of a closed type:

```
Type a3 = typeof(A<int,int>);
```

The default Generic Value

The default keyword can be used to get the default value given a generic type argument. The default value for a reference type is null, and the default value for a value type is the result of bitwise-zeroing the value type's fields:

```
static void Zap<T> (T[] array)
{
  for (int i = 0; i < array.Length; i++)
    array[i] = default(T);
}
```

Generic Constraints

By default, a generic parameter can be substituted with any type whatsoever. *Constraints* can be applied to a generic parameter to require more specific type arguments. These are the possible constraints:

```
where T : base-class    // Base class constraint
where T : interface     // Interface constraint
where T : class         // Class constraint
where T : struct        // Struct constraint
where T : new()         // Parameterless constructor constraint
where U : T             // Naked type constraint
```

In the following example, GenericClass<T> requires T to derive from SomeClass and implement Interface1:

```
class     SomeClass {}
interface Interface1 {}

class GenericClass<T> where T : SomeClass, Interface1 {}
```

Constraints can be applied wherever generic parameters are defined, in both methods and type definitions.

A *base class constraint* or *interface constraint* specifies that the type parameter must subclass or implement a particular class or interface. This allows instances of that type to be implicitly cast to that class or interface. For example, suppose we want to write a generic Max method, which returns the maximum of two values. We can take advantage of the generic interface defined in the framework called IComparable<T>:

```
public interface IComparable<T>
{
   int CompareTo (T other);
}
```

CompareTo returns a positive number if other is greater than this. Using this interface as a constraint, we can write a Max method as follows (to avoid distraction, null checking is omitted):

```
static T Max <T> (T a, T b) where T : IComparable<T>
{
   return a.CompareTo (b) > 0 ? a : b;
}
```

The Max method can accept arguments of any type implementing IComparable<T> (which includes most built-in types such as int and string):

```
int z = Max (5, 10);              // 10
string last = Max ("ant", "zoo");  // zoo
```

The *class constraint* and *struct constraint* simply specify that T must be a class or a struct. A great example of the struct constraint is the System.Nullable<T> struct (we will discuss this class in depth in the section "Nullable Types" in Chapter 4):

```
struct Nullable<T> where T : struct {...}
```

The *parameterless constructor constraint* requires T to have a public parameterless constructor. If this constraint is defined, you can call new( ) on T:

```
static void Initialize<T> (T[] array) where T : new( )
{
   for (int i = 0; i < array.Length; i++)
      array[i] = new T( );
}
```

The *naked type constraint* requires one generic parameter to derive from *another generic parameter*. In this example, the method FilteredStack returns another Stack, containing only the subset of elements where the generic parameter T is of the generic parameter U:

```
class Stack<T>
{
   Stack<U> FilteredStack<U>( ) where U : T {...}
}
```

Generics and Covariance

Generic types are not covariant. This means that even if B can be cast to A, T<B> cannot be cast to T<A>. For example, suppose Animal and Bear are defined as follows:

```
class Animal {}
class Bear : Animal {}
```

The following is illegal:

```
Stack<Bear> bears = new Stack <Bear>();
Stack<Animal> animals = bears;          // compile-time error
```

Lack of covariance can hinder reusability. Suppose, for instance, we want to write a method to Wash a stack of animals:

```
public class ZooCleaner
{
    public static void Wash (Stack<Animal> animals) {...}
}
```

Calling Wash with a stack of bears would generate a compile-time error. The workaround is to redefine the Wash method with a constraint:

```
public class ZooCleaner
{
    public static void Wash<T> (Stack<T> animals) where T : Animal {}
}
```

We can now call Wash as follows:

```
Stack<Bear> bears = new Stack<Bear>();
ZooCleaner.Wash (bears);
```

A comparison of generic types and array types

Strangely, unlike generic types, array types are covariant. This means that if B can be cast to A, B[] can be cast to A[]. For example:

```
Bear[] bears = new Bear[3];
Animal[] animals = bears;       // ok
```

A corollary of this is that element assignments require runtime type checking. For example:

```
animals[0] = new Camel();          // runtime exception
```

Subclassing Generic Types

A generic class can be subclassed just like a nongeneric class. The subclass can leave the base class's generic parameters open, as in the following example:

```
class Stack <T>                   {...}
class SpecialStack <T> : Stack <T> {...}
```

Or the subclass can close the generic type parameters with a concrete type:

```
class IntStack : Stack<int> { ... }
```

A subtype can also introduce fresh generic arguments:

```
class Single<T> { ... }
class Double<T,U> : Single<T> { ... }
```

Self-Referencing Generic Declarations

A type can name *itself* as the concrete type when closing a generic argument:

```
interface IEquatable<T> { bool Equals (T obj); }

public class Balloon : IEquatable<Balloon>
{
  string color;
  int cc;

  public bool Equals (Balloon b)
  {
    if (b == null) return false;
    return b.color == color && b.cc == cc;
  }
}
```

Static Data

Static data is unique for each closed type:

```
public class Bob<T> { public static int Count; }

class Test
{
  static void Main( )
  {
    Console.WriteLine (++Bob<int>.Count);     // 1
    Console.WriteLine (++Bob<int>.Count);     // 2
    Console.WriteLine (++Bob<string>.Count);  // 1
    Console.WriteLine (++Bob<object>.Count);  // 1
  }
}
```

C# Generics Versus C++ Templates

C# generics are similar in application to C++ templates, but they work very differently. In both cases, a synthesis between the producer and consumer must take place, where the placeholder types of the producer are filled in by the consumer. However, with C# generics, producer types (i.e., open types such as List<T>) can be compiled into a library (such as *mscorlib.dll*). This works because the synthesis between the producer and the consumer that produces closed types doesn't actually happen until runtime. With C++ templates, this synthesis is performed at compile time. This means that in C++ you don't deploy template libraries as *.dlls*—they exist only as source code. It also makes it difficult to dynamically inspect, let alone create, parameterized types on the fly.

To dig deeper into why this is the case, consider the Max method in C#, once more:

```
static T Max <T> (T a, T b) where T : IComparable<T>
{
  return a.CompareTo (b) > 0 ? a : b;
}
```

Why couldn't we have implemented it like this?

```
static T Max <T> (T a, T b)
{
  return a > b ? a : b;              // compile error
}
```

The reason is that Max needs to be compiled once and work for all possible values of T. Compilation cannot succeed, because there is no single meaning for > across all values of T—in fact, not every T even has a > operator. In contrast, the following code shows the same Max method written with C++ templates. This code will be compiled separately for each value of T, taking on whatever semantics > has for a particular T, failing to compile if a particular T does not support the > operator:

```
template <class T> T Max (T a, T b)
{
  return a > b ? a : b;
}
```

4

Advanced C#

In this chapter, we cover advanced C# topics that build on concepts explored in previous chapters. You should read the first four sections sequentially; you can read the remaining sections in any order.

Delegates

A delegate dynamically wires up a method caller to its target method. There are two aspects to a delegate: *type* and *instance*. A *delegate type* defines a *protocol* to which the caller and target will conform, comprising a list of parameter types and a return type. A *delegate instance* refers to one (or more) target methods conforming to that protocol.

A delegate instance literally acts as a delegate for the caller: the caller invokes the delegate, and then the delegate calls the target method. This indirection decouples the caller from the target method.

A delegate type declaration is preceded by the keyword delegate, but otherwise it resembles an (abstract) method declaration. For example:

```
delegate int Transformer (int x);
```

To create a delegate instance, you can assign a method to a delegate variable:

```
class Test
{
  static void Main( )
  {
    Transformer t = Square;          // create delegate instance
    int result = t(3);               // invoke delegate
    Console.WriteLine (result);
  }
  static int Square (int x) { return x * x; }
}
```

Invoking a delegate is just like invoking a method (since the delegate's purpose is merely to provide a level of indirection):

```
t(3);
```

This statement:

```
Transformer t = Square;
```

is shorthand for:

```
Transformer t = new Transformer(Square);
```

 A delegate is similar to a *callback*, a general term that captures constructs such as C function pointers.

Writing Plug-in Methods with Delegates

A delegate variable is assigned a method *dynamically*. This is useful for writing plug-in methods. In this example, we have a utility method named Transform that applies a transform to each element in an integer array. The Transform method has a delegate parameter, for specifying a plug-in transform.

```
public delegate int Transformer (int x);

public class Util
{
  public static void Transform (int[] values, Transformer t)
  {
    for (int i = 0; i < values.Length; i++)
      values[i] = t(values[i]);
  }
}

class Test
{
  static void Main( )
  {
    int[] values = new int[] {1, 2, 3};
    Util.Transform(values, Square);      // dynamically hook in Square
    foreach (int i in values)
      Console.Write (i + " ");           // 1   4   9
  }

  static int Square (int x) { return x * x; }
}
```

Multicast Delegates

All delegate instances have *multicast* capability. This means that a delegate instance can reference not just a single target method, but also a list of target methods. The += operator combines delegate instances. For example:

```
SomeDelegate d = SomeMethod1;
d += SomeMethod2;
```

Invoking d will now call both `SomeMethod1` and `SomeMethod2`. Delegates are invoked in the order they are added.

The `-=` method removes the right delegate operand from the left delegate operand. For example:

```
d -= SomeMethod1;
```

Invoking d will now cause only `SomeMethod2` to be invoked.

Calling `+=` on a delegate variable with a `null` value works, and it is equivalent to assigning the variable to a new value:

```
SomeDelegate d = null;
d += SomeMethod1;        // equivalent (when d is null) to d = SomeMethod1;
```

If a multicast delegate has a nonvoid return type, the caller receives the return value from the last method to be invoked. The preceding methods are still called, but their return values are discarded. In most scenarios in which multicast delegates are used, they have void return types, so this subtlety does not arise.

 All delegate types implicitly inherit `System.MulticastDelegate`, which inherits from `System.Delegate`. C# compiles `+=` and `-=` operations made on a delegate to the static `Combine` and `Remove` methods of the `System.Delegate` class.

Multicast delegate example

Suppose you wrote a routine that took a long time to execute. That routine could regularly report progress to its caller by invoking a delegate. In this example, the `HardWork` routine has a `ProgressReporter` delegate parameter, which it invokes to indicate progress:

```
public delegate void ProgressReporter (int percentComplete);

public class Util
{
  public static void HardWork (ProgressReporter p)
  {
    for (int i = 0; i < 10; i++)
    {
      p (i * 10);                              // Invoke delegate
      System.Threading.Thread.Sleep(100);  // Simulate hard work
    }
  }
}
```

To monitor progress, the `Main` method creates a multicast delegate instance p, such that progress is monitored by two independent methods:

```
class Test
{
  static void Main ()
  {
    ProgressReporter p = WriteProgressToConsole;
    p += WriteProgressToFile;
```

```
  Util.HardWork (p);
}

static void WriteProgressToConsole (int percentComplete)
{
  Console.WriteLine (percentComplete);
}

static void WriteProgressToFile (int percentComplete)
{
  System.IO.File.WriteAllText ("progress.txt", percentComplete.
    ToString( ));
}
}
```

Instance Method Targets

When a delegate instance is assigned to an *instance* method, the delegate instance must maintain a reference not only to the method, but also to the *instance* of that method. The System.Delegate class's Target property represents this instance (and will be null for a delegate referencing a static method). For example:

```
public delegate void ProgressReporter (int percentComplete);

class Test
{
  static void Main() {new Test( );}
  Test ()
  {
    ProgressReporter p = InstanceProgress;
    p(99);                                    // 99
    Console.WriteLine (p.Target == this);     // True
    Console.WriteLine (p.Method);             // Void InstanceProgress(Int32)
  }

  void InstanceProgress (int percentComplete)
  {
    Console.WriteLine(percentComplete);
  }
}
```

Generic Delegate Types

A delegate type may contain generic type parameters. For example:

```
public delegate T Transformer<T> (T arg);
```

With this definition, we can write a generalized Transform utility method that works on any type:

```
public class Util
{
  public static void Transform<T> (T[] values, Transformer<T> t)
```

```
      {
        for (int i = 0; i < values.Length; i++)
          values[i] = t(values[i]);
      }
    }

    class Test
    {
      static void Main()
      {
        int[] values = new int[] {1, 2, 3};
        Util.Transform(values, Square);        // dynamically hook in Square
        foreach (int i in values)
          Console.Write (i + "  ");            // 1   4   9
      }

      static int Square (int x) { return x * x; }
    }
```

Delegates Versus Interfaces

A problem that can be solved with a delegate can also be solved with an interface. For instance, the following explains how to solve our filter problem using an ITransformer interface:

```
    public interface ITransformer
    {
      int Transform (int x);
    }

    public class Util
    {
     public static void TransformAll (int[] values, ITransformer t)
     {
       for (int i = 0; i < values.Length; i++)
         values[i] = t.Transform(values[i]);
     }
    }

    class Test : ITransformer
    {
     static void Main()
     {
       int[] values = new int[] {1, 2, 3};
       Util.TransformAll(values, new Test());
       foreach (int i in values)
         Console.WriteLine (i);
     }

     public int Transform (int x) { return x * x; }
    }
```

A delegate design may be a better choice than an interface design if one or more of these conditions are true:

- The interface defines only a single method.
- Multicast capability is needed.
- The listener needs to implement the interface multiple times.

In the ITransformer example, we don't need to multicast. However, the interface defines only a single method. Furthermore, our listener may need to implement ITransformer multiple times, to support different transforms, such as square or cube. With interfaces, we're forced into writing a separate type per transform, since Test can only implement ITransformer once. This is quite cumbersome:

```
class Test
{
  static void Main()
  {
    int[] values = new int[] {1, 2, 3};
    Util.TransformAll(values, new Cuber());
    foreach (int i in values)
      Console.WriteLine (i);
  }

  class Squarer : ITransformer
  {
    public int Transform (int x) { return x * x; }
  }
  class Cuber : ITransformer
  {
    public int Transform (int x) {return x * x * x; }
  }
}
```

Delegate Compatibility

Type compatibility

Delegate types are all incompatible with each other, even if their signatures are the same:

```
delegate void D1();
delegate void D2();
...

D1 d1 = Method1;
D2 d2 = d1;                          // compile-time error
```

Delegate instances are considered equal if they have the same method targets:

```
delegate void D();
...

D d1 = Method1;
D d2 = Method1;
Console.WriteLine (d1 == d2);        // true
```

Parameter compatibility

When you call a method, you can supply arguments that have more specific types than the parameters of that method. This is ordinary polymorphic behavior. For exactly the same reason, a delegate can have more specific parameter types than its method target. This is called *contravariance*.

Consider the following example:

```
delegate void SpecificDelegate (SpecificClass s);

class SpecificClass {}

class Test
{
  static void Main()
  {
    SpecificDelegate specificDelegate = GeneralHandler;
    specificDelegate (new SpecificClass());
  }

  static void GeneralHandler(object o)
  {
    Console.WriteLine(o.GetType()); // SpecificClass
  }
}
```

A delegate merely calls a method on someone else's behalf. In this case, the SpecificDelegate is invoked with an argument of type SpecificClass. When the argument is then relayed to the target method, the argument gets implicitly upcast to an object.

 The standard event pattern is designed to help you leverage contravariance through its use of the common EventArgs base class. For example, you can have a single method invoked by two different delegates, one passing a MouseEventArgs and the other passing a KeyEventArgs.

Return type compatibility

If you call a method, you may get back a type that is more specific than what you asked for. This is ordinary polymorphic behavior. For exactly the same reason, the return type of a delegate can be less specific than the return type of its target method. This is called *covariance*. Consider the following example:

```
delegate Asset DebtCollector();

class Asset {}

class House : Asset {}

class Test
{
  static void Main()
```

```
    {
        DebtCollector d = new DebtCollector (GetHomeSweetHome);
        Asset a = d( );
        Console.WriteLine(a.GetType( )); // House
    }
    static House GetHomeSweetHome() {return new House( ); }
}
```

A delegate merely calls a method on someone else's behalf. In this case, the DebtCollector expects to get back an Asset—but any Asset will do. Delegate return types are said to be covariant.

Events

When using delegates, two emergent roles commonly appear: *broadcaster* and *subscriber*.

The *broadcaster* is a type that contains a delegate field. The broadcaster decides when to broadcast, by invoking the delegate.

The *subscribers* are the method target recipients. A subscriber decides when to start and stop listening, by calling +- and -= on the broadcaster's delegate. A subscriber does not know about, or interfere with, other subscribers.

Events are a language feature that formalizes this pattern. An event is a wrapper for a delegate that exposes just the subset of delegate features required for the broadcaster/subscriber model. The main purpose of events is to *prevent subscribers from interfering with each other*.

To declare an event member, you put the event keyword in front of a delegate member. For instance:

```
    public class Broadcaster
    {
        public event ProgressReporter Progress;
    }
```

Code within the Broadcaster type has full access to Progress and can treat it as a delegate. Code outside of Broadcaster can only perform += and -= operations on Progress.

Consider the following example. The Stock class invokes its PriceChanged event every time the Price of the Stock changes:

```
    public delegate void PriceChangedHandler (decimal oldPrice,
                                               decimal newPrice);

    public class Stock
    {
        string symbol;
        decimal price;

        public Stock (string symbol) {this.symbol = symbol;}

        public event PriceChanged PriceChanged;

        public decimal Price
```

```
  {
    get { return price; }
    set
    {
      if (price == value) return;      // exit if nothing has changed
      if (PriceChanged != null)        // if invocation list not empty
        PriceChanged (price, value);   // fire event
      price = value;
    }
  }
}
```

If we remove the event keyword from our example so that PriceChanged becomes an ordinary delegate field, our example would give the same results. However, Stock would be less robust, in that subscribers could do the following things to interfere with each other:

- Replace other subscribers by reassigning PriceChanged (instead of using the += operator).
- Clear all subscribers (by setting PriceChanged to null).
- Broadcast to other subscribers by invoking the delegate.

Standard Event Pattern

The .NET Framework defines a standard pattern for writing events. Its purpose is to provide consistency across both Framework and user code. At the core of the standard event pattern is System.EventArgs: a predefined Framework class with no members (other than the static Empty property). EventArgs is a base class for conveying information for an event. In our Stock example, we would subclass EventArgs to convey the old and new prices when a PriceChanged event is fired:

```
public class PriceChangedEventArgs : System.EventArgs
{
  public readonly decimal LastPrice;
  public readonly decimal NewPrice;

  public PriceChangedEventArgs (decimal lastPrice, decimal newPrice)
  {
    LastPrice = lastPrice;
    NewPrice = newPrice;
  }
}
```

For reusability, the EventArgs subclass is named according to the information it contains (rather than the event for which it will be used). It typically exposes data as properties or as read-only fields.

With an EventArgs subclass in place, the next step is to choose or define a delegate for the event. There are three rules:

- It must have a void return type.
- It must accept two arguments: the first of type object, and the second a subclass of EventArgs. The first argument indicates the event broadcaster, and the second argument contains the extra information to convey.

- Its name must end in "EventHandler".

The Framework defines a generic delegate called `System.EventHandler<>` that satisfies these rules:

```
public delegate void EventHandler<TEventArgs>
  (object source, TEventArgs e) where TEventArgs : EventArgs;
```

 Before generics existed in the language (prior to C# 2.0), we would have had to instead write a custom delegate as follows:

```
public delegate void PriceChangedHandler (object sender,
  PriceChangedEventArgs e);
```

For historical reasons, most events within the Framework use delegates defined in this way.

The next step is to define an event of the chosen delegate type. Here, we use the generic `EventHandler` delegate:

```
public class Stock
{
  ...

  public event EventHandler<PriceChangedEventArgs> PriceChanged;
}
```

Finally, the pattern requires that you write a protected virtual method that fires the event. The name must match the name of the event, prefixed with the word "On", and then accept a single `EventArgs` argument:

```
public class Stock
{
  ...

  public event EventHandler<PriceChangedEventArgs> PriceChanged;

  protected virtual void OnPriceChanged (PriceChangedEventArgs e)
  {
    if (PriceChanged != null) PriceChanged (this, e);
  }
}
```

This provides a central point from which subclasses can invoke or override the event.

Here's the complete example:

```
using System;

public class PriceChangedEventArgs : EventArgs
{
  public readonly decimal LastPrice;
  public readonly decimal NewPrice;

  public PriceChangedEventArgs (decimal lastPrice, decimal newPrice)
  {
```

```
      LastPrice = lastPrice; NewPrice = newPrice;
  }
}

public class Stock
{
  string symbol;
  decimal price;

  public Stock (string symbol) {this.symbol = symbol;}

  public event EventHandler<PriceChangedEventArgs> PriceChanged;

  protected virtual void OnPriceChanged (PriceChangedEventArgs e)
  {
    if (PriceChanged != null) PriceChanged (this, e);
  }

  public decimal Price
  {
    get { return price; }
    set
    {
      if (price == value) return;
      OnPriceChanged (new PriceChangedEventArgs (price, value));
      price = value;
    }
  }
}

class Test
{
  static void Main( )
  {
    Stock stock = new Stock ("THPW");
    stock.Price = 27.10M;
    // register with the PriceChanged event
    stock.PriceChanged += stock_PriceChanged;
    stock.Price = 31.59M;
  }

  static void stock_PriceChanged (object sender, PriceChangedEventArgs e)
  {
    if ((e.NewPrice - e.LastPrice) / e.LastPrice > 0.1M)
      Console.WriteLine ("Alert, 10% stock price increase!");
  }
}
```

The predefined nongeneric EventHandler delegate can be used when an event doesn't carry extra information. In this example, we rewrite Stock such that the PriceChanged event is fired after the price changes, and no information about the event is necessary, other than it happened. We also make use of the EventArgs. Empty property, in order to avoid unnecessarily instantiating an instance of EventArgs.

```
public class Stock
{
  string symbol;
  decimal price;

  public Stock (string symbol) {this.symbol = symbol;}

  public event EventHandler PriceChanged;

  protected virtual void OnPriceChanged (EventArgs e)
  {
    if (PriceChanged != null) PriceChanged (this, e);
  }

  public decimal Price
  {
    get { return price; }
    set
    {
      if (price == value) return;
      price = value;
      OnPriceChanged (EventArgs.Empty);
    }
  }
}
```

Event Accessors

An event's *accessors* are the implementations of its += and -= functions. By default, accessors are implemented implicitly by the compiler. Consider this event declaration:

```
public event EventHandler PriceChanged;
```

The compiler converts this to the following:

- A private delegate field
- A public pair of event accessor functions, whose implementations forward the += and -= operations to the private delegate field

You can take over this process by defining *explicit* event accessors. Here's a manual implementation of the PriceChanged event from our previous example:

```
private EventHandler _PriceChanged;       // declare a private delegate

public event EventHandler PriceChanged
{
  add
  {
    _PriceChanged += value;
  }
  remove
  {
    _PriceChanged -= value;
  }
}
```

This example is functionally identical to C#'s default accessor implementation. The `add` and `remove` keywords after the event declaration instruct C# not to generate a default field and accessor logic.

With explicit event accessors, you can apply more complex strategies to the storage and access of the underlying delegate. There are three scenarios where this is useful:

- When the event accessors are merely relays for another class that is broadcasting the event.
- When the class exposes a large number of events, where most of the time very few subscribers exist, such as a Windows control. In such cases, it is better to store the subscriber's delegate instances in a dictionary, since a dictionary will contain less storage overhead than dozens of null delegate field references.
- When explicitly implementing an interface that declares an event.

Here is an example that illustrates the last point:

```
public interface IFoo
{
  event EventHandler Ev;
}

class Foo : IFoo
{
  private EventHandler ev;

  event EventHandler IFoo.Ev
  {
    add    { ev += value; }
    remove { ev -= value; }
  }
}
```

The `add` and `remove` parts of an event are compiled to add_*XXX* and remove_*XXX* methods.

The += and -= operations on an event are compiled to calls to the add_*XXX* and remove_*XXX* methods.

Event Modifiers

Like methods, events can be virtual, overridden, abstract, and sealed. Events can also be static:

```
public class Foo
{
  public static event EventHandler<EventArgs> StaticEvent;
  public virtual event EventHandler<EventArgs> VirtualEvent;
}
```

Lambda Expressions (C# 3.0)

A lambda expression is an unnamed method written in place of a delegate instance. The compiler immediately converts the lambda expression to either:

- A delegate instance.
- An *expression tree*, of type Expression<T>, representing the code inside the lambda expression in a traversable object model. This allows the lambda expression to be interpreted later at runtime (see the section "Building Query Expressions" in Chapter 8).

In the following example, square is assigned the lambda expression x => x * x:

```
delegate int Transformer (int i);

class Test
{
  static void Main( )
  {
    Transformer square = x => x * x;
    Console.WriteLine (square(3));    // 9
  }
}
```

We could rewrite the example by converting the lambda expression into a method, and then call the method through the delegate. In fact, the compiler internally performs that translation for you when you assign a delegate a lambda expression:

```
delegate int Transformer (int i);

class Test
{
  static void Main( )
  {
    Transformer square = Square;
    Console.WriteLine (square(3));    // 9
  }
  static int Square (int x) {return x * x;}
}
```

A lambda expression has the following BNF form:

```
(parameters) => expression-or-statement-block
```

For convenience, you can omit the parentheses if and only if there is exactly one parameter of an inferable type.

In our example, there is a single parameter, x, and the expression is x * x:

```
x => x * x;
```

Each parameter of the lambda expression corresponds to a delegate parameter, and the type of the expression (which may be void) corresponds to the return type of the delegate.

In our example, x corresponds to parameter i, and the expression x * x corresponds to the return type int, therefore being compatible with the Transformer delegate:

```
delegate int Transformer (int i);
```

A lambda expression's code can be a *statement block* instead of an expression. We can rewrite our example as follows:

```
x => {return x * x;};
```

Explicitly Specifying Lambda Parameter Types

The compiler can usually *infer* the type of lambda parameters contextually. When this is not the case, you must specify the type of each parameter explicitly. Consider the following delegate type:

```
delegate int Transformer (int i);
```

The compiler uses type inference to infer that x is an int, by examining Transfomer's parameter type:

```
Transformer d = x => x * x;
```

We could explicitly specify x's type as follows:

```
Transformer d = (int x) => x * x;
```

Generic Lambda Expressions and the Func Delegates

With generic delegates, it becomes possible to write a small set of delegate types that are so general they can work for methods of any return type and any (reasonable) number of arguments. These delegates are the Func and Action delegates, defined in the System namespace:

```
delegate TResult Func <T>                    ();
delegate TResult Func <T,TResult>            (T1 arg1);
delegate TResult Func <T1,T2,TResult>        (T1 arg1, T2 arg2);
delegate TResult Func <T1,T2,T3,TResult>     (T1 arg1, T2 arg2, T3 arg3);
delegate TResult Func <T1,T2,T3,T4,TResult>  (T1 arg1, T2 arg2, T3 arg3,
                                              T4 arg4);

delegate void Action                         ();
delegate void Action  <T>                    (T1 arg1);
delegate void Action  <T1,T2>                (T1 arg1, T2 arg2);
delegate void Action  <T1,T2,T3>             (T1 arg1, T2 arg2, T3 arg3);
delegate void Action  <T1,T2,T3,T4>          (T1 arg1, T2 arg2, T3 arg3,
                                              T4 arg4);
```

These delegates are extremely general. The Transformer delegate in our previous example can be replaced with a Func delegate that takes a single int argument and returns an int value:

```
class Test
{
  static void Main( )
  {
```

```
      Func<int,int> square = x => x * x;
      Console.WriteLine (square(3));      // 9
  }
}
```

Outer Variables

A lambda expression can reference the local variables and parameters of the method in which it's defined. For example:

```
delegate int NumericSequence ();

class Test
{
  static void Main()
  {
    int seed = 0;
    NumericSequence natural = () => seed++;
    Console.WriteLine (natural());         // 0
    Console.WriteLine (natural());         // 1
  }
}
```

Local variables and parameters referenced by a lambda expression are called *outer variables*. In our example, seed is an outer variable referenced by the lambda expression () => seed++. Outer variables are *captured*, meaning their lifetime is extended to that of the lambda expression. Let's refactor the example to make the effect of capturing more striking:

```
delegate int NumericSequence ();

class Test
{
  static NumericSequence Natural ()
  {
    int seed = 0;            // executes once  (per call to Natural())
    return () => seed++;  // executes twice (per call to delegate instance
                          //                 returned by Natural())
  }

  static void Main()
  {
    NumericSequence natural = Natural ();
    Console.WriteLine (natural());         // 0
    Console.WriteLine (natural());         // 1
  }
}
```

The local variable seed would ordinarily just pop off the stack when the Natural method exits. However, seed is captured by the lambda expression of the delegate instance returned by Natural. This means the lifetime of seed is extended to the lifetime of that delegate instance. Subsequent invocations of that same delegate instance will reuse the same seed variable.

Capturing is internally implemented by "lifting" the captured variables into fields of a private class. When the method is called, the class is instantiated and lifetime-bound to the delegate instance.

A local variable *instantiated* within a lambda expression is unique per invocation of the delegate instance. If we refactor our previous example to instantiate seed *within* the lambda expression, we get a different (in this case, undesirable) result:

```
delegate int NumericSequence ( );

class Test
{
  static NumericSequence Natural ( )
  {
    return ( ) => {int seed = 0; return seed++; };
  }

  static void Main( )
  {
    NumericSequence natural = Natural ( );
    Console.WriteLine (natural( ));          // 0
    Console.WriteLine (natural( ));          // 0
  }
}
```

Anonymous Methods

Anonymous methods are a C# 2.0 feature that has been subsumed by C# 3.0 lambda expressions. An anonymous method is like a lambda expression, but it lacks the following features:

- Implicitly typed parameters
- Expression syntax (an anonymous method must always be a statement block)
- The ability to compile to an expression tree, by assigning to Expression<T>

To write an anonymous method, you include the delegate keyword followed by a parameter declaration and then a method body. For example:

```
delegate int Transformer (int i);

class Test
{
  static void Main( )
  {
    Transformer square = delegate (int x) {return x * x;};
    Console.WriteLine (square(3));     // 9
  }
}
```

The following line:

```
Transformer square = delegate (int x)    {return x * x;};
```

is semantically equivalent to the following lambda expression:

```
Transformer square =         (int x) => {return x * x;};
```

Or simply:

```
Transformer square =         x => x * x;
```

Anonymous methods capture outer variables in the same way lambda expressions do.

try Statements and Exceptions

A try statement specifies a code block subject to error-handling or cleanup code. The try *block* must be followed by a catch *block*, a finally *block*, or both. The catch block executes when an error occurs in the try block. The finally block executes after execution leaves the try block (or if present, the catch block), to perform cleanup code, whether or not an error occurred.

A catch block has access to an Exception object that contains information about the error. You use a catch block to either compensate for the error or *rethrow* the exception. You rethrow an exception if you merely want to log the problem, or if you want to rethrow a new, higher-level exception type.

A finally block adds determinism to your program, by always executing no matter what. It's useful for cleanup tasks such as closing network connections.

A try statement looks like this:

```
try
{
  ... // exception may get thrown within execution of this block
}
catch (ExceptionA ex)
{
  ... // handle exception of type ExceptionA
}
catch (ExceptionB ex)
{
  ... // handle exception of type ExceptionB
}
finally
{
  ... // cleanup code
}
```

Consider the following program:

```
class Test
{
  static int Calc (int x) {return 10 / x;}

  static void Main()
```

```
  {
    int y = Calc (0);
    Console.WriteLine (y);
  }
}
```

Because x is zero, the runtime throws a DivideByZeroException, and our program terminates. We can prevent this by catching the exception as follows:

```
class Test
{
  static int Calc (int x) {return 10 / x;}

  static void Main( )
  {
    try
    {
      int y = Calc (0);
      Console.WriteLine (y);
    }
    catch (DivideByZeroException ex)
    {
      Console.WriteLine("x cannot be zero");
    }
    Console.WriteLine ("program completed");
  }
}

OUTPUT:
x cannot be zero
program completed
```

When an exception is thrown, the CLR performs a test:

Is execution currently within a try statement that can catch the exception?

- If so, execution is passed to the compatible catch block. If the catch block successfully finishes executing, execution moves to the next statement after the try statement (if present, executing the finally block first).

- If not, execution jumps back to the caller of the function, and the test is repeated (after executing any finally blocks that wrap the statement).

If no function takes responsibility for the exception, an error dialog is displayed to the user, and the program terminates.

The catch Clause

A catch clause specifies what type of exception to catch. This must either be System.Exception or a subclass of System.Exception.

Catching System.Exception catches all possible errors. This is useful when:

- Your program can potentially recover regardless of the specific exception type.
- You plan to rethrow the exception (perhaps after logging it).
- Your error handler is the last resort, prior to termination of the program.

More typically, though, you catch *specific exception types*, in order to avoid having to deal with circumstances for which your handler wasn't designed (e.g., an OutOfMemoryException).

You can handle multiple exception types with multiple catch clauses:

```
class Test
{
  static void Main (string[] args)
  {
    try
    {
      byte b = byte.Parse (args[0]);
      Console.WriteLine (b);
    }
    catch (IndexOutOfRangeException ex)
    {
      Console.WriteLine ("Please provide at least one argument");
    }
    catch (FormatException ex)
    {
      Console.WriteLine ("That's not a number!");
    }
    catch (OverflowException ex)
    {
      Console.WriteLine ("You've given me more than a byte!");
    }
  }
}
```

Only one catch clause executes for a given exception. If you want to include a safety net to catch more general exceptions (such as System.Exception), you must put the more specific handlers *first*.

An exception can be caught without specifying a variable, if you don't need to access its properties:

```
catch (StackOverflowException)   // no variable
{
  ...
}
```

Furthermore, you can omit both the variable and the type (meaning that all exceptions will be caught):

```
catch { ... }
```

In languages other than C#, it is possible (though not recommended) to throw an object that does not derive from Exception. The CLR automatically wraps that object in a RuntimeWrapped-Exception class (which does derive from Exception).

The finally Block

A finally block always executes—whether or not an exception is thrown and whether or not the try block runs to completion. finally blocks are typically used for cleanup code.

A finally block executes either:

- After a catch block finishes
- After control leaves the try block because of a jump statement (e.g., return or goto)
- After the try block ends

A finally block helps add determinism to a program. In the following example, the file that we open *always* gets closed, regardless of whether:

- The try block finishes normally.
- Execution returns early because the file is empty (EndOfStream).
- An IOException is thrown while reading the file.

```
using System;
using System.IO;

class Test
{
  static void Main ()
  {
    StreamReader reader = null;
    try
    {
      reader = File.OpenText ("file.txt");
      if (reader.EndOfStream) return;
      Console.WriteLine (reader.ReadToEnd ());
    }
    finally
    {
      if (reader != null) reader.Dispose ();
    }
  }
}
```

In this example, we closed the file by calling Dispose on the StreamReader. Calling Dispose on an object, within a finally block, is a standard convention throughout the .NET Framework and is supported explicitly in C# through the using statement.

The using statement

Many classes encapsulate unmanaged resources, such as file handles, graphics handles, or database connections. These classes implement System.IDisposable, which defines a single parameterless method named Dispose to clean up these resources. The using statement provides an elegant syntax for instantiating an IDisposable object and then calling its Dispose method within a finally block.

The following:

```
using (StreamReader reader = File.OpenText ("file.txt"))
{
  ...
}
```

is precisely equivalent to:

```
StreamReader reader = File.OpenText ("file.txt");
try
{
  ...
}
finally
{
  if (reader != null)
    ((IDisposable)reader).Dispose();
}
```

We cover the disposal pattern in more detail in Chapter 12.

Throwing Exceptions

Exceptions can be thrown either by the runtime or in user code. In this example, Display throws a System.ArgumentNullException:

```
class Test
{
  static void Display (string name)
  {
    if (name == null)
      throw new ArgumentNullException ("name");

    Console.WriteLine (name);
  }

  static void Main()
  {
    try { Display (null); }
    catch (ArgumentNullException ex)
    {
      Console.WriteLine ("Caught the exception");
    }
  }
}
```

Rethrowing an exception

You can capture and rethrow an exception as follows:

```
try { ... }
catch (Exception ex)
{
```

```
// Log error
...
throw;           // Rethrow same exception
}
```

Rethrowing in this manner lets you log an error without *swallowing* it. It also lets you back out of handling an exception should circumstances turn out to be outside what you expected:

```
using System.Net;        // (See Chapter 14)
...

string s;
using (WebClient wc = new WebClient())
  try { s = wc.DownloadString ("http://albahari.com/");  }
  catch (WebException ex)
  {
    if (ex.Status == WebExceptionStatus.NameResolutionFailure)
      Console.WriteLine ("Bad domain name");
    else
      throw;        // Can't handle other sorts of WebException, so rethrow
  }
```

The other common scenario is to rethrow a more specific exception type. For example:

```
try
{
  ... // parse a date of birth from XML element data
}
catch (FormatException ex)
{
  throw new XmlException ("Invalid date of birth", ex);
}
```

Rethrowing an exception does not affect the StackTrace property of the exception (see the next section). When rethrowing a different exception, you can set the InnerException property with the original exception if doing so could aid debugging. Nearly all types of exceptions provide a constructor for this purpose.

Key Properties of System.Exception

The most important properties of System.Exception are the following:

StackTrace
:   A string representing all the methods that are called from the origin of the exception to the catch block.

Message
:   A string with a description of the error.

InnerException
:   The inner exception (if any) that caused the outer exception. This, itself, may have another InnerException.

All exceptions in C# are runtime exceptions—there is no equivalent to Java's compile-time checked exceptions.

Common Exception Types

The following exception types are used widely throughout the CLR and .NET Framework. You can throw these yourself or use them as base classes for deriving custom exception types.

System.ArgumentException
> Thrown when a function is called with a bogus argument. This generally indicates a program bug.

System.ArgumentNullException
> Subclass of ArgumentException that's thrown when a function argument is (unexpectedly) null.

System.ArgumentOutOfRangeException
> Subclass of ArgumentException that's thrown when a (usually numeric) argument is too big or too small. For example, this is thrown when passing a negative number into a function that accepts only positive values.

System.InvalidOperationException
> Thrown when the state of an object is unsuitable for a method to successfully execute, regardless of any particular argument values. Examples include reading an unopened file or getting the next element from an enumerator where the underlying list has been modified partway through the iteration.

System.NotSupportedException
> Thrown to indicate that a particular functionality is not supported. A good example is calling the Add method on a collection for which IsReadOnly returns true.

System.NotImplementedException
> Thrown to indicate that a function has not yet been implemented.

System.ObjectDisposedException
> Thrown when the object upon which the function is called has been disposed.

Common Patterns

The try method pattern

When writing a method, you have a choice, when something goes wrong, to return some kind of failure code or throw an exception. In general, you throw an exception when the error is outside the normal workflow—or if you expect that the immediate caller won't be able to cope with it. Occasionally, though, it can be best to offer both choices to the consumer. An example of this is the int type, which defines two versions of its Parse method:

```
public int Parse    (string input);
public bool TryParse (string input, out int returnValue);
```

If parsing fails, Parse throws an exception; TryParse returns false.

You can implement this pattern by having the *XXX* method call the Try*XXX* method as follows:

```
public return-type XXX (input-type input)
{
  return-type returnValue;
  if (! TryXXX (input, out returnValue))
    throw new YYYException (...)
  return returnValue;
}
```

The atomicity pattern

It can be desirable for an operation to be *atomic*, where it either successfully completes or fails without affecting state. An object becomes unusable when it enters an indeterminate state that is the result of a half-finished operation. finally blocks facilitate writing atomic operations.

In the following example, we use an Accumulator class that has an Add method that adds an array of integers to its field Total. The Add method will cause an OverflowException if Total exceeds the maximum value for an int. The Add method is atomic, either successfully updating Total or failing, which leaves Total with its former value.

```
class Test
{
  static void Main( )
  {
    Accumulator a = new Accumulator ( );
    try
    {
      a.Add (4, 5);             // a.Total is now 9
      a.Add (1, int.MaxValue);  // will cause OverflowException
    }
    catch (OverflowException)
    {
      Console.WriteLine (a.Total);  // a.Total is still 9
    }
  }
}
```

In the implementation of Accumulator, the Add method affects the Total field as it executes. However, if *anything goes wrong* during the method (e.g., a numeric overflow, a stack overflow, etc.), Total is restored to its initial value at the start of the method.

```
public class Accumulator
{
  public int Total;

  public void Add(params int[] ints)
  {
    bool success = false;
```

```
      int totalSnapshot = Total;
      try
      {
        foreach (int i in ints)
        {
          checked
          {
            Total += i;
          }
        }
        success = true;
      }
      finally
      {
        if (! success)
          Total = totalSnapshot;
      }
    }
  }
```

Alternatives to exceptions

As with int.TryParse, a function can communicate failure by sending an error code back to the calling function via a return type or parameter. Although this can work with simple and predictable failures, it becomes clumsy when extended to all errors, polluting method signatures and creating unnecessary complexity and clutter. It also cannot generalize to functions that are not methods, such as operators (e.g., the division operator) or properties. An alternative is to place the error in a common place where all functions in the call stack can see it (e.g., a static method that stores the current error per thread). This, though, requires each function to participate in an error-propagation pattern that is cumbersome and, ironically, itself error-prone.

Enumeration and Iterators

Enumeration

An *enumerator* is a read-only, forward-only cursor over a *sequence of values*. An enumerator is an object that either:

- Implements IEnumerator or IEnumerator<T>
- Has a method named MoveNext for iterating the sequence, and a property called Current for getting the current element in the sequence

The foreach statement iterates over an *enumerable* object. An enumerable object is the logical representation of a sequence. It is not itself a cursor, but an object that produces cursors over itself. An enumerable object either:

- Implements IEnumerable or IEnumerable<T>
- Has a method named GetEnumerator that returns an *enumerator*

IEnumerator and IEnumerable are defined in System.Collections.
IEnumerator<T> and IEnumerable<T> are defined in System.Collections.Generic.

The enumeration pattern is as follows:

```
class Enumerator    // typically implements IEnumerator or IEnumerator<T>
{
  public IteratorVariableType Current { get {...} }
  public bool MoveNext( )          {...}
}

class Enumerable    // typically implements IEnumerable or IEnumerable<T>
{
  public Enumerator GetEnumerator( ) {...}
}
```

Here is the high-level way of iterating through the characters in the word "beer" using a foreach statement:

```
foreach (char c in "beer")
  Console.WriteLine (c);
```

Here is the low-level way of iterating through the characters in "beer" without using a foreach statement:

```
var enumerator = "beer".GetEnumerator( );

while (enumerator.MoveNext( ))
{
  var element = enumerator.Current;
  Console.WriteLine (element);
}
```

The foreach statement also acts as a using statement, implicitly disposing the enumerator object.

Chapter 7 explains the enumeration interfaces in further detail.

Iterators

Whereas a foreach statement is a *consumer* of an enumerator, an iterator is a *producer* of an enumerator. In this example, we use an iterator to return a sequence of Fibonacci numbers (where each number is the sum of the previous two):

```
using System;
using System.Collections.Generic;

class Test
{
  static void Main( )
```

```
   {
     foreach (int fib in Fibs(6))
       Console.Write (fib + "  ");
   }

   static IEnumerable<int> Fibs(int fibCount)
   {
     for (int i = 0, prevFib = 1, curFib = 1; i < fibCount; i++)
     {
       yield return prevFib;
       int newFib = prevFib+curFib;
       prevFib = curFib;
       curFib = newFib;
     }
   }
 }

OUTPUT: 1  1  2  3  5  8
```

Whereas a return statement expresses "Here's the value you asked me to return from this method," a yield return statement expresses "Here's the next element you asked me to yield from this enumerator." On each yield statement, control is returned to the caller, but the callee's state is maintained so that the method can continue executing as soon as the caller enumerates the next element. The lifetime of this state is bound to the enumerator, such that the state can be released when the caller has finished enumerating.

Iterator Semantics

An iterator is a method, property, or indexer that contains one or more yield statements. An iterator must return one of the following four interfaces (otherwise, the compiler will generate an error):

```
// Enumerable interfaces
System.Collections.IEnumerable
System.Collections.Generic.IEnumerable<T>

// Enumerator interfaces
System.Collections.IEnumerator
System.Collections.Generic.IEnumerator<T>
```

An iterator has different semantics, depending on whether it returns an *enumerable* interface or an *enumerator* interface. We describe this in Chapter 7.

Multiple yield statements are permitted. For example:

```
class Test
{
  static void Main()
  {
    foreach (string s in Foo())
      Console.WriteLine(s);         // prints "One","Two","Three"
  }

  static IEnumerable<string> Foo()
```

```
    {
        yield return "One";
        yield return "Two";
        yield return "Three";
    }
}
```

The yield break statement indicates that the iterator block should exit early, without returning more elements. We can modify Foo as follows to demonstrate:

```
static IEnumerable<string> Foo(bool breakEarly)
{
    yield return "One";
    yield return "Two";

    if (breakEarly)
        yield break;

    yield return "Three";
}
```

 A return statement is illegal in an iterator block. Instead, a yield break statement is used to terminate the iteration.

Composing Sequences

Iterators are highly composable. We can extend our example, this time to output even Fibonacci numbers only:

```
using System;
using System.Collections.Generic;

class Test
{
    static void Main()
    {
        foreach (int fib in EvenNumbersOnly(Fibs(6)))
            Console.WriteLine(fib);
    }

    static IEnumerable<int> Fibs(int fibCount)
    {
        for (int i = 0, prevFib = 1, curFib = 1; i < fibCount; i++)
        {
            yield return prevFib;
            int newFib = prevFib+curFib;
            prevFib = curFib;
            curFib = newFib;
        }
    }

    static IEnumerable<int> EvenNumbersOnly(IEnumerable<int> sequence)
    {
```

```
    foreach(int x in sequence)
      if ((x % 2) == 0)
        yield return x;
  }
}
```

Each element is not calculated until the last moment—when requested by a MoveNext( ) operation. Figure 4-1 shows the data requests and data output over time.

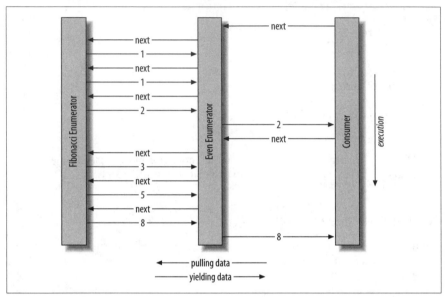

Figure 4-1. Composing sequences

The composability of the iterator pattern is extremely useful in LINQ; we will discuss the subject again in Chapter 8.

Constructing an Enumerable Object

You can instantiate and populate an enumerable object in a single step. For example:

```
using System.Collections.Generic;
...

List<int> list = new List<int> {1, 2, 3};
```

The compiler translates this to the following:

```
using System.Collections.Generic;
...

List<int> list = new List<int>();
list.Add (1);
list.Add (2);
list.Add (3);
```

This requires that the enumerable object implements the System.Collections.IEnumerable interface, and that it has an Add method that takes a single argument.

Nullable Types

Null Basics

Reference types can represent a nonexistent value with a null reference. Value types, however, cannot ordinarily represent null values. For example:

```
string s = null;      // OK, Reference Type
int i = null;         // Compile Error, Value Type cannot be null
```

To represent null in a value type, you must use a special construct called a *nullable type*. A nullable type is denoted with a value type followed by the ? symbol:

```
int? i = null;                    // OK, Nullable Type
Console.WriteLine (i == null);    // True
```

Nullable<T> struct

T? translates into System.Nullable<T>. Nullable<T> is a lightweight immutable structure, having only two fields, to represent Value and HasValue. The essence of System.Nullable<T> is very simple:

```
public struct Nullable<T> where T : struct
{
  public T Value {get;}
  public bool HasValue {get;}
  public T GetValueOrDefault();
  public T GetValueOrDefault(T defaultValue);
  ...
}
```

The code:

```
int? i = null;
Console.WriteLine (i == null);           // true
```

translates to:

```
Nullable<int> i = new Nullable<int>();
Console.WriteLine (! i.HasValue);        // true
```

Attempting to retrieve Value when HasValue is false throws an InvalidOperationException. GetValueOrDefault() returns Value if HasValue is true; otherwise, it returns new T() or a specified custom default value.

The default value of T? is null.

Implicit and explicit nullable conversions

The conversion from T to T? is implicit, and from T? to T is explicit. For example:

```
int? x = 5;       // implicit
int y = (int)x;   // explicit
```

The explicit cast is directly equivalent to calling the nullable object's `Value` property. Hence, an `InvalidOperationException` is thrown if `HasValue` is false.

Boxing and unboxing nullable values

When `T?` is boxed, the boxed value on the heap contains `T`, not `T?`. This optimization is possible because a boxed value is a reference type that can already express null.

Lifted Operators

The `Nullable<T>` struct does not define operators such as `<`, `>`, or even `==`. Despite this, the following code compiles and executes correctly:

```
int? x = 5;
int? y = 10;
bool b = x < y;      // true
```

This works because the compiler steals or "lifts" the less-than operator from the underlying value type. Semantically, it translates the preceding comparison expression into this:

```
bool b = (x.HasValue && y.HasValue) ? (x.Value < y.Value) : false;
```

In other words, if both x and y have values, it compares via int's less-than operator; otherwise, it returns `false`.

Operator lifting means you can implicitly use T's operators on T?. You can define operators for T? in order to provide special-purpose null behavior, but in the vast majority of cases, it's best to rely on the compiler automatically applying systematic nullable logic for you. Here are some examples:

```
int? x = 5;
int? y = null;

// equality operator examples
Console.WriteLine(x == y);     // false
Console.WriteLine(x == null);  // false
Console.WriteLine(x == 5);     // true
Console.WriteLine(y == null);  // true
Console.WriteLine(y == 5);     // false
Console.WriteLine(y != 5);     // true

// relational operator examples
Console.WriteLine(x < 6);      // true
Console.WriteLine(y < 6);      // false
Console.WriteLine(y > 6);      // false

// all other operator examples
Console.WriteLine(x + 5);      // 10
Console.WriteLine(x + y);      // null (prints empty line)
```

The compiler performs null logic differently depending on the category of operator. The following sections explain these different rules.

Equality operators (== !=)

The equality operators work on the principle that the behavior for nullable types works exactly as it does for reference types. This means a nonnull value is not equal to a null value, but two null values are equal.

```
bool a = x == y;    // translation:
bool a = (x != null && y != null) ? (x.Value == y.Value) :
                                     (x != null ^ y != null);

// a is true
```

Relational operators (< <= >= >)

The relational operators work on the principle that it is meaningless to compare null operands. This means comparing a null value to either a null or nonnull value returns false.

```
bool b = x < y;    // translation:
bool b = (x == null || y == null) ? false : (x.Value < y.Value);

// b is false
```

All other operators (+ - * / % & | ^ << >> + ++ --- ! ~)

These operators work on the principle to always return "I don't know" (i.e., null) when fed any operands that are null. This means that if any operand is null, the result is also null. This pattern should be familiar to SQL users.

```
int? c = x + y;    // translation:
int? c = (x == null || y == null) ? null : (int?)(x.Value + y.Value);

// c is null
```

Mixing nullable and nonnullable operators

You can mix and match nullable and nonnullable types (this works because there is an implicit conversion from T to T?):

```
int? x = null;
int y = 2;
int? z = x + y; // equivalent to x + (int?)y

// z is null
```

bool?

When supplied operands of type bool?, the & and | operators treat null as an *unknown value*. So, null | true is true, because:

- If the unknown value is false, the result would be true.
- If the unknown value is true, the result would be true.

Similarly, null & false is false. This behavior would be familiar to SQL users. The following example enumerates other combinations:

```
bool? n = null;
bool? f = false;
```

```
bool? t = true;
Console.WriteLine (n | n);    // (null)
Console.WriteLine (n | f);    // (null)
Console.WriteLine (n | t);    // True
Console.WriteLine (n & n);    // (null)
Console.WriteLine (n & f);    // False
Console.WriteLine (n & t);    // (null)
```

Null Coalescing Operator

The ?? operator is the null coalescing operator, and it can be used with both nullable types and reference types. It says "If the operand is nonnull, give it to me; otherwise, give me a default value." For example:

```
int? x = null;
int y = x ?? 5;       // y is 5
```

The ?? operator is equivalent to calling GetValueOrDefault with an explicit default value.

Scenarios for Nullable Types

One of the most common scenarios for nullable types is to represent unknown values. This frequently occurs in database programming, where a class is mapped to a table with nullable columns. If these columns are strings (e.g., an Email-Address column on a Customer table), there is not a problem as string is a reference type in the CLR, which can be null. However, most other SQL column types map to CLR struct types, making nullable types very useful when mapping SQL to the CLR. For example:

```
// maps to a Customer table in a database
public class Customer
{
  ...
  public decimal? AccountBalance;
}
```

A nullable type can also be used to represent the backing field of an *ambient property*. An ambient property, if null, returns the value of its parent. For example:

```
public class Row
{
  ...
  Grid parent;
  Color? backColor;

  public Color BackColor
  {
    get { return backColor ?? parent.BackColor; }
    set { backColor = backColor == parent.BackColor ? null : value; }
  }
}
```

Alternatives to Nullable Types

Before nullable types were part of the C# language (i.e., before C# 2.0), there were many strategies to deal with nullable value types, examples of which still appear in the .NET Framework for historical reasons. One of these strategies is to designate a particular nonnull value as the "null value"; an example is in the string and array classes. String.IndexOf returns the magic value of -1 when the character is not found:

```
int i = "Pink".IndexOf ('b');
Console.WriteLine(s);          // outputs -1
```

However, Array.IndexOf returns -1 only if the index is 0-bounded. The more general formula is that IndexOf returns 1 less than the minimum bound of the array. In the next example, IndexOf returns 0 when an element is not found:

```
// Create an array whose lower bound is 1 instead of 0:

Array a = Array.CreateInstance (typeof(string),
                       new int[] {2}, new int[] {1});
a.SetValue("a", 1);
a.SetValue("b", 2);
Console.WriteLine(Array.IndexOf(a, "c")); // outputs 0
```

Nominating a "magic value" is problematic for several reasons:

- It means that each value type has a different representation of null. In contrast, nullable types provide one common pattern that works for all value types.

- There may be no reasonable designated value. In the previous example, −1 could not always be used. The same is true for our earlier examples representing an unknown account balance and an unknown temperature.

- Forgetting to test for the magic value results in an incorrect value that may go unnoticed until later in execution—when it pulls an unintended magic trick. Forgetting to test HasValue on a null value, however, throws an InvalidOperationException on the spot.

- The ability for a value to be null is not captured in the *type*. Types communicate the intention of a program, allow the compiler to check for correctness, and enable a consistent set of rules enforced by the compiler.

Operator Overloading

Overview

Operators can be overloaded to provide more natural syntax for custom types. Operator overloading is most appropriately used for implementing custom structs that represent fairly primitive data types. For example, a custom numeric type is an excellent candidate for operator overloading.

Table 4-1 lists the overloadable symbolic operators.

Table 4-1. Overloadable symbolic operators

+ (unary)	- (unary)	!	~	++
--	+	-	*	/
%	&	|	^	<<
>>	==	!=	>	<
>=	<=			

The following operators are also overloadable:

- Implicit and explicit conversions (with the implicit and explicit keywords)
- The literals true and false

The following operators are indirectly overloaded:

- The compound assignment operators (e.g., +=, /=) are implicitly overridden by overriding the noncompound operators (e.g., +, =).
- The conditional operators && and || are implicitly overridden by overriding the bitwise operators & and |.

Operator Functions

An operator is overloaded by declaring an *operator function*. An operator function has the following rules:

- The name of the function is specified with the operator keyword followed by an operator symbol.
- The operator function must be marked static.
- The parameters of the operator function represent the operands.
- The return type of an operator function represents the result of an expression.
- At least one of the operands must be the type in which the operator function is declared.

In the following example, we define a struct called Note representing a musical note, and then overload the + operator:

```
public struct Note
{
  int value;
  public Note (int semitonesFromA) { value = semitonesFromA; }

  public static Note operator + (Note x, int semitones)
  {
    return new Note (x.value + semitones);
  }
}
```

This overload allows us to add an int to a Note:

```
Note B = new Note(2);
Note CSharp = B + 2;
```

Overloading an assignment operator automatically supports the corresponding compound assignment operator. In our example, since we overrode +, we can use += too:

```
CSharp += 2;
```

Overloading Equality and Comparison Operators

Equality and comparison operators are sometimes overridden when writing structs, and in rare cases when writing classes. Special rules and obligations come with overloading the equality and comparison operators, which we explain in Chapter 6. A summary of these rules is as follows:

Pairing
> The C# compiler enforces operators that are logical pairs to both be defined. These operators are (== !=), (< >), and (<= >=).

Equals *and* GetHashCode
> In most cases, if you overload (==) and (!=), you need to override the Equals and GetHashCode methods defined on object in order to get meaningful behavior. The C# compiler will give a warning if you do not do this. (See the section "Equality comparison" in Chapter 6 for more details.)

IComparable *and* IComparable<T>
> If you overload (< >) and (<= >=), you should implement IComparable and IComparable<T>.

Custom Implicit and Explicit Conversions

Implicit and explicit conversions are overloadable operators. These conversions are typically overloaded to make converting between strongly related types (such as numeric types) concise and natural.

To convert between weakly related types, the following strategies are more suitable:

- Write a constructor that has a parameter of the type to convert from.
- Write To*XXX* and From*XXX* methods to convert between types.

As explained in the discussion on types, the rationale behind implicit conversions is that they are guaranteed to succeed and do not lose information during the conversion. Conversely, an explicit conversion should be required either when runtime circumstances will determine whether the conversion will succeed or if information may be lost during the conversion.

In this example, we define conversions between our musical Note type and a double (which represents the frequency in hertz of that note):

```
...
// Convert to hertz
public static implicit operator double(Note x)
{
  return 440 * Math.Pow (2,(double) x.value / 12 );
}
```

```
// Convert from hertz (only accurate to nearest semitone)
public static explicit operator Note(double x)
{
  return new Note ((int) (0.5 + 12 * (Math.Log(x/440) / Math.Log(2)) ));
}
...

Note n =(Note)554.37;  // explicit conversion
double x = n;          // implicit conversion
```

 Following our own guidelines, this example might be better implemented with a ToFrequency method (and a static FromFrequency
method) instead of implicit and explicit operators.

Overloading true and false

The true and false operators are used in the extremely rare case of operators
defining types with three-state logic to enable these types to work seamlessly with
conditional statements and operators—namely, the if, do, while, for, and ?:. The
System.Data.SqlTypes.SqlBoolean struct provides this functionality. For example:

```
class Test
{
  static void Main( )
  {
    SqlBoolean a = SqlBoolean.Null;
    if (a)
      Console.WriteLine("True");
    else if (! a)
      Console.WriteLine("False");
    else
      Console.WriteLine("Null");
  }
}

OUTPUT:
Null
```

The following code is a reimplementation of the parts of SqlBoolean necessary to
demonstrate the true and false operators:

```
public struct SqlBoolean
{
  public static bool operator true (SqlBoolean x)
  {
    return x.m_value == True.m_value;
  }

  public static bool operator false (SqlBoolean x)
  {
    return x.m_value == False.m_value;
  }

  public static SqlBoolean operator !(SqlBoolean x)
```

```
  {
    if (x.m_value == Null.m_value)  return Null;
    if (x.m_value == False.m_value) return True;
    return False;
  }

  public static readonly SqlBoolean Null  =  new SqlBoolean(0);
  public static readonly SqlBoolean False =  new SqlBoolean(1);
  public static readonly SqlBoolean True  =  new SqlBoolean(2);

  private SqlBoolean (byte value) {m_value = value;}
  private byte m_value;
}
```

Extension Methods (C# 3.0)

Extension methods allow an existing type to be extended with new methods without altering the definition of the original type. An extension method is a static method of a static class, where the this modifier is applied to the first parameter. The type of the first parameter will be the type that is extended. For example:

```
public static class StringHelper
{
  public static bool IsCapitalized (this string s)
  {
    if (string.IsNullOrEmpty(s)) return false;
    return char.IsUpper(s[0]);
  }
}
```

The IsCapitalized extension method can be called as though it were an instance method on a string, as follows:

```
Console.WriteLine("Perth".IsCapitalized());
```

An extension method call, when compiled, is translated back into an ordinary static method call:

```
Console.WriteLine(StringHelper.IsCapitalized("Perth"));
```

The translation works as follows:

```
arg0.Method(arg1, arg2, ...);              // extension method call
StaticClass.Method(arg0, arg1, arg2, ...); // static method call
```

Extension Method Chaining

Extension methods, like instance methods, provide a tidy way to chain functions. Consider the following two functions:

```
public static class StringHelper
{
  public static string Pluralize (this string s) {...}
  public static string Capitalize (this string s) {...}
}
```

x and y are equivalent and both evaluate to "Sausages", but x uses extension methods, whereas y uses static methods:

```
string x = "sausage".Pluralize().Capitalize();
string y = StringHelper.Capitalize (StringHelper.Pluralize("sausage")));
```

Ambiguity and Resolution

Namespaces

An extension method cannot be accessed unless the namespace is in scope. Consider the extension method IsCapitalized in the following example:

```
using System;

namespace Utils
{
  public static class StringHelper
  {
    public static bool IsCapitalized (this string s)
    {
      if (string.IsNullOrEmpty(s)) return false;
      return char.IsUpper(s[0]);
    }
  }
}
```

To use IsCapitalized, the following application must import Utils, in order to avoid a compile-time error:

```
namespace MyApp
{
  using Utils;

  class Test
  {
    static void Main()
    {
      Console.WriteLine("Perth".IsCapitalized());
    }
  }
}
```

Extension methods versus instance methods

Any compatible instance method will always take precedence over an extension method. In the following example, Test's Foo method will always take precedence—even when called with an argument x of type int:

```
class Test
{
  public void Foo (object x) { }    // This method always wins
}

static class Extensions
```

```
    {
      public static void Foo (this Test t, int x) { }
    }
```

The only way to call the extension method in this case is via normal static syntax; in other words, Extensions.Foo(...).

Extension methods versus extension methods

If two extension methods have the same signature, the extension method must be called as an ordinary static method to disambiguate the method to call. If one extension method has more specific arguments than another, the more specific extension method takes precedence over the less one. For example:

```
    static class StringHelper
    {
      public static bool IsCapitalized (this string s)
      {
        if (string.IsNullOrEmpty (s)) return false;
        return char.IsUpper (s[0]);
      }
    }

    static class ObjectHelper
    {
      public static bool IsCapitalized (this object s)
      {
        return true;
      }
    }
```

Usage:

```
    // Calls StringHelper.IsCapitalized
    Console.WriteLine("Perth".IsCapitalized( ));

    // Explictly calling ObjectHelper.IsCapitalized
    Console.WriteLine(ObjectHelper.IsCapitalized("Perth"));
```

Extension Methods on Interfaces

Extension methods can apply to interfaces:

```
    using System;
    using System.Collections.Generic;

    static class Test
    {
      static void Main( )
      {
        var strings = new string[] { "a", "b", null, "c"};
        foreach (string s in strings.StripNulls( ))
          Console.WriteLine(s);
      }
```

```
static IEnumerable<T> StripNulls<T> (this IEnumerable<T> seq)
{
  foreach (T t in seq)
    if (t != null)
      yield return t;
}
}
```

Anonymous Types (C# 3.0)

An anonymous type is a simple class created on the fly to store a set of values. To create an anonymous type, use the new keyword followed by an object initializer, specifying the properties and values the type will contain. For example:

```
var dude = new { Name = "Bob", Age = 1 };
```

The compiler translates this to the following:

```
internal class AnonymousGeneratedTypeName
{
  private string name;  // actual field name is irrelevant
  private int     age;  // actual field name is irrelevant

  public string  Name get {return name;} {set {name = value;}}
  public int     Age  get {return age; } {set {age = value; }}
}
...

AnonymousGeneratedTypeName dude = new AnonymousGeneratedTypeName ( );
dude.Name = "Bob";
dude.Age = 1;
```

You must use the var keyword to reference an anonymous type, because the name of the type is anonymous.

The property name of an anonymous type can be inferred from an expression that is itself an identifier. For example:

```
int Age = 1;
var dude = new { Name = "Bob", Age };
```

is equivalent to:

```
var dude = new { Name = "Bob", Age = Age };
```

Anonymous types are used primarily when writing LINQ queries (see Chapter 8).

Attributes

You're already familiar with the notion of attributing code elements of a program with modifiers, such as virtual or ref. These constructs are built into the language. *Attributes* are an extensible mechanism for adding custom information to code elements (assemblies, types, members, return values, and parameters). This extensibility is useful for services that integrate deeply into the type system, without requiring special keywords or constructs in the C# language.

A good scenario for attributes is serialization—the process of converting arbitrary objects to and from a particular format. In this scenario, an attribute on a field can specify the translation between C#'s representation of the field and the format's representation of the field.

Attribute Classes

An attribute is defined by a class that inherits (directly or indirectly) from the abstract class `System.Attribute`. To attach an attribute to a code element, specify the attribute's type name in square brackets, before the code element. For example, the following attaches the `ObsoleteAttribute` to the `Foo` class:

```
[ObsoleteAttribute]
public class Foo {...}
```

This attribute is recognized by the compiler and will cause compiler warnings if a type or member marked obsolete is referenced. By convention, all attribute types end in the word "Attribute". C# recognizes this and allows you to omit the suffix when attaching an attribute:

```
[Obsolete]
public class Foo {...}
```

`ObsoleteAttribute` is a type declared in the `System` namespace as follows (simplified for brevity):

```
public sealed class SerializableAttribute : Attribute {...}
```

The C# language and the .NET Framework include a number of predefined attributes. We describe how to write your own attributes in Chapter 17.

Named and Positional Parameters

Attributes may have parameters. In the following example, we apply the `XmlElement` attribute to a class. The `XmlElement` attribute tells the `System.Xml.Linq` model how an object is represented in XML. The `XmlElement` attribute accepts several *attribute parameters*. The following attribute maps the `CustomerEntity` class to an XML element named `Customer`, belonging to the `http://oreilly.com` namespace:

```
[XmlElement ("Customer", Namespace="http://blah")]
public class CustomerEntity { ... }
```

Attribute parameters fall into one of two categories: positional and named. In the preceding example, the first argument is a *positional parameter*; the second is a *named parameter*. Positional parameters correspond to parameters of the attribute type's public constructors. Named parameters correspond to public fields or public properties on the attribute type.

When specifying an attribute, you must include positional parameters that correspond to one of the attribute's constructors. Named parameters are optional.

In Chapter 17, we describe the valid parameter types and rules for their evaluation.

Attribute Targets

Implicitly, the target of an attribute is the code element it immediately precedes, which is typically a type or type member. You can also attach attributes, however, to an assembly. This requires that you explicitly specify the attribute's target.

Here is an example of using the CLSCompliant attribute to specify CLS compliance for an entire assembly:

```
[assembly:CLSCompliant(true)]
```

Specifying Multiple Attributes

Multiple attributes can be specified for a single code element. Each attribute can be listed either within the same pair of square brackets (separated by a comma) or in separate pairs of square brackets (or a combination of the two). The following three examples are semantically identical:

```
[Serializable, Obsolete, CLSCompliant(false)]
public class Bar {...}

[Serializable] [Obsolete] [CLSCompliant(false)]
public class Bar {...}

[Serializable, Obsolete]
[CLSCompliant(false)]
public class Bar {...}
```

Unsafe Code and Pointers

C# supports direct memory manipulation via pointers within blocks of code marked unsafe and compiled with the /unsafe compiler option. Pointer types are primarily useful for interoperability with C APIs, but may also be used for accessing memory outside the managed heap or for performance-critical hotspots.

Pointer Basics

For every value type or pointer type V, there is a corresponding pointer type V^*. A pointer instance holds the address of a value. This is considered to be of type V, but pointer types can be (unsafely) cast to any other pointer type. Table 4-2 shows the main pointer operators.

Table 4-2. Pointer operators

Operator	Meaning
&	The *address-of* operator returns a pointer to the address of a value.
*	The *dereference* operator returns the value at the address of a pointer.
->	The *pointer-to-member* operator is a syntactic shortcut, in which x->y is equivalent to (*x).y.

Unsafe Code

By marking a type, type member, or statement block with the unsafe keyword, you're permitted to use pointer types and perform C++ style pointer operations on memory within that scope. Here is an example of using pointers to quickly process a bitmap:

```
unsafe void RedFilter(int[,] bitmap)
{
  int length = bitmap.Length;
  fixed (int* b = bitmap)
  {
    int* p = b;
    for(int i = 0; i < length; i++)
      *p++ &= 0xFF;
  }
}
```

Unsafe code can run faster than a corresponding safe implementation. In this case, the code would have required a nested loop with array indexing and bounds checking. An unsafe C# method may also be faster than calling an external C function, since there is no overhead associated with leaving the managed execution environment.

The fixed Statement

The fixed statement is required to pin a managed object, such as the bitmap in the previous example. During the execution of a program, many objects are allocated and deallocated from the heap. In order to avoid unnecessary waste or fragmentation of memory, the garbage collector moves objects around. Pointing to an object is futile if its address could change while referencing it, so the fixed statement tells the garbage collector to "pin" the object and not move it around. This may have an impact on the efficiency of the runtime, so fixed blocks should be used only briefly, and heap allocation should be avoided within the fixed block.

Within a fixed statement, you can get a pointer to any value type, an array of value types, or a string. In the case of arrays and strings, the pointer will actually point to the first element, which is a value type.

Value types declared inline within reference types require the reference type to be pinned, as follows:

```
class Test
{
  int x;
  static void Main( )
  {
    Test test = new Test ( );
    unsafe
    {
      fixed(int* p = &test.x)  // pins test
      {
        *p = 9;
      }
      System.Console.WriteLine(test.x);
    }
  }
}
```

We describe the fixed statement further in the section "Mapping a Struct to Unmanaged Memory" in Chapter 22.

The Pointer-to-Member Operator

In addition to the & and * operators, C# also provides the C++ style -> operator, which can be used on structs:

```
struct Test
{
  int x;
  unsafe static void Main( )
  {
    Test test = new Test( );
    Test* p = &test;
    p->x = 9;
    System.Console.WriteLine(test.x);
  }
}
```

Arrays

The stackalloc keyword

Memory can be allocated in a block on the stack explicitly using the stackalloc keyword. Since it is allocated on the stack, its lifetime is limited to the execution of the method, just as with any other local variable. The block may use the [] operator to index into memory.

```
int* a = stackalloc int [10];
for (int i = 0; i < 10; ++i)
  Console.WriteLine(a[i]); // print raw memory
```

Fixed-size buffers

Memory can be allocated in a block within a struct using the fixed keyword:

```
unsafe struct UnsafeUnicodeString
{
  public short Length;
  public fixed byte Buffer[30];
}

unsafe class UnsafeClass
{
  private UnsafeUnicodeString uus;
  public UnsafeClass (string s)
  {
    uus.Length = (short)s.Length;
    fixed (byte* p = uus.Buffer)
      for (int i = 0; i < s.Length; i++)
        p[i] = (byte)s[i];
  }
}
```

```
class Test
{
  static void Main( ) {new UnsafeClass("Christian Troy");}
}
```

The fixed keyword is also used in this example to pin the object on the heap that contains the buffer (which will be the instance of UnsafeClass).

void*

Rather than pointing to a specific value type, a pointer may make no assumptions about the type of the underlying data. This approach is useful for functions that deal with raw memory. An implicit conversion exists from any pointer type to void*. A void* cannot be dereferenced, and arithmetic operations cannot be performed on void pointers. For example:

```
class Test
{
  unsafe static void Main ()
  {
    short[ ] a = {1,1,2,3,5,8,13,21,34,55};
      fixed (short* p = a)
      {
        //sizeof returns size of value-type in bytes
        Zap (p, a.Length * sizeof (short));
      }
    foreach (short x in a)
      System.Console.WriteLine (x); // prints all zeros
  }

  unsafe static void Zap (void* memory, int byteCount)
  {
    byte* b = (byte*)memory;
      for (int i = 0; i < byteCount; i++)
        *b++ = 0;
  }
}
```

Pointers to Unmanaged Code

Pointers are also useful for accessing data outside the managed heap (such as when interacting with C DLLs or COM), or when dealing with data not in the main memory (such as graphics memory or a storage medium on an embedded device).

Preprocessor Directives

Preprocessor directives supply the compiler with additional information about regions of code. The most common preprocessor directives are the conditional directives, which provide a way to include or exclude regions of code from compilation. For example:

```
#define DEBUG
class MyClass
{
```

```
int x;
void Foo()
{
  # if DEBUG
  Console.WriteLine("Testing: x = {0}", x);
  # endif
}
...
}
```

In this class, the statement in Foo is compiled as conditionally dependent upon the presence of the DEBUG symbol. If we remove the DEBUG symbol, the statement is not compiled. Preprocessor symbols can be defined within a source file (as we have done), and they can be passed to the compiler with the /define: symbol command-line option.

The #error and #warning symbols prevent accidental misuse of conditional directives by making the compiler generate a warning or error given an undesirable set of compilation symbols. See Table 4-3 for a list of preprocessor directives and their actions.

Table 4-3. Preprocessor directives and their actions

Preprocessor directive	Action
#define *symbol*	Defines *symbol*.
#undef *symbol*	Undefines *symbol*.
#if *symbol* [*operator symbol2*] ...	*symbol* to test. *operator*s are = =, ! =, &&, and | | followed by #else, #elif, and #endif.
#else	Executes code to subsequent #endif.
#elif *symbol* [*operator symbol2*]	Combines #else branch and #if test.
#endif	Ends conditional directives.
#warning *text*	*text* of the warning to appear in compiler output.
#error *text*	*text* of the error to appear in compiler output.
#line [*number* ["*file*"] | hidden]	*number* specifies the line in source code; *file* is the filename to appear in computer output; hidden specifies that the compiler should generate debugger information (this feature was added in Visual C# 2003).
#region *name*	Marks the beginning of an outline.
#end *region*	Ends an outline region.

Conditional Attributes

An attribute decorated with the Conditional attribute will be compiled only if a given preprocessor symbol is present. For example:

```
// file1.cs
#define DEBUG
using System;
using System.Diagnostics;
```

```
[Conditional("DEBUG")]
public class TestAttribute : Attribute {}

// file2.cs
#define DEBUG
[Test]
class Foo
{
  [Test]
  private string s;
}
```

The compiler will not incorporate the [Test] attributes if the DEBUG symbol is in scope for *file2.cs*.

Pragma Warning

The compiler generates a warning when it spots something in your code that seems unintentional. Unlike errors, warnings don't ordinarily prevent your application from compiling.

Compiler warnings can be extremely valuable in spotting bugs. Their usefulness, however, is undermined when you get an excessive number of them. In a large application, maintaining a good signal-to-noise ratio is essential if the "real" warnings are to get noticed.

To this effect, the compiler allows you to selectively suppress warnings with the #pragma warning directive. In this example, we instruct the compiler not to warn us about the field Message not being used:

```
public class Foo
{
  static void Main( ) { }

  #pragma warning disable 414
  static string Message = "Hello";
  #pragma warning restore 414
}
```

Omitting the number in the #pragma warning directive disables or restores all warning codes.

If you are thorough in applying this directive, you can compile with the /warnaserror switch—this tells the compiler to treat any residual warnings as errors.

XML Documentation

Documentation comments are composed of embedded XML tags. Documentation comments start with three slashes (///), and apply to a type or type-member definition.

You can also use /** / for documentation comments (notice the extra star), but this format is less supported by the IDE.

The compiler can extract the documentation comments and output an XML file. Since the compiler understands the source code, it is able to validate the comments for consistency and expands cross-references into fully qualified type IDs.

The XML documentation file can be placed in the same directory as the application or library. The Visual Studio .NET IDE will automatically load this XML file, such that the documentation is integrated with IntelliSense. If you're producing a component library, you can use a tool such as NDoc or Sandcastle to produce HTML help files.

Here is an example of documentation comments for a type. If you're using Visual Studio .NET, typing a /// before a member automatically gets the IDE to prepopulate the summary and parameter tags. Within the documentation, starting a tag with < causes IntelliSense to give you a list of built-in XML documentation annotations.

```
// Filename: DocTest.cs
using System;

class Test
{
  /// <summary>
  /// The Foo method is called from
  ///     <see cref="Main">Main</see>
  /// </summary>
  /// <mytag>user defined tag info</mytag>
  /// <param name="s">Description for s</param>
  static void Foo(string s) { Console.WriteLine(s); }

  static void Main() { Foo("42"); }
}
```

When run through the compiler using the /doc:<filename> command-line option, the following XML file is generated:

```
<?xml version="1.0"?>
<doc>
  <assembly>
    <name>DocTest</name>
  </assembly>
  <members>
    <member name="M:Test.Foo(System.String)">
      <summary>
      The Foo method is called from
        <see cref="M:Test.Main">Main</see>
      </summary>
      <mytag>user defined tag info</mytag>
      <param name="s">Description for s</param>
```

```
        </member>
      </members>
    </doc>
```

Every member with a documentation comment has a `<member>` tag with a `name` attribute that uniquely identifies the member. The `cref` attribute in the `<see>` tag has been expanded to correctly refer to another code element. The custom documentation element `<mytag>` is just carried along with the member payload.

Predefined XML Tags

Here is a list of the predefined set of XML tags that can be used to mark up the descriptive text:

`<summary>`
> `<summary>`*description*`</summary>`
> This is the first thing you will see when IntelliSense shows the tool tip for the member.

`<remarks>`
> `<remarks>`*description*`</remarks>`
> This is the additional text you will see when IntelliSense shows the tool tip for the member. This tag provides additional information regarding a particular member. Information about side effects within the method, or particular behavior that may not otherwise be intuitive (such as the idea that this method may throw an `ArrayOutOfBoundsException` if a parameter is greater than 5) is listed here.

`<param>`
> `<param name="`*name*`">`*description*`</param>`
> This tag describes a parameter on a method. If this tag is applied to any parameter on a method, all of the parameters on that method must be documented.

`<returns>`
> `<returns>`*description*`</returns>`
> This tag describes the return value for a method.

`<exception>`
> `<exception [cref="`*type*`"]>`*description*`</exception>`
> This tag documents the exceptions a method may throw. If present, the optional `cref` attribute should refer to the type of the exception. The type name must be enclosed in double quotation marks ("").

`<permission>`
> `<permission [cref="`*type*`"]>`*description*`</permission>`
> This tag documents the permissions requirement for a type or member. If present, the optional `cref` attribute should refer to the type that represents the permission set required by the member, although the compiler does not validate this. The type name must be enclosed in double quotation marks ("").

<example>

> <example>*description*</example>

This tag provides a description and sample source code explaining the use of a type or member. Typically, the <example> tag provides the description and contains the <c> and <code> tags, although they can also be used independently.

<c>

> <c>*code*</c>

This tag indicates an inline code snippet. Typically, this tag is used inside an <example> block (described previously).

<code>

> <code>*code*</code>

This tag is used to indicate multiline code snippets. Again, this is typically used inside an <example> block (described previously).

<see>

> <see cref="*member*">*text*</see>

This tag identifies cross-references in the documentation to other types or members. Typically, the <see> tag is used inline within a description (as opposed to the <seealso> tag, which is broken out into a separate "See Also" section). This tag is useful because it allows tools to generate cross-references, indexes, and hyperlinked views of the documentation. Member names must be enclosed by double quotation marks ("").

<seealso>

> <seealso cref="*member*">*text*</seealso>

This tag identifies cross-references in the documentation to other types or members. Typically, <seealso> tags are broken out into a separate "See Also" section. This tag is useful because it allows tools to generate cross-references, indexes, and hyperlinked views of the documentation. Member names must be enclosed by double quotation marks ("").

<value>

> <value>*description*</value>

This tag describes a property on a class.

<paramref>

> <paramref name="*name*"/>

This tag identifies the use of a parameter name within descriptive text, such as <remarks>. The name must be enclosed by double quotation marks ("").

<list>

> <list type=[bullet | number | table]>
>   <listheader>
>   <term>*name*</term>
>   <description>*description*</description>
>   </listheader>
>   <item>
>   <term>*name*</term>
>   <description>*description*</description>
>   </item>
> </list>

This tag provides hints to documentation generators about how to format the documentation—in this case, as a list of items.

`<para>`
> `<para>`*text*`</para>`
> This tag sets off the text as a paragraph to documentation generators.

`<include>`
> `<include file='`*filename*`' path='`*path-to-element*`'>`
> This tag specifies an external file that contains documentation and an XPath path to a specific element in that file. For example, a path of `docs[@id="001"]/*` retrieves whatever is inside `<docs id="001"/>`. The `filename` and `path` must be enclosed by single quotation marks (`' '`), but you must use double quotation marks (`""`) for the `id` attribute within the `path-to-element` expression.

User-Defined Tags

There is little that is special about the predefined XML tags recognized by the C# compiler, and you are free to define your own. The only special processing done by the compiler is on the `<param>` tag (in which it verifies the parameter name and that all the parameters on the method are documented) and the `cref` attribute (in which it verifies that the attribute refers to a real type or member and expands it to a fully qualified type or member ID). The `cref` attribute can also be used in your own tags and is verified and expanded just as it is in the predefined `<exception>`, `<permission>`, `<see>`, and `<seealso>` tags.

Type or Member Cross-References

Type names and type or member cross-references are translated into IDs that uniquely define the type or member. These names are composed of a prefix that defines what the ID represents and a signature of the type or member.

Table 4-4 lists the set of type or member prefixes.

Table 4-4. XML type ID prefixes

XML type prefix	ID prefixes applied to
N	Namespace
T	Type (class, struct, enum, interface, delegate)
F	Field
P	Property (includes indexers)
M	Method (includes special methods)
E	Event
!	Error

The rules describing how the signatures are generated are well documented, although fairly complex.

Here is an example of a type and the IDs that are generated:

```csharp
// Namespaces do not have independent signatures
namespace NS
{
  /// T:NS.MyClass
  class MyClass
  {
    /// F:NS.MyClass.aField
    string aField;

    /// P:NS.MyClass.aProperty
    short aProperty {get {...} set {...}}

    /// T:NS.MyClass.NestedType
    class NestedType {...};

    /// M:NS.MyClass.X()
    void X() {...}

    /// M:NS.MyClass.Y(System.Int32,System.Double@,System.Decimal@)
    void Y(int p1, ref double p2, out decimal p3) {...}

    /// M:NS.MyClass.Z(System.Char[ ],System.Single[0:,0:])
    void Z(char[ ] 1, float[,] p2) {...}

    /// M:NS.MyClass.op_Addition(NS.MyClass,NS.MyClass)
    public static MyClass operator+(MyClass c1, MyClass c2) {...}

    /// M:NS.MyClass.op_Implicit(NS.MyClass)~System.Int32
    public static implicit operator int(MyClass c) {...}

    /// M:NS.MyClass.#ctor
    MyClass() {...}

    /// M:NS.MyClass.Finalize
    ~MyClass() {...}

    /// M:NS.MyClass.#cctor
    static MyClass() {...}
  }
}
```

5

Framework Overview

Almost all the capabilities of the .NET Framework are exposed via a vast set of managed types. These types are organized into hierarchical namespaces and packaged into a set of assemblies, which together with the CLR comprise the .NET platform.

Some of the .NET types are used directly by the CLR and are essential for the managed hosting environment. These types reside in an assembly called *mscorlib.dll* and include C#'s built-in types, as well as the basic collection classes, types for stream processing, serialization, reflection, threading, and native interoperability.

At a level above this are additional types that "flesh out" the CLR-level functionality, providing features such as XML, networking, and LINQ. These reside in *System.dll*, *System.Xml.dll*, and *System.Core.dll*, and together with *mscorlib* they provide a rich programming environment upon which the rest of the Framework is built. This "core framework" largely defines the scope of this book.

The remainder of the .NET Framework consists of applied APIs, most of which cover three areas of functionality:

- User interface technologies
- Backend technologies
- Distributed system technologies

Table 5-1 shows the history of compatibility between each version of C#, CLR, and the .NET Framework. Interestingly, C# 3.0 targets a new Framework version while using the same CLR version as its predecessor. To be precise, C# 3.0 targets an *updated* version of CLR 2.0, which is installed as part of Framework 3.5. This update is designed not to break compatibility with existing applications.

Table 5-1. C#, CLR, and .NET Framework versions

C# version	CLR version	Framework versions
1.0	1.0	1.0
1.1	1.1	1.1
2.0	2.0	2.0
		3.0
3.0	2.0 (updated)	3.5

This chapter skims all key areas of the .NET Framework—starting with the core types covered in this book and finishing with an overview of the applied technologies.

> Assemblies and namespaces in the .NET Framework *cross cut*. The most extreme examples are *mscorlib.dll* and *System.Core.dll*, both defining types in dozens of namespaces, none of which is prefixed with "mscorlib" or "System.Core". The less obvious cases are the more confusing ones, however, such as the types in System.Security.Cryptography. Most types in this namespace reside in *System.dll*, except for a handful, which reside in *System. Security.dll*. Appendix B lists a complete mapping of Framework namespaces to assemblies.

The CLR and Core Framework

System Types

The most fundamental types live directly in the System namespace. These include C#'s built-in types, the Exception base class, the Enum, Array, and Delegate base classes, and Nullable, Type, DateTime, TimeSpan, and Guid. The System namespace also includes types for performing mathematical functions (Math), generating random numbers (Random), and converting between various types (Convert and BitConverter).

Chapter 6 describes these types—as well as the interfaces that define standard protocols used across the .NET Framework for such tasks as formatting (IFormattable) and order comparison (IComparable).

The System namespace also defines the IDisposable interface and the GC class for interacting with the garbage collector. These topics are saved for Chapter 12.

Text Processing

The System.Text namespace contains the StringBuilder class (the editable or *mutable* cousin of string), and the types for working with text encodings, such as UTF-8 (Encoding and its subtypes). We cover this in Chapter 6.

The System.Text.RegularExpressions namespace contains types that perform advanced pattern-based search and replace operations. It is described in Chapter 24.

What's New in .NET Framework 3.5

Much of what's new in Framework 3.5 centers on LINQ. This includes:

- The standard query operators, in `System.Linq`
- The object model for expression trees, in `System.Linq.Expressions`
- The LINQ to SQL API, in `System.Data.Linq`
- The LINQ to XML document object model, in `System.Xml.Linq`
- A set of general-purpose generic `Action<>` and `Func<>` delegates in the `System` namespace

Framework 3.5 also features the following new core types:

- `System.DateTimeOffset`, for representing a point in time as UTC+offset
- `System.TimeZoneInfo`, for obtaining the offset and daylight saving data of any time zone
- `HashSet<T>`, in `System.Collections.Generic`, for representing a *set* (a dictionary with keys and no values)
- `ReaderWriterLockSlim` in `System.Threading`—an improved version of the former `ReaderWriterLock`
- `PipeStream` and a set of associated types in `System.IO.Pipes`, for stream-based interprocess communication via Windows pipes

There is also a plethora of specialized new APIs and types:

- A PNRP implementation for peer-to-peer communication via that protocol (`System.Net.PeerToPeer`)
- A hosting model for extensibility (`System.AddIn`)
- A managed provider for WMI 2.0 (`System.Management.Instrumentation`)
- An ETW trace listener (`EventProviderTraceListener`) and a schema-aware `EventSchemaTraceListener`
- A managed interface to the performance counters supported by Windows Vista and higher (`System.Diagnostics.PerformanceData`)

In addition, `System.Security.Cryptography` has been supplemented with types to support the "Suite B" set of cryptography algorithms, defined by the National Security Agency.

Framework 3.5 also features enhancements to the four APIs introduced in .NET Framework 3.0:

- Windows Presentation Foundation (WPF)
- Windows Communication Foundation (WCF)
- Windows Workflow
- Windows CardSpace

Most of the new core features of Framework 3.5 have been isolated to a new assembly called *System.Core.dll* to minimize the impact of the CLR 2.0 upgrade (a notable exception is `DateTimeOffset` which is in the [updated] *mscorlib.dll*).

Collections

The .NET Framework offers a variety of classes for managing collections of items. These include both list- and dictionary-based structures, and work in conjunction with a set of standard interfaces that unify their common characteristics. All collection types are defined in the following namespaces, covered in Chapter 7:

```
System.Collections              // Nongeneric collections
System.Collections.Generic      // Generic collections
System.Collections.Specialized  // Strongly typed collections
System.Collections.ObjectModel  // Bases for your own collections
```

Queries

New to C# 3.0 is Language Integrated Query, or LINQ. LINQ allows you to perform type-safe queries over local and remote collections (e.g., SQL Server tables) and is described in Chapters 8–10. A big advantage of LINQ is that it presents a consistent querying API across a variety of domains. The types for resolving LINQ queries reside in these namespaces:

```
System.Linq
System.Xml.Linq          // LINQ to XML
System.Data.Linq         // LINQ to SQL
System.Linq.Expressions  // For building expressions manually
```

The LINQ to SQL API leverages lower-level ADO.NET types in the System.Data namespace.

XML

XML is used widely within the .NET Framework, and so is supported extensively. Chapter 10 focuses entirely on LINQ to XML—a lightweight XML document object model that can be constructed and queried through LINQ. Chapter 11 describes the older W3C DOM, as well as the performant low-level reader/writer classes and the Framework's support for XML schemas, stylesheets, and XPath. The XML namespaces are:

```
System.Xml               // XmlReader, XmlWriter + the old W3C DOM
System.Xml.Linq          // The LINQ to XML DOM
System.Xml.Schema        // Support for XSD
System.Xml.XPath         // XPath query language
System.Xml.Xsl           // Stylesheet support
System.Xml.Serialization // Declarative XML serialization for .NET types
```

Streams and I/O

The Framework provides a stream-based model for low-level input/output. Streams are typically used to read and write directly to files and network connections, and can be chained or wrapped in decorator streams to add compression or encryption functionality. Chapter 13 describes .NET's stream architecture, as well as the specific support for working with files and directories, compression, and isolated storage. The Stream and I/O types are defined in these namespaces:

```
System.IO
System.IO.Pipes
```

```
System.IO.Compression
System.IO.IsolatedStorage
```

Networking

You can directly access standard network protocols such as HTTP, FTP, TCP/IP, and SMTP via the types in `System.Net`. In Chapter 14, we demonstrate how to communicate using each of these protocols, starting with simple tasks such as downloading from a web page, and finishing with using TCP/IP directly to retrieve POP3 email. Here are the namespaces we cover:

```
System.Net
System.Net.Mail          // For sending mail via SMTP
System.Net.Sockets       // TCP, UDP, and IP
```

Serialization

The Framework provides several systems for saving and restoring objects to a binary or text representation. Such systems are required for distributed application technologies, such as WCF, Web Services, and Remoting, and also to save and restore objects to a file. In Chapter 15, we cover all three serialization engines: the data contract serializer, the binary serializer, and the XML serializer. The types for serialization reside in the following namespaces:

```
System.Runtime.Serialization
System.Runtime.Serialization.Formatters.Binary
System.Runtime.Serialization.Formatters.SOAP
System.Xml.Serialization
```

Assemblies, Reflection, and Attributes

The assemblies into which C# programs compile comprise executable instructions (stored as intermediate language or IL) and metadata, which describes the program's types, members, and attributes. Through reflection, you can inspect this metadata at runtime, and do such things as dynamically invoke methods. With `Reflection.Emit`, you can construct new code on the fly.

In Chapter 16, we describe the makeup of assemblies and how to sign them, use the global assembly cache and resources, and resolve file references. In Chapter 17, we cover reflection and attributes—describing how to inspect metadata, dynamically invoke functions, write custom attributes, emit new types, and parse raw IL. The types for using reflection and working with assemblies reside in the following namespaces:

```
System
System.Reflection
System.Reflection.Emit
```

Security

The .NET Framework provides its own security layer, allowing you to both sandbox other assemblies and be sandboxed yourself. In Chapter 18, we cover code access, role, and identity security, and describe how operating system security impacts .NET applications. We then describe cryptography in the Framework, covering encryption, hashing, and data protection. The types for this are defined in:

```
System.Security
System.Security.Permissions
System.Security.Policy
System.Security.Cryptography
```

Threading and Asynchronous Methods

Multithreading allows you to execute code in parallel. Chapter 19 explores this subject in detail, describing both the Framework's support for multithreading and the strategies for writing multithreaded applications. In Chapter 20, we describe how to use asynchronous methods to write highly concurrent server-based applications.

All types for threading are in the System.Threading namespace.

Application Domains

The CLR provides an additional level of isolation within a process, called an *application domain*. In Chapter 21, we examine the properties of an application domain with which you can interact, and demonstrate how to create and use additional application domains within the same process for such purposes as unit testing. We also describe how to use Remoting to communicate with these application domains. The AppDomain type is defined in the System namespace.

Native Interoperability

You can interoperate with native and Win32 code through the P/Invoke system. The .NET runtime allows you to call native functions, register callbacks, map data structures, and interoperate with native data types. The types that support this are in System.Runtime.InteropServices, and we cover them in Chapter 22.

The System.Runtime.InteropServices namespace also defines types for COM interoperability. We don't discuss COM interoperability in this book; however, the chapters from previous editions of *C# in a Nutshell* featuring this topic are available free of charge from the companion web site, *http://www.albahari.com/nutshell/*.

Diagnostics

In Chapter 23, we cover .NET's logging and assertion facilities, and describe how to interact with other processes, write to the Windows event log, and use performance counters for monitoring. The types for this are defined in System.Diagnostics.

Applied Technologies

User Interface Technologies

The .NET Framework provides three APIs for user-interface-based applications:

ASP.NET (System.Web.UI)
: For writing thin client applications that run over a standard web browser

Windows Presentation Foundation (System.Windows)
: For writing rich client applications that target the .NET Framework 3.0

Windows Forms (System.Windows.Forms)
: For writing rich client applications that target the classic Windows API, supported in all versions of the .NET Framework

In general, a thin client application amounts to a web site; a rich client application is a program the end user must download or install on the client computer.

ASP.NET

Applications written using ASP.NET host under Windows IIS and can be accessed from almost any web browser. Here are its advantages over rich client technologies:

- Zero deployment at the client end.
- Clients can run a non-Windows platform.
- Updates are easily deployed.

Further, because most of what you write in an ASP.NET application runs on the server, you design your data access layer to run in the same application domain—without limiting security or scalability. In contrast, a rich client that does the same is not generally as secure or scalable. (The solution, with the rich client, is to insert a *middle tier* between the client and database. The middle tier runs on a remote application server [often alongside the database server] and communicates with the rich clients via WCF, Web Services, or Remoting.)

Another benefit of ASP.NET is that it's mature—it was introduced with the first version of .NET and has been refined with each subsequent .NET release.

The limitations of ASP.NET are largely a reflection of the limitations of thin client systems in general:

- A web browser interface significantly restricts what you can do.
- Maintaining state on the client—or on behalf of the client—is cumbersome.

You can improve the interactivity and responsiveness, however, through client-side scripting or technologies such as AJAX: a good resource for this is *http://ajax.asp.net/*.

The types for writing ASP.NET applications are in the System.Web.UI namespace and its subnamespaces, and are packed in the *System.Web.dll* assembly.

Windows Presentation Foundation (WPF)

WPF is a rich client technology new to Framework 3.0. Framework 3.0 comes preinstalled on Windows Vista—and is available as a separate download for Windows XP SP2.

The benefits of WPF are as follows:

- It supports sophisticated graphics, such as arbitrary transformations, 3D rendering, and true transparency.
- Its primary measurement unit is not pixel-based, so applications display correctly at any DPI (dots per inch).
- It has extensive dynamic layout support, which means you can localize an application without danger of elements overlapping.
- Rendering uses DirectX and is fast, taking good advantage of graphics hardware acceleration.
- User interfaces can be described declaratively in XAML files that can be maintained independently of the "code-behind" files—this helps to separate appearance from functionality.

Here are its limitations:

- The technology is less mature than Windows Forms or ASP.NET.
- Its size and complexity make for a steep learning curve.
- Your clients must run Windows Vista—or Windows XP with Framework 3.0 or later.

The types for writing WPF applications are in the System.Windows namespace and all subnamespaces except for System.Windows.Forms.

Windows Forms

Windows Forms is a rich client API that—like ASP.NET—is as old as the .NET Framework. Compared to WPF, Windows Forms is a relatively simple technology that provides most of the features you need in writing a typical Windows application. It also has significant relevancy in maintaining legacy applications. It has a number of drawbacks, though, compared to WPF:

- Controls are positioned and sized in pixels, making it easy to write applications that break on clients whose DPI settings differ from the developer's.
- The API for drawing nonstandard controls is GDI+, which, although reasonably flexible, is slow in rendering large areas (and without double buffering, flickers horribly).
- Controls lack true transparency.
- Dynamic layout is difficult to get right reliably.

The last point is an excellent reason to favor WPF over Windows Forms—even if you're writing a business application that needs just a user interface and not a "user experience." The layout elements in WPF, such as Grid, make it easy to assemble labels and text boxes such that they always align—even after language changing localization—without messy logic and without any flickering. Further, you don't have to bow to the lowest common denominator in screen resolution—WPF layout elements have been designed from the outset to adapt properly to resizing.

On the subject of speed, it was originally thought that graphics card manufacturers would incorporate GDI+ hardware accelerators. This never happened; their focus was instead on DirectX. Consequently, GDI+ is considerably slower than even its predecessor, GDI, let alone WPF.

On the positive side, Windows Forms is relatively simple to learn and has a wealth of support in third-party controls.

The Windows Forms types are in the `System.Windows.Forms` (in *System.Windows.Forms.dll*) and `System.Drawing` (in *System.Drawing.dll*) namespaces. The latter also contains the GDI+ types for drawing custom controls.

Backend Technologies

ADO.NET

ADO.NET is the managed data access API. Although the name is derived from ADO (ActiveX Data Objects), the technology is completely different. ADO.NET comprises two major components:

Provider layer
> The provider model defines common classes and interfaces for low-level access to database providers. These interfaces comprise connections, commands, adapters, and readers (forward-only, read-only cursors over a database). The Framework ships with native support for Microsoft SQL Server and Oracle and has OLE-DB and ODBC providers.

DataSet model
> A DataSet is a structured cache of data. It resembles a primitive in-memory database, which defines SQL constructs such as tables, rows, columns, relationships, constraints, and views. By programming against a cache of data, you can reduce the number of trips to the server, increasing server scalability and the responsiveness of a rich-client user interface. DataSets are serializable and are designed to be sent across the wire between client and server applications.

LINQ to SQL sits above the provider layer, leveraging the lower-level connection and reader types. With LINQ to SQL, you avoid having to manually construct and parameterize SQL statements, reducing the volume of code in an application's data access layer and improving its type safety. LINQ to SQL also partially avoids the need for DataSets through its object-relational mapping system. DataSets have some advantages, though, such as being able to serialize state-changes to XML (something particularly useful in multitier applications). LINQ and DataSets can interoperate, however; for instance, you can use LINQ to perform type-safe queries over DataSet objects.

Windows Workflow

Windows Workflow is a framework for modeling and managing potentially long-running business processes. Workflow targets a standard runtime library, providing consistency and interoperability. Workflow also helps reduce coding for dynamically controlled decision-making trees.

Windows Workflow is not strictly a backend technology—you can use it anywhere (an example is page flow, in the UI).

Workflow is another part of the shipment of assemblies that came with the .NET Framework 3.0, so like WPF it leverages services that require the operating system support of Windows Vista—or Windows XP after a Framework 3.0 installation. The Workflow types are defined in, and are below, the `System.WorkFlow` namespace.

COM+ and MSMQ

The Framework allows you to interoperate with COM+ for services such as distributed transactions, via types in the `System.EnterpriseServices` namespace. It also supports MSMQ (Microsoft Message Queuing) for asynchronous, one-way messaging through types in `System.Messaging`.

Distributed System Technologies

Windows Communication Foundation (WCF)

WCF is the communications infrastructure new to Framework 3.0. WCF is flexible and configurable enough to make both of its predecessors—Remoting and (.ASMX) Web Services—*mostly* redundant.

WCF, Remoting, and Web Services are all alike in that they implement the following basic model in allowing a client and server application to communicate:

- On the server, you indicate what methods you'd like remote client applications to be able to call.
- On the client, you specify or infer the *signatures* of the server methods you'd like to call.
- On both the server and the client, you choose a transport and communication protocol (in WCF, this is done through a *binding*).
- The client establishes a connection to the server.
- The client calls a remote method, which executes transparently on the server.

WCF further decouples the client and server through service contracts and data contracts. Conceptually, the client sends an (XML) message to an endpoint on a remote *service*, rather than directly invoking a remote *method*. One of the benefits of this decoupling is that clients have no dependency on the .NET platform or on any proprietary communication protocols.

WCF is highly configurable and provides the most extensive support for standardized messaging protocols, including WS-*. This lets you communicate with parties running different software—possibly on different platforms—while still supporting advanced features such as encryption. Another benefit of WCF is that you can change protocols without needing to change other aspects of your client or server applications.

The types for communicating with WCF are in, and are below, the System. ServiceModel namespace.

Remoting and Web Services

Remoting and .ASMX Web Services are WCF's predecessors and are almost redundant in WCF's wake—although Remoting still has a niche in communicating between application domains within the same process (see Chapter 20).

Remoting's functionality is geared toward tightly coupled applications. A typical example is when the client and server are both .NET applications written by the same company (or companies sharing common assemblies). Communication typically involves exchanging potentially complex custom .NET objects that the Remoting infrastructure serializes and deserializes without needing intervention.

The functionality of Web Services is geared toward loosely coupled or SOA-style applications. A typical example is a server designed to accept simple SOAP-based messages that originate from clients running a variety of software—on a variety of platforms. Web Services can only use HTTP and SOAP as transport and formatting protocols, and applications are normally hosted under IIS. The benefits of interoperability come at a performance cost—a Web Services application is typically slower, in both execution and development time, than a well-designed Remoting application.

The types for Remoting are in or under System.Runtime.Remoting; the types for Web Services are under System.Web.Services.

CardSpace

CardSpace comprises the final new piece of the .NET 3.0 shipment. CardSpace is a token-based authentication and identity management protocol designed to simplify password management for end users. CardSpace builds on open XML standards, and parties can participate independently of Microsoft.

With CardSpace, a user can hold multiple identities, which are maintained by a third party (the *identity provider*). When a user wants to access a resource at site X, the user authenticates to the identity provider, which then issues a token to site X. This avoids having to provide a password directly to site X and reduces the number of identities that the user needs to maintain.

WCF allows you to specify a CardSpace identity when connecting through a secure HTTP channel, through types in the System.IdentityModel.Claims and System.IdentityModel.Policy namespaces.

6

Framework Fundamentals

Many of the core facilities that you need when programming are provided not by the C# language, but by types in the .NET Framework. In this chapter, we cover the Framework's role in fundamental programming tasks, such as virtual equality comparison, order comparison, and type conversion. We also cover the basic Framework types, such as String, DateTime, and Enum.

The types in this section reside in the System namespace, with the following exceptions:

- StringBuilder is defined in System.Text, as are the types for *text encodings*.
- CultureInfo and associated types are defined in System.Globalization.
- XmlConvert is defined in System.Xml.

String and Text Handling

char

A C# char represents a single Unicode character and aliases the System.Char struct. In Chapter 2, we described how to express char literals. For example:

```
char c = 'A';
char newLine = '\n';
```

System.Char defines a range of static methods for working with characters, such as ToUpper, ToLower, and IsWhiteSpace. You can call these through either the System.Char type or its char alias:

```
Console.WriteLine (System.Char.ToUpper ('c'));    // C
Console.WriteLine (char.IsWhiteSpace ('\t'));     // True
```

Most of char's static methods are related to categorizing characters and are listed in Table 6-1.

Table 6-1. Static methods for categorizing characters

Static method	Characters included	Unicode categories included
IsLetter	A–Z, a–z, and letters of other alphabets	UpperCaseLetter LowerCaseLetter TitleCaseLetter ModifierLetter OtherLetter
IsUpper	Uppercase letters	UpperCaseLetter
IsLower	Lowercase letters	LowerCaseLetter
IsDigit	0–9 plus digits of other alphabets	DecimalDigitNumber
IsLetterOrDigit	Letters plus digits	Sum of IsLetter and IsDigit
IsNumber	All digits plus Unicode fractions and Roman numeral symbols	DecimalDigitNumber LetterNumber OtherNumber
IsSeparator	Space plus all Unicode separator characters	LineSeparator ParagraphSeparator
IsWhiteSpace	All separators plus /n, /r, /t, /f, and /v	LineSeparator ParagraphSeparator
IsPunctuation	Symbols used for punctuation in Western and other alphabets	DashPunctuation ConnectorPunctuation InitialQuotePunctuation FinalQuotePunctuation
IsSymbol	Most other printable symbols	MathSymbol ModifierSymbol OtherSymbol
IsControl	Nonprintable "control" characters below 0x20, such as /r, /n, /t, /0, and characters between 0x7F and 0x9A	(None)

For more granular categorization, char provides a static method called GetUnicodeCategory; this returns a UnicodeCategory enumeration whose members are shown in the rightmost column of Table 6-1.

> By explicitly casting from an integer, it's possible to produce a char outside of the allocated Unicode set. To test a character's validity, call char.GetUnicodeCategory: if the result is UnicodeCategory. OtherNotAssigned, the character is invalid.

A char is 16 bits wide—enough to represent any Unicode character in the *Basic Multilingual Plane*. To go outside of this, you must use surrogate pairs: the methods for doing this are described later in this chapter in the section "Text Encodings and Unicode."

String

A C# string (== System.String) is an immutable (unchangeable) sequence of characters. In Chapter 2, we described how to express string literals, perform equality comparisons, and concatenate two strings. This section covers the remaining functions for working with strings, exposed through the static and instance members of the System.String class.

Constructing strings

The simplest way to construct a string is to assign a literal, as we saw in Chapter 2:

```
string s1 = "Hello";
string s2 = "First Line\r\nSecond Line";
string s3 = @"\\server\fileshare\helloworld.cs";
```

To create a repeating sequence of characters you can use string's constructor:

```
Console.Write (new string ('*', 10));      // **********
```

You can also construct a string from a char array. The ToCharArray method does the reverse:

```
char[] ca = "Hello".ToCharArray();
string s = new string (ca);                // s = "Hello"
```

string's constructor is also overloaded to accept various (unsafe) pointer types, in order to create strings from types such as char*.

Null and empty strings

An empty string has a length of zero. To create an empty string, you can use either a literal or the static string.Empty field; to test for an empty string, you can either perform an equality comparison or test its Length property:

```
string empty = "";
Console.WriteLine (empty == "");             // True
Console.WriteLine (empty == string.Empty);   // True
Console.WriteLine (empty.Length == 0);       // True
```

Because strings are reference types, they can also be null:

```
string nullString = null;
Console.WriteLine (nullString == null);       // True
Console.WriteLine (nullString == "");         // False
Console.WriteLine (nullString.Length == 0);   // NullReferenceException
```

The static string.IsNullOrEmpty method is a useful shortcut for testing whether a given string is either null or empty.

Accessing characters within a string

A string's indexer returns a single character at the given index. As with all functions that operate on strings, this is zero-indexed:

```
string str = "abcde";
char letter = str[1];        // letter == 'b'
```

string also implements IEnumerable<char>, meaning you can foreach over its characters:

```
foreach (char c in "123") Console.Write (c + ",");     // 1,2,3,
```

Searching within strings

The simplest methods for searching within strings are Contains, StartsWith, and EndsWith. These all return true or false:

```
Console.WriteLine ("quick brown fox".Contains ("brown"));    // True
Console.WriteLine ("quick brown fox".EndsWith ("fox"));      // True
```

IndexOf is more powerful: it returns the first position of a given character or substring (or −1 if the substring isn't found):

```
Console.WriteLine ("abcde".IndexOf ("cd"));    // 2
```

IndexOf is overloaded to accept a startPosition (an index from which to begin searching) and a StringComparison enum. The latter allows you to perform case-insensitive searches:

```
Console.WriteLine ("abcde".IndexOf ("CD",
                     StringComparison.CurrentCultureIgnoreCase));    // 2
```

LastIndexOf is like IndexOf, but works backward through the string.

IndexOfAny returns the first matching position of any one of a set of characters:

```
Console.Write ("ab,cd ef".IndexOfAny (new char[] {' ', ','} ));    // 2
Console.Write ("pas5w0rd".IndexOfAny ("0123456789".ToCharArray() ));  // 3
```

LastIndexOfAny does the same in the reverse direction.

Manipulating strings

Because String is immutable, all the methods that "manipulate" a string return a new one, leaving the original untouched (the same goes for when you reassign a string variable).

Substring extracts a portion of a string:

```
string left3 = "12345".Substring (0, 3);     // left3 = "123";
string mid3  = "12345".Substring (1, 3);     // mid3 = "234";
```

If you omit the length, you get the remainder of the string:

```
string end3  = "12345".Substring (2);        // end3 = "345";
```

Insert and Remove insert or remove characters at a specified position:

```
string s1 = "helloworld".Insert (5, ", ");    // s1 = "hello, world"
string s2 = s1.Remove (5, 2);                 // s2 = "helloworld";
```

PadLeft and PadRight pad a string to a given length with a specified character (or a space if unspecified):

```
Console.WriteLine ("12345".PadLeft (9, '*'));  // ****12345
Console.WriteLine ("12345".PadLeft (9));       //     12345
```

If the input string is longer than the padding length, the original string is returned unchanged.

Framework
Fundamentals

TrimStart and TrimEnd remove specified characters from the beginning or end of a string; Trim does both. By default, these functions remove whitespace characters (including spaces, tabs, new lines, and Unicode variations of these):

```
Console.WriteLine ("  abc \t\r\n ".Trim( ).Length);    // 3
```

Replace replaces all occurrences of a particular character or substring:

```
Console.WriteLine ("to be done".Replace (" ", " | ") );  // to | be | done
Console.WriteLine ("to be done".Replace (" ", "")    );  // tobedone
```

ToUpper and ToLower return upper- and lowercase versions of the input string. By default, they honor the user's current language settings; ToUpperInvariant and ToLowerInvariant always apply English alphabet rules.

Splitting and joining strings

Split takes a sentence and returns an array of words:

```
string[] words = "The quick brown fox".Split( );

foreach (string word in words)
  Console.Write (word + "|");      // The|quick|brown|fox|
```

By default, Split uses whitespace characters as delimiters; it's also overloaded to accept a params char[] of custom delimiters. Split also optionally accepts a StringSplitOptions enum, which has an option to remove empty entries: this is useful when words are separated by several delimiters in a row.

The static Join method does the reverse of Split. It requires a delimiter and string array:

```
string[] words = "The quick brown fox".Split( );
string together = string.Join (" ", words);      // The quick brown fox
```

The static Concat method is similar to Join but accepts only a params string array and applies no separator. Concat is exactly equivalent to the + operator (the compiler, in fact, translates + to Concat):

```
string sentence     = string.Concat ("The", " quick", " brown", " fox");
string sameSentence = "The" + " quick" + " brown" + " fox";
```

String.Format and composite format strings

The static Format method provides a convenient way to build strings that embed variables. The embedded variables can be of any type; the Format simply calls ToString on them.

The master string that includes the embedded variables is called a *composite format string*. When calling String.Format, you provide a composite format string followed by each of the embedded variables. For example:

```
string composite = "It's {0} degrees in {1} on this {2} morning";
string s = string.Format (composite, 35, "Perth", DateTime.Now.DayOfWeek);

// s == "It's 35 degrees in Perth on this Friday morning"
```

(And that's Celsius!)

Each number in curly braces is called a *format item*. The number corresponds to the argument position and is optionally followed by:

- A comma and a *minimum width* to apply
- A colon and a *format string*

The minimum width is useful for aligning columns. If the value is negative, the data is left-aligned; otherwise, it's right-aligned. For example:

```
string composite = "Name={0,-20} Credit Limit={1,15:C}";

Console.WriteLine (string.Format (composite, "Mary", 500));
Console.WriteLine (string.Format (composite, "Elizabeth", 20000));
```

Here's the result:

```
Name=Mary               Credit Limit=       $500.00
Name=Elizabeth          Credit Limit=    $20,000.00
```

The equivalent without using `string.Format` is this:

```
string s = "Name=" + "Mary".PadRight (20) +
           " Credit Limit=" + 500.ToString ("C").PadLeft (15);
```

The credit limit is formatted as currency by virtue of the "C" format string. Format strings are described in detail later, in the section "Formatting and Parsing."

A disadvantage of composite format strings is that it's easier to make a mistake that goes unnoticed until runtime—such as having greater or fewer format items than values. Such a mistake is harder to make when the format items and values are together.

Comparing Strings

In comparing two values, the .NET Framework differentiates the concepts of *equality comparison* and *order comparison*. Equality comparison tests whether two instances are semantically the same; order comparison tests which of two (if any) instances comes first when arranging them in ascending or descending sequence.

Equality comparison is not a *subset* of order comparison; the two systems have different purposes. It's legal, for instance, to have two unequal values in the same ordering position. We resume this topic later, in the section "Equality comparison."

For string equality comparison, you can use the `==` operator or one of `string`'s `Equals` methods. The latter are more versatile because they allow you to specify options such as case insensitivity.

For string order comparison, you can use either the `CompareTo` instance method or the static `Compare` and `CompareOrdinal` methods: these return a positive or negative number—or zero—depending on whether the first value comes before, after, or alongside the second.

Before going into the details of each, we need to examine .NET's underlying string comparison algorithms.

Ordinal versus culture comparison

There are two basic algorithms for string comparison: *ordinal* and *culture-sensitive*. Ordinal comparisons interpret characters simply as numbers (according to their numeric Unicode value); culture-sensitive comparisons interpret characters with reference to a particular alphabet. There are two special cultures: the "current culture," which is based on settings picked up from the computer's control panel, and the "invariant culture," which, by default, is the same on every computer (and closely maps American culture).

For equality comparison, both ordinal and culture-specific algorithms are useful. For ordering, however, culture-specific comparison is nearly always preferable: to order strings alphabetically, you need an alphabet. Ordinal relies on the numeric Unicode point values, which happen to put English characters in alphabetical order—but even then not exactly as you might expect. For example, assuming case sensitivity, consider the strings "Atom", "atom", and "Zamia". The invariant culture puts them in the following order:

```
"Atom", "atom", "Zamia"
```

Ordinal arranges them instead as follows:

```
"Atom", "Zamia", "atom"
```

This is because the invariant culture encapsulates an alphabet, which considers uppercase characters adjacent to their lowercase counterparts (AaBbCcDd...). The ordinal algorithm, however, puts all the uppercase characters first, and then all lowercase characters (A..Z, a..z). This is essentially a throwback from the ASCII character set invented in the 1960s.

Equality comparison

Despite ordinal's limitations, string's == operator always performs *ordinal case-sensitive* comparison. The same goes for the instance version of string.Equals when called without arguments; this defines the "default" equality comparison behavior for the string type.

> The ordinal algorithm was chosen for string's == and Equals functions because it's both highly efficient and *deterministic*. String equality comparison is considered fundamental and is performed far more frequently than order comparison.
>
> A "strict" notion of equality is also consistent with the general use of the == operator.

The following methods allow culture-aware or case-insensitive comparisons:

```
public bool Equals(string value, StringComparison comparisonType);

public static bool Equals (string a, string b,
                           StringComparison comparisonType);
```

The static version is advantageous in that it still works if one or both of the strings are null. StringComparison is an enum defined as follows:

```
public enum StringComparison
{
  CurrentCulture,              // Case-sensitive
  CurrentCultureIgnoreCase,
  InvariantCulture,            // Case-sensitive
  InvariantCultureIgnoreCase,
  Ordinal,                     // Case-sensitive
  OrdinalIgnoreCase
}
```

For example:

```
Console.WriteLine (string.Equals ("foo", "FOO",
                   StringComparison.OrdinalIgnoreCase));    // True

Console.WriteLine ("ü" == "ü");                    // False

Console.WriteLine (string.Equals ("ü", "ü",
                   StringComparison.CurrentCulture));      // ?
```

(The result of the final comparison is determined by the computer's current language settings.)

Order comparison

String's CompareTo instance method performs *culture-sensitive*, *case-sensitive* order comparison. Unlike the == operator, CompareTo does not use ordinal comparison: for ordering, a culture-sensitive algorithm is much more useful.

Here's the method's definition:

```
public int CompareTo (string strB);
```

> The CompareTo instance method implements the generic IComparable interface, a standard comparison protocol used across the .NET Framework. This means string's CompareTo defines the default ordering behavior strings, in such applications as sorted collections, for instance. For more information on IComparable, see the section "Order Comparison" later in this chapter.

For other kinds of comparison, you can call the static Compare and CompareOrdinal methods:

```
public static int Compare (string strA, string strB,
                           StringComparison comparisonType);

public static int Compare (string strA, string strB, bool ignoreCase,
                           CultureInfo culture);

public static int Compare (string strA, string strB, bool ignoreCase);

public static int CompareOrdinal (string strA, string strB);
```

The last two methods are simply shortcuts for calling the first two methods.

All of the order comparison methods return a positive number, a negative number, or zero, depending on whether the first value comes after, before, or alongside the second value:

```
Console.WriteLine ("Boston".CompareTo ("Austin"));    // 1
Console.WriteLine ("Boston".CompareTo ("Boston"));    // 0
Console.WriteLine ("Boston".CompareTo ("Chicago"));   // -1
Console.WriteLine ("ŭ".CompareTo ("ŭ"));    // 0
Console.WriteLine ("foo".CompareTo ("FOO"));          // -1
```

The following performs a case-insensitive comparison using the current culture:

```
Console.WriteLine (string.Compare ("foo", "FOO", true));   // 0
```

By supplying a CultureInfo object, you can plug in any alphabet:

```
// CultureInfo is defined in the System.Globalization namespace

CultureInfo german = CultureInfo.GetCultureInfo ("de-DE");
int i = string.Compare ("Müller", "Muller", false, german);
```

StringBuilder

The StringBuilder class (System.Text namespace) represents a mutable (editable) string. With a StringBuilder, you can Append, Insert, Remove, and Replace substrings without replacing the whole StringBuilder.

StringBuilder's constructor optionally accepts an initial string value, as well as a starting size for its internal capacity (default is 16 bytes). If you go above this, StringBuilder automatically resizes its internal structures to accommodate (at a slight performance cost) up to its maximum capacity (default is 2 billion bytes).

A popular use of StringBuilder is to build up a long string by repeatedly calling Append. This approach is much more efficient than repeatedly concatenating ordinary string types:

```
StringBuilder sb = new StringBuilder();
for (int i = 0; i < 50; i++) sb.Append (i + ",");
```

To get the final result, call ToString():

```
Console.WriteLine (sb.ToString());

0,1,2,3,4,5,6,7,8,9,10,11,12,13,14,15,16,17,18,19,20,21,22,23,24,25,26,
27,28,29,30,31,32,33,34,35,36,37,38,39,40,41,42,43,44,45,46,47,48,49,
```

AppendLine performs an Append that adds a new line sequence ("\r\n" in Windows). AppendFormat accepts a composite format string, just like String. Format.

As well as the Insert, Remove, and Replace methods (Replace functions such as string's Replace), StringBuilder defines a Length property and a writable indexer for getting/setting individual characters.

To clear the contents of a StringBuilder, either instantiate a new one or set its Length to zero.

Setting a `StringBuilder`'s Length to zero doesn't shrink its *internal* capacity. So, if the `StringBuilder` previously contained 1 million characters, it will continue to occupy around 2 MB of memory after zeroing its Length. If you want to release the memory, you must create a new `StringBuilder` and allow the old one to drop out of scope (and be garbage-collected).

Text Encodings and Unicode

A *character set* is an allocation of characters, each with a numeric code or *code point*. There are two character sets in common use: Unicode and ASCII. Unicode has an address space of approximately 1 million characters, of which about 100,000 are currently allocated. Unicode covers most spoken world languages, as well as some historical languages and special symbols. The ASCII set is simply the first 128 characters of the Unicode set, which covers most of what you see on a U.S.-style keyboard. ASCII predates Unicode by 30 years and is still sometimes used for its simplicity and efficiency: each character is represented by one byte.

The .NET type system is designed to work with the Unicode character set. ASCII is implicitly supported, though, by virtue of being a subset of Unicode.

A *text encoding* maps characters from their numeric code point to a binary representation. In .NET, text encodings come into play primarily when dealing with text files or streams. When you read a text file into a string, a *text encoder* translates the file data from binary into the internal Unicode representation that the char and string types expect. A text encoding can restrict what characters can be represented, as well as impacting storage efficiency.

There are two categories of text encoding in .NET:

- Those that map Unicode characters to another character set
- Those that use standard Unicode encoding schemes

The first category contains legacy encodings such as IBM's EBCDIC and 8-bit character sets with extended characters in the upper-128 region that were popular prior to Unicode (identified by a code page). The ASCII encoding is also in this category: it encodes the first 128 characters and drops everything else. This category contains the *nonlegacy* GB18030 as well, which is the mandatory standard for applications written in China—or sold to China—since 2000.

In the second category are UTF-8, UTF-16, and UTF-32 (and the obsolete UTF-7). Each differs in space efficiency. UTF-8 is the most space-efficient: it uses *between one and four bytes* to represent each character. The first 128 characters require only a single byte, making it compatible with ASCII. UTF-8 is the most popular encoding for text files and streams (particularly on the Internet), and it is the default for stream I/O in .NET.

UTF-16 uses one or two 16-bit words to represent each character, and is what .NET uses internally to represent characters and strings. Some programs also write files in UTF-16.

UTF-32 is the least space-efficient: it maps each code point directly to 32 bits, so every character consumes 4 bytes. UTF-32 is rarely used for this reason.

Obtaining an Encoding object

The Encoding class in System.Text is the common base type for classes that encapsulate text encodings. There are several subclasses—their purpose is to encapsulate families of encodings with similar features. You can ignore their presence, however, and obtain the correct encoding object by calling Encoding.GetEncoding with a standard IANA name:

```
Encoding utf8 = Encoding.GetEncoding ("utf-8");
Encoding chinese = Encoding.GetEncoding ("GB18030");
```

The most common encodings can also be obtained through dedicated static properties on Encoding:

Encoding name	Static property on Encoding
UTF-8	Encoding.UTF8
UTF-16	Encoding.Unicode (*not* UTF16)
UTF-32	Encoding.UTF32
ASCII	Encoding.ASCII

The static GetEncodings method returns a list of all supported encodings, with their standard IANA names:

```
foreach (EncodingInfo info in Encoding.GetEncodings())
  Console.WriteLine (info.Name);
```

Encoding for file and stream I/O

The most common application for an Encoding object is to control how text is read and written to a file or stream. For example, the following writes "Testing…" to a file called *data.txt* in UTF-16 encoding:

```
System.IO.File.WriteAllText ("data.txt", "Testing...", Encoding.Unicode);
```

If you omit the final argument, WriteAllText applies the ubiquitous UTF-8 encoding. UTF-8 is the default text encoding for all file and stream I/O.

We resume this subject in Chapter 13, in the section "Stream Adapters."

Encoding to byte arrays

You can also use an Encoding object to go to and from a byte array. The GetBytes method converts from string to byte[] with the given encoding; GetString converts from byte[] to string:

```
byte[] utf8Bytes  = System.Text.Encoding.UTF8.GetBytes    ("0123456789");
byte[] utf16Bytes = System.Text.Encoding.Unicode.GetBytes ("0123456789");
byte[] utf32Bytes = System.Text.Encoding.UTF32.GetBytes   ("0123456789");

Console.WriteLine (utf8Bytes.Length);    // 10
Console.WriteLine (utf16Bytes.Length);   // 20
Console.WriteLine (utf32Bytes.Length);   // 40

string original1 = System.Text.Encoding.UTF8.GetString    (utf8Bytes);
```

```
string original2 = System.Text.Encoding.Unicode.GetString (utf16Bytes);
string original3 = System.Text.Encoding.UTF32.GetString  (utf32Bytes);

Console.WriteLine (original1);        // 0123456789
Console.WriteLine (original2);        // 0123456789
Console.WriteLine (original3);        // 0123456789
```

UTF-16 and strings

Recall that .NET stores characters and strings in UTF-16. Because UTF-16 requires 1 or two 2 16-bit words per character, and a char is only 16 bits in length, some Unicode characters require 2 chars to represent. This has a couple of consequences:

- A string's Length property may be greater than its real character count.
- A single char is not always enough to fully represent a Unicode character.

Most applications ignore this, because nearly all commonly used characters fit into a section of Unicode called the *Basic Multilingual Plane*, which requires only one 16-bit word in UTF-16. The BMP covers several dozen world languages and includes more than 30,000 Chinese characters. Excluded are characters of some ancient languages, symbols for musical notation, and some less common Chinese characters.

If you need to support two-word characters, the following static methods in char convert a 32-bit code point to a string of two chars, and back again:

```
string ConvertFromUtf32 (int utf32)
int    ConvertToUtf32   (char highSurrogate, char lowSurrogate)
```

Two-word characters are called *surrogates*. They are easy to spot because each word is in the range 0xD800 to 0xDFFF. You can use the following static methods in char to assist:

```
bool IsSurrogate     (char c)
bool IsHighSurrogate (char c)
bool IsLowSurrogate  (char c)
bool IsSurrogatePair (char highSurrogate, char lowSurrogate)
```

The StringInfo class in the System.Globalization namespace also provides a range of methods and properties for working with two-word characters.

Characters outside the BMP typically require special fonts and have limited operating system support.

Dates and Times

Three immutable structs in the System namespace do the job of representing dates and times: DateTime, DateTimeOffset, and TimeSpan. C# doesn't define any special keywords that map to these types.

TimeSpan

A TimeSpan represents an interval of time—or a time of the day. In the latter role, it's simply the interval of time since midnight. A TimeSpan has a resolution of

100 ns, has a maximum value of about 10 million days, and can be positive or negative.

There are three ways to construct a TimeSpan:

- Through one of the constructors
- By calling one of the static From... methods
- By subtracting one DateTime from another

Here are the constructors:

```
public TimeSpan (int hours, int minutes, int seconds);
public TimeSpan (int days, int hours, int minutes, int seconds);
public TimeSpan (int days, int hours, int minutes, int seconds,
                                                int milliseconds);
public TimeSpan (long ticks);   // Each tick = 100ns
```

The static From... methods are more convenient when you want to specify an interval in just a single unit, such as minutes, hours, and so on:

```
public static TimeSpan FromDays (double value);
public static TimeSpan FromHours (double value);
public static TimeSpan FromMinutes (double value);
public static TimeSpan FromSeconds (double value);
public static TimeSpan FromMilliseconds (double value);
```

For example:

```
Console.WriteLine (new TimeSpan (2, 30, 0));        // 02:30:00
Console.WriteLine (TimeSpan.FromHours (2.5));        // 02:30:00
Console.WriteLine (TimeSpan.FromHours (-2.5));       // -02:30:00
```

TimeSpan overloads the < and > operators, as well as the + and - operators. The following expression evaluates to a TimeSpan of 2.5 hours:

```
TimeSpan.FromHours(2) + TimeSpan.FromMinutes(30);
```

The next expression evaluates to 1 second short of 10 days:

```
TimeSpan.FromDays(10) - TimeSpan.FromSeconds(1);   // 9.23:59:59
```

Using this expression, we can illustrate the integer properties Days, Hours, Minutes, Seconds, and Milliseconds:

```
TimeSpan nearlyTenDays = TimeSpan.FromDays(10) - TimeSpan.FromSeconds(1);

Console.WriteLine (nearlyTenDays.Days);          // 9
Console.WriteLine (nearlyTenDays.Hours);         // 23
Console.WriteLine (nearlyTenDays.Minutes);       // 59
Console.WriteLine (nearlyTenDays.Seconds);       // 59
Console.WriteLine (nearlyTenDays.Milliseconds);  // 0
```

In contrast, the Total... properties return values of type double describing the entire time span:

```
Console.WriteLine (nearlyTenDays.TotalDays);          // 9.99998842592593
Console.WriteLine (nearlyTenDays.TotalHours);         // 239.999722222222
Console.WriteLine (nearlyTenDays.TotalMinutes);       // 14399.9833333333
Console.WriteLine (nearlyTenDays.TotalSeconds);       // 863999
Console.WriteLine (nearlyTenDays.TotalMilliseconds);  // 863999000
```

The static Parse method does the opposite of ToString, converting a string to a TimeSpan. TryParse does the same, but returns false rather than throwing an exception if the conversion fails. The XmlConvert class also provides TimeSpan/string conversion methods that follow standard XML formatting protocols.

The default value for a TimeSpan is TimeSpan.Zero.

TimeSpan can also be used to represent the time of the day. To obtain the current time of day, call DateTime.Now.TimeOfDay.

DateTime and DateTimeOffset

DateTime and DateTimeOffset are immutable structs for representing a date, and optionally, a time. They have a resolution of 100 ns, and a range covering the years 0001 through 9999.

DateTimeOffset is new to Framework 3.5 and is functionally similar to DateTime. Its distinguishing feature is that it also stores a UTC offset; this allows more meaningful results when comparing values across different time zones.

> An excellent article on the rationale behind the introduction of DateTimeOffset is available on the MSDN BCL blogs. The title is "A Brief History of DateTime," by Anthony Moore.

Choosing between DateTime and DateTimeOffset

DateTime and DateTimeOffset differ in how they handle time zones. A DateTime incorporates a three-state flag indicating whether the DateTime is relative to:

- The local time on the current computer
- UTC (the modern equivalent of Greenwich Mean Time)
- Unspecified

A DateTimeOffset is more specific—it stores the offset from UTC as a TimeSpan:

```
July 01 2007 03:00:00 -06:00
```

This influences equality comparisons, which is the main factor in choosing between DateTime and DateTimeOffset. Specifically:

- DateTime ignores the three-state flag in comparisons and considers two values equal if they have the same year, month, day, hour, minute, and so on.
- DateTimeOffset considers two values equal if they refer to the *same point in time*.

> Daylight saving can make this distinction important even if your application doesn't need to handle multiple geographic time zones.

So, DateTime considers the following two values different, whereas DateTimeOffset considers them equal:

```
July 01 2007 09:00:00 +00:00 (GMT)
July 01 2007 03:00:00 -06:00 (local time, Central America)
```

In most cases, DateTimeOffset's equality logic is preferable. For example, in calculating which of two international events is more recent, a DateTimeOffset implicitly gives the right answer. Similarly, a hacker plotting a distributed denial of service attack would reach for a DateTimeOffset! To do the same with DateTime requires standardizing on a single time zone (typically UTC) throughout your application. This is problematic for two reasons:

- To be friendly to the end user, UTC DateTimes require explicit conversion to local time prior to formatting.
- It's easy to forget and incorporate a local DateTime.

DateTime is better, though, at specifying a value relative to the local computer at runtime—for example, if you want to schedule an archive at each of your international offices for next Sunday, at 3 A.M. local time (when there's least activity). Here, DateTime would be more suitable because it would respect each site's local time.

Internally, DateTimeOffset uses a short integer to store the UTC offset in minutes. It doesn't store any regional information, so there's nothing present to indicate whether an offset of +08:00, for instance, refers to Singapore time or Perth time.

We revisit time zones and equality comparison in more depth in the section "Dates and Time Zones."

SQL Server 2008 introduces direct support for DateTimeOffset through a new data type of the same name.

Constructing a DateTime

DateTime defines constructors that accept integers for the year, month, and day—and optionally, the hour, minute, second, and millisecond:

```
public DateTime (int year, int month, int day);
```

```
public DateTime (int year, int month, int day,
                 int hour, int minute, int second, int millisecond);
```

If you specify only a date, the time is implicitly set to midnight (0:00).

The DateTime constructors also allow you to specify a DateTimeKind—an enum with the following values:

```
Unspecified, Local, Utc
```

This corresponds to the three-state flag described in the preceding section. Unspecified is the default, and it means that the DateTime is time zone agnostic. Local means relative to the local time zone on the current computer. A local DateTime does not include information about *which particular time zone* it refers to, nor, unlike DateTimeOffset, the numeric offset from UTC.

A DateTime's Kind property returns its DateTimeKind.

DateTime's constructors are also overloaded to accept a `Calendar` object as well—this allows you to specify a date using any of the `Calendar` subclasses defined in `System.Globalization`. For example:

```
DateTime d = new DateTime (5767, 1, 1,
                    new System.Globalization.HebrewCalendar( ));

Console.WriteLine (d);     // 12/12/2006 12:00:00 AM
```

(The formatting of the date in this example depends on your computer's control panel settings.) A `DateTime` always uses the default Gregorian calendar—this example, a one-time conversion, takes place during construction. To perform computations using another calendar, you must use the methods on the `Calendar` subclass itself.

You can also construct a `DateTime` with a single *ticks* value of type `long`, where *ticks* is the number of 100 ns intervals from midnight 01/01/0001.

For interoperability, `DateTime` provides the static `FromFileTime` and `FromFileTimeUtc` methods for converting from a Windows file time (specified as a `long`) and `FromOADate` for converting from an OLE automation date/time (specified as a `double`).

To construct a `DateTime` from a string, call the static `Parse` or `ParseExact` method. Both methods accept optional flags and format providers; `ParseExact` also accepts a format string. We discuss parsing in greater detail in the section "Formatting and Parsing."

Constructing a DateTimeOffset

`DateTimeOffset` has a similar set of constructors. The difference is that you also specify a UTC offset as a `TimeSpan`:

```
public DateTimeOffset (int year, int month, int day,
                    int hour, int minute, int second,
                    TimeSpan offset);

public DateTimeOffset (int year, int month, int day,
                    int hour, int minute, int second, int millisecond,
                    TimeSpan offset);
```

The `TimeSpan` must amount to a whole number of minutes, or an exception is thrown.

`DateTimeOffset` also has constructors that accept a `Calendar` object, a `long` *ticks* value, and static `Parse` and `ParseExact` methods that accept a string.

You can construct a `DateTimeOffset` from an existing `DateTime` either by using these constructors:

```
public DateTimeOffset (DateTime dateTime);
public DateTimeOffset (DateTime dateTime, TimeSpan offset);
```

or with an implicit cast:

```
DateTimeOffset dt = new DateTime (2000, 2, 3);
```

The implicit cast from `DateTime` to `DateTimeOffset` is handy because most of the .NET Framework supports `DateTime`—not `DateTimeOffset`.

If you don't specify an offset, it's inferred from the `DateTime` value using these rules:

- If the `DateTime` has a `DateTimeKind` of `Utc`, the offset is zero.
- If the `DateTime` has a `DateTimeKind` of `Local` or `Unspecified` (the default), the offset is taken from the current local time zone.

To convert in the other direction, `DateTimeOffset` provides three properties that return values of type `DateTime`:

- The `UtcDateTime` property returns a `DateTime` in UTC time.
- The `LocalDateTime` property returns a `DateTime` in the current local time zone (converting it if necessary).
- The `DateTime` property returns a `DateTime` in whatever zone it was specified; in other words, it returns the UTC time plus the offset.

The current DateTime/DateTimeOffset

Both `DateTime` and `DateTimeOffset` have a static `Now` property that returns the current date and time:

```
Console.WriteLine (DateTime.Now);          // 11/11/2007 1:23:45 PM
Console.WriteLine (DateTimeOffset.Now);    // 11/11/2007 1:23:45 PM -06:00
```

`DateTime` also provides a `Today` property that returns just the date portion:

```
Console.WriteLine (DateTime.Today);        // 11/11/2007 12:00:00 AM
```

The static `UtcNow` property returns the current date and time in UTC:

```
Console.WriteLine (DateTime.UtcNow);           // 11/11/2007 7:23:45 AM
Console.WriteLine (DateTimeOffset.UtcNow);     // 11/11/2007 7:23:45 AM +00:00
```

The precision of all these methods depends on the operating system and is typically in the 10–20 milliseconds region.

Working with dates and times

`DateTime` and `DateTimeOffset` provide a similar set of instance properties that return various date/time elements:

```
DateTime dt = new DateTime (2000, 2, 3,
                            10, 20, 30);

Console.WriteLine (dt.Year);          // 2000
Console.WriteLine (dt.Month);         // 2
Console.WriteLine (dt.Day);           // 3
Console.WriteLine (dt.DayOfWeek);     // Thursday
Console.WriteLine (dt.DayOfYear);     // 34

Console.WriteLine (dt.Hour);          // 10
```

```
Console.WriteLine (dt.Minute);        // 20
Console.WriteLine (dt.Second);        // 30
Console.WriteLine (dt.Millisecond);   // 0
Console.WriteLine (dt.Ticks);         // 630851700300000000
Console.WriteLine (dt.TimeOfDay);     // 10:20:30  (returns a TimeSpan)
```

DateTimeOffset also has an Offset property of type TimeSpan.

Both types provide the following instance methods to perform computations (most accept an argument of type double or int):

```
AddYears   AddMonths   AddDays
AddHours   AddMinutes  AddSeconds  AddMilliseconds  AddTicks
```

These all return a new DateTime or DateTimeOffset, and they take into account such things as leap years. You can pass in a negative value to subtract.

The Add method adds a TimeSpan to a DateTime or DateTimeOffset. The + operator is overloaded to do the same job:

```
TimeSpan ts = TimeSpan.FromMinutes (90);
Console.WriteLine (dt.Add (ts));        // 3/02/2000 11:50:30 AM
Console.WriteLine (dt + ts);            // 3/02/2000 11:50:30 AM
```

You can also subtract a TimeSpan from a DateTime/DateTimeOffset and subtract one DateTime/DateTimeOffset from another. The latter gives you a TimeSpan:

```
DateTime thisYear = new DateTime (2007, 1, 1);
DateTime nextYear = thisYear.AddYears (1);
TimeSpan oneYear = nextYear - thisYear;
```

Formatting and parsing

Calling ToString on a DateTime formats the result as a *short date* (all numbers) followed by a *long time* (including seconds). For example:

```
3/02/2000 11:50:30 AM
```

The operating system's control panel, by default, determines such things as whether the day, month, or year comes first, the use of leading zeros, and whether 12- or 24-hour time is used.

Calling ToString on a DateTimeOffset is the same, except that the offset is returned also:

```
3/02/2000 11:50:30 AM -06:00
```

The ToShortDateString and ToLongDateString methods return just the date portion. The long date format is also determined by the control panel; an example is "Saturday, 17 February 2007". ToShortTimeString and ToLongTimeString return just the time portion, such as 17:10:10 (the former excludes seconds).

These four methods just described are actually shortcuts to four different *format strings*. ToString is overloaded to accept a format string and provider, allowing you to specify a wide range of options and control how regional settings are applied. We describe this in the section "Formatting and Parsing" later in this chapter.

DateTimes and DateTimeOffsets can be misparsed if the culture settings differ from those in force when formatting takes place. You can avoid this problem by using ToString in conjunction with a format string that ignores culture settings (such as "o"):

```
DateTime dt1 = DateTime.Now;
string cannotBeMisparsed = dt1.ToString ("o");
DateTime dt2 = DateTime.Parse (cannotBeMisparsed);
```

The static Parse and ParseExact methods do the reverse of ToString, converting a string to a DateTime or DateTimeOffset. The Parse method is also overloaded to accept a format provider.

Null DateTime and DateTimeOffset values

Because DateTime and DateTimeOffset are structs, they are not intrinsically nullable. When you need nullability, there are two ways around this:

- Use a Nullable type (i.e., DateTime? or DateTimeOffset?).
- Use the static field DateTime.MinValue or DateTimeOffset.MinValue (the *default values* for these types).

A nullable type is usually the best approach because the compiler helps to prevent mistakes. DateTime.MinValue is useful for backward compatibility with code written prior to C# 2.0 (when nullable types were introduced).

Calling ToUniversalTime or ToLocalTime on a DateTime.MinValue can result in it no longer being DateTime.MinValue (depending on which side of GMT you are on). If you're right on GMT (England, outside daylight saving), the problem won't arise at all because local and UTC times are the same. This is your compensation for the English winter!

Dates and Time Zones

In this section, we examine in more detail how time zones influence DateTime and DateTimeOffset. We also look at the TimeZone and TimeZoneOffset types, which provide information on time zone offsets and daylight saving.

DateTime and Time Zones

DateTime is simplistic in its handling of time zones. Internally, it stores a DateTime using two pieces of information:

- A 62-bit number, indicating the number of ticks since 1/1/0001
- A 2-bit enum, indicating the DateTimeKind (Unspecified, Local, or Utc)

When you compare two DateTime instances, only their *ticks* values are compared; their DateTimeKinds are ignored:

```
DateTime dt1 = new DateTime (2000, 1, 1, 10, 20, 30, DateTimeKind.Local);
DateTime dt2 = new DateTime (2000, 1, 1, 10, 20, 30, DateTimeKind.Utc);
Console.WriteLine (dt1 == dt2);          // True
```

```
DateTime local = DateTime.Now;
DateTime utc = local.ToUniversalTime( );
Console.WriteLine (local == utc);          // False
```

The instance methods ToUniversalTime/ToLocalTime convert to universal/local time. These apply the computer's current time zone settings and return a new DateTime with a DateTimeKind of Utc or Local. No conversion happens if you call ToUniversalTime on a DateTime that's already Utc, or ToLocalTime on a DateTime that's already Local. You will get a conversion, however, if you call ToUniversal-Time or ToLocalTime on a DateTime that's Unspecified.

You can construct a DateTime that differs from another only in Kind with the static DateTime.SpecifyKind method:

```
DateTime d = new DateTime (2000, 12, 12);  // Unspecified
DateTime utc = DateTime.SpecifyKind (d, DateTimeKind.Utc);
Console.WriteLine (utc);               // 12/12/2000 12:00:00 AM
```

DateTimeOffset and Time Zones

Internally, DateTimeOffset comprises a DateTime field whose value is always in UTC, and a 16-bit integer field for the UTC offset in minutes. Comparisons look only at the (UTC) DateTime; the Offset is used primarily for formatting.

The ToUniversalTime/ToLocalTime methods return a DateTimeOffset representing the same point in time, but with a UTC or local offset. Unlike with DateTime, these methods don't affect the underlying date/time value, only the offset:

```
DateTimeOffset local = DateTimeOffset.Now;
DateTimeOffset utc   = local.ToUniversalTime( );

Console.WriteLine (local.Offset);   // -06:00:00 (in Central America)
Console.WriteLine (utc.Offset);     // 00:00:00

Console.WriteLine (local == utc);                  // True
```

To include the Offset in the comparison, you must use the EqualsExact method:

```
Console.WriteLine (local.EqualsExact (utc));       // False
```

TimeZone and TimeZoneInfo

The TimeZone and TimeZoneInfo classes provide information on time zone names, UTC offsets, and daylight saving rules. TimeZoneInfo is the more powerful of the two and is new to Framework 3.5.

The biggest difference between the two types is that TimeZone lets you access only the current local time zone, whereas TimeZoneInfo provides access to all the world's time zones. Further, TimeZoneInfo exposes a richer (although at times, more awkward) rules-based model for describing daylight saving.

TimeZone

The static TimeZone.CurrentTimeZone method returns a TimeZone object based on the current local settings. The following demonstrates the result if run in Western Australia.

```
TimeZone zone = TimeZone.CurrentTimeZone;
Console.WriteLine (zone.StandardName);     // W. Australia Standard Time
Console.WriteLine (zone.DaylightName);     // W. Australia Daylight Time
```

The IsDaylightSavingTime and GetUtcOffset methods work as follows:

```
DateTime dt1 = new DateTime (2008, 1, 1);
DateTime dt2 = new DateTime (2008, 6, 1);
Console.WriteLine (zone.IsDaylightSavingTime (dt1));     // True
Console.WriteLine (zone.IsDaylightSavingTime (dt2));     // False
Console.WriteLine (zone.GetUtcOffset (dt1));             // 09:00:00
Console.WriteLine (zone.GetUtcOffset (dt2));             // 08:00:00
```

The GetDaylightChanges method returns specific daylight saving information for a
given year:

```
DaylightTime day = zone.GetDaylightChanges (2008);
Console.WriteLine (day.Start);    // 26/10/2008 2:00:00 AM   (Note D/M/Y)
Console.WriteLine (day.End);      // 30/03/2008 3:00:00 AM
Console.WriteLine (day.Delta);    // 01:00:00
```

TimeZoneInfo

The TimeZoneInfo class works in a similar manner. TimeZoneInfo.Local returns the
current local time zone:

```
TimeZoneInfo zone = TimeZoneInfo.Local;
Console.WriteLine (zone.StandardName);     // W. Australia Standard Time
Console.WriteLine (zone.DaylightName);     // W. Australia Daylight Time
```

TimeZoneInfo also provides IsDaylightSavingTime and GetUtcOffset methods—the
difference is that they accept either a DateTime or DateTimeOffset.

You can obtain a TimeZoneInfo for any of the world's time zones by calling
FindSystemTimeZoneById with the zone ID. This feature is unique to TimeZoneInfo,
as is everything else that we demonstrate from this point on. We'll stick with
Western Australia for reasons that will soon become clear:

```
TimeZoneInfo wa = TimeZoneInfo.FindSystemTimeZoneById
                  ("W. Australia Standard Time");

Console.WriteLine (wa.Id);                          // W. Australia Standard Time
Console.WriteLine (wa.DisplayName);                 // (GMT+08:00) Perth
Console.WriteLine (wa.BaseUtcOffset);               // 08:00:00
Console.WriteLine (wa.SupportsDaylightSavingTime);  // True
```

The Id property corresponds to the value passed to FindSystemTimeZoneById. The
static GetSystemTimeZones method returns all world time zones; hence, you can list
all valid zone ID strings as follows:

```
foreach (TimeZoneInfo z in TimeZoneInfo.GetSystemTimeZones())
    Console.WriteLine (z.Id);
```

You can also create a custom time zone by calling `TimeZoneInfo.CreateCustomTimeZone`. Because `TimeZoneInfo` is immutable, you must pass in all the relevant data as method arguments.

You can serialize a predefined or custom time zone to a (semi) human-readable string by calling `ToSerializedString`—and deserialize it by calling `TimeZoneInfo.FromSerializedString`.

The static `ConvertTime` method converts a `DateTime` or `DateTimeOffset` from one time zone to another. You can include either just a destination `TimeZoneInfo`—or both source and destination `TimeZoneInfo` objects. You can also convert directly from or to UTC with the methods `ConvertTimeFromUtc` and `ConvertTimeToUtc`.

For working with daylight saving, `TimeZoneInfo` provides the following additional methods:

- `IsInvalidTime` returns true if a `DateTime` is within the hour (or delta) that's skipped when the clocks move forward.
- `IsAmbiguousTime` returns true if a `DateTime` or `DateTimeOffset` is within the hour (or delta) that's repeated when the clocks move back.
- `GetAmbiguousTimeOffsets` returns an array of `TimeSpans` representing the valid offset choices for an ambiguous `DateTime` or `DateTimeOffset`.

Unlike with `TimeZone`, you can't obtain simple dates from a `DateZoneInfo` indicating the start and end of daylight saving. Instead, you must call `GetAdjustmentRules`, which returns a declarative summary of all daylight saving rules that apply to all years. Each rule has a `DateStart` and `DateEnd` indicating the date range within which the rule is valid:

```
foreach (TimeZoneInfo.AdjustmentRule rule in wa.GetAdjustmentRules())
    Console.WriteLine ("Rule: applies from " + rule.DateStart +
                       " to " + rule.DateEnd);
```

Western Australia first introduced daylight saving in 2006, *midseason*. This required a special rule for the first year; hence, there are two rules:

```
Rule: applies from 1/01/2006 12:00:00 AM to 31/12/2006 12:00:00 AM
Rule: applies from 1/01/2007 12:00:00 AM to 31/12/9999 12:00:00 AM
```

Each `AdjustmentRule` has a `DaylightDelta` property of type `TimeSpan` (this is one hour in almost every case) and properties called `DaylightTransitionStart` and `DaylightTransitionEnd`. The latter two are of type `TimeZoneInfo.TransitionTime`, which has the following properties:

```
public bool IsFixedDateRule { get; }
public DayOfWeek DayOfWeek { get; }
public int Week { get; }
public int Day { get; }
public int Month { get; }
public DateTime TimeOfDay { get; }
```

A transition time is somewhat complicated in that it needs to represent both fixed and floating dates. An example of a floating date is "the last Sunday in March." Here are the rules for interpreting a transition time:

1. If, for an end transition, IsFixedDateRule is true, Day is 1, Month is 1, and TimeOfDay is DateTime.MinValue, there is no end to daylight saving in that year (this can happen only in the southern hemisphere, upon the initial introduction of daylight saving to a region).

2. Otherwise, if IsFixedDateRule is true, the Month, Day, and TimeOfDay properties determine the start or end of the adjustment rule.

3. Otherwise, if IsFixedDateRule is false, the Month, DayOfWeek, Week, and TimeOfDay properties determine the start or end of the adjustment rule.

In the last case, Week refers to the week of the month, with "5" meaning the last week. We can demonstrate this by enumerating the adjustment rules for our wa time zone:

```
foreach (TimeZoneInfo.AdjustmentRule rule in wa.GetAdjustmentRules())
{
  Console.WriteLine ("Rule: applies from " + rule.DateStart +
                                " to " + rule.DateEnd);

  Console.WriteLine ("   Delta: " + rule.DaylightDelta);

  Console.WriteLine ("   Start: " + FormatTransitionTime
                              (rule.DaylightTransitionStart, false));

  Console.WriteLine ("   End:   " + FormatTransitionTime
                              (rule.DaylightTransitionEnd, true));
  Console.WriteLine();
}
```

In FormatTransitionTime, we honor the rules just described:

```
static string FormatTransitionTime (TimeZoneInfo.TransitionTime tt,
                                    bool endTime)
{
  if (endTime && tt.IsFixedDateRule
            && tt.Day == 1 && tt.Month == 1
            && tt.TimeOfDay == DateTime.MinValue)
    return "-";

  string s;
  if (tt.IsFixedDateRule)
    s = tt.Day.ToString();
  else
    s = "The " +
        "first second third fourth last".Split() [tt.Week - 1] +
        " " + tt.DayOfWeek + " in";

  return s + " " + DateTimeFormatInfo.CurrentInfo.MonthNames [tt.Month-1]
          + " at " + tt.TimeOfDay.TimeOfDay;
}
```

The result with Western Australia is interesting in that it demonstrates both fixed and floating date rules—as well as an absent end date:

```
Rule: applies from 1/01/2006 12:00:00 AM to 31/12/2006 12:00:00 AM
    Delta: 01:00:00
    Start: 3 December at 02:00:00
    End:   -

Rule: applies from 1/01/2007 12:00:00 AM to 31/12/9999 12:00:00 AM
    Delta: 01:00:00
    Start: The last Sunday in October at 02:00:00
    End:   The last Sunday in March at 03:00:00
```

 Western Australia is actually unique in this regard: here's how we found it:

```
from zone in TimeZoneInfo.GetSystemTimeZones()
let rules = zone.GetAdjustmentRules()
where
  rules.Any
    (r => r.DaylightTransitionEnd.IsFixedDateRule) &&
  rules.Any
    (r => !r.DaylightTransitionEnd.IsFixedDateRule)
select zone
```

Daylight Saving and DateTime

If you use a DateTimeOffset or a UTC DateTime, equality comparisons are unimpeded by the effects of daylight saving. But with local DateTimes, daylight saving can be problematic.

The rules can be summarized as follows:

- Daylight saving impacts local time but not UTC time.
- When the clocks turn back, comparisons that rely on time moving forward will break if (and only if) they use local DateTimes.
- You can always reliably round-trip between UTC and local times (on the same computer)—even as the clocks turn back.

The IsDaylightSavingTime tells you whether a given local DateTime is subject to daylight saving. UTC times always return false:

```
Console.Write (DateTime.Now.IsDaylightSavingTime());    // True or False
Console.Write (DateTime.UtcNow.IsDaylightSavingTime()); // Always False
```

If dto were a DateTimeOffset, you could use the following expression:

```
dto.LocalDateTime.IsDaylightSavingTime
```

The end of daylight saving presents a particular complication for algorithms that use local time. When the clocks go back, the same hour (or more precisely, Delta) repeats itself. We can demonstrate this by instantiating a DateTime right in the "twilight zone" on your computer, and then subtracting Delta (this example requires that you have daylight saving to be interesting!):

```
DaylightTime changes = TimeZone.CurrentTimeZone.GetDaylightChanges (2008);
TimeSpan halfDelta = new TimeSpan (changes.Delta.Ticks / 2);
```

```
DateTime utc1 = changes.End.ToUniversalTime( ) - halfDelta;
DateTime utc2 = utc1 - changes.Delta;
```

Converting these variables to local times demonstrates why you should use UTC and not local time if your code relies on time moving forward:

```
DateTime loc1 = utc1.ToLocalTime( );   // (Pacific Standard Time)
DateTime loc2 = utc2.ToLocalTime( );
Console.WriteLine (loc1);              // 2/11/2008 1:30:00 AM
Console.WriteLine (loc2);              // 2/11/2008 1:30:00 AM
Console.WriteLine (loc1 == loc2);      // True
```

Despite loc1 and loc2 reporting as equal, they are different inside. DateTime reserves a special bit for indicating on which side of the twilight zone an ambiguous local date lies! This bit is ignored in comparison—as we just saw—but comes into play when you format the DateTime unambiguously:

```
Console.Write (loc1.ToString ("o"));   // 2008-11-02T02:30:00.0000000-08:00
Console.Write (loc2.ToString ("o"));   // 2008-11-02T02:30:00.0000000-07:00
```

This bit also is read when you convert back to UTC, ensuring perfect round-tripping between local and UTC times:

```
Console.WriteLine (loc1.ToUniversalTime( ) == utc1);   // True
Console.WriteLine (loc2.ToUniversalTime( ) == utc2);   // True
```

 You can reliably compare any two DateTimes by first calling ToUniversalTime on each. This strategy fails if (and only if) exactly one of them has a DateTimeKind of Unspecified. This potential for failure is another reason for favoring DateTimeOffset.

Formatting and Parsing

Formatting means converting *to* a string; parsing means converting *from* a string. The need to format or parse arises frequently in programming, in a variety of situations. Hence, the .NET Framework provides a variety of mechanisms:

ToString *and* Parse
>   These methods provide default functionality for many types.

Format providers
>   These manifest as additional ToString (and Parse) methods that accept a *format string* and/or a *format provider*. Format providers are highly flexible and culture-aware. The .NET Framework includes format providers for the numeric types and DateTime.

XmlConvert
>   This is a static class with methods that format and parse while honoring XML standards. XmlConvert is also useful for general-purpose conversion when you need culture independence or you want to preempt misparsing. XmlConvert supports the numeric types, bool and DateTime, TimeSpan, and Guid.

Type converters
>   These target designers and XAML parsers.

In this section, we discuss the first two mechanisms, focusing particularly on format providers. In the section following, we describe XmlConvert and type converters, as well as other conversion mechanisms.

ToString and Parse

The simplest formatting mechanism is the ToString method. It gives meaningful output on all simple value types (bool, DateTime, TimeSpan, Guid, and all the numeric types). For the reverse operation, each of these types defines a static Parse method. For example:

```
string s = true.ToString( );     // s = "True"
bool b = bool.Parse (s);         // b = true
```

If the parsing fails, a FormatException is thrown. Many types also define a TryParse method, which returns false if the conversion fails, rather than throwing an exception:

```
int i;
bool failure = int.TryParse ("qwerty", out i);
bool success = int.TryParse ("123", out i);
```

If you anticipate an error, calling TryParse is faster than calling Parse in an exception handling block.

Format Providers

Sometimes you need more control over how formatting and parsing take place. There are dozens of ways to format a DateTime, for instance. Format providers allow extensive control over formatting and parsing, and are supported for numeric types and DateTimes. Format providers are also used by user interface controls for formatting and parsing.

The gateway to using a format provider is IFormattable. All numeric types—and System.DateTime—implement this interface:

```
public interface IFormattable
{
  string ToString (string format, IFormatProvider formatProvider);
}
```

The first argument is the *format string*; the second is the *format provider*. The format string provides instructions; the format provider determines how the instructions are translated. For example:

```
NumberFormatInfo f = new NumberFormatInfo( );
f.CurrencySymbol = "$$";
Console.WriteLine (3.ToString ("C", f));          // $$ 3.00
```

Here, "C" is a format string that indicates *currency*, and the NumberFormatInfo object is a format provider that determines how currency—and other numeric representations—are rendered. This mechanism allows for globalization.

All format strings for numbers and dates are listed in the section "Standard Format Strings and Parsing Flags" later in this chapter.

If you specify a null format string or provider, a default is applied. The default format provider is CultureInfo.CurrentCulture, which, unless reassigned, reflects the computer's runtime control panel settings. For example, on this computer:

```
Console.WriteLine (10.3.ToString ("C", null));   // $10.30
```

For convenience, most types overload ToString such that you can omit a null provider:

```
Console.WriteLine (10.3.ToString ("C"));     // $10.30
Console.WriteLine (10.3.ToString ("F4"));    // 10.3000 (Fix to 4 D.P.)
```

Calling ToString on a DateTime or a numeric type with no arguments is equivalent to using a (default) format provider, with an empty format string.

The .NET Framework defines three format providers (all of which implement IFormatProvider):

```
NumberFormatInfo
DateTimeFormatInfo
CultureInfo
```

All enum types are also formattable, though there's no special IFormatProvider class.

Format providers and CultureInfo

Within the context of format providers, CultureInfo acts as an indirection mechanism for the other two format providers, returning a NumberFormatInfo or DateTimeFormatInfo object applicable to the culture's regional settings.

In the following example, we request a specific culture (*english* language in *Great Britain*):

```
CultureInfo uk = CultureInfo.GetCultureInfo ("en-GB");
Console.WriteLine (3.ToString ("C", uk));      // £3.00
```

This executes using the default NumberFormatInfo object applicable to the en-GB culture.

The next example formats a DateTime with *invariant culture*. Invariant culture is always the same, regardless of the computer's settings:

```
DateTime dt = new DateTime (2000, 1, 2);
CultureInfo iv = CultureInfo.InvariantCulture;
Console.WriteLine (dt.ToString (iv));         // 01/02/2000 00:00:00
Console.WriteLine (dt.ToString ("d", iv));    // 01/02/2000
```

Invariant culture is based on American culture, with the following differences:

- The currency symbol is ☼ instead of $.
- Dates and times are formatted with leading zeros (though still with the month first).
- Time uses the 24-hour format rather than an AM/PM designator.

Using NumberFormatInfo or DateTimeFormatInfo

In the next example, we instantiate a `NumberFormatInfo` and change the group separator from a comma to a space. We then use it to format a number to three decimal places:

```
NumberFormatInfo f = new NumberFormatInfo ();
f.NumberGroupSeparator = " ";
Console.WriteLine (12345.6789.ToString ("N3", f));   // 12 345.679
```

The initial settings for a `NumberFormatInfo` or `DateTimeFormatInfo` are based on the invariant culture. Sometimes, however, it's more useful to choose a different starting point. To do this, you can `Clone` an existing format provider:

```
NumberFormatInfo f = (NumberFormatInfo)
                       CultureInfo.CurrentCulture.NumberFormat.Clone();
...
```

Composite formatting

Composite format strings allow you to combine variable substitution with format strings. The static `string.Format` method accepts a composite format string—we illustrated this earlier, in the section "String and Text Handling":

```
string composite = "Credit={0:C}";
Console.WriteLine (string.Format (composite, 500));   // Credit=$500.00
```

The `Console` class itself overloads its `Write` and `WriteLine` methods to accept composite format strings, allowing us to shorten this example slightly:

```
Console.WriteLine ("Credit={0:C}", 500);   // Credit=$500.00
```

You can also append a composite format string to a `StringBuilder` (via `AppendFormat`), and to a `StreamWriter` for I/O (see Chapter 13).

`string.Format` accepts an optional format provider. A simple application for this is to call `ToString` on an arbitrary object while passing in a format provider. For example:

```
string s = string.Format (CultureInfo.InvariantCulture, "{0}", someObject);
```

This is equivalent to:

```
string s;
if (someObject is IFormattable)
  s = ((IFormattable)someObject).ToString (null,
                                    CultureInfo.InvariantCulture);
else
  s = someObject.ToString();
```

Parsing with format providers

There's no standard interface for parsing through a format provider. Instead, each participating type overloads its static `Parse` (and `TryParse`) method to accept a format provider, and optionally, a `NumberStyles` or `DateTimeStyles` enum.

`NumberStyles` and `DateTimeStyles` are parsing's equivalent of format strings, and they let you specify such things as whether parentheses or a currency symbol can appear in the input string. (By default, the answer to both of these questions is *no*.) For example:

```
int error = int.Parse ("(2)");    // Exception thrown

int minusTwo = int.Parse ("(2)", NumberStyles.Integer |
                        NumberStyles.AllowParentheses);    // OK

  decimal fivePointTwo = decimal.Parse ("£5.20", NumberStyles.Currency,
                        CultureInfo.GetCultureInfo ("en-GB"));
```

The next section lists all `NumberStyles` and `DateTimeStyles` members—as well as the default parsing rules for each type.

IFormatProvider and ICustomFormatter

All format providers implement `IFormatProvider`:

```
public interface IFormatProvider { object GetFormat (Type formatType); }
```

The purpose of this method is to provide indirection—this is what allows `CultureInfo` to defer to an appropriate `NumberFormatInfo` or `DateTimeInfo` object to do the work.

By implementing `IFormatProvider`—along with `ICustomFormatter`—you can also write your own format provider that works in conjunction with existing types. `ICustomFormatter` defines a single method as follows:

```
string Format (string format, object arg, IFormatProvider formatProvider);
```

The following custom format provider writes numbers as words:

```
// Program can be downloaded from http://www.albahari.com/nutshell/

public class WordyFormatProvider : IFormatProvider, ICustomFormatter
{
  static readonly string[] _numberWords =
   "zero one two three four five six seven eight nine minus point".Split();

  IFormatProvider _parent;   // Allows consumers to chain format providers

  public WordyFormatProvider () : this (CultureInfo.CurrentCulture) { }
  public WordyFormatProvider (IFormatProvider parent)
  {
    _parent = parent;
  }

  public object GetFormat (Type formatType)
  {
    if (formatType == typeof (ICustomFormatter)) return this;
    return null;
  }

  public string Format (string format, object arg, IFormatProvider prov)
  {
    // If it's not our format string, defer to the parent provider:
    if (arg == null || format != "W")
```

```
            return string.Format (_parent, "{0:" + format + "}", arg);

        StringBuilder result = new StringBuilder( );
        string digitList = string.Format (CultureInfo.InvariantCulture,
                                            "{0}", arg);
        foreach (char digit in digitList)
        {
          int i = "0123456789-.".IndexOf (digit);
          if (i == -1) continue;
          if (result.Length > 0) result.Append (' ');
          result.Append (_numberWords[i]);
        }
        return result.ToString( );
      }
    }
```

Notice that in the `Format` method we used `string.Format` to convert the input number to a string—with `InvariantCulture`. It would have been much simpler just to call `ToString( )` on `arg`, but then `CurrentCulture` would have been used instead. The reason for needing the invariant culture is evident a few lines later:

```
    int i = "0123456789-.".IndexOf (digit);
```

It's critical here that the number string comprises only characters `0123456789-.` and not any internationalized versions of these.

Here's an example of using `WordyFormatProvider`:

```
    double n = -123.45;
    IFormatProvider fp = new WordyFormatProvider( );
    Console.WriteLine (string.Format (fp, "{0:C} in words is {0:W}", n));

    // -$123.45 in words is one two three point four five
```

Custom format providers can be used only in composite format strings.

Standard Format Strings and Parsing Flags

The standard format strings control how a numeric type or `DateTime` is converted to a string. There are two kinds of format strings:

Standard format strings
> With these, you provide general guidance. A standard format string consists of a single letter, followed, optionally, by a digit (whose meaning depends on the letter). An example is `"C"` or `"F2"`.

Custom format strings
> With these, you micromanage every character with a template. An example is `"0:#.000E+00"`.

Custom format strings are unrelated to custom format providers.

Numeric Format Strings

Table 6-2 lists all standard numeric format strings.

Table 6-2. Standard numeric format strings

Letter	Meaning	Sample input	Result	Notes
G or g	"General"	1.2345, "G"	1.2345	Switches to exponential notation for small or large numbers.
		0.00001, "G"	1E-05	
		0.00001, "g"	1e-05	
		1.2345, "G3"	1.23	G3 limits precision to three digits in *total* (before + after point).
		12345, "G3"	1.23E04	
F	Fixed point	2345.678, "F2"	2345.68	F2 rounds to two decimal places.
		2345.6, "F2"	2345.60	
N	Fixed point with *group separator* ("Numeric")	2345.678, "N2"	2,345.68	As above, with group (1000s) separator (details from format provider).
		2345.6, "F2"	2,345.60	
D	Pad with leading zeros	123, "D5"	00123	For integral types only.
		123, "D1"	123	D5 pads left to five digits; does not truncate.
E or e	Force exponential notation	56789, "E"	5.678900E+004	Six-digit default precision.
		56789, "e"	5.678900e+004	
		56789, "E2"	5.68E+004	
C	Currency	1.2, "C"	$1.20	C with no digit uses default number of D.P. from format provider.
		1.2, "C4"	$1.2000	
P	Percent	.503, "P"	50.30 %	Uses symbol and layout from format provider.
		.503, "P0"	50 %	Decimal places can optionally be overridden.
X or x	Hexadecimal	47, "X"	2F	X for uppercase hex digits; x for lowercase hex digits.
		47, "x"	2f	
		47, "X4"	002F	Integrals only.
R	Round-trip	1f / 3f, "R"	0.333333**43**	For the float and double types, R squeezes out all digits to ensure exact round-tripping.

Supplying no numeric format string (or a null or blank string) is equivalent to using the "G" standard format string followed by no digit. This exhibits the following behavior:

- Numbers smaller than 10^{-4} or larger than the type's precision are expressed in exponential (scientific) notation.
- The two decimal places at the limit of float or double's precision are rounded away to mask the inaccuracies inherent in conversion to decimal from their underlying binary form.

The automatic rounding just described is usually beneficial and goes unnoticed. However, it can cause trouble if you need to round-trip a number; in other words, convert it to a string and back again (maybe repeatedly) while preserving value equality. For this reason, the "R" format string exists to circumvent this implicit rounding.

Table 6-3 lists custom numeric format strings.

Table 6-3. Custom numeric format strings

Specifier	Meaning	Sample input	Result	Notes
#	Digit placeholder	12.345, ".##" 12.345, ".####"	12.35 12.345	Limits digits after D.P.
0	Zero placeholder	12.345, ".00" 12.345, ".0000" 99, "000.00"	12.35 12.3500 099.00	As above, but also pads with zeros before and after D.P.
.	Decimal point			Indicates D.P. Actual symbol comes from NumberFormat-Info.
,	Group separator	1234, "#,###,###" 1234, "0,000,000"	1,234 0,001,234	Symbol comes from NumberFormat-Info.
, (as above)	Multiplier	1000000, "#," 1000000, "#,,"	1000 1	If comma is at end or before D.P., it acts as a multiplier—dividing result by 1,000, 1,000,000, etc.
%	Percent notation	0.6, "00%"	60%	First multiplies by 100 and then substitutes percent symbol obtained from NumberFormat-Info.
E0, e0, E+0, e+0 E-0, e-0	Exponent notation	1234, "0E0" 1234, "0E+0" 1234, "0.00E00" 1234, "0.00e00"	1E0 1E+3 1.25E03 1.25e03	
\	Literal character quote	50, @"\#0"	#50	Use in conjunction with a @ prefix on the string—or use \\.
'xx' 'xx'	Literal string quote	50, "0 '...' "	50 ...	

Table 6-3. Custom numeric format strings (continued)

Specifier	Meaning	Sample input	Result	Notes
;	Section separator	15, "#;(#);zero"	15	(If positive)
		-5, "#;(#);zero"	-5	(If negative)
		0, "#;(#);zero"	zero	(If zero)
Any other char	Literal	35.2, "$0 . 00c"	$35 . 00c	

NumberStyles

Each numeric type defines a static Parse method that accepts a NumberStyles argument. NumberStyles is a flags enum that lets you determine how the string is read as it's converted to a numeric type. It has the following combinable members:

```
AllowLeadingWhite      AllowTrailingWhite
AllowLeadingSign       AllowTrailingSign
AllowParentheses       AllowDecimalPoint
AllowThousands         AllowExponent
AllowCurrencySymbol    AllowHexSpecifier
```

NumberStyles also defines these composite members:

```
None  Integer  Float  Number  HexNumber  Currency  Any
```

Except for None, all composite values include AllowLeadingWhite and AllowTrailingWhite. Their remaining makeup is shown in Figure 6-1, with the most useful three emphasized.

Figure 6-1. Composite NumberStyles

When you call Parse without specifying any flags, the defaults in Figure 6-2 are applied.

The gaps in Figure 6-2 create the use cases for NumberStyles. For example:

```
int thousand = int.Parse ("3E8", NumberStyles.HexNumber);
int minusTwo = int.Parse ("(2)", NumberStyles.Integer |
```

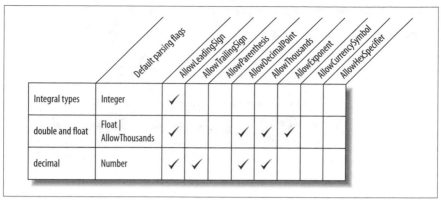

Figure 6-2. Default parsing flags for numeric types

```
                                    NumberStyles.AllowParentheses);
    double aMillion = double.Parse ("1,000,000", NumberStyles.Any);
    decimal threeMillion = decimal.Parse ("3e6", NumberStyles.Any);
    decimal fivePointTwo = decimal.Parse ("$5.20", NumberStyles.Currency);
```

Because we didn't specify a format provider, this example works with your local currency symbol, group separator, decimal point, and so on. The next example is hardcoded to work with the euro sign and a blank group separator for currencies:

```
    NumberFormatInfo ni = new NumberFormatInfo( );
    ni.CurrencySymbol = "€";
    ni.CurrencyGroupSeparator = " ";
    double million = double.Parse ("€1 000 000", NumberStyles.Currency, ni);
```

DateTime Format Strings

DateTime format strings can be divided into two groups, based on whether they honor culture and format provider settings. Those that do are listed in Table 6-4; those that don't are listed in Table 6-5. The sample output comes from formatting the following DateTime (with *invariant culture*, in the case of Table 6-4):

```
    new DateTime (2000, 1, 2,  17, 18, 19);
```

Table 6-4. Culture-sensitive DateTime format strings

Format string	Meaning	Sample output
d	Short date	01/02/2000
D	Long date	Sunday, 02 January 2000
t	Short time	17:18
T	Long time	17:18:19
f	Long date + short time	Sunday, 02 January 2000 17:18
F	Long date + long time	Sunday, 02 January 2000 17:18:19
g	Short date + short time	01/02/2000 17:18
G (default)	Short date + long time	**01/02/2000 17:18:19**

Table 6-4. Culture-sensitive DateTime format strings (continued)

Format string	Meaning	Sample output
m, M	Month and day	January 02
y, Y	Year and month	2000 January

Table 6-5. Culture-insensitive DateTime format strings

Format string	Meaning	Sample output	Notes
o	Round-trippable	2000-01-02T17:11:30.0000000	Will append time zone information unless DateTimeKind is Unspecified
r, R	RFC 1123 standard	Sun, 02 Jan 2000 17:11:30 GMT	You must explicitly convert to UTC with DateTime.ToUniversalTime
s	Sortable; ISO 8601	2000-01-02T17:11:30	Compatible with text-based sorting
u	"Universal" Sortable	2000-01-02 17:11:30Z	Similar to above; must explicitly convert to UTC
U	UTC	Sunday, 02 January 2000 08:11:30	Long date + short time, converted to UTC

The format strings "r", "R", and "u" emit a suffix that implies UTC; yet they don't automatically convert a local to a UTC DateTime (so you must do the conversion yourself). Ironically, "U" automatically converts to UTC, but doesn't write a time zone suffix! In fact, "o" is the only format specifier in the group that can write an unambiguous DateTime without intervention.

DateTimeFormatInfo also supports custom format strings: these are analogous to numeric custom format strings. The list is fairly exhaustive and you can find it in the MSDN. An example of a custom format string is:

```
yyyy-MM-dd HH:mm:ss
```

Parsing and misparsing DateTimes

DateTime strings that put the month or day first are ambiguous and can easily be misparsed—particularly if you or any of your customers live outside America and Canada. This is not a problem in user interface controls because the same settings are in force when parsing as when formatting. But when writing to a file, for instance, day/month misparsing can be a real problem. There are two solutions:

- Always state the same explicit culture when formatting and parsing (e.g., invariant culture).
- Format DateTimes in a manner *independent* of culture.

The second approach is more robust—particularly if you choose a format that puts the four-digit year first: such strings are much harder to misparse by another party. Further, strings formatted with a *standards-compliant* year-first format (such as "o") can parse correctly alongside locally formatted strings—rather like a "universal donor."

To illustrate, suppose we generate a culture-insensitive DateTime string s as follows:

```
string s = DateTime.Now.ToString ("o");
```

We can reparse this in two ways. ParseExact demands strict compliance with the specified format string:

```
DateTime dt1 = DateTime.ParseExact (s, "o", null);
```

(You can achieve a similar result with XmlConvert's ToString and ToDateTime methods.)

Parse, however, implicitly accepts both the "o" format and the CurrentCulture format:

```
DateTime dt2 = DateTime.Parse (s);
```

The "o" format string includes milliseconds in the output. The following custom format string gives the same result as "o", but without milliseconds:

```
yyyy-MM-ddTHH:mm:ss K
```

This works with both DateTime and DateTimeOffset.

DateTimeStyles

DateTimeStyles is a flags enum that provides additional instructions when calling DateTime.Parse. Here are its members:

```
None,
AllowLeadingWhite, AllowTrailingWhite, AllowInnerWhite,
AssumeLocal, AssumeUniversal, AdjustToUniversal,
NoCurrentDateDefault, RoundTripKind
```

There is also a composite member, AllowWhiteSpaces:

```
AllowWhiteSpaces = AllowLeadingWhite | AllowTrailingWhite | AllowInnerWhite
```

The default is None. This means that extra whitespace is normally prohibited (whitespace that's part of a standard DateTime pattern is exempt).

AssumeLocal and AssumeUniversal apply if the string doesn't have a time zone suffix (such as Z or +9:00). AdjustToUniversal still honors time zone suffixes, but then converts to UTC using the current regional settings.

If you parse a string comprising a time but no date, today's date is applied by default. If you apply the NoCurrentDateDefault flag, however, it instead uses 1st January 0001.

Enum Format Strings

In the section "Enums" in Chapter 3, we describe formatting and parsing enum values. Table 6-6 lists each format string and the result of applying it to the following expression:

```
Console.WriteLine (System.ConsoleColor.Red.ToString (formatString));
```

Table 6-6. Enum format strings

Format string	Meaning	Sample output	Notes
G or g	"General"	Red	Default
F or f	Treat as though Flags attribute were present	Red	Works on combined members even if enum has no Flags attribute
D or d	Decimal value	12	Retrieves underlying integral value
X or x	Hexadecimal value	0000000C	Retrieves underlying integral value

Other Conversion Mechanisms

In the previous two sections, we covered format providers—.NET's primary mechanism for formatting and parsing. There are other important conversion mechanisms scattered through various types and namespaces. Some convert to and from string, and some do other kinds of conversions. In this section, we discuss the following topics:

- The Convert class and its functions:
  - — Real to integral conversions that round rather than truncate
  - — Parsing numbers in base 2, 8, and 16
  - — Dynamic conversions
  - — Base 64 translations
- XmlConvert and its role in formatting and parsing for XML
- Type converters and their role in formatting and parsing for designers and XAML
- BitConverter, for binary conversions

Convert

The .NET Framework calls the following types *base types*:

- bool, char, string, and System.DateTime
- All of the C# numeric types

The static Convert class defines methods for converting every base type to every other base type. Unfortunately, most of these methods are useless: either they throw exceptions or they are redundant alongside implicit casts. Among the clutter, however, are some useful methods, listed in the following sections.

> All base types (explicitly) implement IConvertible, which defines methods for converting to every other base type. In most cases, the implementation of each of these methods simply calls a method in Convert. On rare occasions, it can be useful to write a method that accepts an argument of type IConvertible.

Rounding real to integral conversions

In Chapter 2, we saw how implicit and explicit casts allow you to convert between numeric types. In summary:

- Implicit casts work for nonlossy conversions (e.g., int to double).
- Explicit casts are required for lossy conversions (e.g., double to int).

Casts are optimized for efficiency; hence, they *truncate* data that won't fit. This can be a problem when converting from a real number to an integer, because you more often want to *round* than truncate. Convert's numerical conversion methods address just this issue; they always *round*:

```
double d = 3.9;
int i = Convert.ToInt32 (d);    // i == 4
```

Convert uses banker's rounding, which snaps midpoint values to even integers (this avoids positive or negative bias). If banker's rounding is a problem, first call Math.Round on the real number: this accepts an additional argument that allows you to control midpoint rounding.

Parsing numbers in base 2, 8, and 16

Hidden among the To(*integral-type*) methods are overloads that parse numbers in another base:

```
int thirty = Convert.ToInt32  ("1E", 16);    // parse in hexadecimal
uint five  = Convert.ToUInt32 ("101", 2);    // parse in binary
```

The second argument specifies the base. It can be any base you like—as long as it's 2, 8, 10, or 16!

Dynamic conversions

Occasionally, you need to convert from one type to another—but you don't know what the types are until runtime. For this, the Convert class provides a ChangeType method:

```
public static object ChangeType (object value, Type conversionType);
```

The source and target types must be one of the "base" types. ChangeType also accepts an optional IFormatProvider argument. Here's an example:

```
Type targetType = typeof (int);
object source = "42";

object result = Convert.ChangeType (source, targetType);

Console.WriteLine (result);            // 42
Console.WriteLine (result.GetType()); // System.Int32
```

An example of when this might be useful is in writing a deserializer that can work with multiple types. It can also convert any enum to its integral type (see "Enums" in Chapter 3).

A limitation of ChangeType is that you cannot specify a format string or parsing flag.

Base 64 conversions

Sometimes you need to include binary data such as a bitmap within a text document such as an XML file or email message. Base 64 is a ubiquitous means of encoding binary data as readable characters, using 64 characters from the ASCII set.

Convert's ToBase64String method converts from a byte array to base 64; FromBase64String does the reverse.

XmlConvert

If you're dealing with data that's originated from or destined for an XML file, XmlConvert (the System.Xml namespace) provides the most suitable methods for formatting and parsing. The methods in XmlConvert handle the nuances of XML formatting without needing special format strings. For instance, true in XML is "true" and not "True". The .NET Framework internally uses XmlConvert extensively. XmlConvert is also good for general-purpose culture-independent serialization.

The formatting methods in XmlConvert are all provided as overloaded ToString methods; the parsing methods are called ToBoolean, ToDateTime, and so on. For example:

```
string s = XmlConvert.ToString (true);        // s = "true"
bool isTrue = XmlConvert.ToBoolean (s);
```

The methods that convert to and from DateTime accept an XmlDateTime-SerializationMode argument. This is an enum with the following values:

```
Unspecified, Local, Utc, RoundtripKind
```

Local and Utc cause a conversion to take place when formatting (if the DateTime is not already in that time zone). The time zone is then appended to the string:

```
2007-02-22T14:08:30.9375          // Unspecified
2007-02-22T14:07:30.9375+09:00    // Local
2007-02-22T05:08:30.9375Z         // Utc
```

Unspecified strips away any time zone information embedded in the DateTime (i.e., DateTimeKind) before formatting. RoundtripKind honors the DateTime's DateTimeKind—so when it's reparsed, the resultant DateTime struct will be exactly as it was originally.

Type Converters

Type converters are designed to format and parse in design-time environments. They also parse values in XAML (Extensible Application Markup Language) documents—as used in Windows Presentation Foundation and Workflow Foundation.

In the .NET Framework, there are more than 100 type converters—covering such things as colors, images, and URIs. In contrast, format providers are implemented only for a handful of simple value types.

Type converters typically parse strings in a variety of ways—without needing hints. For instance, in an ASP.NET application in Visual Studio, if you assign a control a BackColor by typing l**"Beige"** into the property window, Color's type converter figures out that you're referring to a color name and not an RGB string or system color. This flexibility can sometimes make type converters useful in contexts outside of designers and XAML documents.

All type converters subclass TypeConverter in System.ComponentModel. To obtain a TypeConverter, call TypeDescriptor.GetConverter. The following obtains a Type-Converter for the Color type (in System.Drawing namespace, *System.Drawing.dll*):

```
TypeConverter cc = TypeDescriptor.GetConverter (typeof (Color));
```

Among many other methods, TypeConverter defines methods to ConvertToString and ConvertFromString. We can call these as follows:

```
Color beige  = (Color) cc.ConvertFromString ("Beige");
Color purple = (Color) cc.ConvertFromString ("#800080");
Color window = (Color) cc.ConvertFromString ("Window");
```

By convention, type converters have names ending in "Converter" and are usually in the same namespace as the type they're converting. A type links to its converter via a TypeConverterAttribute—this allows designers to pick up converters automatically.

Type converters can also provide design-time services such as generating standard value lists for populating a drop-down list in a designer or assisting with code serialization.

BitConverter

Most base types can be converted to a byte array, by calling BitConverter. GetBytes:

```
foreach (byte b in BitConverter.GetBytes (3.5))
    Console.Write (b + " ");                        // 0 0 0 0 0 0 12 64
```

BitConverter also provides methods for converting in the other direction, such as ToDouble.

The decimal and DateTime types are not supported by BitConverter. You can, however, convert a decimal to an int array by calling decimal.GetBits. To go the other way around, decimal provides a constructor that accepts an int array.

In the case of DateTime, you can call ToBinary on an instance—this returns a long (upon which you can then use BitConverter). The static DateTime.FromBinary method does the reverse.

Working with Numbers

Conversions

We covered numeric conversions in previous chapters and sections; Table 6-7 summarizes all the options.

Table 6-7. Summary of numeric conversions

Task	Functions	Examples

Parsing base-10 numbers	Parse
	TryParse
		`double d = double.Parse ("3.5");`
		`int i;`
		`bool ok = int.TryParse ("3", out i);`

Parsing from base 2, 8, or 16	`Convert.ToIntegral`	`int i = Convert.ToInt32 ("1E", 16);`
Formatting to hexadecimal	`ToString ("X")`	`string hex = 45.ToString ("X");`
Lossless numeric conversion	Implicit cast	`int i = 23;` `double d = d;`
Truncating numeric conversion	Explicit cast	`double d = 23.5;` `int i = (int) d;`
Rounding numeric conversion (real to integral)	`Convert.ToIntegral`	`double d = 23.5;` `int i = Convert.ToInt32 (d);`

Math

Table 6-8 lists the members of the static Math class. The trigonometric functions accept arguments of type double; other methods such as Max are overloaded to operate on all numeric types. The Math class also defines the mathematical constants E (*e*) and PI.

Table 6-8. Methods in the static Math class

Category	Methods
Rounding	`Round, Truncate, Floor, Ceiling`
Maximum/minimum	`Max, Min`
Absolute value and sign	`Abs, Sign`
Square root	`Sqrt`
Raising to a power	`Pow, Exp`
Logarithm	`Log, Log10`

Trigonometric	`Sin, Cos, Tan`
	`Sinh, Cosh, Tanh`
	`Asin, Acos, Atan`

The Round method lets you specify the number of decimal places with which to round, as well as how to handle midpoints (away from zero, or with banker's rounding). Floor and Ceiling round to the nearest integer: Floor always rounds down and Ceiling always rounds up—even with negative numbers.

Max and Min accept only two arguments. If you have an array or sequence of numbers, use the Max and Min extension methods in System.Linq.Enumerable.

Random

The Random class generates a pseudorandom sequence of random bytes, integers, or doubles.

To use Random, first instantiate it, optionally providing a seed to initiate the random number series. Using the same seed guarantees the same series of numbers, which is sometimes useful when you want reproducibility:

```
Random r1 = new Random (1);
Random r2 = new Random (1);
Console.WriteLine (r1.Next (100) + ", " + r1.Next (100));     // 24, 11
Console.WriteLine (r2.Next (100) + ", " + r2.Next (100));     // 24, 11
```

If you don't want reproducibility, you can construct Random with no seed—then it uses the current time to make one up.

Calling Next(*n*) generates a random integer between 0 and *n*-1. NextDouble generates a random double between 0 and 1. NextBytes fills a byte array with random values.

Even without a seed, Random is not considered random enough for high-security applications, such as cryptography. For this, the .NET Framework provides a *cryptographically strong* random number generator, in the System.Security.Cryptography namespace. Here's how it's used:

```
var rand = System.Security.Cryptography.RandomNumberGenerator.Create( );
byte[] bytes = new byte [32];
rand.GetBytes (bytes);          // Fill the byte array with random numbers.
```

The downside is that it's less flexible: filling a byte array is the only means of obtaining random numbers. To obtain an integer, you must use BitConverter:

```
byte[] bytes = new byte [4];
rand.GetBytes (bytes);
int i = BitConverter.ToInt32 (bytes, 0);
```

Enums

In Chapter 3, we described C#'s enum type, and showed how to combine members, test equality, use logical operators, and perform conversions. The Framework extends C#'s support for enums through the System.Enum type. This type has two roles:

- Providing type unification for all enum types
- Defining static utility methods

Type unification means you can implicitly cast any enum member to a System.Enum instance:

```
enum Nut  { Walnut, Hazelnut, Macadamia }
enum Size { Small, Medium, Large }

static void Demo( )
{
  Display (Nut.Macadamia);    // Nut.Macadamia
  Display (Size.Large);       // Size.Large
}

static void Display (Enum value)
{
  Console.WriteLine (value.GetType().Name + "." + value.ToString( ));
}
```

The static utility methods on System.Enum are primarily related to performing conversions and obtaining lists of members.

Enum Conversions

There are three ways to represent an enum value:

- As an enum member
- As its underlying integral value
- As a string

In this section, we describe how to convert between each.

enum to integral conversions

Recall that an explicit cast converts between an enum member and its integral value. An explicit cast is the correct approach if you know the enum type at compile time:

```
[Flags] public enum BorderSides { Left=1, Right=2, Top=4, Bottom=8 }
...
int i = (int) BorderSides.Top;            // i == 4
BorderSides side = (BorderSides) i;       // side == BorderSides.Top
```

You can cast a System.Enum instance to its integral type in the same way. The trick is to first cast to an object, and then the integral type:

```
static int GetIntegralValue (Enum anyEnum)
{
  return (int) (object) anyEnum;
}
```

This relies on you knowing the integral type: the method we just wrote would crash if passed an enum whose integral type was long. To write a method that works with an enum of any integral type, you can take one of three approaches. The first is to call Convert.ToDecimal:

```
static decimal GetIntegralValue (Enum anyEnum)
{
  return Convert.ToDecimal (anyEnum);
}
```

This works because every integral type (including ulong) can be converted to decimal without loss of information. The second approach is to call Enum.GetUnderlyingType in order to obtain the enum's integral type, and then call Convert.ChangeType:

```
static object GetBoxedIntegralValue (Enum anyEnum)
{
  Type integralType = Enum.GetUnderlyingType (anyEnum.GetType( ));
  return Convert.ChangeType (anyEnum, integralType);
}
```

This preserves the original integral type, as the following example shows:

```
object result = GetBoxedIntegralValue (BorderSides.Top);
Console.WriteLine (result);                    // 4
Console.WriteLine (result.GetType( ));         // System.Int32
```

Our method `GetBoxedIntegralType` in fact performs no value conversion; rather, it *reboxes* the same value in another type. It translates an integral value in *enum-type* clothing to an integral value in *integral-type* clothing. We describe this further in the section "How Enums Work," later in this chapter.

The third approach is to call `Format` or `ToString` specifying the "d" or "D" format string. This gives you the enum's integral value as a string, and it is useful when writing custom serialization formatters:

```
static string GetIntegralValueAsString (Enum anyEnum)
{
  return anyEnum.ToString ("D");      // returns something like "4"
}
```

Integral to enum conversions

`Enum.ToObject` converts an integral value to an enum instance of the given type:

```
object bs = Enum.ToObject (typeof (BorderSides), 3);
Console.WriteLine (bs);                       // Left, Right
```

This is the dynamic equivalent of this:

```
BorderSides bs = (BorderSides) 3;
```

`ToObject` is overloaded to accept all integral types, as well as `object`. (The latter works with any boxed integral type.)

String conversions

To convert an enum to a string, you can either call the static `Enum.Format` method or call `ToString` on the instance. Each method accepts a format string, which can be "G" for default formatting behavior, "D" to emit the underlying integral value as a string, "X" for the same in hexadecimal, or "F" to format combined members of an enum without the `Flags` attribute. We listed examples of these in the section "Standard Format Strings and Parsing Flags" earlier in this chapter.

`Enum.Parse` converts a string to an enum. It accepts the enum type and a string that can include multiple members:

```
BorderSides leftRight = (BorderSides) Enum.Parse (typeof (BorderSides),
                                                  "Left, Right");
```

An optional third argument lets you perform case-insensitive parsing. A `Format-Exception` is thrown if the member is not found.

Enumerating Enum Values

`Enum.GetValues` returns an array comprising all members of a particular enum type:

```
foreach (Enum value in Enum.GetValues (typeof (BorderSides)))
    Console.WriteLine (value);
```

Composite members such as `LeftRight = Left | Right` are included too.

`Enum.GetNames` performs the same function, but returns an array of *strings*.

Internally, the CLR implements GetValues and GetNames by reflecting over the fields in the enum's type. The results are cached for efficiency.

How Enums Work

The semantics of enums are enforced largely by the compiler. In the CLR, there's no runtime difference between an enum instance (when unboxed) and its underlying integral value. Further, an enum definition in the CLR is merely a subtype of System.Enum with static integral-type fields for each member. This makes the ordinary use of an enum highly efficient, with a runtime cost matching that of integral constants.

The downside of this strategy is that enums can provide *static* but not *strong* type safety. We saw an example of this in Chapter 3:

```
public enum BorderSides { Left=1, Right=2, Top=4, Bottom=8 }
...
BorderSides b = BorderSides.Left;
b += 1234;                          // No error!
```

When the compiler is unable to perform validation (as in this example), there's no backup from the runtime to throw an exception.

What we said about there being no runtime difference between an enum instance and its integral value might seem at odds with the following:

```
[Flags] public enum BorderSides { Left=1, Right=2, Top=4, Bottom=8 }
...
Console.WriteLine (BorderSides.Right.ToString());       // Right
Console.WriteLine (BorderSides.Right.GetType().Name);   // BorderSides
```

Given the nature of an enum instance at runtime you'd expect this to print 2 and Int32! The reason for its behavior is down to some more compile-time trickery. C# explicitly *boxes* an enum instance before calling its virtual methods—such as ToString or GetType. And when an enum instance is boxed, it gains a runtime wrapping that references its enum type.

The Guid Struct

The Guid struct represents a globally unique identifier: a 16-byte value that if randomly generated, will almost certainly be unique in the world. Guids are often used for keys of various sorts—in applications and databases. There are 2^{128} or 3.4 $\times 10^{38}$ unique Guids.

To create a new random Guid, you call the static Guid.NewGuid method:

```
Guid g = Guid.NewGuid ();
Console.WriteLine (g.ToString());  // 0d57629c-7d6e-4847-97cb-9e2fc25083fe
```

To instantiate an existing value, you use one of the constructors. The two most useful constructors are:

```
public Guid (byte[] b);     // Accepts a 16-byte array
public Guid (string g);     // Accepts a formatted string
```

When represented as a string, a Guid is formatted as a 32-digit hexadecimal number, with optional hyphens after the 8th, 12th, 16th, and 20th digits. The whole string can also be optionally wrapped in brackets or braces:

```
Guid g1 = new Guid ("{0d57629c-7d6e-4847-97cb-9e2fc25083fe}");
Guid g2 = new Guid ("0d57629c7d6e484797cb9e2fc25083fe");
Console.WriteLine (g1 == g2);  // True
```

Being a struct, a Guid honors value type semantics; hence, the equality operator works in the preceding example.

The ToByteArray method converts a Guid to a byte array.

The static Guid.Empty property returns an empty Guid (all zeros). This is often used in place of null.

Equality Comparison

Until now, we've assumed that the == and != operators are all there is to equality comparison. The issue of equality, however, is more complex and subtler, sometimes requiring the use of additional methods and interfaces. This section explores the standard C# and .NET protocols for equality, focusing particularly on two questions:

- When are == and != adequate—and inadequate—for equality comparison, and what are the alternatives?
- How and when should you customize a type's equality logic?

Referential Versus Value Equality

There are two kinds of equality:

Value equality
    Two variables are equal if they have the same value.

Referential equality
    Two variables are equal if they refer to the same storage location.

By default:

- Value types use *value equality*.
- Reference types use *referential equality*.

Value types, in fact, can *only* use value equality (unless boxed). For composite value types (i.e., structs), the default algorithm for determining equality performs a value comparison on each of the fields.

Standard Equality Protocols

There are three standard protocols for equality comparison:

- The == and != operators
- The virtual Equals method in object
- The IEquatable<T> interface

(This excludes the pluggable protocols described in Chapter 7.)

== and !=

We've already seen in many examples how the standard == and != operators perform equality/inequality comparisons. The subtleties with == and != arise because they are *operators*, and so are statically resolved (in fact, they are implemented as static functions). So, when you use == or !=, C# makes a *compile-time* decision as to which type will perform the comparison, and no virtual behavior comes into play. This is normally desirable: in the following example, the compiler hard-wires == to the int type because x and y are both int:

```
int x = 5;
int y = 5;
Console.WriteLine (x == y);    // True
```

But in the next example, the compiler wires the == operator to the object type:

```
object x = 5;
object y = 5;
Console.WriteLine (x == y);    // False
```

Because object is a class (and so a reference type), object's == operator uses *referential equality* to compare x and y. The result is false, because x and y each refer to different boxed objects on the heap.

The virtual Object.Equals method

To correctly equate x and y in the preceding example, we can use the virtual Equals method. Equals is defined in System.Object, and so is available to all types:

```
object x = 5;
object y = 5;
Console.WriteLine (x.Equals (y));    // True
```

Equals is resolved at runtime—according to the object's actual type. In this case, it calls Int32's Equals method, which applies *value equality* to the operands, returning true.

> *Why the complexity?*
>
> You might wonder why the designers of C# didn't avoid the problem by making == virtual, and so functionally identical to Equals. There are three reasons for this:
>
> - If the first operand is null, Equals fails with a NullReferenceException; a static operator does not.
> - Because the == operator is statically resolved, it executes extremely quickly. This means that you can write computationally intensive code without penalty—and without needing to learn another language such as C++.
> - Occasionally, it can be useful to have == and Equals apply different definitions of equality. We describe this scenario later in this section.

Hence, Equals is suitable for equating two objects in a type-agnostic fashion. The following method equates two objects of any type:

```
public static bool AreEqual (object obj1, object obj2)
{
  return obj1.Equals (obj2);
}
```

There is one case, however, in which this fails. If the first argument is null, you get a NullReferenceException. Here's the fix:

```
public static bool AreEqual (object obj1, object obj2)
{
  if (obj1 == null) return obj2 == null;
  return obj1.Equals (obj2);
}
```

The static object.Equals method

The object class provides a static helper method that does the work of AreEqual in the preceding example. Its name is Equals—just like the virtual method—but there's no conflict because it accepts *two* arguments:

```
public static bool Equals (object objA, object objB)
```

Equals returns true if both objA and objB are null or if they reference the same object. If *only* objA or objB is null, it returns false; otherwise, it calls the virtual Equals method on objA. This is a fail-safe algorithm for equality comparison when the types are unknown at compile time.

Here's a simple example:

```
object x = 3, y = 3;
Console.WriteLine (object.Equals (x, y));   // True
x = null;
Console.WriteLine (object.Equals (x, y));   // False
y = null;
Console.WriteLine (object.Equals (x, y));   // True
```

A useful application is when writing generic types. The following code will not compile if object.Equals is replaced with the == or != operator:

```
class Test <T>
{
  T _value;
  public void SetValue (T newValue)
  {
    if (!object.Equals (newValue, _value))
    {
      _value = newValue;
      OnValueChanged( );
    }
  }
  protected virtual void OnValueChanged( ) { ... }
}
```

Operators are prohibited here because the compiler cannot bind to the static method of an unknown type.

The static object.ReferenceEquals method

Occasionally, you need to force referential equality comparison. The static
object.ReferenceEquals method does just this:

```
class Widget { ... }

class Test
{
  static void Main( )
  {
    Widget w1 = new Widget( );
    Widget w2 = new Widget( );
    Console.WriteLine (object.ReferenceEquals (w1, w2));     // False;
  }
}
```

The reason you might want to do this is that it's possible for Widget to override
the virtual Equals method, such that w1.Equals(w2) would return true. Further,
it's possible for Widget to overload the == operator so that w1==w2 would also
return true. In such cases, calling object.ReferenceEquals guarantees normal
referential equality semantics.

 Another way to force referential equality comparison is to cast the
first value to an object and then apply the == operator.

The IEquatable<T> interface

A consequence of calling object.Equals is that it forces boxing on value types.
This is undesirable in highly performance-sensitive scenarios because boxing is
relatively expensive compared to the actual comparison. A solution was introduced in C# 2.0, with the IEquatable<T> interface:

```
public interface IEquatable<T>
{
  bool Equals (T other);
}
```

The idea is that IEquatable<T>, when implemented, gives the same result as calling
object's virtual Equals method—but faster. Most basic .NET types implement
IEquatable<T>. You can use IEquatable<T> as a constraint in a generic type:

```
class Test<T> where T : IEquatable<T>
{
  bool IsEqual (T a, T b)
  {
    return a.Equals (b);     // No boxing with generic T
  }
}
```

If we remove the generic constraint, the class would still compile, but a.Equals(b)
would instead bind to the slower object.Equals (slower assuming T was a value
type).

When Equals and == are not equal

We said earlier that it's occasionally useful for == and Equals to apply different definitions of equality. For example:

```
double x = double.NaN;
Console.WriteLine (x == x);          // False
Console.WriteLine (x.Equals (x));    // True
```

The double type's == operator applies three-valued logic, which enforces that one NaN can never equal another. This is most natural from a mathematical perspective, and it reflects the underlying processor behavior. The Equals method, however, cannot follow this because it would violate an axiom:

x.Equals (x) must *always* return true.

Collections and dictionaries rely on Equals behaving this way—otherwise, they could not find an item they previously stored.

Equality and Custom Types

Recall default equality comparison behavior:

- Value types use *value equality*.
- Reference types use *referential equality*.

Further:

- For structs, value equality means comparing each field.

Sometimes it makes sense to override this behavior when writing a type. There are two cases for doing so:

- To change the meaning of equality
- To speed up equality comparisons for structs

The first case can arise when the default behavior of == and Equals is unnatural for your type and is *not what a consumer would expect*. An example is DateTimeOffset, a struct with two private fields: a UTC DateTime and a numeric integer offset. If you were writing this type, you'd want to ensure that equality comparisons considered only the UTC DateTime field and not the offset field. Another example is numeric types that support NaN values such as float and double. If you were implementing such types yourself, you'd want to ensure that three-value logic was supported in equality comparisons.

The second case arises because the default equality comparison algorithm for structs is relatively slow: in simple cases, overriding Equals can improve performance by a factor of five. Overloading the == operator and implementing IEquatable<T> allows unboxed equality comparisons that execute up to five times faster *again*.

Equality customization is much more applicable to structs than to classes. With a class, there's no potential for improving performance because the default reference-type comparison is already highly efficient. Instead, there is potential to confuse the consumer of the class, who will in most cases expect reference-type equality semantics. There are some exceptions—for example, when writing a type for which a consumer *would* expect value equality—but for performance or other reasons, must be a class. Such types are generally small and immutable; an example is System.String. Another exception is when writing an internally or privately scoped class for a specialized purpose.

> In general, you should avoid messing with the equality semantics of classes. For instance, if you have a Customer class with fields such as ID, FirstName, LastName, and so on, it would be inappropriate to change the equality semantics such that two Customer instances with the same ID or name reported as being equal.

There's actually another, rather peculiar case for customizing equality, and that's to improve a struct's hashing algorithm for better performance in a hashtable. This comes of the fact that equality comparison and hashing are joined at the hip. We'll examine hashing in a moment.

How to override equality semantics

Here is a summary of the steps:

1. Override GetHashCode( ) and Equals( ).
2. Overload != and ==.
3. (Optionally) implement IEquatable<T>.

Overriding GetHashCode

It might seem odd that System.Object—with its small footprint of members—defines a method with a specialized and narrow purpose. GetHashCode is a virtual method in Object that fits this description—it exists primarily for the benefit of just the following two types:

```
System.Collections.Hashtable
System.Collections.Generic.Dictionary<TKey,TValue>
```

These are *hashtables*—collections where each element has a key used for storage and retrieval. A hashtable applies a very specific strategy for efficiently allocating elements based on their key. This requires that each key have an Int32 number, or *hash code*. The hash code need not be unique for each key, but should be as varied as possible for good hashtable performance. Hashtables are considered important enough that GetHashCode is defined in System.Object—so that every type can emit a hash code.

> We describe hashtables in detail in the section "Dictionaries" in Chapter 7.

Both reference and value types have default implementations of GetHashCode, meaning you don't need to override this method—*unless you override* Equals. The converse is also true: override GetHashCode and you must also override Equals.

Here are the other rules for overriding `object.GetHashCode`:

- It must return the same value if called repeatedly on the same object.
- It must return the same value on two objects for which `Equals` returns `true` (hence, `GetHashCode` and `Equals` are overridden together).
- It must not throw exceptions.

For maximum performance in hashtables, `GetHashCode` should be written so as to minimize the likelihood of two different values returning the same hashcode. This gives rise to the third reason for overriding `Equals` and `GetHashCode` on structs, which is to provide a more efficient hashing algorithm than the default. The default for structs simply performs a bitwise exclusive OR on each of the fields, which typically generates more duplicate codes than if you wrote the algorithm yourself.

In contrast, the default `GetHashCode` implementation for *classes* is based on an internal object token, which is always unique.

When overriding `GetHashCode` in a class, the calculations should be based on immutable fields. In other words, a reference type object's hashcode should not change throughout its life—*otherwise, hashtables that use it as a key will break.*

A complete example illustrating how to override `GetHashCode` is listed shortly.

Overriding Equals

The axioms for `object.Equals` are as follows:

- An object equals itself.
- An object cannot equal `null` (unless it's a nullable type).
- Equality is commutative and associative.
- Equality operations are repeatable and reliable (they don't throw exceptions).

Overloading == and !=

For consistency, it's a good idea to overload the equality and inequality operators when overriding `Equals`. The consequences of overriding `Equals` while *failing* to overload `==` and `!=` depend on whether you're writing a struct or a class:

- With a struct, `==` and `!=` will simply not work on your type.
- With a class, `==` and `!=` will work, but will be functionally out of line with the `Equals` method.

Although it's possible to overload `!=` such that it means something other than `!(==)`, this is almost never done in practice, except when implementing three-value logic.

Implementing IEquatable<T>

For completeness, it's also good to implement IEquatable<T> when overriding Equals. Its results should always match those of the overridden object's Equals method. Implementing IEquatable<T> comes at no programming cost if you structure your Equals method implementation, as in the following example.

An example: The Area struct

Imagine we need a struct to represent an area whose width and height are interchangeable. In other words, 5×10 is equal to 10×5. (Such a type would be suitable in an algorithm that arranges rectangular shapes.)

Here's the complete code:

```
public struct Area : IEquatable <Area>
{
  public readonly int Measure1;
  public readonly int Measure2;

  public Area (int m1, int m2)
  {
    Measure1 = m1;
    Measure2 = m2;
  }

  public override bool Equals (object other)
  {
    if (!(other is Area)) return false;
    return Equals ((Area) other);        // Calls method below
  }

  public bool Equals (Area other)        // Implements IEquatable<Area>
  {
    return Measure1 == other.Measure1 && Measure2 == other.Measure2
        || Measure1 == other.Measure2 && Measure2 == other.Measure1;
  }

  public override int GetHashCode( )
  {
    if (Measure1 > Measure2)
      return Measure1 * 37 + Measure2;    // 37 = a prime number
    else
      return Measure2 * 37 + Measure1;
  }

  public static bool operator == (Area a1, Area a2)
  {
    return a1.Equals (a2);
  }
}
```

```
    public static bool operator != (Area a1, Area a2)
    {
      return !a1.Equals (a2);
    }
  }
```

In implementing GetHashCode, we have to ensure that the same value is returned regardless of the order of Measure1 and Measure2—hence, the if statement. To increase the likelihood of uniqueness, we multiply the larger measure by some prime number (ignoring any overflow) before adding the two together.

Here's a demo of the Area struct:

```
  Area a1 = new Area (5, 10);
  Area a2 = new Area (10, 5);
  Console.WriteLine (a1.Equals (a2));    // True
  Console.WriteLine (a1 == a2);          // True
```

Pluggable equality comparers

If you want a type to take on different equality semantics just for a particular scenario, you can use a pluggable IEqualityComparer. This is particularly useful in conjunction with the standard collection classes, and we describe it in the following chapter, in the section "Plugging in Equality and Order."

Order Comparison

As well as defining standard protocols for equality, C# and .NET define standard protocols for determining the order of one object relative to another. The basic protocols are:

- The IComparable interfaces (IComparable and IComparable<T>)
- The > and < operators

The IComparable interfaces are used by general-purpose sorting algorithms. In the following example, the static Array.Sort method works because System.String implements the IComparable interfaces:

```
  string[] colors = { "Green", "Red", "Blue" };
  Array.Sort (colors);
  foreach (string c in colors) Console.Write (c + " ");    // Blue Green Red
```

The < and > operators are more specialized, and they are intended mostly for numeric types. Because they are statically resolved, they can translate to highly efficient bytecode, suitable for computationally intensive algorithms.

The .NET Framework also provides pluggable ordering protocols, via the IComparer interfaces. We describe these in the final section of Chapter 7.

IComparable

The IComparable interfaces are defined as follows:

```
  public interface IComparable    { int CompareTo (object other); }
  public interface IComparable<T> { int CompareTo (T other);      }
```

The two interfaces represent the same functionality. With value types, the generic type-safe interface is faster than the nongeneric interface. In both cases, the CompareTo method works as follows:

- If a comes after b, a.CompareTo(b) returns a positive number.
- If a is the same as b, a.CompareTo(b) returns 0.
- If a comes before b, a.CompareTo(b) returns a negative number.

For example:

```
Console.WriteLine ("Beck".CompareTo ("Anne"));    // 1
Console.WriteLine ("Beck".CompareTo ("Beck"));    // 0
Console.WriteLine ("Beck".CompareTo ("Chris"));   // -1
```

Most of the base types implement both IComparable interfaces. These interfaces are also sometimes implemented when writing custom types. An example is given shortly.

IComparable versus Equals

Consider a type that both overrides Equals and implements the IComparable interfaces. You'd expect that when Equals returns true, CompareTo should return 0. And you'd be right. But here's the catch:

> When Equals returns false CompareTo can return what it likes!

In other words, equality can be "fussier" than comparison, but not vice versa (violate this and sorting algorithms will break). So, CompareTo can say "All objects are equal" while Equals says "But some are more equal than others!"

A great example of this is System.String. String's Equals method and == operator use *ordinal* comparison, which compares the Unicode point values of each character. Its CompareTo method, however, uses a less fussy *culture-dependent* comparison. On most computers, for instance, the strings "ǔ" and "ū" are different according to Equals, but the same according to CompareTo.

In Chapter 7, we discuss the pluggable ordering protocol, IComparer, which allows you to specify an alternative ordering algorithm when sorting or instantiating a sorted collection. A custom IComparer can further extend the gap between CompareTo and Equals—a case-insensitive string comparer, for instance, will return 0 when comparing "A" and "a". The reverse rule still applies, however: CompareTo can never be fussier than Equals.

 When implementing the IComparable interfaces in a custom type, you can avoid running afoul of this rule by writing the first line of CompareTo as follows:

```
if (Equals (other)) return 0;
```

After that, it can return what it likes, as long as it's consistent!

< and >

Some types define < and > operators. For instance:

```
bool after2008 = DateTime.Now > new DateTime (2008, 1, 1);
```

You can expect the < and > operators, when implemented, to be functionally consistent with the IComparable interfaces. This is standard practice across the .NET Framework.

It's also standard practice to implement the IComparable interfaces whenever < and > are overloaded; although the reverse is not true. In fact, most .NET types that implement IComparable *do not* overload < and >. This differs from the situation with equality, where it's normal to overload == when overriding Equals.

Typically, > and < are overloaded only when:

- A type has a strong intrinsic concept of "greater than" and "less than" (versus IComparable's broader concepts of "comes before" and "comes after").
- There is only one way *or context* in which to perform the comparison.
- The result is invariant across cultures.

System.String doesn't satisfy the last point: the results of string comparisons can vary according to language. Hence, string doesn't support the > and < operators:

```
bool error = "Beck" > "Anne";        // Compile-time error
```

Implementing the IComparable Interfaces

In the following struct, representing a musical note, we implement the IComparable interfaces, as well as overloading the < and > operators. For completeness, we also override Equals/GetHashCode and overload == and !=:

```
public struct Note : IComparable<Note>, IEquatable<Note>, IComparable
{
  int _semitonesFromA;

  public Note (int semitonesFromA)
  {
    _semitonesFromA = semitonesFromA;
  }

  public int CompareTo (Note other)           // Generic IComparable<T>
  {
    if (Equals (other)) return 0;   // Fail-safe check
    return _semitonesFromA.CompareTo (other._semitonesFromA);
  }

  int IComparable.CompareTo (object other)     // Nongeneric IComparable
  {
    if (!(other is Note))
      throw new InvalidOperationException ("CompareTo: Not a note");
    return CompareTo ((Note) other);
  }

  public static bool operator < (Note n1, Note n2)
  {
    return n1.CompareTo (n2) < 0;
  }
```

```csharp
    public static bool operator > (Note n1, Note n2)
    {
      return n1.CompareTo (n2) > 0;
    }

    public bool Equals (Note other)     // for IEquatable<Note>
    {
      return _semitonesFromA == other._semitonesFromA;
    }

    public override bool Equals (object other)
    {
      if (!(other is Note)) return false;
      return Equals ((Note) other);
    }

    public override int GetHashCode()
    {
      return _semitonesFromA.GetHashCode();
    }

    public static bool operator == (Note n1, Note n2)
    {
        return n1.Equals (n2);
    }

    public static bool operator != (Note n1, Note n2)
    {
        return !(n1 == n2);
    }
}
```

Utility Classes

Console

The static Console class handles standard input/output for console-based applications. In a command-line (Console) application, the input comes from the keyboard via Read, ReadKey, and ReadLine, and the output goes to the text window via Write and WriteLine. You can control the window's position and dimensions with the properties WindowLeft, WindowTop, WindowHeight, and WindowWidth. You can also change the BackgroundColor and ForegroundColor properties and manipulate the cursor with the CursorLeft, CursorTop, and CursorSize properties:

```csharp
Console.WindowWidth = Console.LargestWindowWidth;
Console.ForegroundColor = ConsoleColor.Green;
Console.Write ("test... 50%");
Console.CursorLeft -= 3;
Console.Write ("90%");     // test... 90%
```

The Write and WriteLine methods are overloaded to accept a composite format string (see String.Format in the earlier section "String and Text Handling").

However, neither method accepts a format provider, so you're always stuck with CultureInfo.CurrentCulture.

You can redirect the Console's input and output streams via the SetIn and SetOut methods:

```
// First save existing output writer:
System.IO.TextWriter oldOut = Console.Out;

// Redirect the console's output to a file:
using (System.IO.TextWriter w = System.IO.File.CreateText
                                ("e:\\output.txt"))
{
  Console.SetOut (w);
  Console.WriteLine ("Hello world");
}

// Restore standard console output
Console.SetOut (oldOut);

// Open the output.txt file in Notepad:
System.Diagnostics.Process.Start ("e:\\output.txt");
```

In Chapter 13, we describe how streams and text writers work.

> In a Visual Studio Windows application, the Console's output is automatically redirected to Visual Studio's output window (in debug mode). This can make Console.Write useful for diagnostic purposes; although in most cases the Debug and Trace classes in the System. Diagnostics namespace are more appropriate (see Chapter 23).

Environment

The static System.Environment class provides a range of useful properties:

Files and folders
    CurrentDirectory, SystemDirectory, CommandLine

Computer and operating system
    MachineName, ProcessorCount, OSVersion

User logon
    UserName, UserInteractive, UserDomainName

Diagnostics
    TickCount, StackTrace, WorkingSet, Version

You can obtain additional folders by calling GetFolderPath; we describe this in the section "File and Directory Operations" in Chapter 13.

You can access OS environment variables (what you see when you type "set" at the command prompt) with the following three methods: GetEnvironmentVariable, GetEnvironmentVariables, and SetEnvironmentVariable.

The ExitCode property lets you set the return code, for when your program is called from a command or batch file, and the FailFast method terminates a program immediately, without performing cleanup.

Process

The Process class in System.Diagnostics allows you to launch a new process.

The static Process.Start method has a number of overloads; the simplest accepts a simple filename with optional arguments:

```
Process.Start ("notepad.exe");
Process.Start ("notepad.exe", "e:\\file.txt");
```

You can also specify just a filename and the registered program for its extension will be launched:

```
Process.Start ("e:\\file.txt");
```

The most flexible overload accepts a ProcessStartInfo instance. With this, you can capture and redirect the launched process's input, output, and error output (if you set UseShellExecute to false). The following captures the output of calling ipconfig:

```
ProcessStartInfo psi = new ProcessStartInfo ();
psi.FileName = "cmd.exe";
psi.Arguments = "/c ipconfig /all";
psi.RedirectStandardOutput = true;
psi.UseShellExecute = false;
Process p = Process.Start (psi);
string result = p.StandardOutput.ReadToEnd();
Console.WriteLine (result);
```

You can do the same to invoke the csc compiler, if you set Filename to the following:

```
psi.FileName = System.IO.Path.Combine (
   System.Runtime.InteropServices.RuntimeEnvironment.GetRuntimeDirectory(),
   "csc.exe");
```

If you don't redirect output, Process.Start executes in a nonblocking fashion, meaning that it returns immediately while the new process executes in parallel. If you want to wait for the new process to complete, you can call WaitForExit on the Process object, with an optional timeout.

The Process class also allows you to query and interact with other processes running on the computer (see Chapter 23).

7

Collections

The .NET Framework provides a standard set of types for storing and managing collections of objects. These include resizable lists, linked lists, sorted and unsorted dictionaries as well as arrays. Of these, only arrays form part of the C# language; the remaining collections are just classes you instantiate like any other. In this, C# differs from languages such as Perl and Python, which incorporate key/value data structures and dynamically sized arrays into the language itself.

The types in the Framework for collections can be divided into the following categories:

- Interfaces that define standard collection protocols
- Ready-to-use collection classes (lists, dictionaries, etc.)
- Base classes for writing application-specific collections

This chapter covers each of these categories, with an additional section on the types used in determining equality and order within collections. Where applicable, both generic and nongeneric versions of each collection type are described, with less emphasis on older Framework types in cases when they've been largely superseded. Table 7-1 lists collection namespaces.

Table 7-1. Collection namespaces

Namespace	Contains
System.Collections	Nongeneric collection classes and interfaces
System.Collections.Specialized	Strongly typed nongeneric collection classes
System.Collections.Generic	Generic collection classes and interfaces
System.Collections.ObjectModel	Proxies and bases for custom collections

Enumeration

In computing, there are many different kinds of collections ranging from simple data structures, such as arrays or linked lists, to more complex ones, such as red/black trees and priority queues. Although the internal implementation and external characteristics of these data structures vary widely, the ability to traverse the contents of the collection is an almost universal need. The Framework supports this need via a pair of interfaces (IEnumerable, IEnumerator, and their generic counterparts) that allow different data structures to expose a common traversal API. These are part of a larger set of collection interfaces illustrated in Figure 7-1.

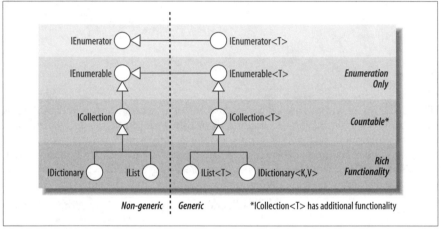

Figure 7-1. Collection interfaces

IEnumerable and IEnumerator

The IEnumerator interface defines the basic low-level protocol by which elements in a collection are traversed—or enumerated—in a forward-only matter. Its declaration is as follows:

```
public interface IEnumerator
{
  bool MoveNext( );
  object Current { get; }
  void Reset( );
}
```

MoveNext advances the current element or "cursor" to the next position, returning false if there are no more elements in the collection. Current returns the element at the current position (usually cast from object to a more specific type). MoveNext must be called before retrieving the first element—this is to allow for an empty collection. The Reset method, if implemented, moves back to the start, allowing the collection to be re-iterated. (Calling Reset is generally avoided because it's not supported by all enumerators.)

Collections do not *implement* enumerators; instead, they *provide* enumerators, via the interface IEnumerable:

```
public interface IEnumerable
{
  IEnumerator GetEnumerator();
}
```

By defining a single method retuning an enumerator, IEnumerable provides flexibility in that the iteration logic can be farmed off to another class. IEnumerable can be thought of as "IEnumeratorProvider," and it is the most basic interface that collection classes implement.

The following example illustrates low-level use of IEnumerable and IEnumerator:

```
string s = "Hello";

// Because string implements IEnumerable, we can call GetEnumerator():
IEnumerator rator = s.GetEnumerator();

while (rator.MoveNext())
{
  char c = (char) rator.Current;
  Console.Write (c + ".");
}

// Output:  H.e.l.l.o.
```

However, it's rare to call methods on enumerators directly in this manner, because C# provides a syntactic shortcut: the foreach statement. Here's the same example rewritten using foreach:

```
string s = "Hello";       // The String class implements IEnumerable

foreach (char c in s)
  Console.Write (c + ".");
```

IEnumerable<T> and IEnumerator<T>

IEnumerator and IEnumerable are nearly always implemented in conjunction with their extended generic versions:

```
public interface IEnumerator<T> : IEnumerator, IDisposable
{
  T Current { get; }
}

public interface IEnumerable<T> : IEnumerable
{
  IEnumerator<T> GetEnumerator();
}
```

By defining a typed version of Current and GetEnumerator, these interfaces strengthen static type safety, avoid the overhead of boxing with value type elements, and are more convenient to the consumer. The following code generates a compiler warning because n is of type byte and not int:

```
public static int CountNumbers (IEnumerable<int> numbers)
{
```

```
    int total = 0;
    foreach (byte n in numbers) total += n;
    return total;
}
```

Had numbers been declared of type IEnumerable, there would be no compiler warning, only a runtime error.

Arrays automatically implement IEnumerable<T> (where T is the member type of the array). If we correct our CountNumbers method by changing byte to int, we can call it as follows:

```
int[] data = { 1, 2, 3 };
Console.WriteLine (CountNumbers (data));    // 6
```

The compiler further helps by preventing us from calling CountNumbers with an array of characters.

It's standard practice for collection classes to publicly expose IEnumerable<T>, while "hiding" the nongeneric IEnumerable through explicit interface implementation. This is so that if you directly call GetEnumerator( ), you get back the type-safe generic IEnumerator<T>. There are times, though, when this rule is broken for reasons of backward compatibility (generics did not exist prior to C# 2.0). A good example is arrays—these must return the nongeneric (the nice way of putting it is "classic") IEnumerator to avoid breaking earlier code. In order to get a generic IEnumerator<T>, you must cast to expose the explicit interface:

```
int[] data = { 1, 2, 3 };
IEnumerator<int> rator = ((IEnumerable <int>)data).GetEnumerator( );
```

Fortunately, you rarely need to write this sort of code, thanks to the foreach statement.

Implementing the Enumeration Interfaces

You might want to implement IEnumerable or IEnumerable<T> for one or more of the following reasons:

*   To support the foreach statement
*   To interoperate with anything expecting a standard collection
*   As part of implementing a more sophisticated collection interface

To implement IEnumerable/IEnumerable<T>, you must provide an enumerator. This can be done in one of three ways:

*   If the class is "wrapping" another collection, by returning the wrapped collection's enumerator
*   Via an iterator using yield return
*   By instantiating your own IEnumerator/IEnumerator<T> implementation

Returning another collection's enumerator is just a matter of calling GetEnumerator on the inner collection. However, this is viable only in the simplest scenarios, where the items in the inner collection are exactly what are required. A more flexible approach is to write an iterator, using C#'s yield return statement. An *iterator* is a C# language feature that assists in writing collections, in the same way the foreach statement assists in consuming collections. An iterator automatically handles the implementation of IEnumerable and IEnumerator—or their generic versions. Here's a simple example:

```
public class MyCollection : IEnumerable
{
  int[] data = {1, 2, 3};

  public IEnumerator GetEnumerator()
  {
    foreach (int i in data)
      yield return i;
  }
}
```

Notice the "black magic": GetEnumerator doesn't appear to return an enumerator at all! The compiler, upon parsing the yield return statement, writes "behind the scenes," a hidden nested enumerator class, and then refactors GetEnumerator to instantiate and return that class. Iterators are powerful and simple.

Keeping with this approach, we can also implement the generic interface IEnumerable<T>:

```
public class MyGenCollection : IEnumerable<int>
{
  int[] data = {1, 2, 3};

  public IEnumerator<int> GetEnumerator()
  {
    foreach (int i in data)
      yield return i;
  }

  IEnumerator IEnumerable.GetEnumerator()      // Explicit implementation
  {                                            // keeps it hidden.
    return GetEnumerator ();
  }
}
```

Because IEnumerable<T> implements IEnumerable, we must implement both the generic and nongeneric versions of GetEnumerator. In accordance with standard practice, we've implemented the nongeneric version explicitly. It can simply call the generic GetEnumerator because IEnumerator<T> implements IEnumerator.

The class we've just written would be suitable as a basis from which to write a more sophisticated collection. However, if we need nothing above a simple IEnumerable<T> implementation, the yield return statement allows for an easier variation. Rather than writing a class, you can move the iteration logic into a method returning a generic IEnumerable<T> and let the compiler take care of the rest. Here's an example:

```
public class Test
{
  public static IEnumerable <int> GetSomeIntegers()
  {
```

```
      yield return 1;
      yield return 2;
      yield return 3;
    }
}
```

Here's our method in use:

```
foreach (int i in Test.GetSomeIntegers())
  Console.WriteLine (i);

// Output
1
2
3
```

The final approach in writing GetEnumerator is to write a class that implements IEnumerator directly. This is exactly what the compiler does behind the scenes, in resolving iterators. The following example defines a collection that's hardcoded to contain the integers 1, 2, and 3:

```
public class MyIntList : IEnumerable
{
  int[] data = { 1, 2, 3 };

  public IEnumerator GetEnumerator ()
  {
    return new Enumerator (this);
  }

  class Enumerator : IEnumerator        // Define an inner class
  {                                      // for the enumerator.
    MyIntList collection;
    int currentIndex = -1;

    internal Enumerator (MyIntList collection)
    {
      this.collection = collection;
    }

    public object Current
    {
      get {
        if (currentIndex == collection.data.Length)
          throw new InvalidOperationException ("Past end of list!");
        return collection.data [currentIndex];
      }
    }

    public bool MoveNext()
    {
      if (currentIndex > collection.data.Length)
        throw new InvalidOperationException ("Past end of list!");
      return ++currentIndex < collection.data.Length;
    }
```

```
    public void Reset() { currentIndex = -1; }
  }
}
```

 Implementing Reset is optional—you can instead throw a NotSupportedException.

Note that the first call to MoveNext should move to the first (and not the second) item in the list.

To get on par with an iterator in functionality, we must also implement IEnumerator<T>. Here's an example with bounds checking omitted for brevity:

```
class MyIntList : IEnumerable<int>
{
  int[] data = { 1, 2, 3 };

  // The generic enumerator is compatible with both IEnumerable and
  // IEnumerable<T>. We implement the nongeneric GetEnumerator method
  // explicitly to avoid a naming conflict.

  public IEnumerator<int> GetEnumerator() { return new Enumerator(this); }
  IEnumerator IEnumerable.GetEnumerator() { return new Enumerator(this); }

  class Enumerator : IEnumerator<int>
  {
    int currentIndex = -1;
    MyIntList collection;

    internal Enumerator (MyIntList collection)
    {
      this.collection = collection;
    }

    public int Current { get { return collection.data [currentIndex]; } }
    object IEnumerator.Current { get { return Current; } }

    public bool MoveNext()
    {
      return ++currentIndex < collection.data.Length;
    }

    public void Reset() { currentIndex = -1; }

    // Given we don't need a Dispose method, it's good practice to
    // implement it explicitly, so it's hidden from the public interface.

    void IDisposable.Dispose() {}
  }
}
```

The example with generics is faster because IEnumerator<int>.Current doesn't require casting from integer to object, and so avoids the overhead of boxing.

IDictionaryEnumerator

Later in this chapter, we discuss the use of dictionary data structures. IDictionaryEnumerator is the standard nongeneric interface used to enumerate over the contents of a dictionary, in which each element is a *dictionary entry*—a structure having both a key and a value. IDictionaryEnumerator is simply a specialized version of IEnumerator, with an Entry property (a typed version of Current that returns a dictionary entry) and Key/Value properties (to provide direct access to the dictionary entry's key and value properties). The interface looks like this:

```
public interface IDictionaryEnumerator : IEnumerator
{
    DictionaryEntry Entry { get; }
    object Key { get; }
    object Value { get; }
}
```

The generic equivalent of this interface is as follows: IEnumerator <KeyValuePair<TKey,TValue>>.

The ICollection and IList Interfaces

Although the enumeration interfaces provide a protocol for forward-only iteration over a collection, they don't provide a mechanism to determine the size of the collection, access a member by index, search, or modify the collection. The .NET Framework defines additional interfaces for such functionality via a set of six interfaces: ICollection, IList, IDictionary, and their generic counterparts.

The inheritance hierarchy for these interfaces is shown in Figure 7-1, earlier in the chapter. The easiest way to summarize them is as follows:

IEnumerable *and* IEnumerable<T>
   Provides minimum functionality (enumeration only)

ICollection *and* ICollection<T>
   Provides medium functionality (e.g., the Count property)

IList/IDictionary *and their generic counterparts*
   Provides maximum functionality (including "random" access by index/key)

The generic and nongeneric versions differ in ways over and above what you might expect, particularly in the case of ICollection. The reasons for this are mostly historical: because generics came later, the generic interfaces were developed with the benefit of hindsight. For this reason, ICollection<T> does not extend ICollection; IList<T> does not extend IList, and IDictionary<TKey, TValue> does not extend IDictionary. Of course, a collection class itself is free to implement both versions of an interface if beneficial (which, often, it is).

There is no *consistent* rationale in the way the words "collection" and "list" are applied throughout the .NET Framework. For instance, since IList<T> is a more functional version of ICollection<T>, you might expect the class List<T> to be correspondingly more functional than the class Collection<T>. This is not the case. It's best to consider the terms "collection" and "list" as broadly synonymous, except when a specific type is involved.

This section covers ICollection, IList, and their generic versions; the later section "Dictionaries" covers the dictionary interfaces.

ICollection and ICollection<T>

ICollection is the standard interface for countable collections of objects. It provides the ability to determine the size of a collection, to determine whether it can be modified or is synchronized (thread-safe), and to copy the collection into an array for more sophisticated processing. Since ICollection extends IEnumerable, types that implement ICollection can also be traversed via IEnumerable and IEnumerator.

ICollection<T> is similar in that it provides a countable collection, but allows items to be added and removed from the list as well. The generic interface differs also in that it doesn't define properties to assist with synchronization (Chapter 19)—thread safety is no longer considered intrinsic to the list.

The ICollection interfaces look like this:

```
public interface ICollection : IEnumerable
{
   void CopyTo (Array array, int index);
   int Count {get;}
   bool IsSynchronized {get;}
   object SyncRoot {get;}
}

public interface ICollection<T> : IEnumerable<T>, IEnumerable
{
   void Add(T item);
   void Clear();
   bool Contains (T item);
   void CopyTo (T[] array, int arrayIndex);
   int Count { get; }
   bool IsReadOnly { get; }
   bool Remove (T item);
}
```

The nongeneric ICollection is fairly straightforward to implement. If wrapping another collection, the IsSynchronized and SyncRoot properties should be implemented by calling through to the wrapped collection's methods. Otherwise, you can make IsSynchronized return false and SyncRoot return null—this disables built-in support for synchronization wrappers, which is consistent with the modern pattern for writing collection classes (see the section "Thread Safety" in Chapter 19).

ICollection<T> is similarly straightforward to implement, the only caveat being that there's nothing to prevent the Add or Remove method being called on a collection where IsReadOnly returns true. Standard practice is to throw an exception within the implementation of the Add, Remove, and Clear methods if the collection is read-only.

The ICollection interfaces are usually implemented in conjunction with either the IList or the IDictionary interfaces.

IList and IList<T>

IList is the standard interface for array-indexable collections. In addition to the functionality inherent in ICollection and IEnumerable, it also provides the ability to index directly into the collection by position (using the overloaded indexer), to add, remove, and change elements in the collection by position, and to search for elements in the collection. The nongeneric interface definition looks like this:

```
public interface IList : ICollection, IEnumerable
{
  object this [int index] { get; set }
  bool IsFixedSize { get; }
  bool IsReadOnly  { get; }
  int  Add       (object value);
  void Clear( );
  bool Contains (object value);
  int  IndexOf  (object value);
  void Insert   (int index, object value);
  void Remove   (object value);
  void RemoveAt (int index);
}
```

The generic interface IList<T> is functionally very similar to IList. Its definition is shorter because it inherits much of its functionality from ICollection<T>:

```
public interface IList<T> : ICollection<T>, IEnumerable<T>, IEnumerable
{
  T this [int index] { get; set; }
  int IndexOf (T item);
  void Insert (int index, T item);
  void RemoveAt (int index);
}
```

The Add method on the nongeneric IList interface returns an integer—this is the index of the newly added item. In contrast, the Add method on ICollection<T> has a void return type.

The IndexOf methods perform a linear search on the list, returning -1 if the specified item is not found.

IList and IList<T> each have advantages. IList<T> provides better type safety and ease of use, and requires no boxing when used with value types. IList is more interoperable—partly because it has been around longer, and partly because the lack of type restrictions can sometimes be helpful. Suppose U is a subclass of T. Although U is type-compatible with T, IList<U> is not type-compatible with IList<T>, because generics are not variant. The nongeneric IList doesn't suffer from this issue, so it can actually be more versatile. Collections often implement both IList and IList<T>.

The general-purpose List<T> class is the quintessential implementation of both IList and IList<T>. C# arrays also implement both the generic and nongeneric ILists (although the methods that add or remove elements are hidden via explicit interface implementation and throw a NotSupportedException if called).

The Array Class

The Array class is the implicit base class for all single and multidimensional arrays, and it is one of the most fundamental types implementing the standard collection interfaces. The Array class provides type unification, so a common set of methods is available to all arrays, regardless of their declaration or underlying element type.

Since arrays are so fundamental, C# provides explicit syntax for their declaration and initialization, described in Chapters 2 and 3. When an array is declared using C#'s syntax, the CLR implicitly subtypes the Array class—synthesizing a *pseudotype* appropriate to the array's dimensions and element types. This pseudotype implements the typed generic collection interfaces, such as IList<string>.

The CLR also treats array types specially upon construction, assigning them a contiguous space in memory. This makes indexing into arrays highly efficient, but prevents them from being resized later on.

Array implements the collection interfaces up to IList in both their generic and nongeneric forms. IList itself is implemented explicitly, though, to keep Array's public interface clean of methods such as Add or Remove, which throw an exception on fixed-length collections such as arrays. The Array class does actually offer a static Resize method, although this works by creating a new array and then copying over each element. As well as being inefficient, references to the array elsewhere in the program will still point to the original version. A better solution for resizable collections is to use the List class (described in the following section).

An array can contain value type or reference type elements. Value type elements are stored in place in the array, so an array of three long integers (each 8 bytes) will occupy 24 bytes of contiguous memory. A reference type element, however, occupies only as much space in the array as a reference (4 bytes on a 32-bit machine). Figure 7-2 illustrates the effect, in memory, of the following program.

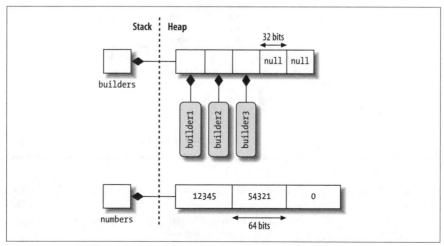

Figure 7-2. Arrays in memory

```
static void Main( )
{
  StringBuilder[] builders = new StringBuilder [5];
  builders [0] = new StringBuilder ("builder1");
  builders [1] = new StringBuilder ("builder2");
  builders [2] = new StringBuilder ("builder3");

  long[] numbers = new long [3];
  numbers [0] = 12345;
  numbers [1] = 54321;
}
```

Because Array is a class, arrays are always (themselves) reference types—regardless of the array's element type. This means that the statement arrayB = arrayA results in two objects that reference the same array. Arrays can be duplicated with the Clone method: arrayB = arrayA.Clone( ). However, this results in a shallow clone, meaning that only the memory represented by the array itself is copied. If the array contains value type objects, the values themselves are copied; if the array contains reference type objects, just the references are copied (resulting in two arrays whose members reference the same subobjects). Figure 7-3 demonstrates the effect of adding the following code to our example:

```
StringBuilder[] builders2 = builders;
StringBuilder[] shallowClone = (StringBuilder[]) builders.Clone( );
```

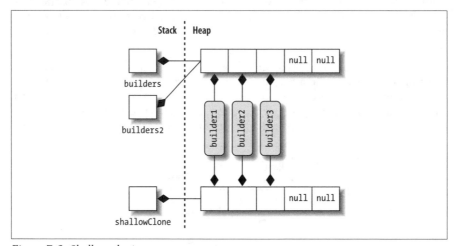

Figure 7-3. Shallow-cloning an array

To create a deep copy—where reference type subobjects are duplicated—you must loop through the array and clone each element manually. The same rules apply to other .NET collection types.

Although Array is designed primarily for use with 32-bit indexers, it also has limited support for 64-bit indexers (allowing an array to address up to 2^{64} possible elements). As a result, several methods, in particular Copy( ), CopyTo( ), GetValue( ), and SetValue( ), accept either Int32 or Int64 parameters.

Many of the methods on the Array class that you expect to be instance methods are in fact static methods. This is perhaps the result of an odd design decision, and it means you should check for both static and instance methods when looking for a method on Array.

Construction and Indexing

The easiest way to create and index arrays is through C#'s language constructs:

```
int[] myArray = new int[] { 1, 2, 3};
int first = myArray [0];
int last = myArray [myArray.Length - 1];
```

Alternatively, you can instantiate an array dynamically by calling Array. CreateInstance. This allows you to specify element type and rank (number of dimensions) at runtime—as well as allowing nonzero-based arrays through specifying a lower bound. Nonzero-based arrays are not CLS (Common Language Specification)-compliant.

The static GetValue and SetValue methods let you access elements in a dynamically created array (they also work on ordinary arrays):

```
// Create a string array 2 elements in length:
Array a = Array.CreateInstance (typeof(string), 2);
a.SetValue ("hi", 0);                   // → a[0] = "hi";
a.SetValue ("there", 1);                // → a[1] = "there";
string s = (string) a.GetValue (0);     // → s = a[0];

// We can also cast to a C# array as follows:
string[] cSharpArray = (string[]) a;
string s2 = cSharpArray [0];
```

Arrays created dynamically can be cast to a C# array of a matching or compatible type (compatible by standard array-variance rules). For example, if Apple subclasses Fruit, Apple[] can be cast to Fruit[]. This leads to the issue of why object[] was not used as the unifying array type rather the Array class. The answer is that object[] is incompatible with both multidimensional and value type arrays. An int[] array cannot be cast to object[]. Hence, we require the Array class for full type unification.

GetValue and SetValue also work on compiler-created arrays, and they are useful when writing methods that can deal with an array of any type and rank. For multi-dimensional arrays, they accept an *array* of indexers:

```
public object GetValue (params int[] indices)
public void   SetValue (object value, params int[] indices)
```

The following method prints the first element of any array, regardless of rank:

```
void WriteFirstValue (Array a)
{
    Console.Write (a.Rank + "-dimensional; ");

    // The indexers array will automatically initialize to all zeros, so
    // passing it into GetValue or SetValue will get/set the zero-based
```

```
    // (i.e., first) element in the array.

    int[] indexers = new int[a.Rank];
    Console.WriteLine ("First value is " + a.GetValue (indexers));
}

void Demo()
{
    int[]  oneD = new int[] { 1, 2, 3 };
    int[,] twoD = new int[,] { { 5, 6 }, { 8, 9 } };

    WriteFirstValue (oneD);   // 1-dimensional; first value is 1
    WriteFirstValue (twoD);   // 2-dimensional; first value is 5
}
```

 For working with arrays of unknown type but known rank, generics provide an easier and more efficient solution:

```
void WriteFirstValue<T> (T[] array)
{
    Console.WriteLine (array[0]);
}
```

SetValue throws an exception if the element is of an incompatible type for the array.

When an array is instantiated, whether via language syntax or Array.CreateInstance, its elements are automatically initialized. For arrays with reference type elements, this means writing nulls; for arrays with value type elements, this means calling the value type's default constructor (effectively "zeroing" the members). The Array class also provides this functionality on demand via the Clear method:

```
public static void Clear (Array array, int index, int length);
```

This method doesn't affect the size of the array. This is in contrast to the usual use of Clear (such as in IList.Clear) where the collection is reduced to zero elements.

Enumeration

Arrays are easily enumerated with a foreach statement:

```
int[] myArray = { 1, 2, 3};
foreach (int val in myArray)
  Console.WriteLine (val);
```

You can also enumerate using the static Array.ForEach method, defined as follows:

```
public static void ForEach<T> (T[] array, Action<T> action);
```

This uses an Action delegate, with this signature:

```
public delegate void Action<T> (T obj);
```

Here's the first example rewritten with Array.ForEach:

```
Array.ForEach (new[] { 1, 2, 3 }, Console.WriteLine);
```

Length and Rank

Array provides the following methods and properties for querying length and rank:

```
public int  GetLength     (int dimension);
public long GetLongLength (int dimension);

public int  Length        { get; }
public long LongLength     { get; }

public int GetLowerBound (int dimension);
public int GetUpperBound (int dimension);

public int Rank { get; }    // Returns number of dimensions in array
```

GetLength and GetLongLength return the length for a given dimension (0 for a single-dimensional array), and Length and LongLength return the total number of elements in the array—all dimensions included.

GetLowerBound and GetUpperBound are useful with nonzero indexed arrays. GetUpperBound returns the same result as adding GetLowerBound to GetLength for any given dimension.

Searching

The Array class provides a range of methods for finding elements within a one-dimensional array:

```
public static int BinarySearch<T> (T[] array,   object value);
public static int BinarySearch<T> (T[] array,   object value, IComparer<T>
                                                               comparer);
public static int BinarySearch    (Array array, object value);
public static int BinarySearch    (Array array, object value, IComparer
                                                               comparer);
public static int IndexOf<T>      (T[] array,   T value);
public static int IndexOf         (Array array, object value);
public static int LastIndexOf<T>  (T[] array,   T value);
public static int LastIndexOf     (Array array, object value);

// Predicate-based searching:

public static T   Find<T>         (T[] array, Predicate<T> match);
public static T   FindLast<T>     (T[] array, Predicate<T> match);
public static T[] FindAll<T>      (T[] array, Predicate<T> match);

public static bool Exists<T>      (T[] array, Predicate<T> match);
public static bool TrueForAll<T>  (T[] array, Predicate<T> match);

public static int  FindIndex<T>     (T[] array, Predicate<T> match);
public static int  FindLastIndex<T> (T[] array, Predicate<T> match);
```

The methods shown in bold are also overloaded to accept the following additional arguments:

```
int index   // starting index at which to begin searching
int length  // maximum number of elements to search
```

None of these methods throws an exception if the specified value is not found. Instead, if an item is not found, methods returning an integer return –1 (assuming a zero-indexed array), and methods returning a generic type return the type's default value (e.g., 0 for an integer, or null for a string).

The binary search methods are fast, but they work only on sorted arrays and require that the elements be compared for *order*, rather than simply *equality*. To this effect, the binary search methods can accept an IComparer or IComparer<T> object to arbitrate on ordering decisions (see the section "Plugging in Equality and Order" later in this chapter). This must be consistent with any comparer used in originally sorting the array. If no comparer is provided, the type's default ordering algorithm will be applied, based on its implementation of IComparable/IComparable<T>.

The IndexOf and LastIndexOf methods perform a simple enumeration over the array, returning the position of the first (or last) element that matches the given value.

The predicate-based searching methods allow a method delegate or lambda expression to arbitrate on whether a given element is a "match." A predicate is simply a delegate accepting an object and returning true or false:

```
public delegate bool Predicate<T> (T object);
```

In the following example, we search an array of strings for a name containing the letter "a":

```
static void Main()
{
  string[] names = { "Rodney", "Jack", "Jill" };
  string match = Array.Find (names, new Predicate <string> (ContainsA));
  Console.WriteLine (match);      // Jack
}
static bool ContainsA (string name) { return name.Contains ("a"); }
```

Here's the same code shortened with an anonymous method:

```
string[] names = { "Rodney", "Jack", "Jill" };
string match = Array.Find (names, delegate (string name)
  { return name.Contains ("a"); } );
```

A lambda expression shortens it further:

```
string[] names = { "Rodney", "Jack", "Jill" };
string match = Array.Find (names, n => n.Contains ("a"));      // Jack
```

FindAll returns an array of all items satisfying the predicate. It's in fact equivalent to Enumerable.Where in the System.Linq namespace except that FindAll returns an array of matching items rather than an IEnumerable<T> of the same.

Exists returns true if any array member satisfies the given predicate, and is equivalent to Any in System.Linq.Enumerable.

TrueForAll returns true if all items satisfy the predicate, and is equivalent to All in System.Linq.Enumerable.

Sorting

Array has the following built-in sorting methods:

```
// For sorting a single array:

public static void Sort<T> (T[] array);
public static void Sort     (Array array);

// For sorting a pair of arrays:

public static void Sort<TKey,TValue> (TKey[] keys, TValue[] items);
public static void Sort              (Array keys, Array items);
```

Each of these methods is additionally overloaded to also accept:

```
int index               // starting index at which to begin sorting
int length              // number of elements to sort
IComparer comparer      // object making ordering decisions
Comparison<T> comparison  // method making ordering decisions
```

The following illustrates the simplest use of Sort:

```
int[] numbers = { 3, 2, 1 };
Array.Sort (numbers);                    // array is now { 1, 2, 3 }
```

The methods accepting a pair of arrays work by rearranging the items of each array in tandem, basing the ordering decisions on the first array. In the next example, both the numbers and their corresponding words are sorted into numerical order:

```
int[] numbers = { 3, 2, 1 };
string[] words = new string[] { "three", "two", "one" };
Array.Sort (numbers, words);

// numbers array is now { 1, 2, 3 }
// words   array is now { "one", "two", "three" }
```

Array.Sort requires that the elements in the array implement IComparable (see the section "Order Comparison" in Chapter 6). This means that most primitive C# types (such as integers, as in the preceding example) can be sorted. If the elements are not intrinsically comparable, or you want to override the default ordering, you must provide Sort with a custom comparison method that reports on the relative position of two elements. There are ways to do this:

- Via a helper object that implements IComparer/IComparer<T> (see the section "Plugging in Equality and Order" later in this chapter)
- Via a Comparison delegate:

```
public delegate int Comparison<T> (T x, T y);
```

The Comparison delegate follows the same semantics as IComparer<T>.CompareTo: if x comes before y, a negative integer is returned; if x comes after y, a positive integer is returned; if x and y have the same sorting position, 0 is returned.

In the following example, we sort an array of integers such that the odd numbers come first:

```
int[] numbers = { 1, 2, 3, 4, 5 };
Array.Sort (numbers, (x, y) => x % 2 == y % 2 ? 0 : x % 2 == 1 ? -1 : 1);

// numbers array is now { 3, 5, 1, 2, 4 }
```

 As an alternative to calling Sort, you can use LINQ's OrderBy and ThenBy operators. Unlike Array.Sort, the LINQ operators don't alter the original array, instead emitting the sorted result in a fresh IEnumerable<T> sequence.

Reversing Elements

The following Array methods reverse the order of all—or a portion of—elements in an array:

```
public static void Reverse (Array array);
public static void Reverse (Array array, int index, int length);
```

Copying, Converting, and Resizing

Array provides shallow copying and cloning methods as follows:

```
// Instance methods:

public object Clone( );
public void CopyTo (Array array, int index);

// Static methods:

public static void Copy (Array sourceArray,
                         Array destinationArray,
                         int length);

public static void Copy (Array sourceArray,      int sourceIndex,
                         Array destinationArray, int destinationIndex,
                         int length);

public static void ConstrainedCopy (
                         Array sourceArray,      int sourceIndex,
                         Array destinationArray, int destinationIndex,
                         int length);

public static ReadOnlyCollection<T> AsReadOnly<T> (T[] array)

public static TOutput[] ConvertAll<TInput, TOutput>
    (TInput[] array, Converter<TInput, TOutput> converter)

public static void Resize<T> (ref T[] array, int newSize);
```

The Copy and CopyTo methods are overloaded to accept Int64 index arguments.

The Clone method returns a whole new (shallow-copied) array. The Copy and CopyTo methods copy a contiguous subset of the array. Copying a multidimensional rectangular array requires you to map the multidimensional index to a linear index. For example, the middle square (position[1,1]) in a 3×3 array is represented with the index 4, from the calculation: 1*3 + 1. The source and destination ranges can overlap without causing a problem.

ConstrainedCopy performs an *atomic* operation: if all of the requested elements cannot be successfully copied (due to a type error, for instance), the operation is rolled back.

AsReadOnly returns a wrapper that prevents elements from being reassigned. ConvertAll creates and returns a new array of element type TOutput, calling the supplied Converter delegate to copy over the elements. Converter is defined as follows:

```
public delegate TOutput Converter<TInput,TOutput> (TInput input)
```

The following converts an array of floats to an array of integers:

```
float[] reals = { 1.3f, 1.5f, 1.8f };

int[] wholes = Array.ConvertAll <float, int> (
  reals, delegate (float from) { return Convert.ToInt32 (from); } );

// wholes array is { 1, 2, 2 }
```

The Resize method works by creating a new array and copying over the elements, returning the new array via the reference parameter. However, any references to the original array in other objects will remain unchanged.

 (C# 3.0) The System.Linq namespace offers an additional buffet of extension methods suitable for array conversion. These methods return an IEnumerable<T>, which you can convert back to an array via Enumerable's ToArray method.

Lists, Queues, Stacks, and Sets

The Framework provides a reasonably comprehensive set of concrete collection classes that implement the interfaces described in this chapter. This section concentrates on the *list-like* collections (versus the *dictionary-like* collections covered later in this chapter in the section "Dictionaries"). As with the interfaces we discussed previously, you usually have a choice of generic or nongeneric versions of each type. In terms of flexibility and performance, the generic classes win in nearly all situations, making their nongeneric counterparts largely redundant, other than for backward compatibility. This differs from the situation with collection interfaces, where both the generic and nongeneric versions are useful.

Of the classes described in this section, the generic List class is the most commonly used.

List<T> and ArrayList

The generic List and nongeneric ArrayList classes provide a dynamically sized array of objects and are among the most commonly used of the collection classes. ArrayList implements IList, whereas List<T> implements both IList and IList<T>. Unlike with arrays, all interfaces are implemented publicly, and methods such as Add and Remove are exposed and work as you would expect.

Internally, List<T> and ArrayList work by maintaining an internal array of objects, replaced with a larger array upon reaching capacity. Appending elements is efficient (since there is usually a free slot at the end), but inserting elements can be slow (since all elements have to be shifted to make a free slot). As with arrays, searching is efficient if the BinarySearch method is used on a list that has been sorted, but is otherwise inefficient because each item must be individually checked.

List<T> is up to several times faster than ArrayList if T is a value type, because List<T> avoids the overhead of boxing and unboxing elements.

List<T> and ArrayList provide constructors that accept an existing collection of elements: these copy each element from the existing collecting into the new List<T> or ArrayList:

```
public class List <T> : IList <T>
{
  public List ();
  public List (IEnumerable<T> collection);
  public List (int capacity);

  // Add+Insert
  public void Add          (T item);
  public void AddRange     (IEnumerable<T> collection);
  public void Insert       (int index, T item);
  public void InsertRange  (int index, IEnumerable<T> collection);

  // Remove
  public bool Remove       (T item);
  public void RemoveAt     (int index);
  public void RemoveRange  (int index, int count);
  public int  RemoveAll    (Predicate<T> match);

  // Indexing
  public T this [int index] { get; set; }
  public List<T> GetRange (int index, int count);
  public Enumerator<T> GetEnumerator();

  // Exporting, copying and converting:
  public T[] ToArray();
  public void CopyTo (T[] array);
  public void CopyTo (T[] array, int arrayIndex);
  public void CopyTo (int index, T[] array, int arrayIndex, int count);
```

```
    public ReadOnlyCollection<T> AsReadOnly();
    public List<TOutput> ConvertAll<TOutput> (Converter <T,TOutput>
                                                      converter);
    // Other:
    public void Reverse();            // Reverses order of elements in list.
    public int Capacity { get;set; }  // Forces expansion of internal array.
    public void TrimExcess();         // Trims internal array back to size.
    public void Clear();              // Removes all elements, so Count=0.
}

    public delegate TOutput Converter <TInput, TOutput> (TInput input);
```

In addition to these members, List<T> provides instance versions of all of Array's searching and sorting methods.

The following code demonstrates List's properties and methods. See the section "The Array Class" earlier in this chapter for examples on searching and sorting.

```
List<string> words = new List<string>();    // New string-typed list

words.Add ("melon");
words.Add ("avocado");
words.AddRange (new string[] { "banana", "plum" } );
words.Insert (0, "lemon");                                  // insert at
words.InsertRange (0, new string[] { "peach", "nashi" });   // start

words.Remove ("melon");
words.RemoveAt (3);                          // Remove the 4th element
words.RemoveRange (0, 2);                     // Remove first 2 elements

// Remove all strings starting in 'n':
words.RemoveAll (delegate (string s) { return s.StartsWith ("n"); });

Console.WriteLine (words [0]);                      // first word
Console.WriteLine (words [words.Count - 1]);        // last word
foreach (string s in words) Console.WriteLine (s);  // all words
List<string> subset = words.GetRange (1, 2);        // 2nd->3rd words

string[] wordsArray = words.ToArray();     // Creates a new typed array

// Copy first two elements to the end of an existing array:
string[] existing = new string [1000];
words.CopyTo (0, existing, 998, 2);

List<string> bigWords = words.ConvertAll <string>     // Converts to
  (delegate (string s) { return s.ToUpper (); } );    // uppercase

List<int> lengths = words.ConvertAll <int>
  (delegate (string s) { return s.Length; } );
```

The ArrayList class is the nongeneric version of List<T>, used mainly for backward compatibility. Clumsy casts are usually required, as the following example demonstrates:

```
ArrayList al = new ArrayList ();
al.Add ("hello");
```

```
string first = (string) al [0];
string[] strArr = (string[]) al.ToArray (typeof (string));
```

Such casts cannot be verified by the compiler; the following compiles successfully but then fails at runtime:

```
int first = (int) al [0];    // Runtime exception
```

 An ArrayList is functionally similar to List<object>. Both are useful when you need a list of mixed-type elements that share no common base type. The advantage of choosing an ArrayList, in this case, would be if you need to deal with the list using reflection (see Chapter 17). Reflection and dynamic binding are easier with a non-generic ArrayList than a List<object>.

(C# 3.0) If you import the System.Linq namespace, you can convert an ArrayList to a generic List by calling OfType and then ToList:

```
ArrayList al = new ArrayList();
al.AddRange ( new[] { 1, 5, 9 } );
List <int> list = al.OfType <int>().ToList();
```

OfType and ToList are extension methods in the System.Linq.Enumerable class, supported from .NET Framework 3.5.

LinkedList<T>

LinkedList<T> is a generic doubly linked list (see Figure 7-4). A doubly linked list is a chain of nodes in which each references the node before, the node after, and the actual element. Its main benefit is that an element can always be inserted efficiently anywhere in the list, since it just involves creating a new node and updating a few references. However, finding where to insert the node in the first place can be slow as there's no intrinsic mechanism to index directly into a linked list; each node must be traversed, and binary-chop searches are not possible.

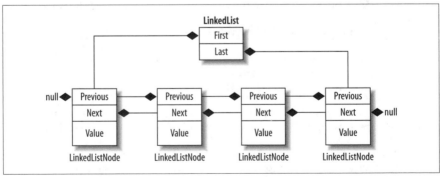

Figure 7-4. LinkedList<T>

LinkedList<T> implements IEnumerable<T> and ICollection<T> (and their nongeneric versions), but not IList<T> since access by index is not supported. List nodes are implemented via the following class:

```
public sealed class LinkedListNode<T>
{
  public LinkedList<T> List { get; }
  public LinkedListNode<T> Next { get; }
  public LinkedListNode<T> Previous { get; }
  public T Value { get; set; }
}
```

When adding a node, you can specify its position either relative to another node or at the start/end of the list. LinkedList<T> provides the following methods for this:

```
public void AddFirst(LinkedListNode<T> node);
public LinkedListNode<T> AddFirst (T value);

public void AddLast (LinkedListNode<T> node);
public LinkedListNode<T> AddLast (T value);

public void AddAfter (LinkedListNode<T> node, LinkedListNode<T> newNode);
public LinkedListNode<T> AddAfter (LinkedListNode<T> node, T value);

public void AddBefore (LinkedListNode<T> node, LinkedListNode<T> newNode);
public LinkedListNode<T> AddBefore (LinkedListNode<T> node, T value);
```

Similar methods are provided to remove elements:

```
public void Clear();

public void RemoveFirst();
public void RemoveLast();

public bool Remove (T value);
public void Remove (LinkedListNode<T> node);
```

LinkedList<T> has internal fields to keep track of the number of elements in the list, as well as the head and tail of the list. These are exposed in the following public properties:

```
public int Count { get; }                    // Fast
public LinkedListNode<T> First { get; }       // Fast
public LinkedListNode<T> Last { get; }        // Fast
```

LinkedList<T> also supports the following searching methods (each requiring that the list be internally enumerated):

```
public bool Contains (T value);
public LinkedListNode<T> Find (T value);
public LinkedListNode<T> FindLast (T value);
```

Finally, LinkedList<T> supports copying to an array for indexed processing and obtaining an enumerator to support the foreach statement:

```
public void CopyTo (T[] array, int index);
public Enumerator<T> GetEnumerator();
```

Here's a demonstration on the use of LinkedList<string>:

```
LinkedList<string> tune = new LinkedList<string>();
tune.AddFirst ("do");                         // do
```

```
tune.AddLast ("so");                                    // do - so

tune.AddAfter (tune.First, "re");                       // do - re - so
tune.AddAfter (tune.First.Next, "mi");                  // do - re - mi - so
tune.AddBefore (tune.Last, "fa");                       // do - re - mi - fa - so

tune.RemoveFirst( );                                    // re - mi - fa - so
tune.RemoveLast( );                                     // re - mi - fa

LinkedListNode<string> miNode = tune.Find ("mi");
tune.Remove (miNode);                                   // re - fa
tune.AddFirst (miNode);                                 // mi - re - fa

foreach (string s in tune) Console.WriteLine (s);
```

Queue and Queue<T>

Queue and Queue<T> are standard first-in first-out (FIFO) data structures, providing methods to Enqueue (add an item to the tail of the queue) and Dequeue (retrieve and remove the item at the head of the queue). A Peek method is also provided to return the element at the head of the queue without removing it, and a Count property (useful in checking that elements are present before dequeuing).

Although queues are enumerable, they do not implement IList or IList<T>, since members cannot be accessed directly by index. A ToArray method is provided, however, for copying the elements to an array where they can be randomly accessed:

```
public class Queue<T> : IEnumerable<T>, ICollection, IEnumerable
{
  public Queue( );
  public Queue (IEnumerable<T> collection);    // Copies existing elements
  public Queue (int capacity);                 // To lessen auto-resizing
  public void Clear();
  public bool Contains (T item);
  public void CopyTo (T[] array, int arrayIndex);
  public int Count { get; }
  public T Dequeue( );
  public void Enqueue (T item);
  public Enumerator<T> GetEnumerator( );       // To support foreach
  public T Peek( );
  public T[] ToArray( );
  public void TrimExcess( );
}
```

The following is an example of using Queue<int>:

```
Queue<int> q = new Queue<int> ( );
q.Enqueue (10);
q.Enqueue (20);
int[] data = q.ToArray ( );       // Exports to an array
Console.WriteLine (q.Count);      // "2"
Console.WriteLine (q.Peek());     // "10"
Console.WriteLine (q.Dequeue());  // "10"
Console.WriteLine (q.Dequeue());  // "20"
Console.WriteLine (q.Dequeue());  // throws an exception (queue empty)
```

Queues are implemented internally using an array that's resized as required—much like the generic List class. The queue maintains indexes that point directly to the head and tail elements; therefore, enqueuing and dequeuing are extremely quick operations (except when an internal resize is required).

Stack and Stack<T>

Stack and Stack<T> are standard last-in first-out (LIFO) data structures, providing methods to Push (add an item to the top of the stack) and Pop (retrieve and remove an element from the top of the stack). A nondestructive Peek method is also provided, as is a Count property and a ToArray method for exporting the data for random access.

```
public class Stack<T> : IEnumerable<T>, ICollection, IEnumerable
{
  public Stack();
  public Stack (IEnumerable<T> collection);    // Copies existing elements
  public Stack (int capacity);                 // Lessens auto-resizing
  public void Clear();
  public bool Contains (T item);
  public void CopyTo (T[] array, int arrayIndex);
  public int Count { get; }
  public Enumerator<T> GetEnumerator();        // To support foreach
  public T Peek();
  public T Pop();
  public void Push (T item);
  public T[] ToArray();
  public void TrimExcess();
}
```

The following example demonstrates Stack<int>:

```
Stack<int> s = new Stack<int>();
s.Push (1);                      //                Stack = 1
s.Push (2);                      //                Stack = 1,2
s.Push (3);                      //                Stack = 1,2,3
Console.WriteLine (s.Count);     // Prints 3
Console.WriteLine (s.Peek());    // Prints 3,  Stack = 1,2,3
Console.WriteLine (s.Pop());     // Prints 3,  Stack = 1,2
Console.WriteLine (s.Pop());     // Prints 2,  Stack = 1
Console.WriteLine (s.Pop());     // Prints 1,  Stack = <empty>
Console.WriteLine (s.Pop());     // throws exception
```

Stacks are implemented internally with an array that's resized as required, as with Queue<T> and List<T>.

BitArray

A BitArray is a dynamically sized list of bool values. It is more memory-efficient than both a simple array of bool and a generic List of bool, because it uses only one bit for each value, whereas the bool type otherwise occupies one byte for each value:

```
public sealed class BitArray : ICollection, IEnumerable, ICloneable
{
  // Constructors
```

Collections

```
public BitArray (BitArray bits);    // An existing BitArray to copy
public BitArray (int length);       // Capacity, in bits
public BitArray (bool[] values);
public BitArray (byte[] bytes);
public BitArray (int[] values);
public BitArray (int length, bool defaultValue);

// To get/set value
public bool this [int index] { get; set; }
public bool Get  (int index);
public void Set  (int index, bool value);
public void SetAll (bool value);

// Bitwise operators
public BitArray Not( );
public BitArray And (BitArray value);
public BitArray Or  (BitArray value);
public BitArray Xor (BitArray value);

// Copying
public void CopyTo (Array array, int index);
public object Clone( );

// Other
public IEnumerator GetEnumerator( );
public int  Count          { get; }
public int  Length         { get; set; }
public bool IsReadOnly     { get; }
public bool IsSynchronized { get; }
public object SyncRoot     { get; }
}
```

The following is an example of using the BitArray class:

```
BitArray bits = new BitArray(2);
bits[1] = true;
bits.Xor (bits);                  // Bitwise exclusive-OR bits with itself
Console.WriteLine (bits[1]);   // False
```

HashSet<T>

HashSet<T> is a generic collection introduced with .NET Framework 3.5. A HashSet has the following distinguishing features:

- Its Contains method executes quickly using a hash-based lookup.
- It does not store duplicate elements and silently ignores requests to add duplicates.
- You cannot access an element by position.

HashSet<T> is implemented using a hashtable that stores only keys, no values.

Here's its definition:

```
public class HashSet<T> : ICollection<T>, IEnumerable<T>, IEnumerable
{
  // Constructors
```

```
public HashSet( );
public HashSet (IEnumerable<T> collection);
public HashSet (IEqualityComparer<T> comparer);
public HashSet (IEnumerable<T> collection, IEqualityComparer<T> comparer);

// Testing for membership
public bool Contains (T item);

// Adding / removing
public bool Add     (T item);
public bool Remove (T item);
public int RemoveWhere (Predicate<T> match);
public void Clear( );

// Set operations - destructive
public void UnionWith           (IEnumerable<T> other);    // Adds
public void IntersectWith        (IEnumerable<T> other);    // Removes
public void ExceptWith           (IEnumerable<T> other);    // Removes
public void SymmetricExceptWith (IEnumerable<T> other);    // Removes

// Set operations - bool
public bool IsSubsetOf          (IEnumerable<T> other);
public bool IsProperSubsetOf    (IEnumerable<T> other);
public bool IsSupersetOf        (IEnumerable<T> other);
public bool IsProperSupersetOf (IEnumerable<T> other);
public bool Overlaps            (IEnumerable<T> other);
public bool SetEquals           (IEnumerable<T> other);

// Other
public int Count { get; }
public IEqualityComparer<T> Comparer { get; }
public void CopyTo (T[] array);
public void CopyTo (T[] array, int arrayIndex);
public void CopyTo (T[] array, int arrayIndex, int count);
public void TrimExcess( );
public static IEqualityComparer<HashSet<T>> CreateSetComparer( );
}
```

The following constructs a HashSet<char> from an existing collection, tests for membership, and then enumerates the collection (notice the absence of duplicates):

```
HashSet<char> letters = new HashSet<char> ("the quick brown fox");

Console.WriteLine (letters.Contains ('t'));      // true
Console.WriteLine (letters.Contains ('j'));      // false

foreach (char c in letters) Console.Write (c);   // the quickbrownfx
```

The reason we can pass a string into HashSet<char>'s constructor is because string implements IEnumerable<char>.

The destructive set operators modify the original collection. UnionWith adds all the elements in the second set to the original set (excluding duplicates). IntersectsWith removes the elements that are not in both sets. We remove all the vowels from our set of characters in the following code.

```
HashSet<char> letters = new HashSet<char> ("the quick brown fox");
letters.IntersectWith ("aeiou");
foreach (char c in letters) Console.Write (c);    // euio
```

ExceptWith removes the specified elements from the source set. Here, we strip all vowels from the set:

```
HashSet<char> letters = new HashSet<char> ("the quick brown fox");
letters.ExceptWith ("aeiou");
foreach (char c in letters) Console.Write (c);    // th qckbrwnfx
```

SymmetricExceptWith removes all but the elements that are unique to one set or the other:

```
HashSet<char> letters = new HashSet<char> ("the quick brown fox");
letters.SymmetricExceptWith ("the lazy brown fox");
foreach (char c in letters) Console.Write (c);    // quicklazy
```

Because HashSet<T> implements IEnumerable<T>, you can use another set as the argument to any of the set operation methods.

You must reference *System.Core.dll* in order to use HashSet<T>.

Dictionaries

A dictionary is a collection in which each element is a key/value pair. Dictionaries are most commonly used for lookups and sorted lists.

The framework defines a standard protocol for dictionaries, via the interfaces IDictionary and IDictionary <TKey, TValue>, as well as a set of general-purpose dictionary classes. The classes each differ in the following regards:

- Whether or not items are stored in sorted sequence
- Whether or not items can be accessed by position (index) as well as by key
- Whether generic or nongeneric
- Their performance when large

Table 7-2 summarizes each of the dictionary classes and how they differ in these respects. The performance times are in milliseconds, to perform 50,000 operations on a dictionary with integer keys and values, on a 1.5 GHz PC. (The differences in performance between generic and nongeneric counterparts using the same underlying collection structure are due to boxing, and show up only with value type elements.)

Table 7-2. Dictionary classes

Type	Underlying structure	Retrieve by index?	Memory overhead (avg. bytes per item)	Speed: random insertion	Speed: sequential insertion	Speed: retrieval by key
Unsorted						
Dictionary <K,V>	Hashtable	No	22	30	30	20
Hashtable	Hashtable	No	38	50	50	30

Table 7-2. Dictionary classes (continued)

Type	Underlying structure	Retrieve by index?	Memory overhead (avg. bytes per item)	Speed: random insertion	Speed: sequential insertion	Speed: retrieval by key
ListDictionary	Linked list	No	36	50,000	50,000	50,000
OrderedDictionary	Hashtable + array	Yes	59	70	70	40
Sorted						
SortedDictionary <K,V>	Red/black tree	No	20	130	100	120
SortedList <K,V>	2xArray	Yes	2	3,300	30	40
SortedList	2xArray	Yes	27	4,500	100	180

IDictionary and IDictionary<TKey,TValue>

IDictionary and IDictionary<TKey,TValue> define the standard protocol for all key/value-based collections. They extend ICollection/ICollection<T> by adding methods and properties to access elements based on a key of arbitrary type.

IDictionary and IDictionary<TKey,TValue> differ in behavior when you retrieve an item through the indexer, for a key that doesn't exist in the dictionary. The nongeneric indexer returns null; the generic indexer throws an exception. If you want to avoid an exception when retrieving by key with the generic interface, you have two choices: either first test for membership with ContainsKey or use the TryGetValue method, which tests for membership and retrieves the item in one step.

To test for membership by key:

- With IDictionary, call ContainsKey.
- With IDictionary<TKey,TValue>, call Contains.

With both interfaces, it's acceptable to use the indexer property's set method on a key that doesn't exist—and the key will be automatically added. Duplicate keys are forbidden in all dictionary implementations.

Their interface definitions are as follows:

```
public interface IDictionary : ICollection, IEnumerable
{
    IDictionaryEnumerator GetEnumerator();

    bool Contains (object key);
    void Add      (object key, object value);
    void Remove   (object key);
    void Clear();

    object this [object key] { get; set; }
    bool IsFixedSize         { get; }
    bool IsReadOnly          { get; }
    ICollection Keys         { get; }     // Returns all keys as a list
    ICollection Values       { get; }     // Returns all values as a list
}
```

```
public interface IDictionary <TKey, TValue> :
  ICollection <KeyValuePair <TKey, TValue>>, IEnumerable
{
  bool ContainsKey (TKey key);
  bool TryGetValue (TKey key, out TValue value);
  void Add        (TKey key, TValue value);
  bool Remove     (TKey key);

  TValue this [TKey key]      { get; set; }  // Main indexer - by key
  ICollection <TKey> Keys     { get; }       // Returns just keys
  ICollection <TValue> Values { get; }       // Returns just values
}
```

Enumerating directly over an `IDictionary` returns a sequence of `DictionaryEntry` structs:

```
public struct DictionaryEntry
{
  public object Key   { get; set; }
  public object Value { get; set; }
}
```

Enumerating directly over a generic dictionary interface returns a sequence of `KeyValuePair` structs:

```
public struct KeyValuePair <TKey, TValue>
{
  public TKey Key     { get; }
  public TValue Value { get; }
}
```

We demonstrate the use of these interfaces with the `Dictionary` class in the following section.

Dictionary<TKey,TValue> and Hashtable

The generic `Dictionary` class is one of the most commonly used collections (along with the `List` collection). It uses a hashtable data structure to store keys and values, and it is fast and efficient.

> The nongeneric version of `Dictionary<TKey,TValue>` is called `Hashtable`; there is no nongeneric class called `Dictionary`. When we refer simply to `Dictionary`, we mean the generic `Dictionary<TKey,TValue>` class.

`Dictionary` implements both the generic and nongeneric `IDictionary` interfaces, the generic `IDictionary` being exposed publicly. `Dictionary` is, in fact, a "textbook" implementation of the generic `IDictionary`.

Here's how to use it:

```
var d = new Dictionary<string, int> ();

d.Add("One", 1);
d["Two"] = 2;      // adds to dictionary because "two" not already present
```

```
d["Two"] = 22;      // updates dictionary because "two" is now present
d["Three"] = 3;

Console.WriteLine (d["Two"]);             // Prints "22"
Console.WriteLine (d.ContainsKey ("One"));   // true (fast operation)
Console.WriteLine (d.ContainsValue (3));     // true (slow operation)
int val = 0;
if (!d.TryGetValue ("onE", out val))
  Console.WriteLine ("No val");              // "No val" (case sensitive)

// Three different ways to enumerate the dictionary:

foreach (KeyValuePair<string, int> kv in d)   // One ; 1
  Console.WriteLine (kv.Key + "; " + kv.Value);  // Two ; 22
                                                 // Three ; 3

foreach (string s in d.Keys) Console.Write (s);   // OneTwoThree
Console.WriteLine();
foreach (int i in d.Values) Console.Write (i);    // 1223
```

Its underlying hashtable works by converting each element's key into an integer hashcode—a pseudounique value—and then applying an algorithm to convert the hashcode into a hash key. This hash key is used internally to determine which "bucket" an entry belongs to. If the bucket contains more than one value, a linear search is performed on the bucket. A hashtable typically starts out maintaining a 1:1 ratio of buckets to values (a 1:1 *load factor*), meaning that each bucket contains only one value. However, as more items are added to the hashtable, the load factor dynamically increases, in a manner designed to optimize insertion and retrieval performance as well as memory requirements.

A dictionary can work with keys of any type, providing it's able to determine equality between keys and obtain hashcodes. By default, equality is determined via the key's object.Equals method, and the pseudounique hashcode is obtained via the key's GetHashCode method. This behavior can be changed, either by overriding these methods or by providing an IEqualityComparer object when constructing the dictionary. A common application of this is to specify a case-insensitive equality comparer when using string keys:

```
var d = new Dictionary<string, int> (StringComparer.OrdinalIgnoreCase);
```

We discuss this further in the section "Plugging in Equality and Order" later in this chapter.

As with many other types of collections, the performance of a dictionary can be improved slightly by specifying the collection's expected size in the constructor, avoiding or lessening the need for internal resizing operations.

The nongeneric version is (more aptly) named Hashtable and is functionally similar apart from differences stemming from it exposing the nongeneric IDictionary interface discussed previously.

The downside to Dictionary and Hashtable is that the items are not sorted. Furthermore, the original order in which the items were added is not retained. As with all dictionaries, duplicate keys are not allowed.

OrderedDictionary

An `OrderedDictionary` is a nongeneric dictionary that maintains elements in the same order that they were added. With an `OrderedDictionary`, you can access elements both by index and by key.

 An `OrderedDictionary` is not a *sorted* dictionary.

An `OrderedDictionary` is a combination of a `Hashtable` and an `ArrayList`. This means it has all the functionality of a `Hashtable`, plus functions such as `RemoveAt`, as well as an integer indexer. It also exposes `Keys` and `Values` properties that return elements in their original order.

This class was introduced in .NET 2.0, yet peculiarly, there's no generic version.

ListDictionary and HybridDictionary

`ListDictionary` uses a singly linked list to store the underlying data. It doesn't provide sorting, although it does preserve the original entry order of the items. `ListDictionary` is extremely slow with large lists. Its only real "claim to fame" is its efficiency with very small lists (less than 10 items).

`HybridDictionary` is a `ListDictionary` that automatically converts to a `Hashtable` upon reaching a certain size, to address `ListDictionary`'s problems with performance. The idea is to get a low memory footprint when the dictionary is small, and good performance when the dictionary is large. However, given the overhead in converting from one to the other—and the fact that a hashtable is not excessively heavy or slow in either scenario—you wouldn't suffer unreasonably by using a `Hashtable` (or better still, a generic `Dictionary`) to begin with.

Both classes come only in nongeneric form.

Sorted Dictionaries

The Framework provides three dictionary classes internally structured such that their content is always sorted by key:

- `SortedDictionary<TKey,TValue>`
- `SortedList`
- `SortedList<TKey,TValue>` (a generic version of `SortedList`)

(In this section, we will abbreviate `<TKey,TValue>` to `<,>`.)

`SortedDictionary<,>` uses a red/black tree: a data structure designed to perform consistently well in any insertion or retrieval scenario.

`SortedList` and `SortedList<,>` are functionally similar. Internally, they use an ordered array pair, providing fast retrieval (via a binary-chop search) but poor insertion performance (because existing values have to be shifted to make room for a new entry).

SortedDictionary<,> is much faster than SortedList or SortedList<,> at inserting elements in a random sequence (particularly with large lists). The SortedList classes, however, have an extra ability: to access items by index as well as by key. With a sorted list, you can go directly to the *n*th element in the sorting sequence (via the indexer on the Keys/Values properties). To do the same with a SortedDictionary<,>, you must manually enumerate over *n* items. (Alternatively, you could write a class that combines a sorted dictionary with a list class.)

None of the three collections allows duplicate keys (as is the case with all dictionaries).

The following example uses reflection to load all the methods defined in System. Object into a sorted list keyed by name, and then enumerates their keys and values:

```
// MethodInfo is in the System.Reflection namespace

var sorted = new SortedList <string, MethodInfo>();

foreach (MethodInfo m in typeof (object).GetMethods())
  sorted [m.Name] = m;

foreach (string name in sorted.Keys)
  Console.WriteLine (name);

foreach (MethodInfo m in sorted.Values)
  Console.WriteLine (m.Name + " returns a " + m.ReturnType);
```

Here's the result of the first enumeration:

```
Equals
GetHashCode
GetType
ReferenceEquals
ToString
```

Here's the result of the second enumeration:

```
Equals returns a System.Boolean
GetHashCode returns a System.Int32
GetType returns a System.Type
ReferenceEquals returns a System.Boolean
ToString returns a System.String
```

Notice that we populated the dictionary through its indexer. If we instead used the Add method, it would throw an exception because the object class upon which we're reflecting overloads the Equals method, and you can't add the same key twice to a dictionary. By using the indexer, the later entry overwrites the earlier entry, preventing this error.

 You can store multiple members of the same key by making each value element a list:

```
SortedList <string, List<MethodInfo>>
```

Extending our example, the following retrieves the MethodInfo whose key is "GetHashCode", just as with an ordinary dictionary:

```
Console.WriteLine (sorted ["GetHashCode"]);       // Int32 GetHashCode( )
```

So far, everything we've done would also work with a SortedDictionary<,>. The following two lines, however, which retrieve the last key and value, work only with a sorted list:

```
Console.WriteLine (sorted.Keys [sorted.Count - 1]);        // ToString
Console.WriteLine (sorted.Values[sorted.Count - 1].IsVirtual); // True
```

Customizable Collections and Proxies

The collection classes discussed in previous sections are convenient in that they can be directly instantiated, but they don't allow you to control what happens when an item is added to or removed from the collection. With strongly typed collections in an application, you sometimes need this control—for instance:

- To fire an event when an item is added or removed
- To update properties because of the added or removed item
- To detect an "illegal" add/remove operation and throw an exception (for example, if the operation violates a business rule)

The .NET Framework provides collection classes for this exact purpose, in System.Collections (for the nongeneric versions) and in System.Collections. ObjectModel (for the generic versions). These are essentially proxies or wrappers that implement IList or IDictionary by forwarding the methods through to an underlying collection. Each Add, Remove, or Clear operation is routed via a virtual method which acts as a "gateway" when overridden.

Customizable collection classes are commonly used for publicly exposed collections; for instance, a collection of controls exposed publicly on a System.Windows. Form class.

Collection<T> and CollectionBase

The generic Collection<T> class is a customizable wrapper for List<T>.

As well as implementing IList and IList<T>, it defines four additional virtual methods and a protected property as follows:

```
public class Collection<T> :
  IList<T>, ICollection<T>, IEnumerable<T>, IList, ICollection, IEnumerable
{
  // ...

  protected virtual void ClearItems( );
  protected virtual void InsertItem (int index, T item);
  protected virtual void RemoveItem (int index);
  protected virtual void SetItem (int index, T item);

  protected IList<T> Items { get; }
}
```

The virtual methods provide the gateway by which you can "hook in" to change or enhance the list's normal behavior. The protected Items property allows the implementer to directly access the "inner list"—this is used to make changes internally without the virtual methods firing.

The virtual methods need not be overridden; they can be left alone until there's a requirement to alter the list's default behavior. The following example demonstrates the typical "skeleton" use of Collection<T>:

```
public class Animal
{
  public string Name;
  public int Popularity;

  public Animal (string name, int popularity)
  {
    Name = name; Popularity = popularity;
  }
}

public class AnimalCollection : Collection <Animal>
{
  // AnimalCollection is already a fully functioning list of animals.
  // No extra code is required.
}

public class Zoo    // The class that will expose AnimalCollection.
{                   // This would typically have additional members.

  public readonly AnimalCollection Animals = new AnimalCollection( );
}

class Program
{
  static void Main( )
  {
    Zoo zoo = new Zoo( );
    zoo.Animals.Add (new Animal ("Kangaroo", 10));
    zoo.Animals.Add (new Animal ("Mr Sea Lion", 20));
    foreach (Animal a in zoo.Animals) Console.WriteLine (a.Name);
  }
}
```

As it stands, AnimalCollection is no more functional than a simple List<Animal>; its role is to provide a base for future extension. To illustrate, we'll now add a Zoo property to Animal, so it can reference the Zoo in which it lives and override each of the virtual methods in Collection<Animal> to maintain that property automatically:

```
public class Animal
{
  public string Name;
  public int Popularity;
  public Zoo Zoo { get; internal set; }
```

```
  public Animal(string name, int popularity)
  {
    Name = name; Popularity = popularity;
  }
}

public class AnimalCollection : Collection <Animal>
{
  Zoo zoo;
  public AnimalCollection (Zoo zoo) { this.zoo = zoo; }

  protected override void InsertItem (int index, Animal item)
  {
    base.InsertItem (index, item);
    item.Zoo = zoo;
  }
  protected override void SetItem (int index, Animal item)
  {
    base.SetItem (index, item);
    item.Zoo = zoo;
  }
  protected override void RemoveItem (int index)
  {
    this [index].Zoo = null;
    base.RemoveItem (index);
  }
  protected override void ClearItems()
  {
    foreach (Animal a in this) a.Zoo = null;
    base.ClearItems();
  }
}

public class Zoo
{
  public readonly AnimalCollection Animals;
  public Zoo() { Animals = new AnimalCollection (this); }
}
```

Collection<T> also has a constructor accepting an existing IList<T>. Unlike with other collection classes, the supplied list is *proxied* rather than *copied*, meaning that subsequent changes will be reflected in the wrapping Collection<T> (although *without* Collection<T>'s virtual methods firing). Conversely, changes made via the Collection<T> will change the underlying list.

A nongeneric version of Collection<T> is also available, called CollectionBase. This is an older and clumsier version, providing most of the same features. Instead of the template methods InsertItem, RemoveItem, SetItem, and ClearItem, CollectionBase has "hook" methods that double the number of methods required: OnInsert, OnInsertComplete, OnSet, OnSetComplete, OnRemove, OnRemoveComplete, OnClear, and OnClearComplete. Because CollectionBase is nongeneric, you must also implement typed methods when subclassing it—at a minimum, a typed indexer and Add method.

KeyedCollection<TKey,TItem> and DictionaryBase

KeyedCollection<TKey,TItem> subclasses Collection<TItem>. It both adds and subtracts functionality. What it adds is the ability to access items by key, much like with a dictionary. What it subtracts is the ability to proxy your own inner list.

A keyed collection has some resemblance to an OrderedDictionary in that it combines a linear list with a hashtable. However, unlike OrderedDictionary, it doesn't implement IDictionary and doesn't support the concept of a key/value *pair*. Keys are obtained instead from the items themselves: via the abstract GetItemForKey method. This means enumerating a keyed collection is just like enumerating an ordinary list.

KeyedCollection<TKey,TItem> is best thought of as Collection<TItem> plus fast lookup by key.

Because it subclasses Collection<>, a keyed collection inherits all of Collection<>'s functionality, except for the ability to specify an existing list in construction. The additional members it defines are as follows:

```
public abstract class KeyedCollection <TKey, TItem> : Collection <TItem>

  // ...

  protected abstract TKey GetKeyForItem(TItem item);
  protected void ChangeItemKey(TItem item, TKey newKey);

  // Fast lookup by key - this is in addition to lookup by index.
  public TItem this[TKey key] { get; }

  protected IDictionary<TKey, TItem> Dictionary { get; }
}
```

GetItemForKey is what the implementer overrides to obtain an item's key from the underlying object. The ChangeItemForKey method must be called if the item's key property changes, in order to update the internal dictionary. The Dictionary property returns the internal dictionary used to implement the lookup, which is created when the first item is added. This behavior can be changed by specifying a creation threshold in the constructor, delaying the internal dictionary from being created until the threshold is reached (in the interim, a linear search is performed if an item is requested by key). A good reason not to specify a creation threshold is that having a valid dictionary can be useful in obtaining an ICollection<> of keys, via the Dictionary's Keys property. This collection can then be passed on to a public property.

The most common use for KeyedCollection<,> is in providing a collection of items accessible both by index and by name. To demonstrate this, we'll revisit the zoo, this time implementing AnimalCollection as a KeyedCollection<string,Animal>:

```
public class Animal
{
  string name;
  public string Name
  {
    get { return name; }
```

```
      set {
        if (Zoo != null) Zoo.NotifyNameChange (this, value);
        name = value;
      }
    }
    public int Popularity;
    public Zoo Zoo { get; internal set; }

    public Animal (string name, int popularity)
    {
      Name = name; Popularity = popularity;
    }
  }
}

public class AnimalCollection : KeyedCollection <string, Animal>
{
  Zoo zoo;
  public AnimalCollection (Zoo zoo) { this.zoo = zoo; }

  internal void NotifyNameChange (Animal a, string newName)
  {
    this.ChangeItemKey (a, newName);
  }

  protected override string GetKeyForItem (Animal item)
  {
    return item.Name;
  }

  // The following methods would be implemented as in the previous example
  protected override void InsertItem (int index, Animal item)...
  protected override void SetItem (int index, Animal item)...
  protected override void RemoveItem (int index)...
  protected override void ClearItems ()...
}

public class Zoo
{
  public readonly AnimalCollection Animals;
  public Zoo() { Animals = new AnimalCollection (this); }
}

class Program
{
  static void Main()
  {
    Zoo zoo = new Zoo ();
    zoo.Animals.Add (new Animal ("Kangaroo", 10));
    zoo.Animals.Add (new Animal ("Mr Sea Lion", 20));
    Console.WriteLine (zoo.Animals [0].Popularity);              // 10
    Console.WriteLine (zoo.Animals ["Mr Sea Lion"].Popularity);  // 20
```

```
      zoo.Animals ["Kangaroo"].Name = "Mr Roo";
      Console.WriteLine (zoo.Animals ["Mr Roo"].Popularity);         // 10
    }
  }
```

The nongeneric version of KeyedCollection is DictionaryBase. DictionaryBase is very different in its approach: it implements IDictionary and uses clumsy hook methods like CollectionBase: OnInsert, OnInsertComplete, OnSet, OnSetComplete, OnRemove, OnRemoveComplete, OnClear, and OnClearComplete (and additionally, OnGet). The primary advantage of implementing IDictionary over taking the KeyedCollection approach is that you don't need to subclass it in order to obtain keys. But since the very purpose of DictionaryBase is to be subclassed, it's no advantage at all. The improved model in KeyedCollection is almost certainly due to the fact that it was written some years later, with the benefit of hindsight. DictionaryBase is best considered useful for backward compatibility.

ReadOnlyCollection<T>

ReadOnlyCollection<T> is a wrapper, or *proxy*, that provides a read-only view of a collection. This is useful in allowing a class to publicly expose read-only access to a collection that the class can still update internally.

A read-only collection accepts the input collection in its constructor, to which it maintains a permanent reference. It doesn't take a static copy of the input collection, so subsequent changes to the input collection are visible through the read-only wrapper.

To illustrate, suppose your class wants to provide read-only public access to a list of strings called Names:

```
public class Test
{
  public List<string> Names { get; private set; }
}
```

This does only half the job. Although other types cannot reassign the Names property, they can still call Add, Remove, or Clear on the list. The ReadOnlyCollection<T> class resolves this:

```
public class Test
{
  List<string> names;
  public ReadOnlyCollection<string> Names { get; private set; }

  public Test()
  {
    names = new List<string>();
    Names = new ReadOnlyCollection<string> (names);
  }

  public void AddInternally() { names.Add ("test"); }
}
```

Only members within the Test class can now alter the list of names:

```
Test t = new Test( );

Console.WriteLine (t.Names.Count);        // 0
t.AddInternally( );
Console.WriteLine (t.Names.Count);        // 1

t.Names.Add ("test");                     // Compiler error
((IList<string>) t.Names).Add ("test");   // NotSupportedException
```

Plugging in Equality and Order

In the sections "Equality comparison" and "Order comparison" in Chapter 6, we described the standard .NET protocols that make a type equatable, hashable, and comparable. A type that implements these protocols can function correctly in a dictionary or sorted list "out of the box." More specifically:

- A type for which Equals and GetHashCode return meaningful results can be used as a key in a Dictionary or Hashtable.
- A type that implements IComparable/IComparable<T> can be used as a key in any of the *sorted* dictionaries or lists.

A type's default equating or comparison implementation typically reflects what is most "natural" for that type. Sometimes, however, the default behavior is not what you want. You might need a dictionary whose string-type key is treated case-insensitively. Or you might want a sorted list of customers, sorted by each customer's postcode. For this reason, the .NET Framework also defines a matching set of "plug-in" protocols. The plug-in protocols achieve two things:

- They allow you to switch in alternative equating or comparison behavior.
- They allow you to use a dictionary or sorted collection with a key type that's not intrinsically equatable or comparable.

The plug-in protocols consist of the following interfaces:

IEqualityComparer *and* IEqualityComparer<T>
- Performs plug-in *equality comparison and hashing*
- Recognized by Hashtable and Dictionary

IComparer *and* IComparer<T>
- Performs plug-in *order comparison*
- Recognized by the sorted dictionaries and collections; also, Array.Sort

Each interface comes in both generic and nongeneric forms. The IEquality-Comparer interfaces also have a default implementation in a class called EqualityComparer.

IEqualityComparer and EqualityComparer

An equality comparer switches in nondefault equality and hashing behavior, primarily for the Dictionary and Hashtable classes.

Recall the requirements of a hashtable-based dictionary. It needs answers to two questions for any given key:

- Is it the same as another?
- What is its integer hashcode?

An equality comparer answers these questions by implementing the IEquality-Comparer interfaces:

```
public interface IEqualityComparer<T>
{
   bool Equals (T x, T y);
   int GetHashCode (T obj);
}

public interface IEqualityComparer        // Nongeneric version
{
   bool Equals (object x, object y);
   int GetHashCode (object obj);
}
```

To write a custom comparer, you must implement at least the nongeneric IEqualityComparer, and ideally, both interfaces. As this is somewhat tedious, an alternative is to subclass the abstract EqualityComparer class, defined as follows:

```
public abstract class EqualityComparer<T> : IEqualityComparer,
                                            IEqualityComparer<T>
{
   public abstract bool Equals (T x, T y);
   public abstract int GetHashCode (T obj);

   bool IEqualityComparer.Equals (object x, object y);
   int IEqualityComparer.GetHashCode (object obj);

   public static EqualityComparer<T> Default { get; }
}
```

EqualityComparer implements both interfaces; your job is simply to override the two abstract methods.

The semantics for Equals and GetHashCode follow the same rules for object.Equals and object.GetHashCode, described in Chapter 6. In the following example, we define a Customer class with two fields, and then write an equality comparer that matches both the first and last names:

```
public class Customer
{
   public string LastName;
   public string FirstName;

   public Customer (string last, string first)
   {
     LastName = last;
     FirstName = first;
   }
}
```

```
public class LastFirstEqComparer : EqualityComparer <Customer>
{
  public override bool Equals (Customer x, Customer y)
  {
    return x.LastName == y.LastName && x.FirstName == y.FirstName;
  }

  public override int GetHashCode (Customer obj)
  {
    return (obj.LastName + ";" + obj.FirstName).GetHashCode( );
  }
}
```

To illustrate how this works, we'll create two customers:

```
Customer c1 = new Customer ("Bloggs", "Joe");
Customer c2 = new Customer ("Bloggs", "Joe");
```

Because we've not overridden object.Equals, normal reference type equality semantics apply:

```
Console.WriteLine (c1 == c2);             // false
Console.WriteLine (c1.Equals (c2));       // false
```

The same default equality semantics apply when using these customers in a Dictionary without specifying an equality comparer:

```
Dictionary<Customer, string> d = new Dictionary<Customer, string>( );
d [c1] = "Joe";
Console.WriteLine (d.ContainsKey (c2));        // false
```

Now with the custom equality comparer:

```
LastFirstEqComparer eq = new LastFirstEqComparer( );
Dictionary<Customer, string> d = new Dictionary<Customer, string> (eq);
d [c1] = "Joe";
Console.WriteLine (d.ContainsKey (c2));        // true
```

In this example, we would have to be careful not to change the customer's FirstName or LastName while it was in use in the dictionary. Otherwise, its hash-code would change and the Dictionary would break.

IComparer and Comparer

Comparers are used to switch in custom ordering logic for sorted dictionaries and collections.

Note that a comparer is useless to the unsorted dictionaries such as Dictionary and Hashtable—these require an IEqualityComparer to get hashcodes. Similarly, an equality comparer is useless for sorted dictionaries and collections.

Here are the IComparer interface definitions:

```
public interface IComparer
{
  int Compare(object x, object y);
}
```

```
public interface IComparer<T>
{
  int Compare(T x, T y);
}
```

As with equality comparers, there's an abstract class you can subtype instead of implementing the interfaces:

```
public abstract class Comparer<T> : IComparer, IComparer<T>
{
    public static Comparer<T> Default { get; }

    public abstract int Compare (T x, T y);        // Implemented by you
    int IComparer.Compare (object x, object y);    // Implemented for you
}
```

The following example illustrates a class that describes a wish, and a comparer that sorts wishes by priority:

```
class Wish
{
  public string Name;
  public int Priority;

  public Wish (string name, int priority)
  {
    Name = name;
    Priority = priority;
  }
}

class PriorityComparer : Comparer <Wish>
{
  public override int Compare (Wish x, Wish y)
  {
    if (object.Equals (x, y)) return 0;          // Fail-safe check
    return x.Priority.CompareTo (y.Priority);
  }
}
```

The object.Equals check ensures that we can never contradict the Equals method. Calling the static object.Equals method in this case is better than calling x.Equals because it still works if x is null!

Here's how our PriorityComparer is used to sort a List:

```
List<Wish> wishList = new List<Wish> ();
wishList.Add (new Wish ("Peace", 2));
wishList.Add (new Wish ("Wealth", 3));
wishList.Add (new Wish ("Love", 2));
wishList.Add (new Wish ("3 more wishes", 1));

wishList.Sort (new PriorityComparer());
foreach (Wish w in wishList) Console.Write (w.Name + " | ");

// OUTPUT: 3 more wishes | Love | Peace | Wealth |
```

In the next example, SurnameComparer allows you to sort surname strings in an order suitable for a phonebook listing:

```
class SurnameComparer : Comparer <string>
{
  string Normalize (string s)
  {
    s = s.Trim ().ToUpper();
    if (s.StartsWith ("MC")) s = "MAC" + s.Substring (2);
    return s;
  }

  public override int Compare (string x, string y)
  {
    return Normalize (x).CompareTo (Normalize (y));
  }
}
```

Here's SurnameComparer in use in a sorted dictionary:

```
SortedDictionary<string,string> dic = new SortedDictionary<string,string>
                              (new SurnameComparer());
dic.Add ("MacPhail", "second!");
dic.Add ("MacWilliam", "third!");
dic.Add ("McDonald", "first!");

foreach (string s in dic.Values)
  Console.Write (s + " ");                    // first! second! third!
```

StringComparer

StringComparer is a predefined plug-in class for equating and comparing strings, allowing you to specify language and case sensitivity. StringComparer implements both IEqualityComparer and IComparer (and their generic versions), so it can be used with any type of dictionary or sorted collection:

```
// CultureInfo is defined in System.Globalization

public abstract class StringComparer : IComparer, IComparer <string>,
                                       IEqualityComparer,
                                       IEqualityComparer <string>
{
  public abstract int Compare (string x, string y);
  public abstract bool Equals (string x, string y);
  public abstract int GetHashCode (string obj);

  public static StringComparer Create (CultureInfo culture,
                                       bool ignoreCase);
  public static StringComparer CurrentCulture { get; }
  public static StringComparer CurrentCultureIgnoreCase { get; }
  public static StringComparer InvariantCulture { get; }
  public static StringComparer InvariantCultureIgnoreCase { get; }
  public static StringComparer Ordinal { get; }
  public static StringComparer OrdinalIgnoreCase { get; }
}
```

Because `StringComparer` is abstract, you obtain instances via its static methods and properties. `StringComparer.Ordinal` mirrors the default behavior for string equality comparison and `StringComparer.CurrentCulture` for order comparison.

In the following example, an ordinal case-insensitive dictionary is created, such that dict["Joe"] and dict["JOE"] mean the same thing:

```
Dictionary<string, int> dict = new Dictionary<string, int>
  (StringComparer.OrdinalIgnoreCase);
```

In the next example, an array of names is sorted, using Australian English:

```
string [] names = new string [] { "Tom", "HARRY", "sheila" };
CultureInfo ci = new CultureInfo ("en-AU");
Array.Sort<string> (names, StringComparer.Create (ci, false));
```

The final example is a culture-aware version of the `SurnameComparer` we wrote in the previous section (to compare names suitable for a phonebook listing):

```
class SurnameComparer : Comparer <string>
{
  StringComparer strCmp;

  public SurnameComparer (CultureInfo ci)
  {
    // Create a case-sensitive, culture-sensitive string comparer
    strCmp = StringComparer.Create (ci, false);
  }

  string Normalize (string s)
  {
    s = s.Trim ();
    if (s.ToUpper().StartsWith ("MC")) s = "MAC" + s.Substring (2);
    return s;
  }

  public override int Compare (string x, string y)
  {
    // Directly call Compare on our culture-aware StringComparer
    return strCmp.Compare (Normalize (x), Normalize (y));
  }
}
```

8

LINQ Queries

LINQ, or Language Integrated Query, is a set of C# 3.0 language and framework features for writing structured type-safe queries over local object collections and remote data sources.

LINQ enables you to query any collection implementing IEnumerable<>, whether an array, list, or XML DOM, as well as remote data sources, such as tables in SQL Server. LINQ offers the benefits of both compile-time type checking and dynamic query composition.

This chapter describes the LINQ architecture and the fundamentals of writing queries. All core types are defined in the System.Linq and System.Linq. Expressions namespaces.

 The examples in this and the following two chapters are pre-loaded into an interactive querying tool called LINQPad. You can download LINQPad from the companion web site at *http://www. albahari.com/nutshell/.*

Getting Started

The basic units of data in LINQ are *sequences* and *elements*. A sequence is any object that implements the generic IEnumerable interface and an element is each item in the sequence. In the following example, names is a sequence, and Tom, Dick, and Harry are elements:

```
string[] names = { "Tom", "Dick", "Harry" };
```

We call this a *local sequence* because it represents a local collection of objects in memory.

A *query operator* is a method that transforms a sequence. A typical query operator accepts an *input sequence* and emits a transformed *output sequence*. In the

Enumerable class in `System.Linq`, there are around 40 query operators—all implemented as static extension methods. These are called *standard query operators*.

> LINQ also supports sequences that can be dynamically fed from a remote data source such as a SQL Server. These sequences additionally implement the `IQueryable<>` interface and are supported through a matching set of standard query operators in the `Queryable` class. We discuss this further in the section "Interpreted Queries" later in this chapter.

A query is an expression that transforms sequences with query operators. The simplest query comprises one input sequence and one operator. For instance, we can apply the `Where` operator on a simple array to extract those whose length is at least four characters as follows:

```
string[] names = { "Tom", "Dick", "Harry" };

IEnumerable<string> filteredNames = System.Linq.Enumerable.Where
                                    (names, n => n.Length >= 4);
foreach (string n in filteredNames)
  Console.Write (n + "|");            // Dick|Harry|
```

Because the standard query operators are implemented as extension methods, we can call `Where` directly on names—as though it were an instance method:

```
IEnumerable<string> filteredNames = names.Where (n => n.Length >= 4);
```

For this to compile, you must import the `System.Linq` namespace. Here's a complete example:

```
using System;
using System.Linq;

class LinqDemo
{
  static void Main()
  {
    string[] names = { "Tom", "Dick", "Harry" };
    IEnumerable<string> filteredNames = names.Where (n => n.Length >= 4);
    foreach (string name in filteredNames) Console.Write (name + "|");
  }
}
```

```
RESULT: Dick|Harry|
```

> We could further shorten our query by implicitly typing filteredNames:
>
> ```
> var filteredNames = names.Where (n => n.Length >= 4);
> ```
>
> This can hinder readability, however, particularly outside of an IDE, where there are no tool tips to help.
>
> In this chapter, we avoid implicitly typing query results except when it's mandatory (as we'll see later, in the section "Projection Strategies"), or when a query's type is irrelevant to an example.

LINQ Queries

Most query operators accept a lambda expression as an argument. The lambda expression helps guide and shape the query. In our example, the lambda expression is as follows:

```
n => n.Length >= 4
```

The input argument corresponds to an input element. In this case, the input argument n represents each name in the array and is of type string. The Where operator requires that the lambda expression return a bool value, which if true, indicates that the element should be included in the output sequence. Here's its signature:

```
public static IEnumerable<TSource> Where<TSource>
  (this IEnumerable<TSource> source, Func<TSource,bool> predicate)
```

The following query retrieves all names that contain the letter "a":

```
IEnumerable<string> filteredNames = names.Where (n => n.Contains ("a"));

foreach (string name in query) Console.Write (name + "|");    // Harry|
```

So far, we've composed queries using extension methods and lambda expressions. In this book, we refer to these as *lambda queries*. C# also defines a special syntax for writing queries, called *query comprehension syntax*. Here's our preceding query expressed in comprehension syntax:

```
IEnumerable<string> filteredNames = from n in names
                                    where n.Contains ("a")
                                    select n;
```

Lambda syntax and comprehension syntax are complementary. In the following two sections, we explore each in more detail.

Lambda Queries

Lambda queries are the most flexible and fundamental. In this section, we describe how to chain operators in order to form more complex queries and show why extension method syntax is important to this process. We also describe how to formulate lambda expressions for a query operator and introduce several new query operators.

Chaining Query Operators

In the preceding section, we showed two basic lambda queries, each comprising a single query operator. To build more complex queries, you add additional query operators, creating a chain. For example, the following query extracts all strings containing the letter "a", sorts them by length, and then converts the results to uppercase:

```
using System;
using System.Linq;

class LinqDemo
{
  static void Main()
  {
```

```
        string[] names = { "Tom", "Dick", "Harry", "Mary", "Jay" };

        IEnumerable<string> query = names
          .Where    (n => n.Contains ("a"))
          .OrderBy (n => n.Length)
          .Select  (n => n.ToUpper());

        foreach (string name in query) Console.Write (name + "|");
      }
    }
```

RESULT: JAY|MARY|HARRY|

 The variable, n, in our example, is privately scoped to each of the
lambda expressions. We can reuse n for the same reason we can
reuse c in the following method:

```
    void Test()
    {
      foreach (char c in "string1") Console.Write (c);
      foreach (char c in "string2") Console.Write (c);
      foreach (char c in "string3") Console.Write (c);
    }
```

Where, OrderBy, and Select are all standard query operators that resolve to extension methods in the Enumerable class.

We already introduced the Where operator, which emits a filtered version of the input sequence. The OrderBy operator emits a sorted version of its input sequence; the Select method emits a sequence where each input element is transformed or *projected* with a given lambda expression (n.ToUpper(), in this case). Data flows from left to right through the chain of operators, so the data is first filtered, then sorted, then projected.

 A query operator never alters the input sequence; instead, it returns
a new sequence. This is consistent with the *functional programming* paradigm, from which LINQ was inspired.

Here are the signatures of each of these extension methods (with the OrderBy signature simplified slightly):

```
    public static IEnumerable<TSource> Where<TSource>
      (this IEnumerable<TSource> source, Func<TSource,bool> predicate)

    public static IEnumerable<TSource> OrderBy<TSource,TKey>
      (this IEnumerable<TSource> source, Func<TSource,TKey> keySelector)

    public static IEnumerable<TResult> Select<TSource,TResult>
      (this IEnumerable<TSource> source, Func<TSource,TResult> selector)
```

When query operators are chained as in this example, the output sequence of one operator is the input sequence of the next. The end result resembles a production line of conveyor belts, as illustrated in Figure 8-1.

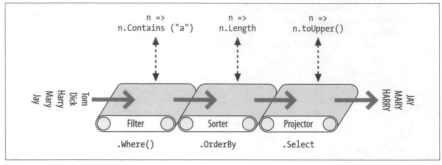

Figure 8-1. Chaining query operators

We can construct the identical query *progressively*, as follows:

```
// You must import the System.Linq namespace for this to compile:

IEnumerable<string> filtered   = names   .Where  (n => n.Contains ("a"));
IEnumerable<string> sorted     = filtered.OrderBy (n => n.Length);
IEnumerable<string> finalQuery = sorted  .Select  (n => n.ToUpper( ));
```

finalQuery is compositionally identical to the query we had constructed previously. Further, each intermediate step also comprises a valid query that we can execute:

```
foreach (string name in filtered)
  Console.Write (name + "|");         // Harry|Mary|Jay|

Console.WriteLine( );
foreach (string name in sorted)
  Console.Write (name + "|");         // Jay|Mary|Harry|

Console.WriteLine( );
foreach (string name in finalQuery)
  Console.Write (name + "|");         // JAY|MARY|HARRY|
```

Why extension methods are important

Instead of using extension method syntax, you can use conventional static method syntax to call the query operators. For example:

```
IEnumerable<string> filtered = Enumerable.Where (names,
                                          n => n.Contains ("a"));
IEnumerable<string> sorted = Enumerable.OrderBy (filtered, n => n.Length);
IEnumerable<string> finalQuery = Enumerable.Select (sorted,
                                          n => n.ToUpper( ));
```

This is, in fact, how the compiler translates extension method calls. Shunning extension methods comes at a cost, however, if you want to write a query in a single statement as we did earlier. Let's revisit the single-statement query—first in extension method syntax:

```
IEnumerable<string> query = names.Where  (n => n.Contains ("a"))
                                 .OrderBy (n => n.Length)
                                 .Select  (n => n.ToUpper( ));
```

Its natural linear shape reflects the left-to-right flow of data, as well as keeping lambda expressions alongside their query operators (*infix* notation). Without extension methods, the query becomes an untidy nest:

```
IEnumerable<string> query =
  Enumerable.Select (
    Enumerable.OrderBy (
      Enumerable.Where (
        names, n => n.Contains ("a")
      ), n => n.Length
    ), n => n.ToUpper ( )
  );
```

Composing Lambda Expressions

In previous examples, we fed the following lambda expression to the `Where` operator:

```
n => n.Contains ("a")      // Input type=string, return type=bool.
```

 An expression returning a bool value is called a *predicate*.

The purpose of the lambda expression depends on the particular query operator. With the `Where` operator, it indicates whether an element should be included in the output sequence. In the case of the `OrderBy` operator, the lambda expression maps each element in the input sequence to its sorting key. With the `Select` operator, the lambda expression determines how each element in the input sequence is transformed before being fed to the output sequence.

 A lambda expression in a query operator always works on individual elements in the input sequence—not the sequence as a whole.

You can think of the lambda expression you supply as a *callback*. The query operator evaluates your lambda expression upon demand—typically once per element in the input sequence. Lambda expressions allow you to feed your own logic into the query operators. This makes the query operators versatile—as well as being simple under the hood. Here's the complete implementation of `Enumerable.Where`, exception handling aside:

```
public static IEnumerable<TSource> Where<TSource>
  (this IEnumerable<TSource> source, Func<TSource,bool> predicate)
{
  foreach (TSource element in source)
    if (predicate (element))
      yield return element;
}
```

Lambda expressions and Func signatures

The standard query operators utilize generic Func delegates. Func is a family of general-purpose generic delegates in System.Linq, defined with the following intent:

> The type arguments in Func appear in the same order they do in lambda expressions.

Hence, Func<TSource,bool> matches a TSource=>bool lambda expression: one that accepts a TSource argument and returns a bool value.

Similarly, Func<TSource,TResult> matches a TSource=>TResult lambda expression.

The Func delegates are listed in the section "Lambda Expressions (C# 3.0)" in Chapter 4.

Lambda expressions and element typing

The standard query operators use the following generic type names:

Generic type letter	Meaning
TSource	Element type for the input sequence
TResult	Element type for the output sequence—if different from TSource
TKey	Element type for the *key* used in sorting, grouping, or joining

TSource is determined by the input sequence. TResult and TKey are *inferred from your lambda expression.*

For example, consider the signature of the Select query operator:

```
public static IEnumerable<TResult> Select<TSource,TResult>
   (this IEnumerable<TSource> source, Func<TSource,TResult> selector)
```

Func<TSource,TResult> matches a TSource=>TResult lambda expression: one that maps an *input element* to an *output element*. TSource and TResult are different types, so the lambda expression can change the type of each element. Further, the lambda expression *determines the output sequence type*. The following query uses Select to transform string type elements to integer type elements:

```
string[] names = { "Tom", "Dick", "Harry", "Mary", "Jay" };
IEnumerable<int> query = names.Select (n => n.Length);

foreach (int length in query) Console.Write (length);        // 34543
```

The compiler *infers* the type of TResult from the return value of the lambda expression. In this case, TResult is inferred to be of type int.

The Where query operator is simpler and requires no type inference for the output, since input and output elements are of the same type. This makes sense because the operator merely filters elements; it does not *transform* them:

```
public static IEnumerable<TSource> Where<TSource>
   (this IEnumerable<TSource> source, Func<TSource,bool> predicate)
```

Finally, consider the signature of the OrderBy operator:

```
// Slightly simplified:
public static IEnumerable<TSource> OrderBy<TSource,TKey>
    (this IEnumerable<TSource> source, Func<TSource,TKey> keySelector)
```

Func<TSource,TKey> maps an input element to a *sorting key*. TKey is inferred from your lambda expression and is separate from the input and output element types. For instance, we could choose to sort a list of names by length (int key) or alphabetically (string key):

```
string[] names = { "Tom", "Dick", "Harry", "Mary", "Jay" };
IEnumerable<string> sortedByLength, sortedAlphabetically;
sortedByLength       = names.OrderBy (n => n.Length);   // int key
sortedAlphabetically = names.OrderBy (n => n);          // string key
```

 You can call the query operators in Enumerable with traditional delegates that refer to methods instead of lambda expressions. This approach is effective in simplifying certain kinds of local queries—particularly with LINQ to XML—and is demonstrated in Chapter 10. It doesn't work with IQueryable<>-based sequences, however (e.g., LINQ to SQL tables), because the operators in Queryable require lambda expressions in order to emit expression trees. We discuss this later in the section "Interpreted Queries."

Natural Ordering

The original ordering of elements within an input sequence is significant in LINQ. Some query operators rely on this behavior, such as Take, Skip, and Reverse.

The Take operator outputs the first x elements, discarding the rest:

```
int[] numbers  = { 10, 9, 8, 7, 6 };
IEnumerable<int> firstThree = numbers.Take (3);     // { 10, 9, 8 }
```

The Skip operator ignores the first x elements and outputs the rest:

```
IEnumerable<int> lastTwo      = numbers.Skip (3);     // { 7, 6 }
```

Reverse does exactly as it says:

```
IEnumerable<int> reversed    = numbers.Reverse();    // { 6, 7, 8, 9, 10 }
```

Operators such as Where and Select preserve the original ordering of the input sequence. LINQ preserves the ordering of elements in the input sequence wherever possible.

Other Operators

Not all query operators return a sequence. The *element* operators extract one element from the input sequence; examples are First, Last, Single, and ElementAt:

```
int[] numbers      = { 10, 9, 8, 7, 6 };
int firstNumber  = numbers.First();                         // 10
int lastNumber   = numbers.Last();                          // 6
int secondNumber = numbers.ElementAt(1);                    // 9
int lowestNumber = numbers.OrderBy (n => n).First();        // 6
```

The *aggregation* operators return a scalar value; usually of numeric type:

```
int count = numbers.Count();         // 5;
int min = numbers.Min();             // 6;
```

The *quantifiers* return a bool value:

```
bool hasTheNumberNine = numbers.Contains (9);        // true
bool hasMoreThanZeroElements = numbers.Any();        // true
bool hasAnOddElement = numbers.Any (n => n % 2 == 1); // true
```

Because these operators don't return a collection, you can't call further operators on their result. In other words, they must appear as the last operator in a query.

Some query operators accept two input sequences. Examples are Concat, which appends one sequence to another, and Union, which does the same but with duplicates removed:

```
int[] seq1 = { 1, 2, 3 };
int[] seq2 = { 3, 4, 5 };
IEnumerable<int> concat = seq1.Concat (seq2);    // { 1, 2, 3, 3, 4, 5 }
IEnumerable<int> union  = seq1.Union (seq2);     // { 1, 2, 3, 4, 5 }
```

The joining operators also fall into this category. Chapter 9 covers all the query operators in detail.

Comprehension Queries

C# provides a syntactic shortcut for writing LINQ queries, called *query comprehension syntax*.

In the preceding section, we wrote a query to extract strings containing the letter "a", sorted by length and converted to uppercase. Here's the same query in comprehension syntax:

```
using System;
using System.Collections.Generic;
using System.Linq;

class LinqDemo
{
  static void Main()
  {
    string[] names = { "Tom", "Dick", "Harry", "Mary", "Jay" };

    IEnumerable<string> query =
      from    n in names
      where   n.Contains ("a")    // Filter elements
      orderby n.Length            // Sort elements
      select  n.ToUpper();        // Translate each element (project)

    foreach (string name in query) Console.Write (name + "/");
  }
}

JAY/MARY/HARRY/
```

A comprehension query always starts with a from clause and ends with either a select or group clause. The from clause declares an *iteration variable* (in this case, n), which you can think of as traversing the input collection—rather like foreach. Figure 8-2 illustrates the complete syntax.

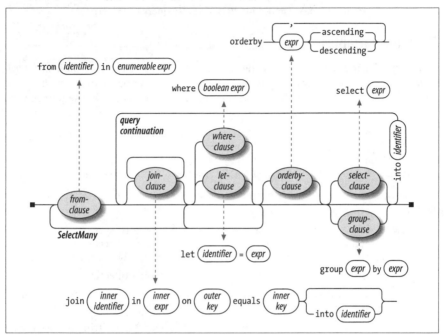

Figure 8-2. Query comprehension syntax

The compiler processes comprehension queries by translating them to lambda syntax. It does this in a fairly mechanical fashion—much like it translates foreach statements into calls to GetEnumerator and MoveNext. This means that anything you can write in comprehension syntax you can also write in lambda syntax. The compiler translates our example query into the following:

```
IEnumerable<string> query = names.Where  (n => n.Contains ("a"))
                                  .OrderBy (n => n.Length)
                                  .Select  (n => n.ToUpper());
```

The Where, OrderBy, and Select operators then resolve using the same rules that would apply if the query were written in lambda syntax. In this case, they bind to extension methods in the Enumerable class, because the System.Linq namespace is imported and names implements IEnumerable<string>. The compiler doesn't specifically favor the Enumerable class, however, when translating comprehension queries. You can think of the compiler as mechanically injecting the words "Where," "OrderBy," and "Select" into the statement, and then compiling it as though you'd typed the method names yourself. This offers flexibility in how they resolve. The operators in the LINQ to SQL queries that we'll write in later sections, for instance, will bind instead to extension methods in Queryable.

If we remove the using System.Linq directive from our program, the comprehension query would not compile, because the Where, OrderBy, and Select methods would have nowhere to bind. Comprehension queries *cannot compile* unless you import a namespace (or write an instance method for every query operator!).

Iteration Variables

The identifier immediately following the from keyword syntax is called the *iteration variable*. In our examples, the iteration variable n appears in every clause in the query. And yet, the variable actually enumerates over a *different* sequence with each clause:

```
from    n in names         // n is our iteration variable
where   n.Contains ("a")   // n = directly from the array
orderby n.Length           // n = subsequent to being filtered
select  n.ToUpper( )       // n = subsequent to being sorted
```

This becomes clear when we examine the compiler's mechanical translation to lambda syntax:

```
names.Where   (n => n.Contains ("a"))   // Privately scoped n
     .OrderBy (n => n.Length)           // Privately scoped n
     .Select  (n => n.ToUpper( ))       // Privately scoped n
```

- Where enumerates n over the array, emitting a filtered collection.
- OrderBy enumerates a fresh n over the filtered collection, emitting a sorted collection.
- Select enumerates a fresh n over the sorted collection, emitting an uppercase version.

Hence, the iteration variable always enumerates over the results of the *preceding clause* in the query. The only exception to this rule is when a clause introduces a *new variable*. There are three such cases:

- let
- into
- An additional from clause

We cover these later in this chapter in the section "Composition Strategies," and also in Chapter 9, in the sections "Projecting" and "Joining."

Comprehension Syntax Versus SQL Syntax

LINQ comprehension syntax looks superficially like SQL syntax, yet the two are very different. A LINQ query boils down to a C# expression, and so follows standard C# rules. For example, with LINQ, you cannot use a variable before you declare it. In SQL, you reference a table alias in the SELECT clause before defining it in a FROM clause.

A subquery in LINQ is just another C# expression and so requires no special syntax. Subqueries in SQL are subject to special rules.

With LINQ, data logically flows from left to right through the query. With SQL, the order is more random.

A LINQ query comprises a conveyor belt or *pipeline* of operators that accept and emit *ordered sequences*. A SQL query comprises a *network* of clauses that work mostly with *unordered sets*.

LINQ queries are "close to the metal" of their underlying implementation; SQL queries are more abstracted.

Comprehension Syntax Versus Lambda Syntax

Comprehension and lambda syntax each have advantages.

Comprehension syntax is much simpler for queries that involve any of the following:

- A let clause for introducing a new variable alongside the iteration variable
- SelectMany, Join, or GroupJoin, followed by an outer iteration variable reference

(We describe the let clause in the later section, "Composition Strategies"; we describe SelectMany, Join, and GroupJoin in Chapter 9.)

The middle ground is queries that involve the simple use of Where, OrderBy, and Select. Either syntax works well; the choice here is largely personal.

For queries that comprise a single operator, lambda syntax is shorter and less cluttered.

Finally, there are many operators that have no query comprehension keyword. These require that you use lambda syntax—at least in part. This means any operator outside of the following:

```
Where, Select, SelectMany
OrderBy, ThenBy, OrderByDescending, ThenByDescending
Group, Join, GroupJoin
```

Mixed Syntax Queries

If a query operator has no comprehension support, you can mix comprehension and lambda syntax. The only restriction is that each comprehension component must be complete (i.e., start with a from clause and end with a select or group clause).

Assuming this array declaration:

```
string[] names = { "Tom", "Dick", "Harry", "Mary", "Jay" };
```

the following example counts the number of names containing the letter "a":

```
int matches = (from n in names where n.Contains ("a") select n).Count();
// 3
```

The next query obtains the first name in alphabetical order:

```
string first = (from n in names orderby n select n).First();    // Dick
```

The mixed syntax approach is sometimes beneficial in more complex queries. With these simple examples, however, we could stick to lambda syntax throughout without penalty:

```
int matches = names.Where (n => n.Contains ("a")).Count( );    // 3
string first = names.OrderBy (n => n).First( );                // Dick
```

 There are times when mixed syntax queries offer by far the highest "bang for the buck" in terms of function and simplicity. It's important not to unilaterally favor either comprehension or lambda syntax; otherwise, you'll be unable to write mixed syntax queries without feeling a sense of failure!

The remainder of this chapter, where applicable, will show key concepts in both lambda and comprehension syntax.

Deferred Execution

An important feature of most query operators is that they execute not when constructed, but when *enumerated* (in other words, when MoveNext is called on its enumerator). Consider the following query:

```
var numbers = new List<int>( );
numbers.Add (1);

IEnumerable<int> query = numbers.Select (n => n * 10);    // Build query

numbers.Add (2);                        // Sneak in an extra element

foreach (int n in query)
  Console.Write (n + "|");              // 10|20|
```

The extra number that we sneaked into the list *after* constructing the query is included in the result, because it's not until the foreach statement runs that any filtering or sorting takes place. This is called *deferred* or *lazy* evaluation. All standard query operators provide deferred execution, with the following exceptions:

* Operators that return a single element or scalar value, such as First or Count
* The following *conversion operators*:

    ToArray, ToList, ToDictionary, ToLookup

These operators cause immediate query execution because their result types have no mechanism for providing deferred execution. The Count method, for instance, returns a simple integer, which doesn't then get enumerated. The following query is executed immediately:

```
int matches = numbers.Where (n => n < 2).Count( );    // 1
```

Deferred execution is important because it decouples query *construction* from query *execution*. This allows you to construct a query in several steps, as well as making LINQ to SQL queries possible.

Subqueries provide another level of indirection. Everything in a subquery is subject to deferred execution—including aggregation and conversion methods. We describe this in the section "Subqueries later in this chapter.

Reevaluation

Deferred execution has another consequence: a deferred execution query is reevaluated when you reenumerate:

```
var numbers = new List<int>() { 1, 2 };

IEnumerable<int> query = numbers.Select (n => n * 10);
foreach (int n in query) Console.Write (n + "|");   // 10|20|

numbers.Clear();
foreach (int n in query) Console.Write (n + "|");   // <nothing>
```

There are a couple of reasons why reevaluation is sometimes disadvantageous:

- Sometimes you want to "freeze" or cache the results at a certain point in time.
- Some queries are computationally intensive (or rely on querying a remote database), so you don't want to unnecessarily repeat them.

You can defeat reevaluation by calling a conversion operator, such as ToArray or ToList. ToArray copies the output of a query to an array; ToList copies to a generic List<>:

```
var numbers = new List<int>() { 1, 2 };

List<int> timesTen = numbers
  .Select (n => n * 10)
  .ToList();                    // Executes immediately into a List<int>

numbers.Clear();
Console.WriteLine (timesTen.Count);       // Still 2
```

Outer Variables

Deferred execution also has a sinister effect. If your query's lambda expressions reference local variables, these variables are subject to *outer variable* semantics. This means that if you later change their value, the query changes as well:

```
int[] numbers = { 1, 2 };

int factor = 10;
IEnumerable<int> query = numbers.Select (n => n * factor);

factor = 20;
foreach (int n in query) Console.Write (n + "|");   // 20|40|
```

LINQ Queries

This can be a real trap when building up a query within a foreach loop. For example, suppose we wanted to remove all vowels from a string. The following, although inefficient, gives the correct result:

```
IEnumerable<char> query = "Not what you might expect";

query = query.Where (c => c != 'a');
query = query.Where (c => c != 'e');
query = query.Where (c => c != 'i');
query = query.Where (c => c != 'o');
query = query.Where (c => c != 'u');

foreach (char c in query) Console.Write (c);   // Nt wht y mght xpct
```

Now watch what happens when we refactor this with a foreach loop:

```
IEnumerable<char> query = "Not what you might expect";

foreach (char vowel in "aeiou")
  query = query.Where (c => c != vowel);

foreach (char c in query) Console.Write (c);    // Not what yo might expect
```

Only the 'u' is stripped! This is because the compiler translates the foreach loop into something like this:

```
IEnumerable<char> vowels = "aeiou";
IEnumerator<char> rator = vowels.GetEnumerator ();
char vowel;
while (rator.MoveNext())
{
  vowel = rator.Current;
  query = query.Where (c => c != vowel);
}
```

Because vowel is declared outside the loop, the *same* variable is repeatedly updated, so each lambda expression captures the same vowel. When we later enumerate the query, all lambda expressions reference that single variable's current value, which is 'u'. To solve this, you must assign the loop variable to another variable declared *inside* the statement block:

```
foreach (char vowel in "aeiou")
{
  char temp = vowel;
  query = query.Where (c => c != temp);
}
```

This forces a fresh variable to be used on each loop iteration.

How Deferred Execution Works

Query operators provide deferred execution by returning *decorator* sequences.

Unlike a traditional collection class such as an array or linked list, a decorator sequence has no backing structure of its own to store elements. Instead, it wraps another sequence that you supply at runtime, to which it maintains a permanent dependency. Whenever you request data from a decorator, it in turn must request data from the wrapped input sequence.

The query operator's transformation constitutes the "decoration." If the output sequence performed no transformation, it would be a *proxy* rather than a decorator.

Calling Where merely constructs the decorator wrapper sequence, holding a reference to the input sequence, the lambda expression, and any other arguments supplied. The input sequence is enumerated only when the decorator is enumerated.

Figure 8-3 illustrates the composition of the following query:

```
IEnumerable<int> lessThanTen = new int[] { 5, 12, 3 }.Where (n => n < 10);
```

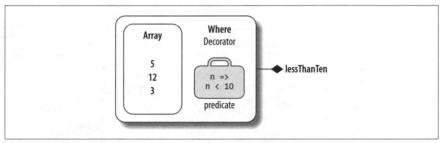

Figure 8-3. Decorator sequence

When you enumerate lessThanTen, you're, in effect, querying the array through the Where decorator.

The good news—if you ever want to write your own query operator—is that implementing a decorator sequence is easy with a C# iterator. Here's how you can write your own Select method:

```
public static IEnumerable<TResult> Select<TSource,TResult>
  (this IEnumerable<TSource> source, Func<TSource,TResult> selector)
{
  foreach (TSource element in source)
    yield return selector (element);
}
```

This method is an iterator by virtue of the yield return statement. Functionally, it's a shortcut for the following:

```
public static IEnumerable<TResult> Select<TSource,TResult>
  (this IEnumerable<TSource> source, Func<TSource,TResult> selector)
{
  return new SelectSequence (source, selector);
}
```

where *SelectSequence* is a (compiler-written) class whose enumerator encapsulates the logic in the iterator method.

Hence, when you call an operator such as Select or Where, you're doing nothing more than instantiating an enumerable class that decorates the input sequence.

LINQ Queries

Chaining Decorators

Chaining query operators creates a layering of decorators. Consider the following query:

```
IEnumerable<int> query = new int[] { 5, 12, 3 }.Where  (n => n < 10)
                                              .OrderBy (n => n)
                                              .Select  (n => n * 10);
```

Each query operator instantiates a new decorator that wraps the previous sequence (rather like a Russian doll). The object model of this query is illustrated in Figure 8-4. Note that this object model is fully constructed prior to any enumeration.

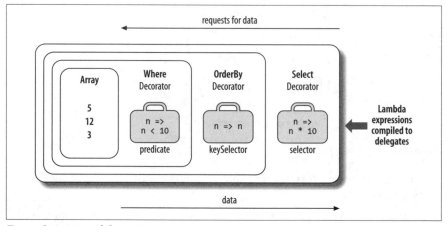

Figure 8-4. Layered decorator sequences

When you enumerate query, you're querying the original array, transformed through a layering or chain of decorators.

 Adding ToList onto the end of this query would cause the preceding operators to execute right away, collapsing the whole object model into a single list.

Figure 8-5 shows the same object composition in UML syntax. Select's decorator references the OrderBy decorator, which references Where's decorator, which references the array. A feature of deferred execution is that you build the identical object model if you compose the query progressively:

```
IEnumerable<int>
  source   = new int[] { 5, 12, 3 },
  filtered = source   .Where  (n => n < 10),
  sorted   = filtered .OrderBy (n => n),
  query    = sorted   .Select  (n => n * 10);
```

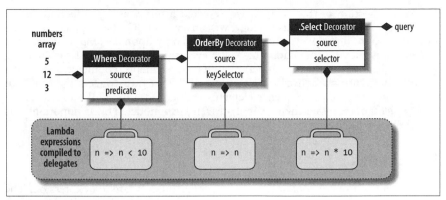

Figure 8-5. UML decorator composition

How Queries Are Executed

Here are the results of enumerating the preceding query:

```
foreach (int n in query) Console.WriteLine (n);
```

```
30
50
```

Behind the scenes, the foreach calls GetEnumerator on Select's decorator (the last or outermost operator), which kicks everything off. The result is a chain of enumerators that structurally mirrors the chain of decorator sequences. Figure 8-6 illustrates the flow of execution as enumeration proceeds.

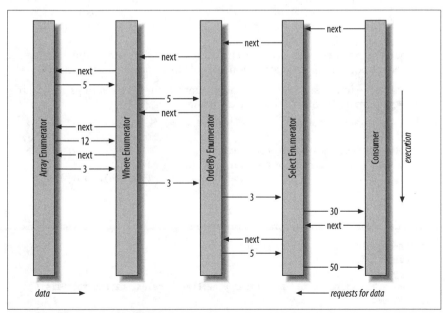

Figure 8-6. Execution of a local query

In the first section of this chapter, we depicted a query as a production line of conveyor belts. Extending this analogy, we can say a LINQ query is a lazy production line, where the conveyor belts roll elements only upon *demand*. Constructing a query constructs a production line—with everything in place—but with nothing rolling. Then when the consumer requests an element (enumerates over the query), the rightmost conveyor belt activates; this in turn triggers the others to roll—as and when input sequence elements are needed. LINQ follows a demand-driven *pull* model, rather than a supply-driven *push* model. This is important—as we'll see later—in allowing LINQ to scale to querying SQL databases.

Subqueries

A subquery is a query contained within another query's lambda expression. The following example uses a subquery to sort musicians by their last name:

```
string[] musos = { "David Gilmour", "Roger Waters", "Rick Wright" };
IEnumerable<string> query = musos.OrderBy (m => m.Split( ).Last( ));
```

m.Split converts each string into a collection of words, upon which we then call the Last query operator. Last is the subquery; query references the *outer query*.

Subqueries are permitted because you can put any valid C# expression on the righthand side of a lambda. A subquery is simply another C# expression. This means that the rules for subqueries are a consequence of the rules for lambda expressions (and the behavior of query operators in general).

> The term *subquery*, in the general sense, has a broader meaning. For the purpose of describing LINQ, we use the term only for a query referenced from within the lambda expression of another query. In comprehension syntax, a subquery amounts to a query referenced from an expression in any clause except the from clause.

A subquery is privately scoped to the enclosing expression and is able to reference the outer lambda argument (or iteration variable in comprehension syntax).

Last is a very simple subquery. The next query retrieves all strings in an array whose length matches that of the shortest string:

```
string[] names = { "Tom", "Dick", "Harry", "Mary", "Jay" };

IEnumerable<string> outerQuery = names
  .Where (n => n.Length == names.OrderBy (n2 => n2.Length)
                                .Select (n2 => n2.Length).First( ));

Tom, Jay
```

Here's the same thing in comprehension syntax:

```
IEnumerable<string> comprehension =
  from   n in names
  where  n.Length ==
          (from n2 in names orderby n2.Length select n2.Length).First( )
  select n;
```

Because the outer iteration variable (n) is in scope for a subquery, we cannot reuse n as the subquery's iteration variable.

A subquery is executed whenever the enclosing lambda expression is evaluated. This means a subquery is executed upon demand, at the discretion of the outer query. You could say that execution proceeds from the *outside in*. Local queries follow this model literally; interpreted queries (e.g., LINQ to SQL queries) follow this model *conceptually*.

The subquery executes as and when required, to feed the outer query. In our example, the subquery (the top conveyor belt in Figure 8-7) executes once for every outer loop iteration. This is illustrated in Figures 8-7 and 8-8.

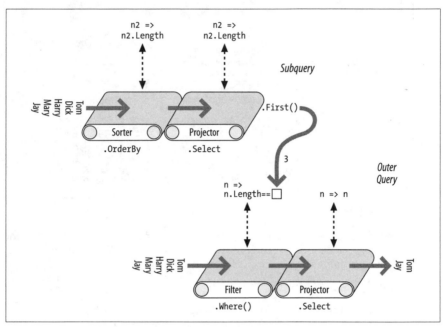

Figure 8-7. Subquery composition

We can express our preceding subquery more succinctly as follows:

```
IEnumerable<string> query =
    from  n in names
    where n.Length == names.OrderBy (n2 => n2.Length).First( ).Length
    select n;
```

With the Min aggregation function, we can simplify the query further:

```
IEnumerable<string> query =
    from  n in names
    where n.Length == names.Min (n2 => n2.Length)
    select n;
```

In the later section "Interpreted Queries," we'll describe how remote sources such as SQL tables can be queried. Our example makes an ideal LINQ to SQL query, because it would be processed as a unit, requiring only one round trip to the data-

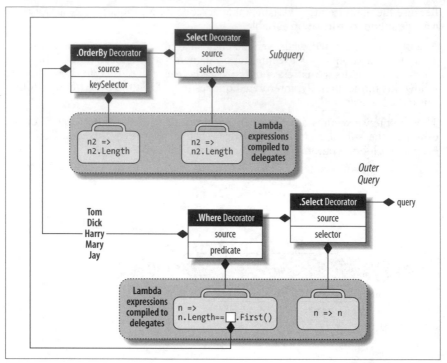

Figure 8-8. UML subquery composition

base server. This query, however, is inefficient for a local collection because the subquery is recalculated on each outer loop iteration. We can avoid this inefficiency by running the subquery separately (so that it's no longer a subquery):

```
int shortest = names.Min (n => n.Length);

IEnumerable<string> query = from    n in names
                            where   n.Length == shortest
                            select n;
```

 Factoring out subqueries in this manner is nearly always desirable when querying local collections. An exception is when the sub-query is *correlated*, meaning that it references the outer iteration variable. We explore correlated subqueries in the following chapter, in the section "Projecting."

Subqueries and Deferred Execution

An element or aggregation operator such as `First` or `Count` in a subquery doesn't force the *outer* query into immediate execution—deferred execution still holds for the outer query. This is because subqueries are called *indirectly*—through a delegate in the case of a local query, or through an expression tree in the case of an interpreted query.

An interesting case arises when you include a subquery within a Select expression. In the case of a local query, you're actually *projecting a sequence of queries*—each itself subject to deferred execution. The effect is generally transparent, and it serves to further improve efficiency. We revisit Select subqueries in some detail in Chapter 9.

Composition Strategies

In this section, we describe three strategies for building more complex queries:

- Progressive query construction
- Using the into keyword
- Wrapping queries

All are *chaining* strategies and produce identical runtime queries.

Progressive Query Building

At the start of the chapter, we demonstrated how you could build a lambda query progressively:

```
var filtered  = names    .Where   (n => n.Contains ("a"));
var sorted    = filtered .OrderBy (n => n);
var query     = sorted   .Select  (n => n.ToUpper( ));
```

Because each of the participating query operators returns a decorator sequence, the resultant query is the same chain or layering of decorators that you would get from a single-expression query. There are a couple of potential benefits, however, to building queries progressively:

- It can make queries easier to write.
- You can add query operators *conditionally*. For example:

  ```
  if (includeFilter) query = query.Where (...)
  ```

A progressive approach is often useful in comprehension queries. To illustrate, imagine we want to remove all vowels from a list of names, and then present in alphabetical order those whose length is still more than two characters. In lambda syntax, we could write this query as a single expression—by projecting *before* we filter:

```
IEnumerable<string> query = names
  .Select  (n => n.Replace ("a", "").Replace ("e", "").Replace ("i", "")
                  .Replace ("o", "").Replace ("u", ""))
  .Where   (n => n.Length > 2)
  .OrderBy (n => n);

RESULT: { "Dck", "Hrry", "Mry" }
```

 Rather than calling string's Replace method five times, we could remove vowels from a string more efficiently with a regular expression:

```
n => Regex.Replace (n, "[aeiou]", "")
```

string's Replace method has the advantage, though, of also working in LINQ to SQL queries.

Translating this directly to comprehension syntax is troublesome because comprehension clauses must appear in where-orderby-select order, to be recognized by the compiler. And if we rearrange the query so as to project last, the result would be different:

```
IEnumerable<string> query =
  from    n in names
  where   n.Length > 2
  orderby n
  select  n.Replace ("a", "").Replace ("e", "").Replace ("i", "")
            .Replace ("o", "").Replace ("u", "");

RESULT: { "Dck", "Hrry", "Jy", "Mry", "Tm" }
```

Fortunately, there are a number of ways to get the original result in comprehension syntax. The first is by querying progressively:

```
IEnumerable<string> query =
  from   n in names
  select n.Replace ("a", "").Replace ("e", "").Replace ("i", "")
           .Replace ("o", "").Replace ("u", "");

query = from n in query where n.Length > 2 orderby n select n;

RESULT: { "Dck", "Hrry", "Mry" }
```

The into Keyword

The into keyword is interpreted in two very different ways in comprehension syntax, depending on context. The meaning we're describing now is for signaling *query continuation* (the other is for signaling a GroupJoin).

The into keyword lets you "continue" a query after a projection and is a shortcut for progressively querying. With into, we can rewrite the preceding query as:

```
IEnumerable<string> query =
  from   n in names
  select n.Replace ("a", "").Replace ("e", "").Replace ("i", "")
           .Replace ("o", "").Replace ("u", "")
  into noVowel
    where noVowel.Length > 2 orderby noVowel select noVowel;
```

The only place you can use into is after a select or group clause. into "restarts" a query, allowing you to introduce fresh where, orderby, and select clauses.

Although it's easiest to think of into as restarting a query from the perspective of comprehension syntax, it's *all one query* when translated to its final lambda form. Hence, there's no intrinsic performance hit with into. Nor do you lose any points for its use!

The equivalent of into in lambda syntax is simply a longer chain of operators.

Scoping rules

All query variables are out of scope following an into keyword. The following will not compile:

```
var query =
  from n1 in names
  select n1.ToUpper()
  into n2                            // Only n2 is visible from here on.
    where n1.Contains ("x")          // Illegal: n1 is not in scope.
    select n2;
```

To see why, consider how this maps to lambda syntax:

```
var query = names
  .Select (n1 => n1.ToUpper())
  .Where  (n2 => n1.Contains ("x"));      // Error: n1 no longer in scope
```

The original name (n1) is lost by the time the Where filter runs. Where's input sequence contains only uppercase names, so it cannot filter based on n1.

Wrapping Queries

A query built progressively can be formulated into a single statement by wrapping one query around another. In general terms:

```
var tempQuery = tempQueryExpr
var finalQuery = from ... in tempQuery ...
```

can be reformulated as:

```
var finalQuery = from ... in (tempQueryExpr)
```

Wrapping is semantically identical to progressive query building or using the into keyword (without the intermediate variable). The end result in all cases is a linear chain of query operators. For example, consider the following query:

```
IEnumerable<string> query =
  from   n in names
  select n.Replace ("a", "").Replace ("e", "").Replace ("i", "")
         .Replace ("o", "").Replace ("u", "");

query = from n in query where n.Length > 2 orderby n select n;
```

Reformulated in wrapped form, it's the following:

```
IEnumerable<string> query =
  from n1 in
  (
    from   n2 in names
    select n2.Replace ("a", "").Replace ("e", "").Replace ("i", "")
           .Replace ("o", "").Replace ("u", "")
  )
  where n1.Length > 2 orderby n1 select n1;
```

When converted to lambda syntax, the result is the same linear chain of operators as in previous examples.

```
IEnumerable<string> query = names
  .Select  (n => n.Replace ("a", "").Replace ("e", "").Replace ("i", "")
                  .Replace ("o", "").Replace ("u", ""))
  .Where   (n => n.Length > 2)
  .OrderBy (n => n);
```

(The compiler does not emit the final .Select (n => n) because it's redundant.)

Wrapped queries can be confusing because they resemble the *subqueries* we wrote earlier. Both have the concept of an inner and outer query. When converted to lambda syntax, however, you can see that wrapping is simply a strategy for sequentially chaining operators. The end result bears no resemblance to a subquery, which embeds an inner query within the *lambda expression* of another.

Returning to a previous analogy: when wrapping, the "inner" query amounts to the *preceding conveyor belts*. In contrast, a subquery rides above a conveyor belt and is activated upon demand through the conveyor belt's lambda worker (as illustrated in Figure 8-7).

Projection Strategies

Object Initializers

So far, all our select clauses have projected scalar element types. With C# object initializers, you can project into more complex types. For example, suppose, as a first step in a query, we want to strip vowels from a list of names while still retaining the original versions alongside, for the benefit of subsequent queries. We can write the following class to assist:

```
class TempProjectionItem
{
  public string Original;   // Original name
  public string Vowelless;  // Vowel-stripped name
}
```

and then project into it with object initializers:

```
string[] names = { "Tom", "Dick", "Harry", "Mary", "Jay" };

IEnumerable<TempProjectionItem> temp =
  from n in names
  select new TempProjectionItem
  {
    Original  = n,
    Vowelless = n.Replace ("a", "").Replace ("e", "").Replace ("i", "")
                 .Replace ("o", "").Replace ("u", "")
  };
```

The result is of type IEnumerable<TempProjectionItem>, which we can subsequently query:

```
IEnumerable<string> query = from    item in temp
                            where   item.Vowelless.Length > 2
                            select  item.Original;
```

```
Dick
Harry
Mary
```

Anonymous Types

Anonymous types allow you to structure your intermediate results without writing special classes. We can eliminate the `TempProjectionItem` class in our previous example with anonymous types:

```
var intermediate = from n in names
  select new
  {
    Original = n,
    Vowelless = n.Replace ("a", "").Replace ("e", "").Replace ("i", "")
                .Replace ("o", "").Replace ("u", "")
  };

IEnumerable<string> query = from   item in intermediate
                            where  item.Vowelless.Length > 2
                            select item.Original;
```

This gives the same result as the previous example, but without needing to write a one-off class. The compiler does the job instead, writing a temporary class with fields that match the structure of our projection. This means, however, that the intermediate query has the following type:

```
IEnumerable <random-compiler-produced-name>
```

The only way we can declare a variable of this type is with the var keyword. In this case, var is more than just a clutter reduction device; it's a necessity.

We can write the whole query more succinctly with the into keyword:

```
var query = from n in names
  select new
  {
     Original = n,
     Vowelless = n.Replace ("a", "").Replace ("e", "").Replace ("i", "")
                 .Replace ("o", "").Replace ("u", "")
  }
  into temp
  where temp.Vowelless.Length > 2
  select temp.Original;
```

Query comprehension syntax provides a shortcut for writing this kind of query: the let keyword.

The let Keyword

The let keyword introduces a new variable alongside the iteration variable.

With let, we can write a query extracting strings whose length excluding vowels exceeds two characters as follows:

```
string[] names = { "Tom", "Dick", "Harry", "Mary", "Jay" };

IEnumerable<string> query =
```

```
from n in names
let vowelless = n.Replace ("a", "").Replace ("e", "").Replace ("i", "")
                .Replace ("o", "").Replace ("u", "")
where vowelless.Length > 2
orderby vowelless
select n;      // Thanks to let, n is still in scope.
```

The compiler resolves a let clause by projecting into a temporary anonymous
type that contains both the iteration variable and the new expression variable. In
other words, the compiler translates this query into the preceding example.

let accomplishes two things:

- It projects new elements alongside existing elements.
- It allows an expression to be used repeatedly in a query without being
  rewritten.

The let approach is particularly advantageous in this example, because it allows
the select clause to project either the original name (n) or its vowel-removed
version (v).

You can have any number of let statements, before or after a where statement (see
Figure 8-2). A let statement can reference variables introduced in earlier let statements (subject to the boundaries imposed by an into clause). let *reprojects* all
existing variables transparently.

A let expression need not evaluate a scalar type: sometimes it's useful to have it
evaluate to a subsequence, for instance.

Interpreted Queries

LINQ provides two parallel architectures: *local* queries for local object collections, and *interpreted* queries for remote data sources. So far, we've examined the
architecture of local queries, which operate over collections implementing
IEnumerable<>. Local queries resolve to query operators in the Enumerable class,
which in turn resolve to chains of decorator sequences. The delegates that they
accept—whether expressed in comprehension syntax, lambda syntax, or traditional delegates—are fully local to Intermediate Language (IL) code just as any
other C# method.

By contrast, interpreted queries are *descriptive*. They operate over sequences that
implement IQueryable<>, and they resolve to the query operators in the Queryable
class, which emit *expression trees* that are interpreted at runtime.

The query operators in Enumerable can actually work with
IQueryable<> sequences. The difficulty is that the resultant queries
always execute locally on the client—this is why a second set of
query operators is provided in the Queryable class.

There are two IQueryable implementations in the .NET Framework:

- LINQ to SQL
- LINQ to Entities

In addition, the AsQueryable extension method generates an IQueryable wrapper around an ordinary enumerable collection. We describe AsQueryable in the section "Building Query Expressions" later in this chapter.

In this section, we'll use LINQ to SQL to illustrate interpreted query architecture.

 IQueryable<> is an extension of IEnumerable<> with additional methods for constructing expression trees. Most of the time you can ignore the details of these methods; they're called indirectly by the Framework. The "Building Query Expressions" section covers IQueryable<> in more detail.

Suppose we create a simple customer table in SQL Server and populate it with a few names using the following SQL script:

```
create table Customer
(
  ID int not null primary key,
  Name varchar(30)
)
insert Customer values (1, 'Tom')
insert Customer values (2, 'Dick')
insert Customer values (3, 'Harry')
insert Customer values (4, 'Mary')
insert Customer values (5, 'Jay')
```

With this table in place, we can write an interpreted LINQ query in C# to retrieve customers whose name contains the letter "a" as follows:

```
using System;
using System.Linq;
using System.Data.Linq;
using System.Data.Linq.Mapping;

[Table] public class Customer
{
  [Column(IsPrimaryKey=true)] public int ID;
  [Column]                    public string Name;
}

class Test
{
  static void Main( )
  {
    DataContext dataContext = new DataContext ("connection string");
    Table<Customer> customers = dataContext.GetTable <Customer>( );

    IQueryable<string> query = from c in customers
      where   c.Name.Contains ("a")
      orderby c.Name.Length
      select  c.Name.ToUpper( );

    foreach (string name in query) Console.WriteLine (name);
  }
}
```

LINQ to SQL translates this query into the following SQL:

```
SELECT UPPER([t0].[Name]) AS [value]
FROM [Customer] AS [t0]
WHERE [t0].[Name] LIKE '%a%'
ORDER BY LEN([t0].[Name])
```

with the following end result:

```
JAY
MARY
HARRY
```

How Interpreted Queries Work

Let's examine how the preceding query is processed.

First, the compiler converts the query from comprehension to lambda syntax. This is done exactly as with local queries:

```
IQueryable<string> query = customers.Where  (n => n.Name.Contains ("a"))
                                    .OrderBy (n => n.Name.Length)
                                    .Select  (n => n.Name.ToUpper( ));
```

Next, the compiler resolves the query operator methods. Here's where local and interpreted queries differ—interpreted queries resolve to query operators in the Queryable class instead of the Enumerable class.

To see why, we need to look at the customers variable, the source upon which the whole query builds. customers is of type Table<>, which implements IQueryable<> (a subtype of IEnumerable<>). This means the compiler has a choice in resolving Where: it could call the extension method in Enumerable or the following extension method in Queryable:

```
public static IQueryable<TSource> Where<TSource> (this
    IQueryable<TSource> source, Expression <Func<TSource,bool>> predicate)
```

The compiler chooses Queryable.Where because its signature is a *more specific match*.

Queryable.Where accepts a predicate wrapped in an Expression<TDelegate> type. This instructs the compiler to translate the supplied lambda expression—in other words, n=>n.Name.Contains("a")—to an *expression tree* rather than a compiled delegate. An expression tree is an object model based on the types in System.Linq. Expressions that can be inspected at runtime (so that LINQ to SQL can later translate it to a SQL statement).

Because Queryable.Where also returns IQueryable<>, the same process follows with the OrderBy and Select operators. The end result is illustrated in Figure 8-9. In the shaded box, there is an *expression tree* describing the entire query, which can be traversed at runtime.

Execution

Interpreted queries follow a deferred execution model—just like local queries. This means that the SQL statement is not generated until you start enumerating

---

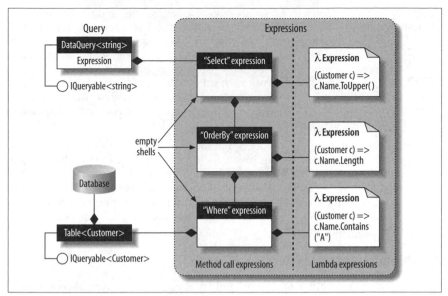

Figure 8-9. Interpreted query composition

the query. Further, enumerating the same query twice results in the database being queried twice.

Under the covers, interpreted queries differ from local queries in how they execute. When you enumerate over an interpreted query, the outermost sequence runs a program that traverses the entire expression tree, processing it as a unit. In our example, LINQ to SQL translates the expression tree to a SQL statement, which it then executes, yielding the results as a sequence.

 To work, LINQ to SQL needs some clues as to the schema of the database. The Table and Column attributes that we applied to the Customer class serve just this function. The section "LINQ to SQL," later in this chapter, describes these attributes in more detail.

We said previously that a LINQ query is like a production line. When you enumerate an IQueryable conveyor belt, though, it doesn't start up the whole production line, like with a local query. Instead, just the IQueryable belt starts up, with a special enumerator that calls upon a production manager. The manager reviews the entire production line—which consists not of compiled code, but of *dummies* (method call expressions) with instructions pasted to their *foreheads* (lambda expression trees). The manager then traverses all the expressions, in this case transcribing them to a single piece of paper (a SQL statement), which it then executes, feeding the results back to the consumer. Only one belt turns; the rest of the production line is a network of empty shells, existing just to describe what has to be done.

This has some practical implications. For instance, with local queries, you can write your own query methods (fairly easily, with iterators) and then use them to supplement the predefined set. With remote queries, this is difficult, and even undesirable. If you wrote a MyWhere extension method accepting IQueryable<>, it would be like putting your own dummy into the production line. The production manager wouldn't know what to do with your dummy. Even if you intervened at this stage, your solution would be hard-wired to a particular provider, such as LINQ to SQL, and would not work with other IQueryable implementations. Part of the benefit of having a standard set of methods in Queryable is that they define a *standard vocabulary* for querying *any* remote collection. As soon as you try to extend the vocabulary, you're no longer interoperable.

Another consequence of this model is that an IQueryable provider may be unable to cope with some queries—even if you stick to the standard methods. LINQ to SQL, for instance, is limited by the capabilities of the database server; some LINQ queries have no SQL translation. If you're familiar with SQL, you'll have a good intuition for what these are, although at times you have to experiment to see what causes a runtime error; it can be surprising what *does* work! Your chances with LINQ to SQL are best with the latest version of Microsoft SQL Server.

Combining Interpreted and Local Queries

A query can include both interpreted and local operators. A typical pattern is to have the local operators on the *outside* and the interpreted components on the *inside*; in other words, the interpreted queries feed the local queries. This pattern works well with LINQ to SQL queries.

For instance, suppose we write a custom extension method to pair up strings in a collection:

```
public static IEnumerable<string> Pair (this IEnumerable<string> source)
{
  string firstHalf = null;
  foreach (string element in source)
    if (firstHalf == null)
      firstHalf = element;
    else
    {
      yield return firstHalf + ", " + element;
      firstHalf = null;
    }
}
```

We can use this extension method in a query that mixes LINQ to SQL and local operators:

```
DataContext dataContext = new DataContext ("connection string");
Table<Customer> customers = dataContext.GetTable <Customer>();

IEnumerable<string> q = customers
  .Select (c => c.Name.ToUpper())
  .Pair()                         // Local from this point on.
  .OrderBy (n => n);

foreach (string element in q) Console.WriteLine (element);

HARRY, MARY
TOM, DICK
```

Because customers is of a type implementing IQueryable<>, the Select operator resolves to Queryable.Select. This returns an output sequence also of type IQueryable. But the next query operator, Pair, has no overload accepting IQueryable<>—only the less specific IEnumerable<>. So, it resolves to our local Pair method—wrapping the interpreted query in a local query. Pair also emits IEnumerable, so OrderBy wraps another local operator.

On the LINQ to SQL side, here's the resulting SQL statement:

```
SELECT UPPER (Name) FROM Customer
```

The remaining work is done locally. Figure 8-10 shows the query diagrammatically. In effect, we have a local query (on the outside), whose source is an interpreted query (the inside).

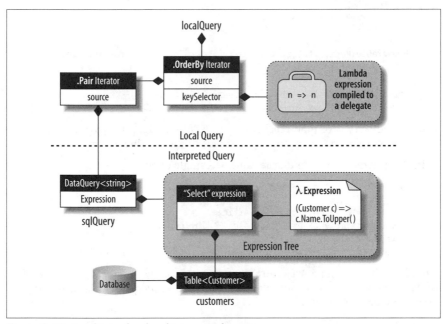

Figure 8-10. Combining local and interpreted queries

AsEnumerable

Enumerable.AsEnumerable is the simplest of all query operators. Here's its complete definition:

```
public static IEnumerable<TSource> AsEnumerable<TSource>
            (this IEnumerable<TSource> source)
{
    return source;
}
```

Its purpose is to cast an IQueryable<T> sequence to IEnumerable<T>, forcing subsequent query operators to bind to Enumerable operators instead of Queryable operators. This causes the remainder of the query to execute locally.

To illustrate, suppose we had a `MedicalArticles` table in SQL Server and wanted to use LINQ to SQL to retrieve all articles on influenza whose abstract contained less than 100 words. For the latter predicate, we need a regular expression:

```
Regex wordCounter = new Regex (@"\b(\w|[-'])+\b");

var query = dataContext.MedicalArticles
  .Where (article => article.Topic == "influenza" &&
                wordCounter.Matches (article.Abstract).Count < 100);
```

The problem is that SQL Server doesn't support regular expressions, so LINQ to SQL throws an exception, complaining that the query cannot be translated to SQL. We can solve this by querying in two steps: first retrieving all articles on influenza through a LINQ to SQL query, and then filtering *locally* for abstracts of less than 100 words:

```
Regex wordCounter = new Regex (@"\b(\w|[-'])+\b");

IEnumerable<MedicalArticle> sqlQuery = dataContext.MedicalArticles
  .Where (article => article.Topic == "influenza");

IEnumerable<MedicalArticle> localQuery = sqlQuery
  .Where (article => wordCounter.Matches (article.Abstract).Count < 100);
```

Because `sqlQuery` is of type `IEnumerable<MedicalArticle>`, the second query binds to the local query operators, forcing that part of the filtering to run on the client.

With `AsEnumerable`, we can do the same in a single query:

```
Regex wordCounter = new Regex (@"\b(\w|[-'])+\b");

var query = dataContext.MedicalArticles
  .Where (article => article.Topic == "influenza")
  .AsEnumerable()
  .Where (article => wordCounter.Matches (article.Abstract).Count < 100);
```

An alternative to calling `AsEnumerable` is to call `ToArray` or `ToList`. The advantage of `AsEnumerable` is that it doesn't force immediate query execution, nor does it create any storage structure.

> Moving query processing from the database server to the client can hurt performance, especially if it means retrieving more rows. A more efficient (though more complex) way to solve our example would be to use SQL CLR integration to expose a function on the database that implemented the regular expression.

We demonstrate combined interpreted and local queries further in Chapter 10.

LINQ to SQL

Throughout this and the following chapter, we rely on LINQ to SQL to demonstrate interpreted queries. This section examines the key features of this technology.

LINQ to SQL Entity Classes

LINQ to SQL allows you to use any class to represent data, as long as you decorate it with appropriate attributes. Here's a simple example:

```
[Table]
public class Customer
{
  [Column(IsPrimaryKey=true)]
  public int ID;

  [Column]
  public string Name;
}
```

The [Table] attribute, in the System.Data.Linq.Mapping namespace, tells LINQ to SQL that an object of this type represents a row in a database table. By default, it assumes the table name matches the class name; if this is not the case, you can specify the table name as follows:

```
[Table (Name="Customers")]
```

A class decorated with the [Table] attribute is called an *entity* in LINQ to SQL. To be useful, its structure must closely—or exactly—match that of a database table, making it a low-level construct.

The [Column] attribute flags a field or property that maps to a column in a table. If the column name differs from the field or property name, you can specify the column name as follows:

```
[Column (Name="FullName")]
public string Name;
```

The IsPrimaryKey property in the [Column] attribute indicates that the column partakes in the table's primary key and is required for maintaining object identity, as well as allowing updates to be written back to the database.

Instead of defining public fields, you can define public properties in conjunction with private fields. This allows you to write validation logic into the property accessors. If you take this route, you can optionally instruct LINQ to SQL to bypass your property accessors and write to the field directly when populating from the database:

```
string _name;

[Column (Storage="_name")]
public string Name { get { return _name; } set { _name = value; } }
```

Column(Storage="_name") tells LINQ to SQL to write directly to the _name field (rather than the Name property) when populating the entity. LINQ to SQL's use of reflection allows the field to be private—as in this example.

DataContext

Once you've defined entity classes, start querying by instantiating a DataContext object and then calling GetTable on it. The following example uses the Customer class defined originally.

```
DataContext dataContext = new DataContext ("connection string");
Table<Customer> customers = dataContext.GetTable <Customer>( );

Console.WriteLine (customers.Count( ));                 // # of rows in table.

Customer cust = customers.Single (c => c.ID == 2);   // Retrieves Customer
                                                      // with ID of 2.
```

 The Single operator is ideal for retrieving a row by primary key. Unlike First, it throws an exception if more than one element is returned.

A DataContext object does two things. First, it acts as a factory for generating tables that you can query. Second, it keeps track of any changes that you make to your entities so that you can write them back:

```
DataContext dataContext = new DataContext ("connection string");
Table<Customer> customers = dataContext.GetTable <Customer>( );
Customer cust = customers.OrderBy (c => c.Name).First( );
cust.Name = "Updated Name";
dataContext.SubmitChanges( );
```

A DataContext object keeps track of all the entities it instantiates, so it can feed the same ones back to you whenever you request the same rows in a table. In other words, a DataContext object in its lifetime will never emit two separate entities that refer to the same row in a table (where a row is identified by primary key).

 You can disable this behavior by setting ObjectTrackingEnabled to false on the DataContext object. (Disabling object tracking also prevents you from submitting updates to the data.)

To illustrate object tracking, suppose the customer whose name is alphabetically first also has the lowest ID. In the following example, a and b will reference the same object:

```
DataContext dataContext = new DataContext ("connection string");
Table<Customer> customers = dataContext.GetTable <Customer>( );

Customer a = customers.OrderBy (c => c.Name).First( );
Customer b = customers.OrderBy (c => c.ID).First( );
```

This has a couple of interesting consequences. First, consider what happens when LINQ to SQL encounters the second query. It starts by querying the database—and obtaining a single row. It then reads the primary key of this row and performs a lookup in the DataContext's entity cache. Seeing a match, it returns the existing object *without updating any values*. So, if another user had just updated that customer's Name in the database, the new value would be ignored. This is essential for avoiding unexpected side effects (the Customer object could be in use elsewhere) and also for managing concurrency. If you had altered properties on the Customer object and not yet called SubmitChanges, you wouldn't want your properties automatically overwritten.

To get fresh information from the database, you must either instantiate a new `DataContext` or call the `DataContext`'s `Refresh` method, passing in the entity or entities that you want refreshed.

The second consequence is that you cannot explicitly project into an entity type—to select a subset of the row's columns—without causing trouble. For example, if you want to retrieve only a customer's name, any of the following approaches is valid:

```
customers.Select (c => c.Name);
customers.Select (c => new { Name = c.Name } );
customers.Select (c => new MyCustomType { Name = c.Name } );
```

The following, however, is not:

```
customers.Select (c => new Customer { Name = c.Name } );
```

This is because the `Customer` entities will end up partially populated. So, the next time you perform a query that requests *all* customer columns, you get the same cached `Customer` objects with only the `Name` property populated.

 In a multitier application, you cannot use a single static instance of a `DataContext` object in the middle tier to handle all requests, because `DataContext` is not thread-safe. Instead, middle-tier methods must create a fresh `DataContext` object per client request. This is actually beneficial because it shifts the burden in handling simultaneous updates to the database server, which is properly equipped for the job. A database server, for instance, will apply transaction isolation-level semantics.

Automatic Entity Generation

Because LINQ to SQL entity classes need to follow the structure of their underlying tables, it's likely that you'll want to generate them automatically from an existing database schema. You can do this via either the SqlMetal command-line tool or the LINQ to SQL designer in Visual Studio. These tools generate entities as partial classes so that you can incorporate additional logic in separate files.

As a bonus, you also get a strongly typed `DataContext` class. This is simply a subclassed `DataContext` with properties that return tables of each entity type. It saves you calling `GetTable`:

```
var dataContext = new MyTypedDataContext ("connection string");
Table<Customer> customers = dataContext.Customers;
Console.WriteLine (customers.Count( ));
```

or simply:

```
Console.WriteLine (dataContext.Customers.Count( ));
```

The LINQ to SQL designer automatically pluralizes identifiers where appropriate; in this example, it's `dataContext.Customers` and not `dataContext.Customer`—even though the SQL table and entity class are both called `Customer`.

Associations

The entity generation tools perform another useful job. For each relationship defined in your database, properties are automatically generated on each side that query that relationship. For example, suppose we define a customer and purchase table in a one-to-many relationship:

```
create table Customer
(
  ID int not null primary key,
  Name varchar(30) not null
)

create table Purchase
(
  ID int not null primary key,
  CustomerID int references Customer (ID),
  Description varchar(30) not null,
  Price decimal not null
)
```

If we use automatically generated entity classes, we can write these queries as follows:

```
var dataContext = new MyTypedDataContext ("connection string");

// Retrieve all purchases made by the first customer (alphabetically):

Customer cust1 = dataContext.Customers.OrderBy (c => c.Name).First();
foreach (Purchase p in cust1.Purchases)
  Console.WriteLine (p.Price);

// Retrieve the customer who made the lowest value purchase:

Purchase cheapest = dataContext.Purchases.OrderBy (p => p.Price).First();
Customer cust2 = cheapest.Customer;
```

Further, if cust1 and cust2 happened to refer to the same customer, c1 and c2 would *refer to the same object*: cust1==cust2 would return true.

Let's examine the signature of the automatically generated Purchases property on the Customer entity:

```
[Association (Storage="_Purchases", OtherKey="CustomerID")]
public EntitySet <Purchase> Purchases { get {...} set {...} }
```

An EntitySet is like a predefined query, with a built-in Where clause that extracts related entities. The [Association] attribute gives LINQ to SQL the information it needs to write the query. As with any other type of query, you get deferred execution. This means that with an EntitySet, the query doesn't execute until you enumerate over the related collection.

Here's the Purchases.Customer property, on the other side of the relationship:

```
[Association (Storage="_Customer",ThisKey="CustomerID",IsForeignKey=true)]
public Customer Customer { get {...} set {...} }
```

Although the property is of type Customer, its underlying field (_Customer) is of type EntityRef. The EntityRef type implements deferred loading, so the related Customer is not retrieved from the database until you actually ask for it.

Deferred Execution with LINQ to SQL

LINQ to SQL queries are subject to deferred execution, just like local queries. This allows you to build queries progressively. There is one aspect, however, in which LINQ to SQL has special deferred execution semantics, and that is when a subquery appears inside a Select expression:

- With local queries, you get double deferred execution, because from a functional perspective, you're selecting a sequence of *queries*. So, if you enumerate the outer result sequence, but never enumerate the inner sequences, the subquery will never execute.

- With LINQ to SQL, the subquery is executed at the same time as the main outer query. This avoids excessive round-tripping.

For example, the following query executes in a single round trip upon reaching the first foreach statement:

```
var dataContext = new MyTypedDataContext ("connection string");

var query = from c in dataContext.Customers
            select
                from p in c.Purchases
                select new { c.Name, p.Price };

foreach (var customerPurchaseResults in query)
  foreach (var namePrice in customerPurchaseResults)
    Console.WriteLine (namePrice.Name + " spent " + namePrice.Price);
```

Any EntitySets that you explicitly project are fully populated in a single round trip:

```
var query = from c in dataContext.Customers
            select new { c.Name, c.Purchases };

foreach (var row in query)
  foreach (Purchase p in row.Purchases)    // No extra round-tripping
    Console.WriteLine (row.Name + " spent " + p.Price);
```

But if we enumerate EntitySet properties without first having projected, deferred execution rules apply. In the following example, LINQ to SQL executes another Purchases query on each loop iteration:

```
foreach (Customer c in dataContext.Customers)
  foreach (Purchase p in c.Purchases)    // Another SQL round-trip
    Console.WriteLine (c.Name + " spent " + p.Price);
```

This model is advantageous when you want to *selectively* execute the inner loop, based on a test that can be performed only on the client:

```
foreach (Customer c in dataContext.Customers)
  if (myWebService.HasBadCreditHistory (c.ID))
    foreach (Purchase p in c.Purchases)    // Another SQL round trip
      Console.WriteLine (...);
```

LINQ Queries

In Chapter 9, we explore `Select` subqueries in more detail, in the section "Projecting."

DataLoadOptions

The `DataLoadOptions` class has two distinct uses:

- It lets you specify, in advance, a filter for `EntitySet` associations (`AssociateWith`).
- It lets you request that certain `EntitySets` be eagerly loaded, to lessen round-tripping (`LoadWith`).

Specifying a filter in advance

Let's refactor our previous example as follows:

```
foreach (Customer c in dataContext.Customers)
  if (myWebService.HasBadCreditHistory (c.ID))
    ProcessCustomer (c);
```

We'll define `ProcessCustomer` like this:

```
void ProcessCustomer (Customer c)
{
  Console.WriteLine (c.ID + " " + c.Name);
  foreach (Purchase p in c.Purchases)
    Console.WriteLine ("  - purchased a " + p.Description);
}
```

Now suppose we want to feed `ProcessCustomer` only a *subset* of each customer's purchases; say, the high-value ones. Here's one solution:

```
foreach (Customer c in dataContext.Customers)
  if (myWebService.HasBadCreditHistory (c.ID))
    ProcessCustomer (c.ID,
                     c.Name,
                     c.Purchases.Where (p => p.Price > 1000));
...
void ProcessCustomer (int custID, string custName,
                      IEnumerable<Purchase> purchases)
{
  Console.WriteLine (custID + " " + custName);
  foreach (Purchase p in purchases)
    Console.WriteLine ("  - purchased a " + p.Description);
}
```

This is messy. It would get messier still if `ProcessCustomer` required more `Customer` fields. A better solution is to use `DataLoadOptions`'s `AssociateWith` method:

```
DataLoadOptions options = new DataLoadOptions();
options.AssociateWith <Customer>
  (c => c.Purchases.Where (p => p.Price > 1000));
dataContext.LoadOptions = options;
```

This instructs our DataContext instance always to filter a `Customer`'s `Purchases` using the given predicate. We can now use the original version of `ProcessCustomer`.

AssociateWith doesn't change deferred execution semantics. When a particular relationship is used, it simply instructs to implicitly add a particular filter to the equation.

Eager loading

The second use for a `DataLoadOptions` is to request that certain `EntitySets` be eagerly loaded with their parent. For instance, suppose you want to load all customers and their purchases in a single SQL round trip. The following does exactly this:

```
DataLoadOptions options = new DataLoadOptions();
options.LoadWith <Customer> (c => c.Purchases);
dataContext.LoadOptions = options;

foreach (Customer c in dataContext.Customers)      // One round trip:
  foreach (Purchase p in c.Purchases)
    Console.WriteLine (c.Name + " bought a " + p.Description);
```

This instructs that whenever a `Customer` is retrieved, its `Purchases` should be also at the same time. You can also request that grandchildren be included:

```
options.LoadWith <Customer> (c => c.Purchases);
options.LoadWith <Purchase> (p => p.PurchaseItems);
```

You can combine `LoadWith` with `AssociateWith`. The following instructs that whenever a customer is retrieved, its *high-value* purchases should be retrieved in the same round trip:

```
options.LoadWith <Customer> (c => c.Purchases);
options.AssociateWith <Customer>
  (c => c.Purchases.Where (p => p.Price > 1000));
```

Updates

LINQ to SQL also keeps track of changes that you make to your entities and allows you to write them back to the database by calling `SubmitChanges` on the `DataContext` object. The `Table<>` class provides `InsertOnSubmit` and `DeleteOnSubmit` methods for inserting and deleting rows in a table. Here's how to insert a row:

```
var dataContext = new MyTypedDataContext ("connection string");

Customer cust = new Customer { ID=1000, Name="Bloggs" };
dataContext.Customers.InsertOnSubmit (cust);
dataContext.SubmitChanges();
```

We can later retrieve that row, update it, and then delete it:

```
var dataContext = new MyTypedDataContext ("connection string");

Customer cust = dataContext.Customers.Single (c => c.ID == 1000);
cust.Name = "Bloggs2";
dataContext.SubmitChanges();                     // Updates the customer

dataContext.Customers.DeleteOnSubmit (cust);
dataContext.SubmitChanges();                     // Deletes the customer
```

`DataContext.SubmitChanges` gathers all the changes that were made to its entities since the `DataContext`'s creation (or the last `SubmitChanges`), and then executes a SQL statement to write them to the database. Any `TransactionScope` is honored; if none is present it wraps all statements in a new transaction.

You can also add new or existing rows to an `EntitySet` by calling `Add`. LINQ to SQL automatically populates the foreign keys when you do this:

```
Purchase p1 = new Purchase { ID=100, Description="Bike", Price=500 };
Purchase p2 = new Purchase { ID=101, Description="Tools", Price=100 };

Customer cust = dataContext.Customers.Single (c => c.ID == 1);

cust.Purchases.Add (p1);
cust.Purchases.Remove (p2);

dataContext.SubmitChanges();          // Inserts the two purchases
```

 If you don't want the burden of allocating unique keys, you can use either an auto-incrementing field (IDENTITY in SQL Server) or a Guid for the primary key.

In this example, LINQ to SQL automatically writes 100 into the `CustomerID` column of each of the new purchases (it knows to do this because of the association that we defined on the `Purchases` property):

```
[Association (Storage="_Purchases", OtherKey="CustomerID")]
public EntitySet <Purchase> Purchases { get {...} set {...} }
```

If the `Customer` and `Purchase` entities were generated by the Visual Studio designer or SqlMetal, the generated classes would include further code to keep the two sides of each relationship in sync. In other words, assigning the `Purchase.Customer` property would automatically add the new customer to the `Customer.Purchases` entity set—and vice versa. We can illustrate this by rewriting the preceding example as follows:

```
var dataContext = new MyTypedDataContext ("connection string");

Customer cust = dataContext.Customers.Single (c => c.ID == 1);
new Purchase { ID=100, Description="Bike", Price=500, Customer=cust };
new Purchase { ID=101, Description="Tools", Price=100, Customer=cust };

dataContext.SubmitChanges();          // Inserts the two purchases
```

When you remove a row from an `EntitySet`, its foreign key field is automatically set to `null`. The following disassociates our two recently added purchases from their customer:

```
var dataContext = new MyTypedDataContext ("connection string");

Customer cust = dataContext.Customers.Single (c => c.ID == 1);

cust.Purchases.Remove (cust.Purchases.Single (p => p.ID == 100));
cust.Purchases.Remove (cust.Purchases.Single (p => p.ID == 101));

dataContext.SubmitChanges();          // Submit SQL to database
```

Because this tries to set each purchase's CustomerID field to null, Purchase.CustomerID must be nullable in the database-otherwise an exception is thrown. (Further, the CustomerID field or property in the entity class must be a nullable type.)

To delete child entities entirely, remove them from the Table<> instead:

```
Customer cust = dataContext.Customers.Single (c => c.ID == 1);

var dc = dataContext;
dc.Purchases.DeleteOnSubmit (dc.Purchases.Single (p => p.ID == 100));
dc.Purchases.DeleteOnSubmit (dc.Purchases.Single (p => p.ID == 101));

dataContext.SubmitChanges();          // Submit SQL to database
```

Building Query Expressions

So far in this chapter, when we've needed to dynamically compose queries, we've done so by conditionally chaining query operators. Although this is adequate in many scenarios, sometimes you need to work at a more granular level and dynamically compose the lambda expressions that feed the operators.

In this section, we'll assume the following Product class:

```
[Table] public partial class Product
{
  [Column(IsPrimaryKey=true)]  public int ID;
  [Column]                     public string Description;
  [Column]                     public bool Discontinued;
  [Column]                     public DateTime LastSale;
}
```

Delegates Versus Expression Trees

Recall that:

- Local queries, which use Enumerable operators, take delegates.
- Interpreted queries, which use Queryable operators, take expression trees.

We can see this by comparing the signature of the Where operator in Enumerable and Queryable:

```
public static IEnumerable<TSource> Where<TSource> (this
    IEnumerable<TSource> source, Func<TSource,bool> predicate)

public static IQueryable<TSource> Where<TSource> (this
    IQueryable<TSource> source, Expression<Func<TSource,bool>> predicate)
```

When embedded within a query, a lambda expression looks identical whether it binds to Enumerable's operators or Queryable's operators:

```
IEnumerable<Product> q1 = localProducts.Where (p => !p.Discontinued);
IQueryable<Product>  q2 = sqlProducts.Where  (p => !p.Discontinued);
```

When you assign a lambda expression to an intermediate variable, however, you must be explicit on whether to resolve to a delegate (i.e., Func<>) or an expression

LINQ Queries

tree (i.e., Expression<Func<>>). In the following example, predicate1 and predicate2 are not interchangeable:

```
Func <Product, bool> predicate1 = p => !p.Discontinued;
IEnumerable<Product> q1 = localProducts.Where (predicate1);

Expression <Func <Product, bool>> predicate2 = p => !p.Discontinued;
IQueryable<Product> q2 = sqlProducts.Where (predicate2);
```

Compiling expression trees

You can convert an expression tree to a delegate by calling Compile. This is of particular value when writing methods that return reusable expressions. To illustrate, we'll add a static method to the Product class that returns a predicate evaluating to true if a product is not discontinued and has sold in the past 30 days:

```
public partial class Product
{
  public static Expression<Func<Product, bool>> IsSelling()
  {
    return p => !p.Discontinued && p.LastSale > DateTime.Now.AddDays (-30);
  }
}
```

(We've defined this in a separate partial class to avoid being overwritten by an automatic DataContext generator such as Visual Studio's LINQ to SQL designer.)

The method just written can be used both in interpreted and in local queries as follows:

```
void Test()
{
  var dataContext = new MyTypedDataContext ("connection string");
  Product[] localProducts = dataContext.Products.ToArray();

  IQueryable<Product> sqlQuery =
    dataContext.Products.Where (Product.IsSelling());

  IEnumerable<Product> localQuery =
    localProducts.Where (Product.IsSelling.Compile());
}
```

 You cannot convert in the reverse direction, from a delegate to an expression tree. This makes expression trees more versatile.

AsQueryable

The AsQueryable operator lets you write whole *queries* that can run over either local or remote sequences:

```
IQueryable<Product> FilterSortProducts (IQueryable<Product> input)
{
    return from p in input
           where ...
           order by ...
           select p;
}

void Test()
{
    var dataContext = new MyTypedDataContext ("connection string");
    Product[] localProducts = dataContext.Products.ToArray();

    var sqlQuery   = FilterSortProducts (dataContext.Products);
    var localQuery = FilterSortProducts (localProducts.AsQueryable());
    ...
}
```

AsQueryable wraps IQueryable<> clothing around a local sequence so that subsequent query operators resolve to expression trees. When you later enumerate over the result, the expression trees are implicitly compiled, and the local sequence enumerates as it would ordinarily.

Expression Trees

We said previously, that assigning a lambda expression to a variable of type Expression<TDelegate> causes the C# compiler to emit an expression tree. With some programming effort, you can do the same thing manually at runtime—in other words, dynamically build an expression tree from scratch. The result can be cast to an Expression<TDelegate> and used in LINQ to SQL queries, or compiled into an ordinary delegate by calling Compile.

The Expression DOM

An expression tree is a miniature code DOM. Each node in the tree is represented by a type in the System.Linq.Expressions namespace; these types are illustrated in Figure 8-11.

The base class for all nodes is the (nongeneric) Expression class. The generic Expression<TDelegate> class actually means "typed lambda expression" and might have been named LambdaExpression<TDelegate> if it wasn't for the clumsiness of this:

```
LambdaExpression<Func<Customer,bool>> f = ...
```

Expression<>'s base type is the (nongeneric) LambdaExpression class. LamdbaExpression provides type unification for lambda expression trees: any typed Expression<> can be cast to a LambdaExpression.

The thing that distinguishes LambdaExpressions from ordinary Expressions is that lambda expressions have *parameters*.

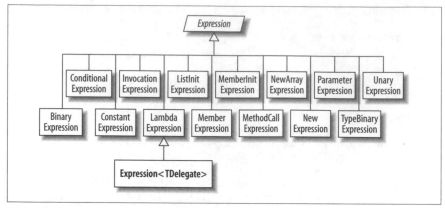

Figure 8-11. Expression types

To create an expression tree, don't instantiate node types directly; rather, you call static methods provided on the Expression class. Here are all the methods:

Add	ElementInit	MakeMemberAccess	Or
AddChecked	Equal	MakeUnary	OrElse
And	ExclusiveOr	MemberBind	Parameter
AndAlso	Field	MemberInit	Power
ArrayIndex	GreaterThan	Modulo	Property
ArrayLength	GreaterThanOrEqual	Multiply	PropertyOrField
Bind	Invoke	MultiplyChecked	Quote
Call	Lambda	Negate	RightShift
Coalesce	LeftShift	NegateChecked	Subtract
Condition	LessThan	New	SubtractChecked
Constant	LessThanOrEqual	NewArrayBounds	TypeAs
Convert	ListBind	NewArrayInit	TypeIs
ConvertChecked	ListInit	Not	UnaryPlus
Divide	MakeBinary	NotEqual	

Figure 8-12 shows the expression tree that the following assignment creates:

```
Expression<Func<string, bool>> f = s => s.Length < 5;
```

We can demonstrate this as follows:

```
Console.WriteLine (f.Body.NodeType);                      // LessThan
Console.WriteLine (((BinaryExpression) f.Body).Right);    // 5
```

Let's now build this expression from scratch. The principle is that you start from the bottom of the tree and work your way up. The bottommost thing in our tree is a ParameterExpression, the lambda expression parameter called "s" of type string:

```
ParameterExpression p = Expression.Parameter (typeof (string), "s");
```

The next step is to build the MemberExpression and ConstantExpression. In the former case, we need to access the Length *property* of our parameter, "s":

```
MemberExpression stringLength = Expression.Property (p, "Length");
ConstantExpression five = Expression.Constant (5);
```

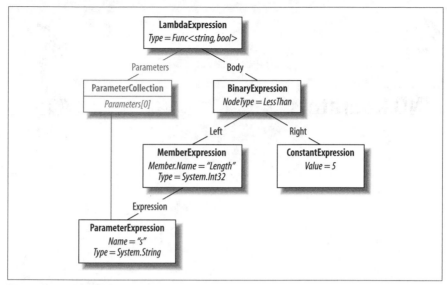

Figure 8-12. Expression tree

Next is the `LessThan` comparison:

```
BinaryExpression comparison = Expression.LessThan (stringLength, five);
```

The final step is to construct the lambda expression, which links an expression Body to a collection of parameters:

```
Expression<Func<string, bool>> lambda
    = Expression.Lambda<Func<string, bool>> (comparison, p);
```

A convenient way to test our lambda is by compiling it to a delegate:

```
Func<string, bool> runnable = lambda.Compile( );

Console.WriteLine (runnable ("kangaroo"));        // False
Console.WriteLine (runnable ("dog"));             // True
```

 The easiest way to figure out which expression type to use is to examine an existing lambda expression in the Visual Studio debugger.

We continue this discussion online, at *http://www.albahari.com/expressions/*.

9

LINQ Operators

This chapter describes each of the LINQ query operators. As well as serving as a reference, two of the sections, "Projection" and "Joining," cover a number of conceptual areas:

- Projecting object hierarchies
- Joining with Select, SelectMany, Join, and GroupJoin
- Outer iteration variables in query comprehension syntax

All of the examples in this chapter assume that a names array is defined as follows:

```
string[] names = { "Tom", "Dick", "Harry", "Mary", "Jay" };
```

Examples that use LINQ to SQL assume a typed DataContext variable called dataContext:

```
var dataContext = new DemoDataContext();

...

public class DemoDataContext : DataContext
{
  public DemoDataContext (string cxString) : base (cxString) {}

  public Table<Customer> Customers { get { return GetTable<Customer>(); } }
  public Table<Purchase> Purchases { get { return GetTable<Purchase>(); } }
}

[Table] public class Customer
{
  [Column(IsPrimaryKey=true)]  public int ID;
  [Column]                     public string Name;

  [Association (OtherKey="CustomerID")]
  public EntitySet<Purchase> Purchases = new EntitySet<Purchase>();
```

```
    }

    [Table] public class Purchase
    {
        [Column(IsPrimaryKey=true)]  public int ID;
        [Column]                     public int? CustomerID;
        [Column]                     public string Description;
        [Column]                     public decimal Price;
        [Column]                     public DateTime Date;

        EntityRef<Customer> custRef;

        [Association (Storage="custRef",ThisKey="CustomerID",IsForeignKey=true)]
        public Customer Customer
        {
          get { return custRef.Entity; } set { custRef.Entity = value; }
        }
    }
```

 The LINQ to SQL entity classes shown are a simplified version of what automated tools typically produce, and do not include code to update the opposing side in a relationship when their entities have been reassigned.

Here are their corresponding SQL table definitions:

```
create table Customer
(
  ID int not null primary key,
  Name varchar(30) not null
)
create table Purchase
(
  ID int not null primary key,
  CustomerID int references Customer (ID),
  Description varchar(30) not null,
  Price decimal not null
)
```

Overview

In this section, we provide an overview of the query operators supported by C# 3.0. C# query operators tend to fall into one of three categories, and this is a convenient way to present them:

- Collection in, collection out (collection to collection)
- Collection, single element or scalar value out
- Single element or scalar value in, and collection out

We first present each of the three categories and the query operators they include, and then we take up each individual query operator in detail.

Collection → Collection

Most query operators accept one or more input collections and emit one or more output collections. Figure 9-1 illustrates those operators that restructure the shape of the collections.

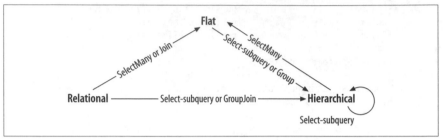

Figure 9-1. Shape-changing operators

Filtering

```
IEnumerable<TSource> → IEnumerable<TSource>
```

Returns a subset of the original elements.

> Where, Take, TakeWhile, Skip, SkipWhile, Distinct

Projecting

```
IEnumerable<TSource> → IEnumerable<TResult>
```

Transforms each element with a lambda function. SelectMany flattens nested collections; Select and SelectMany perform inner joins, left outer joins, cross joins, and non-equi joins with LINQ to SQL.

> Select, SelectMany

Joining

```
IEnumerable<TOuter>, IEnumerable<TInner> → IEnumerable<TResult>
```

Meshes elements of one collection with another. The joining operators are designed to be efficient with local queries and support inner and left outer joins.

> Join, GroupJoin

Ordering

```
IEnumerable<TSource> → IOrderedEnumerable<TSource>
```

Returns a reordering of a collection.

> OrderBy, ThenBy, Reverse

Grouping

```
IEnumerable<TSource> → IEnumerable<IGrouping<TSource,TElement>>
```

Groups a collection into subcollections.

    GroupBy

Set operators

IEnumerable<TSource>, IEnumerable<TSource> → IEnumerable<TSource>

Takes two same-typed collections and returns their commonality, sum, or difference.

    Concat, Union, Intersect, Except

Conversion methods: Import

IEnumerable → IEnumerable<TResult>

    OfType, Cast

Conversion methods: Export

IEnumerable<TSource> → An array, list, dictionary, lookup, or sequence

    ToArray, ToList, ToDictionary, ToLookup, AsEnumerable, AsQueryable

Collection → Noncollection

The following query operators accept an input collection and emit a single element or scalar value.

Element operators

IEnumerable<TSource> → TSource

Picks a single element from a collection.

    First, FirstOrDefault, Last, LastOrDefault, Single, SingleOrDefault,
    ElementAt, ElementAtOrDefault, DefaultIfEmpty

Aggregation methods

IEnumerable<TSource> → *scalar*

Performs a computation across a collection, returning a scalar value (typically a number).

    Aggregate, Average, Count, LongCount, Sum, Max, Min

Quantifiers

IEnumerable<TSource> → *bool*

An aggregation returning true or false.

    All, Any, Contains, SequenceEqual

Noncollection → Collection

In the third and final category are query operators that accept no input collection and produce an output collection from scratch.

Generation methods

void → IEnumerable<TResult>

Manufactures a simple collection.

    Empty, Range, Repeat

Filtering

IEnumerable<TSource> → IEnumerable<TSource>

Method	Description	SQL equivalents
Where	Returns a subset of elements that satisfy a given condition	WHERE
Take	Returns the first count elements and discards the rest	WHERE ROW_NUMBER( )... *or* TOP *n* subquery
Skip	Ignores the first count elements and returns the rest	WHERE ROW_NUMBER( )... *or* NOT IN (SELECT TOP *n*...)
TakeWhile	Emits elements from the input sequence until the predicate is true	Exception thrown
SkipWhile	Ignores elements from the input sequence until the predicate is true, and then emits the rest	Exception thrown
Distinct	Returns a collection that excludes duplicates	SELECT DISTINCT...

The "SQL equivalents" column in the reference tables in this chapter do not necessarily correspond to what an IQueryable implementation such as LINQ to SQL will produce. Rather, it indicates what you'd typically use to do the same job if you were writing the SQL query yourself. Where there is no simple translation, the column is left blank. Where there is no translation at all, the column reads "Exception thrown".

Enumerable implementation code, when shown, excludes checking for null arguments and indexing predicates.

With each of the filtering methods, you always end up with either the same number or fewer elements than you started with. You can never get more! The elements are also identical when they come out; they are not transformed in any way.

Where

Argument	Type
Source sequence	IEnumerable<TSource>
Predicate	TSource => bool or (TSource,int) => bool[a]

[a] Prohibited with LINQ to SQL

Comprehension syntax

```
where bool-expression
```

Enumerable.Where implementation

The internal implementation of Enumerable.Where, null checking aside, is functionally equivalent to the following:

```
public static IEnumerable<TSource> Where<TSource>
  (this IEnumerable<TSource> source, Func <TSource, bool> predicate)
{
  foreach (TSource element in source)
    if (predicate (element))
      yield return element;
}
```

Overview

Where returns the elements from the input sequence that satisfy the given predicate.

For instance:

```
string[] names = { "Tom", "Dick", "Harry", "Mary", "Jay" };
IEnumerable<string> query = names.Where (name => name.EndsWith ("y"));

// Result: { "Harry", "Mary", "Jay" }
```

In comprehension syntax:

```
IEnumerable<string> query = from n in names
                            where n.EndsWith ("y")
                            select n;
```

A where clause can appear more than once in a query and be interspersed with let clauses:

```
from n in names
where n.Length > 3
let u = n.ToUpper( )
where u.EndsWith ("Y")
select u;                    // Result: { "HARRY", "MARY" }
```

Standard C# scoping rules apply to such queries. In other words, you cannot refer to a variable prior to declaring it with an iteration variable or a let clause.

Indexed filtering

Where's predicate optionally accepts a second argument, of type int. This is fed with the position of each element within the input sequence, allowing the predicate to use this information in its filtering decision. For example, the following skips every second element:

```
IEnumerable<string> query = names.Where ((n, i) => i % 2 == 0);

// Result: { "Tom", "Harry", "Jay" }
```

An exception is thrown if you use indexed filtering in LINQ to SQL.

Where in LINQ to SQL

The following methods on string translate to SQL's LIKE operator:

```
Contains, StartsWith, EndsWith
```

For instance, c.Name.Contains ("abc") translates to customer.Name LIKE '%abc%' (or more accurately, a parameterized version of this). You can perform more complex comparisons by calling SqlMethods.Like—this method maps directly to SQL's LIKE operator. You can also perform *order* comparison on strings with string's CompareTo method; this maps to SQL's < and > operators:

```
dataContext.Purchases.Where (p => p.Description.CompareTo ("C") < 0)
```

LINQ to SQL also allows you to apply the Contains operator to a local collection within a filter predicate. For instance:

```
string[] chosenOnes = { "Tom", "Jay" };

from c in dataContext.Customers
where chosenOnes.Contains (c.Name)
...
```

This maps to SQL's IN operator—in other words:

```
WHERE customer.Name IN ("Tom", "Jay")
```

If the local collection is an array of entities or nonscalar types, LINQ to SQL may instead emit an EXISTS clause.

Take and Skip

Argument	Type
Source sequence	IEnumerable<TSource>
Number of elements to take or skip	int

Take emits the first *n* elements and discards the rest; Skip discards the first *n* elements and emits the rest. The two methods are useful together when implementing a web page allowing a user to navigate through a large set of matching records. For instance, suppose a user searches a book database for the term "mercury," and there are 100 matches. The following returns the first 20:

```
IQueryable<Book> query = dataContext.Books
    .Where   (b => b.Title.Contains ("mercury"))
    .OrderBy (b => b.Title)
    .Take (20);
```

The next query returns books 21 to 40:

```
IQueryable<Book> query = dataContext.Books
    .Where   (b => b.Title.Contains ("mercury"))
    .OrderBy (b => b.Title)
    .Skip (20).Take (20);
```

LINQ to SQL translates Take and Skip to the ROW_NUMBER function in SQL Server 2005, or a TOP *n* subquery in earlier versions of SQL Server.

TakeWhile and SkipWhile

Argument	Type
Source sequence	IEnumerable<TSource>
Predicate	TSource => bool or (TSource,int) => bool

TakeWhile enumerates the input sequence, emitting each item, until the given predicate is true. It then ignores the remaining elements:

```
int[] numbers    = { 3, 5, 2, 234, 4, 1 };
var takeWhileSmall = numbers.TakeWhile (n => n < 100);   // { 3, 5, 2 }
```

SkipWhile enumerates the input sequence, ignoring each item until the given predicate is true. It then emits the remaining elements:

```
int[] numbers    = { 3, 5, 2, 234, 4, 1 };
var skipWhileSmall = numbers.SkipWhile (n => n < 100);   // { 234, 4, 1 }
```

TakeWhile and SkipWhile have no translation to SQL and cause a runtime error if used in a LINQ to SQL query.

Distinct

Distinct returns the input sequence, stripped of duplicates. Only the default equality comparer can be used for equality comparison. The following returns distinct letters in a string:

```
char[] distinctLetters = "HelloWorld".Distinct().ToArray();
string s = new string (distinctLetters);                // HeloWrd
```

We can call LINQ methods directly on a string, because string implements IEnumerable<char>.

Projecting

IEnumerable<TSource> → IEnumerable<TResult>

Method	Description	SQL equivalents
Select	Transforms each input element with the given lambda expression	SELECT
SelectMany	Transforms each input element, and then flattens and concatenates the resultant subsequences	INNER JOIN, LEFT OUTER JOIN, CROSS JOIN

 For LINQ to SQL queries, Select and SelectMany are the most versatile joining constructs; for local queries, Join and GroupJoin are the most *efficient* joining constructs.

Select

Argument	Type
Source sequence	IEnumerable<TSource>
Result selector	TSource => TResult or (TSource,int) => TResult[a]

[a] Prohibited with LINQ to SQL

Comprehension syntax

```
select projection-expression
```

Enumerable implementation

```
public static IEnumerable<TResult> Select<TSource,TResult>
  (this IEnumerable<TSource> source, Func<TSource,TResult> selector)
{
  foreach (TSource element in source)
    yield return selector (element);
}
```

Overview

With Select, you always get the same number of elements that you started with. Each element, however, can be transformed in any manner by the lambda function.

The following selects the names of all fonts installed on the computer (from System.Drawing):

```
IEnumerable<string> query = from f in FontFamily.Families
                            select f.Name;

foreach (string name in query) Console.WriteLine (name);
```

In this example, the select clause converts a FontFamily object to its name. Here's the lambda equivalent:

```
IEnumerable<string> query = FontFamily.Families.Select (f => f.Name);
```

Select statements are often used to project into anonymous types:

```
var query =
  from f in FontFamily.Families
  select new { f.Name, LineSpacing = f.GetLineSpacing (FontStyle.Bold) };
```

A projection with no transformation is sometimes used in comprehension queries, in order to satisfy the requirement that the query end in a select or group clause. The following selects fonts supporting strikeout:

```
IEnumerable<FontFamily> query =
  from f in FontFamily.Families
  where f.IsStyleAvailable (FontStyle.Strikeout)
  select f;

foreach (FontFamily ff in query) Console.WriteLine (ff.Name);
```

In such cases, the compiler omits the projection when translating to lambda syntax.

Indexed projection

The selector expression can optionally accept an integer argument, which acts as an indexer, providing the expression with the position of each input in the input sequence. This works only with local queries:

```
string[] names = { "Tom", "Dick", "Harry", "Mary", "Jay" };

IEnumerable<string> query = names
  .Select ((s,i) => i + "=" + s);      //  { "0=Tom", "1=Dick", ... }
```

Select subqueries and object hierarchies

You can nest a subquery in a select clause to build an object hierarchy. The following example returns a collection describing each directory under *D:\source*, with a subcollection of files under each directory:

```
DirectoryInfo[] dirs = new DirectoryInfo (@"d:\source").GetDirectories();

var query =
  from d in dirs
  where (d.Attributes & FileAttributes.System) == 0
  select new
  {
    DirectoryName = d.FullName,
    Created = d.CreationTime,
    Files = from f in d.GetFiles()
            where (f.Attributes & FileAttributes.Hidden) == 0
            select new { FileName = f.Name, f.Length, }
  };

foreach (var dirFiles in query)
{
  Console.WriteLine ("Directory: " + dirFiles.DirectoryName);
  foreach (var file in dirFiles.Files)
    Console.WriteLine ("   " + file.FileName + "Len: " + file.Length);
}
```

The inner portion of this query can be called a *correlated subquery*. A subquery is correlated if it references an object in the outer query—in this case, it references d, the directory being enumerated.

 A subquery inside a Select allows you to map one object hierarchy to another, or map a relational object model to a hierarchical object model.

With local queries, a subquery within a Select causes double-deferred execution. In our example, the files don't get filtered or projected until the inner foreach statement enumerates.

Subqueries and joins in LINQ to SQL

Subquery projections work well in LINQ to SQL and can be used to do the work of SQL-style joins. Here's how we retrieve each customer's name along with their high-value purchases:

```
var query =
    from c in dataContext.Customers
    select new {
                c.Name,
                Purchases = from p in dataContext.Purchases
                            where p.CustomerID == c.ID && p.Price > 1000
                            select new { p.Description, p.Price }
            };

foreach (var namePurchases in query)
{
    Console.WriteLine ("Customer: " + namePurchases.Name);
    foreach (var purchaseDetail in namePurchases.Purchases)
        Console.WriteLine ("  - $$$: " + purchaseDetail.Price);
}
```

 This style of query is ideally suited to interpreted queries. LINQ to SQL processes the outer query and subquery as a unit, avoiding unnecessary round-tripping. With local queries, however, it's inefficient because every combination of outer and inner elements must be enumerated to get the few matching combinations. A better choice for local queries is Join or GroupJoin, described in the following sections.

This query matches up objects from two disparate collections, and it can be thought of as a "join." The difference between this and a conventional database join (or subquery) is that we're not flattening the output into a single two-dimensional result set. We're mapping the relational data to hierarchical data, rather than to flat data.

Here's the same query simplified by using the Purchases association property on the Customer entity:

```
from c in dataContext.Customers
select new
{
```

```
        c.Name,
    Purchases = from p in c.Purchases      // Purchases is EntitySet<Purchase>
                where p.Price > 1000
                select new { p.Description, p.Price }
};
```

Both queries are analogous to a left outer join in SQL in the sense that we get all customers in the outer enumeration, regardless of whether they have any purchases. To emulate an inner join—where customers without high-value purchases are excluded—we would need to add a filter condition on the purchases collection:

```
from c in dataContext.Customers
where c.Purchases.Any (p => p.Price > 1000)
select new {
            c.Name,
            Purchases = from p in c.Purchases
                        where p.Price > 1000
                        select new { p.Description, p.Price }
        };
```

This is slightly untidy, however, in that we've written the same predicate (Price > 1000) twice. We can avoid this duplication with a let clause:

```
from c in dataContext.Customers
let highValueP = from p in c.Purchases
                 where p.Price > 1000
                 select new { p.Description, p.Price }
where highValueP.Any( )
select new { c.Name, Purchases = highValueP };
```

This style of query is flexible. By changing Any to Count, for instance, we can modify the query to retrieve only customers with at least two high-value purchases:

```
...
where highValueP.Count( ) >= 2
select new { c.Name, Purchases = highValueP };
```

Projecting into concrete types

Projecting into anonymous types is useful in obtaining intermediate results, but not so useful if you want to send a result set back to a client, for instance, because anonymous types can exist only as local variables within a method. An alternative is to use concrete types for projections, such as DataSets or custom business entity classes. A custom business entity is simply a class that you write with some properties, similar to a LINQ to SQL [Table] annotated class, but designed to hide lower-level (database-related) details. You might exclude foreign key fields from business entity classes, for instance. Assuming we wrote custom entity classes called CustomerEntity and PurchaseEntity, here's how we could project into them:

```
IQueryable<CustomerEntity> query =
    from c in dataContext.Customers
    select new CustomerEntity
    {
      Name = c.Name,
```

```
    Purchases =
      (from p in c.Purchases
      where p.Price > 1000
      select new PurchaseEntity {
                                Description = p.Description,
                                Value = p.Price
                              }
      ).ToList()
  };

  // Force query execution, converting output to a more convenient List:
  List<CustomerEntity> result = query.ToList();
```

Notice that so far, we've not had to use a Join or SelectMany statement. This is because we're maintaining the hierarchical shape of the data, as illustrated in Figure 9-2. With LINQ, you can often avoid the traditional SQL approach of flattening tables into a two-dimensional result set.

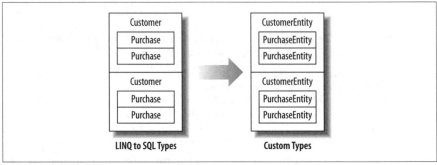

Figure 9-2. Projecting an object hierarchy

SelectMany

Argument	Type
Source sequence	IEnumerable<TSource>
Result selector	TSource => IEnumerable<TResult>
	or (TSource, int) => IEnumerable<TResult>[a]

[a] Prohibited with LINQ to SQL

Comprehension syntax

```
from identifier1 in enumerable-expression1
from identifier2 in enumerable-expression2
...
```

Enumerable implementation

```
public static IEnumerable<TResult> SelectMany<TSource,TResult>
  (IEnumerable<TSource> source,
   Func <TSource,IEnumerable<TResult>> selector)
{
  foreach (TSource element in source)
```

```
    foreach (TResult subElement in selector (element))
        yield return subElement;
}
```

Overview

SelectMany concatenates subsequences into a single flat output sequence.

Recall that for each input element, Select yields exactly one output element. In contrast, SelectMany yields *0..n* output elements. The *0..n* elements come from a subsequence or child sequence that the lambda expression must emit.

SelectMany can be used to expand child sequences, flatten nested collections, and join two collections into a flat output sequence. Using the conveyor belt analogy, SelectMany funnels fresh material onto a conveyor belt. With SelectMany, each input element is the *trigger* for the introduction of fresh material. The fresh material is emitted by the selector lambda expression and must be a sequence. In other words, the lambda expression must emit a *child sequence* per input *element*. The final result is a concatenation of the child sequences emitted for each input element.

Starting with a simple example, suppose we have an array of names as follows:

```
string[] fullNames = { "Anne Williams", "John Fred Smith", "Sue Green" };
```

which we wish to convert to a single flat collection of words—in other words:

```
"Anne", "Williams", "John", "Fred", "Smith", "Sue", Green"
```

SelectMany is ideal for this task, because we're mapping each input element to a variable number of output elements. All we must do is come up with a selector expression that converts each input element to a child sequence. string.Split does the job nicely: it takes a string and splits it into words, emitting the result as an array:

```
string testInputElement = "Anne Williams";
string[] childSequence  = testInputElement.Split( );

// childSequence is { "Anne", "Williams" };
```

So, here's our SelectMany query and the result:

IEnumerable<string> query = fullNames.SelectMany (name => name.Split( ));

```
foreach (string name in query)
    Console.Write (name + "|");   // Anne|Williams|John|Fred|Smith|Sue|Green|
```

If you replace SelectMany with Select, you get the same results in hierarchical form. The following emits a sequence of string *arrays*, requiring nested foreach statements to enumerate:

```
        IEnumerable<string[]> query =
            fullNames.Select (name => name.Split( ));

        foreach (string[] stringArray in query)
            foreach (string name in stringArray)
                Console.Write (name + "/");
```

The benefit of SelectMany is that it yields a single *flat* result sequence.

SelectMany is supported in query comprehension syntax and is invoked by having an *additional generator*—in other words, an extra from clause in the query. The from keyword has two meanings in comprehension syntax. At the start of a query, it introduces the original iteration variable and input sequence. *Anywhere else* in the query, it translates to SelectMany. Here's our query in comprehension syntax:

```
IEnumerable<string> query =
    from fullName in fullNames
    from name in fullName.Split()      // Translates to SelectMany
    select name;
```

Note that the additional generator introduces a new query variable—in this case, name. The new query variable becomes the iteration variable from then on, and the old iteration variable is demoted to an *outer iteration variable*.

Outer iteration variables

In the preceding example, fullName becomes an outer iteration variable after SelectMany. Outer iteration variables remain in scope until the query either ends or reaches an into clause. The extended scope of these variables is *the* killer scenario for comprehension syntax over lambda syntax.

To illustrate, we can take the preceding query and include fullName in the final projection:

```
IEnumerable<string> query =
    from fullName in fullNames        // fullName = outer variable
    from name in fullName.Split()     // name = iteration variable
    select name + " came from " + fullName;

Anne came from Anne Williams
Williams came from Anne Williams
John came from John Fred Smith
...
```

Behind the scenes, the compiler must pull some tricks to resolve outer references. A good way to appreciate this is to try writing the same query in lambda syntax. It's tricky! It gets harder still if you insert a where or orderby clause before projecting:

```
from fullName in fullNames
from name in fullName.Split()
orderby fullName, name
select name + " came from " + fullName;
```

The problem is that SelectMany emits a flat sequence of child elements—in our case, a flat collection of words. The original outer element from which it came (fullName) is lost. The solution is to "carry" the outer element with each child, in a temporary anonymous type:

```
from fullName in fullNames
from x in fullName.Split().Select (name => new { name, fullName } )
orderby x.fullName, x.name
select x.name + " came from " + x.fullName;
```

The only change here is that we're wrapping each child element (name) in an anonymous type that also contains its fullName. This is similar to how a let clause is resolved. Here's the final conversion to lambda syntax:

```
IEnumerable<string> query = fullNames
  .SelectMany (fName => fName.Split( )
                  .Select (name => new { name, fName } ))
  .OrderBy (x => x.fName)
  .ThenBy  (x => x.name)
  .Select  (x => x.name + " came from " + x.fName);
```

Thinking in comprehension syntax

As we just demonstrated, there are good reasons to use comprehension syntax if you need the outer iteration variable. In such cases, it helps not only to use comprehension syntax, but also to think directly in its terms.

There are two basic patterns when writing additional generators. The first is *expanding and flattening subsequences*. To do this, you call a property or method on an existing query variable in your additional generator. We did this in the previous example:

```
from fullName in fullNames
from name in fullName.Split( )
```

Here, we've expanded from enumerating full names to enumerating words. An analogous query in LINQ to SQL is when you expand child association properties. The following query lists all customers along with their purchases:

```
IEnumerable<string> query = from c in dataContext.Customers
                            from p in c.Purchases
                            select c.Name + " bought a " + p.Description;

Tom bought a Bike
Tom bought a Holiday
Dick bought a Phone
Harry bought a Car
...
```

Here, we've expanded each customer into a subsequence of purchases.

The second pattern is performing a *cross product* or *cross join*—where every element of one sequence is matched with every element of another. To do this, introduce a generator whose selector expression returns a sequence unrelated to an iteration variable:

```
int[] numbers = { 1, 2, 3 };  string[] letters = { "a", "b" };

IEnumerable<string> query = from n in numbers
                            from l in letters
                            select n.ToString() + l;

RESULT: { "1a", "1b", "2a", "2b", "3a", "3b" }
```

This style of query is the basis of SelectMany-style *joins*.

Joining with SelectMany

You can use `SelectMany` to join two sequences, simply by filtering the results of a cross product. For instance, suppose we wanted to match players for a game. We could start as follows:

```
string[] players = { "Tom", "Jay", "Mary" };

IEnumerable<string> query = from name1 in players
                            from name2 in players
                            select name1 + " vs " + name2;

RESULT: { "Tom vs Tom", "Tom vs Jay", "Tom vs Mary",
          "Jay vs Tom", "Jay vs Jay", "Jay vs Mary",
          "Mary vs Tom", "Mary vs "Jay", "Mary vs Mary" }
```

The query reads: "For every player, reiterate every player, selecting player 1 vs player 2". Although we got what we asked for (a cross join), the results are not useful until we add a filter:

```
IEnumerable<string> query = from name1 in players
                            from name2 in players
                            where name1.CompareTo (name2) < 0
                            orderby name1, name2
                            select name1 + " vs " + name2;

RESULT: { "Jay vs Mary", "Jay vs Tom", "Mary vs Tom" }
```

The filter predicate constitutes the *join condition*. Our query can be called a *non-equi join*, because the join condition doesn't use an equality operator.

We'll demonstrate the remaining types of joins with LINQ to SQL.

SelectMany in LINQ to SQL

SelectMany in LINQ to SQL can perform cross joins, non-equi joins, inner joins, and left outer joins. You can use `SelectMany` with both predefined associations and ad hoc relationships—just as with `Select`. The difference is that `SelectMany` returns a flat rather than a hierarchical result set.

A cross join in LINQ to SQL is written just as in the preceding section. The following query matches every customer to every purchase (a cross join):

```
var query = from c in dataContext.Customers
            from p in dataContext.Purchases
            select c.Name + " might have bought a " + p.Description;
```

More typically, though, you'd want to match customers to their own purchases only. You achieve this by adding a `where` clause with a joining predicate. This results in a standard SQL-style equi-join:

```
var query = from c in dataContext.Customers
            from p in dataContext.Purchases
            where c.ID == p.CustomerID
            select c.Name + " bought a " + p.Description;
```

This translates well to SQL. In the next section, we'll see how it extends to support outer joins. Reformulating such queries with LINQ's Join operator actually makes them *less* extensible—LINQ is opposite to SQL in this sense.

If you have association properties for relationships in your LINQ to SQL entities, you can express the same query by expanding the subcollection instead of filtering the cross product:

```
from c in dataContext.Customers
from p in c.Purchases
select new { c.Name, p.Description };
```

The advantage is that we've eliminated the joining predicate. We've gone from filtering a cross product to expanding and flattening. Both queries, however, will result in the same SQL.

You can add where clauses to such a query for additional filtering. For instance, if we wanted only customers whose names started with "T", we could filter as follows:

```
from c in dataContext.Customers
where c.Name.StartsWith ("T")
from p in c.Purchases
select new { c.Name, p.Description };
```

This LINQ to SQL query would work equally well if the where clause is moved one line down. If it is a local query, however, moving the where clause down would make it less efficient. With local queries, you should filter *before* joining.

You can introduce new tables into the mix with additional from clauses. For instance, if each purchase had purchase item child rows, you could produce a flat result set of customers with their purchases, each with their purchase detail lines as follows:

```
from c in dataContext.Customers
from p in c.Purchases
from pi in p.PurchaseItems
select new { c.Name, p.Description, pi.DetailLine };
```

Each from clause introduces a new *child* table. To include data from a *parent* table (via an association property), you don't add a from clause—you simply navigate to the property. For example, if each customer has a salesperson whose name you want to query, just do this:

```
from c in dataContext.Customers
select new { Name = c.Name, SalesPerson = c.SalesPerson.Name };
```

You don't use SelectMany in this case because there's no subcollection to flatten. Parent association properties return a single item.

Outer joins with SelectMany

We saw previously that a Select subquery yields a result analogous to a left outer join.

LINQ Operators

```
from c in dataContext.Customers
select new {
            c.Name,
            Purchases = from p in c.Purchases
                        where p.Price > 1000
                        select new { p.Description, p.Price }
          };
```

In this example, every outer element (customer) is included, regardless of whether the customer has any purchases. But suppose we rewrite this query with SelectMany, so we can obtain a single flat collection rather than a hierarchical result set:

```
from c in dataContext.Customers
from p in c.Purchases
where p.Price > 1000
select new { c.Name, p.Description, p.Price };
```

In the process of flattening the query, we've switched to an inner join: customers are now included only for whom one or more high-value purchases exist. To get a left outer join with a flat result set, we must apply the DefaultIfEmpty query operator on the inner sequence. This method returns null if its input sequence has no elements. Here's such a query, price predicate aside:

```
from c in dataContext.Customers
from p in c.Purchases.DefaultIfEmpty()
select new { c.Name, p.Description, Price = (decimal?) p.Price };
```

This works perfectly with LINQ to SQL, returning all customers, even if they have no purchases. But if we were to run this as a local query, it would crash, because when p is null, p.Description and p.Price throw a NullReferenceException. We can make our query robust in either scenario as follows:

```
from c in dataContext.Customers
from p in c.Purchases.DefaultIfEmpty()
select new {
            c.Name,
            Descript = p == null ? null : p.Description,
            Price = p == null ? (decimal?) null : p.Price
          };
```

Let's now reintroduce the price filter. We cannot use a where clause as we did before, because it would execute *after* DefaultIfEmpty:

```
from c in dataContext.Customers
from p in c.Purchases.DefaultIfEmpty()
where p.Price > 1000...
```

The correct solution is to splice the Where clause *before* DefaultIfEmpty with a subquery:

```
from c in dataContext.Customers
from p in c.Purchases.Where (p => p.Price > 1000).DefaultIfEmpty()
select new {
            c.Name,
            Descript = p == null ? null : p.Description,
            Price = p == null ? (decimal?) null : p.Price
          };
```

This translates to a left outer join in LINQ to SQL, and is an effective pattern for writing this type of query.

 If you're used to writing outer joins in SQL, you might be tempted to overlook the simpler option of a Select subquery for this style of query, in favor of the awkward but familiar SQL-centric flat approach. The hierarchical result set from a Select subquery is often better suited to outer join-style queries because there are no additional nulls to deal with.

Joining

IEnumerable<TOuter>, IEnumerable<TInner> → IEnumerable<TResult>

Method	Description	SQL equivalents
Join	Applies a lookup strategy to match elements from two collections, emitting a flat result set	INNER JOIN
GroupJoin	As above, but emits a *hierarchical* result set	INNER JOIN, LEFT OUTER JOIN

Join and GroupJoin

Join arguments

Argument	Type
Outer sequence	IEnumerable<TOuter>
Inner sequence	IEnumerable<TInner>
Outer key selector	TOuter => TKey
Inner key selector	TInner => TKey
Result selector	(TOuter,TInner) => TResult

GroupJoin arguments

Argument	Type
Outer sequence	IEnumerable<TOuter>
Inner sequence	IEnumerable<TInner>
Outer key selector	TOuter => TKey
Inner key selector	TInner => TKey
Result selector	(TOuter,**IEnumerable<TInner>**) => TResult

Comprehension syntax

```
from outer-var in outer-enumerable
join inner-var in inner-enumerable on outer-key-expr equals inner-key-expr
 [ into identifier ]
```

Overview

Join and GroupJoin mesh two input sequences into a single output sequence. Join emits flat output; GroupJoin emits hierarchical output.

Join and GroupJoin provide an alternative strategy to Select and SelectMany. The advantage of Join and GroupJoin is that they execute efficiently over local in-memory collections, since they first load the inner sequence into a keyed lookup, avoiding the need to repeatedly enumerate over every inner element. The disadvantage is that they offer the equivalent of inner and left outer joins only; cross joins and non-equi joins must still be done with Select/SelectMany. With LINQ to SQL queries, Join and GroupJoin offer no real benefits over Select and SelectMany.

Table 9-1 summarizes the differences between each of the joining strategies.

Table 9-1. Joining strategies

Strategy	Result shape	Local query efficiency	Inner joins	Left outer joins	Cross joins	Non-equal joins
Select + SelectMany	Flat	Bad	Yes	Yes	Yes	Yes
Select + Select	Nested	Bad	Yes	Yes	Yes	Yes
Join	Flat	Good	Yes	-	-	-
GroupJoin	Nested	Good	Yes	Yes	-	-
GroupJoin + SelectMany	Flat	Good	Yes	Yes	-	-

Join

The Join operator performs an inner join, emitting a flat output sequence.

The simplest way to demonstrate Join is with LINQ to SQL. The following query lists all customers alongside their purchases, without using an association property:

```
IQueryable<string> query =
  from c in dataContext.Customers
  join p in dataContext.Purchases on c.ID equals p.CustomerID
  select c.Name + " bought a " + p.Description;
```

The results match what we would get from a SelectMany-style query:

```
Tom bought a Bike
Tom bought a Holiday
Dick bought a Phone
Harry bought a Car
```

To see the benefit of Join over SelectMany, we must convert this to a local query. We can demonstrate this by first copying all customers and purchases to arrays, and then querying the arrays:

```
Customer[] customers = dataContext.Customers.ToArray();
Purchase[] purchases = dataContext.Purchases.ToArray();
```

```
var slowQuery = from c in customers
                from p in purchases where c.ID == p.CustomerID
                select c.Name + " bought a " + p.Description;

var fastQuery = from c in customers
                join p in purchases on c.ID equals p.CustomerID
                select c.Name + " bought a " + p.Description;
```

Although both queries yield the same results, the Join query is considerably faster because its implementation in Enumerable preloads the inner collection (purchases) into a keyed lookup.

The comprehension syntax for join can be written in general terms as follows:

```
join inner-var in inner-sequence on outer-key-expr equals inner-key-expr
```

Join operators in LINQ differentiate between the *outer sequence* and *inner sequence*. Syntactically, as follows:

The outer sequence
  The input sequence (in this case, customers).

The inner sequence
  The new collection you introduce (in this case, purchases).

Join performs inner joins, meaning customers without purchases are excluded from the output. With inner joins, you can swap the inner and outer sequences in the query and still get the same results:

```
from p in purchases                              // p is now outer
join c in customers on p.CustomerID equals c.ID  // c is now inner
...
```

You can add further join clauses to the same query. If each purchase, for instance, has one or more purchase items, you could join the purchase items as follows:

```
from c in customers
join p in purchases on c.ID equals p.CustomerID    // first join
join pi in purchaseItems on p.ID equals pi.PurchaseID  // second join
...
```

purchases acts as the *inner* sequence in the first join and as the *outer* sequence in the second join. You could obtain the same results (inefficiently) using nested foreach statements as follows:

```
foreach (Customer c in customers)
  foreach (Purchase p in purchases)
    if (c.ID == p.CustomerID)
      foreach (PurchaseItem pi in purchaseItems)
        if (p.ID == pi.PurchaseID)
          Console.WriteLine (c.Name + "," + p.Price + "," + pi.Detail);
```

In query comprehension syntax, variables from earlier joins remain in scope—just as outer iteration variables do with SelectMany-style queries. You're also permitted to insert where and let clauses in between join clauses.

Joining on multiple keys

You can join on multiple keys with anonymous types as follows:

```
from x in sequenceX
join y in sequenceY on new { K1 = x.Prop1, K2 = x.Prop2 }
                equals new { K1 = y.Prop3, K2 = y.Prop4 }
...
```

For this to work, the two anonymous types must be structured identically. The compiler then implements each with the same internal type, making the joining keys compatible.

Joining in lambda syntax

The following comprehension syntax join:

```
from c in customers
join p in purchases on c.ID equals p.CustomerID
select new { c.Name, p.Description, p.Price };
```

in lambda syntax is as follows:

```
customers.Join (                            // outer collection
    purchases,                              // inner collection
    c => c.ID,                              // outer key selector
    p => p.CustomerID,                      // inner key selector
    (c, p) => new
        { c.Name, p.Description, p.Price }    // result selector
);
```

The result selector expression at the end creates each element in the output sequence. If you have additional clauses prior to projecting, such as orderby in this example:

```
from c in customers
join p in purchases on c.ID equals p.CustomerID
orderby p.Price
select c.Name + " bought a " + p.Description;
```

you must manufacture a temporary anonymous type in the result selector in lambda syntax. This keeps both c and p in scope following the join:

```
customers.Join (                            // outer collection
    purchases,                              // inner collection
    c => c.ID,                              // outer key selector
    p => p.CustomerID,                      // inner key selector
    (c, p) => new { c, p } )                // result selector
    .OrderBy (x => x.p.Price)
    .Select (x => x.c.Name + " bought a " + x.p.Description);
```

Comprehension syntax is usually preferable when joining; it's less fiddly.

GroupJoin

GroupJoin does the same work as Join, but instead of yielding a flat result, it yields a hierarchical result, grouped by each outer element. It also allows left outer joins.

The comprehension syntax for GroupJoin is the same as for Join, but is followed by the into keyword.

Here's the most basic example:

```
IEnumerable<IEnumerable<Purchase>> query =
  from c in customers
  join p in purchases on c.ID equals p.CustomerID
  into custPurchases
  select custPurchases;   // custPurchases is a sequence
```

 An into clause translates to GroupJoin only when it appears directly after a join clause. After a select or group clause, it means *query continuation*. The two uses of the into keyword are quite different, although they have one feature in common: they both introduce a new query variable.

The result is a sequence of sequences, which we could enumerate as follows:

```
foreach (IEnumerable<Purchase> purchaseSequence in query)
  foreach (Purchase p in purchaseSequence)
    Console.WriteLine (p.Description);
```

This isn't very useful, however, because outerSeq has no reference to the outer customer. More commonly, you'd reference the outer iteration variable in the projection:

```
from c in customers
join p in purchases on c.ID equals p.CustomerID
into custPurchases
select new { CustName = c.Name, custPurchases };
```

This gives the same results as the following (inefficient) Select subquery:

```
from c in customers
select new
{
  CustName = c.Name,
  custPurchases = purchases.Where (p => c.ID == p.CustomerID)
};
```

By default, GroupJoin does the equivalent of a left outer join. To get an inner join—where customers without purchases are excluded—you need to filter on custPurchases:

```
from c in customers join p in purchases on c.ID equals p.CustomerID
into custPurchases
where custPurchases.Any()
select ...
```

Clauses after a group-join into operate on *subsequences* of inner child elements, not *individual* child elements. This means that to filter individual purchases, you'd have to call Where *before* joining:

```
from c in customers
join p in purchases.Where (p2 => p2.Price > 1000)
  on c.ID equals p.CustomerID
into custPurchases ...
```

You can construct lambda queries with GroupJoin as you would with Join.

Flat outer joins

You run into a dilemma if you want both an outer join and a flat result set. GroupJoin gives you the outer join; Join gives you the flat result set. The solution is to first call GroupJoin, and then DefaultIfEmpty on each child sequence, and then finally SelectMany on the result:

```
from c in customers
join p in purchases on c.ID equals p.CustomerID into custPurchases
from cp in custPurchases.DefaultIfEmpty()
select new
{
  CustName = c.Name,
  Price = cp == null ? (decimal?) null : cp.Price
};
```

DefaultIfEmpty emits a null value if a subsequence of purchases is empty. The second from clause translates to SelectMany. In this role, it *expands and flattens* all the purchase subsequences, concatenating them into a single sequence of purchase *elements*.

Joining with lookups

The Join and GroupJoin methods in Enumerable work in two steps. First, they load the inner sequence into a *lookup*. Second, they query the outer sequence in combination with the lookup.

A *lookup* is a sequence of groupings that can be accessed directly by key. Another way to think of it is as a dictionary of sequences—a dictionary that can accept many elements under each key. Lookups are read-only and defined by the following interface:

```
public interface ILookup<TKey,TElement> :
    IEnumerable<IGrouping<TKey,TElement>>, IEnumerable
{
  int Count { get; }
  bool Contains (TKey key);
  IEnumerable<TElement> this [TKey key] { get; }
}
```

 The joining operators—like other sequence-emitting operators—honor deferred or lazy execution semantics. This means the lookup is not built until you begin enumerating the output sequence.

You can create and query lookups manually as an alternative strategy to using the joining operators, when dealing with local collections. There are a couple of benefits in doing so:

- You can reuse the same lookup over multiple queries—as well as in ordinary imperative code.
- Querying a lookup is an excellent way of understanding how Join and GroupJoin work.

The `ToLookupTT` extension method creates a lookup. The following loads all purchases into a lookup—keyed by their `CustomerID`:

```
ILookup<int?,Purchase> purchLookup =
    purchases.ToLookup (p => p.CustomerID, p => p);
```

The first argument selects the key; the second argument selects the objects that are to be loaded as values into the lookup.

Reading a lookup is rather like reading a dictionary, except that the indexer returns a *sequence* of matching items, rather than a *single* matching item. The following enumerates all purchases made by the customer whose ID is 1:

```
foreach (Purchase p in purchLookup [1])
    Console.WriteLine (p.Description);
```

With a lookup in place, you can write `SelectMany`/`Select` queries that execute as efficiently as `Join`/`GroupJoin` queries. `Join` is equivalent to using `SelectMany` on a lookup:

```
from c in customers
from p in purchLookup [c.ID]
select new { c.Name, p.Description, p.Price };

Tom Bike 500
Tom Holiday 2000
Dick Bike 600
Dick Phone 300
...
```

Adding a call to `DefaultIfEmpty` makes this into an outer join:

```
from c in customers
from p in purchLookup [c.ID].DefaultIfEmpty()
 select new {
            c.Name,
            Descript = p == null ? null : p.Description,
            Price = p == null ? (decimal?) null : p.Price
        };
```

`GroupJoin` is equivalent to reading the lookup inside a projection:

```
from c in customers
select new {
            CustName = c.Name,
            CustPurchases = purchLookup [c.ID]
        };
```

Enumerable implementations

Here's the simplest valid implementation of `Enumerable.Join`, null checking aside:

```
public static IEnumerable <TResult> Join
                                   <TOuter,TInner,TKey,TResult> (
    this IEnumerable <TOuter>    outer,
    IEnumerable <TInner>         inner,
    Func <TOuter,TKey>           outerKeySelector,
    Func <TInner,TKey>           innerKeySelector,
```

```
      Func <TOuter,TInner,TResult>  resultSelector)
    {
      ILookup <TKey, TInner> lookup = inner.ToLookup (innerKeySelector);
      return
        from outerItem in outer
        from innerItem in lookup [outerKeySelector (outerItem)]
        select resultSelector (outerItem, innerItem);
    }
```

GroupJoin's implementation is like that of Join, but simpler:

```
    public static IEnumerable <TResult> GroupJoin
                                     <TOuter,TInner,TKey,TResult> (
      this IEnumerable <TOuter>      outer,
      IEnumerable <TInner>           inner,
      Func <TOuter,TKey>             outerKeySelector,
      Func <TInner,TKey>             innerKeySelector,
      Func <TOuter,IEnumerable<TInner>,TResult>  resultSelector)
    {
      ILookup <TKey, TInner> lookup = inner.ToLookup (innerKeySelector);
      return
        from outerItem in outer
        select resultSelector
          (outerItem, lookup [outerKeySelector (outerItem)]);
    }
```

Ordering

IEnumerable<TSource> → IOrderedEnumerable<TSource>

Method	Description	SQL equivalents
OrderBy, ThenBy	Sorts a sequence in ascending order	ORDER BY ...
OrderByDescending, ThenByDescending	Sorts a sequence in descending order	ORDER BY ... DESC
Reverse	Returns a sequence in reverse order	Exception thrown

Ordering operators return the same elements in a different order.

OrderBy, OrderByDescending, ThenBy, and ThenByDescending

OrderBy and OrderByDescending arguments

Argument	Type
Input sequence	IEnumerable<TSource>
Key selector	TSource => TKey

Return type = IOrderedEnumerable<TSource>

ThenBy and ThenByDescending arguments

Argument	Type
Input sequence	IOrderedEnumerable<TSource>
Key selector	TSource => TKey

Comprehension syntax

```
orderby expression1 [descending] [, expression2 [descending] ... ]
```

Overview

OrderBy returns a sorted version of the input sequence, using the keySelector expression to make comparisons. The following query emits a sequence of names in alphabetical order:

```
IEnumerable<string> query = names.OrderBy (s => s);
```

The following sorts names by length:

```
IEnumerable<string> query = names.OrderBy (s => s.Length);

// Result: { "Jay", "Tom", "Mary", "Dick", "Harry" };
```

The relative order of elements with the same sorting key (in this case, Jay/Tom and Mary/Dick) is indeterminate—unless you append a ThenBy operator:

```
IEnumerable<string> query = names.OrderBy (s => s.Length).ThenBy (s => s);

// Result: { "Jay", "Tom", "Dick", "Mary", "Harry" };
```

ThenBy reorders only elements that had the same sorting key in the preceding sort. You can chain any number of ThenBy operators. The following sorts first by length, then by the second character, and finally by the first character:

```
names.OrderBy (s => s.Length).ThenBy (s => s[1]).ThenBy (s => s[0]);
```

The equivalent in comprehension syntax is this:

```
from s in names
orderby s.Length, s[1], s[0]
select s;
```

LINQ also provides OrderByDescending and ThenByDescending operators, which do the same things, emitting the results in reverse order. The following LINQ to SQL query retrieves purchases in descending order of price, with those of the same price listed alphabetically:

```
dataContext.Purchases.OrderByDescending (p => p.Price)
                .ThenBy (p => p.Description);
```

In comprehension syntax:

```
from p in dataContext.Purchases
orderby p.Price descending, p.Description
select p;
```

Comparers and collations

In a local query, the key selector objects themselves determine the ordering algorithm via their default `IComparable` implementation (see Chapter 7). You can override the sorting algorithm by passing in an `IComparer` object. The following performs a case-insensitive sort:

```
names.OrderBy (n => n, StringComparer.CurrentCultureIgnoreCase);
```

Passing in a comparer is not supported in comprehension syntax, nor in any way by LINQ to SQL. In LINQ to SQL, the comparison algorithm is determined by the participating column's collation. If the collation is case-sensitive, you can request a case-insensitive sort by calling `ToUpper` in the key selector:

```
from p in dataContext.Purchases
orderby p.Description.ToUpper( )
select p;
```

IOrderedEnumerable and IOrderedQueryable

The ordering operators return special subtypes of `IEnumerable<T>`. Those in `Enumerable` return `IOrderedEnumerable`; those in `Queryable` return `IOrderedQueryable`. These subtypes allow a subsequent `ThenBy` operator to refine rather than replace the existing ordering.

The additional members that these subtypes define are not publicly exposed, so they present like ordinary sequences. The fact that they are different types comes into play when building queries progressively:

```
IOrderedEnumerable<string> query1 = names.OrderBy (s => s.Length);
IOrderedEnumerable<string> query2 = query1.ThenBy (s => s);
```

If we instead declare query1 of type `IEnumerable<string>`, the second line would not compile—`ThenBy` requires an input of type `IOrderedEnumerable<string>`. You can avoid worrying about this by implicitly typing query variables:

```
var query1 = names.OrderBy (s => s.Length);
var query2 = query1.ThenBy (s => s);
```

Implicit typing can create problems of its own, though. The following will not compile:

```
var query = names.OrderBy (s => s.Length);
query = query.Where (n => n.Length > 3);        // Compile-time error
```

The compiler infers query to be of type `IOrderedEnumerable<string>`, based on `OrderBy`'s output sequence type. However, the `Where` on the next line returns an ordinary `IEnumerable<string>`, which cannot be assigned back to query. You can work around this either with explicit typing or by calling `AsEnumerable( )` after `OrderBy`:

```
var query = names.OrderBy (s => s.Length).AsEnumerable( );
query = query.Where (n => n.Length > 3);                 // OK
```

The equivalent in interpreted queries is to call `AsQueryable`.

Grouping

```
IEnumerable<TSource> → IEnumerable<IGrouping<TSource,TElement>>
```

Method	Description	SQL equivalents
GroupBy	Groups a sequence into subsequences	GROUP BY

GroupBy

Argument	Type
Input sequence	IEnumerable<TSource>
Key selector	TSource => TKey
Element selector (optional)	TSource => TElement
Comparer (optional)	IEqualityComparer<TKey>

Comprehension syntax

```
group element-expression by key-expression
```

Overview

GroupBy organizes a flat input sequence into sequences of *groups*. For example, the following organizes all the files in *c:\temp* by extension:

```
string[] files = Directory.GetFiles ("c:\\temp");

IEnumerable<IGrouping<string,string>> query =
  files.GroupBy (file => Path.GetExtension (file));
```

Or if you're comfortable with implicit typing:

```
var query = files.GroupBy (file => Path.GetExtension (file));
```

Here's how to enumerate the result:

```
foreach (IGrouping<string,string> grouping in query)
{
  Console.WriteLine ("Extension: " + grouping.Key);

  foreach (string filename in grouping)
    Console.WriteLine ("   - " + filename);
}

Extension: .pdf
  -- chapter03.pdf
  -- chapter04.pdf
Extension: .doc
  -- todo.doc
  -- menu.doc
  -- Copy of menu.doc
...
```

Enumerable.GroupBy works by reading the input elements into a temporary dictionary of lists so that all elements with the same key end up in the same sublist. It then emits a sequence of *groupings*. A grouping is a sequence with a Key property:

```
public interface IGrouping <TKey,TElement> : IEnumerable<TElement>,
                                             IEnumerable
{
  TKey Key { get; }      // Key applies to the subsequence as a whole
}
```

By default, the elements in each grouping are untransformed input elements, unless you specify an elementSelector argument. The following projects each input element to uppercase:

```
files.GroupBy (file => Path.GetExtension (file), file => file.ToUpper());
```

An elementSelector is independent of the keySelector. In our case, this means that the Key on each grouping is still in its original case:

```
Extension: .pdf
  -- CHAPTER03.PDF
  -- CHAPTER04.PDF
Extension: .doc
  -- TODO.DOC
```

Note that the subcollections are not emitted in alphabetical order of key. GroupBy groups only; it does not *sort*; in fact, it preserves the original ordering. To sort, you must add an OrderBy operator:

```
files.GroupBy (file => Path.GetExtension (file), file => file.ToUpper())
     .OrderBy (grouping => grouping.Key);
```

GroupBy has a simple and direct translation in comprehension syntax:

```
group element-expr by key-expr
```

Here's our example in comprehension syntax:

```
from file in files
group file.ToUpper() by Path.GetExtension (file);
```

As with select, group "ends" a query—unless you add a query continuation clause:

```
from file in files
group file.ToUpper() by Path.GetExtension (file) into grouping
orderby grouping.Key
select grouping;
```

Query continuations are often useful in a group by query. The next query filters out groups that have fewer than five files in them:

```
from file in files
group file.ToUpper() by Path.GetExtension (file) into grouping
where grouping.Count() < 5
select grouping;
```

A *where* after a *group by* is equivalent to HAVING in SQL. It applies to each subsequence or grouping as a whole, rather than the individual elements.

Sometimes you're interested purely in the result of an aggregation on a grouping and so can abandon the subsequences:

```
string[] votes = { "Bush", "Gore", "Gore", "Bush", "Bush" };

IEnumerable<string> query = from vote in votes
                            group vote by vote into g
                            orderby g.Count( ) descending
                            select g.Key;

string winner = query.First( );    // Bush
```

GroupBy in LINQ to SQL

Grouping works in the same way with interpreted queries. If you have association properties set up in LINQ to SQL, you'll find, however, that the need to group arises less frequently than with standard SQL. For instance, to select customers with at least two purchases, you don't need to group; the following query does the job nicely:

```
from c in dataContext.Customers
where c.Purchases.Count >= 2
select c.Name + " has made " + c.Purchases.Count + " purchases";
```

An example of when you might use grouping is to list total sales by year:

```
from p in dataContext.Purchases
group p.Price by p.Date.Year into salesByYear
select new {
            Year       = salesByYear.Key,
            TotalValue = salesByYear.Sum( )
          };
```

LINQ's grouping operators expose a superset of SQL's "GROUP BY" functionality.

Another departure from traditional SQL comes in there being no obligation to project the variables or expressions used in grouping or sorting.

Grouping by multiple keys

You can group by a composite key, using an anonymous type:

```
from n in names
group n by new { FirstLetter = n[0], Length = n.Length };
```

Custom equality comparers

You can pass a custom equality comparer into GroupBy, in a local query, to change the algorithm for key comparison. Rarely is this required, though, because changing the key selector expression is usually sufficient. For instance, the following creates a case-insensitive grouping:

```
group name by name.ToUpper( )
```

Set Operators

IEnumerable<TSource>, IEnumerable<TSource> → IEnumerable<TSource>

Method	Description	SQL equivalents
Concat	Returns a concatenation of elements in each of the two sequences	UNION ALL
Union	Returns a concatenation of elements in each of the two sequences, excluding duplicates	UNION
Intersect	Returns elements present in both sequences	WHERE ... IN (...)
Except	Returns elements present in the first, but not the second sequence	EXCEPT *or* WHERE ... NOT IN (...)

Concat and Union

Contact returns all the elements of the first sequence, followed by all the elements of the second. Union does the same, but removes any duplicates:

```
int[] seq1 = { 1, 2, 3 }, seq2 = { 3, 4, 5 };

IEnumerable<int>
  concat = seq1.Concat (seq2),    // { 1, 2, 3, 3, 4, 5 }
  union  = seq1.Union  (seq2);    // { 1, 2, 3, 4, 5 }
```

Intersect and Except

Intersect returns the elements that two sequences have in common. Except returns the elements in the first input sequence that are *not* present in the second:

```
int[] seq1 = { 1, 2, 3 }, seq2 = { 3, 4, 5 };

IEnumerable<int>
  commonality = seq1.Intersect (seq2),    // { 3 }
  difference1 = seq1.Except    (seq2),    // { 1, 2 }
  difference2 = seq2.Except    (seq1);    // { 4, 5 }
```

Enumerable.Except works internally by loading all of the elements in the first collection into a dictionary, then removing from the dictionary all elements present in the second sequence. The equivalent in SQL is a NOT EXISTS or NOT IN subquery:

```
SELECT number FROM numbers1Table
WHERE number NOT IN (SELECT number FROM numbers2Table)
```

Conversion Methods

LINQ deals primarily in sequences—in other words, collections of type IEnumerable<T>. The conversion methods convert to and from other types of collections:

Method	Description
OfType	Converts IEnumerable to IEnumerable<T>, discarding wrongly typed elements
Cast	Converts IEnumerable to IEnumerable<T>, throwing an exception if there are any wrongly typed elements
ToArray	Converts IEnumerable<T> to T[ ]
ToList	Converts IEnumerable<T> to List<T>
ToDictionary	Converts IEnumerable<T> to Dictionary<TKey,TValue>
ToLookup	Converts IEnumerable<T> to ILookup<TKey,TElement>
AsEnumerable	Downcasts to IEnumerable<T>
AsQueryable	Casts or converts to IQueryable<T>

OfType and Cast

OfType and Cast accept a nongeneric IEnumerable collection and emit a generic IEnumerable<T> sequence that you can subsequently query:

```
ArrayList classicList = new ArrayList();        // in System.Collections
classicList.AddRange ( new int[] { 3, 4, 5 } );
IEnumerable<int> sequence1 = classicList.Cast<int>();
```

Cast and OfType differ in their behavior when encountering an input element that's of an incompatible type. Cast throws an exception; OfType ignores the incompatible element. Continuing the preceding example:

```
DateTime offender = DateTime.Now;
classicList.Add (offender);
IEnumerable<int>
  sequence2 = classicList.OfType<int>(), // OK - ignores offending DateTime
  sequence3 = classicList.Cast<int>();   // Throws exception
```

The rules for element compatibility exactly follow those of C#'s is operator. We can see this by examining the internal implementation of OfType:

```
public static IEnumerable<TSource> OfType <TSource> (IEnumerable source)
{
  foreach (object element in source)
    if (element is TSource)
      yield return (TSource)element;
}
```

Cast has an identical implementation, except that it omits the type compatibility test:

```
public static IEnumerable<TSource> Cast <TSource> (IEnumerable source)
{
  foreach (object element in source)
    yield return (TSource)element;
}
```

A consequence of these implementations is that you cannot use Cast to convert elements from one value type to another (for this, you must perform a Select operation instead). In other words, Cast is not as flexible as C#'s cast operator, which also allows static type conversions such as the following:

```
int i = 3;
long l = i;        // Static conversion int->long
int i2 = (int) l;  // Static conversion long->int
```

We can demonstrate this by attempting to use OfType or Cast to convert a sequence of ints to a sequence of longs:

```
int[] integers = { 1, 2, 3 };

IEnumerable<long> test1 = integers.OfType<long>();
IEnumerable<long> test2 = integers.Cast<long>();
```

When enumerated, test1 emits zero elements and test2 throws an exception. Examining OfType's implementation, it's fairly clear why. After substituting TSource, we get the following expression:

```
(element is long)
```

which returns false for an int element, due to the lack of an inheritance relationship.

 The reason for test2 throwing an exception, when enumerated, is subtler. Notice in Cast's implementation that element is of type object. When TSource is a value type, the CLR synthesizes a method that reproduces the scenario described in the section "Boxing and Unboxing" in Chapter 4:

```
int value = 123;
object element = value;
long result = (long) element;  // exception
```

Because the element variable is declared of type object, an object-to-long cast is performed (an unboxing) rather than an int-to-long numeric conversion. Unboxing operations require an exact type match, so the object-to-long unbox fails when given an int.

As we suggested previously, the solution is to use an ordinary Select:

```
IEnumerable<long> castLong = integers.Select (s => (long) s);
```

OfType and Cast are also useful in downcasting elements in a generic input sequence. For instance, if you have an input sequence of type IEnumerable<Fruit>, OfType<Apple> would return just the apples. This is particularly useful in LINQ to XML (see Chapter 10).

ToArray, ToList, ToDictionary, and ToLookup

ToArray and ToList emit the results into an array or generic list. These operators force the immediate enumeration of the input sequence (unless indirected via a subquery or expression tree). For examples, refer to the section "Deferred Execution" in Chapter 8.

`ToDictionary` and `ToLookup` accept the following arguments:

Argument	Type
Input sequence	`IEnumerable<TSource>`
Key selector	`TSource => TKey`
Element selector (optional)	`TSource => TElement`
Comparer (optional)	`IEqualityComparer<TKey>`

`ToDictionary` also forces immediate execution of a sequence, writing the results to a generic `Dictionary`. The `keySelector` expression you provide must evaluate to a unique value for each element in the input sequence; otherwise, an exception is thrown. In contrast, `ToLookup` allows many elements of the same key. We describe lookups in the earlier section "Joining with lookups."

AsEnumerable and AsQueryable

`AsEnumerable` upcasts a sequence to `IEnumerable<T>`, forcing the compiler to bind subsequent query operators to methods in `Enumerable`, instead of `Queryable`. For an example, see the section "Combining Interpreted and Local Queries" in Chapter 8.

`AsQueryable` downcasts a sequence to `IQueryable<T>` if it implements that interface. Otherwise, it instantiates an `IQueryable<T>` wrapper over the local query.

Element Operators

`IEnumerable<TSource>` → `TSource`

Method	Description	SQL equivalents
`First`, `FirstOrDefault`	Returns the first element in the sequence, optionally satisfying a predicate	SELECT TOP 1 ... ORDER BY ...
`Last`, `LastOrDefault`	Returns the last element in the sequence, optionally satisfying a predicate	SELECT TOP 1 ... ORDER BY ... DESC
`Single`, `SingleOrDefault`	Equivalent to `First`/`FirstOrDefault`, but throws an exception if there is more than one match	
`ElementAt`, `ElementAtOrDefault`	Returns the element at the specified position	Exception thrown
`DefaultIfEmpty`	Returns null or `default(TSource)` if the sequence has no elements	OUTER JOIN

Methods ending in "OrDefault" return `default(TSource)` rather than throwing an exception if the input sequence is empty or if no elements match the supplied predicate.

default(TSource) = null for reference type elements, or "blank" (usually zero) for value type elements.

First, Last, and Single

Argument	Type
Source sequence	IEnumerable<TSource>
Predicate (optional)	TSource => bool

The following example demonstrates First and Last:

```
int[] numbers   = { 1, 2, 3, 4, 5 };
int first       = numbers.First();                  // 1
int last        = numbers.Last();                   // 5
int firstEven   = numbers.First  (n => n % 2 == 0);  // 2
int lastEven    = numbers.Last   (n => n % 2 == 0);  // 4
```

The following demonstrates First versus FirstOrDefault:

```
int firstBigError  = numbers.First        (n => n > 10);   // Exception
int firstBigNumber = numbers.FirstOrDefault (n => n > 10);   // 0
```

To avoid an exception, Single requires exactly one matching element; SingleOrDefault requires one *or zero* matching elements:

```
int onlyDivBy3 = numbers.Single (n => n % 3 == 0);   // 3
int divBy2Err  = numbers.Single (n => n % 2 == 0);   // Error: 2 & 4 match

int singleError = numbers.Single        (n => n > 10);      // Error
int noMatches   = numbers.SingleOrDefault (n => n > 10);      // 0
int divBy2Error = numbers.SingleOrDefault (n => n % 2 == 0);  // Error
```

Single is the "fussiest" in this family of element operators. FirstOrDefault and LastOrDefault are the most tolerant.

In LINQ to SQL, Single is often used to retrieve a row from a table by primary key:

```
Customer cust = dataContext.Customers.Single (c => c.ID == 3);
```

ElementAt

Argument	Type
Source sequence	IEnumerable<TSource>
Index of element to return	int

ElementAt picks the *n*th element from the sequence:

```
int[] numbers   = { 1, 2, 3, 4, 5 };
int third       = numbers.ElementAt (2);          // 3
int tenthError  = numbers.ElementAt (9);          // Exception
int tenth       = numbers.ElementAtOrDefault (9); // 0
```

Enumerable.ElementAt is written such that if the input sequence happens to implement IList<T>, it calls IList<T>'s indexer. Otherwise, it enumerates *n* times, and then returns the next element. ElementAt is not supported in LINQ to SQL.

DefaultIfEmpty

DefaultIfEmpty converts empty sequences to null/default( ). This is used in writing flat outer joins: see the earlier sections "Outer joins with SelectMany" and "Flat Outer Joins."

Aggregation Methods

IEnumerable<TSource> → *scalar*

Method	Description	SQL equivalents
Count, LongCount	Returns the number of elements in the input sequence, optionally satisfying a predicate	COUNT (...)
Min, Max	Returns the smallest or largest element in the sequence	MIN (...), MAX (...)
Sum, Average	Calculates a numeric sum or average over elements in the sequence	SUM (...), AVG (...)
Aggregate	Performs a custom aggregation	Exception thrown

Count and LongCount

Argument	Type
Source sequence	IEnumerable<TSource>
Predicate (optional)	TSource => bool

Count simply enumerates over a sequence, returning the number of items:

```
int fullCount = new int[] { 5, 6, 7 }.Count();    // 3
```

The internal implementation of Enumerable.Count tests the input sequence to see whether it happens to implement ICollection<T>. If it does, it simply calls ICollection<T>.Count. Otherwise, it enumerates over every item, incrementing a counter.

You can optionally supply a predicate:

```
int digitCount = "pa55w0rd".Count (c => char.IsDigit (c));    // 3
```

LongCount does the same job as Count, but returns a 64-bit integer, allowing for sequences of greater than 2 billion elements.

Min and Max

Argument	Type
Source sequence	IEnumerable<TSource>
Result selector (optional)	TSource => TResult

LINQ Operators

Min and Max return the smallest or largest element from a sequence:

```
int[] numbers = { 28, 32, 14 };
int smallest = numbers.Min( );  // 14;
int largest  = numbers.Max( );  // 32;
```

If you include a selector expression, each element is first projected:

```
int smallest = numbers.Max (n => n % 10);  // 8;
```

A selector expression is mandatory if the items themselves are not intrinsically comparable—in other words, if they do not implement IComparable<T>:

```
Purchase runtimeError = dataContext.Purchases.Min ( );          // Error
decimal? lowestPrice = dataContext.Purchases.Min (p => p.Price);  // OK
```

A selector expression determines not only how elements are compared, but also the final result. In the preceding example, the final result is a decimal value, not a purchase object. To get the cheapest purchase, you need a subquery:

```
Purchase cheapest = dataContext.Purchases
  .Where (p => p.Price == dataContext.Purchases.Min (p2 => p2.Price))
  .FirstOrDefault( );
```

In this case, you could also formulate the query without an aggregation—using an OrderBy followed by FirstOrDefault.

Sum and Average

Argument	Type
Source sequence	IEnumerable<TSource>
Result selector (optional)	TSource => TResult

Sum and Average are aggregation operators that are used in a similar manner to Min and Max:

```
decimal[] numbers  = { 3, 4, 8 };
decimal sumTotal   = numbers.Sum( );          // 15
decimal average    = numbers.Average( );      // 5   (mean value)
```

The following returns the total length of each of the strings in the names array:

```
int combinedLength = names.Sum (s => s.Length);  // 19
```

Sum and Average are fairly restrictive in their typing. Their definitions are hard-wired to each of the numeric types (int, long, float, double, decimal, and their nullable versions). In contrast, Min and Max can operate directly on anything that implements IComparable<T>—such as a string, for instance.

Further, Average always returns either decimal or double, according to the following table:

Selector type	Result type
decimal	decimal
int, long, float, double	double

This means the following does not compile ("cannot convert double to int"):

```
int avg = new int[] { 3, 4 }.Average();
```

But this will compile:

```
double avg = new int[] { 3, 4 }.Average();    // 3.5
```

Average implicitly upscales the input values to avoid loss of precision. In this example, we averaged integers and got 3.5, without needing to resort to an input element cast:

```
double avg = numbers.Average (n => (double) n);
```

In LINQ to SQL, Sum and Average translate to the standard SQL aggregations. The following query returns customers whose average purchase was more than $500:

```
from c in dataContext.Customers
where c.Purchases.Average (p => p.Price) > 500
select c.Name;
```

Aggregate

Aggregate allows you to plug a custom accumulation algorithm, for implementing unusual aggregations. Aggregate is not supported in LINQ to SQL, and is somewhat specialized in its use cases. The following demonstrates how Aggregate can do the work of Sum:

```
int[] numbers = { 1, 2, 3 };
int sum = numbers.Aggregate (0, (seed, n) => seed + n);   // 6
```

The first argument to Aggregate is the *seed*, from which accumulation starts. The second argument is an expression to update the accumulated value, given a fresh element. You can optionally supply a third argument to project the final result value from the accumulated value.

The difficulty with Aggregate is that a simple scalar type rarely serves the job as a useful accumulator. To calculate an average, for instance, you need to keep a running tally of the number of the elements—as well as the sum. Writing a custom accumulator type solves the problem, but is uneconomical in effort, compared to the conventional approach of using a simple foreach loop to calculate the aggregation.

Quantifiers

IEnumerable<TSource> → *bool*

Method	Description	SQL equivalents
Contains	Returns true if the input sequence contains the given element	WHERE ... IN (...)
Any	Returns true if any elements satisfy the given predicate	WHERE ... IN (...)
All	Returns true if all elements satisfy the given predicate	WHERE (...)
SequenceEqual	Returns true if the second sequence has identical elements to the input sequence	

Contains and Any

The Contains method accepts an argument of type TSource; Any accepts an optional *predicate*.

Contains returns true if the given element is present:

```
bool hasAThree = new int[] { 2, 3, 4 }.Contains (3);        // true;
```

Any returns true if the given expression is true for at least one element. We can rewrite the preceding query with Any as follows:

```
bool hasAThree = new int[] { 2, 3, 4 }.Any (n => n == 3);  // true;
```

Any can do everything that Contains can do, and more:

```
bool hasABigNumber = new int[] { 2, 3, 4 }.Any (n => n > 10);  // false;
```

Calling Any without a predicate returns true if the sequence has one or more elements. Here's another way to write the preceding query:

```
bool hasABigNumber = new int[] { 2, 3, 4 }.Where (n => n > 10).Any( );
```

Any is particularly useful in subqueries.

All and SequenceEqual

All returns true if all elements satisfy a predicate. The following returns customers whose purchases are less than $100:

```
dataContext.Customers.Where (c => c.Purchases.All (p => p.Price < 100));
```

SequenceEqual compares two sequences. To return true, each sequence must have identical elements, in the identical order.

Generation Methods

void → IEnumerable<TResult>

Method	Description
Empty	Creates an empty sequence
Repeat	Creates a sequence of repeating elements
Range	Creates a sequence of integers

Empty, Repeat, and Range are static (nonextension) methods that manufacture simple local sequences.

Empty

Empty manufactures an empty sequence and requires just a type argument:

```
foreach (string s in Enumerable.Empty<string>())
  Console.Write (s);                            // <nothing>
```

In conjunction with the ?? operator, Empty does the reverse of DefaultIfEmpty. For example, suppose we have a jagged array of integers, and we want to get all the integers into a single flat list. The following SelectMany query fails if any of the inner arrays is null:

```
int[][] numbers =
{
  new int[] { 1, 2, 3 },
  new int[] { 4, 5, 6 },
  null                    // this null makes the query below fail.
};

IEnumerable<int> flat = numbers.SelectMany (innerArray => innerArray);
```

Empty in conjunction with ?? fixes the problem:

```
IEnumerable<int> flat = numbers
  .SelectMany (innerArray => innerArray ?? Enumerable.Empty <int>() );

foreach (int i in flat)
  Console.Write (i + " ");      // 1 2 3 4 5 6
```

Range and Repeat

Range and Repeat work only with integers. Range accepts a starting index and count:

```
foreach (int i in Enumerable.Range (5, 5))
  Console.Write (i + " ");                  // 5 6 7 8 9
```

Repeat accepts the number to repeat, and the number of iterations:

```
foreach (int i in Enumerable.Repeat (5, 3))
  Console.Write (i + " ");                  // 5 5 5
```

10

LINQ to XML

The .NET Framework provides a number of APIs for working with XML data. From Framework 3.5, the primary choice for general-purpose XML document processing is *LINQ to XML*. LINQ to XML comprises a lightweight LINQ-friendly XML document object model, and a set of supplementary query operators. In most scenarios, it can be considered a complete replacement for the preceding W3C-compliant DOM, a.k.a. `XmlDocument`.

In this chapter, we concentrate entirely on LINQ to XML. In the following chapter, we cover the more specialized XML types and APIs, including the forward-only reader/writer, the types for working with schemas, stylesheets and XPaths, and the legacy W3C-compliant DOM.

The LINQ to XML DOM is extremely well designed and highly performant. Even without LINQ, the LINQ to XML DOM is valuable as a lightweight façade over the low-level `XmlReader` and `XmlWriter` classes.

All LINQ to XML types are defined in the `System.Xml.Linq` namespace.

Architectural Overview

This section starts with a very brief introduction to the concept of a DOM, and then explains the rationale behind LINQ to XML's DOM.

What Is a DOM?

Consider the following XML file:

```xml
<?xml version="1.0" encoding="utf-8" standalone="yes"?>
<customer id="123" status="archived">
  <firstname>Joe</firstname>
  <lastname>Bloggs</lastname>
</customer>
```

As with all XML files, we start with a *declaration*, and then a root *element*, whose name is `customer`. The `customer` element has two *attributes*, each with a name (`id` and `status`) and value ("123" and "archived"). Within `customer`, there are two child elements, `firstname` and `lastname`, each having simple text content ("Joe" and "Bloggs").

Each of these constructs—declaration, element, attribute, value, and text content—can be represented with a class. And if such classes have collection properties for storing child content, we can assemble a *tree* of objects to fully describe a document. This is called a *document object model*, or DOM.

The LINQ to XML DOM

LINQ to XML comprises two things:

- An XML DOM, which we call the *X-DOM*
- A set of about 10 supplementary query operators

As you might expect, the X-DOM consists of types such as `XDocument`, `XElement`, and `XAttribute`. Interestingly, the X-DOM types are not tied to LINQ—you can load, instantiate, update, and save an X-DOM without ever writing a LINQ query.

Conversely, you could use LINQ to query a DOM created of the older W3C-compliant types. However, this would be frustrating and limiting. The distinguishing feature of the X-DOM is that it's *LINQ-friendly*. This means:

- It has methods that emit useful `IEnumerable` sequences, upon which you can query.
- Its constructors are designed such that you can build an X-DOM tree through a LINQ projection.

X-DOM Overview

Figure 10-1 shows the core X-DOM types. The most frequently used of these types is `XElement`. `XObject` is the root of the *inheritance* hierarchy; `XElement` and `XDocument` are roots of the *containership* hierarchy.

Figure 10-2 shows the X-DOM tree created from the following code:

```
string xml = @"<customer id='123' status='archived'>
                <firstname>Joe</firstname>
                <lastname>Bloggs<!--nice name--></lastname>
              </customer>";

XElement customer = XElement.Parse (xml);
```

`XObject` is the abstract base class for all XML content. It defines a link to the `Parent` element in the containership tree as well as an optional `XDocument`.

`XNode` is the base class for most XML content excluding attributes. The distinguishing feature of `XNode` is that it can sit in an ordered collection of mixed-type `XNode`s. For instance, consider the following XML:

```
<data>
  Hello world
```

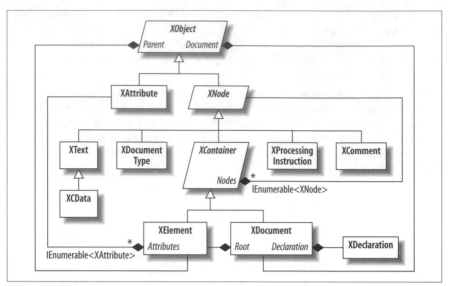

Figure 10-1. Core X-DOM types

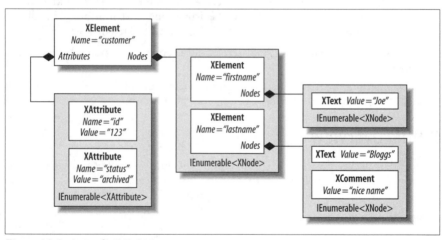

Figure 10-2. A simple X-DOM tree

```
    <subelement1/>
    <!--comment-->
    <subelement2/>
</data>
```

Within the parent element <data>, there's first an XText node (Hello world), then an XElement node, then an XComment node, and then a second XElement node. In contrast, an XAttribute will tolerate only other XAttributes as peers.

Although an XNode can access its parent XElement, it has no concept of *child* nodes: this is the job of its subclass XContainer. XContainer defines members for dealing with children and is the abstract base class for XElement and XDocument.

XElement introduces members for managing attributes—as well as a Name and Value. In the (fairly common) case of an element having a single XText child node, the Value property on XElement encapsulates this child's content for both get and set operations, cutting unnecessary navigation. Thanks to Value, you can mostly avoid working directly with XText nodes.

XDocument represents the root of an XML tree. More precisely, it *wraps* the root XElement, adding an XDeclaration, processing instructions, and other root-level "fluff." Unlike with the W3C DOM, its use is optional: you can load, manipulate, and save an X-DOM without ever creating an XDocument! The nonreliance on XDocument also means you can efficiently and easily move a node subtree to another X-DOM hierarchy.

Loading and Parsing

Both XElement and XDocument provide static Load and Parse methods to build an X-DOM tree from an existing source:

- Load builds an X-DOM from a file, URI, TextReader, or XmlReader.
- Parse builds an X-DOM from a string.

For example:

```
XDocument fromWeb = XDocument.Load ("http://albahari.com/sample.xml");

XElement fromFile = XElement.Load (@"e:\media\somefile.xml");

XElement config = XElement.Parse (
@"<configuration>
   <client enabled='true'>
     <timeout>30</timeout>
   </client>
 </configuration>");
```

In later sections, we describe how to traverse and update an X-DOM. As a quick preview, here's how to manipulate the config element we just populated:

```
foreach (XElement child in config.Elements( ))
    Console.WriteLine (child.Name);                 // client

XElement client = config.Element ("client");

bool enabled = (bool) client.Attribute ("enabled");   // Read attribute
Console.WriteLine (enabled);                           // True
client.Attribute ("enabled").SetValue (!enabled);      // Update attribute

int timeout = (int) client.Element ("timeout");        // Read element
Console.WriteLine (timeout);                           // 30
client.Element ("timeout").SetValue (timeout * 2);     // Update element

client.Add (new XElement ("retries", 3));              // Add new elememt

Console.WriteLine (config);          // Implicitly call config.ToString( )
```

Here's the result of that last `Console.WriteLine`:

```
<configuration>
  <client enabled="false">
    <timeout>60</timeout>
    <retries>3</retries>
  </client>
</configuration>
```

 XNode also provides a static `ReadFrom` method that instantiates and populates any type of node from an `XmlReader`. Unlike `Load`, it stops after reading one (complete) node, so you can continue to read manually from the `XmlReader` afterward.

You can also do the reverse and use an `XmlReader` or `XmlWriter` to read or write an `XNode`, via its `CreateReader` and `CreateWriter` methods.

We describe XML readers and writers and how to use them with the X-DOM in Chapter 11.

Saving and Serializing

Calling `ToString` on any node converts its content to an XML string—formatted with line breaks and indentation as we just saw. (You can disable the line breaks and indentation by specifying `SaveOptions.DisableFormatting` when calling `ToString`.)

`XElement` and `XDocument` also provide a `Save` method that writes an X-DOM to a file, `TextWriter`, or `XmlWriter`. If you specify a file, an XML declaration is automatically written. There is also a `WriteTo` method defined in the `XNode` class, which accepts just an `XmlWriter`.

We describe the handling of XML declarations when saving in more detail in the section "Documents and Declarations" later in this chapter.

Instantiating an X-DOM

Rather than using the `Load` or `Parse` methods, you can build an X-DOM tree by manually instantiating objects and adding them to a parent via `XContainer`'s `Add` method.

To construct an `XElement` and `XAttribute`, simply provide a name and value:

```
XElement lastName = new XElement ("lastname", "Bloggs");
lastName.Add (new XComment ("nice name"));

XElement customer = new XElement ("customer");
customer.Add (new XAttribute ("id", 123));
customer.Add (new XElement ("firstname", "Joe"));
customer.Add (lastName);

Console.WriteLine (customer.ToString());
```

The result:

```
<customer id="123">
  <firstname>Joe</firstname>
  <lastname>Bloggs<!--nice name--></lastname>
</customer>
```

A value is optional when constructing an XElement—you can provide just the element name and add content later. Notice that when we did provide a value, a simple string sufficed—we didn't need to explicitly create and add an XText child node. The X-DOM does this work automatically, so you can deal simply with "values."

Functional Construction

In our preceding example, it's hard to glean the XML structure from the code. X-DOM supports another mode of instantiation, called *functional construction* (from functional programming). With functional construction, you build an entire tree in a single expression:

```
XElement customer =
  new XElement ("customer", new XAttribute ("id", 123),
    new XElement ("firstname", "joe"),
    new XElement ("lastname", "bloggs",
      new XComment ("nice name")
    )
  );
```

This has two benefits. First, the code resembles the shape of the XML. Second, it can be incorporated into the select clause of a LINQ query. For example, the following LINQ to SQL query projects directly into an X-DOM:

```
XElement query =
  new XElement ("customers",
    from c in dataContext.Customers
    select
      new XElement ("customer", new XAttribute ("id", c.ID),
        new XElement ("firstname", c.FirstName),
        new XElement ("lastname", c.LastName,
          new XComment ("nice name")
        )
      )
  );
```

More on this later in this chapter, in the section "Projecting into an X-DOM."

Specifying Content

Functional construction is possible because the constructors for XElement (and XDocument) are overloaded to accept a params object array:

```
public XElement (XName name, params object[] content)
```

The same holds true for the Add method in XContainer:

```
public void Add (params object[] content)
```

Hence, you can specify any number of child objects of any type, when building or appending an X-DOM. This works because *anything* counts as legal content. To see how, we need to examine how each content object is processed internally. Here are the decisions made by XContainer, in order:

1. If the object is null, it's ignored.

2. If the object is based on XNode or XStreamingElement, it's added as is to the Nodes collection.

3. If the object is an XAttribute, it's added to the Attributes collection.

4. If the object is a string, it gets wrapped in an XText node and added to Nodes.*

5. If the object implements IEnumerable, it's enumerated, and the same rules are applied to each element.

6. Otherwise, the object is converted to a string, wrapped in an XText node, and then added to Nodes.†

Everything ends up in one of two buckets: Nodes or Attributes. Furthermore, any object is valid content because it can always ultimately call ToString on it and treat it as an XText node.

> Before calling ToString on an arbitrary type, XContainer first tests whether it is one of the following types:
>
> ```
> float, double, decimal, bool,
> DateTime, DateTimeOffset, TimeSpan
> ```
>
> If so, it calls an appropriate typed ToString method on the XmlConvert helper class instead of calling ToString on the object itself. This ensures that the data is round-trippable and compliant with standard XML formatting rules.

Automatic Deep Cloning

When a node or attribute is added to an element (whether via functional construction or an Add method) the node or attribute's Parent property is set to that element. A node can have only one parent element: if you add an already parented node to a second parent, the node is automatically *deep-cloned*. In the following example, each customer has a separate copy of address:

```
var address = new XElement ("address",
                new XElement ("street", "Lawley St"),
                new XElement ("town", "North Beach")
            );
var customer1 = new XElement ("customer1", address);
var customer2 = new XElement ("customer2", address);
```

---

* The X-DOM actually optimizes this step internally by storing simple text content in a string. The XTEXT node is not actually created until you call Nodes( ) on the XContainer.

† See footnote 1.

```
customer1.Element ("address").Element ("street").Value = "Another St";
Console.WriteLine (
   customer2.Element ("address").Element ("street").Value);   // Lawley St
```

This automatic duplication keeps X-DOM object instantiation free of side effects—another hallmark of functional programming.

Navigating and Querying

As you might expect, the XNode and XContainer classes define methods and properties for traversing the X-DOM tree. Unlike a conventional DOM, however, these functions don't return a collection that implements IList<T>. Instead, they return either a single value or a *sequence* that implements IEnumerable<T>—upon which you are then expected to execute a LINQ query (or enumerate with a foreach). This allows for advanced queries as well as simple navigation tasks—using familiar LINQ query syntax.

Element and attribute names are case-sensitive in the X-DOM—just as they are in XML.

Child Node Navigation

Return type	Members	Works on
XNode	FirstNode { get; }	XContainer
	LastNode { get; }	XContainer
IEnumerable<XNode>	Nodes( )	XContainer*
	DescendantNodes( )	XContainer*
	DescendantNodesAndSelf( )	XElement*
XElement	Element (XName)	XContainer
IEnumerable<XElement>	Elements( )	XContainer*
	Elements (XName)	XContainer*
	Descendants( )	XContainer*
	Descendants (XName)	XContainer*
	DescendantsAndSelf( )	XElement*
	DescendantsAndSelf (XName)	XElement*
bool	HasElements { get; }	XElement

Functions marked with an asterisk in the third column of this and other tables also operate on *sequences* of the same type. For instance, you can call Nodes on either an XContainer or a sequence of XContainer objects. This is possible because of extension methods defined in System.Xml.Linq—the supplementary query operators we talked about in the overview.

FirstNode, LastNode, and Nodes

FirstNode and LastNode give you direct access to the first or last child node; Nodes returns all children as a sequence. All three functions consider only direct descendants. For example:

```
var bench = new XElement ("bench",
            new XElement ("toolbox",
              new XElement ("handtool", "Hammer"),
              new XElement ("handtool", "Rasp")
            ),
            new XElement ("toolbox",
              new XElement ("handtool", "Saw"),
              new XElement ("powertool", "Nailgun")
            ),
            new XComment ("Be careful with the nailgun")
          );
foreach (XNode node in bench.Nodes())
  Console.WriteLine (node.ToString (SaveOptions.DisableFormatting) + ".");
```

This is the output:

```
<toolbox><handtool>Hammer</handtool><handtool>Rasp</handtool></toolbox>.
<toolbox><handtool>Saw</handtool><powertool>Nailgun</powertool></toolbox>.
<!--Be careful with the nailgun-->.
```

Retrieving elements

The Elements method returns just the child nodes of type XElement:

```
foreach (XElement e in bench.Elements())
  Console.WriteLine (e.Name + "=" + e.Value);    // toolbox=HammerRasp
                                                  // toolbox=SawNailgun
```

The following LINQ query finds the toolbox with the nail gun:

```
IEnumerable<string> query =
  from toolbox in bench.Elements()
  where toolbox.Elements().Any (tool => tool.Value == "Nailgun")
  select toolbox.Value;

RESULT: { "SawNailgun" }
```

The next example uses a SelectMany query to retrieve the hand tools in all toolboxes:

```
IEnumerable<string> query =
  from toolbox in bench.Elements()
  from tool in toolbox.Elements()
  where tool.Name == "handtool"
  select tool.Value;

RESULT: { "Hammer", "Rasp", "Saw" }
```

Elements itself is equivalent to a LINQ query on Nodes. Our preceding query could be started as follows:

```
from toolbox in bench.Nodes().OfType<XElement>()
where ...
```

Elements can also return just the elements of a given name. For example:

```
int x = bench.Elements ("toolbox").Count();     // 2
```

This is equivalent to:

```
int x = bench.Elements().Where (e => e.Name == "toolbox").Count();  // 2
```

Elements is also defined as an extension method accepting IEnumerable<XContainer> or, more precisely, it accepts an argument of this type:

```
IEnumerable<T> where T : XContainer
```

This allows it to work with sequences of elements too. Using this method, we can rewrite the query that finds the hand tools in all toolboxes as follows:

```
from tool in bench.Elements ("toolbox").Elements ("handtool")
select tool.Value.ToUpper();
```

The first call to Elements binds to XContainer's instance method; the second call to Elements binds to the extension method.

Retrieving a single element

The method Element (singular) returns the first matching element of the given name. Element is useful for simple navigation, as follows:

```
XElement settings = XElement.Load ("databaseSettings.xml");
string cx = settings.Element ("database").Element ("connectString").Value;
```

Element is equivalent to calling Elements() and then applying LINQ's FirstOr-Default query operator with a name-matching predicate. Element returns null if the requested element doesn't exist.

Element("xyz").Value will throw a NullReferenceException if element xyz does not exist. If you'd prefer a null rather than an exception, cast the XElement to a string instead of querying its Value property. In other words:

```
string xyz = (string) settings.Element ("xyz");
```

This works because XElement defines an explicit string conversion—just for this purpose!

Recursive functions

XContainer also provides Descendants and DescendantNodes methods that return child elements or nodes, *recursively*. Descendants accepts an optional element name. Returning to our earlier example, we can use Descendants to find all the hand tools as follows:

```
Console.WriteLine (bench.Descendants ("handtool").Count());  // 3
```

Both parent and leaf nodes are included, as the following example demonstrates:

```
foreach (XNode node in bench.DescendantNodes())
  Console.WriteLine (node.ToString (SaveOptions.DisableFormatting));
```

```
<toolbox><handtool>Hammer</handtool><handtool>Rasp</handtool></toolbox>
<handtool>Hammer</handtool>
Hammer
<handtool>Rasp</handtool>
Rasp
<toolbox><handtool>Saw</handtool><powertool>Nailgun</powertool></toolbox>
<handtool>Saw</handtool>
Saw
<powertool>Nailgun</powertool>
Nailgun
<!--Be careful with the nailgun-->
```

The next query extracts all comments anywhere within the X-DOM that contain the word "careful":

```
IEnumerable<string> query =
  from c in bench.DescendantNodes().OfType<XComment>()
  where c.Value.Contains ("careful")
  orderby c.Value
  select c.Value;
```

Parent Navigation

All XNodes have a Parent property and AncestorXXX methods for parent navigation. A parent is always an XElement:

Return type	Members	Works on
XElement	Parent { get; }	XNode*
Enumerable<XElement>	Ancestors()	XNode*
	Ancestors (XName)	XNode*
	AncestorsAndSelf()	XElement*
	AncestorsAndSelf (XName)	XElement*

If x is an XElement, the following always prints true:

```
foreach (XNode child in x.Nodes())
  Console.WriteLine (child.Parent == x);
```

The same is not the case, however, if x is an XDocument. XDocument is peculiar: it can have children, but can never be anyone's parent! To access the XDocument, you instead use the Document property—this works on any object in the X-DOM tree.

Ancestors returns a sequence whose first element is Parent, and whose next element is Parent.Parent, and so on, until the root element.

> You can navigate to the root element with the LINQ query AncestorsAndSelf().Last().
>
> Another way to achieve the same thing is to call Document.Root— although this works only if an XDocument is present.

Peer Node Navigation

Return type	Members	Defined in
bool	IsBefore (XNode node)	XNode
	IsAfter (XNode node)	XNode
XNode	PreviousNode { get; }	XNode
	NextNode { get; }	XNode
IEnumerable<XNode>	NodesBeforeSelf( )	XNode
	NodesAfterSelf( )	XNode
IEnumerable<XElement>	ElementsBeforeSelf( )	XNode
	ElementsBeforeSelf (XName name)	XNode
	ElementsAfterSelf( )	XNode
	ElementsAfterSelf (XName name)	XNode

With PreviousNode and NextNode (and FirstNode/LastNode), you can traverse nodes with the feel of a linked list. This is noncoincidental: internally, nodes are stored in a linked list.

XNode internally uses a *singly* linked list, so PreviousNode is not performant.

Attribute Navigation

Return type	Members	Defined in
bool	HasAttributes { get; }	XElement
XAttribute	Attribute (XName name)	XElement
	FirstAttribute { get; }	XElement
	LastAttribute { get; }	XElement
IEnumerable<XAttribute>	Attributes( )	XElement
	Attributes (XName name)	XElement

In addition, XAttribute defines PreviousAttribute and NextAttribute properties, as well as Parent.

The Attributes method that accepts a name returns a sequence with either zero or one element; an element cannot have duplicate attribute names in XML.

Updating an X-DOM

You can update elements and attributes in the following ways:

- Call SetValue or reassign the Value property.
- Call SetElementValue or SetAttributeValue.
- Call one of the Remove*XXX* methods.
- Call one of the Add*XXX* or Replace*XXX* methods, specifying fresh content.

You can also reassign the Name property on XElement objects.

Simple Value Updates

Members	Works on
SetValue (object value)	XElement, XAttribute
Value { get; set }	XElement, XAttribute

The SetValue method replaces an element or attribute's content with a simple value. Setting the Value property does the same, but accepts string data only. We describe both of these functions in detail later in this chapter (see the section "Working with Values").

An effect of calling SetValue (or reassigning Value) is that it replaces all child nodes:

```
XElement settings = new XElement ("settings",
                    new XElement ("timeout", 30)
                );
settings.SetValue ("blah");
Console.WriteLine (settings.ToString( ));  // <settings>blah</settings>
```

Updating Child Nodes and Attributes

Category	Members	Works on
Add	Add (params object[] content)	XContainer
	AddFirst (params object[] content)	XContainer
Remove	RemoveNodes( )	XContainer
	RemoveAttributes( )	XElement
	RemoveAll( )	XElement
Update	ReplaceNodes (params object[] content)	XContainer
	ReplaceAttributes (params object[] content)	XElement
	ReplaceAll (params object[] content	XElement
	SetElementValue (XName name, object value)	XElement
	SetAttributeValue (XName name, object value)	XElement

The most convenient methods in this group are the last two: SetElementValue and SetAttributeValue. They serve as shortcuts for instantiating an XElement or XAttribute and then Adding it to a parent, replacing any existing element or attribute of that name:

```
XElement settings = new XElement ("settings");
settings.SetElementValue ("timeout", 30);    // Adds child node
settings.SetElementValue ("timeout", 60);    // Update it to 60
```

Add appends a child node to an element or document. AddFirst does the same thing, but inserts at the beginning of the collection rather than the end.

You can remove all child nodes or attributes in one hit with RemoveNodes or RemoveAttributes. RemoveAll is equivalent to calling both of these methods.

The ReplaceXXX methods are equivalent to Removing and then Adding. They take a snapshot of the input, so e.ReplaceNodes(e.Nodes()) works as expected.

Updating Through the Parent

Members		Works on
AddBeforeSelf	(params object[] content)	XNode
AddAfterSelf	(params object[] content)	XNode
Remove()		XNode*, XAttribute*
ReplaceWith	(params object[] content)	XNode

The methods AddBeforeSelf, AddAfterSelf, Remove, and ReplaceWith don't operate on the node's children. Instead, they operate on the collection in which the node itself is in. This requires that the node have a parent element—otherwise, an exception is thrown. AddBeforeSelf and AddAfterSelf are useful for inserting a node into an arbitrary position:

```
XElement items = new XElement ("items",
                new XElement ("one"),
                new XElement ("three")
            );
items.FirstNode.AddAfterSelf (new XElement ("two"));
```

Here's the result:

```
<items><one /><two /><three /></items>
```

Inserting into an arbitrary position within a long sequence of elements is actually quite efficient, because nodes are stored internally in a linked list.

The Remove method removes the current node from its parent. ReplaceWith does the same—and then inserts some other content at the same position. For instance:

```
XElement items = XElement.Parse ("<items><one/><two/><three/></items>");
items.FirstNode.ReplaceWith (new XComment ("One was here"));
```

Here's the result:

```
<items><!--one was here--><two /><three /></items>
```

Removing a sequence of nodes or attributes

Thanks to extension methods in System.Xml.Linq, you can also call Remove on a *sequence* of nodes or attributes. Consider this X-DOM:

```
XElement contacts = XElement.Parse (
@"<contacts>
    <customer name='Mary'/>
    <customer name='Chris' archived='true'/>
    <supplier name='Susan'>
      <phone archived='true'>012345678<!--confidential--></phone>
    </supplier>
  </contacts>");
```

The following removes all customers:

```
contacts.Elements ("customer").Remove();
```

The next statement removes all archived contacts (so *Chris* disappears):

```
contacts.Elements().Where (e => (bool?) e.Attribute ("archived") == true)
                   .Remove();
```

If we replaced Elements() with Descendants(), all archived elements throughout the DOM would disappear, with this result:

```
<contacts>
  <customer name="Mary" />
  <supplier name="Susan" />
</contacts>
```

The next example removes all contacts that feature the comment "confidential" anywhere in their tree:

```
contacts.Elements().Where (e => e.DescendantNodes()
                                 .OfType<XComment>()
                                 .Any (c => c.Value == "confidential")
                           ).Remove();
```

This is the result:

```
<contacts>
  <customer name="Mary" />
  <customer name="Chris" archived="true" />
</contacts>
```

Contrast this with the following simpler query, which strips all comment nodes from the tree:

```
contacts.DescendantNodes().OfType<XComment>().Remove();
```

 Internally, the Remove methods first read all matching elements into a temporary list, and then enumerate over the temporary list to perform the deletions. This avoids errors that could otherwise result from deleting and querying at the same time.

Working with Values

XElement and XAttribute both have a Value property of type string. If an element has a single XText child node, XElement's Value property acts as a convenient shortcut to the content of that node. With XAttribute, the Value property is simply the attribute's value.

Despite the storage differences, the X-DOM provides a consistent set of operations for working with element and attribute values.

Setting Values

There are two ways to assign a value: call SetValue or assign the Value property. SetValue is more flexible because it accepts not just strings, but other simple data types too:

```
var e = new XElement ("date", DateTime.Now);
e.SetValue (DateTime.Now.AddDays(1));
Console.Write (e.Value);              // 2007-03-02T16:39:10.734375+09:00
```

We could have instead just set the element's Value property, but this would mean manually converting the DateTime to a string. This is more complicated than calling ToString—it requires the use of XmlConvert for an XML-compliant result.

When you pass a *value* into XElement or XAttribute's constructor, the same automatic conversion takes place for nonstring types. This ensures that DateTimes are correctly formatted; true is written in lowercase, and double.NegativeInfinity is written as "-INF".

Getting Values

To go the other way around and parse a Value back to a base type, you simply cast the XElement or XAttribute to the desired type. It sounds like it shouldn't work—but it does! For instance:

```
XElement e = new XElement ("now", DateTime.Now);
DateTime dt = (DateTime) e;

XAttribute a = new XAttribute ("resolution", 1.234);
double res = (double) a;
```

An element or attribute doesn't store DateTimes or numbers natively—they're always stored as text, and then parsed as needed. It also doesn't "remember" the original type, so you must cast it correctly to avoid a runtime error. To make your code robust, you can put the cast in a try/catch block, catching a FormatException.

Explicit casts on XElement and XAttribute can parse to the following types:

- All standard numeric types
- string, bool, DateTime, DateTimeOffset, TimeSpan, and Guid
- Nullable<> versions of the aforementioned value types

Casting to a nullable type is useful in conjunction with the Element and Attribute methods, because if the requested name doesn't exist, the cast still works. For instance, if x has no timeout element, the first line generates a runtime error and the second line does not:

```
int timeout = (int) x.Element ("timeout");     // Error
int? timeout = (int?) x.Element ("timeout");    // OK; timeout is null.
```

You can factor away the nullable type in the final result with the ?? operator. The following evaluates to 1.0 if the resolution attribute doesn't exist:

```
double resolution = (double?) x.Attribute ("resolution") ?? 1.0;
```

Casting to a nullable type won't get you out of trouble, though, if the element or attribute *exists* and has an empty (or improperly formatted) value. For this, you must catch a FormatException.

You can also use casts in LINQ queries. The following returns "John":

```
var data = XElement.Parse (
  @"<data>
```

```
            <customer id='1' name='Mary' credit='100' />
            <customer id='2' name='John' credit='150' />
            <customer id='3' name='Anne' />
          </data>");

    IEnumerable<string> query = from cust in data.Elements()
                                where (int?) cust.Attribute ("credit") > 100
                                select cust.Attribute ("name").Value;
```

Casting to a nullable int avoids a NullReferenceException in the case of Anne, who has no credit attribute. Another solution would be to add a predicate to the where clause:

```
    where cust.Attributes ("credit").Any( ) && (int) cust.Attribute...
```

The same principles apply in querying element values.

Values and Mixed Content Nodes

Given the value of Value, you might wonder when you'd ever need to deal directly with XText nodes. The answer is when you have mixed content. For example:

```
    <summary>An XAttribute is <bold>not</bold> an XNode</summary>
```

A simple Value property is not enough to capture summary's content. The summary element contains three children: an XText node followed by an XElement, followed by another XText node. Here's how to construct it:

```
    XElement summary = new XElement ("summary",
                         new XText ("An XAttribute is "),
                         new XElement ("bold", "not"),
                         new XText (" an XNode")
                       );
```

Interestingly, we can still query summary's Value—without getting an exception. Instead, we get a concatenation of each child's value:

```
    An XAttribute is not an XNode
```

It's also legal to reassign summary's Value, at the cost of replacing all previous children with a single new XText node.

Automatic XText Concatenation

When you add simple content to an XElement, the X-DOM appends to the existing XText child rather than creating a new one. In the following examples, e1 and e2 end up with just one child XText element whose value is HelloWorld:

```
    var e1 = new XElement ("test", "Hello"); e1.Add ("World");
    var e2 = new XElement ("test", "Hello", "World");
```

If you specifically create XText nodes, however, you end up with multiple children:

```
    var e = new XElement ("test", new XText ("Hello"), new XText ("World"));
    Console.WriteLine (e.Value);            // HelloWorld
    Console.WriteLine (e.Nodes().Count( ));  // 2
```

XElement doesn't concatenate the two XText nodes, so the nodes' object identities are preserved.

Documents and Declarations

XDocument

As we said previously, an XDocument wraps a root XElement and allows you to add an XDeclaration, processing instructions, a document type, and root-level comments. An XDocument is optional and can be ignored or omitted: unlike with the W3C DOM, it does not serve as glue to keep everything together.

An XDocument provides the same functional constructors as XElement. And because it's based on XContainer, it also supports the AddXXX, RemoveXXX, and ReplaceXXX methods. Unlike XElement, however, an XDocument can accept only limited content:

- A single XElement object (the "root")
- A single XDeclaration object
- A single XDocumentType object (to reference a DTD)
- Any number of XProcessingInstruction objects
- Any number of XComment objects

 Of these, only the root XElement is mandatory in order to have a valid XDocument. The XDeclaration is optional—if omitted, default settings are applied during serialization.

The simplest valid XDocument has just a root element:

```
var doc = new XDocument (
        new XElement ("test", "data")
    );
```

Notice that we didn't include an XDeclaration object. The file generated by calling doc.Save would still contain an XML declaration, however, because one is generated by default.

The next example produces a simple but correct XHTML file, illustrating all the constructs that an XDocument can accept:

```
var styleInstruction = new XProcessingInstruction (
  "xml-stylesheet", "href='styles.css' type='text/css'");

var docType = new XDocumentType ("html",
  "-//W3C//DTD XHTML 1.0 Strict//EN",
  "http://www.w3.org/TR/xhtml1/DTD/xhtml1-strict.dtd", null);

XNamespace ns = "http://www.w3.org/1999/xhtml";
var root =
  new XElement (ns + "html",
    new XElement (ns + "head",
      new XElement (ns + "title", "An XHTML page")),
```

```
    new XElement (ns + "body",
      new XElement (ns + "p", "This is the content"))
  );

var doc =
  new XDocument (
    new XDeclaration ("1.0", "utf-8", "no"),
    new XComment ("Reference a stylesheet"),
    styleInstruction,
    docType,
    root);

doc.Save ("test.html");
```

The resultant *test.html* reads as follows:

```
<?xml version="1.0" encoding="utf-8" standalone="no"?>
<!--Reference a stylesheet-->
<?xml-stylesheet href='styles.css' type='text/css'?>
<!DOCTYPE html PUBLIC "-//W3C//DTD XHTML 1.0 Strict//EN"
                      "http://www.w3.org/TR/xhtml1/DTD/xhtml1-strict.dtd">
<html xmlns="http://www.w3.org/1999/xhtml">
  <head>
    <title>An XHTML page</title>
  </head>
  <body>
    <p>This is the content</p>
  </body>
</html>
```

XDocument has a Root property that serves as a shortcut for accessing a document's single XElement. The reverse link is provided by XObject's Document property, which works for all objects in the tree:

```
Console.WriteLine (doc.Root.Name.LocalName);       // html
XElement bodyNode = doc.Root.Element (ns + "body");
Console.WriteLine (bodyNode.Document == doc);       // True
```

Recall that a document's children have no Parent:

```
Console.WriteLine (doc.Root.Parent == null);       // True
foreach (XNode node in doc.Nodes())
  Console.Write (node.Parent == null);              // TrueTrueTrueTrue
```

 An XDeclaration is not an XNode and does not appear in the document's Nodes collection—unlike comments, processing instructions, and the root element. Instead, it gets assigned to a dedicated property called Declaration. This is why "True" is repeated four and not five times in the last example.

XML Declarations

A standard XML file starts with a declaration such as the following:

```
<?xml version="1.0" encoding="utf-8" standalone="yes"?>
```

An XML declaration ensures that the file will be correctly parsed and understood by a reader. XElement and XDocument follow these rules in emitting XML declarations:

- Calling Save with a filename always writes a declaration.
- Calling Save with an XmlWriter writes a declaration unless the XmlWriter is instructed otherwise.
- The ToString method never emits an XML declaration.

> You can instruct an XmlWriter not to produce a declaration by setting the OmitXmlDeclaration and ConformanceLevel properties of an XmlWriterSettings object when constructing the XmlWriter. We describe this in Chapter 11.

The presence or absence of an XDeclaration object has no effect on whether an XML declaration gets written. The purpose of an XDeclaration is instead to *hint the XML serialization*—in two ways:

- What text encoding to use
- What to put in the XML declaration's encoding and standalone attributes (should a declaration be written)

XDeclaration's constructor accepts three arguments, which correspond to the attributes version, encoding, and standalone. In the following example, *test.xml* is encoded in UTF-16:

```
var doc = new XDocument (
           new XDeclaration ("1.0", "utf-16", "yes"),
           new XElement ("test", "data")
         );
doc.Save ("test.xml");
```

> Whatever you specify for the XML version is ignored by the XML writer: it always writes "1.0".

The encoding must use an IETF code such as "utf-16"—just as it would appear in the XML declaration.

Writing a declaration to a string

Suppose we want to serialize an XDocument to a string—including the XML declaration. Because ToString doesn't write a declaration, we'd have to use an XmlWriter instead:

```
var doc = new XDocument (
           new XDeclaration ("1.0", "utf-8", "yes"),
           new XElement ("test", "data")
         );
var output = new StringBuilder();
var settings = new XmlWriterSettings { Indent = true };
using (XmlWriter xw = XmlWriter.Create (output, settings))
  doc.Save (xw);
Console.WriteLine (output.ToString());
```

This is the result:

```
<?xml version="1.0" encoding="utf-16" standalone="yes"?>
<test>data</test>
```

Notice that we got UTF-16 in the output—even though we explicitly requested UTF-8 in an XDeclaration! This might look like a bug, but in fact, XmlWriter is being remarkably smart. Because we're writing to a string and not a file or stream, it's impossible to apply any encoding other than UTF-16—the format in which strings are internally stored. Hence, XmlWriter writes "utf-16"—so as not to lie.

This also explains why the ToString method doesn't emit an XML declaration. Imagine that instead of calling Save, you did the following to write an XDocument to a file:

```
File.WriteAllText ("data.xml", doc.ToString());
```

As it stands, *data.xml* would lack an XML declaration, making it incomplete but still parsable (you can infer the text encoding). But if ToString( ) emitted an XML declaration, *data.xml* would actually contain an *incorrect* declaration (encoding="utf-16"), which might prevent it from being read at all, because WriteAllText encodes using UTF-8.

Names and Namespaces

Just as .NET types can have namespaces, so too can XML elements and attributes.

XML namespaces achieve two things. First, rather like namespaces in C#, they help avoid naming collisions. This can become an issue when you merge data from one XML file into another. Second, namespaces assign *absolute* meaning to a name. The name "nil," for instance, could mean anything. Within the *http://www.w3.org/2001/XMLSchema-instance* namespace, however, "nil" means something equivalent to null in C# and comes with specific rules on how it can be applied.

Because XML namespaces are a significant source of confusion, we'll cover the topic first in general, and then move on to how they're used in LINQ to XML.

Namespaces in XML

Suppose we want to define a customer element in the namespace OReilly.Nutshell.CSharp. There are two ways to proceed. The first is to use the xmlns attribute as follows:

```
<customer xmlns="OReilly.Nutshell.CSharp"/>
```

xmlns is a special reserved attribute. When used in this manner, it performs two functions:

- It specifies a namespace for the element in question.
- It specifies a default namespace for all descendant elements.

This means that in the following example, address and postcode implicitly live in the OReilly.Nutshell.CSharp namespace:

```
<customer xmlns="OReilly.Nutshell.CSharp">
  <address>
```

```
      <postcode>02138</postcode>
    </address>
  </customer>
```

If we want address and postcode to have *no* namespace, we'd have to do this:

```
<customer xmlns="OReilly.Nutshell.CSharp">
  <address xmlns="">
    <postcode>02138</postcode>      <!-- postcode now inherits empty ns -->
  </address>
</customer>
```

Prefixes

The other way to specify a namespace is with a *prefix*. A prefix is an alias that you assign to a namespace to save typing. There are two steps in using a prefix—*defining* the prefix and *using* it. You can do both together as follows:

```
<nut:customer xmlns:nut="OReilly.Nutshell.CSharp"/>
```

Two distinct things are happening here. On the right, xmlns:nut="..." defines a prefix called nut and makes it available to this element and all its descendants. On the left, nut:customer assigns the newly allocated prefix to the customer element.

A prefixed element *does not* define a default namespace for descendants. In the following XML, firstname has an empty namespace:

```
<nut:customer nut:xmlns="OReilly.Nutshell.CSharp">
  <firstname>Joe</firstname>
</customer>
```

To give firstname the OReilly.Nutshell.CSharp prefix, we must do this:

```
<nut:customer xmlns:nut="OReilly.Nutshell.CSharp">
  <nut:firstname>Joe</firstname>
</customer>
```

You can also define a prefix—or prefixes—for the convenience of your descendants, without assigning any of them to the parent element itself. The following defines two prefixes, i and z, while leaving the customer element itself with an empty namespace:

```
<customer xmlns:i="http://www.w3.org/2001/XMLSchema-instance"
          xmlns:z="http://schemas.microsoft.com/2003/10/Serialization/">
  ...
</customer>
```

If this was the root node, the whole document would have i and z at its fingertips. Prefixes are convenient when elements need to draw from a number of namespaces.

Notice that both namespaces in this example are URIs. Using URIs (that you own) is standard practice: it ensures namespace uniqueness. So, in real life, our customer element would more likely be:

```
<customer xmlns="http://oreilly.com/schemas/nutshell/csharp"/>
```

or:

```
<nut:customer xmlns:nut="http://oreilly.com/schemas/nutshell/csharp"/>
```

Attributes

You can assign namespaces to attributes too. The main difference is that it always requires a prefix. For instance:

```
<customer xmlns:nut="OReilly.Nutshell.CSharp" nut:id="123" />
```

Another difference is that an unqualified attribute always has an empty namespace: it never inherits a default namespace from a parent element.

Attributes tend not to need namespaces because their meaning is usually local to the element. An exception is with general-purpose or metadata attributes, such as the nil attribute defined by W3C:

```
<customer xmlns:xsi="http://www.w3.org/2001/XMLSchema-instance">
  <firstname>Joe</firstname>
  <lastname xsi:nil="true"/>
</customer>
```

This indicates unambiguously that lastname is nil (null in C#) and not an empty string. Because we've used the standard namespace, a general-purpose parsing utility could know with certainty our intention.

Specifying Namespaces in the X-DOM

So far in this chapter, we've used just simple strings for XElement and XAttribute names. A simple string corresponds to an XML name with an empty namespace—rather like a .NET type defined in the global namespace.

There are a couple of ways to specify an XML namespace. The first is to enclose it in braces, before the local name. For example:

```
var e = new XElement ("{http://domain.com/xmlspace}customer", "Bloggs");
Console.WriteLine (e.ToString());
```

Here's the resulting XML:

```
<customer xmlns="http://domain.com/xmlspace">Bloggs</customer>
```

The second (and more performant) approach is to use the XNamespace and XName types. Here are their definitions:

```
public sealed class XNamespace
{
  public string NamespaceName { get; }
}

public sealed class XName     // A local name with optional namespace
{
  public string LocalName { get; }
  public XNamespace Namespace { get; }   // Optional
}
```

Both types define implicit casts from string, so the following is legal:

```
XNamespace ns   = "http://domain.com/xmlspace";
XName localName = "customer";
XName fullName  = "{http://domain.com/xmlspace}customer";
```

XName also overloads the + operator, allowing you to combine a namespace and name without using braces:

```
XNamespace ns = "http://domain.com/xmlspace";
XName fullName = ns + "customer";
Console.WriteLine (fullName);      // {http://domain.com/xmlspace}customer
```

All constructors and methods in the X-DOM that accept an element or attribute name actually accept an XName object rather than a string. The reason you can substitute a string—as in all our examples to date—is because of the implicit cast.

Specifying a namespace is the same whether for an element or an attribute:

```
XNamespace ns = "http://domain.com/xmlspace";
var data = new XElement (ns + "data",
               new XAttribute (ns + "id", 123)
           );
```

The X-DOM and Default Namespaces

The X-DOM ignores the concept of default namespaces until it comes time to actually output XML. This means that when you construct a child XElement, you must give it a namespace explicitly if needed: it *will not* inherit from the parent:

```
XNamespace ns = "http://domain.com/xmlspace";
var data = new XElement (ns + "data",
               new XElement (ns + "customer", "Bloggs"),
               new XElement (ns + "purchase", "Bicycle")
           );
```

The X-DOM does, however, apply default namespaces when reading and outputting XML:

```
Console.WriteLine (data.ToString());
```

OUTPUT:
```
<data xmlns="http://domain.com/xmlspace">
  <customer>Bloggs</customer>
  <purchase>Bicycle</purchase>
</data>
```

```
Console.WriteLine (data.Element (ns + "customer").ToString());
```

OUTPUT:
```
<customer xmlns="http://domain.com/xmlspace">Bloggs</customer>
```

If you construct XElement children without specifying namespaces—in other words:

```
XNamespace ns = "http://domain.com/xmlspace";
var data = new XElement (ns + "data",
               new XElement ("customer", "Bloggs"),
               new XElement ("purchase", "Bicycle")
           );
Console.WriteLine (data.ToString());
```

you get this result instead:

```
<data xmlns="http://domain.com/xmlspace">
  <customer xmlns="">Bloggs</customer>
  <purchase xmlns="">Bicycle</purchase>
</data>
```

Another trap is failing to include a namespace when navigating an X-DOM:

```
XNamespace ns = "http://domain.com/xmlspace";
var data = new XElement (ns + "data",
             new XElement (ns + "customer", "Bloggs"),
             new XElement (ns + "purchase", "Bicycle")
           );
XElement x = data.Element (ns + "customer");    // ok
XElement y = data.Element ("customer");          // null
```

If you build an X-DOM tree without specifying namespaces, you can subsequently assign every element to a single namespace as follows:

```
foreach (XElement e in data.DescendantsAndSelf( ))
  if (e.Name.Namespace == "")
    e.Name = ns + e.Name.LocalName;
```

Prefixes

The X-DOM treats prefixes just as it treats namespaces: purely as a serialization function. This means you can choose to completely ignore the issue of prefixes—and get by! The only reason you might want to do otherwise is for efficiency when outputting to an XML file. For example, consider this:

```
XNamespace ns1 = "http://domain.com/space1";
XNamespace ns2 = "http://domain.com/space2";

var mix = new XElement (ns1 + "data",
            new XElement (ns2 + "element", "value"),
            new XElement (ns2 + "element", "value"),
            new XElement (ns2 + "element", "value")
          );
```

By default, XElement will serialize this as follows:

```
<data xmlns="http://domain.com/space1">
  <element xmlns="http://domain.com/space2">value</element>
  <element xmlns="http://domain.com/space2">value</element>
  <element xmlns="http://domain.com/space2">value</element>
</data>
```

As you can see, there's a bit of unnecessary duplication. The solution is *not* to change the way you construct the X-DOM, but instead to hint the serializer prior to writing the XML. Do this by adding attributes defining prefixes that you want to see applied. This is typically done on the root element:

```
mix.SetAttributeValue (XNamespace.Xmlns + "ns1", ns1);
mix.SetAttributeValue (XNamespace.Xmlns + "ns2", ns2);
```

This assigns the prefix "ns1" to our XNamespace variable ns1, and "ns2" to ns2. The X-DOM automatically picks up these attributes when serializing and uses them to condense the resulting XML. Here's the result now of calling ToString on mix:

```
<ns1:data xmlns:ns1="http://domain.com/space1"
          xmlns:ns2="http://domain.com/space2">
  <ns2:element>value</ns2:element>
  <ns2:element>value</ns2:element>
  <ns2:element>value</ns2:element>
</ns1:data>
```

Prefixes don't change the way you construct, query, or update the X-DOM—for these activities, you ignore the presence of prefixes and continue to use full names. Prefixes come into play only when converting to and from XML files or streams.

Prefixes are also honored in serializing attributes. In the following example, we record a customer's date of birth and credit as "nil" using the W3C-standard attribute. The highlighted line ensures that the prefix is serialized without unnecessary namespace repetition:

```
XNamespace xsi = "http://www.w3.org/2001/XMLSchema-instance";
var nil = new XAttribute (xsi + "nil", true);

var cust = new XElement ("customers",
             new XAttribute (XNamespace.Xmlns + "xsi", xsi),
             new XElement ("customer",
               new XElement ("lastname", "Bloggs"),
               new XElement ("dob", nil),
               new XElement ("credit", nil)
             )
           );
```

This is its XML:

```
<customers xmlns:xsi="http://www.w3.org/2001/XMLSchema-instance">
  <customer>
    <lastname>Bloggs</lastname>
    <dob xsi:nil="true" />
    <credit xsi:nil="true" />
  </customer>
</customers>
```

For brevity, we predeclared the nil XAttribute so that we could use it twice in building the DOM. You're allowed to reference the same attribute twice because it's automatically duplicated as required.

Annotations

You can attach custom data to any XObject with an annotation. Annotations are intended for your own private use and are treated as black boxes by X-DOM. If you've ever used the Tag property on a Windows Forms or WPF control, you'll be familiar with the concept—the difference is that you have multiple annotations, and your annotations can be *privately scoped*. You can create an annotation that other types cannot even see—let alone overwrite.

The following methods on XObject add and remove annotations:

```
public void AddAnnotation (object annotation)
public void RemoveAnnotations<T>()     where T : class
```

The following methods retrieve annotations:

```
public T Annotation<T>()               where T : class
public IEnumerable<T> Annotations<T>() where T : class
```

Each annotation is keyed by its *type*, which must be a reference type. The following adds and then retrieves a string annotation:

```
XElement e = new XElement ("test");
e.AddAnnotation ("Hello");
Console.WriteLine (e.Annotation<string>());    // Hello
```

You can add multiple annotations of the same type, and then use the Annotations method to retrieve a *sequence* of matches.

A public type such as string doesn't make a great key, however, because code in other types can interfere with your annotations. A better approach is to use an internal or (nested) private class:

```
class X
{
  class CustomData { internal string Message; }    // Private nested type

  static void Test()
  {
    XElement e = new XElement ("test");
    e.AddAnnotation (new CustomData { Message = "Hello" } );
    Console.Write (e.Annotations<CustomData>().First().Message);   // Hello
  }
}
```

To remove annotations, you must also have access to the key's type:

```
e.RemoveAnnotations<CustomData>();
```

Projecting into an X-DOM

So far, we've shown how to use LINQ to get data *out* of an X-DOM. You can also use LINQ queries to project *into* an X-DOM. The source can be anything over which LINQ can query, such as:

- LINQ to SQL Tables
- A local collection
- Another X-DOM

Regardless of the source, the strategy is the same in using LINQ to emit an X-DOM: first write a *functional construction* expression that produces the desired X-DOM shape, and then build a LINQ query around the expression.

For instance, suppose we want to retrieve customers from a database into the following XML:

```
<customers>
  <customer id="1">
    <name>Sue</name>
    <buys>3</buys>
  </customer>
  ...
</customers>
```

We start by writing a functional construction expression for the X-DOM using simple literals:

```
var customers =
  new XElement ("customers",
    new XElement ("customer", new XAttribute ("id", 1),
      new XElement ("name", "Sue"),
      new XElement ("buys", 3)
    )
  );
```

We then turn this into a projection and build a LINQ query around it:

```
var customers =
  new XElement ("customers",
    from c in dataContext.Customers
    select
      new XElement ("customer", new XAttribute ("id", c.ID),
        new XElement ("name", c.Name),
        new XElement ("buys", c.Purchases.Count)
      )
  );
```

Here's the result:

```
<customers>
  <customer id="1">
    <name>Tom</firstname>
    <buys>3</buys>
  </customer>
  <customer id="2">
    <name>Harry</firstname>
    <buys>2</buys>
  </customer>
  ...
</customers>
```

We can see how this works more clearly by constructing the same query in two steps. First:

```
IEnumerable<XElement> sqlQuery =
  from c in dataContext.Customers
  select
    new XElement ("customer", new XAttribute ("id", c.ID),
      new XElement ("name", c.Name),
      new XElement ("buys", c.Purchases.Count)
    );
```

This inner portion is a normal LINQ to SQL query that projects into custom types (from LINQ to SQL's perspective). Here's the second step:

```
var customers = new XElement ("customers", sqlQuery);
```

This constructs the root XElement. The only thing unusual is that the content, sqlQuery, is not a single XElement but an IQueryable<XElement>—which implements IEnumerable<XElement>. Remember that in the processing of XML content, collections are automatically enumerated. So, each XElement gets added as a child node.

This outer query also defines the line at which the query transitions from being a remote LINQ to SQL query to a local LINQ to enumerable query. XElement's constructor doesn't know about IQueryable<>, so it forces enumeration of the LINQ to SQL query—and execution of the SQL statement.

Eliminating Empty Elements

Suppose in the preceding example that we also wanted to include details of the customer's most recent high-value purchase. We could do this as follows:

```
var customers =
  new XElement ("customers",
    from c in dataContext.Customers
    let lastBigBuy = (from p in c.Purchases
                      where p.Price > 1000
                      orderby p.Date descending
                      select p).FirstOrDefault()
    select
      new XElement ("customer", new XAttribute ("id", c.ID),
        new XElement ("name", c.Name),
        new XElement ("buys", c.Purchases.Count),
        new XElement ("lastBigBuy",
          new XElement ("description",
            lastBigBuy == null ? null : lastBigBuy.Description),
          new XElement ("price",
            lastBigBuy == null ? 0m : lastBigBuy.Price)
        )
      )
  );
```

This emits empty elements, though, for customers with no high-value purchases. (If it was a local query rather than a LINQ to SQL query, it would throw a NullReferenceException.) In such cases, it would be better to omit the lastBigBuy node entirely. We can achieve this by wrapping the constructor for the lastBigBuy element in a conditional operator:

```
select
  new XElement ("customer", new XAttribute ("id", c.ID),
    new XElement ("name", c.Name),
    new XElement ("buys", c.Purchases.Count),
    lastBigBuy == null ? null :
      new XElement ("lastBigBuy",
        new XElement ("description", lastBigBuy.Description),
        new XElement ("price", lastBigBuy.Price)
```

For customers with no `lastBigBuy`, a null is emitted instead of an empty `XElement`. This is what we want, because null content is simply ignored.

Streaming a Projection

If you're projecting into an X-DOM only to Save it (or call `ToString` on it), you can improve memory efficiency through an `XStreamingElement`. An `XStreamingElement` is a cut-down version of `XElement` that applies *deferred loading* semantics to its child content. To use it, you simply replace the outer `XElement`s with `XStreamingElement`s:

```
var customers =
  new XStreamingElement ("customers",
    from c in dataContext.Customers
    select
      new XStreamingElement ("customer", new XAttribute ("id", c.ID),
        new XElement ("name", c.Name),
        new XElement ("buys", c.Purchases.Count)
      )
  );
customers.Save ("data.xml");
```

The queries passed into an `XStreamingElement`'s constructor are not enumerated until you call Save, `ToString`, or `WriteTo` on the element; this avoids loading the whole X-DOM into memory at once. The flipside is that the queries are reevaluated, should you re-Save. Also, you cannot traverse an `XStreamingElement`'s child content—it does not expose methods such as `Elements` or `Attributes`.

`XStreamingElement` is not based on `XObject`—or any other class—because it has such a limited set of members. The only members it has, besides Save, `ToString`, and `WriteTo`, are:

- An `Add` method, which accepts content like the constructor
- A `Name` property

`XStreamingElement` does not allow you to *read* content in a streamed fashion—for this, you must use an `XmlReader` in conjunction with the X-DOM. We describe how to do this in the section "Patterns for Using XmlReader/XmlWriter" in Chapter 11.

Transforming an X-DOM

You can transform an X-DOM by reprojecting it. For instance, suppose we want to transform an *msbuild* XML file, used by the C# compiler and Visual Studio to describe a project, into a simple format suitable for generating a report. An msbuild file looks like this:

```
<Project DefaultTargets="Build" xmlns="http://schemas.microsoft.com/dev...">
  <PropertyGroup>
    <Platform Condition=" '$(Platform)' == '' ">AnyCPU</Platform>
    <ProductVersion>9.0.11209</ProductVersion>
    ...
  </PropertyGroup>
  <ItemGroup>
```

```
    <Compile Include="ObjectGraph.cs" />
    <Compile Include="Program.cs" />
    <Compile Include="Properties\AssemblyInfo.cs" />
    <Compile Include="Tests\Aggregation.cs" />
    <Compile Include="Tests\Advanced\RecursiveXml.cs" />
  </ItemGroup>
  <ItemGroup>
    ...
  </ItemGroup>
  ...
</Project>
```

Let's say we want to include only files, as follows:

```
<ProjectReport>
  <File>ObjectGraph.cs</File>
  <File>Program.cs</File>
  <File>Properties\AssemblyInfo.cs</File>
  <File>Tests\Aggregation.cs</File>
  <File>Tests\Advanced\RecursiveXml.cs</File>
</ProjectReport>
```

The following query performs this transformation:

```
XElement project = XElement.Load ("myProjectFile.csproj");
XNamespace ns = project.Name.Namespace;
var query =
  new XElement ("ProjectReport",
    from compileItem in
      project.Elements (ns + "ItemGroup").Elements (ns + "Compile")
    let include = compileItem.Attribute ("Include")
    where include != null
    select new XElement ("File", include.Value)
  );
```

The query first extracts all ItemGroup elements, and then uses the Elements exten-sion method to obtain a flat sequence of all their Compile subelements. Notice that we had to specify an XML namespace—everything in the original file inherits the namespace defined by the Project element—so a local element name such as ItemGroup won't work on its own. Then, we extracted the Include attribute value and projected its value as an element.

Advanced transformations

When querying a local collection such as an X-DOM, you're free to write custom query operators to assist with more complex queries.

Suppose in the preceding example that we instead wanted a hierarchical output, based on folders:

```
<Project>
  <File>ObjectGraph.cs</File>
  <File>Program.cs</File>
  <Folder name="Properties">
    <File>AssemblyInfo.cs</File>
  </Folder>
```

```
<Folder name="Tests">
  <File>Aggregation.cs</File>
  <Folder name="Advanced">
    <File>RecursiveXml.cs</File>
  </Folder>
</Folder>
</Project>
```

To produce this, we need to process path strings such as *Tests\Advanced\ RecursiveXml.cs* recursively. The following method does just this: it accepts a sequence of path strings and emits an X-DOM hierarchy consistent with our desired output:

```
static IEnumerable<XElement> ExpandPaths (IEnumerable<string> paths)
{
  var brokenUp = from path in paths
                 let split = path.Split (new char[] { '\\' }, 2)
                 orderby split[0]
                 select new
                 {
                   name = split[0],
                   remainder = split.ElementAtOrDefault (1)
                 };

  IEnumerable<XElement> files = from b in brokenUp
                                where b.remainder == null
                                select new XElement ("file", b.name);

  IEnumerable<XElement> folders = from b in brokenUp
                                  where b.remainder != null
                                  group b.remainder by b.name into grp
                                  select new XElement ("folder",
                                    new XAttribute ("name", grp.Key),
                                    ExpandPaths (grp)
                                  );

  return files.Concat (folders);
}
```

The first query splits each path string at the first backslash, into a name + remainder:

```
Tests\Advanced\RecursiveXml.cs -> Tests + Advanced\RecursiveXml.cs
```

If remainder is null, we're dealing with a straight filename. The files query extracts these cases.

If remainder is not null, we've got a folder. The folders query handles these cases. Because other files can be in the same folder, it must group by folder name to bring them all together. For each group, it then executes the same function for the subelements.

The final result is a concatenation of files and folders. The Concat operator preserves order, so all the files come first, alphabetically, then all the folders, alphabetically.

With this method in place, we can complete the query in two steps. First, we extract a simple sequence of path strings:

```
IEnumerable<string> paths =
  from compileItem in
    project.Elements (ns + "ItemGroup").Elements (ns + "Compile")
  let include = compileItem.Attribute ("Include")
  where include != null
  select include.Value;
```

Then, we feed this into our ExpandPaths method for the final result:

```
var query = new XElement ("Project", ExpandPaths (paths));
```

11

Other XML Technologies

The System.Xml namespace comprises the following namespaces and core classes:

System.Xml.*

XmlReader *and* XmlWriter
> High-performance, forward-only cursors for reading or writing an XML stream

XmlDocument
> Represents an XML document in a W3C-style DOM

System.Xml.XPath
> Infrastructure and API (XPathNavigator) for XPath, a string-based language for querying XML

System.Xml.XmlSchema
> Infrastructure and API for (W3C) XSD schemas

System.Xml.Xsl
> Infrastructure and API (XslCompiledTransform) for performing (W3C) XSLT transformations of XML

System.Xml.Serialization
> Supports the serialization of classes to and from XML (see Chapter 15)

System.Xml.XLinq
> Modern, simplified, LINQ-centric version of XmlDocument (see Chapter 10)

W3C is an abbreviation for World Wide Web Consortium, where the XML standards are defined.

XmlConvert, the static class for parsing and formatting XML strings, is covered in Chapter 6.

XmlReader

XmlReader is a high-performance class for reading an XML stream in a low-level, forward-only manner.

Consider the following XML file:

```
<?xml version="1.0" encoding="utf-8" standalone="yes"?>
<customer id="123" status="archived">
  <firstname>Jim</firstname>
  <lastname>Bo</lastname>
</customer>
```

To instantiate an XmlReader, you call the static XmlReader.Create method, passing in a Stream, a TextReader, or a URI string. For example:

```
using (XmlReader reader = XmlReader.Create ("customer.xml"))
  ...
```

To construct an XmlReader that reads from a string:

```
XmlReader reader = XmlReader.Create (
  new System.IO.StringReader (myString));
```

You can also pass in an XmlReaderSettings object to control parsing and validation options. The following three properties on XmlReaderSettings are particularly useful for skipping over superfluous content:

```
bool IgnoreComments                // Skip over comment nodes?
bool IgnoreProcessingInstructions  // Skip over processing instructions?
bool IgnoreWhitespace              // Skip over whitespace?
```

In the following example, we instruct the reader not to emit whitespace nodes, which are a distraction in typical scenarios:

```
XmlReaderSettings settings = new XmlReaderSettings( );
settings.IgnoreWhitespace = true;

using (XmlReader reader = XmlReader.Create ("customer.xml", settings))
  ...
```

Another useful property on XmlReaderSettings is ConformanceLevel. Its default value of Document instructs the reader to assume a valid XML document with a single root node. This is a problem if you want to read just an inner portion of XML, containing multiple nodes:

```
<firstname>Jim</firstname>
<lastname>Bo</lastname>
```

To read this without throwing an exception, you must set ConformanceLevel to Fragment.

XmlReaderSettings also has a property called CloseInput, which indicates whether to close the underlying stream when the reader is closed (there's an analogous property on XmlWriterSettings called CloseOutput). The default value for Close-Input and CloseOutput is true.

Reading Nodes

The units of an XML stream are *XML nodes*. The reader traverses the stream in textual (depth-first) order. The Depth property of the reader returns the current depth of the cursor.

The most primitive way to read from an XmlReader is to call Read. It advances to the next node in the XML stream, rather like MoveNext in IEnumerator. The first call to Read positions the cursor at the first node. When Read returns false, it means the cursor has advanced *past* the last node, at which point the XmlReader should be closed and abandoned.

In this example, we read every node in the XML stream, outputting each node type as we go:

```
XmlReaderSettings settings = new XmlReaderSettings( );
settings.IgnoreWhitespace = true;

using (XmlReader reader = XmlReader.Create ("customer.xml", settings))
  while (reader.Read( ))
  {
    Console.Write (new string (' ',reader.Depth*2));  // Write indentation
    Console.WriteLine (reader.NodeType);
  }
```

The output is as follows:

```
XmlDeclaration
Element
  Element
    Text
  EndElement
  Element
    Text
  EndElement
EndElement
```

 Attributes are not included in Read-based traversal (see the section "Reading Attributes" later in this chapter).

NodeType is of type XmlNodeType, which is an enum with these members:

None	Comment	Document
XmlDeclaration	Entity	DocumentType
Element	EndEntity	DocumentFragment
EndElement	EntityReference	Notation
Text	ProcessingInstruction	Whitespace
Attribute	CDATA	SignificantWhitespace

Two string properties on XmlReader provide access to a node's content: Name and Value. Depending on the node type, either Name or Value (or both) is populated:

```
XmlReaderSettings settings = new XmlReaderSettings( );
settings.IgnoreWhitespace = true;
```

```
settings.ProhibitDtd = false;        // Must set this to read DTDs

using (XmlReader r = XmlReader.Create ("customer.xml", settings))
  while (r.Read( ))
  {
    Console.Write (r.NodeType.ToString( ).PadRight (17, '-'));
    Console.Write ("> ".PadRight (r.Depth * 3));

    switch (r.NodeType)
    {
      case XmlNodeType.Element:
      case XmlNodeType.EndElement:
        Console.WriteLine (r.Name); break;

      case XmlNodeType.Text:
      case XmlNodeType.CDATA:
      case XmlNodeType.Comment:
      case XmlNodeType.XmlDeclaration:
        Console.WriteLine (r.Value); break;

      case XmlNodeType.DocumentType:
        Console.WriteLine (r.Name + " - " + r.Value); break;

      default: break;
    }
  }
```

To demonstrate this, we'll expand our XML file to include a document type, entity, CDATA, and comment:

```
<?xml version="1.0" encoding="utf-8" ?>
<!DOCTYPE customer [ <!ENTITY tc "Top Customer"> ]>
<customer id="123" status="archived">
  <firstname>Jim</firstname>
  <lastname>Bo</lastname>
  <quote><![CDATA[C#'s operators include: < > &]]></quote>
  <notes>Jim Bo is a &tc;</notes>
  <!-- That wasn't so bad! -->
</customer>
```

An entity is like a macro; a CDATA is like a verbatim string (@"...") in C#. Here's the result:

```
XmlDeclaration---> version="1.0" encoding="utf-8"
DocumentType-----> customer -  <!ENTITY tc "Top Customer">
Element----------> customer
Element----------> firstname
Text------------>     Jim
EndElement------->  firstname
Element----------> lastname
Text------------>     Bo
EndElement------->  lastname
Element----------> quote
CDATA------------>     C#'s operators include: < > &
EndElement------->  quote
```

```
Element----------->   notes
Text------------->      Jim Bo is a Top Customer
EndElement------->    notes
Comment---------->      That wasn't so bad!
EndElement------->    customer
```

XmlReader automatically resolves entities, so in our example, the entity reference
&tc; expands into Top Customer.

Reading Elements

Often, you already know the structure of the XML document that you're reading.
To help with this, XmlReader provides a range of methods that read while
presuming a particular structure. This simplifies your code, as well as performing
some validation at the same time.

> XmlReader throws an XmlException if any validation fails. Xml-
> Exception has LineNumber and LinePosition properties indicating
> where the error occurred—logging this information is essential if
> the XML file is large!

ReadStartElement verifies that the current NodeType is StartElement, and then calls
Read. If you specify a name, it verifies that it matches that of the current element.

ReadEndElement verifies that the current NodeType is EndElement, and then calls
Read.

For instance, we could read this:

```
<firstname>Jim</firstname>
```

as follows:

```
reader.ReadStartElement ("firstname");
Console.WriteLine (reader.Value);
reader.ReadEndElement();
```

The ReadElementContentAsString method does all of this in one hit. It reads a start
element, a text node, and an end element, returning the content as a string:

```
string firstName = reader.ReadElementContentAsString ("firstname", "");
```

The second argument refers to the namespace, which is blank in this example.
There are also typed versions of this method, such as ReadElementContentAsInt,
which parse the result. Returning to our original XML document:

```
<?xml version="1.0" encoding="utf-8" standalone="yes"?>
<customer id="123" status="archived">
  <firstname>Jim</firstname>
  <lastname>Bo</lastname>
  <creditlimit>500.00</creditlimit>    <!-- OK, we sneaked this in! -->
</customer>
```

We could read it in as follows:

```
XmlReaderSettings settings = new XmlReaderSettings();
settings.IgnoreWhitespace = true;
```

```
using (XmlReader r = XmlReader.Create ("customer.xml", settings))
{
  r.MoveToContent( );                    // Skip over the XML declaration
  r.ReadStartElement ("customer");
  string firstName   = r.ReadElementContentAsString ("firstname", "");
  string lastName    = r.ReadElementContentAsString ("lastname", "");
  decimal creditLimit = r.ReadElementContentAsDecimal ("creditlimit", "");

  r.MoveToContent( );       // Skip over that pesky comment
  r.ReadEndElement( );      // Read the closing customer tag
}
```

 The MoveToContent method is really useful. It skips over all the fluff: XML declarations, whitespace, comments, and processing instructions. You can also instruct the reader to do most of this automatically through the properties on XmlReaderSettings.

Optional elements

In the previous example, suppose that <lastname> was optional. The solution to this is straightforward:

```
r.ReadStartElement ("customer");
string firstName   = r. ReadElementContentAsString ("firstname", "");
string lastName    = r.Name == "lastname"
                     ? r.ReadElementContentAsString( ) : null;
decimal creditLimit = r.ReadElementContentAsDecimal ("creditlimit", "");
```

Random element order

The examples in this section rely on elements appearing in the XML file in a set order. If you need to cope with elements appearing in any order, the easiest solution is to read that section of the XML into an X-DOM. We describe how to do this later in the section "Patterns for Using XmlReader/XmlWriter."

Empty elements

The way that XmlReader handles empty elements presents a horrible trap. Consider the following element:

```
<customerList></customerList>
```

In XML, this is equivalent to:

```
<customerList/>
```

And yet, XmlReader treats the two differently. In the first case, the following code works as expected:

```
reader.ReadStartElement ("customerList");
reader.ReadEndElement( );
```

In the second case, ReadEndElement throws an exception, because there is no separate "end element" as far as XmlReader is concerned. The workaround is to check for an empty element as follows:

```
bool isEmpty = reader.IsEmptyElement;
reader.ReadStartElement ("customerList");
if (!isEmpty) reader.ReadEndElement( );
```

In reality, this is a nuisance only when the element in question may contain child elements (such as a customer list). With elements that wrap simple text (such as firstname), you can avoid the whole issue by calling a method such as Read-ElementContentAsString. The ReadElement*XXX* methods handle both kinds of empty elements correctly.

Other ReadXXX methods

Table 11-1 summarizes all Read*XXX* methods in XmlReader. Most of these are designed to work with elements. The sample XML fragment shown in bold is the section read by the method described.

Table 11-1. Read methods

Members	Works on NodeType	Sample XML fragment	Input parameters	Data returned
ReadContentAs*XXX*	Text	<a>**x**</a>		x
ReadString	Text	<a>**x**</a>		x
ReadElementString	Element	**<a>x</a>**		x
ReadElementContentAs*XXX*	Element	**<a>x</a>**		x
ReadInnerXml	Element	**<a>x</a>**		x
ReadOuterXml	Element	**<a>x</a>**		<a>x</a>
ReadStartElement	Element	**<a>**x</a>		
ReadEndElement	Element	<a>x**</a>**		
ReadSubtree	Element	**<a>x</a>**		<a>x</a>
ReadToDescendent	Element	**<a>**x<b></b></a>	"b"	
ReadToFollowing	Element	**<a>**x<b></b></a>	"b"	
ReadToNextSibling	Element	**<a>x</a>**<b></b>	"b"	
ReadAttributeValue	Attribute	See "Reading Attributes"		

The ReadContentAs*XXX* methods parse a text node into type *XXX*. Internally, the XmlConvert class performs the string-to-type conversion. The text node can be within an element or an attribute.

The ReadElementContentAs*XXX* methods are wrappers around corresponding ReadContentAs*XXX* methods. They apply to the *element* node, rather than the *text* node enclosed by the element.

> The typed Read*XXX* methods also include versions that read base 64 and BinHex formatted data into a byte array.

ReadInnerXml is typically applied to an element, and it reads and returns an element and all its descendents. When applied to an attribute, it returns the value of the attribute.

ReadOuterXml is the same as ReadInnerXml, except it includes rather than excludes the element at the cursor position.

ReadSubtree returns a proxy reader that provides a view over just the current element (and its descendents). The proxy reader must be closed before the original reader can be safely read again. At the point the proxy reader is closed, the cursor position of the original reader moves to the end of the subtree.

ReadToDescendent moves the cursor to the start of the first descendent node with the specified name/namespace.

ReadToFollowing moves the cursor to the start of the first node—regardless of depth—with the specified name/namespace.

ReadToNextSibling moves the cursor to the start of the first sibling node with the specified name/namespace.

ReadString and ReadElementString behave like ReadContentAsString and ReadElementContentAsString, except that they throw an exception if there's more than a *single* text node within the element. In general, these methods should be avoided, as they throw an exception if an element contains a comment.

Reading Attributes

XmlReader provides an indexer giving you direct (random) access to an element's attributes—by name or position. Using the indexer is equivalent to calling GetAttribute.

Given the following XML fragment:

```
<customer id="123" status="archived"/>
```

we could read its attributes as follows:

```
Console.WriteLine (reader ["id"]);              // 123
Console.WriteLine (reader ["status"]);          // archived
Console.WriteLine (reader ["bogus"] == null);   // True
```

> The XmlReader must be positioned *on a start element* in order to read attributes. *After* calling ReadStartElement, the attributes are gone forever!

Although attribute order is semantically irrelevant, you can access attributes by their ordinal position. We could rewrite the preceding example as follows:

```
Console.WriteLine (reader [0]);              // 123
Console.WriteLine (reader [1]);              // archived
```

The indexer also lets you specify the attribute's namespace—if it has one.

AttributeCount returns the number of attributes for the current node.

Attribute nodes

To explicitly traverse attribute nodes, you must make a special diversion from the normal path of just calling Read. A good reason to do so is if you want to parse attribute values into other types, via the ReadContentAs*XXX* methods.

The diversion must begin from a *start element*. To make the job easier, the forward-only rule is relaxed during attribute traversal: you can jump to any attribute (forward or backward) by calling MoveToAttribute.

 MoveToElement returns you to the start element from anyplace within the attribute node diversion.

Returning to our previous example:

```
<customer id="123" status="archived"/>
```

we can do this:

```
reader.MoveToAttribute ("status");
string status = ReadContentAsString();

reader.MoveToAttribute ("id");
int id = ReadContentAsInt();
```

MoveToAttribute returns false if the specified attribute doesn't exist.

You can also traverse each attribute in sequence by calling the MoveToFirstAttribute and then the MoveToNextAttribute methods:

```
if (reader.MoveToFirstAttribute())
  do
  {
    Console.WriteLine (reader.Name + "=" + reader.Value);
  }
  while (reader.MoveToNextAttribute());

// OUTPUT:
id=123
status=archived
```

Namespaces and Prefixes

XmlReader provides two parallel systems for referring to element and attribute names:

- Name
- NamespaceURI and LocalName

Whenever you read an element's Name property or call a method that accepts a single name argument, you're using the first system. This works well if no namespaces or prefixes are present; otherwise, it acts in a crude and literal manner. Namespaces are ignored, and prefixes are included exactly as they were written. For example:

Sample fragment	Name
<customer ...>	customer
<customer xmlns='blah' ...>	customer
<x:customer ...>	x:customer

The following code works with the first two cases:

```
reader.ReadStartElement ("customer");
```

The following is required to handle the third case:

```
reader.ReadStartElement ("x:customer");
```

The second system works through two *namespace-aware* properties: `NamespaceURI` and `LocalName`. These properties take into account prefixes and default namespaces defined by parent elements. Prefixes are automatically expanded. This means that `NamespaceURI` always reflects the semantically correct namespace for the current element, and `LocalName` is always free of prefixes.

When you pass two name arguments into a method such as `ReadStartElement`, you're using this same system. For example, consider the following XML:

```
<customer xmlns="DefaultNamespace" xmlns:other="OtherNamespace">
  <address>
    <other:city>
      ...
```

We could read this as follows:

```
reader.ReadStartElement ("customer", "DefaultNamespace");
reader.ReadStartElement ("address",  "DefaultNamespace");
reader.ReadStartElement ("city",     "OtherNamespace");
```

Abstracting away prefixes is usually exactly what you want. If necessary, you can see what prefix was used through the `Prefix` property and convert it into a namespace by calling `LookupNamespace`.

XmlWriter

`XmlWriter` is a forward-only writer of an XML stream. The design of `XmlWriter` is symmetrical to `XmlReader`.

As with `XmlTextReader`, you construct an `XmlWriter` by calling `Create` with an optional settings object. In the following example, we enable indenting to make the output more human-readable, and then write a simple XML file:

```
XmlWriterSettings settings = new XmlWriterSettings();
settings.Indent = true;

using (XmlWriter writer = XmlWriter.Create ("..\\..\\foo.xml", settings))
{
  writer.WriteStartElement ("customer");
  writer.WriteElementString ("firstname", "Jim");
  writer.WriteElementString ("lastname"," Bo");
  writer.WriteEndElement();
}
```

This produces the following document (the same as the file we read in the first example of `XmlReader`):

```
<?xml version="1.0" encoding="utf-8" ?>
<customer>
```

```
<firstname>Jim</firstname>
<lastname>Bo</lastname>
</customer>
```

XmlWriter automatically writes the declaration at the top unless you indicate otherwise in XmlWriterSettings, by setting OmitXmlDeclaration to true or ConformanceLevel to Fragment. The latter also permits writing multiple root nodes—something that otherwise throws an exception.

The WriteValue method writes a single text node. It accepts both string and nonstring types such as bool and DateTime, internally calling XmlConvert to perform XML-compliant string conversions:

```
writer.WriteStartElement ("birthdate");
writer.WriteValue (DateTime.Now);
writer.WriteEndElement( );
```

In contrast, if we call:

```
WriteElementString ("birthdate", DateTime.Now.ToString( ));
```

the result would be both non-XML-compliant and vulnerable to incorrect parsing

WriteString is equivalent to calling WriteValue with a string. XmlWriter automatically escapes characters that would otherwise be illegal within an attribute or element, such as & < >, and extended Unicode characters.

Writing Attributes

You can write attributes immediately after writing a start element:

```
writer.WriteStartElement ("customer");
writer.WriteAttributeString ("id", "1");
writer.WriteAttributeString ("status", "archived");
```

To write nonstring values, call WriteStartAttribute, WriteValue, and then WriteEndAttribute.

Writing Other Node Types

XmlWriter also defines the following methods for writing other kinds of nodes:

```
WriteBase64          // for binary data
WriteBinHex          // for binary data
WriteCData
WriteComment
WriteDocType
WriteEntityRef
WriteProcessingInstruction
WriteRaw
WriteWhitespace
```

WriteRaw directly injects a string into the output stream. There is also a WriteNode method that accepts an XmlReader, echoing everything from the given XmlReader.

Namespaces and Prefixes

The overloads for the Write* methods allow you to associate an element or attribute with a namespace. Let's rewrite the contents of the XML file in our previous example. This time we will associate all the elements with the *http://oreilly.com* namespace, declaring the prefix o at the customer element:

```
writer.WriteStartElement ("o", "customer", "http://oreilly.com");
writer.WriteElementString ("o", "firstname", "http://oreilly.com", "Jim");
writer.WriteElementString ("o", "firstname", "http://oreilly.com", "Bo");
writer.WriteEndElement( );
```

The output is now as follows:

```
<?xml version="1.0" encoding="utf-8" standalone="yes"?>
<o:customer xmlns:o='http://oreilly.com'>
  <o:firstname>Jim</o:firstname>
  <o:lastname>Bo</o:lastname>
</o:customer>
```

Notice how for brevity XmlWriter omits the child element's namespace declarations when they are already declared by the parent element.

Patterns for Using XmlReader/XmlWriter

Working with Hierarchical Data

Consider the following classes:

```
public class Contacts
{
  public IList<Customer> Customers = new List<Customer>( );
  public IList<Supplier> Suppliers = new List<Supplier>( );
}

public class Customer { public string FirstName, LastName; }
public class Supplier { public string Name;               }
```

Suppose you want to use XmlReader and XmlWriter to serialize a Contacts object to XML as in the following:

```
<?xml version="1.0" encoding="utf-8" standalone="yes"?>
<contacts>
  <customer id="1">
    <firstname>Jay</firstname>
    <lastname>Dee</lastname>
  </customer>
  <customer>                    <!-- we'll assume id is optional -->
    <firstname>Kay</firstname>
    <lastname>Gee</lastname>
  </customer>
  <supplier>
    <name>X Technologies Ltd</name>
  </supplier>
</contacts>
```

The best approach is not to write one big method, but to encapsulate XML functionality in the Customer and Supplier types themselves by writing ReadXml and WriteXml methods on these types. The pattern in doing so is straightforward:

- ReadXml and WriteXml leave the reader/writer at the same depth when they exit.

- ReadXml reads the outer element, whereas WriteXml writes only its inner content.

Here's how we would write the Customer type:

```
public class Customer
{
  public const string XmlName = "customer";
  public int? ID;
  public string FirstName, LastName;

  public Customer () { }
  public Customer (XmlReader r) { ReadXml (r); }

  public void ReadXml (XmlReader r)
  {
    if (r.MoveToAttribute ("id")) ID = r.ReadContentAsInt( );
    r.ReadStartElement( );
    FirstName = r.ReadElementContentAsString ("firstname", "");
    LastName = r.ReadElementContentAsString ("lastname", "");
    r.ReadEndElement( );
  }

  public void WriteXml (XmlWriter w)
  {
    if (ID.HasValue) w.WriteAttributeString ("id", "", ID.ToString( ));
    w.WriteElementString ("firstname", FirstName);
    w.WriteElementString ("lastname", LastName);
  }
}
```

Notice that ReadXml reads the outer start and end element nodes. If its caller did this job instead, Customer couldn't read its own attributes. The reason for not making WriteXml symmetrical in this regard is twofold:

- The caller might need to choose how the outer element is named.

- The caller might need to write extra XML attributes, such as the element's *subtype* (which could then be used to decide which class to instantiate when reading back the element).

Another benefit of following this pattern is that it makes your implementation compatible with IXmlSerializable (see Chapter 15).

The Supplier class is analogous:

```
public class Supplier
{
  public const string XmlName = "supplier";
  public string Name;
```

```
   public Supplier () { }
   public Supplier (XmlReader r) { ReadXml (r); }

   public void ReadXml (XmlReader r)
   {
     r.ReadStartElement( );
     Name = r.ReadElementContentAsString ("name", "");
     r.ReadEndElement( );
   }

   public void WriteXml (XmlWriter w)
   {
     w.WriteElementString ("name", Name);
   }
 }
```

With the Contacts class, we must enumerate the customers element in ReadXml, checking whether each subelement is a customer or a supplier. We also have to code around the empty element trap:

```
public void ReadXml (XmlReader r)
{
  bool isEmpty = r.IsEmptyElement;      // This ensures we don't get
  r.ReadStartElement( );                // snookered by an empty
  if (isEmpty) return;                  // <contacts/> element!
  while (r.NodeType == XmlNodeType.Element)
  {
    if (r.Name == Customer.XmlName)     Customers.Add (new Customer (r));
    else if (r.Name == Supplier.XmlName) Suppliers.Add (new Supplier (r));
    else
      throw new XmlException ("Unexpected node: " + r.Name);
  }
  r.ReadEndElement( );
}

public void WriteXml (XmlWriter w)
{
  foreach (Customer c in Customers)
  {
    w.WriteStartElement (Customer.XmlName);
    c.WriteXml (w);
    w.WriteEndElement( );
  }
  foreach (Supplier s in Suppliers)
  {
    w.WriteStartElement (Supplier.XmlName);
    s.WriteXml (w);
    w.WriteEndElement( );
  }
}
```

Mixing XmlReader/XmlWriter with an X-DOM

You can fly in an X-DOM at any point in the XML tree where XmlReader or XmlWriter becomes too cumbersome. Using the X-DOM to handle inner elements is an excellent way to combine X-DOM's ease of use with the low-memory footprint of XmlReader and XmlWriter.

Using XmlReader with XElement

To read the current element into an X-DOM, you call XNode.ReadFrom, passing in the XmlReader. Unlike XElement.Load, this method is not "greedy" in that it doesn't expect to see a whole document. Instead, it reads just the end of the current subtree.

For instance, suppose we have an XML logfile structured as follows:

```
<log>
  <logentry id="1">
    <date>...</date>
    <source>...</source>
    ...
  </logentry>
  ...
</log>
```

If there were 1 million logentry elements, reading the whole thing into an X-DOM would waste memory. A better solution is to traverse each logentry with an XmlReader, and then use XElement to process the elements individually:

```
XmlReaderSettings settings = new XmlReaderSettings( );
settings.IgnoreWhitespace = true;

using (XmlReader r = XmlReader.Create ("logfile.xml", settings))
{
  r.ReadStartElement ("log");
  while (r.Name == "logentry")
  {
    XElement logEntry = (XElement) XNode.ReadFrom (r);
    int id = (int) logEntry.Attribute ("id");
    DateTime date = (DateTime) logEntry.Element ("date");
    string source = (string) logEntry.Element ("source");
    ...
  }
  r.ReadEndElement( );
}
```

If you follow the pattern described in the previous section, you can slot an XElement into a custom type's ReadXml or WriteXml method without the caller ever knowing you've cheated! For instance, we could rewrite Customer's ReadXml method as follows:

```
public void ReadXml (XmlReader r)
{
  XElement x = (XElement) XNode.ReadFrom (r);
  FirstName = (string) x.Element ("firstname");
  LastName = (string) x.Element ("lastname");
}
```

XElement collaborates with XmlReader to ensure that namespaces are kept intact and prefixes are properly expanded—even if defined at an outer level. So, if our XML file read like this:

```
<log xmlns="http://loggingspace">
  <logentry id="1">
    ...
```

the XElements we constructed at the logentry level would correctly inherit the outer namespace.

Using XmlWriter with XElement

You can use an XElement just to write inner elements to an XmlWriter. The following code writes 1 million logentry elements to an XML file using XElement—without storing the whole thing in memory:

```
using (XmlWriter w = XmlWriter.Create ("log.xml"))
{
  w.WriteStartElement ("log");
  for (int i = 0; i < 1000000; i++)
  {
    XElement e = new XElement ("logentry",
                  new XAttribute ("id", i),
                  new XElement ("date", DateTime.Today.AddDays (-1)),
                  new XElement ("source", "test"));
    e.WriteTo (w);
  }
  w.WriteEndElement ();
}
```

Using an XElement incurs minimal execution overhead. If we amend this example to use XmlWriter throughout, there's no measurable difference in execution time.

XmlDocument

XmlDocument is an in-memory representation of an XML document. Its object model and the methods that its types expose conform to a pattern defined by the W3C. So, if you're familiar with another W3C-compliant XML DOM (e.g., in Java), you'll be at home with XmlDocument. When compared to the X-DOM, however, the W3C model is much "clunkier."

The base type for all objects in an XmlDocument tree is XmlNode. The following types derive from XmlNode:

```
XmlNode
  XmlDocument
  XmlDocumentFragment
  XmlEntity
  XmlNotation
  XmlLinkedNode
```

XmlLinkedNode exposes NextSibling and PreviousSibling properties and is an abstract base for the following subtypes:

```
XmlLinkedNode
  XmlCharacterData
  XmlDeclaration
  XmlDocumentType
  XmlElement
  XmlEntityReference
  XmlProcesingInstruction
```

Loading and Saving an XmlDocument

To load an XmlDocument from an existing source, you instantiate an XmlDocument and then call Load or LoadXml:

- Load accepts a filename, Stream, TextReader, or XmlReader.
- LoadXml accepts a literal XML string.

To save a document, call Save with a filename, Stream, TextWriter, or XmlWriter:

```
XmlDocument doc = new XmlDocument( );
doc.Load ("customer1.xml");
doc.Save ("customer2.xml");
```

Traversing an XmlDocument

To illustrate traversing an XmlDocument, we'll use the following XML file:

```
<?xml version="1.0" encoding="utf-8" standalone="yes"?>
<customer id="123" status="archived">
  <firstname>Jim</firstname>
  <lastname>Bo</lastname>
</customer>
```

The ChildNodes property (defined in XNode) allows you to descend into the tree structure. This returns an indexable collection:

```
XmlDocument doc = new XmlDocument( );
doc.Load ("customer.xml");

Console.WriteLine (doc.DocumentElement.ChildNodes[0].InnerText);   // Jim
Console.WriteLine (doc.DocumentElement.ChildNodes[1].InnerText);   // Bo
```

With the ParentNode property, you can ascend back up the tree:

```
Console.WriteLine (
  doc.DocumentElement.ChildNodes[1].ParentNode.Name);        // customer
```

The following properties also help traverse the document (all of which return null if the node does not exist):

```
FirstChild
LastChild
NextSibling
PreviousSibling
```

The following two statements both output firstname:

```
Console.WriteLine (doc.DocumentElement.FirstChild.Name);
Console.WriteLine (doc.DocumentElement.LastChild.PreviousSibling.Name);
```

XmlNode exposes an Attributes property for accessing attributes either by name (and namespace) or by ordinal position. For example:

```
Console.WriteLine (doc.DocumentElement.Attributes ["id"].Value);
```

InnerText and InnerXml

The InnerText property represents the concatenation of all child text nodes. The following two lines both output Jim, since our XML document contains only a single text node:

```
Console.WriteLine (doc.DocumentElement.ChildNodes[0].InnerText);
Console.WriteLine (doc.DocumentElement.ChildNodes[0].FirstChild.Value);
```

Setting the InnerText property replaces *all* child nodes with a single text node. Be careful when setting InnerText to not accidentally wipe over element nodes. For example:

```
doc.DocumentElement.ChildNodes[0].InnerText = "Jo";            // wrong
doc.DocumentElement.ChildNodes[0].FirstChild.InnerText = "Jo";   // right
```

The InnerXml property represents the XML fragment *within* the current node. You typically use InnerXml on elements:

```
Console.WriteLine (doc.DocumentElement.InnerXml);

// OUTPUT:
<firstname>Jim</firstname><lastname>Bo</lastname>
```

InnerXml throws an exception if the node type cannot have children.

Creating and Manipulating Nodes

To create and add new nodes:

1. Call one of the Create*XXX* methods on the XmlDocument, such as CreateElement.
2. Add the new node into the tree by calling AppendChild, PrependChild, InsertBefore, or InsertAfter on the desired parent node.

 Creating nodes requires that you first have an XmlDocument—you cannot simply instantiate an XmlElement on its own like with the X-DOM. Nodes rely on a host XmlDocument for sustenance.

For example:

```
XmlDocument doc = new XmlDocument( );
XmlElement customer = doc.CreateElement ("customer");
doc.AppendChild (customer);
```

The following creates a document matching the XML we started with earlier in this chapter in the section "XmlReader":

```
XmlDocument doc = new XmlDocument ( );
doc.AppendChild (doc.CreateXmlDeclaration ("1.0", null, "yes"));

XmlAttribute id      = doc.CreateAttribute ("id");
```

```
XmlAttribute status = doc.CreateAttribute ("status");
id.Value    = "123";
status.Value = "archived";

XmlElement firstname = doc.CreateElement ("firstname");
XmlElement lastname  = doc.CreateElement ("lastname");
firstname.AppendChild (doc.CreateTextNode ("Jim"));
lastname.AppendChild  (doc.CreateTextNode ("Bo"));

XmlElement customer = doc.CreateElement ("customer");
customer.Attributes.Append (id);
customer.Attributes.Append (status);
customer.AppendChild (lastname);
customer.AppendChild (firstname);

doc.AppendChild (customer);
```

You can construct the tree in any order. In the previous example, it doesn't matter if you rearrange the order of the lines that append child nodes.

To remove a node, you call RemoveChild, ReplaceChild, or RemoveAll.

Namespaces

 See Chapter 10 for an introduction to XML namespaces and prefixes.

The CreateElement and CreateAttribute methods are overloaded to let you specify a namespace and prefix:

```
CreateXXX (string name);
CreateXXX (string name, string namespaceURI);
CreateXXX (string prefix, string localName, string namespaceURI);
```

The name parameter refers to either a local name (i.e., no prefix) or a name qualified with a prefix. The namespaceURI parameter is used if and only if *declaring* (rather than merely referring to) a namespace.

Here is an example of *declaring* a namespace with a prefix while creating an element:

```
XmlElement customer = doc.CreateElement ("o", "customer",
                                         "http://oreilly.com");
```

Here is an example of *referring* to a namespace with a prefix while creating an element:

```
XmlElement customer = doc.CreateElement ("o:firstname");
```

In the next section, we will explain how to deal with namespaces when writing XPath queries.

XPath

XPath is the W3C standard for XML querying. In the .NET Framework, XPath can query an XmlDocument rather like LINQ queries an X-DOM. XPath has a wider scope, though, in that it's also used by other XML technologies, such as XML schema, XLST, and XAML.

 XPath queries are expressed in terms of the XPath 2.0 Data Model. Both the DOM and the XPath Data Model represent an XML document as a tree. The difference is that the XPath Data Model is purely data-centric, abstracting away the formatting aspects of XML text. For example, CDATA sections are not required in the XPath Data Model, since the only reason CDATA sections exist is to enable text to contain markup character sequences. The XPath specification is at *http://www.w3.org/TR/xpath20/*.

The examples in this section all use the following XML file:

```
<?xml version="1.0" encoding="utf-8" standalone="yes"?>
<customers>
  <customer id="123" status="archived">
    <firstname>Jim</firstname>
    <lastname>Bo</lastname>
  </customer>
  <customer>
    <firstname>Thomas</firstname>
    <lastname>Jefferson</lastname>
  </customer>
</customers>
```

You can write XPath queries within code in the following ways:

- Call one of the Select*XXX* methods on an XmlDocument or XmlNode.
- Spawn an XPathNavigator from either:
  — An XmlDocument
  — An XPathDocument
- Call an XPath*XXX* extension method on an XNode.

The Select*XXX* methods accept an XPath query string. For example, the following finds the firstname node of an XmlDocument:

```
XmlDocument doc = new XmlDocument( );
doc.Load ("customers.xml");
XmlNode n = doc.SelectSingleNode ("customers/customer[firstname='Jim']");
Console.WriteLine (n.InnerText);  // JimBo
```

The Select*XXX* methods delegate their implementation to XPathNavigator, which you can also use directly—over either an XmlDocument or a read-only XPathDocument.

You can also execute XPath queries over an X-DOM, via extension methods defined in System.Xml.XPath:

```
XDocument doc = XDocument.Load (@"Customers.xml");
XElement e = e.XPathSelectElement ("customers/customer[firstname='Jim']");
Console.WriteLine (e.Value);   // JimBo
```

The extension methods for use with XNodes are:

```
CreateNavigator
XPathEvaluate
XPathSelectElement
XPathSelectElements
```

Common XPath Operators

The XPath specification is huge. However, you can get by knowing just a few operators (see Table 11-2), just as you can play a lot of songs knowing just three chords.

Table 11-2. Common XPath operators

Operator	Description
/	Children
//	Recursively children
.	Current node (usually implied)
..	Parent node
*	Wildcard
@	Attribute
[]	Filter
:	Namespace separator

To find the customers node:

```
XmlNode node = doc.SelectSingleNode ("customers");
```

The / symbol queries child nodes. To select the customer nodes:

```
XmlNode node = doc.SelectSingleNode ("customers/customer");
```

The // operator includes all child nodes, regardless of nesting level. To select all lastname nodes:

```
XmlNodeList nodes = doc.SelectNodes ("//lastname");
```

The .. operator selects parent nodes. This example is a little silly because we're starting from the root anyway, but it serves to illustrate the functionality:

```
XmlNodeList nodes = doc.SelectNodes ("customers/customer..customers");
```

The * operator selects nodes regardless of name. The following selects the child nodes of customer, regardless of name:

```
XmlNodeList nodes = doc.SelectNodes ("customers/customer/*");
```

The @ operator selects attributes. * can be used as a wildcard. Here is how to select the id attribute:

```
XmlNode node = doc.SelectSingleNode ("customers/customer/@id");
```

The [] operator filters a selection, in conjunction with the operators =, !=, <, >, not( ), and, and or. In this example, we filter on firstname:

```
XmlNode n = doc.SelectSingleNode ("customers/customer[firstname='Jim']");
```

The : operator qualifies a namespace. Had the customers element been qualified with the x namespace, we would access it as follows:

```
XmlNode node = doc.SelectSingleNode ("x:customers");
```

XPathNavigator

XPathNavigator is a cursor over the XPath Data Model representation of an XML document. It is loaded with primitive methods that move the cursor around the tree (e.g., move to parent, move to first child, etc.). The XPathNavigator's Select* methods take an XPath string to express more complex navigations or queries that return multiple nodes.

Spawn instances of XPathNavigator from an XmlDocument, an XPathDocument, or another XPathNavigator. Here is an example of spawning an XPathNavigator from an XmlDoument:

```
XPathNavigator nav = doc.CreateNavigator( );
XPathNavigator jim = nav.SelectSingleNode
  (
     "customers/customer[firstname='Jim']"
  );

Console.WriteLine (jim.Value);                        // JimBo
```

In the XPath Data Model, the value of a node is the concatenation of the text elements, equivalent to XmlDocument's InnerText property.

The SelectSingleNode method returns a single XPathNavigator. The Select method returns an XPathNodeIterator, which simply iterates over multiple XPathNavigators. For example:

```
XPathNavigator nav = doc.CreateNavigator( );
string xPath = "customers/customer/firstname/text( )";
foreach (XPathNavigator navC in nav.Select (xPath))
  Console.WriteLine (navC.Value);

OUTPUT:
Jim
Thomas
```

To perform faster queries, you can compile an XPath query into an XPathExpression. You then pass the compiled expression to a Select* method, instead of a string. For example:

```
XPathNavigator nav = doc.CreateNavigator( );
XPathExpression expr = nav.Compile ("customers/customer/firstname");
foreach (XPathNavigator a in nav.Select (expr))
  Console.WriteLine (a.Value);

OUTPUT:
Jim
Thomas
```

Querying with Namespaces

Querying elements and attributes that contain namespaces requires some extra unintuitive steps. Consider the following XML file:

```
<?xml version="1.0" encoding="utf-8" standalone="yes"?>

<o:customers xmlns:o='http://oreilly.com'>
  <o:customer id="123" status="archived">
    <firstname>Jim</firstname>
    <lastname>Bo</lastname>
  </o:customer>
  <o:customer>
    <firstname>Thomas</firstname>
    <lastname>Jefferson</lastname>
  </o:customer>
</o:customers>
```

The following query will fail, despite qualifying the nodes with the prefix o:

```
XmlDocument doc = new XmlDocument();
doc.Load ("customers.xml");
XmlNode n = doc.SelectSingleNode ("o:customers/o:customer");
Console.WriteLine (n.InnerText);  // JimBo
```

To make this query work, you must first create an XmlNamespaceManager instance as follows:

```
XmlNamespaceManager xnm = new XmlNamespaceManager (doc.NameTable);
```

You can treat NameTable as a black box (XmlNamespaceManager uses it internally to cache and reuse strings). Once we create the namespace manager, we can add prefix/namespace pairs to it as follows:

```
xnm.AddNamespace ("o", "http://oreilly.com");
```

The Select* methods on XmlDocument and XPathNavigator have overloads that accept an XmlNamespaceManager. We can successfully rewrite the previous query as follows:

```
XmlNode n = doc.SelectSingleNode ("o:customers/o:customer", xnm);
```

XPathDocument

XPathDocument is used for read-only XML documents that conform to the W3C XPath Data Model. An XPathNavigator backed by an XPathDocument is faster than an XmlDocument, but it cannot make changes to the underlying document:

```
XPathDocument doc = new XPathDocument ("customers.xml");
XPathNavigator nav = doc.CreateNavigator();
foreach (XPathNavigator a in nav.Select ("customers/customer/firstname"))
  Console.WriteLine (a.Value);

OUTPUT:
Jim
Thomas
```

XSD and Schema Validation

The content of a particular XML document is nearly always domain-specific, such as a Microsoft Word document, an application configuration document, or a web service. For each domain, the XML file conforms to a particular pattern. There are several standards for describing the schema of such a pattern, to standardize and automate the interpretation and validation of XML documents. The most widely accepted standard is *XSD*, short for *XML Schema Definition*. Its precursors, DTD and XDR, are also supported by System.Xml.

Consider the following XML document:

```xml
<?xml version="1.0"?>
<customers>
  <customer id="1" status="active">
    <firstname>Jim</firstname>
    <lastname>Bo</lastname>
  </customer>
  <customer id="1" status="archived">
    <firstname>Thomas</firstname>
    <lastname>Jefferson</lastname>
  </customer>
</customers>
```

We can write an XSD for this document as follows:

```xml
<?xml version="1.0" encoding="utf-8"?>
<xs:schema attributeFormDefault="unqualified"
           elementFormDefault="qualified"
           xmlns:xs="http://www.w3.org/2001/XMLSchema">
  <xs:element name="customers">
    <xs:complexType>
      <xs:sequence>
        <xs:element maxOccurs="unbounded" name="customer">
          <xs:complexType>
            <xs:sequence>
              <xs:element name="firstname" type="xs:string" />
              <xs:element name="lastname" type="xs:string" />
            </xs:sequence>
            <xs:attribute name="id" type="xs:int" use="required" />
            <xs:attribute name="status" type="xs:string" use="required" />
          </xs:complexType>
        </xs:element>
      </xs:sequence>
    </xs:complexType>
  </xs:element>
</xs:schema>
```

As you can see, XSD documents are themselves written in XML. Furthermore, an XSD document is describable with XSD—you can find that definition at *http://www.w3.org/2001/XMLSchema.xsd*.

Performing Schema Validation

You can validate an XML file or document against one or more schemas before reading or processing it. There are a number of reasons to do so:

- You can get away with less error checking and exception handling.
- Schema validation picks up errors you might otherwise overlook.
- Error messages are detailed and informative.

To perform validation, plug a schema into an `XmlReader`, an `XmlDocument`, or an X-DOM object, and then read or load the XML as you would normally. Schema validation happens automatically as content is read, so the input stream is not read twice.

Validating with an XmlReader

Here's how to plug a schema from the file *customers.xsd* into an `XmlReader`:

```
XmlReaderSettings settings = new XmlReaderSettings( );
settings.ValidationType = ValidationType.Schema;
settings.Schemas.Add (null, "customers.xsd");

using (XmlReader r = XmlReader.Create ("customers.xml", settings))
  ...
```

If the schema is inline, set the following flag instead of adding to `Schemas`:

```
settings.ValidationFlags |= XmlSchemaValidationFlags.ProcessInlineSchema;
```

You then `Read` as you would normally. If schema validation fails at any point, an `XmlSchemaValidationException` is thrown.

> Calling `Read` on its own validates both elements and attributes: you don't need to navigate to each individual attribute for it to be validated.

If you want *only* to validate the document, you can do this:

```
using (XmlReader r = XmlReader.Create ("customers.xml", settings))
  try { while (r.Read()) ; }
  catch (XmlSchemaValidationException ex)
  {
    ...
  }
```

`XmlSchemaValidationException` has properties for the error `Message`, `LineNumber`, and `LinePosition`. In this case, it only tells you about the first error in the document. If you want to report on all errors in the document, you instead must handle the `ValidationEventHandler` event:

```
XmlReaderSettings settings = new XmlReaderSettings( );
settings.ValidationType = ValidationType.Schema;
settings.Schemas.Add (null, "customers.xsd");
settings.ValidationEventHandler += ValidationHandler;
```

```
using (XmlReader r = XmlReader.Create ("customers.xml", settings))
  while (r.Read()) ;
```

When you handle this event, schema errors no longer throw exceptions. Instead, they fire your event handler:

```
static void ValidationHandler (object sender, ValidationEventArgs e)
{
  Console.WriteLine ("Error: " + e.Exception.Message);
}
```

The Exception property of ValidationEventArgs contains the XmlSchema-
ValidationException that would have otherwise been thrown.

 The System.Xml namespace also contains a class called Xml-
ValidatingReader. This was used to perform schema validation
prior to Framework 2.0, and it is now deprecated.

Validating an X-DOM or XmlDocument

To validate an XML file or stream while reading into an X-DOM or XmlDocument, you create an XmlReader, plug in the schemas, and then use the reader to load the DOM:

```
XmlReaderSettings settings = new XmlReaderSettings();
settings.ValidationType = ValidationType.Schema;
settings.Schemas.Add (null, "customers.xsd");

XDocument doc;
using (XmlReader r = XmlReader.Create ("customers.xml", settings))
  try { doc = XDocument.Load (r); }
  catch (XmlSchemaValidationException ex) { ... }

XmlDocument xmlDoc = new XmlDocument();
using (XmlReader r = XmlReader.Create ("customers.xml", settings))
  try { xmlDoc.Load (r); }
  catch (XmlSchemaValidationException ex) { ... }
```

You can also validate an XDocument or XElement that's already in memory, by calling extension methods in System.Xml.Schema. These methods accept an XmlSchemaSet (a collection of schemas) and a validation event handler:

```
XDocument doc = XDocument.Load (@"customers.xml");
XmlSchemaSet set = new XmlSchemaSet ();
set.Add (null, @"customers.xsd");
StringBuilder errors = new StringBuilder ();
doc.Validate (set, (sender, args) => { errors.AppendLine
                                      (args.Exception.Message); }
            );
Console.WriteLine (errors.ToString());
```

To validate an XmlDocument already in memory, add the schema(s) to the XmlDocument's Schemas collection and then call the document's Validate method, passing in a ValidationEventHandler to process the errors.

XSLT

XSLT stands for *Extensible Stylesheet Language Transformations*. It is an XML language that describes how to transform one XML language into another. The quintessential example of such a transformation is transforming an XML document (that typically describes data) into an XHTML document (that describes a formatted document).

Consider the following XML file:

```
<customer>
  <firstname>Jim</firstname>
  <lastname>Bo</lastname>
</customer>
```

The following XSLT file describes such a transformation:

```
<?xml version="1.0" encoding="UTF-8"?>
  <xsl:stylesheet xmlns:xsl="http://www.w3.org/1999/XSL/Transform"
      version="1.0">
  <xsl:template match="/">
    <html>
      <p><xsl:value-of select="//firstname"/></p>
      <p><xsl:value-of select="//lastname"/></p>
    </html>
  </xsl:template>
</xsl:stylesheet>
```

The output is as follows:

```
<html>
  <p>Jim</p>
  <p>Bo</p>
</html>
```

The `System.Xml.Xsl.XslCompiledTransform` transform class efficiently performs XLST transforms. It renders `XmlTransform` obsolete. `XmlTransform` works very simply:

```
XslCompiledTransform transform = new XslCompiledTransform( );
transform.Load ("test.xslt");
transform.Transform ("input.xml", "output.xml");
```

Generally, it's more useful to use the overload of `Transform` that accepts an `XmlWriter` rather than an output file, so you can control the formatting.

12

Disposal and Garbage Collection

Some objects require explicit tear-down code to release resources such as open files, locks, operating system handles, and unmanaged objects. In .NET parlance, this is called *disposal*, and it is supported through the IDisposable interface. The managed memory occupied by unused objects must also be reclaimed at some point; this function is known as *garbage collection* and is performed by the CLR.

Disposal differs from garbage collection in that disposal is usually explicitly instigated; garbage collection is totally automatic. In other words, the programmer takes care of such things as releasing file handles, locks, and operating system resources while the CLR takes care of releasing memory.

This chapter discusses both disposal and garbage collection, also describing C# finalizers and the pattern by which they can provide a backup for disposal. Lastly, the intricacies of the garbage collector are explored in detail, and other memory management options are discussed.

IDisposable, Dispose, and Close

The .NET Framework defines a special interface for types requiring a tear-down method:

```
public interface IDisposable
{
  void Dispose( );
}
```

C#'s using statement provides a syntactic shortcut for calling Dispose on objects that implement IDisposable, using a try/finally block. For example:

```
using (FileStream fs = new FileStream ("myFile.txt", FileMode.Open))
{
  // ... Write to the file ...
}
```

The compiler converts this to:

```
FileStream fs = new FileStream ("myFile.txt", FileMode.Open);
try
{
  // ... Write to the file ...
}
finally
{
  if (fs != null) fs.Dispose();
}
```

The `finally` block ensures that the `Dispose` method is called even when an exception is thrown, or the code exits the block early.

Writing your own disposable type is simple: implement `IDisposable` and write a `Dispose` method:

```
public class Demo : IDisposable
{
  public virtual void Dispose()
  {
    // Perform cleanup / tear-down.
    ...
  }
}
```

`Dispose` is generally declared virtual (on nonsealed classes) so that subtypes can override the method to add their own tear-down logic. When you override a `Dispose` method, you nearly always call `base.Dispose`.

Standard Disposal Semantics

The Framework follows a de facto set of rules in its disposal logic. These rules are not hard-wired to the framework or C# language in any way; their purpose is to define a consistent protocol to consumers. Here they are:

- Once disposed, an object is beyond redemption. It cannot be reactivated, and calling its methods or properties may throw exceptions or give incorrect results.
- Calling an object's `Dispose` method repeatedly causes no error.
- If disposable object x contains or "wraps" or "possesses" disposable object y, x's `Dispose` method automatically calls y's `Dispose` method—unless instructed otherwise.

These rules are also helpful when writing your own types, though not mandatory. Nothing prevents you from writing an "Undispose" method, other than, perhaps, the flak you might cop from colleagues!

According to rule 3, a container object automatically disposes its child objects. A good example is a Windows container control such as a `Form` or `Panel`. The container may host many child controls, yet you don't dispose every one of them explicitly: closing or disposing the parent control or form takes care of the whole lot. Another example is when you wrap a `FileStream` in a `DeflateStream`.

Disposing the `DeflateStream` also disposes the `FileStream`—unless you instructed otherwise in the constructor.

Close and Stop

Some types define a method called `Close` in addition to `Dispose`. The Framework is not completely consistent on the semantics of a `Close` method, although in nearly all cases it's either:

- Functionally identical to `Dispose`
- A functional *subset* of `Dispose`

An example of the latter is `IDbConnection`: a `Closed` connection can be re-`Opened`; a `Disposed` connection cannot. Another example is a Windows `Form` activated with `ShowDialog`: `Close` hides it; `Dispose` releases its resources.

Some classes define a `Stop` method (e.g., `Timer` or `HttpListener`). A `Stop` method typically releases unmanaged resources such as `Dispose`, but unlike `Dispose`, allows for re-Starting.

When to Dispose

A safe rule to follow (in nearly all cases) is "if in doubt, dispose." A disposable object—if it could talk—would say the following:

> When you've finished with me, let me know. If simply abandoned, I might cause trouble for other object instances, the application domain, the computer, the network, or the database!

Objects wrapping an unmanaged resource handle will nearly always require disposal, in order to free the handle. Examples include Windows Forms controls, file or network streams, network sockets, GDI+ pens, brushes, and bitmaps. Conversely, if a type is disposable, it will often (but not always) reference an unmanaged handle, directly or indirectly. This is because unmanaged handles provide the gateway to the "outside world" of operating system resources, network connections, database locks—the primary means by which objects can create trouble outside of themselves if improperly abandoned.

There are, however, scenarios for *not* disposing. These can be grouped into two categories:

- Cases where calling `Dispose` causes harm
- Cases where calling `Dispose` causes inconvenience

The first category is rare. The main cases are in the `System.Drawing` namespace: the GDI+ objects obtained through *static fields or properties* (such as `Brushes.Blue`) must never be disposed because the same instance is used throughout the life of the application. Instances that you obtain through constructors, however (such as `new SolidBrush`), *should* be disposed, as should instances obtained through static *methods* (such as `Font.FromHdc`).

The second category is more common. There are some good examples in the `System.IO` namespace:

Type	Disposal function	When not to dispose
`MemoryStream`	Prevents further I/O	When you later need to read/write the stream
`StreamReader, Stream-Writer`	Flushes the reader/writer and closes the underlying stream	When you want to keep the underlying stream open (you must instead call `Flush` on a `StreamWriter` when you're done)
`IDbConnection`	Releases a database connection and clears the connection string	If you need to re-`Open` it, you should call `Close` instead of `Dispose`

`MemoryStream`'s `Dispose` method disables only the object; it doesn't perform any critical cleanup because a `MemoryStream` holds no unmanaged handles or other such resources. The same applies to `StringReader`, `StringWriter`, and `Background-Worker` (in `System.ComponentModel`). These types are disposable under the duress of their base class rather than through a genuine need to perform essential cleanup.

Opt-in Disposal

Because `IDisposable` makes a type tractable with C#'s using construct, there's a temptation to extend the reach of `IDisposable` to nonessential activities. For instance:

```
public class HouseManager : IDisposable
{
  public virtual void Dispose( )
  {
    CheckTheMail( );
  }
  ...
}
```

The idea is that a consumer of this class can choose to circumvent the nonessential cleanup—simply by not calling `Dispose`. This, however, relies on the consumer knowing what's inside Demo's `Dispose` method. It also breaks if *essential* cleanup activity is later added:

```
public virtual void Dispose( )
{
  CheckTheMail( );    // Nonessential
  LockTheHouse( );    // Essential
}
```

The solution to this problem is the opt-in disposal pattern:

```
public class Demo : IDisposable
{
  public bool CheckMailOnDispose;

  public Demo (bool checkMailOnDispose)
  {
    CheckMailOnDispose = checkMailOnDispose;
  }

  public virtual void Dispose( )
```

```
    {
      if (CheckMailOnDispose) CheckTheMail( );
      LockTheHouse( );
    }
    ...
  }
```

The consumer can then always call Dispose—providing simplicity and avoiding the need for special documentation or reflection. An example of where this pattern is implemented is in the DeflateStream class, in System.IO.Compression. Here's its constructor:

```
public DeflateStream (Stream stream, CompressionMode mode, bool leaveOpen)
```

The nonessential activity is closing the inner stream (the first parameter) upon disposal. There are times when you want to leave the inner stream open and yet still dispose the DeflateStream to perform its *essential* tear-down activity (flushing buffered data).

This pattern might look simple; yet it escaped StreamReader and StreamWriter (System.IO namespace). The result is messy: StreamWriter must expose another method (Flush) to perform essential cleanup for consumers not calling Dispose. The CryptoStream class in System.Security.Cryptography suffers a similar problem and requires that you call FlushFinalBlock to tear it down while keeping the inner stream open.

Garbage Collection and Finalizers

Regardless of whether an object requires a Dispose method for custom tear-down logic, at some point, the memory it occupies must be freed. The CLR handles this side of it entirely automatically, via an automatic garbage collector. You never deallocate managed memory yourself. For example, consider the following method:

```
public void Test( )
{
  byte[] myArray = new byte[1000];
  ...
}
```

When Test executes, an array to hold 1,000 bytes is allocated on the memory heap. The array is referenced by the variable myArray, stored on the local variable stack. When the method exits, this local variable myArray pops out of scope, meaning that nothing is left to reference the array on the memory heap. The orphaned array then becomes eligible to be reclaimed in garbage collection.

Garbage collection does not happen immediately after an object is orphaned. Rather like garbage collection on the street, it happens periodically, although (unlike garbage collection on the street) not to a fixed schedule. The CLR bases its decision on when to collect upon a number of factors, such as the available memory, the number of memory allocations made, and the time since the last collection. This means that there's an indeterminate delay between an object being orphaned and being released from memory. Theoretically, it can range from nanoseconds to days.

A consequence of automatic garbage collection is that applications can consume more memory than they need, particularly if large temporary arrays are constructed.

The problem can look worse than it is, though, if you judge memory consumption by the "Memory Usage" figure reported by the Task Manager in Windows XP. This figure includes memory that a process has internally deallocated and is willing to rescind immediately to the operating system should another process need it. (The reason it doesn't return the memory to the operating system immediately is to avoid the overhead of asking for it back, should it be required a short while later. It reasons: "If the computer has plenty of free memory, why not use it to lessen allocation/deallocation overhead?")

You can determine your process's real memory consumption by querying a performance counter (System.Diagnostics):

```
string procName = Process.GetCurrentProcess().ProcessName;
using (PerformanceCounter pc = new PerformanceCounter
    ("Process", "Private Bytes", procName))
  Console.WriteLine (pc.NextValue());
```

Reading performance counters requires administrative privileges.

When the garbage collector releases an object from memory, it calls the type's *finalizer*, if it has one. A finalizer is declared in the same way as a constructor, but it is prefixed by the ~ symbol:

```
class Test
{
  ~Test()
  {
    // Finalizer logic...
  }
}
```

Finalizers can be useful, but they come with some provisos:

- Finalizers can slow the allocation and collection of memory and prolong the life of referred objects unnecessarily.
- It's impossible to predict in what order the finalizers for a set of objects will be called.
- You have limited control over when the finalizer for an object will be called.
- If code in a finalizer blocks, other objects cannot get finalized.
- Finalizers may be circumvented altogether if an application fails to unload cleanly.

In summary, finalizers are somewhat like lawyers—although there are cases in which you really need them, in general you don't want to use them unless absolutely necessary. If you do use them, you need to be 100 percent sure you understand what they are doing for you.

Here are some guidelines for implementing finalizers:

- Ensure that your finalizer executes quickly.
- Never block in your finalizer.
- Don't reference other objects.
- Don't throw exceptions.

Calling Dispose from a Finalizer

One excellent use for finalizers is to provide a backup for cases when you forget to call `Dispose` on a disposable object; it's usually better to have an object disposed late than never! There's a standard pattern for implementing this, as follows:

```
class Test : IDisposable
{
  public void Dispose( )            // NOT virtual
  {
    Dispose (true);
    GC.SuppressFinalize (this);     // Prevent finalizer from running
  }

  protected virtual void Dispose (bool disposing)
  {
    if (disposing)
    {
      // The full disposal treatment
      // ...
    }

    // Bare-bones disposal
    // ...
  }

  ~Test( )
  {
    Dispose (false);
  }
}
```

`Dispose` is overloaded to accept a `bool disposing` flag. The original version (without arguments) is no longer declared `virtual` and simply calls the enhanced version.

The enhanced version contains the actual disposal logic and is `protected` and `virtual`. The `disposing` flag means it's being called "properly" from the `Dispose` method rather than in "last-resort mode" from the finalizer. The idea is that when called with `disposing` false, this method should not perform any disposal tasks that involve referencing other objects (because other objects may no longer exist). This rules out quite a lot! Here are a couple of tasks it can still perform in last-resort mode, when `disposing` is false:

- Releasing any *direct references* to operating system resources (obtained, perhaps, via a P/Invoke call to the Win32 API)
- Deleting a temporary file created on construction

To make this robust, any code capable of throwing an exception should be wrapped in a try/catch block, and the exception, ideally, logged. Any logging should itself be in another try/catch block with an empty catch.

 This pattern is intended more as a backup than a replacement for calling Dispose. A difficulty with relying on it completely is that you couple resource deallocation to memory deallocation—two things with potentially divergent interests. You also increase the burden on the finalization thread.

How the Garbage Collector Works

The CLR uses a generational mark-and-compact garbage collector (GC) that performs automatic memory management for type instances stored on the managed heap. The GC is considered to be a *tracing* garbage collector in that it doesn't interfere with every access to an object, but rather wakes up intermittently and traces the graph of objects stored on the managed heap to determine which objects can be considered garbage and therefore collected.

The GC initiates a garbage collection upon performing a memory allocation (via the new keyword) either when memory is too low to fulfill the request, or at other times to reduce the application's memory footprint. This process can also be initiated manually by calling System.GC.Collect. Initiating a garbage collection may freeze all threads in the process to allow the GC time to examine the managed heap (this depends on the CLR version and configuration).

The GC begins with the set of object references considered roots, and walks the object graph, marking all the objects it touches as reachable. Once this process is complete, all objects that have not been marked are considered to be garbage.

Objects that are considered garbage and don't have finalizers are immediately discarded, and the memory is reclaimed. Objects that are considered garbage and do have finalizers are flagged for additional asynchronous processing on a separate thread to invoke their Finalize methods before they can be considered garbage and reclaimed at the next collection.

Objects considered live are then shifted down to the bottom of the heap (compacted), hopefully freeing space to allow the memory allocation to succeed. At this point, the memory allocation is attempted again, the threads in the process are unfrozen, and either normal processing continues or an OutOfMemoryException is thrown.

Optimization Techniques

Although this may sound like an inefficient process compared to managing memory manually, the GC incorporates various optimization techniques to reduce the garbage collection time.

The most important of these optimizations is one that makes the GC generational. This technique takes advantage of the fact that although many objects tend to be allocated and discarded rapidly, certain objects are long-lived and thus don't need to be traced during every collection.

Basically, the GC divides the managed heap into three generations. Objects that have just been allocated are considered to be in Gen0, objects that have survived one collection cycle are considered to be in Gen1, and all other objects are considered to be in Gen2.

When it performs a collection, the GC initially collects only Gen0 objects. If not enough memory is reclaimed to fulfill the request, both Gen0 and Gen1 objects are collected; if that fails as well, a full collection of the Gen0, Gen1, and Gen2 objects is attempted.

Forcing Garbage Collection

You can manually force a garbage collection at any time, by calling GC.Collect. Calling GC.Collect without an argument instigates a full collection, which includes objects in all generations. If you pass in an integer value, generations to that value are collected only, so GC.Collect(0) performs only a (relatively fast) Gen0 collection.

In general, you get the best performance by allowing the garbage collector to decide when to collect—although there are exceptions. The most common case for intervention is when an application goes to sleep for a while: a good example is a Windows Service that performs a daily activity (checking for updates, perhaps). Such an application might use a System.Timers.Timer to initiate the activity every 24 hours. After completing the activity, no further code executes for 24 hours, which means that for this period, no memory allocations are made and so the garbage collector has no opportunity to activate. Whatever memory the service consumed in performing its activity, it will continue to consume for the following 24 hours—even with an empty object graph! The solution is to call GC.Collect right after the daily activity completes.

To ensure the collection of objects for which collection is delayed by finalizers, you can take the additional step of calling WaitForPendingFinalizers and re-collecting:

```
GC.Collect();
GC.WaitForPendingFinalizers();
GC.Collect();
```

Alternatives to Garbage Collection

Automatic garbage collection has major benefits. It's convenient, and it rules out the possibility of memory leaks. It also means there's minimal performance overhead when objects are allocated, when references are changed, and when objects fall out of scope. The only cost is when garbage collection is performed, at which point the whole application may freeze, typically for 10–100 milliseconds. This is rarely noticed in most applications, but it can matter in programs that perform such activities as real-time hardware communication. You then have the following choices:

- Write in an unmanaged language such as C++.
- Prevent garbage collection from taking place.

In order to suppress garbage collection, you must ensure that no new objects are allocated on the heap once the application reaches the "critical" stage when garbage collection should not take place. This means preallocating all required objects, and then calling GC.Collect to release any temporary objects allocated in the process. If this is impractical, and the program needs to allocate memory throughout, another option is to obtain unmanaged memory by calling Marshal. AllocHGlobal and then directly mapping an explicit-layout struct into the memory returned (we describe this in Chapter 22). Memory allocated in this fashion must be freed manually by calling Marshal.FreeHGlobal; otherwise, a memory leak will result. This approach works fairly well, once you get used to pointer semantics. Perhaps the only other disadvantage is that you're at times restricted by the lack of inheritance on structs.

13

Streams and I/O

This chapter describes the fundamental types for input and output in .NET, with emphasis on the following topics:

- The .NET stream architecture and how it provides a consistent programming interface for reading and writing across a variety of I/O types
- Manipulating files and directories on disk
- Isolated storage and its role in segregating data by program and user

This chapter concentrates on the types in the System.IO namespace, the home of lower-level I/O functionality. The .NET Framework also provides higher-level I/O functionality in the form of SQL connections and commands, LINQ to SQL and LINQ to XML, Web Services, Remoting, and Windows Communication Foundation.

Stream Architecture

The .NET stream architecture centers on three concepts: backing stores, decorators, and adapters, as shown in Figure 13-1.

A *backing store* is the endpoint that makes input and output useful, such as a file or network connection. Precisely, it is either or both of the following:

- A source from which bytes can be sequentially read
- A destination to which bytes can be sequentially written

A backing store is of no use, though, unless exposed to the programmer. A *stream* is the standard .NET class for this purpose; it exposes a standard set of methods for reading, writing, and positioning. Unlike an array, where all the backing data exists in memory at once, a stream deals with data serially—either one byte at a time or in blocks of a manageable size. Hence, a stream can use little memory regardless of the size of its backing store.

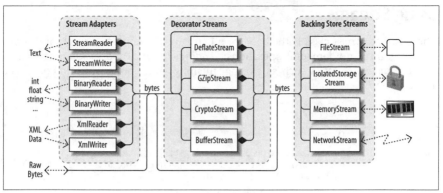

Figure 13-1. Stream architecture

Streams fall into two categories:

Backing store streams
> These are hard-wired to a particular type of backing store, such as `FileStream` or `NetworkStream`

Decorator streams
> These feed off another stream, transforming the data in some way, such as `DeflateStream` or `CryptoStream`

Decorator streams have the following architectural benefits:

- They liberate backing store streams from needing to implement such features as compression and encryption themselves.
- Streams don't suffer a change of interface when decorated.
- You connect decorators at runtime.
- You can chain decorators together (e.g., a compressor followed by an encryptor).

Both backing store and decorator streams deal exclusively in bytes. Although this is flexible and efficient, applications often work at higher levels such as text or XML. *Adapters* bridge this gap by wrapping a stream in a class with specialized methods typed to a particular format. For example, a text reader exposes a `ReadLine` method; an XML writer exposes a `WriteAttributes` method.

 An adapter wraps a stream, just as a decorator. Unlike a decorator, however, an adapter is not *itself* a stream; it typically hides the byte-oriented methods completely.

To summarize, backing store streams provide the raw data; decorator streams provide transparent binary transformations such as encryption; adapters offer typed methods for dealing in higher-level types such as strings and XML. Figure 13-1 illustrates their associations. To compose a chain, you simply pass one object into another's constructor.

Using Streams

The abstract Stream class is the base for all streams. It defines methods and properties for three fundamental operations: *reading*, *writing*, and *seeking*, as well as for administrative tasks such as closing, flushing, and configuring timeouts (see Table 13-1).

Table 13-1. Stream class members

Category	Members

Reading	`public abstract bool CanRead { get; }`
	`public abstract int  Read (byte[] buffer, int offset, int count)`
	`public virtual  int  ReadByte();`

Writing	`public abstract bool CanWrite { get; }`
	`public abstract void Write (byte[] buffer, int offset, int count);`
	`public virtual  void WriteByte (byte value);`

Seeking	`public abstract bool CanSeek { get; }`
	`public abstract long Position { get; set; }`
	`public abstract void SetLength (long value);`
	`public abstract long Length { get; }`
	`public abstract long Seek (long offset, SeekOrigin origin);`

Closing/flushing	`public virtual void Close();`
	`public void Dispose();`
	`public abstract void Flush();`

Timeouts	`public abstract bool CanTimeout { get; }`
	`public override int ReadTimeout { get; set; }`
	`public override int WriteTimeout { get; set; }`

Other	`public static readonly Stream Null;  // "Null" stream` `public static Stream Synchronized (Stream stream);`

In the following example, we use a file stream to read, write, and seek:

```
using System;
using System.IO;

class Program
{
  static void Main()
  {
    // Create a file called test.txt in the current directory:
    using (Stream s = new FileStream ("test.txt", FileMode.Create))
    {
      Console.WriteLine (s.CanRead);       // true
      Console.WriteLine (s.CanWrite);      // true
      Console.WriteLine (s.CanSeek);       // true

      s.WriteByte (101);
      s.WriteByte (102);
      byte[] block = { 1, 2, 3, 4, 5 };
      s.Write (block, 0, block.Length);    // Write block of 5 bytes
```

```
            Console.WriteLine (s.Length);          // 7
            Console.WriteLine (s.Position);        // 7
            s.Position = 0;                         // Move back to the start

            Console.WriteLine (s.ReadByte( ));      // 101
            Console.WriteLine (s.ReadByte( ));      // 102

            // Read from the stream back into the block array:
            Console.WriteLine (s.Read (block, 0, block.Length));    // 5

            // Assuming the last Read returned 5, we'll be at
            // the end of the file, so Read will now return 0:
            Console.WriteLine (s.Read (block, 0, block.Length));    // 0
      }
    }
  }
```

Reading and Writing

A stream may support reading, writing, or both. If CanWrite returns false, the
stream is read-only; if CanRead returns false, the stream is write-only.

Read receives a block of data from the stream into an array. It returns the number
of bytes received, which is always either less than or equal to the count argument.
If it's less than count, it means either that the end of the stream has been reached
or the stream is giving you the data in smaller chunks (as is often the case with
network streams). In either case, the balance of bytes in the array will remain
unwritten, their previous values preserved.

With Read, you can be certain you've reached the end of the stream
only when the method returns 0. So, if you have a 1,000-byte
stream, the following code may fail to read it all into memory:

```
// Assuming s is a stream:
byte[] data = new byte [1000];
s.Read (data, 0, data.Length);
```

The Read method could read anywhere from 1 to 1,000 bytes, leaving the balance of the stream unread.

Here's the correct way to read a 1,000-byte stream:

```
byte[] data = new byte [1000];

// bytesRead will always end up at 1000, unless the stream is
// itself smaller in length:

int bytesRead = 0;
int chunkSize = 1;
while (bytesRead < data.Length && chunkSize > 0)
  bytesRead +=
    chunkSize = s.Read (data, bytesRead, data.Length - bytesRead);
```

Fortunately, the BinaryReader type provides a simpler way to achieve the same result:

```
byte[] data = new BinaryReader (s).ReadBytes (1000);
```

If the stream is less than 1,000 bytes long, the byte array returned reflects the actual stream size. If the stream is seekable, you can read its entire contents by replacing 1000 with (int)s.Length.

We describe the BinaryReader type further in the setion "Stream Adapters," later in this chapter.

The ReadByte method is simpler: it reads just a single byte, returning –1 to indicate the end of the stream.

The Write and WriteByte methods send data to the stream. If they are unable to send the specified bytes, an exception is thrown.

In the Read and Write methods, the offset argument refers to the index in the buffer array at which reading or writing begins; not the position within the stream.

Streams also support asynchronous reading and writing through the methods BeginRead and BeginWrite. Asynchronous methods are intended for high-throughput server applications, and we describe them in Chapter 19.

Seeking

A stream is seekable if CanSeek returns true. With a seekable stream (such as a file stream), you can query or modify its Length, and at any time change the Position at which you're reading or writing. The Position property is relative to the beginning of the stream; the Seek method, however, allows you to move relative to the current position or the end of the stream.

With a nonseekable stream (such as an encryption stream), the only way to determine its length is to read it right through. Furthermore, if you need to reread a previous section, you must close the stream and start afresh with a new one.

Closing and Flushing

Streams must be closed or disposed after use to release underlying resources such as file and socket handles. A simple way to guarantee this is by instantiating streams within using blocks. Streams follow standard disposal semantics:

- Dispose and Close are identical in function.
- Closing a stream repeatedly causes no error.

Closing a decorator stream closes both the decorator and its backing store stream. With a chain of decorators, closing the outermost decorator (at the head of the chain) closes the whole lot.

MemoryStream is unusual in that closing it is optional.

Some streams internally buffer data to and from the backing store to lessen round-tripping and so improve performance (file streams are a good example of this). This means data you write to a stream may not hit the backing store immediately; it can be delayed as the buffer fills up. The Flush method forces any internally buffered data to be written immediately. Flush is called automatically when a stream is closed, so you never need to do the following:

```
s.Flush(); s.Close( );
```

Timeouts

A stream supports read and write timeouts if CanTimeout returns true. Network streams support timeouts; file and memory streams do not. The ReadTimeout and WriteTimeout properties determine the desired timeout in milliseconds, where 0 means no timeout. The Read and Write methods indicate that a timeout has occurred by throwing an exception.

Thread Safety

As a rule, streams are not thread-safe, meaning that two threads cannot concurrently read or write to the same stream without possible error. The Stream class offers a simple workaround via the static Synchronized method. This method accepts a stream of any type and returns a thread-safe wrapper. The wrapper works by obtaining an exclusive lock around each read, write, or seek, ensuring that only one thread can perform such an operation at a time. In practice, this allows multiple threads to simultaneously append data to the same stream—other kinds of activities (such as concurrent reading) require additional locking to ensure that each thread accesses the desired portion of the stream. We discuss thread safety fully in Chapter 19.

Backing Store Streams

Figure 13-2 shows the key backing store streams provided by the .NET Framework. A "null stream" is also available, via the Stream's static Null field.

In the following sections, we describe FileStream and MemoryStream; in the final section in this chapter, we describe IsolatedStorageStream. In Chapter 14, we cover NetworkStream.

FileStream

Earlier in this section, we demonstrated the basic use of a FileStream to read and write bytes of data. We'll now examine the special features of this class.

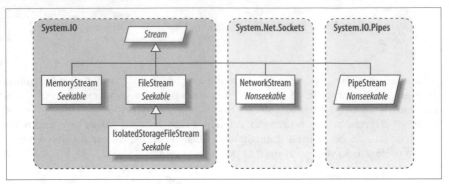

Figure 13-2. Backing store streams

Constructing a FileStream

The simplest way to instantiate a `FileStream` is to use one of the following static façade methods on the `File` class:

```
FileStream fs1 = File.OpenRead  ("readme.bin");            // Read-only
FileStream fs2 = File.OpenWrite (@"c:\temp\writeme.tmp");  // Write-only
FileStream fs3 = File.Create    (@"c:\temp\writeme.tmp");  // Read/write
```

`OpenWrite` and `Create` differ in behavior if the file already exists. `Create` truncates any existing content; `OpenWrite` leaves existing content intact with the stream positioned at zero. If you write fewer bytes than were previously in the file, `OpenWrite` leaves you with a mixture of old and new content.

 The following static methods read an entire file into memory in one step:

- `File.ReadAllText` (returns a string)
- `File.ReadAllLines` (returns an array of strings)
- `File.ReadAllBytes` (returns a byte array)

The following static methods write an entire file in one step:

- `File.WriteAllText`
- `File.WriteAllLines`
- `File.WriteAllBytes`
- `File.AppendAllText` (great for appending to a log file)

You can also instantiate a `FileStream` directly. Its constructors provide access to every feature, allowing you to specify a filename or low-level file handle, file creation and access modes, and options for sharing, buffering, and security.

Specifying a filename

A filename can be either absolute (e.g., *c:\temp\test.txt*) or relative to the current directory (e.g., *test.txt* or *temp\test.txt*). You can access or change the current directory via the static `Environment.CurrentDirectory` property.

When a program starts, the current directory may or may not coincide with that of the program's executable. For this reason, you should never rely on the current directory for locating additional runtime files packaged along with your executable.

`AppDomain.CurrentDomain.BaseDirectory` returns the *application base directory*, which in normal cases contains the program's executable. To specify a filename relative to this directory, you can call `Path.Combine`:

```
string baseFolder = AppDomain.CurrentDomain.BaseDirectory;
string logoPath = Path.Combine (baseFolder, "logo.jpg");
Console.WriteLine (File.Exists (logoPath));
```

You can read and write across a network via a UNC path, such as *\\JoesPC\ PicShare\pic.jpg* or *\\10.1.1.2\PicShare\pic.jpg*.

Specifying a FileMode

All of `FileStream`'s constructors that accept a filename also require a `FileMode` enum argument. Figure 13-3 shows how to choose a `FileMode`, and the choices yield results akin to calling a static method on the `File` class.

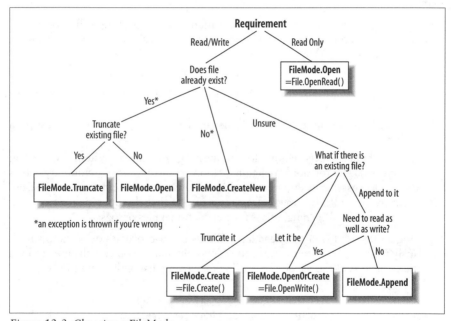

Figure 13-3. Choosing a FileMode

`File.Create`, `FileMode.Create`, and `FileMode.Truncate` will throw an exception if used on hidden files. To overwrite a hidden file, you must first delete it:

```
if (File.Exists ("hidden.txt")) File.Delete ("hidden.txt");
```

Constructing a `FileStream` with just a filename, and `FileMode` gives you (with just one exception) a readable writable stream. You can request a downgrade if you also supply a `FileAccess` argument:

```
[Flags]
public enum FileAccess { Read = 1, Write = 2, ReadWrite = 3 }
```

The following returns a read-only stream, equivalent to calling `File.OpenRead`:

```
FileStream fs = new FileStream ("x.bin", FileMode.Open, FileAccess.Read);
```

`FileMode.Append` is the odd one out: with this mode, you get a *write-only* stream. To append with read-write support, you must instead use `FileMode.Open` or `FileMode.OpenOrCreate`, and then seek the end of the stream:

```
using (FileStream fs = new FileStream ("myFile.bin", FileMode.Open))
{
  fs.Seek (0, SeekOrigin.End);
  ...
```

Advanced FileStream features

Here are other optional arguments you can include when constructing a `FileStream`:

- A `FileShare` enum describing how much access to grant other processes wanting to dip into the same file before you've finished (`None`, `Read` [default], `ReadWrite`, or `Write`).
- The size, in bytes, of the internal buffer (default is 4 KB).
- A flag indicating whether to defer to the operating system for asynchronous I/O.
- A `FileSecurity` object describing what user and role permissions to assign a new file.
- A `FileOptions` flags enum for requesting operating system encryption (`Encrypted`), automatic deletion upon closure for temporary files (`DeleteOnClose`), and optimization hints (`RandomAccess` and `SequentialScan`). There is also a `WriteThrough` flag that requests that the operating system disable write-behind caching; this is for transactional files or logs.

Opening a file with `FileShare.ReadWrite` allows other processes or users to simultaneously read and write to the same file. To avoid chaos, you can all agree to lock specified portions of the file before reading or writing, using these methods:

```
// Defined on the FileStream class:
public virtual void Lock   (long position, long length);
public virtual void Unlock (long position, long length);
```

Lock throws an exception if part or all of the requested file section has already been locked. This is the system used in file-based databases such as Access and FoxPro.

MemoryStream

`MemoryStream` uses an array as a backing store. This partly defeats the purpose of having a stream, because the entire backing store must reside in memory at once.

MemoryStream still has uses, however; an example is when you need random access to a nonseekable stream. If you know the source stream will be of a manageable size, you can copy it into a MemoryStream as follows:

```
static MemoryStream ToMemoryStream (Stream input, bool closeInput)
{
  try
  {                                         // Read and write in
    byte[] block = new byte [0x1000];       // blocks of 4K.
    MemoryStream ms = new MemoryStream( );
    while (true)
    {
      int bytesRead = input.Read (block, 0, block.Length);
      if (bytesRead == 0) return ms;
      ms.Write (block, 0, bytesRead);
    }
  }
  finally { if (closeInput) input.Close ( ); }
}
```

The reason for the closeInput argument is to avoid a situation where the method author and consumer each think the other will close the stream.

You can convert a MemoryStream to a byte array by calling ToArray. The GetBuffer method does the same job more efficiently by returning a direct reference to the underlying storage array; unfortunately, this array is usually longer than the stream's real length.

 Closing and flushing a MemoryStream is optional. If you close a MemoryStream, you can no longer read or write to it, but you are still permitted to call ToArray to obtain the underlying data. Flush does absolutely nothing on a memory stream.

You can find further MemoryStream examples in the section "Compression" later in this chapter, and in the section "Cryptography" in Chapter 18.

PipeStream

PipeStream is new to Framework 3.5. It provides a simple means by which one process can communicate with another through the Windows *pipes* protocol. There are two kinds of pipe:

Anonymous pipe
 Allows one-way communication between a parent and child process on the same computer.

Named pipe
 Allows two-way communication between arbitrary processes on the same computer—or different computers across a Windows network.

A pipe is particularly suited to interprocess communication (IPC) on a single computer because it doesn't rely on a network transport. This equates to good performance and no issues with firewalls.

A pipe is a low-level construct that allows just the sending and receiving of bytes (or *messages*, which are groups of bytes). The WCF and Remoting APIs offer higher-level messaging frameworks with the option of using an IPC channel for communication.

PipeStream is an abstract class with four concrete subtypes. Two are used for anonymous pipes and the other two for named pipes:

Anonymous pipes
    AnonymousPipeServerStream and AnonymousPipeClientStream

Named pipes
    NamedPipeServerStream and NamedPipeClientStream

Named pipes are simpler to use, so we'll describe them first.

Named pipes

With named pipes, the parties communicate through a pipe of the same name. The protocol defines two distinct roles: the client and server. Communication happens between the client and server as follows:

- The server instantiates a NamedPipeServerStream and then calls Wait-ForConnection.
- The client instantiates a NamedClientStream and then calls Connect (with an optional timeout).

The two parties then read and write the streams to communicate.

The following example demonstrates a server that sends a single byte (100), and then waits to receive a single byte:

```
using (var s = new NamedPipeServerStream ("pipedream")
{
  s.WaitForConnection( );
  s.WriteByte (100);
  Console.WriteLine (s.ReadByte( ));
}
```

Here's the corresponding client code:

```
using (var s = new NamedPipeClientStream ("pipedream"))
{
  s.Connect( );
  Console.WriteLine (s.ReadByte( ));
  s.WriteByte (200);                    // Send the value 200 back.
}
```

Named pipe streams are bidirectional by default, so either party can read or write their stream. This means the client and server must agree on some protocol to coordinate their actions, so both parties don't end up sending or receiving at once.

There also needs to be agreement on the length of each transmission. Our example was trivial in this regard, because we bounced just a single byte in each direction. To help with messages longer than one byte, pipes provide a *message transmission* mode. If this is enabled, a party calling Read can know when a message is complete by checking the IsMessageComplete property. To demonstrate, we'll start by writing a helper method that reads a whole message from a message-enabled PipeStream—in other words, reads until IsMessageComplete is false:

```
static byte[] ReadMessage (PipeStream s)
{
  MemoryStream ms = new MemoryStream( );
  byte[] buffer = new byte [0x1000];      // Read in 4 KB blocks

  do    { ms.Write (buffer, 0, s.Read (buffer, 0, buffer.Length)); }
  while (!s.IsMessageComplete);

  return ms.ToArray( );
}
```

 You cannot determine whether a PipeStream has finished reading a message simply by waiting for Read to return 0. This is because, unlike most other kinds of stream, pipe streams and network streams have no definite end. Instead, they temporarily "dry up" between message transmissions.

Now we can activate message transmission mode. On the server, this is done by specifying PipeTransmissionMode.Message when constructing the stream:

```
using (var s = new NamedPipeServerStream ("pipedream", PipeDirection.InOut,
                                     1, PipeTransmissionMode.Message))
{
  s.WaitForConnection( );

  byte[] msg = Encoding.UTF8.GetBytes ("Hello");
  s.Write (msg, 0, msg.Length);

  Console.WriteLine (Encoding.UTF8.GetString (ReadMessage (s)));
}
```

On the client, we activate message transmission mode by setting ReadMode after calling Connect:

```
using (var s = new NamedPipeClientStream ("pipedream"))
{
  s.Connect( );
  s.ReadMode = PipeTransmissionMode.Message;

  Console.WriteLine (Encoding.UTF8.GetString (ReadMessage (s)));

  byte[] msg = Encoding.UTF8.GetBytes ("Hello right back!");
  s.Write (msg, 0, msg.Length);
}
```

Anonymous pipes

An anonymous pipe provides a one-way communication stream between a parent and child process. Instead of using a system-wide name, anonymous pipes tune in through a private handle.

As with named pipes, there are distinct client and server roles. The system of communication is a little different, however, and proceeds as follows:

1. The server instantiates an AnonymousPipeServerStream, committing to a PipeDirection of In or Out.

2. The server calls GetClientHandleAsString to obtain an identifier for the pipe, which it then passes to the client (typically as an argument when starting the child process).

3. The child process instantiates an AnonymousPipeClientStream, specifying the opposite PipeDirection.

4. The server releases the local handle that was generated in step 2, by calling DisposeLocalCopyOfClientHandle.

5. The parent and child processes communicate by reading/writing the stream.

Because anonymous pipes are unidirectional, a server must create two pipes for bidirectional communication. The following demonstrates a server that sends a single byte to the child process, and then receives a single byte back from that process:

```
string clientExe = "d:\PipeDemo\ClientDemo.exe";

HandleInheritability inherit = HandleInheritability.Inheritable;

using (var tx = new AnonymousPipeServerStream (PipeDirection.Out, inherit))
using (var rx = new AnonymousPipeServerStream (PipeDirection.In, inherit))
{
  string txID = tx.GetClientHandleAsString( );
  string rxID = rx.GetClientHandleAsString( );

  var startInfo = new ProcessStartInfo (clientExe, txID + " " + rxID);
  startInfo.UseShellExecute = false;    // Required for child process
  Process p = Process.Start (startInfo);

  tx.DisposeLocalCopyOfClientHandle( );    // Release unmanaged
  rx.DisposeLocalCopyOfClientHandle( );    // handle resources.

  tx.WriteByte (100);
  Console.WriteLine ("Server received: " + rx.ReadByte( ));

  p.WaitForExit( );
}
```

Here's the corresponding client code that would be compiled to *d:\PipeDemo\ ClientDemo.exe*:

```
static void Main (string[] args)
{
  string rxID = args[0];    // Note we're reversing the
  string txID = args[1];    // receive and transmit roles.
```

```
using (var rx = new AnonymousPipeClientStream (PipeDirection.In, rxID))
using (var tx = new AnonymousPipeClientStream (PipeDirection.Out, txID))
{
  Console.WriteLine ("Client received: " + rx.ReadByte());
  tx.WriteByte (200);
}
}
```

As with named pipes, the client and server must coordinate their sending and receiving and agree on the length of each transmission. Anonymous pipes don't, unfortunately, support message mode, so you must implement your own protocol for message length agreement. One solution is to send, in the first four bytes of each transmission, an integer value defining the length of the message to follow. The BitConverter class provides methods for converting between an integer and an array of four bytes.

BufferedStream

BufferedStream decorates, or wraps, another stream with buffering capability, and it is one of a number of decorator stream types, all of which are illustrated in Figure 13-4.

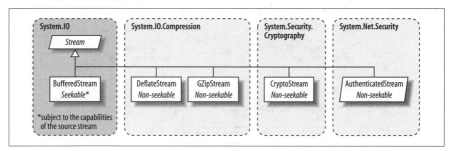

Figure 13-4. Decorator streams

Buffering improves performance by reducing round trips to the backing store. Here's how we wrap a FileStream in a 20 KB BufferedStream:

```
// Write 100K to a file:
File.WriteAllBytes ("myFile.bin", new byte [100000]);

using (FileStream fs = File.OpenRead ("myFile.bin"))
using (BufferedStream bs = new BufferedStream (fs, 20000))  //20K buffer
{
  bs.ReadByte();
  Console.WriteLine (fs.Position);         // 20000
}
```

In this example, the underlying stream advances 20,000 bytes after reading just 1 byte, thanks to the read-ahead buffering. We could call ReadByte another 19,999 times before the FileStream would be hit again.

Coupling a BufferedStream to a FileStream, as in this example, is of limited value because FileStream already has built-in buffering. Its only use might be in enlarging the buffer on an already constructed FileStream.

Closing a `BufferedStream` automatically closes the underlying backing store stream.

Stream Adapters

A `Stream` deals only in bytes; to read or write data types such as strings, integers, or XML elements you must plug in an adapter. Here's what the Framework provides:

Text adapters (for string and character data)

> TextReader, TextWriter
>
> StreamReader, StreamWriter
>
> StringReader, StringWriter

Binary adapters (for primitive types such as int, bool, string, *and* float*)*

> BinaryReader, BinaryWriter

XML adapters (covered in Chapter 11)

> XmlReader, XmlWriter

The relationships between these types are illustrated in Figure 13-5.

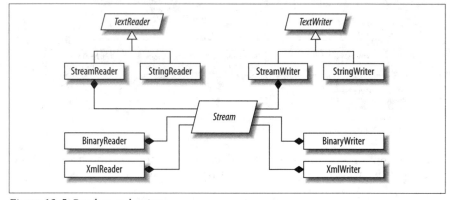

Figure 13-5. Readers and writers

Text Adapters

`TextReader` and `TextWriter` are the abstract base classes for adapters that deal exclusively with characters and strings. Each has two general-purpose implementations in the framework:

`StreamReader`/`StreamWriter`
> Uses a `Stream` for its raw data store, translating the stream's bytes into characters or strings

`StringReader`/`StringWriter`
> Implements `TextReader`/`TextWriter` using in-memory strings

Table 13-2 lists TextReader's members by category. Peek returns the next character in the stream without advancing the position. Both Peek and the zero-argument version of Read return −1 if at the end of the stream; otherwise, they return an integer that can be cast directly to a char. The overload of Read that accepts a char[] buffer is identical in functionality to the ReadBlock method. ReadLine reads until reaching either a CR (character 13) or LF (character 10), or a CR+LF pair in sequence. It then returns a string, discarding the CR/LF characters.

Table 13-2. TextReader members

Category	Members
Reading one char	`public virtual int Peek();` // Cast the result to a char `public virtual int Read();` // Cast the result to a char

Reading many chars	`public virtual int Read      (char[] buffer, int index, int count);`
	`public virtual int ReadBlock (char[] buffer, int index, int count);`
	`public virtual string ReadLine();`
	`public virtual string ReadToEnd();`

Closing	`public virtual void Close();` `public void Dispose();` // Same as Close
Other	`public static readonly TextReader Null;` `public static TextReader Synchronized (TextReader reader);`

The new line sequence in Windows is loosely modeled on a mechanical typewriter: a carriage return (character 13) followed by a line feed (character 10). The C# string is "\r\n" (think "ReturN"). Reverse the order and you'll get either two new lines or none!

TextWriter has analogous methods for writing, as shown in Table 13-3. The Write and WriteLine methods are additionally overloaded to accept every primitive type, plus the object type. These methods simply call the ToString method on whatever is passed in (optionally through an IFormatProvider specified either when calling the method or when constructing the TextWriter).

Table 13-3. TextWriter members

Category	Members
Writing one char	`public virtual void Write (char value);`

Writing many chars	`public virtual void Write (string value);`
	`public virtual void Write (char[] buffer, int index, int count);`
	`public virtual void Write (string format, params object[] arg);`
	`public virtual void WriteLine (string value);`

Closing and flushing	`public virtual void Close();`
	`public void Dispose();` // Same as Close
	`public virtual void Flush();`

Formatting and encoding	`public virtual IFormatProvider FormatProvider { get; }`
	`public virtual string NewLine { get; set; }`
	`public abstract Encoding Encoding { get; }`

Other	`public static readonly TextWriter Null;` `public static TextWriter Synchronized (TextWriter writer);`

WriteLine simply appends the given text with CR+LF. You can change this via the
NewLine property.

StreamReader and StreamWriter

In the following example, a StreamWriter writes two lines of text to a file, and then
a StreamReader reads the file back:

```
using (FileStream fs = File.Create ("test.txt"))
using (TextWriter writer = new StreamWriter (fs))
{
  writer.WriteLine ("Line1");
  writer.WriteLine ("Line2");
}

using (FileStream fs = File.OpenRead ("test.txt"))
using (TextReader reader = new StreamReader (fs))
{
  Console.WriteLine (reader.ReadLine());      // Line1
  Console.WriteLine (reader.ReadLine());      // Line2
}
```

Because text adapters are so often coupled with files, the File class provides the
static methods CreateText, AppendText, and OpenText to shortcut the process:

```
using (TextWriter writer = File.CreateText ("test.txt"))
{
  writer.WriteLine ("Line1");
  writer.WriteLine ("Line2");
}
using (TextWriter writer = File.AppendText ("test.txt"))
  writer.WriteLine ("Line3");

using (TextReader reader = File.OpenText ("test.txt"))
  while (reader.Peek() > -1)
    Console.WriteLine (reader.ReadLine());      // Line1
                                                // Line2
                                                // Line3
```

This also illustrates the easiest way to test for the end of a file (viz. reader.Peek()).

You can also read and write other types such as integers, but because TextWriter
invokes ToString on your type, you must parse a string when reading it back:

```
using (TextWriter w = File.CreateText ("data.txt"))
{
  w.WriteLine (123);          // Writes "123"
  w.WriteLine (true);         // Writes the word "true"
}
using (TextReader r = File.OpenText ("data.txt"))
{
  int myInt = int.Parse (r.ReadLine());      // myInt == 123
  bool yes = bool.Parse (r.ReadLine());      // yes == true
}
```

Character encodings

TextReader and TextWriter are by themselves just abstract classes with no connection to a stream or backing store. The StreamReader and StreamWriter types, however, are connected to an underlying byte-oriented stream, so they must convert between characters and bytes. They do so through an Encoding class from the System.Text namespace, which you choose when constructing the StreamReader or StreamWriter. If you choose none, the default UTF-8 encoding is used.

 A StreamReader or StreamWriter will throw an exception if it encounters bytes that do not have a valid string translation for their encoding.

The simplest of the encodings is ASCII, because characters and bytes translate 1:1. The ASCII encoding maps the first 127 characters of the Unicode set into its single byte, covering what you see on a U.S.-style keyboard. Most other characters, including specialized symbols and non-English characters, cannot be represented and are converted to the □ character. The default UTF-8 encoding can map all allocated Unicode characters, but it is more complex. The first 127 characters encode to a single byte, for ASCII compatibility; the remaining characters encode to a variable number of bytes (most commonly two or three). Consider this:

```
using (TextWriter w = File.CreateText ("but.txt"))    // Use default UTF-8
  w.WriteLine ("but–");                                // encoding.

using (Stream s = File.OpenRead ("but.txt"))
  for (int b; (b = s.ReadByte()) > -1;)
    Console.WriteLine (b);
```

The word "but" is followed not by a stock-standard hyphen, but by the longer em dash (—) character, U+2014. This is the one that won't get you into trouble with your book editor! Let's examine the output:

```
98     // b
117    // u
116    // t
226    // em dash byte 1      Note that the byte values
128    // em dash byte 2      are >= 128 for each part
148    // em dash byte 3      of the multibyte sequence.
13     // <CR>
10     // <LF>
```

Because the em dash is outside the first 127 characters of the Unicode set, it requires more than a single byte to encode in UTF-8 (in this case, three). UTF-8 is efficient with the Western alphabet as most popular characters consume just one byte. It also downgrades easily to ASCII simply by ignoring all bytes above 127. Its disadvantage is that seeking within a stream is troublesome, since a character's position does not correspond to its byte position in the stream. An alternative is UTF-16 (labeled just "Unicode" in the Encoding class). Here's how we write the same string with UTF-16:

```
using (Stream s = File.Create ("but.txt"))
using (TextWriter w = new StreamWriter (s, Encoding.Unicode))
  w.WriteLine ("but–");
```

```
foreach (byte b in File.ReadAllBytes ("but.txt"))
  Console.WriteLine (b);
```

The output is then:

```
255    // Byte-order mark 1
254    // Byte-order mark 2
98     // 'b' byte 1
0      // 'b' byte 2
117    // 'u' byte 1
0      // 'u' byte 2
116    // 't' byte 1
0      // 't' byte 2
20     // '–' byte 1
32     // '–' byte 2
13     // <CR> byte 1
0      // <CR> byte 2
10     // <LF> byte 1
0      // <LF> byte 2
```

Technically, UTF-16 uses either two or four bytes per character (there are close to a million Unicode characters allocated or reserved, so 2 bytes is not always enough). However, because the C# char type is itself only 16 bits wide, a UTF-16 encoding will always use exactly two bytes per .NET char. This makes it easy to jump to a particular character index within a stream.

UTF-16 uses a two-byte prefix to identify whether the byte pairs are written in a "little-endian" or "big-endian" order (the least significant byte first or the most significant byte first). The default little-endian order is standard for Windows-based systems.

StringReader and StringWriter

The StringReader and StringWriter adapters don't wrap a stream at all; instead, they use a string or StringBuilder as the underlying data source. This means no byte translation is required—in fact, the classes do nothing you couldn't easily achieve with a string or StringBuilder coupled with an index variable. Their advantage, though, is that they share a base class with StreamReader/StringWriter. For instance, suppose we have a string containing XML and want to parse it with an XmlReader. The XmlReader.Create method accepts one of the following:

- A URI
- A Stream
- A TextReader

So, how do we XML-parse our string? Because StringReader is a subclass of TextReader, we're in luck. We can instantiate and pass in a StringReader as follows:

```
XmlReader r = XmlReader.Create (new StringReader (myString));
```

Binary Adapters

BinaryReader and BinaryWriter read and write native data types: bool, byte, char, decimal, float, double, short, int, long, sbyte, ushort, uint, and ulong, as well as strings and arrays of the primitive data types.

Unlike StreamReader and StreamWriter, binary adapters store primitive data types efficiently, as they are represented in memory. So, an int uses four bytes; a double eight bytes. Strings are written through a text encoding (as with StreamReader and StreamWriter) but are length-prefixed, in order to make it possible to read back a series of strings without needing special delimiters.

Imagine we have a simple type, defined as follows:

```
public class Person
{
  public string Name;
  public int    Age;
  public double Height;
}
```

We can add the following methods to Person to save/load its data to/from a stream using binary adapters:

```
public void SaveData (Stream s)
{
  BinaryWriter w = new BinaryWriter (s);
  w.Write (Name);
  w.Write (Age);
  w.Write (Height);
  w.Flush( );        // Ensure the BinaryWriter buffer is cleared.
                     // We won't dispose/close it, so more data
}                    // can to be written to the stream.

public void LoadData (Stream s)
{
  BinaryReader r = new BinaryReader (s);
  Name   = r.ReadString( );
  Age    = r.ReadInt32( );
  Height = r.ReadDouble( );
}
```

BinaryReader can also read into byte arrays. The following reads the entire contents of a seekable stream:

```
byte[] data = new BinaryReader (s).ReadBytes ((int) s.Length);
```

This is more convenient than reading directly from a stream, because it doesn't require a loop to ensure that all data has been read.

Closing and Disposing Stream Adapters

You have four choices in tearing down stream adapters:

- Close the adapter only.
- Close the adapter, and then close the stream.
- (For writers) Flush the adapter, and then close the stream.
- (For readers) Close just the stream.

Close and Dispose are synonymous with adapters, just as they are with streams.

Options 1 and 2 are semantically identical, because closing an adapter automatically closes the underlying stream. Whenever you nest using statements, you're implicitly taking option 2:

```
using (FileStream fs = File.Create ("test.txt"))
using (TextWriter writer = new StreamWriter (fs))
  writer.WriteLine ("Line");
```

Because the nest disposes from the inside out, the adapter is first closed, and then the stream. Furthermore, if an exception is thrown within the adapter's constructor, the stream still closes. It's hard to go wrong with nested using statements!

Never close a stream before closing or flushing its writer—you'll amputate any data that's buffered in the adapter.

Options 3 and 4 work because adapters are in the unusual category of *optionally* disposable objects. An example of when you might choose not to dispose an adapter is when you've finished with the adapter, but you want to leave the underlying stream open for subsequent use:

```
using (FileStream fs = new FileStream ("test.txt", FileMode.Create))
{
  StreamWriter writer = new StreamWriter (fs);
  writer.WriteLine ("Hello");
  writer.Flush( );

  fs.Position = 0;
  Console.WriteLine (fs.ReadByte( ));
}
```

Here we write to a file, reposition the stream, and then read the first byte before closing the stream. If we disposed the StreamWriter, it would also close the underlying FileStream, causing the subsequent read to fail. The proviso is that we call Flush to ensure that the StreamWriter's buffer is written to the underlying stream.

Stream adapters—with their optional disposal semantics—do not implement the extended disposal pattern where the finalizer calls Dispose. This allows an abandoned adapter to evade automatic disposal when the garbage collector catches up with it.

File and Directory Operations

The System.IO namespace provides a set of types for performing "utility" file and directory operations, such as copying and moving, creating directories, and setting file attributes and permissions. For most features, you can choose between either of two classes, one offering static methods and the other instance methods:

Static classes
    File and Directory

Instance method classes (constructed with a file or directory name)
    FileInfo and DirectoryInfo

Additionally, there's a static class called Path. This does nothing to files or directories; instead, it provides string manipulation methods for filenames and directory paths. Path also assists with temporary files.

The File Class

File is a static class whose methods all accept a filename. The filename can be either relative to the current directory or fully qualified with a directory. Here are its methods (all public and static):

```
bool Exists (string path);      // Returns true if the file is present

void Delete  (string path);
void Copy    (string sourceFileName, string destFileName);
void Move    (string sourceFileName, string destFileName);
void Replace (string sourceFileName, string destinationFileName,
                                     string destinationBackupFileName);

FileAttributes GetAttributes (string path);
void SetAttributes           (string path, FileAttributes fileAttributes);

void Decrypt (string path);
void Encrypt (string path);

DateTime GetCreationTime   (string path);      // UTC versions are
DateTime GetLastAccessTime (string path);      // also provided.
DateTime GetLastWriteTime  (string path);

void SetCreationTime   (string path, DateTime creationTime);
void SetLastAccessTime (string path, DateTime lastAccessTime);
void SetLastWriteTime  (string path, DateTime lastWriteTime);

FileSecurity GetAccessControl (string path);
FileSecurity GetAccessControl (string path,
                               AccessControlSections includeSections);
void SetAccessControl (string path, FileSecurity fileSecurity);
```

Move throws an exception if the destination file already exists; Replace does not. Both methods allow the file to be renamed as well as moved to another directory.

Delete throws an UnauthorizedAccessException if the file is marked read-only; you can tell this in advance by calling GetAttributes. Here are all the members of the FileAttribute enum that GetAttributes returns:

```
Archive, Compressed, Device, Directory, Encrypted,
Hidden, Normal, NotContentIndexed, Offline, ReadOnly,
ReparsePoint, SparseFile, System, Temporary
```

Members in this enum are combinable. Here's how to toggle a single file attribute without upsetting the rest:

```
string filePath = "c:\\temp\\test.txt";

FileAttributes fa = File.GetAttributes (filePath);
if ((fa & FileAttributes.ReadOnly) > 0)
{
    fa ^= FileAttributes.ReadOnly;
    File.SetAttributes (filePath, fa);
}

// Now we can delete the file, for instance:
File.Delete (filePath);
```

 FileInfo offers an easier way to change a file's read-only flag:

```
new FileInfo (@"c:\temp\test.txt").IsReadOnly = false;
```

Compression and encryption attributes

The Compressed and Encrypted file attributes correspond to the compression and encryption checkboxes on a file or directory's *properties* dialog in Windows Explorer. This type of compression and encryption is *transparent* in that the operating system does all the work behind the scenes, allowing you to read and write plain data.

To change a file's Compressed or Encrypted attributes, you cannot use SetAttributes—it fails silently if you try! The workaround is simple in the latter case: you instead call the Encrypt( ) and Decrypt( ) methods in the File class. With compression, it's more complicated; one solution is to use the Windows Management Instrumentation (WMI) API in System.Management. The following method compresses a directory, returning 0 if successful (or a WMI error code if not):

```
static uint CompressFolder (string folder, bool recursive)
{
  string path = "Win32_Directory.Name='" + folder + "'";
  using (ManagementObject dir = new ManagementObject (path))
  using (ManagementBaseObject p = dir.GetMethodParameters ("CompressEx"))
  {
    p ["Recursive"] = recursive;
    using (ManagementBaseObject result = dir.InvokeMethod ("CompressEx",
                                                            p, null))
      return (uint) result.Properties ["ReturnValue"].Value;
  }
}
```

To uncompress, replace CompressEx with UncompressEx.

Transparent encryption relies on a key seeded from the logged-in-user's password. The system is robust to password changes performed by the authenticated user, but if a password is reset via an administrator, data in encrypted files is unrecoverable.

Transparent encryption and compression require special filesystem support. NTFS (used most commonly on hard drives) supports these features; CDFS (on CD-ROMs) and FAT (on removable media cards) do not.

You can determine whether a volume supports compression and encryption with Win32 interop:

```
using System;
using System.IO;
using System.Text;
using System.Runtime.InteropServices;

class SupportsCompressionEncryption
{
  const int SupportsCompression = 0x10;
  const int SupportsEncryption = 0x20000;

  [DllImport ("Kernel32.dll", SetLastError = true)]
  extern static bool GetVolumeInformation (string vol, StringBuilder name,
    int nameSize, out uint serialNum, out uint maxNameLen, out uint flags,
    StringBuilder fileSysName, int fileSysNameSize);

  static void Main( )
  {
    uint serialNum, maxNameLen, flags;
    bool ok = GetVolumeInformation (@"C:\", null, 0, out serialNum,
                                    out maxNameLen, out flags, null, 0);
    if (!ok)
      throw new Exception
        ("Error: Win32 code=" + Marshal.GetLastWin32Error( ));

    bool canCompress = (flags & SupportsCompression) > 0;
    bool canEncrypt = (flags & SupportsEncryption) > 0;
  }
}
```

File security

The GetAccessControl and SetAccessControl methods allow you to query and change the operating system permissions assigned to users and roles via a FileSecurity object (namespace System.Security.AccessControl). You can also pass a FileSecurity object to a FileStream's constructor to specify permissions when creating a new file.

In this example, we list a file's existing permissions, and then assign execution permission to the "Users" group:

```
using System;
using System.IO;
using System.Security.AccessControl;
using System.Security.Principal;

...
```

```
FileSecurity sec = File.GetAccessControl (@"c:\temp\test.txt");
AuthorizationRuleCollection rules = sec.GetAccessRules (true, true,
                                               typeof (NTAccount));
foreach (FileSystemAccessRule rule in rules)
{
  Console.WriteLine (rule.AccessControlType);        // Allow or Deny
  Console.WriteLine (rule.FileSystemRights);         // e.g., FullControl
  Console.WriteLine (rule.IdentityReference.Value);  // e.g., MyDomain/Joe
}

FileSystemAccessRule newRule = new FileSystemAccessRule
  ("Users", FileSystemRights.ExecuteFile, AccessControlType.Allow);
sec.AddAccessRule (newRule);
File.SetAccessControl (@"c:\temp\test.txt", sec);
```

The Directory Class

The static Directory class provides a set of methods analogous to those in the File class—for checking whether a directory exists (Exists), moving a directory (Move), deleting a directory (Delete), getting/setting times of creation or last access, and getting/setting security permissions. Furthermore, Directory exposes the following static methods:

```
string GetCurrentDirectory ();
void   SetCurrentDirectory (string path);

DirectoryInfo CreateDirectory  (string path);
DirectoryInfo GetParent        (string path);
string        GetDirectoryRoot (string path);

string[] GetLogicalDrives();

// The following methods all return full paths:
string[] GetFiles             (string path);
string[] GetFiles             (string path, string searchPattern);
string[] GetDirectories       (string path);
string[] GetDirectories       (string path, string searchPattern);
string[] GetFileSystemEntries (string path);
string[] GetFileSystemEntries (string path, string searchPattern);
```

GetFiles and GetDirectories are also overloaded to accept a SearchOption; if you specify SearchAllSubDirectories, a recursive subdirectory search is performed. GetFileSystemEntries combines the results of GetFiles with GetDirectories.

Here's how to create a directory if it doesn't already exist:

```
if (!Directory.Exists (@"c:\temp"))
  Directory.CreateDirectory (@"c:\temp");
```

FileInfo and DirectoryInfo

The static methods on File and Directory are convenient for executing a single file or directory operation. If you need to call a series of methods in a row, the

FileInfo and DirectoryInfo classes provide an object model that makes the job easier.

FileInfo offers most of the File's static methods in instance form—with some additional properties such as Extension, Length, IsReadOnly, and Directory—for returning a DirectoryInfo object. For example:

```
FileInfo fi = new FileInfo (@"c:\temp\FileInfo.txt");
Console.WriteLine (fi.Exists);          // false

using (TextWriter w = fi.CreateText())
  w.Write ("Some text");

Console.WriteLine (fi.Exists);          // false (still)
fi.Refresh();
Console.WriteLine (fi.Exists);          // true

Console.WriteLine (fi.Name);            // FileInfo.txt
Console.WriteLine (fi.FullName);        // c:\temp\FileInfo.txt
Console.WriteLine (fi.DirectoryName);   // c:\temp
Console.WriteLine (fi.Directory.Name);  // temp
Console.WriteLine (fi.Extension);       // .txt
Console.WriteLine (fi.Length);          // 9

fi.Encrypt();
fi.Attributes ^= FileAttributes.Hidden;   // (Toggle hidden flag)
fi.IsReadOnly = true;

Console.WriteLine (fi.Attributes);      // ReadOnly,Archive,Hidden,Encrypted
Console.WriteLine (fi.CreationTime);

fi.MoveTo (@"c:\temp\FileInfoX.txt");

DirectoryInfo di = fi.Directory;
Console.WriteLine (di.Name);              // temp
Console.WriteLine (di.FullName);          // c:\temp
Console.WriteLine (di.Parent.FullName);   // c:\
di.CreateSubdirectory ("SubFolder");
```

Here's how to use DirectoryInfo to enumerate files and subdirectories:

```
DirectoryInfo di = new DirectoryInfo (@"e:\photos");

foreach (FileInfo fi in di.GetFiles ("*.jpg"))
  Console.WriteLine (fi.Name);

foreach (DirectoryInfo subDir in di.GetDirectories())
  Console.WriteLine (subDir.FullName);
```

Path

The static Path class defines methods and fields for working with paths and filenames.

Streams & I/O

Assuming this setup code:

```
string dir  = @"c:\mydir";
string file = "myfile.txt";
string path = @"c:\mydir\myfile.txt";

Directory.SetCurrentDirectory (@"k:\demo");
```

Table 13-4 demonstrates all of Path's methods and fields.

Table 13-4. Path methods and fields

Expression	Result
Directory.GetCurrentDirectory( )	k:\demo\
Path.IsPathRooted (file)	False
Path.IsPathRooted (path)	True
Path.GetPathRoot (path)	c:\
Path.GetDirectoryName (path)	c:\mydir
Path.GetFileName (path)	myfile.txt
Path.GetFullPath (file)	k:\demo\myfile.txt
Path.Combine (dir, file)	c:\mydir\myfile.txt
File extensions:	
Path.HasExtension (file)	True
Path.GetExtension (file)	.txt
Path.GetFileNameWithoutExtension (file)	myfile
Path.ChangeExtension (file, ".log")	myfile.log
Separators and characters:	
Path.AltDirectorySeparatorChar	/
Path.PathSeparator	;
Path.VolumeSeparatorChar	:
Path.GetInvalidPathChars( )	chars 0 to 31 and "<>|
Path.GetInvalidFileNameChars( )	chars 0 to 31 and "<>|:*?\/
Temporary files:	
Path.GetTempPath( )	*<local user folder>*\Temp
Path.GetRandomFileName( )	*d2dwuzjf.dnp*
Path.GetTempFileName( )	*<local user folder>*\Temp*tmp14B.tmp*

Combine is particularly useful: it allows you to combine a directory and filename—or two directories—without first having to check whether a trailing backslash is present.

GetFullPath converts a path relative to the current directory to an absolute path. It accepts values such as ..\..*file.txt*.

GetRandomFileName returns a genuinely unique 8.3 character filename, without actually creating any file. GetTempFileName generates a temporary filename using an auto-incrementing counter that repeats every 65,000 files. It then creates a zero-byte file of this name in the local temporary directory.

You must delete the file generated by GetTempFileName when you're done; otherwise, it will eventually throw an exception (after your 65,000th call to GetTempFileName). If this is a problem, you can instead Combine GetTempPath with GetRandomFileName. Just be careful not to fill up the user's hard drive!

Special Folders

One thing missing from Path and Directory is a means to locate folders such as *My Documents*, *Program Files*, *Application Data*, and so on. This is provided instead by the GetFolderPath method in the System.Environment class:

```
string myDocPath = Environment.GetFolderPath
    (Environment.SpecialFolder.MyDocuments);
```

Environment.SpecialFolder is an enum whose values encompass all special directories in Windows:

ApplicationData	Favorites	MyMusic	SendTo
CommonApplication-Data	History	MyPictures	StartMenu
	InternetCache	Personal	Startup
CommonProgramFiles	LocalApplication-Data	ProgramFiles	System
Cookies		Programs	Templates
Desktop	MyComputer	Recent	
DesktopDirectory	MyDocuments		

Of particular value is ApplicationData: this is where you can store settings that travel with a user across a network (if roaming profiles are enabled on the network domain). LocalApplicationData is for nonroaming data; CommonApplicationData is shared by every user of the computer. Writing application data to these folders is considered preferable to using the Windows Registry. A better option still, in most cases, is to use isolated storage (described in the final section of this chapter).

 The simplest place to write configuration and log files is to the application's base directory, which you can obtain with AppDomain.CurrentDomain.BaseDirectory. This is not recommended, however, because the operating system may deny your application permissions to write to this folder after initial installation.

The following method returns the .NET Framework directory:

```
System.Runtime.InteropServices.RuntimeEnvironment.GetRuntimeDirectory()
```

Querying Volume Information

You can query the drives on a computer with the DriveInfo class:

```
DriveInfo c = new DriveInfo ("C");         // Query the C: drive.

long totalSize = c.TotalSize;              // Size in bytes.
long freeBytes = c.TotalFreeSpace;         // Ignores disk quotas.
long freeToMe  = c.AvailableFreeSpace;     // Takes quotas into account.
```

```
foreach (DriveInfo d in DriveInfo.GetDrives())    // All defined drives.
{
  Console.WriteLine (d.Name);            // C:\
  Console.WriteLine (d.DriveType);       // Fixed
  Console.WriteLine (d.RootDirectory);   // C:\

  if (d.IsReady)   // If the drive is not ready, the following two
                   // properties will throw exceptions:
  {
    Console.WriteLine (d.VolumeLabel);   // The Sea Drive
    Console.WriteLine (d.DriveFormat);   // NTFS
  }
}
```

The static `GetDrives` method returns all mapped drives, including CD-ROMs, media cards, and network connections. `DriveType` is an enum with the following values:

```
Unknown, NoRootDirectory, Removable, Fixed, Network, CDRom, Ram
```

Catching Filesystem Events

The `FileSystemWatcher` class lets you monitor a directory (and optionally, subdirectories) for activity. `FileSystemWatcher` has events that fire when files or subdirectories are created, modified, renamed, and deleted, as well as when their attributes change. These events fire regardless of the user or process performing the change. Here's an example:

```
static void Main() { Watch (@"c:\temp", "*.txt", true); }

static void Watch (string path, string filter, bool includeSubDirs)
{
  using (FileSystemWatcher watcher = new FileSystemWatcher (path, filter))
  {
    watcher.Created += FileCreatedChangedDeleted;
    watcher.Changed += FileCreatedChangedDeleted;
    watcher.Deleted += FileCreatedChangedDeleted;
    watcher.Renamed += FileRenamed;
    watcher.Error   += FileError;

    watcher.IncludeSubdirectories = includeSubDirs;
    watcher.EnableRaisingEvents = true;

    Console.WriteLine ("Listening for events - press <enter> to end");
    Console.ReadLine();
  }
  // Disposing the FileSystemWatcher stops further events from firing.
}

static void FileCreatedChangedDeleted (object o, FileSystemEventArgs e)
{
  Console.WriteLine ("File {0} has been {1}", e.FullPath, e.ChangeType);
}
```

```
static void FileRenamed (object o, RenamedEventArgs e)
{
  Console.WriteLine ("Renamed: {0}->{1}", e.OldFullPath, e.FullPath);
}

static void FileError (object o, ErrorEventArgs e)
{
  Console.WriteLine ("Error: " + e.GetException( ).Message);
}
```

The Error event does not inform you of filesystem errors; instead, it indicates that
the FileSystemWatcher's event buffer overflowed because it was overwhelmed by
Changed, Created, Deleted, or Renamed events. You can change the buffer size via
the InternalBufferSize property.

IncludeSubdirectories applies recursively. So, if you create a FileSystemWatcher
on *C:* with IncludeSubdirectories true, its events will fire when a file or directory changes anywhere on the hard drive.

Compression

Two general-purpose compression streams are provided in the System.IO.
Compression namespace: DeflateStream and GZipStream. Both use a popular
compression algorithm similar to that of the ZIP format. They differ in that
GZipStream writes an additional protocol at the start and end; this allows
Microsoft to add additional compression formats in the future without breaking
compatibility with data already serialized. Hence, GZipStream is better for
persisting compressed data; DeflateStream is better for *transmitting* compressed
data.

Both streams allow reading and writing, with the following provisos:

- You always *write* to the stream when compressing.
- You always *read* from the stream when decompressing.

DeflateStream and GZipStream are decorators; they compress or decompress data
from another stream that you supply in construction. In the following example,
we compress and decompress a series of bytes, using a FileStream as the backing
store:

```
using (Stream s = File.Create ("compressed.bin"))
using (Stream ds = new DeflateStream (s, CompressionMode.Compress))
  for (byte i = 0; i < 100; i++)
    ds.WriteByte (i);

using (Stream s = File.OpenRead ("compressed.bin"))
using (Stream ds = new DeflateStream (s, CompressionMode.Decompress))
  for (byte i = 0; i < 100; i++)
    Console.WriteLine (ds.ReadByte( ));       // Writes 0 to 99
```

Even with the smaller of the two algorithms, the compressed file is 241 bytes long:
more than double the original! Compression works poorly with "dense,"
nonrepetitive binary files. It works well with most text files; in the next example,
we compress and decompress a text stream composed of 1,000 words chosen

randomly from a small sentence. This also demonstrates chaining a backing store stream, a decorator stream, and an adapter, as depicted at the start of the chapter in Figure 13-1:

```
string[] words = "The quick brown fox jumps over the lazy dog".Split( );
Random rand = new Random( );

using (Stream s = File.Create ("compressed.bin"))
using (Stream ds = new DeflateStream (s, CompressionMode.Compress))
using (TextWriter w = new StreamWriter (ds))
  for (int i = 0; i < 1000; i++)
    w.Write (words [rand.Next (words.Length)] + " ");

Console.WriteLine (new FileInfo ("compressed.bin").Length);        // 1073

using (Stream s = File.OpenRead ("compressed.bin"))
using (Stream ds = new DeflateStream (s, CompressionMode.Decompress))
using (TextReader r = new StreamReader (ds))
  Console.Write (r.ReadToEnd( ));                     // Output below:

lazy lazy the fox the quick The brown fox jumps over fox over fox The
brown brown brown over brown quick fox brown dog dog lazy fox dog brown
over fox jumps lazy lazy quick The jumps fox jumps The over jumps dog...
```

In this case, DeflateStream compresses efficiently to 1,073 bytes—slightly more than 1 byte per word.

Compressing in Memory

Sometimes you need to compress entirely in memory. Here's how to use a MemoryStream for this purpose:

```
byte[] data = new byte[1000];          // We can expect a good compression
                                       // ratio from an empty array!
MemoryStream ms = new MemoryStream( );
using (Stream ds = new DeflateStream (ms, CompressionMode.Compress))
  ds.Write (data, 0, data.Length);

byte[] compressed = ms.ToArray( );
Console.WriteLine (compressed.Length);        // 113

// Decompress back to the data array:
ms = new MemoryStream (compressed);
using (Stream ds = new DeflateStream (ms, CompressionMode.Decompress))
  for (int i = 0; i < 1000; i += ds.Read (data, i, 1000 - i));
```

The using statement around the DeflateStream closes it in a textbook fashion, flushing any unwritten buffers in the process. This also closes the MemoryStream it wraps—meaning we must then call ToArray to extract its data.

Here's an alternative that avoids closing the MemoryStream:

```
byte[] data = new byte[1000];

MemoryStream ms = new MemoryStream( );
using (Stream ds = new DeflateStream (ms, CompressionMode.Compress, true))
  ds.Write (data, 0, data.Length);
```

```
Console.WriteLine (ms.Length);              // 113
ms.Position = 0;
using (Stream ds = new DeflateStream (ms, CompressionMode.Decompress))
   for (int i = 0; i < 1000; i += ds.Read (data, i, 1000 - i));
```

The additional flag sent to DeflateStream's constructor tells it not to follow the usual protocol of taking the underlying stream with it in disposal. In other words, the MemoryStream is left open, allowing us to position it back to zero and reread it.

Isolated Storage

Each .NET program has access to a special filesystem unique to that program, called *isolated storage*. Isolated storage is useful and important for a number of reasons:

- Your application, if subject to code access security, is more likely to be granted permission to isolated storage than any other form of file I/O (by default, even applications running from an Internet URI have some access to isolated storage).
- Data that you create is segregated from other applications.
- Isolated storage is Windows Vista-friendly.

In terms of security, isolated storage is a fence designed more to keep you in than to keep other applications out! Data in isolated storage is strongly protected against intrusion from other .NET applications running under the most restricted permission set (i.e., the "Internet" zone). In other cases, there's no hard security preventing another application from accessing your isolated storage *if it really wants to*. The benefit of using isolated storage over CommonApplicationData is that applications must go out of their way to interfere with each other—it cannot happen through carelessness or by accident.

Applications running in a restricted permission set can have their quota of isolated storage limited through the computer's .NET Framework configuration—preventing partially trusted software from causing trouble by filling up the disk.

Isolated storage also has disadvantages:

- The API is somewhat awkward to use—particularly when accessing roaming stores.
- You can read/write only with an IsolatedStorageStream; you cannot obtain a file or directory path and then use ordinary file I/O.

Isolation Types

Isolated storage can separate by both program and user. This results in three basic types of compartments:

Local user compartments
   One per user, per program, per computer

Roaming user compartments
   One per user, per program

Machine compartments
    One per program, per computer (shared by all users of a program)

The data in a roaming user compartment follows the user across a network—with appropriate operating system and domain support. If this support is unavailable, it behaves like a local user compartment.

So far, we've talked about how isolated storage separates by "program." Isolated storage considers a program to be one of two things, depending on which mode you choose:

- An assembly
- An assembly running within the context of a particular application

The latter is called *domain isolation* and is more commonly used than *assembly isolation*. Domain isolation segregates according to two things: the currently executing assembly and the executable or web application that originally started it. Assembly isolation segregates only according to the currently executing assembly—so different applications calling the same assembly will share the same store.

 Assemblies and applications are identified by their strong name. If no strong name is present, the assembly's full file path or URI is used instead. This means that if you move or rename a weakly named assembly, its isolated storage is reset.

In total, then, there are six kinds of isolated storage compartments. Table 13-5 compares the isolation provided by each.

Table 13-5. Isolated storage containers

Type	Computer?	Application?	Assembly?	User?	Method to obtain store
Domain User (default)	✓	✓	✓	✓	`GetUserStoreForDomain`
Domain Roaming		✓	✓	✓	
Domain Machine	✓	✓	✓		`GetMachineStoreForDomain`
Assembly User	✓		✓	✓	`GetUserStoreForAssembly`
Assembly Roaming			✓	✓	
Assembly Machine	✓		✓		`GetMachineStoreForAssembly`

There is no such thing as domain-only isolation. If you want to share an isolated store across all assemblies within an application, there's a simple workaround, however. Just expose a public method in one of the assemblies that instantiates and returns an `IsolatedStorageFileStream` object. Any assembly can access any isolated store if given an `IsolatedStorageFile` object—isolation restrictions are imposed upon construction, not subsequent use.

Similarly, there's no such thing as machine-only isolation. If you want to share an isolated store across a variety of applications, the workaround is to write a common assembly that all applications reference, and then expose a method on the common assembly that creates and returns an assembly-isolated `IsolatedStorageFileStream`. The common assembly must be strongly named for this to work.

Reading and Writing Isolated Storage

Isolated storage uses streams that work much like ordinary file streams. To obtain an isolated storage stream, you first specify the kind of isolation you want by calling one of the static methods on `IsolatedStorageFile`—as shown previously in Table 13-5. You then use it to construct an `IsolatedStorageFileStream`, along with a filename and `FileMode`:

```
// IsolatedStorage classes live in System.IO.IsolatedStorage

using (IsolatedStorageFile f =
        IsolatedStorageFile.GetMachineStoreForDomain())
using (var s = new IsolatedStorageFileStream ("hi.txt",FileMode.Create,f))
using (var writer = new StreamWriter (s))
  writer.WriteLine ("Hello, World");

// Read it back:

using (IsolatedStorageFile f =
        IsolatedStorageFile.GetMachineStoreForDomain())
using (var s = new IsolatedStorageFileStream ("hi.txt", FileMode.Open, f))
using (var reader = new StreamReader (s))
  Console.WriteLine (reader.ReadToEnd());        // Hello, world
```

(In C# 2.0, replace var x = new *TypeName*( ) with *TypeName* x = new *TypeName*( ).)

You can optionally omit the first step, and then the default isolation (Domain User) is used:

```
using (var s = new IsolatedStorageFileStream ("a.txt", FileMode.Create))
using (var writer = new StreamWriter (s))
  ...
```

 IsolatedStorageFile is poorly named in that it doesn't represent a file, but rather a *container* for files (basically, a directory).

`IsolatedStorageFile` doesn't provide methods to directly access the roaming stores: you must instead call `GetStore` with an `IsolatedStorageScope` argument. `IsolatedStorageScope` is a flags enum whose members you must combine in exactly the right way to get a valid store. Figure 13-6 lists all the valid combinations.

Here's how to write to a store isolated by assembly and roaming user:

```
var flags = IsolatedStorageScope.Assembly
        | IsolatedStorageScope.User
```

	Assembly	Assembly & Domain
Local User	Assembly | User	Assembly | Domain | User
Roaming User	Assembly | User | Roaming	Assembly | Domain | User | Roaming
Machine	Assembly | Machine	Assembly | Domain | Machine

Figure 13-6. Valid IsolatedStorageScope combinations

```
                    | IsolatedStorageScope.Roaming;

  using (IsolatedStorageFile f = IsolatedStorageFile.GetStore (flags,
                                                       null, null))
  using (var s = new IsolatedStorageFileStream ("a.txt", FileMode.Create, f))
  using (var writer = new StreamWriter (s))
    writer.WriteLine ("Hello, World");
```

Store Location

Here's where .NET writes isolated storage files:

Scope	Location
Local user	[LocalApplicationData]*IsolatedStorage*
Roaming user	[ApplicationData]*IsolatedStorage*
Machine	[CommonApplicationData]*IsolatedStorage*

You can obtain the locations of each of the folders in square brackets by calling the Environment.GetFolderPath method. Here are the defaults for Windows Vista:

Scope	Location
Local user	*\Users\<user>\AppData\Local\IsolatedStorage*
Roaming user	*\Users\<user>\AppData\Roaming\IsolatedStorage*
Machine	*\ProgramData\IsolatedStorage*

For Windows XP:

Scope	Location
Local user	*\Documents and Settings\<user>\Local Settings\Application Data\IsolatedStorage*
Roaming user	*\Documents and Settings\<user>\Application Data\IsolatedStorage*
Machine	*\Documents and Settings\All Users\Application Data\IsolatedStorage*

These are merely the base folders; the data files themselves are buried deep in a labyrinth of subdirectories whose names derive from hashed assembly names. This is both a reason to use—and not to use—isolated storage. On the one hand, it makes isolation possible: a permission-restricted application wanting to interfere with another can be stumped by being denied a directory listing—despite having the same filesystem rights as its peers. On the other hand, it makes administration impractical from outside the application. Sometimes it's handy—or essential—to edit an XML configuration file in Notepad so that an application can start up properly. Isolated storage makes this impractical.

Enumerating Isolated Storage

An IsolatedStorageFile object also provides methods for listing files in the store:

```
using (IsolatedStorageFile f = IsolatedStorageFile.GetUserStoreForDomain())
{
  using (var s = new IsolatedStorageFileStream ("f1.x",FileMode.Create,f))
    s.WriteByte (123);

  using (var s = new IsolatedStorageFileStream ("f2.x",FileMode.Create,f))
    s.WriteByte (123);

  foreach (string s in f.GetFileNames ("*.*"))
    Console.Write (s + " ");                      // f1.x f2.x
}
```

You can also create and remove subdirectories, as well as files:

```
using (IsolatedStorageFile f = IsolatedStorageFile.GetUserStoreForDomain())
{
  f.CreateDirectory ("subfolder");

  foreach (string s in f.GetDirectoryNames ("*.*"))
    Console.WriteLine (s);                        // subfolder

  using (var s = new IsolatedStorageFileStream (@"subfolder\sub1.txt",
                                                 FileMode.Create, f))
    s.WriteByte (100);

  f.DeleteFile (@"subfolder\sub1.txt");
  f.DeleteDirectory ("subfolder");
}
```

With sufficient permissions, you can also enumerate over all isolated stores created by the current user, as well as all machine stores. This function can violate program privacy, but not user privacy. Here's an example:

```
System.Collections.IEnumerator rator =
  IsolatedStorageFile.GetEnumerator (IsolatedStorageScope.User);

while (rator.MoveNext())
{
  var isf = (IsolatedStorageFile) rator.Current;

  Console.WriteLine (isf.AssemblyIdentity);     // Strong name or URI
  Console.WriteLine (isf.CurrentSize);
  Console.WriteLine (isf.Scope);                // User + ...
}
```

The GetEnumerator method is unusual in accepting an argument (this makes its containing class foreach-unfriendly). GetEnumerator accepts one of three values:

IsolatedStorageScope.User
    Enumerates all local stores belonging to the current user

IsolatedStorageScope.User | IsolatedStorageScope.Roaming
    Enumerates all roaming stores belonging to the current user

IsolatedStorageScope.Machine
    Enumerates all machine stores on the computer

Once you have the IsolatedStorageFile object, you can list its content by calling GetFiles and GetDirectories.

14

Networking

The Framework offers a variety of classes in the System.Net.* namespaces for communicating via standard network protocols, such as HTTP, TCP/IP, and FTP. Here's a summary of the key components:

- A WebClient façade class for simple download/upload operations via HTTP or FTP
- WebRequest and WebResponse classes for more control over client-side HTTP or FTP operations
- HttpListener for writing an HTTP server
- SmtpClient for constructing and sending mail messages via SMTP
- Dns for converting between domain names and addresses
- TcpClient, UdpClient, TcpListener, and Socket classes for direct access to the transport and network layers

The Framework supports primarily Internet-based protocols, although this doesn't limit applicability to the Internet; protocols such as TCP/IP also dominate local area networks.

The types described in this chapter are defined mostly in the System.Net and System.Net.Sockets namespaces; however, many of the examples also use types in System.IO.

Network Architecture

Figure 14-1 illustrates the .NET networking types and the communication layers in which they reside. Most types reside in the *transport layer* or *application layer*. The transport layer defines basic protocols for sending and receiving bytes (TCP and UDP); the application layer defines higher-level protocols designed for specific applications such as retrieving web pages (HTTP), transferring files (FTP), sending mail (SMTP), and converting between domain names and IP addresses (DNS).

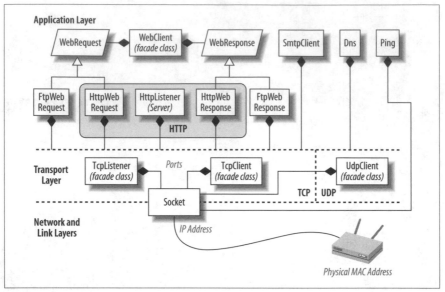

Figure 14-1. Network architecture

It's usually most convenient to program at the application layer; however, there are a couple of reasons you might want to work directly at the transport layer. One is if you need an application protocol not provided in the Framework, such as POP3 for retrieving mail. Another is if you want to invent a custom protocol for a special application such as a peer-to-peer client.

Of the application protocols, HTTP is special in that its use has extended to general-purpose communication. Its basic mode of operation—"give me the web page with this URL"—adapts nicely to "give me the return value from calling this method with these arguments." HTTP has a rich set of features that are useful in multitier business applications and service-oriented architectures, such as protocols for authentication and encryption, message chunking, extensible headers and cookies, and the ability to have many server applications share a single port and IP address. For these reasons, HTTP is well supported in the Framework—both directly, as described in this chapter, and at a higher level, through such technologies as WCF, Web Services, and ASP.NET.

The Framework provides client-side support for FTP, the popular Internet protocol for sending and receiving files. Server-side support comes in the form of IIS or Unix-based server software.

As the preceding discussion makes clear, networking is a field that is awash in acronyms. Table 14-1 is a handy Network TLA (three-letter and more acronym buster).

Table 14-1. Network TLA (three-letter acronym) buster

Acronym	Expansion	Notes
DNS	Domain Name Service	Converts between domain names (e.g., ebay.com) and IP addresses (e.g., 199.54.213.2)
FTP	File Transfer Protocol	Internet-based protocol for sending and receiving files

Table 14-1. *Network TLA (three-letter acronym) buster*

Acronym	Expansion	Notes
HTTP	Hypertext Transfer Protocol	Retrieves web pages and runs web services
IIS	Internet Information Services	Microsoft's web server software
IP	Internet Protocol	Network-layer protocol below TCP and UDP
LAN	Local Area Network	Most LANs use Internet-based protocols such as TCP/IP
POP	Post Office Protocol	Retrieves Internet mail
SMTP	Simple Mail Transfer Protocol	Sends Internet mail
TCP	Transmission and Control Protocol	Transport-layer Internet protocol on top of which most higher-layer services are built
UDP	Universal Datagram Protocol	Transport-layer Internet protocol used for low-overhead services such as VoIP
UNC	Universal Naming Convention	*computer**sharename**filename*
URI	Uniform Resource Identifier	Ubiquitous resource naming system (e.g., *http://www.amazon.com* or *mailto:joe@bloggs.org*)
URL	Uniform Resource Locator	Technical meaning (fading from use): subset of URI; popular meaning: synonym of URI

Addresses and Ports

For communication to work, a computer or device requires an address. The Internet uses two addressing systems:

IPv4
> Currently the dominant addressing system; IPv4 addresses are 32 bits wide. When string-formatted, IPv4 addresses are written as four dot-separated decimals (e.g., 101.102.103.104). An address can be unique in the world—or unique within a particular *subnet* (such as on a corporate network).

IPv6
> The newer 128-bit addressing system. Addresses are string-formatted in hexadecimal with a colon separator (e.g., [3EA0:FFFF:198A:E4A3:4FF2:54f-A:41BC:8D31]). The .NET Framework requires that you add square brackets around the address.

The IPAddress class in the System.Net namespace represents an address in either protocol. It has a constructor accepting a byte array, and a static Parse method accepting a correctly formatted string:

```
IPAddress a1 = new IPAddress (new byte[] { 101, 102, 103, 104 });
IPAddress a2 = IPAddress.Parse ("101.102.103.104");
Console.WriteLine (a1.Equals (a2));              // True
Console.WriteLine (a1.AddressFamily);            // InterNetwork

IPAddress a3 = IPAddress.Parse
  ("[3EA0:FFFF:198A:E4A3:4FF2:54fA:41BC:8D31]");
Console.WriteLine (a3.AddressFamily);   // InterNetworkV6
```

The TCP and UDP protocols break out each IP address into 65,535 ports, allowing a computer on a single address to run multiple applications, each on its own port. Many applications have standard port assignments; for instance, HTTP uses port 80; SMTP uses port 25.

 The TCP and UDP ports from 49152 to 65535 are officially unassigned, so they are good for testing and small-scale deployments.

An IP address and port combination is represented in the .NET Framework by the IPEndPoint class:

```
IPAddress a = IPAddress.Parse ("101.102.103.104");
IPEndPoint ep = new IPEndPoint (a, 222);          // Port 222
Console.WriteLine (ep.ToString( ));               // 101.102.103.104:222
```

 Firewalls block ports. In many corporate environments, only a few ports are in fact open—typically, port 80 (for unencrypted HTTP) and port 443 (for secure HTTP).

URIs

A URI is a specially formatted string that describes a resource on the Internet or a LAN, such as a web page, file, or email address. Examples include *http://www.ietf. org*, *ftp://myisp/doc.txt*, and *mailto:joe@bloggs.com*. The exact formatting is defined by the Internet Engineering Task Force (*http://www.ietf.org/*).

A URI can be broken up into a series of elements—typically, *scheme*, *authority*, and *path*. The Uri class in the System namespace performs just this division, exposing a property for each element. This is illustrated in Figure 14-2.

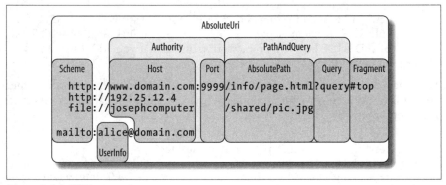

Figure 14-2. URI properties

The Uri class is useful when you need to validate the format of a URI string or to split a URI into its component parts. Otherwise, you can treat a URI simply as a string—most networking methods are overloaded to accept either a Uri object or a string.

You can construct a Uri object by passing any of the following strings into its constructor:

- A URI string, such as *http://www.ebay.com* or *file://janespc/sharedpics/dolphin.jpg*
- An absolute path to a file on your hard disk, such as *c:\myfiles\data.xls*
- A UNC path to a file on the LAN, such as *\\janespc\sharedpics\dolphin.jpg*

File and UNC paths are automatically converted to URIs: the "file:" protocol is added, and backslashes are converted to forward slashes. The Uri constructors also perform some basic cleanup on your string before creating the Uri, including converting the scheme and hostname to lowercase and removing default and blank port numbers. If you supply a URI string without the scheme, such as "www.test.com", a UriFormatException is thrown.

Uri has an IsLoopback property, which indicates whether the Uri references the local host (IP address 127.0.0.1), and an IsFile property, which indicates whether the Uri references a local or UNC (IsUnc) path. If IsFile returns true, the LocalPath property returns a version of AbsolutePath that is friendly to the local operating system (with backslashes), on which you can call File.Open.

Instances of Uri have read-only properties. To modify an existing Uri, instantiate a UriBuilder object—this has writable properties and can be converted back via its Uri property.

Uri also provides methods for comparing and subtracting paths:

```
Uri info = new Uri ("http://www.domain.com:80/info/");
Uri page = new Uri ("http://www.domain.com/info/page.html");

Console.WriteLine (info.Host);      // www.domain.com
Console.WriteLine (info.Port);      // 80
Console.WriteLine (page.Port);      // 80  (Uri knows the default HTTP port)

Console.WriteLine (info.IsBaseOf (page));      // True
Uri relative = info.MakeRelativeUri (page);
Console.WriteLine (relative.IsAbsoluteUri);    // False
Console.WriteLine (relative.ToString( ));      // page.html
```

A relative Uri, such as *page.html* in this example, will throw an exception if you call almost any property or method other than IsAbsoluteUri and ToString( ). You can instantiate a relative Uri directly as follows:

```
Uri u = new Uri ("page.html", UriKind.Relative);
```

A trailing slash is significant in a URI and makes a difference as to how a server processes a request if a path component is present.

For instance, given the URI *http://www.albahari.com/nutshell/*, you can expect an HTTP web server to look in the *nutshell* subdirectory in the site's web folder and return the default document (usually *index.html*).

Without the trailing slash, the web server will instead look for a file called *nutshell* (without an extension) directly in the site's root folder—which is usually not what you want. If no such file exists, most web servers will assume the user mistyped and will return a 301 *Permanent Redirect* error, suggesting the client retries with the trailing slash. A .NET HTTP client, by default, will respond transparently to a 301 in the same way as a web browser—by retrying with the suggested URI. This means that if you omit a trailing slash when it should have been included, your request will still work—but will suffer an unnecessary extra round trip.

The `Uri` class also provides static helper methods such as `EscapeUriString()`, which converts a string to a valid URL by converting all characters with an ASCII value greater than 127 to hexadecimal representation. The `CheckHostName()` and `CheckSchemeName()` methods accept a string and check whether it is syntactically valid for the given property (although they do not attempt to determine whether a host or URI exists).

Request/Response Architecture

`WebRequest` and `WebResponse` are the common base classes for managing both HTTP and FTP client-side activity, as well as the "file:" protocol. They encapsulate the "request/response" model that these protocols all share: the client makes a request, and then awaits a response from a server.

`WebClient` is simply a façade class that does the work of calling `WebRequest` and `WebResponse`, saving you some coding. `WebClient` gives you a choice of dealing in strings, byte arrays, files, or streams; `WebRequest` and `WebResponse` support just streams. Unfortunately, you cannot rely entirely on `WebClient`; some features (such as cookies) are available only through `WebRequest` and `WebResponse`.

WebClient

Here are the steps in using `WebClient`:

1. Instantiate a `WebClient` object.
2. Assign the `Proxy` property.
3. Assign the `Credentials` property if authentication is required.
4. Call a `DownloadXXX` or `UploadXXX` method with the desired URI.

Its download methods are as follows:

```
public void   DownloadFile   (string address, string fileName);
public string DownloadString (string address);
public byte[] DownloadData   (string address);
public Stream OpenRead        (string address);
```

Each is overloaded to accept a `Uri` object instead of a string address. The upload methods are similar; their return values contain the response (if any) from the server:

```
public byte[] UploadFile  (string address, string fileName);
public byte[] UploadFile  (string address, string method, string fileName);
public string UploadString(string address, string data);
public string UploadString(string address, string method, string data);
public byte[] UploadData  (string address, byte[] data);
public byte[] UploadData  (string address, string method, byte[] data);
public byte[] UploadValues(string address, NameValueCollection data);
public byte[] UploadValues(string address, string method,
                                            NameValueCollection data);
public Stream OpenWrite    (string address);
public Stream OpenWrite    (string address, string method);
```

The `UploadValues` methods can be used to post values to an HTTP form, with a method argument of "POST". `WebClient` also has a `BaseAddress` property; this allows you to specify a string to be prefixed to all addresses, such as *http://www. mysite.com/data/*.

Here's how to download the code samples page for this book to a file in the current folder, and then display it in the default web browser:

```
using (WebClient wc = new WebClient())
{
  wc.Proxy = null;
  wc.DownloadFile ("http://www.albahari.com/nutshell/code.html",
                   "code.html");
}
System.Diagnostics.Process.Start ("code.html");
```

You can use the same `WebClient` object to perform many tasks in sequence. It will crash, however, if you try to make it do two things at once with multithreading. Instead, you must create a separate `WebClient` object for each thread.

WebRequest and WebResponse

`WebRequest` and `WebResponse` are more complex to use than `WebClient`, but also more flexible. Here's how to get started:

1. Call `WebRequest.Create` with a URI to instantiate a web request.

2. Assign the `Proxy` property.

3. Assign the `Credentials` property if authentication is required.

To upload data:

4. Call `GetRequestStream` on the request object, and then write to the stream. Go to step 5 if a response is expected.

To download data:

5. Call `GetResponse` on the request object to instantiate a web response.

6. Call `GetResponseStream` on the response object, and then read the stream (a `StreamReader` can help!).

The following downloads and displays the code samples web page (a rewrite of the preceding example):

```
WebRequest req = WebRequest.Create
                ("http://www.albahari.com/nutshell/code.html");
req.Proxy = null;
using (WebResponse res = req.GetResponse())
using (Stream s = res.GetResponseStream())
using (StreamReader sr = new StreamReader(s))
  File.WriteAllText ("code.html", sr.ReadToEnd ());

System.Diagnostics.Process.Start ("code.html");
```

 The web response object has a ContentLength property, indicating the length of the response stream in bytes, as reported by the server. This value comes from the response headers and may be missing or incorrect. In particular, if an HTTP server chooses the "chunked" mode to break up a large response, the ContentLength value is usually −1. The same can apply with dynamically generated pages.

The static Create method instantiates a subclass of the WebRequest type, such as HttpWebRequest or FtpWebRequest. Its choice of subclass depends on the URI's prefix:

Prefix	Web request type
http: or https:	HttpWebRequest
ftp:	FtpWebRequest
file:	FileWebRequest

 Casting a web request object to its concrete type (HttpWebRequest or FtpWebRequest) allows you to access its protocol-specific features.

You can also register your own prefixes by calling WebRequest.RegisterPrefix. This requires a prefix along with a factory object with a Create method that instantiates an appropriate web request object.

The "https:" protocol is for secure (encrypted) HTTP, via Secure Sockets Layer or SSL. Both WebClient and WebRequest activate SSL transparently upon seeing this prefix (see "SSL" under "HTTP-Specific Support" later in this chapter). The "file:" protocol simply forwards requests to a FileStream object. Its purpose is in meeting a consistent protocol for reading a URI, whether it be a web page, FTP site, or file path.

WebRequest has a Timeout property, in milliseconds. If a timeout occurs, a WebException is thrown with a Status property of WebExceptionStatus.Timeout. The default timeout is 100 seconds for HTTP and infinite for FTP.

You cannot recycle a WebRequest object for multiple requests—each instance is good for one job only.

Proxies

A *proxy server* is an intermediary through which HTTP and FTP requests can be routed. Organizations sometimes set up a proxy server as the only means by which employees can access the Internet—primarily because it simplifies security. A proxy has an address of its own and can demand authentication so that only selected users on the local area network can access the Internet.

You can instruct a WebClient or WebRequest object to route requests through a proxy server with a WebProxy object:

```
// Create a WebProxy with the proxy's IP address and port. You can
// optionally set Credentials if the proxy needs a username/password.

WebProxy p = new WebProxy ("192.178.10.49", 808);
p.Credentials = new NetworkCredential ("username", "password");
// or:
p.Credentials = new NetworkCredential ("username", "password", "domain");

using (WebClient wc = new WebClient( ))
{
  wc.Proxy = p;
  ...
}

// Same procedure with a WebRequest object:
WebRequest req = WebRequest.Create ("...");
req.Proxy = p;
```

If you supply a domain when constructing the NetworkCredential, Windows-based authentication protocols are used. To use the currently authenticated Windows user, assign the static CredentialCache.DefaultNetworkCredentials value to the proxy's Credentials property.

If you don't have a proxy, you must set the Proxy property to null on all WebClient and WebRequest objects. Otherwise, the Framework may attempt to "auto-detect" your proxy settings, adding up to 30 seconds to your request. If you're wondering why your web requests execute slowly, this is probably it!

As an alternative to setting the Proxy on every WebClient and WebRequest object, you can set the global default as follows:

```
WebRequest.DefaultWebProxy = myWebProxy;
```

or:

```
WebRequest.DefaultWebProxy = null;
```

Whatever you set applies for the life of the application domain (unless some other code changes it!).

Authentication

You can supply a username and password to an HTTP or FTP site by creating a NetworkCredential object and assigning it to the Credentials property of WebClient or WebRequest:

```
using (WebClient wc = new WebClient())
{
  wc.Proxy = null;
  wc.BaseAddress = "ftp://ftp.albahari.com/incoming/";

  // Authenticate, then upload and download a file to the FTP server.
  // The same approach also works for HTTP and HTTPS.

  string username = "anonymous@albahari.com";
  string password = "";
  wc.Credentials = new NetworkCredential (username, password);

  wc.DownloadFile ("guestbook.txt", "guestbook.txt");

  string data = "Hello from " + Environment.UserName + "!\r\n";
  File.AppendAllText ("guestbook.txt", data);

  wc.UploadFile ("guestbook.txt", "guestbook.txt");
}
```

This works with dialog-based authentication protocols, such as Basic and Digest, and is extensible through the AuthenticationManager class. It also supports Windows NTLM and Kerberos (if you include a domain name when constructing the NetworkCredential object). If you want to use the currently authenticated Windows user, you can leave the Credentials property null and instead set UseDefaultCredentials true.

 Assigning Credentials is useless for getting through forms-based authentication. We discuss forms-based authentication separately, in the section "HTTP-Specific Support."

The authentication is ultimately handled by a WebRequest subtype (in this case, FtpWebRequest), which automatically negotiates a compatible protocol. In the case of HTTP, there can be a choice: if you examine the initial response from a Microsoft Exchange server web mail page, for instance, it might contain the following headers:

```
HTTP/1.1 401 Unauthorized
Content-Length: 83
Content-Type: text/html
Server: Microsoft-IIS/6.0
WWW-Authenticate: Negotiate
WWW-Authenticate: NTLM
WWW-Authenticate: Basic realm="exchange.mydomain.com"
X-Powered-By: ASP.NET
Date: Sat, 05 Aug 2006 12:37:23 GMT
```

The 401 code signals that authorization is required; the "WWW-Authenticate" headers indicate what authentication protocols are understood. If you configure a

WebClient or WebRequest object with the correct username and password, however, this message will be hidden from you because the Framework responds automatically by choosing a compatible authentication protocol, and then resubmitting the original request with an extra header. For example:

```
Authorization: Negotiate TlRMTVNTUAAABAAAt5II2gjACDArAAACAwACACgAAAAQ
ATmKAAAADOlVDRdPUksHUq9VUA==
```

This mechanism provides transparency, but generates an extra round trip with each request. You can avoid the extra round trips on subsequent requests to the same URI by setting the PreAuthenticate property to true. This property is defined on the WebRequest class (and works only in the case of HttpWebRequest). WebClient doesn't support this feature at all.

CredentialCache

You can force a particular authentication protocol with a CredentialCache object. A credential cache contains one or more NetworkCredential objects, each keyed to a particular protocol and URI prefix. For example, you might want to avoid the Basic protocol when logging into an Exchange Server, as it transmits passwords in plain text:

```
CredentialCache cache = new CredentialCache( );
Uri prefix = new Uri ("http://exchange.mydomain.com");
cache.Add (prefix, "Digest",  new NetworkCredential ("joe", "passwd"));
cache.Add (prefix, "Negotiate", new NetworkCredential ("joe", "passwd"));

WebClient wc = new WebClient( );
wc.Credentials = cache;
...
```

An authentication protocol is specified as a string. The valid values are as follows:

```
Basic, Digest, NTLM, Kerberos, Negotiate
```

In this particular example, WebClient will choose Negotiate, because the server didn't indicate that it supported Digest in its authentication headers. Negotiate is a Windows protocol that boils down to either Kerberos or NTLM, depending on the capabilities of the server.

The static CredentialCache.DefaultNetworkCredentials property allows you to add the currently authenticated Windows user to the credential cache without having to specify a password:

```
cache.Add (prefix, "Negotiate", CredentialCache.DefaultNetworkCredentials);
```

Concurrency

Because communicating across a network can be time-consuming, it makes sense to run WebClient or WebRequest on a parallel execution path. This allows you to do other things at the same time, and also maintain a responsive user interface. There are a number of ways to achieve parallel execution:

- Create a new thread.
- Use asynchronous delegates.
- Use BackgroundWorker.

We describe each in Chapter 19. Creating a new thread is simplest, although you must deal with exceptions explicitly on the worker thread:

```
using System;
using System.Net;
using System.Threading;

class ThreadTest
{
  static void Main()
  {
    new Thread (Download).Start();
    Console.WriteLine ("I'm still here while the download's happening!");
    Console.ReadLine();
  }

  static void Download()
  {
    using (WebClient wc = new WebClient())
      try
      {
        wc.Proxy = null;
        wc.DownloadFile ("http://www.oreilly.com", "oreilly.html");
        Console.WriteLine ("Finished!");
      }
      catch (Exception ex)
      {
        // Process exception...
      }
  }
}
```

You can cancel an active WebClient operation from another thread by calling CancelAsync. (This works whether or not you used an "asynchronous" method to initiate the download or upload.) You can cancel a WebRequest in a similar manner, by calling its Abort method from another thread.

> Another way to achieve parallel execution is to call the asynchronous event methods on WebClient (ending in "Asynch"), such as DownloadFileAsynch. In theory, these methods return instantly, allowing the caller to do other things while they run. Unfortunately, these methods are flawed—they block the caller for a portion of the download or upload.
>
> The asynchronous *methods* on WebRequest and WebResponse (starting in "Begin" and "End") should also be avoided if you're simply after parallel execution—these methods serve a subtly different purpose, described in Chapter 20.

When a WebClient or WebRequest is canceled, a WebException is thrown on its thread. The exception has a Status property of WebExceptionStatus.Request-Canceled. You can catch and deal with this exception just as you would any other, such as an invalid domain name.

Exception Handling

WebRequest, WebResponse, WebClient, and their streams all throw a WebException in the case of a network or protocol error. You can determine the specific error via the WebException's Status property; this returns a WebExceptionStatus enum that has the following members:

CacheEntryNotFound	PipelineFailure	SecureChannelFailure
ConnectFailure	ProtocolError	SendFailure
ConnectionClosed	ProxyNameResolution-	ServerProtocolViolation
KeepAliveFailure	Failure	Success
MessageLengthLimitExceeded	ReceiveFailure	Timeout
NameResolutionFailure	RequestCanceled	TrustFailure
Pending	RequestProhibitedBy-	UnknownError
	CachePolicy	
	RequestProhibitedByProxy	

An invalid domain name causes a NameResolutionFailure; a dead network causes a ConnectFailure; a request exceeding WebRequest.Timeout milliseconds causes a Timeout.

Errors such as "Page not found," "Moved Permanently," and "Not Logged In" are specific to the HTTP or FTP protocols, and so are all lumped together under the ProtocolError status. To get a more specific code:

1. Cast the WebException's Response property to HttpWebResponse or Ftp-WebResponse.

2. Examine the response object's Status property (an HttpStatusCode or FtpStatusCode enum) and/or its StatusDescription property (string).

For example:

```
using (WebClient wc = new WebClient())
  try
  {
    wc.Proxy = null;
    string s = wc.DownloadString ("http://www.albahari.com/notthere");
  }
  catch (WebException ex)
  {
    if (ex.Status == WebExceptionStatus.NameResolutionFailure)
      Console.WriteLine ("Bad domain name");
    else if (ex.Status == WebExceptionStatus.ProtocolError)
    {
      HttpWebResponse response = (HttpWebResponse) ex.Response;
      Console.WriteLine (response.StatusDescription);    // "Not Found"
      if (response.StatusCode == HttpStatusCode.NotFound)
        Console.WriteLine ("Not there!");                // "Not there!"
    }
    else throw;
  }
```

If you want the three-digit status code, such as 401 or 404, simply cast the HttpStatusCode or FtpStatusCode enum to an integer.

By default, you'll never get a redirection error because WebClient and WebRequest automatically follow redirection responses. You can switch off this behavior in a WebRequest object by setting AllowAutoRedirect to false.

The redirection errors are 301 (Moved Permanently), 302 (Found/Redirect), and 307 (Temporary Redirect).

If an exception is thrown because you've incorrectly used the WebClient or WebRequest classes, it will more likely be an InvalidOperationException or ProtocolViolationException than a WebException.

HTTP-Specific Support

This section describes HTTP-specific request and response features.

Headers

Both WebClient and WebRequest allow you to add custom HTTP headers, as well as enumerate the headers in a response. A header is simply a key/value pair containing metadata, such as the message content type or server software. Here's how to add a custom header to a request, then list all headers in a response message:

```
using (WebClient wc = new WebClient ())
{
  wc.Proxy = null;
  wc.Headers.Add ("CustomHeader", "JustPlaying/1.0");
  wc.DownloadString ("http://www.oreilly.com");

  foreach (string name in wc.ResponseHeaders.Keys)
    Console.WriteLine (name + "=" + wc.ResponseHeaders [name]);
}

Age=51
X-Cache=HIT from oregano.bp
X-Cache-Lookup=HIT from oregano.bp:3128
Connection=keep-alive
Accept-Ranges=bytes
Content-Length=95433
Content-Type=text/html
...
```

Query Strings

A query string is simply a string appended to a URI with a question mark, used to send simple data to the server. You can specify multiple key/value pairs in a query string with the following syntax:

```
?key1=value1&key2=value2&key3=value3...
```

`WebClient` provides an easy way to add query strings through a dictionary-style property. The following searches Google for the word "WebClient", displaying the result page in French:

```
using (WebClient wc = new WebClient())
{
  wc.Proxy = null;
  wc.QueryString.Add ("q", "WebClient");      // Search for "WebClient"
  wc.QueryString.Add ("hl", "fr");            // Display page in French
  wc.DownloadFile ("http://www.google.com/search", "results.html");
  System.Diagnostics.Process.Start ("results.html");
}
```

To achieve the same result with `WebRequest`, you must manually append a correctly formatted string to the request URI:

```
string requestURI = "http://www.google.com/search?q=WebClient&hl=fr";
```

Uploading Form Data

`WebClient` provides `UploadValues` methods for posting data to an HTML form. Here's how to query the Safari web site for books containing the term "webclient":

```
using (WebClient wc = new WebClient())
{
  wc.Proxy = null;

  var data = new System.Collections.Specialized.NameValueCollection ();
  data.Add ("searchtextbox", "webclient");
  data.Add ("searchmode", "simple");

  byte[] result = wc.UploadValues ("http://safari.oreilly.com/search",
                                   "POST", data);

  System.IO.File.WriteAllBytes ("SearchResults.html", result);
  System.Diagnostics.Process.Start ("SearchResults.html");
}
```

The keys in the `NameValueCollection`, such as `searchtextbox` and `searchMode`, correspond to the names of input boxes on the HTML form.

Uploading form data is more work via `WebRequest`. (You'll need to take this route if you need to use features such as cookies.) Here's the procedure:

1. Set the request's `ContentType` to "application/x-www-form-urlencoded" and its `Method` to "POST".
2. Build a string containing the data to upload, encoded as follows:

       name1=value1&name2=value2&name3=value3...

3. Convert the string to a byte array, with `Encoding.UTF8.GetBytes`.
4. Set the web request's `ContentLength` property to the byte array length.
5. Call `GetRequestStream` on the web request and write the data array.
6. Call `GetResponse` to read the server's response.

Here's the previous example written with `WebRequest`:

```
WebRequest req = WebRequest.Create ("http://safari.oreilly.com/search");

req.Proxy = null;
req.Method = "POST";
req.ContentType = "application/x-www-form-urlencoded";

string reqString
  = "searchtextbox=webclient&searchmode=simple";
byte[] reqData = Encoding.UTF8.GetBytes (reqString);
req.ContentLength = reqData.Length;

using (Stream reqStream = req.GetRequestStream ())
  reqStream.Write (reqData, 0, reqData.Length);

using (WebResponse res = req.GetResponse ())
using (Stream resSteam = res.GetResponseStream ())
using (StreamReader sr = new StreamReader (resSteam))
  File.WriteAllText ("SearchResults.html", sr.ReadToEnd ());

System.Diagnostics.Process.Start ("SearchResults.html");
```

Cookies

A cookie is a name/value string pair that an HTTP server sends to a client in a response header. A web browser client typically remembers cookies, and replays them to the server in each subsequent request (to the same address) until their expiry. A cookie allows a server to know whether it's talking to the same client it was a minute ago—or yesterday—without needing a messy query string in the URI.

By default, `HttpWebRequest` ignores any cookies received from the server. To accept cookies, create a `CookieContainer` object and assign it to the `WebRequest`. The cookies received in a response can then be enumerated:

```
CookieContainer cc = new CookieContainer();

var request = (HttpWebRequest) WebRequest.Create ("http://www.google.com");
request.Proxy = null;
request.CookieContainer = cc;
using (var response = (HttpWebResponse) request.GetResponse())
{
  foreach (Cookie c in response.Cookies)
  {
    Console.WriteLine (" Name:   " + c.Name);
    Console.WriteLine (" Value:  " + c.Value);
    Console.WriteLine (" Path:   " + c.Path);
    Console.WriteLine (" Domain: " + c.Domain);
  }
  // Read response stream...
}

 Name:   PREF
```

```
Value:  ID=6b10df1da493a9c4:TM=1179025486:LM=1179025486:S=EJCZri0aWEHlk4tt
Path:   /
Domain: .google.com
```

 The WebClient façade class does not provide direct support for cookies.

To replay the received cookies in future requests, simply assign the same CookieContainer object to each new WebRequest object. (CookieContainer is serializable, so it can be written to disk—see Chapter 15.) Alternatively, you can start with a fresh CookieContainer, and then add cookies manually as follows:

```
Cookie c = new Cookie ("PREF",
                       "ID=6b10df1da493a9c4:TM=1179...",
                       "/",
                       ".google.com");
freshCookieContainer.Add (c);
```

The third and fourth arguments indicate the path and domain of the originator. A CookieContainer on the client can house cookies from many different places; WebRequest sends only those cookies whose path and domain match those of the server.

Forms Authentication

We saw in the previous section how a NetworkCredentials object can satisfy authentication systems such as Basic or NTLM (that pop up a dialog in a web browser). Most web sites requiring authentication, however, use some type of forms-based approach. Enter your username and password into text boxes that are part of an HTML form decorated in appropriate corporate graphics, press a button to post the data, and then receive a cookie upon successful authentication. The cookie allows you greater privileges in browsing pages in the web site. With WebRequest, you can do all this with the features discussed in the preceding two sections. Here's how to log into *http://www.webshots.com*:

```
string loginUri = "http://www.webshots.com/login";
string username = "username";
string password = "password";
string reqString = "username=" + username + "&password=" + password;
byte[] requestData = Encoding.UTF8.GetBytes (reqString);

CookieContainer cc = new CookieContainer();
var request = (HttpWebRequest)WebRequest.Create (loginUri);
request.Proxy = null;
request.CookieContainer = cc;
request.Method = "POST";

request.ContentType = "application/x-www-form-urlencoded";
request.ContentLength = requestData.Length;
using (Stream s = request.GetRequestStream())
    s.Write (requestData, 0, requestData.Length);
```

```
using (var response = (HttpWebResponse) request.GetResponse( ))
  foreach (Cookie c in response.Cookies)
    Console.WriteLine (c.Name + " = " + c.Value);

// We're now logged in. As long as we assign cc to subsequent WebRequest
// objects, we can do such things as download photos.
```

The request string format matches the HTML form. Here's an extract of the form on the *webshots.com* page for which the example was written:

```
<form action="http://www.webshots.com/login" method="post" id="login-form">
  <input type="text" id="user" name="username">
  <input type="password" id="pass" name="password">
  <button type="submit" id="login-btn">Log In</button>
</form>
```

SSL

Both WebClient and WebRequest use SSL automatically when you specify an "https:" prefix. The only complication that can arise relates to bad X.509 certificates. If the server's site certificate is invalid in any way (for instance, if it's a test certificate), an exception is thrown when you attempt to communicate. To work around this, you can attach a custom certificate validator to the static ServicePointManager class:

```
using System.Net;
using System.Net.Security;
using System.Security.Cryptography.X509Certificates;
...
static void ConfigureSSL( )
{
  ServicePointManager.ServerCertificateValidationCallback = CertChecker;
}
```

ServerCertificateValidationCallback is a delegate. If it returns true, the certificate is accepted:

```
static bool CertChecker (object sender, X509Certificate certificate,
                         X509Chain chain, SslPolicyErrors errors)
{
  // Return true if you're happy with the certificate
  ...
}
```

Writing an HTTP Server

You can write your own HTTP server with the HttpListener class. The following is a simple server that listens on port 51111, waits for a single client request, and then returns a one-line reply.

 HttpListener does not work on operating systems prior to Windows XP.

```
static void Main( )
{
  new System.Threading.Thread (Listen).Start( ); // Run server in parallel.
  Thread.Sleep (500);                            // Wait half a second.

  using (WebClient wc = new WebClient( ))        // Make a client request.
    Console.WriteLine (wc.DownloadString
      ("http://localhost:51111/MyApp/Request.txt"));
}

static void Listen( )
{
  HttpListener listener = new HttpListener ( );
  listener.Prefixes.Add ("http://localhost:51111/MyApp/");  // Listen on
  listener.Start( );                                        // port 51111.

  // Wait for a client request:
  HttpListenerContext context = listener.GetContext( );

  // Respond to the request:
  string msg = "You asked for: " + context.Request.RawUrl;
  context.Response.ContentLength64 = Encoding.UTF8.GetByteCount (msg);
  context.Response.StatusCode = (int) HttpStatusCode.OK;

  using (Stream s = context.Response.OutputStream)
  using (StreamWriter writer = new StreamWriter (s))
    writer.Write (msg);

  listener.Stop( );
}

OUTPUT: You asked for: /MyApp/Request.txt
```

In this example, we sleep for 500 ms to give the server time to start before connecting to it. A better solution would be for the server to signal that it's ready with an EventWaitHandle (described in Chapter 19). An example of when you might consider doing this in real life is if writing a unit testing framework for your HTTP server.

HttpListener does not internally use .NET Socket objects; it instead calls the Windows HTTP Server API. This is supported on Windows XP and above and allows many applications on a computer to listen on the same IP address and port—as long as each registers different address prefixes. In our example, we registered the prefix *http://localhost/MyApp*, so another application would be free to listen on the same IP and port on another prefix such as *http://localhost/AnotherApp*. This is of value because opening new ports on corporate firewalls can be politically arduous.

HttpListener waits for the next client request when you call GetContext, returning an object with Request and Response properties. Each is analogous to a WebRequest and WebResponse object, but from the server's perspective. You can read and write headers and cookies, for instance, to the request and response objects, much as you would at the client end.

Networking

You can choose how fully to support features of the HTTP protocol, based on your anticipated client audience. At a bare minimum, you should set the content length and status code on each request.

Here's a very simple web page server that handles up to 50 concurrent requests:

```
using System;
using System.IO;
using System.Net;
using System.Text;
using System.Threading;

class WebServer
{
  HttpListener _listener;
  string _baseFolder;      // Your web page folder.

  public WebServer (string uriPrefix, string baseFolder)
  {
    System.Threading.ThreadPool.SetMaxThreads (50, 1000);
    System.Threading.ThreadPool.SetMinThreads (50, 50);
    _listener = new HttpListener();
    _listener.Prefixes.Add (uriPrefix);
    _baseFolder = baseFolder;
  }

  public void Start()         // Run this on a separate thread, as
  {                           // we did before.
    _listener.Start();
    while (true)
      try
      {
        HttpListenerContext request = _listener.GetContext();
        ThreadPool.QueueUserWorkItem (ProcessRequest, request);
      }
      catch (HttpListenerException)    { break; }   // Listener stopped.
      catch (InvalidOperationException) { break; }   // Listener stopped.
  }

  public void Stop() { _listener.Stop (); }

  void ProcessRequest (object listenerContext)
  {
    try
    {
      var context = (HttpListenerContext) listenerContext;
      string filename = Path.GetFileName (context.Request.RawUrl);
      string path = Path.Combine (_baseFolder, filename);
      byte[] msg;
      if (!File.Exists (path))
      {
        context.Response.StatusCode = (int) HttpStatusCode.NotFound;
        msg = Encoding.UTF8.GetBytes ("Sorry, that page does not exist");
      }
```

```
      else
      {
        context.Response.StatusCode = (int) HttpStatusCode.OK;
        msg = File.ReadAllBytes (path);
      }
      context.Response.ContentLength64 = msg.Length;
      using (Stream s = context.Response.OutputStream)
        s.Write (msg, 0, msg.Length);
    }
    catch (Exception ex) { Console.WriteLine ("Request error: " + ex); }
  }
}
```

Here's a main method to set things in motion:

```
static void Main()
{
  // Listen on the default port (80), serving files in e:\mydocs\webroot:
  var server = new WebServer ("http://localhost/", @"e:\mydocs\webroot");

  // Start the server on a parallel thread:
  new System.Threading.Thread (server.Start).Start();

  Console.WriteLine ("Server running... press Enter to stop");
  Console.ReadLine();
  server.Stop();
}
```

You can test this at the client end with any web browser; the URI in this case will be *http://localhost/* plus the name of the web page.

Calling `SetMinThreads` instructs the thread pool not to delay the allocation of threads in an attempt to save memory. This results in a responsive and performant server, up to its limit of 50 requests. If you want to go higher, you can— much higher, and without needing more threads—by following the asynchronous method pattern. This means calling `BeginRead` and `BeginWrite` on the request and response streams, each time exiting with a callback (bringing the investment in programming time almost on par with configuring IIS!). We describe this in detail in Chapter 20.

 `HttpListener` will not start if other software is competing for the same port (unless that software also uses the Windows HTTP Server API). Examples of applications that might listen on port 80 include a web server or a peer-to-peer program such as Skype.

Using FTP

For simple FTP upload and download operations, you can use `WebClient` as we did previously:

```
using (WebClient wc = new WebClient())
{
  wc.Proxy = null;
  wc.Credentials = new NetworkCredential ("anonymous@albahari.com", "");
```

```
    wc.BaseAddress = "ftp://ftp.albahari.com/incoming/";

    wc.UploadString ("tempfile.txt", "hello!");
    Console.WriteLine (wc.DownloadString ("tempfile.txt"));   // hello!
  }
```

There's more to FTP, however, than just uploading and downloading files. The protocol also lists a set of commands or "methods," defined as string constants in WebRequestMethods.Ftp:

AppendFile	ListDirectory	Rename
DeleteFile	ListDirectoryDetails	UploadFile
DownloadFile	MakeDirectory	UploadFileWithUniqueName
GetDateTimestamp	PrintWorkingDirectory	
GetFileSize	RemoveDirectory	

To run one of these commands, assign its string constant to the web request's Method property, and then call GetResponse( ). Here's how to get a directory listing:

```
    var req = (FtpWebRequest) WebRequest.Create (
                        "ftp://ftp.albahari.com/incoming");
    req.Proxy = null;
    req.Credentials = new NetworkCredential ("anonymous@albahari.com", "");

    req.Method = WebRequestMethods.Ftp.ListDirectory;

    using (WebResponse resp = req.GetResponse())
    using (StreamReader reader = new StreamReader (resp.GetResponseStream()) )
      Console.WriteLine (reader.ReadToEnd());

    RESULT:
    .
    ..
    guestbook.txt
    tempfile.txt
    test.doc
```

In the case of getting a directory listing, we needed to read the response stream to get the result. Most other commands, however, don't require this step. For instance, to get the result of the GetFileSize command, just query the response's ContentLength property:

```
    var req = (FtpWebRequest) WebRequest.Create (
                        "ftp://ftp.albahari.com/incoming/tempfile.txt");
    req.Proxy = null;
    req.Credentials = new NetworkCredential ("anonymous@albahari.com", "");

    req.Method = WebRequestMethods.Ftp.GetFileSize;

    using (WebResponse resp = req.GetResponse ())
      Console.WriteLine (resp.ContentLength);            // 6
```

The GetDateTimestamp command works in a similar way, except that you query the response's LastModified property. This requires that you cast to FtpWebResponse:

```
...
req.Method = WebRequestMethods.Ftp.GetDateTimestamp;

using (var resp = (FtpWebResponse) req.GetResponse() )
  Console.WriteLine (resp.LastModified);
```

To use the Rename command, you must populate the request's RenameTo property with the new filename (without a directory prefix). For example, to rename a file in the *incoming* directory from *tempfile.txt* to *deleteme.txt*:

```
var req = (FtpWebRequest) WebRequest.Create (
                        "ftp://ftp.albahari.com/incoming/tempfile.txt");
req.Proxy = null;
req.Credentials = new NetworkCredential ("anonymous@albahari.com", "");

req.Method = WebRequestMethods.Ftp.Rename;
req.RenameTo = "deleteme.txt";

req.GetResponse().Close();          // Perform the rename
```

Here's how to delete a file:

```
var req = (FtpWebRequest) WebRequest.Create (
                        "ftp://ftp.albahari.com/incoming/deleteme.txt");
req.Proxy = null;
req.Credentials = new NetworkCredential ("anonymous@albahari.com", "");

req.Method = WebRequestMethods.Ftp.DeleteFile;

req.GetResponse().Close();          // Perform the deletion
```

 In all these examples, you would typically use an exception handling block to catch network and protocol errors. A typical catch block looks like this:

```
catch (WebException ex)
{
  if (ex.Status == WebExceptionStatus.ProtocolError)
  {
    // Obtain more detail on error:
    var response = (FtpWebResponse) ex.Response;
    FtpStatusCode errorCode = response.StatusCode;
    string errorMessage = response.StatusDescription;
    ...
  }
  ...
}
```

Using DNS

The static Dns class encapsulates the Domain Name Service, which converts between a raw IP address, such as 66.135.192.87, and a human-friendly domain name, such as *ebay.com*.

The `GetHostAddresses` method converts from domain name to IP address (or addresses):

```
foreach (IPAddress a in Dns.GetHostAddresses ("ebay.com"))
  Console.WriteLine (a.ToString ());              // 66.135.192.87
```

The `GetHostEntry` method goes the other way around, converting from address to domain name:

```
IPHostEntry entry = Dns.GetHostEntry ("66.135.192.87");
Console.WriteLine (entry.HostName);               // pages.ebay.com
```

`GetHostEntry` also accepts an `IPAddress` object, so you can specify an IP address as a byte array:

```
IPAddress address = new IPAddress (new byte[] { 66, 135, 192, 87 });
IPHostEntry entry = Dns.GetHostEntry (address);
Console.WriteLine (entry.HostName);               // pages.ebay.com
```

Domain names are automatically resolved to IP addresses when you use a class such as `WebRequest` or `TcpClient`. If you plan to make many network requests to the same address over the life of an application, however, you can sometimes improve performance by first using `Dns` to explicitly convert the domain name into an IP address, and then communicating directly with the IP address from that point on. This avoids repeated round-tripping to resolve the same domain name, and it can be of benefit when dealing at the transport layer (via `TcpClient`, `UdpClient`, or `Socket`).

The DNS class also provides asynchronous methods for high-concurrency applications (see Chapter 19).

Sending Mail with SmtpClient

The `SmtpClient` class in the `System.Net.Mail` namespace allows you to send mail messages through the ubiquitous Simple Mail Transfer Protocol. To send a simple text message, instantiate `SmtpClient`, set its `Host` property to your SMTP server address, and then call `Send`:

```
SmtpClient client = new SmtpClient ();
client.Host = "mail.myisp.net";
client.Send ("from@adomain.com", "to@adomain.com", "subject", "body");
```

To frustrate spammers, most SMTP servers on the Internet will accept connections only from the ISP's subscribers, so you need the SMTP address appropriate to the current connection for this to work.

Constructing a `MailMessage` object exposes further options, including the ability to add attachments:

```
SmtpClient client = new SmtpClient ();
client.Host = "mail.myisp.net";
MailMessage mm = new MailMessage ();

mm.Sender = new MailAddress ("kay@domain.com", "Kay");
mm.From   = new MailAddress ("kay@domain.com", "Kay");
mm.To.Add  (new MailAddress ("bob@domain.com", "Bob"));
```

```
mm.CC.Add   (new MailAddress ("dan@domain.com", "Dan"));
mm.Subject = "Hello!";
mm.Body = "Hi there. Here's the photo!";
mm.IsBodyHtml = false;
mm.Priority = MailPriority.High;

Attachment a = new Attachment ("photo.jpg",
                               System.Net.Mime.MediaTypeNames.Image.Jpeg);
mm.Attachments.Add (a);

client.Send (mm);
```

SmtpClient allows you to specify Credentials for servers requiring authentication, EnableSsl if supported, and change the TCP Port to a nondefault value. By changing the DeliveryMethod property, you can instruct the SmtpClient to instead use IIS to send mail messages or simply to write each message to an *.eml* file in a specified directory:

```
SmtpClient client = new SmtpClient( );
client.DeliveryMethod = SmtpDeliveryMethod.SpecifiedPickupDirectory;
client.PickupDirectoryLocation = @"c:\mail";
```

Using TCP

TCP and UDP constitute the transport layer protocols on top of which most Internet—and local area network—services are built. HTTP, FTP, and SMTP use TCP; DNS uses UDP. TCP is connection-oriented and includes reliability mechanisms; UDP is connectionless, has a lower overhead, and supports broadcasting. *BitTorrent* uses UDP, as does Voice over IP.

The transport layer offers greater flexibility—and potentially improved performance—over the higher layers, but it requires that you handle such tasks as authentication and encryption yourself.

 The good news with the TCP and UDP classes is that you don't have to worry about setting Proxy to null. The bad news is that if your only access to the Internet is through a web proxy, you can forget about working directly at the TCP or UDP layer!

With TCP, you have a choice of either the easier-to-use TcpClient and TcpListener façade classes, or the feature-rich Socket class. (In fact, you can mix and match, because TcpClient exposes the underlying Socket object through the Client property.) The Socket class exposes more configuration options and allows direct access to the network layer (IP) and non-Internet-based protocols such as Novell's SPX/IPX.

As with other protocols, TCP differentiates a client and server: the client initiates a request, while the server waits for a request. Here's the basic structure for a TCP client request:

```
using (TcpClient client = new TcpClient ("address", port))
using (NetworkStream n = client.GetStream( ))
```

```
  {
    // Read and write to the network stream...
  }
```

TcpClient immediately establishes a connection upon construction to a server at the given IP or domain name address and port. The constructor blocks until a connection is established. The NetworkStream then provides a means of two-way communication, for both transmitting and receiving bytes of data from a server.

A simple TCP server looks like this:

```
TcpListener listener = new TcpListener (<ip address>, port);
listener.Start( );

while (keepProcessingRequests)
  using (TcpClient c = listener.AcceptTcpClient( ))
  using (NetworkStream n = c.GetStream( ))
  {
    // Read and write to the network stream...
  }

listener.Stop ( );
```

TcpListener requires the local IP address on which to listen (a computer with two network cards, for instance, may have two addresses). You can use IPAddress.Any to tell it to listen on all (or the only) local IP addresses. AcceptTcpClient blocks until a client request is received, at which point we call GetStream, just as on the client side.

When working at the transport layer, you need to decide on a protocol for who talks when—and for how long—rather like with a walkie-talkie. If both parties talk or listen at the same time, communication breaks down!

Let's invent a protocol where the client speaks first, saying "Hello," and then the server responds by saying "Hello right back!" Here's the code:

```
using System;
using System.IO;
using System.Net;
using System.Net.Sockets;
using System.Threading;

class TcpDemo
{
  static void Main( )
  {
    new Thread (Server).Start( );      // Run server method concurrently.
    Thread.Sleep (500);                // Give server time to start.
    Client( );
  }

  static void Client( )
  {
    using (TcpClient client = new TcpClient ("localhost", 51111))
    using (NetworkStream n = client.GetStream( ))
    {
```

```
        BinaryWriter w = new BinaryWriter (n);
        w.Write ("Hello");
        w.Flush();
        Console.WriteLine (new BinaryReader (n).ReadString());
    }
}

static void Server()        // Handles a single client request, then exits.
{
    TcpListener listener = new TcpListener (IPAddress.Any, 51111);
    listener.Start();
    using (TcpClient c = listener.AcceptTcpClient())
    using (NetworkStream n = c.GetStream())
    {
        string msg = new BinaryReader (n).ReadString();
        BinaryWriter w = new BinaryWriter (n);
        w.Write (msg + " right back!");
        w.Flush();                          // Must call Flush because we're not
    }                                       // disposing the writer.
    listener.Stop();
    }
}

Hello
Hello right back!
```

In this example, we're using the localhost loopback to run the client and server on the same machine. We've arbitrarily chosen a port in the unallocated range (above 49152) and used a BinaryWriter and BinaryReader to encode the text messages. We've avoided closing or disposing the readers and writers in order to keep the underlying NetworkStream open until our conversation completes.

BinaryReader and BinaryWriter might seem like odd choices for reading and writing strings. However, they have a major advantage over StreamReader and StreamWriter: they have length-prefix strings, so a BinaryReader always knows exactly how many bytes to read. If you call StreamReader.ReadToEnd you might block indefinitely—because a NetworkStream doesn't have an end! As long as the connection is open, the network stream can never be sure that the client isn't going to send more data.

> StreamReader is in fact completely out of bounds with Network-Stream, even if you plan only to call ReadLine. This is because StreamReader has a read-ahead buffer, which can result in it reading more bytes than are currently available, blocking indefinitely (or until the socket times out). Other streams such as FileStream don't suffer this incompatibility with StreamReader because they have a definite *end*—at which point Read returns immediately with a value of 0.

Concurrency

You'll often want to do other things at the same time as reading or writing a TCP stream. If you need to manage just a few concurrent activities, any multithreading option described in Chapter 19 is viable: a new thread; asynchronous delegates; or `ThreadPool.QueueUserWorkItem` or `BackgroundWorker`. On a highly concurrent server, however, you need to be choosier. As a simple rule of thumb:

- For less than 50 concurrent connections, think *simplicity* and use either `ThreadPool.QueueUserWorkItem` or asynchronous delegates.
- For more than 50 concurrent connections, think *efficiency* and use asynchronous methods.

Chapter 20 describes how to write a TCP server using each of these models.

Receiving POP3 Mail with TCP

The .NET Framework provides no application-layer support for POP3, so you have to write at the TCP layer in order to receive mail from a POP3 server. Fortunately, this is a simple protocol; a POP3 conversation goes like this:

Client	Mail server	Notes
Client connects...	+OK Hello there.	Welcome message
USER joe	+OK Password required.	
PASS password	+OK Logged in.	
LIST	+OK 1 1876 2 5412 3 845 .	Lists the ID and file size of each message on the server
RETR 1	+OK 1876 octets *Content of message #1...* .	Retrieves the message with the specified ID
DELE 1	+OK Deleted.	Deletes a message from the server
QUIT	+OK Bye-bye.	

Each command and response is terminated by a new line (CR + LF) except for the multiline LIST and RETR commands, which are terminated by a single dot on a separate line. Because we can't use `StreamReader` with `NetworkStream`, we can start by writing a helper method to read a line of text in a nonbuffered fashion:

```
static string ReadLine (Stream s)
{
  List<byte> lineBuffer = new List<byte> ();
  while (true)
  {
    int b = s.ReadByte();
    if (b == 10 || b < 0) break;
    if (b != 13) lineBuffer.Add ((byte)b);
  }
  return Encoding.UTF8.GetString (lineBuffer.ToArray());
}
```

We also need a helper method to send a command. Because we always expect to receive a response starting with "+OK," we can read and validate the response at the same time:

```
static void SendCommand (Stream stream, string line)
{
  byte[] data = Encoding.UTF8.GetBytes (line + "\r\n");
  stream.Write (data, 0, data.Length);
  string response = ReadLine (stream);
  if (!response.StartsWith ("+OK"))
    throw new Exception ("POP Error: " + response);
}
```

With these methods written, the job of retrieving mail is easy. We establish a TCP connection on port 110 (the default POP3 port), and then start talking to the server. In this example, we write each mail message to a randomly named file with an *.eml* extension, before deleting the message off the server:

```
using (TcpClient client = new TcpClient ("mail.isp.com ", 110))
using (NetworkStream n = client.GetStream( ))
{
  ReadLine (n);                          // Read the welcome message.
  SendCommand (n, "USER username");
  SendCommand (n, "PASS password");
  SendCommand (n, "LIST");               // Retrieve message IDs
  List<int> messageIDs = new List<int>( );
  while (true)
  {
    string line = ReadLine (n);          // e.g., "1 1876"
    if (line == ".") break;
    messageIDs.Add (int.Parse (line.Split (' ')[0] ));   // Message ID
  }

  foreach (int id in messageIDs)         // Retrieve each message.
  {
    SendCommand (n, "RETR " + id);
    string randomFile = Guid.NewGuid().ToString( ) + ".eml";
    using (StreamWriter writer = File.CreateText (randomFile))
      while (true)
      {
        string line = ReadLine (n);      // Read next line of message.
        if (line == ".") break;          // Single dot = end of message.
        if (line == "..") line = ".";    // "Escape out" double dot.
        writer.WriteLine (line);         // Write to output file.
      }
    SendCommand (n, "DELE " + id);        // Delete message off server.
  }
  SendCommand (n, "QUIT");
}
```

15

Serialization

This chapter introduces serialization and deserialization, the mechanism by which objects can be represented in a flat text or binary form. Unless otherwise stated, the types in this chapter all exist in the following namespaces:

```
System.Runtime.Serialization
System.Xml.Serialization
```

Serialization Concepts

Serialization is the act of taking an in-memory object or *object graph* (set of objects that reference each other) and flattening it into a stream of bytes or XML nodes that can be stored or transmitted. *Deserialization* works in reverse, taking a data stream and reconstituting it into an in-memory object or object graph.

Serialization and deserialization are typically used to:

- Transmit objects across a network or application boundary.
- Store representations of objects within a file or database.

Another, less common use is to deep-clone objects. The data contract and XML serialization engines can also be used as general-purpose tools for loading and saving XML files of a known structure.

The .NET Framework supports serialization and deserialization both from the perspective of clients wanting to serialize and deserialize objects, and from the perspective of types wanting some control over how they are serialized.

Serialization Engines

There are four serialization mechanisms in the .NET Framework:

- The data contract serializer
- The binary serializer

- The (attribute-based) XML serializer (XmlSerializer)
- The IXmlSerializable interface

Of these, the first three are serialization "engines" that do most or all of the serialization work for you. The last is just a hook for doing the serialization yourself, using XmlReader and XmlWriter. IXmlSerializable is designed to work in conjunction with the data contract serializer or XmlSerializer, to handle the more complicated XML serialization tasks.

Table 15-1 compares each of the engines.

Table 15-1. Serialization engine comparison

Feature	Data contract serializer	Binary serializer	XmlSerializer	IXmlSerializable
Level of automation	***	*****	****	*
Type coupling	Choice	Tight	Loose	Loose
Version tolerance	*****	***	*****	*****
Preserves object references	Choice	Yes	No	Choice
Can serialize nonpublic fields	Yes	Yes	No	Yes
Suitability for interoperable messaging	*****	**	****	****
Flexibility in reading/writing XML files	**	-	****	*****
Compact output	**	****	**	**
Performance	***	****	* to ***	***

The scores for IXmlSerializable assume you've (hand) coded optimally using XmlReader and XmlWriter. The XML serialization engine requires that you recycle the same XmlSerializer object for good performance.

Why three engines?

The reason for there being three engines is partly historical. The Framework started out with two distinct goals in serialization:

- Serializing .NET object graphs with type and reference fidelity
- Interoperating with XML and SOAP messaging standards

The first was led by the requirements of Remoting; the second was led by the requirements of Web Services. The job of writing one serialization engine to do both was too daunting, so Microsoft wrote two engines: the binary serializer and the XML serializer.

When Windows Communication Foundation (WCF) was later written, as part of Framework 3.0, part of the goal was to unify Remoting and Web Services. This required a new serialization engine—hence, the *data contract serializer*. The data contract serializer unifies the features of the older two engines *relevant to (interoperable) messaging*. Outside of this context, however, the two older engines are still important.

The data contract serializer

The data contract serializer is the newest and the most versatile of the three serialization engines and is used by WCF. The serializer is particularly strong in two scenarios:

- When exchanging information through standards-compliant messaging protocols
- When you need high-version tolerance plus the option of preserving object references

The data contract serializer supports a *data contract* model that helps you decouple the low-level details of the types you want to serialize from the structure of the serialized data. This provides excellent version tolerance, meaning you can deserialize data that was serialized from an earlier or later version of a type. You can even deserialize types that have been renamed or moved to a different assembly.

The data contract serializer can cope with most object graphs, although it can require more assistance than the binary serializer. It can also be used as a general-purpose tool for reading/writing XML files, if you're flexible on how the XML is structured. (If you need to store data in attributes or cope with XML elements presenting in a random order, you cannot use the data contract serializer.)

The binary serializer

The binary serialization engine is easy to use, highly automatic, and well supported throughout the .NET Framework. Remoting uses binary serialization—including when communicating between two application domains in the same process (see Chapter 21).

The binary serializer is highly automated: quite often, a single attribute is all that's required to make a complex type fully serializable. The binary serializer is also faster than the data contract serializer when full type fidelity is needed. However, it tightly couples a type's internal structure to the format of the serialized data, resulting in poor version tolerance. (Prior to Framework 2.0, even adding a simple field was a version-breaking change.) The binary engine is also not really designed to produce XML, although it offers a formatter for SOAP-based messaging that provides limited interoperability with simple types.

XmlSerializer

The XML serialization engine can *only* produce XML, and it is less powerful than other engines in saving and restoring a complex object graph (it cannot restore shared object references). It's the most flexible of the three, however, in following an arbitrary XML structure. For instance, you can choose whether properties are serialized to elements or attributes and the handling of a collection's outer element. The XML engine also provides excellent version tolerance.

XmlSerializer is used by Web Services.

IXmlSerializable

Implementing `IXmlSerializable` means to do the serialization yourself with an `XmlReader` and `XmlWriter`. The `IXmlSerializable` interface is recognized both by `XmlSerializer` and by the data contract serializer, so it can be used selectively to handle the more complicated types. (It also can be used directly by WCF and Web Services.) We describe `XmlReader` and `XmlWriter` in detail in Chapter 11.

Formatters

The output of the data contract and binary serializers is shaped by a pluggable *formatter*. The role of a formatter is the same with both serialization engines, although they use completely different classes to do the job.

A formatter shapes the final presentation to suit a particular medium or context of serialization. In general, you can choose between XML and binary formatters. An XML formatter is designed to work within the context of an XML reader/writer, text file/stream, or SOAP messaging packet. A binary formatter is designed to work in a context where an arbitrary stream of bytes will do—typically a file/stream or proprietary messaging packet. Binary output is usually smaller than XML—sometimes radically so.

 The term "binary" in the context of a formatter is unrelated to the "binary" serialization engine. Each of the two engines ships with both XML and binary formatters!

In theory, the engines are decoupled from their formatters. In practice, the design of each engine is geared toward one kind of formatter. The data contract serializer is geared toward the interoperability requirements of XML messaging. This is good for the XML formatter but means its binary formatter doesn't always achieve the gains you might hope. In contrast, the binary engine provides a relatively good binary formatter, but its XML formatter is highly limited, offering only crude SOAP interoperability.

Explicit Versus Implicit Serialization

Serialization and deserialization can be initiated in two ways.

The first is *explicitly*, by requesting that a particular object be serialized or deserialized. When you serialize or deserialize explicitly, you choose both the serialization engine and the formatter.

In contrast, *implicit* serialization is initiated by the Framework. This happens when:

- A serializer recurses a child object.
- You use a feature that relies on serialization, such as WCF, Remoting, or Web Services.

WCF always uses the data contract serializer, although it can interoperate with the attributes and interfaces of the other engines.

Remoting always uses the binary serialization engine.

Web Services always uses XmlSerializer.

The Data Contract Serializer

Here are the basic steps in using the data contract serializer:

1. Decide whether to use the DataContractSerializer or the NetDataContract-
   Serializer.
2. Decorate the types and members you want to serialize with [DataContract]
   and [DataMember] attributes, respectively.
3. Instantiate the serializer and call WriteObject or ReadObject.

If you chose the DataContractSerializer, you will also need to register "known
types" (subtypes that can also be serialized), and decide whether to preserve
object references.

You may also need to take special action to ensure that collections are properly
serialized.

 Types for the data contract serializer are defined in the System.
Runtime.Serialization namespace, in an assembly of the same
name.

DataContractSerializer Versus NetDataContractSerializer

There are two data contract serializers:

DataContractSerializer
  Loosely couples .NET types to data contract types

NetDataContractSerializer
  Tightly couples .NET types to data contract types

The DataContractSerializer can produce interoperable standards-compliant XML
such as this:

```
<Person xmlns="...">
  ...
</Person>
```

It requires, however, that you explicitly register serializable subtypes in advance so
that it can map a data contract name such as "Person" to the correct .NET type.
The NetDataContractSerializer requires no such assistance, because it writes the
full type and assembly names of the types it serializes, rather like the binary serialization engine:

```
<Person z:Type="SerialTest.Person" z:Assembly=
  "SerialTest, Version=1.0.0.0, Culture=neutral, PublicKeyToken=null">
  ...
</Person>
```

Such output, however, is proprietary. It also relies on the presence of a specific .NET type in a specific namespace and assembly in order to deserialize.

If you're saving an object graph to a "black box," you can choose either serializer, depending on what benefits are more important to you. If you're communicating through WCF, or reading/writing an XML file, you'll most likely want the `DataContractSerializer`.

Another difference between the two serializers is that `NetDataContractSerializer` always preserves referential equality; `DataContractSerializer` does so only upon request.

We'll go into each of these topics in more detail in the following sections.

Using the Serializers

After choosing a serializer, the next step is to attach attributes to the types and members you want to serialize. At a minimum:

- Add the `[DataContract]` attribute to each type.
- Add the `[DataMember]` attribute to each member that you want to include.

Here's an example:

```
namespace SerialTest
{
  [DataContract] public class Person
  {
    [DataMember] public string Name;
    [DataMember] public int Age;
  }
}
```

These attributes are enough to make a type *implicitly* serializable through the data contract engine.

You can then *explicitly* serialize or deserialize an object instance by instantiating a `DataContractSerializer` or `NetDataContractSerializer` and calling `WriteObject` or `ReadObject`:

```
Person p = new Person { Name = "Stacey", Age = 30 };

DataContractSerializer ds = new DataContractSerializer (typeof (Person));

using (Stream s = File.Create ("person.xml"))
  ds.WriteObject (s, p);                       // Serialize

Person p2;
using (Stream s = File.OpenRead ("person.xml"))
  p2 = (Person) ds.ReadObject (s);             // Deserialize

Console.WriteLine (p2.Name + " " + p2.Age);    // Stacey 30
```

`DataContractSerializer`'s constructor requires the *root object* type (the type of the object you're explicitly serializing). In contrast, `NetDataContractSerializer` does not.

```
NetDataContractSerializer ns = new NetDataContractSerializer( );

// NetDataContractSerializer is otherwise the same to use
// as DataContractSerializer.
...
```

Both types of serializer use the XML formatter by default. With an XmlWriter, you can request that the output be indented for readability:

```
Person p = new Person { Name = "Stacey", Age = 30 };
DataContractSerializer ds = new DataContractSerializer (typeof (Person));

XmlWriterSettings settings = new XmlWriterSettings() { Indent = true };
using (XmlWriter w = XmlWriter.Create ("person.xml", settings))
  ds.WriteObject (w, p);

System.Diagnostics.Process.Start ("person.xml");
```

Here's the result:

```
<Person xmlns="http://schemas.datacontract.org/2004/07/SerialTest"
        xmlns:i="http://www.w3.org/2001/XMLSchema-instance">
  <Age>30</Age>
  <Name>Stacey</Name>
</Person>
```

The XML element name <Person> reflects the *data contract name*, which, by default, is the .NET type name. You can override this and explicitly state a data contract name as follows:

```
[DataContract (Name="Candidate")]
public class Person { ... }
```

The XML namespace reflects the *data contract namespace*, which, by default, is *http://schemas.datacontract.org/2004/07/* plus the .NET type namespace. You can override this in a similar fashion:

```
[DataContract (Namespace="http://oreilly.com/nutshell")]
public class Person { ... }
```

> Specifying a name and namespace decouples the contract identity from the .NET type name. It ensures that, should you later refactor and change the type's name or namespace, serialization is unaffected.

You can also override names for data members:

```
[DataContract (Name="Candidate", Namespace="http://oreilly.com/nutshell")]
public class Person
{
  [DataMember (Name="FirstName")]  public string Name;
  [DataMember (Name="ClaimedAge")] public int Age;
}
```

Here's the output:

```
<?xml version="1.0" encoding="utf-8"?>
<Candidate xmlns="http://oreilly.com/nutshell"
           xmlns:i="http://www.w3.org/2001/XMLSchema-instance" >
```

```
    <ClaimedAge>30</ClaimedAge>
    <FirstName>Stacey</FirstName>
</Candidate>
```

[DataMember] supports both fields and properties—public and private. The field or property's data type can be any of the following:

- Any primitive type
- DateTime, TimeSpan, Guid, Uri, or an Enum value
- Nullable versions of the above
- byte[ ] (serializes in XML to base 64)
- Any "known" type decorated with DataMember
- Any IEnumerable type (see the section "Serializing Collections" later in this chapter)
- Any type with the [Serializable] attribute or implementing ISerializable (see the section "Extending Data Contracts" later in this chapter)
- Any type implementing IXmlSerializable

Specifying a binary formatter

You can use a binary formatter with DataContractSerializer or NetData-ContractSerializer. The process is the same:

```
Person p = new Person { Name = "Stacey", Age = 30 };
DataContractSerializer ds = new DataContractSerializer (typeof (Person));

MemoryStream s = new MemoryStream( );
using (XmlDictionaryWriter w = XmlDictionaryWriter.CreateBinaryWriter (s))
    ds.WriteObject (w, p);

MemoryStream s2 = new MemoryStream (s.ToArray( ));
Person p2;
using (XmlDictionaryReader r = XmlDictionaryReader.CreateBinaryReader (s2,
                               XmlDictionaryReaderQuotas.Max))
    p2 = (Person) ds.ReadObject (r);
```

The output varies between being slightly smaller than that of the XML formatter, and radically smaller if your types contain large arrays.

Serializing Subclasses

You don't need to do anything special to handle the serializing of subclasses with the NetDataContractSerializer. The only requirement is that subclasses have the DataContract attribute. The serializer will write the fully qualified names of the actual types that it serializes as follows:

```
<Person ... z:Type="SerialTest.Person" z:Assembly=
    "SerialTest, Version=1.0.0.0, Culture=neutral, PublicKeyToken=null">
```

A DataContractSerializer, however, must be informed about all subtypes that it may have to serialize or deserialize. To illustrate, suppose we subclass Person as follows:

```
[DataContract] public class Person
{
  [DataMember] public string Name;
  [DataMember] public int Age;
}

[DataContract] public class Student : Person { }
[DataContract] public class Teacher : Person { }
```

and then write a method to clone a Person:

```
static Person DeepClone (Person p)
{
  DataContractSerializer ds = new DataContractSerializer (typeof (Person));
  MemoryStream stream = new MemoryStream( );
  ds.WriteObject (stream, p);
  stream.Position = 0;
  return (Person) ds.ReadObject (stream);
}
```

which we call as follows:

```
Person  person  = new Person  { Name = "Stacey", Age = 30 };
Student student = new Student { Name = "Stacey", Age = 30 };
Teacher teacher = new Teacher { Name = "Stacey", Age = 30 };

Person  p2 =            DeepClone (person);    // OK
Student s2 = (Student) DeepClone (student);    // SerializationException
Teacher t2 = (Teacher) DeepClone (teacher);    // SerializationException
```

DeepClone works if called with a Person but throws an exception with a Student or Teacher, because the deserializer has no way of knowing what .NET type (or assembly) a "Student" or "Teacher" should resolve to. This also helps with security, in that it prevents the deserialization of unexpected types.

The solution is to specify all permitted or "known" subtypes. You can do this either when constructing the DataContractSerializer as follows:

```
DataContractSerializer ds = new DataContractSerializer (typeof (Person),
  new Type[] { typeof (Student), typeof (Teacher) } );
```

or in the type itself, with the KnownType attribute:

```
[DataContract, KnownType (typeof (Student)), KnownType (typeof (Teacher))]
public class Person
...
```

Here's what a serialized Student now looks like:

```
<Person xmlns="..."
        xmlns:i="http://www.w3.org/2001/XMLSchema-instance"
        i:type="Student" >
  ...
<Person>
```

Because we specified `Person` as the root type, the root element still has that name. The actual subclass is described separately—in the type attribute.

The `NetDataContractSerializer` suffers a performance hit when serializing subtypes—with either formatter. It seems that when it encounters a subtype, it has to stop and think for a while!

Serialization performance matters on an application server that's handling many concurrent requests.

Object References

References to other objects are serialized too. Consider the following classes:

```
[DataContract] public class Person
{
  [DataMember] public string Name;
  [DataMember] public int Age;
  [DataMember] public Address HomeAddress;
}

[DataContract] public class Address
{
  [DataMember] public string Street, Postcode;
}
```

Here's the result of serializing this to XML using the `DataContractSerializer`:

```
<Person...>
  <Age>...</Age>
  <HomeAddress>
    <Street>...</Street>
    <Postcode>...</Postcode>
  </HomeAddress>
  <Name>...</Name>
</Person>
```

The `DeepClone` method we wrote in the preceding section would clone `HomeAddress` too—distinguishing it from a simple `Memberwise-Clone`.

If you're using a `DataContractSerializer`, the same rules apply when subclassing `Address` as when subclassing the root type. So, if we define a `USAddress` class, for instance:

```
[DataContract]
public class USAddress : Address { }
```

and assign an instance of it to a `Person`:

```
Person p = new Person { Name = "John", Age = 30 };
p.HomeAddress = new USAddress { Street="Fawcett St", Postcode="02138" };
```

`p` could not be serialized. The solution is either to apply the `KnownType` attribute to `Address`, as shown next.

```
[DataContract, KnownType (typeof (USAddress))]
public class Address
{
  [DataMember] public string Street, Postcode;
}
```

or to tell DataContractSerializer about USAddress in construction:

```
DataContractSerializer ds = new DataContractSerializer (typeof (Person),
  new Type[] { typeof (USAddress) } );
```

(We don't need to tell it about Address because it's the declared type of the HomeAddress data member.)

Preserving object references

The NetDataContractSerializer always preserves referential equality. The DataContractSerializer does not, unless you specifically ask it to.

This means that if the same object is referenced in two different places, a DataContractSerializer ordinarily writes it twice. So, if we modify the preceding example so that Person also stores a work address:

```
[DataContract] public class Person
{
  ...
  [DataMember] public Address HomeAddress, WorkAddress;
}
```

and then serialize an instance as follows:

```
Person p = new Person { Name = "Stacey", Age = 30 };
p.HomeAddress = new Address { Street = "Odo St", Postcode = "6020" };
p.WorkAddress = p.HomeAddress;
```

we would see the same address details twice in the XML:

```
...
<HomeAddress>
  <Postcode>6020</Postcode>
  <Street>Odo St</Street>
</HomeAddress>
...
<WorkAddress>
  <Postcode>6020</Postcode>
  <Street>Odo St</Street>
</WorkAddress>
```

When this was later deserialized, WorkAddress and HomeAddress would be different objects. The advantage of this system is that it keeps the XML simple and standards-compliant. The disadvantages of this system include larger XML, loss of referential integrity, and the inability to cope with cyclical references.

You can request referential integrity by specifying true for preserve-ObjectReferences when constructing a DataContractSerializer:

```
DataContractSerializer ds = new DataContractSerializer (typeof (Person),
                                    null, 1000, false, true, null);
```

The third argument is mandatory when preserveObjectReferences is true: it indicates the maximum number of object references that the serializer should keep track of. The serializer throws an exception if this number is exceeded (this prevents a denial of service attack through a maliciously constructed stream).

Here's what the XML then looks like for a Person with the same home and work addresses:

```
<Person xmlns="http://schemas.datacontract.org/2004/07/SerialTest"
        xmlns:i="http://www.w3.org/2001/XMLSchema-instance"
        xmlns:z="http://schemas.microsoft.com/2003/10/Serialization/"
        z:Id="1">
  <Age>30</Age>
  <HomeAddress z:Id="2">
    <Postcode z:Id="3">6020</Postcode>
    <Street z:Id="4">Odo St</Street>
  </HomeAddress>
  <Name z:Id="5">Stacey</Name>
  <WorkAddress z:Ref="2" i:nil="true" />
</Person>
```

The cost of this is in reduced interoperability (notice the proprietary namespace of the Id and Ref attributes).

Version Tolerance

You can add and remove data members without breaking forward or backward compatibility. By default, the data contract deserializers do the following:

- Skip over data for which there is no [DataMember] in the type.
- Don't complain if any [DataMember] is missing in the serialization stream.

Rather than skipping over unrecognized data, you can instruct the deserializer to store unrecognized data members in a black box, and then replay them should the type later be reserialized. This allows you to correctly round-trip data that's been serialized by a later version of your type. To activate this feature, implement IExtensibleDataObject. This interface really means "IBlackBoxProvider." It requires that you implement a single property, to get/set the black box:

```
[DataContract] public class Person : IExtensibleDataObject
{
    [DataMember] public string Name;
    [DataMember] public int Age;

    ExtensionDataObject IExtensibleDataObject.ExtensionData { get; set; }
}
```

Required members

If a member is essential for a type, you can demand that it be present with IsRequired:

```
[DataMember (IsRequired=true)] public int ID;
```

If that member is not present, an exception is then thrown upon deserialization.

Member Ordering

The data contract serializers are extremely fussy about the ordering of data members. The deserializers, in fact, *skip over any members considered out of sequence*.

Members are written in the following order when serializing:

1. Base class to subclass
2. Low `Order` to high `Order` (for data members whose `Order` is set)
3. Alphabetical order (using *ordinal* string comparison)

So, in the preceding examples, `Age` comes before `Name`. In the following example, `Name` comes before `Age`:

```
[DataContract] public class Person
{
  [DataMember (Order=0)] public string Name;
  [DataMember (Order=1)] public int Age;
}
```

If `Person` has a base class, the base class's data members would all serialize first.

The main reason to specify an order is to comply with a particular XML schema. XML element order equates to data member order.

If you don't need to interoperate with anything else, the easiest approach is *not* to specify a member `Order` and rely purely on alphabetical ordering. A discrepancy will then never arise between serialization and deserialization as members are added and removed. The only time you'll come unstuck is if you move a member between a base class and a subclass.

Null and Empty Values

There are two ways to deal with a data member whose value is null or empty:

1. Explicitly write the null or empty value (the default).
2. Omit the data member from the serialization output.

In XML, an explicit null value looks like this:

```
<Person xmlns="..."
          xmlns:i="http://www.w3.org/2001/XMLSchema-instance">
  <Name i:nil="true" />
</Person>
```

Writing null or empty members can waste space, particularly on a type with lots of fields or properties that are usually left empty. More importantly, you may need to follow an XML schema that expects the use of optional elements (e.g., `minOccurs="0"`) rather than `nil` values.

You can instruct the serializer not to emit data members for null/empty values as follows:

```
[DataContract] public class Person
{
```

```
[DataMember (EmitDefaultValue=false)] public string Name;
[DataMember (EmitDefaultValue=false)] public int Age;
}
```

Name is omitted if its value is null; Age is omitted if its value is 0 (the default value for the int type).

The data contract deserializer, in rehydrating an object, bypasses the type's constructors and field initializers. This allows you to omit data members as described without breaking fields that are assigned nondefault values through an initializer or constructor. To illustrate, suppose we set the default Age for a Person to 30 as follows:

```
[DataMember (EmitDefaultValue=false)]
public int Age = 30;
```

Now suppose that we instantiate Person, explicitly set its Age from 30 to 0, and then serialize it. The output won't include Age, because 0 is the default value for the int type. This means that in deserialization, Age will be ignored and the field will remain at its default value—which fortunately is 0, given that field initializers and constructors were bypassed.

Data Contracts and Collections

The data contract serializers can save and repopulate any enumerable collection. For instance, suppose we define Person to have a List<> of addresses:

```
[DataContract] public class Person
{
    ...
    [DataMember] public List<Address> Addresses;
}

[DataContract] public class Address
{
    [DataMember] public string Street, Postcode;
}
```

Here's the result of serializing a Person with two addresses:

```
<Person ...>
  ...
  <Addresses>
    <Address>
      <Postcode>6020</Postcode>
      <Street>Odo St</Street>
    </Address>
    <Address>
      <Postcode>6152</Postcode>
      <Street>Comer St</Street>
    </Address>
  </Addresses>
  ...
</Person>
```

Notice that the serializer doesn't encode any information about the particular *type* of collection it serialized. If the Addresses field was instead of type Address[], the output would be identical. This allows the collection type to change between serialization and deserialization without causing an error.

Sometimes, though, you need your collection to be of a more specific type than you expose. An extreme example is with interfaces:

```
[DataMember] public IList<Address> Addresses;
```

This would serialize correctly (as before), but a problem would arise in deserialization. There's no way the deserializer can know which concrete type to instantiate, so it chooses the simplest option—an array. The deserializer sticks to this strategy even if you initialize the field with a different concrete type:

```
[DataMember] public IList<Address> Addresses = new List<Address>();
```

(Remember that the deserializer bypasses field initializers.) The workaround is to make the data member a private field and add a public property to access it:

```
[DataMember (Name="Addresses")] List<Address> _addresses;

public IList<Address> Addresses { get { return _addresses; } }
```

In a nontrivial application, you would probably use properties in this manner anyway. The only unusual thing here is that we've marked the private field as the data member, rather than the public property.

Subclassed Collection Elements

The serializer handles subclassed collection elements transparently. You must declare the valid subtypes just as you would if they were used anywhere else:

```
[DataContract, KnownType (typeof (USAddress))]
public class Address
{
  [DataMember] public string Street, Postcode;
}

public class USAddress : Address { }
```

Adding a USAddress to a Person's address list then generates XML like this:

```
...
  <Addresses>
    <Address i:type="USAddress">
      <Postcode>02138</Postcode>
      <Street>Fawcett St</Street>
    </Address>
  </Addresses>
```

Customizing Collection and Element Names

If you subclass a collection class itself, you can customize the XML name used to describe each element by attaching a CollectionDataContract attribute:

```
[CollectionDataContract (ItemName="Residence")]
public class AddressList : Collection<Address> { }

[DataContract] public class Person
{
  ...
  [DataMember] public AddressList Addresses;
}
```

Here's the result:

```
...
  <Addresses>
    <Residence>
      <Postcode>6020</Postcode>
      <Street>Odo St</Street>
    </Residence>
    ...
```

CollectionDataContract also lets you specify a Namespace and Name. The latter is not used when the collection is serialized as a property of another object (such as in this example), but it is when the collection is serialized as the root object.

You can also use CollectionDataContract to control the serialization of dictionaries:

```
[CollectionDataContract (ItemName="Entry",
                         KeyName="Kind",
                         ValueName="Number")]
public class PhoneNumberList : Dictionary <string, string> { }

[DataContract] public class Person
{
  ...
  [DataMember] public PhoneNumberList PhoneNumbers;
}
```

Here's how this formats:

```
...
  <PhoneNumbers>
    <Entry>
      <Kind>Home</Kind>
      <Number>08 1234 5678</Number>
    </Entry>
    <Entry>
      <Kind>Mobile</Kind>
      <Number>040 8765 4321</Number>
    </Entry>
  </PhoneNumbers>
```

Extending Data Contracts

This section describes how you can extend the capabilities of the data contract serializer through serialization hooks, [Serializable] and IXmlSerializable.

Serialization and Deserialization Hooks

You can request that a custom method be executed before or after serialization, by flagging the method with one of the following attributes:

[OnSerializing]
> Indicates a method to be called just *before* serialization

[OnSerialized]
> Indicates a method to be called just *after* serialization

Similar attributes are supported for deserialization:

[OnDeserializing]
> Indicates a method to be called just *before* deserialization

[OnDeserialized]
> Indicates a method to be called just *after* deserialization

The custom method must have a single parameter of type StreamingContext. This parameter is required for consistency with the binary engine, and it is not used by the data contract serializer.

[OnSerializing] and [OnDeserialized] are useful in handling members that are outside the capabilities of the data contract engine, such as a collection that has an extra payload or that does not implement standard interfaces. Here's the basic approach:

```
[DataContract] public class Person
{
  public SerializationUnfriendlyType Addresses;

  [DataMember (Name="Addresses")]
  SerializationFriendlyType _serializationFriendlyAddresses;

  [OnSerializing]
  void PrepareForSerialization (StreamingContext sc)
  {
    // Copy Addresses --> _serializationFriendlyAddresses
    // ...
  }

  [OnDeserialized]
  void CompleteDeserialization (StreamingContext sc)
  {
    // Copy _serializationFriendlyAddresses --> Addresses
    // ...
  }
}
```

An [OnSerializing] method can also be used to conditionally serialize fields:

```
public DateTime DateOfBirth;

[DataMember] public bool Confidential;

[DataMember (Name="DateOfBirth", EmitDefaultValue=false)]
```

```
DateTime? _tempDateOfBirth;

[OnSerializing]
void PrepareForSerialization (StreamingContext sc)
{
  if (Confidential)
    _tempDateOfBirth = DateOfBirth;
  else
    _tempDateOfBirth = null;
}
```

Recall that the data contract deserializers bypass field initializers and constructors. An [OnDeserializing] method acts as a pseudoconstructor for deserialization, and it is useful for initializing fields excluded from serialization:

```
[DataContract] public class Test
{
  bool _editable = true;

  public Test( ) { _editable = true; }

  [OnDeserializing]
  void Init (StreamingContext sc)
  {
    _editable = true;
  }
}
```

If it wasn't for the Init method, _editable would be false in a deserialized instance of Test—despite the other two attempts at making it true.

Methods decorated with these four attributes can be private. If subtypes need to participate, they can define their own methods with the same attributes, and they will get executed too.

Interoperating with [Serializable]

The data contract serializer can also serialize types marked with the binary serialization engine's attributes and interfaces. This ability is important, since support for the binary engine has been woven into much of what was written prior to Framework 3.0—including the .NET Framework itself!

 The following things flag a type as being serializable for the binary engine:

- The [Serializable] attribute
- Implementing ISerializable

Binary interoperability is useful in serializing existing types as well as new types that need to support both engines. It also provides another means of extending the capability of the data contract serializer, because the binary engine's ISerializable is more flexible than the data contract attributes. Unfortunately, the data contract serializer is inefficient in how it formats data added via ISerializable.

A type wanting the best of both worlds cannot define attributes for both engines. This creates a problem for types such as string and DateTime, which for historical reasons cannot divorce the binary engine attributes. The data contract serializer works around this by filtering out these basic types and processing them specially. For all other types marked for binary serialization, the data contract serializer applies similar rules to what the binary engine would use. This means it honors attributes such as NonSerialized or calls ISerializable if implemented. It does not *thunk* to the binary engine itself—this ensures that output is formatted in the same style as if data contract attributes were used.

 Types designed to be serialized with the binary engine expect object references to be preserved. You can enable this option through the DataContractSerializer (or by using the NetDataContract-Serializer).

The rules for registering known types also apply to objects and subobjects serialized through the binary interfaces.

The following example illustrates a class with a [Serializable] data member:

```
[DataContract] public class Person
{
  ...
  [DataMember] public Address MailingAddress;
}

[Serializable] public class Address
{
  public string Postcode, Street;
}
```

Here's the result of serializing it:

```
<Person ...>
  ...
  <MailingAddress>
    <Postcode>6020</Postcode>
    <Street>Odo St</Street>
  </MailingAddress>
  ...
```

Had Address implemented ISerializable, the result would be less efficiently formatted:

```
<MailingAddress>
  <Street xmlns:d3p1="http://www.w3.org/2001/XMLSchema"
    i:type="d3p1:string" xmlns="">str</Street>
  <Postcode xmlns:d3p1="http://www.w3.org/2001/XMLSchema"
    i:type="d3p1:string" xmlns="">pcode</Postcode>
</MailingAddress>
```

Interoperating with IXmlSerializable

A limitation of the data contract serializer is that it gives you little control over the structure of the XML. In a WCF application this can actually be beneficial, in that it makes it easier for the infrastructure to comply with standard messaging protocols.

If you do need precise control over the XML, you can implement IXml-Serializable and then use XmlReader and XmlWriter to manually read and write the XML. The data contract serializer allows you to do this just on the types for which this level of control is required. We describe the IXmlSerializable interface further in the final section of this chapter.

The Binary Serializer

The binary serialization engine is used implicitly by Remoting. It can also be used to perform such tasks as saving and restoring objects to disk. The binary serialization is highly automated and can handle complex object graphs with minimum intervention.

There are two ways to make a type support binary serialization. The first is attribute-based; the second involves implementing ISerializable. Adding attributes is simpler; implementing ISerializable is more flexible. You typically implement ISerializable to:

* Dynamically control what gets serialized.

* Make your serializable type friendly to being subclassed by other parties.

Getting Started

A type can be made serializable with a single attribute:

```
[Serializable] public sealed class Person
{
  public string Name;
  public int Age;
}
```

The [Serializable] attribute instructs the serializer to include all fields in the type. This includes both private and public fields (but not properties). Every field must itself be serializable; otherwise, an exception is thrown. Primitive .NET types such as string and int support serialization (as do many other .NET types).

The Serializable attribute is not inherited, so subclasses are not automatically serializable, unless also marked with this attribute.

With automatic properties, the binary serialization engine serializes the underlying compiler-generated field. The name of this field, unfortunately, can change when its type is recompiled with more properties, breaking compatibility with existing serialized data. The workaround is either to avoid automatic properties in [Serializable] types or to implement ISerializable.

To serialize an instance of Person, instantiate a formatter and call Serialize. There are two formatters for use with the binary engine:

`BinaryFormatter`
> This is the more efficient of the two, producing smaller output in less time. Its namespace is `System.Runtime.Serialization.Formatters.Binary`.

`SoapFormatter`
> This supports basic SOAP-style messaging when used with Remoting. Its namespace is `System.Runtime.Serialization.Formatters.Soap`.

`BinaryFormatter` is contained in *mscorlib*; `SoapFormatter` is contained in *System. Runtime.Serialization.Formatters.Soap.dll*.

 The `SoapFormatter` is less functional than the `BinaryFormatter`. The `SoapFormatter` doesn't support generic types or the filtering of extraneous data necessary for version tolerant serialization.

The two formatters are otherwise exactly the same to use. The following serializes a `Person` with a `BinaryFormatter`:

```
Person p = new Person() { Name = "George", Age = 25 };

IFormatter formatter = new BinaryFormatter();

using (FileStream s = File.Create ("serialized.bin"))
  formatter.Serialize (s, p);
```

All the data necessary to reconstruct the `Person` object is written to the file *serialized.bin*. The `Deserialize` method restores the object:

```
using (FileStream s = File.OpenRead ("serialized.bin"))
{
  Person p2 = (Person) formatter.Deserialize (s);
  Console.WriteLine (p2.Name + " " + p.Age);     // George 25
}
```

 The deserializer bypasses all constructors when re-creating objects. Behind the scenes, it calls `FormatterServices.GetUninitialized-Object` to do this job. You can call this method yourself to implement some very grubby design patterns!

The serialized data includes full type and assembly information, so if we try to cast the result of deserialization to a matching `Person` type in a different assembly, an error would result. The deserializer fully restores object references to their original state upon deserialization. This includes collections, which are just treated as serializable objects like any other (all collection types in `System.Collections.*` are marked as serializable).

 The binary engine can handle large, complex object graphs without special assistance (other than ensuring that all participating members are serializable). One thing to be wary of is that the serializer's performance degrades in proportion to the number of references in your object graph. This can become an issue in a Remoting server that has to process many concurrent requests.

Binary Serialization Attributes

[NonSerialized]

Unlike data contracts, which have an *opt-in* policy in serializing fields, the binary engine has an *opt-out* policy. Fields that you don't want serialized, such as those used for temporary calculations, or for storing file or window handles, you must mark explicitly with the [NonSerialized] attribute:

```
[Serializable] public sealed class Person
{
  public string Name;
  public DateTime DateOfBirth;

  // Age can be calculated, so there's no need to serialize it.
  [NonSerialized] public int Age;
}
```

This instructs the serializer to ignore the Age member.

> Nonserialized members are always empty or null when deserialized—even if field initializers or constructors set them otherwise.

[OnDeserializing] and [OnDeserialized]

Deserialization bypasses all your normal constructors as well as field initializers. This is of little consequence if every field partakes in serialization, but it can be problematic if some fields are excluded via [NonSerialized]. We can illustrate this by adding a bool field called Valid:

```
public sealed class Person
{
  public string Name;
  public DateTime DateOfBirth;

  [NonSerialized] public int Age;
  [NonSerialized] public bool Valid = true;

  public Person() { Valid = true; }
}
```

A deserialized Person will not be Valid—despite the constructor and field initializer.

The solution is the same as with the data contract serializer: to define a special deserialization "constructor" with the [OnDeserializing] attribute. A method that you flag with this attribute gets called just prior to deserialization:

```
[OnDeserializing]
void OnDeserializing (StreamingContext context)
{
  Valid = true;
}
```

We could also write an [OnDeserialized] method to update the calculated Age field (this fires just *after* deserialization):

```
[OnDeserialized]
void OnDeserialized (StreamingContext context)
{
  TimeSpan ts = DateTime.Now - DateOfBirth;
  Age = ts.Days / 365;                    // Rough age in years
}
```

[OnSerializing] and [OnSerialized]

The binary engine also supports the [OnSerializing] and [OnSerialized] attributes. These flag a method for execution before or after serialization. To see how they can be useful, we'll define a Team class that contains a generic List of players:

```
[Serializable] public sealed class Team
{
  public string Name;
  public List<Person> Players = new List<Person>();
}
```

This class serializes and deserializes correctly with the binary formatter but not the SOAP formatter. This is because of an obscure limitation: the SOAP formatter refuses to serialize generic types! An easy solution is to convert Players to an array just prior to serialization, then convert it back to a generic List upon deserialization. To make this work, we can add another field for storing the array, mark the original Players field as [NonSerialized], and then write the conversion code in as follows:

```
[Serializable] public sealed class Team
{
  public string Name;
  Person[] _playersToSerialize;

  [NonSerialized] public List<Person> Players = new List<Person>();

  [OnSerializing]
  void OnSerializing (StreamingContext context)
  {
    _playersToSerialize = Players.ToArray();
  }

  [OnSerialized]
  void OnSerialized (StreamingContext context)
  {
    _playersToSerialize = null;    // Allow it to be freed from memory
  }

  [OnDeserialized]
  void OnDeserialized (StreamingContext context)
  {
```

```
      Players = new List<Person> (_playersToSerialize);
  }
}
```

[OptionalField] and Versioning

By default, adding a field breaks compatibility with data that's already serialized, unless you attach the [OptionalField] attribute to the new field.

To illustrate, suppose we start with a Person class that has just one field. Let's call it Version 1:

```
[Serializable] public sealed class Person        // Version 1
{
  public string Name;
}
```

Later, we realize we need a second field, so we create Version 2 as follows:

```
[Serializable] public sealed class Person        // Version 2
{
  public string Name;
  public DateTime DateOfBirth;
}
```

If two computers were exchanging Person objects via Remoting, deserialization would go wrong unless they both updated to Version 2 at *exactly the same time*. The OptionalField attribute gets around this problem:

```
[Serializable] public sealed class Person        // Version 2 Robust
{
  public string Name;
  [OptionalField (VersionAdded = 2)] public DateTime DateOfBirth;
}
```

This tells the deserializer not to panic if it sees no DateOfBirth in the data stream, and instead to treat the missing field as nonserialized. This means you end up with an empty DateTime (you can assign a different value in an [OnDeserializing] method).

The VersionAdded argument is an integer that you increment each time you augment a type's fields. This serves as documentation, and it has no effect on serialization semantics.

 If versioning robustness is important, avoid renaming and deleting fields and avoid retrospectively adding the NonSerialized attribute. Never change a field's type.

So far we've focused on the backward-compatibility problem: the deserializer failing to find an expected field in the serialization stream. But with two-way communication, a forward-compatibility problem can also arise whereby the deserializer encounters an extraneous field with no knowledge of how to process it. The binary formatter is programmed to automatically cope with this by throwing away the extraneous data; the SOAP formatter instead throws an exception! Hence, you must use the binary formatter if two-way versioning robustness is required; otherwise, manually control the serialization by implementing ISerializable.

Binary Serialization with ISerializable

Implementing ISerializable gives a type complete control over its binary serialization and deserialization.

Here's the ISerializable interface definition:

```
public interface ISerializable
{
  void GetObjectData (SerializationInfo info, StreamingContext context);
}
```

GetObjectData fires upon serialization; its job is to populate the SerializationInfo object (a name-value dictionary) with data from all fields that you want serialized. Here's how we would write a GetObjectData method that serializes two fields, called Name and DateOfBirth:

```
public virtual void GetObjectData (SerializationInfo info,
                                   StreamingContext context)
{
  info.AddValue ("Name", Name);
  info.AddValue ("DateOfBirth", DateOfBirth);
}
```

In this example, we've chosen to name each item according to its corresponding field. This is not required; any name can be used, as long as the same name is used upon deserialization. The values themselves can be of any serializable type; the Framework will recursively serialize as necessary. It's legal to store null values in the dictionary.

It's a good idea to make the GetObjectData method virtual—unless your class is sealed. This allows subclasses to extend serialization without having to reimplement the interface.

SerializationInfo also contains properties that you can use to control the type and assembly that the instance should deserialize as. The StreamingContext parameter is a structure that contains, among other things, an enumeration value indicating to where the serialized instance is heading (disk, Remoting, etc., although this value is not always populated).

In addition to implementing ISerializable, a type controlling its own serialization needs to provide a deserialization constructor that takes the same two parameters as GetObjectData. The constructor can be declared with any accessibility and the runtime will still find it. Typically, though, you would declare it protected so that subclasses can call it.

In the following example, we implement ISerializable in the Team class. When it comes to handling the List of players, we serialize the data as an array rather than a generic list, so as to offer compatibility with the SOAP formatter:

```csharp
[Serializable] public class Team : ISerializable
{
  public string Name;
  public List<Person> Players;

  public virtual void GetObjectData (SerializationInfo si,
                                     StreamingContext sc)
  {
    si.AddValue ("Name", Name);
    si.AddValue ("PlayerData", Players.ToArray( ));
  }

  public Team( ) {}

  protected Team (SerializationInfo si, StreamingContext sc)
  {
    Name = si.GetString ("Name");

    // Deserialize Players to an array to match our serialization:
    Person[] a = (Person[]) si.GetValue ("PlayerData", typeof (Person[]));

    // Construct a new List using this array:
    Players = new List<Person> (a);
  }
}
```

For commonly used types, the SerializationInfo class has typed "Get" methods such as GetString, in order to make writing deserialization constructors easier. If you specify a name for which no data exists, an exception is thrown. This happens most often when there's a version mismatch between the code doing the serialization and deserialization. You've added an extra field, for instance, and then forgotten about the implications of deserializing an old instance. To work around this problem, you can either:

- Add exception handling around code that retrieves a data member added in a later version.

- Implement your own version numbering system. For example:

```csharp
public string MyNewField;

public virtual void GetObjectData (SerializationInfo si,
                                   StreamingContext sc)
{
  si.AddValue ("_version", 2);
  si.AddValue ("MyNewField", MyNewField);
  ...
}

protected Team (SerializationInfo si, StreamingContext sc)
{
  int version = si.GetInt32 ("_version");
  if (version >= 2) MyNewField = si.GetString ("MyNewField");
  ...
}
```

Subclassing Serializable Classes

In the preceding examples, we sealed the classes that relied on attributes for serialization. To see why, consider the following class hierarchy:

```
[Serializable] public class Person
{
  public string Name;
  public int Age;
}

[Serializable] public sealed class Student : Person
{
  public string Course;
}
```

In this example, both Person and Student are serializable, and both classes use the default runtime serialization behavior since neither class implements ISerializable.

Now imagine that the developer of Person decides for some reason to implement ISerializable and provide a deserialization constructor to control Person serialization. The new version of Person might look like this:

```
[Serializable] public class Person : ISerializable
{
  public string Name;
  public int Age;

  public virtual void GetObjectData (SerializationInfo si,
                                     StreamingContext sc)
  {
    si.AddValue ("Name", Name);
    si.AddValue ("Age", Age);
  }

  protected Person (SerializationInfo si, StreamingContext sc)
  {
    Name = si.GetString ("Name");
    Age = si.GetInt32 ("Age");
  }

  public Person() {}
}
```

Although this works for instances of Person, this change breaks serialization of Student instances. Serializing a Student instance would appear to succeed, but the Course field in the Student type isn't saved to the stream because the implementation of ISerializable.GetObjectData on Person has no knowledge of the members of the Student-derived type. Additionally, deserialization of Student instances throws an exception since the runtime is looking (unsuccessfully) for a deserialization constructor on Student.

The solution to this problem is to implement ISerializable from the outset for serializable classes that are public and nonsealed. (With internal classes, it's not so important because you can easily modify the subclasses later if required.)

If we started out by writing Person as in the preceding example, Student would then be written as follows:

```
[Serializable]
public class Student : Person
{
  public string Course;

  public override void GetObjectData (SerializationInfo si,
                                      StreamingContext sc)
  {
    base.GetObjectData (si, sc);
    si.AddValue ("Course", Course);
  }

  protected Student (SerializationInfo si, StreamingContext sc)
    : base (si, sc)
  {
    Course = si.GetString ("Course");
  }

  public Student() {}
}
```

XML Serialization

The Framework provides a dedicated XML serialization engine called XmlSerializer in the System.Xml.Serialization namespace. It's suitable for serializing .NET types to XML files and is also used implicitly by Web Services.

As with the binary engine, there are two approaches you can take:

- Sprinkle attributes throughout your types (defined in System.Xml. Serialization).
- Implement IXmlSerializable.

Unlike with the binary engine, however, implementing the interface (i.e., IXmlSerializable) eschews the engine completely, leaving you to code the serialization yourself with XmlReader and XmlWriter.

Getting Started with Attribute-Based Serialization

To use XmlSerializer, you instantiate it and call Serialize or Deserialize with a Stream and object instance. To illustrate, suppose we define the following class:

```
public class Person
{
  public string Name;
  public int Age;
}
```

The following saves a Person to an XML file, and then restores it:

```
Person p = new Person( );
p.Name = "Stacey"; p.Age = 30;

XmlSerializer xs = new XmlSerializer (typeof (Person));

using (Stream s = File.Create ("person.xml"))
  xs.Serialize (s, p);

Person p2;
using (Stream s = File.OpenRead ("person.xml"))
  p2 = (Person) xs.Deserialize (s);

Console.WriteLine (p2.Name + " " + p2.Age);    // Stacey 30
```

Serialize and Deserialize can work with a Stream, XmlWriter/XmlReader, or TextWriter/TextReader. Here's the resultant XML:

```
<?xml version="1.0"?>
<Person xmlns:xsi="http://www.w3.org/2001/XMLSchema-instance"
        xmlns:xsd="http://www.w3.org/2001/XMLSchema">
  <Name>Stacey</Name>
  <Age>30</Age>
</Person>
```

XmlSerializer can serialize types without any attributes—such as our Person type. By default, it serializes all *public fields and properties* on a type. You can exclude members you don't want serialized with the XmlIgnore attribute:

```
public class Person
{
  ...
  [XmlIgnore] public DateTime DateOfBirth;
}
```

Unlike the other two engines, XmlSerializer does not recognize the [OnDeserializing] attribute and relies instead on a parameterless constructor for deserialization, throwing an exception if one is not present. (In our example, Person has an *implicit* parameterless constructor.) This also means field initializers execute prior to deserialization:

```
public class Person
{
  public bool Valid = true;    // Executes before deserialization
}
```

Although XmlSerializer can serialize almost any type, it recognizes the following types and treats them specially:

- The primitive types, DateTime, TimeSpan, Guid, and nullable versions
- byte[] (which is converted to base 64)
- An XmlAttribute or XmlElement (whose contents are injected into the stream)

- Any type implementing IXmlSerializable
- Any collection type

The deserializer is version-tolerant: it doesn't complain if elements or attributes are missing or if superfluous data is present.

Attributes, names, and namespaces

By default, fields and properties serialize to an XML element. You can request an XML attribute be used instead as follows:

```
[XmlAttribute] public int Age;
```

You can control an element or attribute's name as follows:

```
public class Person
{
  [XmlElement ("FirstName")] public string Name;
  [XmlAttribute ("RoughAge")] public int Age;
}
```

Here's the result:

```
<Person RoughAge="30" ...>
  <FirstName>Stacey</FirstName>
</Person>
```

The default XML namespace is blank (unlike the data contract serializer, which uses the type's namespace). To specify an XML namespace, [XmlElement] and [XmlAttribute] both accept a Namespace argument. You can also assign a name and namespace to the type itself with [XmlRoot]:

```
[XmlRoot ("Candidate", Namespace = "http://mynamespace/test/")]
public class Person { ... }
```

This names the person element "Candidate" as well as assigning a namespace to this element and its children.

XML element order

XmlSerializer writes elements in the order that they're defined in the class. You can change this by specifying an Order in the XmlElement attribute:

```
public class Person
{
  [XmlElement (Order = 2)] public string Name;
  [XmlElement (Order = 1)] public int Age;
}
```

If you use Order at all, you must use it throughout.

The deserializer is not fussy about the order of elements—they can appear in any sequence and the type will properly deserialize.

Subclasses and Child Objects

Subclassing the root type

Suppose your root type has two subclasses as follows:

```
public class Person { public string Name; }

public class Student : Person { }
public class Teacher : Person { }
```

and you write a reusable method to serialize the root type:

```
public void SerializePerson (Person p, string path)
{
  XmlSerializer xs = new XmlSerializer (typeof (Person));
  using (Stream s = File.Create (path))
    xs.Serialize (s, p);
}
```

To make this method work with a Student or Teacher, you must inform
XmlSerializer about the subclasses. There are two ways to do this. The first is to
register each subclass with the XmlInclude attribute:

```
[XmlInclude (typeof (Student))]
[XmlInclude (typeof (Teacher))]
public class Person { public string Name; }
```

The second is to specify each of the subtypes when constructing XmlSerializer:

```
XmlSerializer xs = new XmlSerializer (typeof (Person),
                    new Type[] { typeof (Student), typeof (Teacher) } );
```

In either case, the serializer responds by recording the subtype in the type
attribute (just like with the data contract serializer):

```
<Person xmlns:xsi="http://www.w3.org/2001/XMLSchema-instance"
        xsi:type="Student">
  <Name>Stacey</Name>
</Person>
```

This deserializer then knows from this attribute to instantiate a Student and not a
Person.

> You can control the name that appears in the XML type attribute
> by applying [XmlType] to the subclass:
> ```
> [XmlType ("Candidate")]
> public class Student : Person { }
> ```
> Here's the result:
> ```
> <Person xmlns:xsi="..."
>         xsi:type="Candidate">
> ```

Serializing child objects

XmlSerializer automatically recurses object references such as the HomeAddress
field in Person:

```
public class Person
{
  public string Name;
  public Address HomeAddress = new Address();
}

public class Address { public string Street, PostCode; }
```

To demonstrate:

```
Person p = new Person (); p.Name = "Stacey";
p.HomeAddress.Street = "Odo St";
p.HomeAddress.PostCode = "6020";
```

Here's the XML to which this serializes:

```
<Person ... >
  <Name>Stacey</Name>
  <HomeAddress>
    <Street>Odo St</Street>
    <PostCode>6020</PostCode>
  </HomeAddress>
</Person>
```

If you have two fields or properties that refer to the same object, that object is serialized twice. If you need to preserve referential equality, you must use another serialization engine.

Subclassing child objects

Suppose you need to serialize a Person that can reference *subclasses* of Address as follows:

```
public class Address { public string Street, PostCode; }
public class USAddress : Address {  }
public class AUAddress : Address {  }

public class Person
{
  public string Name;
  public Address HomeAddress = new USAddress();
}
```

There are two distinct ways to proceed, depending on how you want the XML structured. If you want the element name always to match the field or property name with the subtype recorded in a type attribute:

```
<Person ...>
  ...
  <HomeAddress xsi:type="USAddress">
    ...
  </HomeAddress>
</Person>
```

you use [XmlInclude] to register each of the subclasses with Address as follows:

```
[XmlInclude (typeof (AUAddress))]
[XmlInclude (typeof (USAddress))]
```

```
public class Address
{
  public string Street, PostCode;
}
```

If, on the other hand, you want the element name to reflect the name of the subtype, to the following effect:

```
<Person ...>
  ...
  <USAddress>
    ...
  </USAddress>
</Person>
```

you instead stack multiple [XmlElement] attributes onto the field or property in the parent type:

```
public class Person
{
  public string Name;

  [XmlElement ("Address", typeof (Address))]
  [XmlElement ("AUAddress", typeof (AUAddress))]
  [XmlElement ("USAddress", typeof (USAddress))]
  public Address HomeAddress = new USAddress ();
}
```

Each XmlElement maps an element name to a type. If you take this approach, you don't require the [XmlInclude] attributes on the Address type (although their presence doesn't break serialization).

> If you omit the element name in [XmlElement] (and specify just a type), the type's default name is used (which is influenced by [XmlType] but not [XmlRoot]).

Serializing Collections

XmlSerializer recognizes and serializes concrete collection types without intervention:

```
public class Person
{
  public string Name;
  public List<Address> Addresses = new List<Address> ();
}

public class Address { public string Street, PostCode; }
```

Here's the XML to which this serializes:

```
<Person ... >
  <Name>...</Name>
  <Addresses>
    <Address>
      <Street>...</Street>
      <Postcode>...</Postcode>
```

```
    </Address>
    <Address>
      <Street>...</Street>
      <Postcode>...</Postcode>
    </Address>
    ...
  </Addresses>
</Person>
```

The [XmlArray] attribute lets you rename the *outer* element (i.e., Addresses).

The [XmlArrayItem] attribute lets you rename the *inner* elements (i.e., the Address elements).

For instance, the following class:

```
public class Person
{
  public string Name;

  [XmlArray ("PreviousAddresses")]
  [XmlArrayItem ("Location")]
  public List<Address> Addresses = new List<Address> ();
}
```

serializes to this:

```
<Person ... >
  <Name>...</Name>
  <PreviousAddresses>
    <Location>
      <Street>...</Street>
      <Postcode>...</Postcode>
    </Location>
    <Location>
      <Street>...</Street>
      <Postcode>...</Postcode>
    </Location>
    ...
  </PreviousAddresses>
</Person>
```

The XmlArray and XmlArrayItem attributes also allow you to specify XML namespaces.

To serialize collections *without* the outer element, i.e.:

```
<Person ... >
  <Name>...</Name>
  <Address>
    <Street>...</Street>
    <Postcode>...</Postcode>
  </Address>
  <Address>
    <Street>...</Street>
    <Postcode>...</Postcode>
  </Address>
</Person>
```

Serialization

instead add [XmlElement] to the collection field or property:

```
public class Person
{
  ...
  [XmlElement ("Address")]
  public List<Address> Addresses = new List<Address> ();
}
```

Working with subclassed collection elements

The rules for subclassing collection elements follow naturally from the other subclassing rules. To encode subclassed elements with the type attribute, i.e.:

```
<Person ... >
  <Name>...</Name>
  <Addresses>
    <Address xsi:type="AUAddress">
      ...
```

add [XmlInclude] attributes to the base (Address) type as we did before. This works whether or not you suppress serialization of the outer element.

If you want subclassed elements to be named according to their type, i.e.:

```
<Person ... >
  <Name>...</Name>
  <!--start of optional outer element-->
  <AUAddress>
    <Street>...</Street>
    <Postcode>...</Postcode>
  </AUAddress>
  <USAddress>
    <Street>...</Street>
    <Postcode>...</Postcode>
  </USAddress>
  <!--end of optional outer element-->
</Person>
```

you must stack multiple [XmlArrayItem] or [XmlElement] attributes onto the collection field or property.

Stack multiple [XmlArrayItem] attributes if you want to *include* the outer collection element:

```
[XmlArrayItem ("Address",   typeof (Address))]
[XmlArrayItem ("AUAddress", typeof (AUAddress))]
[XmlArrayItem ("USAddress", typeof (USAddress))]
public List<Address> Addresses = new List<Address> ();
```

Stack multiple [XmlElement] attributes if you want to *exclude* the outer collection element:

```
[XmlElement ("Address",   typeof (Address))]
[XmlElement ("AUAddress", typeof (AUAddress))]
[XmlElement ("USAddress", typeof (USAddress))]
public List<Address> Addresses = new List<Address> ();
```

IXmlSerializable

Although attribute-based XML serialization is flexible, it has limitations. For instance, you cannot add serialization hooks—nor can you serialize nonpublic members. It's also awkward to use if the XML might present the same element or attribute in a number of different ways.

On that last issue, you can push the boundaries somewhat by passing an XmlAttributeOverrides object into XmlSerializer's constructor. There comes a point, however, when it's easier to take an imperative approach. This is the job of IXmlSerializable:

```
public interface IXmlSerializable
{
  XmlSchema GetSchema( );
  void ReadXml (XmlReader reader);
  void WriteXml (XmlWriter writer);
}
```

Implementing this interface gives you total control over the XML that's read or written.

 A collection class that implements IXmlSerializable bypasses XmlSerializer's rules for serializing collections. This can be useful if you need to serialize a collection with a payload—in other words, additional fields or properties that would otherwise be ignored.

The rules for implementing IXmlSerializable are as follows:

* ReadXml should read the outer start element, then the content, and then the outer end element.
* WriteXml should write just the content.

For example:

```
using System;
using System.Xml;
using System.Xml.Schema;
using System.Xml.Serialization;

public class Address : IXmlSerializable
{
  public string Street, PostCode;

  public XmlSchema GetSchema( ) { return null; }

  public void ReadXml(XmlReader reader)
  {
    reader.ReadStartElement( );
    Street   = reader.ReadElementContentAsString ("Street", "");
    PostCode = reader.ReadElementContentAsString ("PostCode", "");
    reader.ReadEndElement( );
  }
```

```
    public void WriteXml (XmlWriter writer)
    {
      writer.WriteElementString ("Street", Street);
      writer.WriteElementString ("PostCode", PostCode);
    }
}
```

Serializing and deserializing an instance of Address via XmlSerializer automatically calls the WriteXml and ReadXml methods. Further, if Person was defined as follows:

```
public class Person
{
  public string Name;
  public Address HomeAddress;
}
```

IXmlSerializable would be called upon selectively to serialize the HomeAddress field.

We describe XmlReader and XmlWriter at length in the first section of Chapter 11. Also in Chapter 11, in the section, "Patterns for Using XmlReader/XmlWriter," we provide examples of IXmlSerializable-ready classes.

16

Assemblies

An assembly is the basic unit of deployment in .NET and is also the container for all types. An assembly contains compiled types with their IL code, runtime resources, and information to assist with versioning, security, and referencing other assemblies. An assembly also defines a boundary for type resolution and security permissioning. In general, an assembly comprises a single Windows *Portable Executable* (PE) file—with an *.exe* extension in the case of an application, or a *.dll* extension in the case of a reusable library.

Most of the types in this chapter come from the following namespaces:

```
System.Reflection
System.Resources
System.Globalization
```

What's in an Assembly

An assembly contains four kinds of things:

An assembly manifest
> Provides information to the .NET runtime, such as the assembly's name, version, requested permissions, and other assemblies that it references

An application manifest
> Provides information to the operating system, such as how the assembly should be deployed and whether administrative elevation is required

Compiled types
> The compiled IL code and metadata of the types defined within the assembly

Resources
> Nonexecutable data embedded within the assembly, such as images and localizable text

Of these, only the *assembly manifest* is mandatory, although an assembly nearly always contains compiled types.

Assemblies are structured similarly whether they're executables or libraries. The main difference with an executable is that it defines an entry point.

The Assembly Manifest

The assembly manifest serves two purposes:

- It describes the assembly to the managed hosting environment.
- It acts as a directory to the modules, types, and resources in the assembly.

Assemblies are hence *self-describing*. A consumer can discover all of an assembly's data, types, and functions—without needing additional files.

 An assembly manifest is not something you add explicitly to an assembly—it's automatically embedded into an assembly as part of compilation.

Here's a summary of the functionally significant data stored in the manifest:

- The simple name of the assembly
- A version number (`AssemblyVersion`)
- A public key and signed hash of the assembly, if strongly named
- A list of referenced assemblies, including their version and public key
- A list of modules that comprise the assembly
- A list of types defined in the assembly and the module containing each type
- An optional set of security permissions requested or refused by the assembly (`SecurityPermission`)
- The culture it targets, if a satellite assembly (`AssemblyCulture`)

The manifest can also store the following informational data:

- A full title and description (`AssemblyTitle` and `AssemblyDescription`)
- Company and copyright information (`AssemblyCompany` and `Assembly-Copyright`)
- A display version (`AssemblyInformationalVersion`)
- Additional attributes for custom data

Some of this data is derived from arguments given to the compiler, such as the list of referenced assemblies or the public key with which to sign the assembly. The rest comes from assembly attributes, indicated in parentheses.

 You can view the contents of an assembly's manifest with the .NET tool *ildasm.exe*. In Chapter 17, we describe how to use reflection to do the same programmatically.

Specifying assembly attributes

You can control much of the manifest's content with assembly attributes. For example:

```
[assembly: AssemblyCopyright ("\x00a9 Corp Ltd. All rights reserved.")]
[assembly: AssemblyVersion ("2.3.2.1")]
```

These declarations are usually all defined in one file in your project. Visual Studio automatically creates a file called *AssemblyInfo.cs* with every new C# project for this purpose, prepopulated with a default set of assembly attributes that provide a starting point for further customization.

The Application Manifest

An application manifest is an XML file that communicates information about the assembly to the operating system. An application manifest, if present, is read and processed before the .NET-managed hosting environment loads the assembly—and can influence how the operating system launches an application's process.

An application manifest has a root element called assembly in the XML namespace urn:schemas-microsoft-com:asm.v1:

```
<?xml version="1.0" encoding="utf-8"?>
<assembly manifestVersion="1.0" xmlns="urn:schemas-microsoft-com:asm.v1">
  <!-- contents of manifest -->
</assembly>
```

The following manifest instructs the OS to request administrative elevation when the assembly runs under Windows Vista:

```
<?xml version="1.0" encoding="utf-8"?>
<assembly manifestVersion="1.0" xmlns="urn:schemas-microsoft-com:asm.v1">
  <trustInfo xmlns="urn:schemas-microsoft-com:asm.v2">
    <security>
      <requestedPrivileges>
        <requestedExecutionLevel level="requireAdministrator" />
      </requestedPrivileges>
    </security>
  </trustInfo>
</assembly>
```

We describe the consequences of requesting administrative elevation in "Operating System Security" in Chapter 18.

Deploying an application manifest

You can deploy an application manifest in two ways:

- As a specially named file located in the same folder as the assembly
- Embedded within the assembly itself

As a separate file, its name must match that of the assembly's, plus *.manifest*. So, if an assembly was named *MyApp.exe*, its manifest would be named *MyApp.exe.manifest*.

To embed an application manifest file into an assembly, first build the assembly and then call the .NET mt tool as follows:

```
mt -manifest MyApp.exe.manifest -outputresource:MyApp.exe;#1
```

 The .NET tool *ildasm.exe* is blind to the presence of an embedded application manifest. Visual Studio, however, indicates whether an embedded application manifest is present if you double-click the assembly in Solution Explorer.

Modules

The contents of an assembly are actually packaged within one or more intermediate containers, called *modules*. A module corresponds to a file containing the contents of an assembly. The reason for this extra layer of containership is to allow an assembly to span multiple files—a feature that's useful when building an assembly containing code compiled in a mixture of programming languages.

Figure 16-1 shows the normal case of an assembly with a single module. Figure 16-2 shows a multifile assembly. In a multifile assembly, the "main" module always contains the manifest; additional modules can contain IL and/or resources. The manifest describes the relative location of all the other modules that make up the assembly.

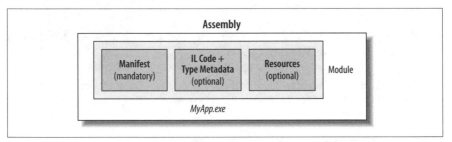

Figure 16-1. Single-file assembly

Multifile assemblies have to be compiled from the command line: there's no support in Visual Studio. To do this, invoke the csc compiler with the /t switch to create each module, and then link them with the assembly linker tool, *al.exe*.

Although the need for multifile assemblies is rare, at times you need to be aware of the extra level of containership that modules impose—even when dealing just with single-module assemblies. The main scenario is with reflection (see the sections "Reflecting Assemblies" and "Emitting Assemblies and Types" in Chapter 17).

The Assembly Class

The Assembly class in System.Reflection is a gateway to accessing assembly metadata at runtime. There are a number of ways to obtain an assembly object: the simplest is via a Type's Assembly property:

```
Assembly a = typeof (Program).Assembly;
```

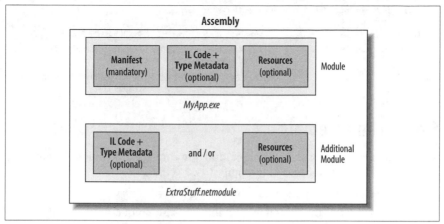

Figure 16-2. Multifile assembly

You can also obtain an `Assembly` object by calling one of `Assembly`'s static methods:

`GetExecutingAssembly`
Returns the assembly of the type that defines the currently executing function

`GetCallingAssembly`
Does the same as `GetExecutingAssembly`, but for the function that called the currently executing function

`GetCallingAssembly`
Returns the assembly defining the application's original entry method

Once you have an `Assembly` object, you can use its properties and methods to query the assembly's metadata and reflect upon its types. Table 16-1 shows a summary of these functions.

Table 16-1. Assembly members

Functions	Purpose	See the section...
FullName, GetName	Returns the fully qualified name or an `AssemblyName` object	"Assembly Names"
CodeBase, Location	Location of the assembly file	"Resolving and Loading Assemblies"
Load, LoadFrom, LoadFile	Manually loads an assembly into the current application domain	"Resolving and Loading Assemblies"
GlobalAssemblyCache	Indicates whether the assembly is defined in the GAC	"The Global Assembly Cache"
GetSatelliteAssembly	Locates the satellite assembly of a given culture	"Resources and Satellite Assemblies"
GetType, GetTypes	Returns a type, or all types, defined in the assembly	"Reflecting and Activating Types" in Chapter 17
EntryPoint	Returns the application's entry method, as a `MethodInfo`	"Reflecting and Invoking Members" in Chapter 17

Table 16-1. Assembly members (continued)

Functions	Purpose	See the section...
GetModules, ManifestModule	Returns all modules, or the main module, of an assembly	"Reflecting Assemblies" in Chapter 17
GetCustomAttributes	Returns the assembly's attributes	"Working with Attributes" in Chapter 17

Signing an Assembly

Signing an assembly gives it a unique and untamperable identity. It works by writing two bits of metadata to the manifest:

- A *unique number* that identifies the signing party
- A *signed hash* of the assembly, proving that the unique number holder produced the assembly

This requires a public/private key pair. The *public key* provides the unique identifying number, and the *private key* facilitates signing. A signed assembly incorporates the public key into its identity and is said to have a *strong name*.

A strong name is valuable in guaranteeing the uniqueness of assembly references. The signature is valuable for security—it prevents a malicious party from tampering with your assembly. Without your private key, no one can release a modified version of the assembly without the signature breaking (causing an error when loaded). Of course, someone could re-sign the assembly with a different key pair—but this would give the assembly a different identity. Any application referencing the original assembly would shun the imposter because public key tokens are written into references.

Adding a strong name to a previously "weak" named assembly changes its identity. For this reason, it pays to give production assemblies strong names from the outset.

A signed assembly can also be registered in the GAC.

How to Sign an Assembly

To sign an assembly, first generate a public/private key pair with the *sn.exe* utility:

```
sn.exe -k MyKeyPair.snk
```

This manufactures a new key pair and stores it to a file called *MyApp.snk*. If you subsequently lose this file, you will permanently lose the ability to recompile your assembly with the same identity.

You then compile with the /keyfile switch:

```
csc.exe /keyfile:MyKeyPair.snk Program.cs
```

Visual Studio assists you with both steps in the Project Properties window.

A strongly named assembly cannot reference a weakly named assembly. This is another compelling reason to strongly name all your production assemblies.

The same key pair can sign multiple assemblies—they'll still have distinct identities if their simple names differ. The choice as to how many key pair files to use within an organization depends on a number of factors. Having a separate key pair for every assembly is advantageous should you later transfer ownership of a particular application (along with its referenced assemblies), in terms of minimum disclosure. But it makes it harder for you to create a security policy that recognizes all of your assemblies (for example, to run with unrestricted permissions over a network path). It also makes it harder to validate dynamically loaded assemblies.

Prior to C# 2.0, the compiler did not support the /keyfile switch and you would specify a key file with the AssemblyKeyFile attribute instead. This presented a minor security risk, because the path to the key file would remain embedded in the assembly's metadata. For instance, with *ildasm*, you can see quite easily that the path to the key file used to sign *mscorlib* was as follows:

```
F:\qfe\Tools\devdiv\EcmaPublicKey.snk
```

Obviously, you need access to that folder on Microsoft's .NET Framework build machine to take advantage of that information!

Delay Signing

In an organization with hundreds of developers, you might want to restrict access to the key pairs used for signing assemblies, for a couple of reasons:

- If a key pair gets leaked, your assemblies are no longer untamperable.
- A test assembly, if signed and leaked, could be maliciously propagated as the real assembly.

Withholding key pairs from developers, though, means they cannot compile and test assemblies with their correct identity. *Delay signing* is a system for working around this problem.

A delay-signed assembly is flagged with the correct public key, but not *signed* with the private key. A delay-signed assembly is equivalent to a tampered assembly and would normally be rejected by the CLR. The developer, however, instructs the CLR to bypass validation for the delay-sign assemblies on *that computer*, allowing the unsigned assemblies to run. When it comes time for final deployment, the private key holder re-signs the assembly with the real key pair.

To delay-sign, you need a file containing *just* the public key. You can extract this from a key pair by calling sn with the -p switch:

```
sn -k KeyPair.snk
sn -p KeyPair.snk PublicKeyOnly.pk
```

KeyPair.snk is kept secure and *PublicKeyOnly.pk* is freely distributed.

You can also obtain *PublicKeyOnly.pk* from an existing signed assembly with the -e switch:

```
sn -e YourLibrary.dll PublicKeyOnly.pk
```

You then delay-sign with *PublicKeyOnly.pk* by calling csc with the /delaysign+ switch:

```
csc /delaysign+ /keyfile: PublicKeyOnly.pk /target:library YourLibrary.cs
```

Visual Studio does the same if you tick the "Delay sign" checkbox.

The next step is to instruct the .NET runtime to skip assembly identity verification on the development computers running the delay-signed assemblies. This can be done on either a per-assembly or a per-public key basis, by calling the sn tool with the Vr switch:

```
sn -Vr YourLibrary.dll
```

Visual Studio does not perform this step automatically. You must disable assembly verification manually from the command line. Otherwise, your assembly will not execute.

The final step is to fully sign the assembly prior to deployment. This is when you replace the null signature with a real signature that can be generated only with access to the private key. To do this, you call sn with the R switch:

```
sn -R YourLibrary.dll KeyPair.snk
```

You can then reinstate assembly verification on development machines as follows:

```
sn -Vu YourLibrary.dll
```

You won't need to recompile any applications that reference the delay-signed assembly, because you've changed only the assembly's signature, not its *identity*.

Assembly Names

An assembly's "identity" comprises four pieces of metadata from its manifest:

- Its simple name
- Its version ("0.0.0.0" if not present)
- Its culture ("neutral" if not a satellite)
- Its public key token ("null" if not signed)

The simple name comes not from any attribute, but from the name of the file to which it was originally compiled (less any extension). So, the simple name of the *System.Xml.dll* assembly is "System.Xml". Renaming a file doesn't change the assembly's simple name.

The version number comes from the AssemblyVersion attribute. It's a string divided into four parts as follows:

```
major.minor.build.revision
```

You can specify a version number as follows:

```
[assembly: AssemblyVersion ("2.5.6.7")]
```

The culture comes from the `AssemblyCulture` attribute and applies to satellite assemblies, described later in the section "Resources and Satellite Assemblies."

The public key token comes from a key pair supplied at compile time via the `/keyfile` switch, as we saw earlier, in the section "Signing an Assembly."

Fully Qualified Names

A fully qualified assembly name is a string that includes all four identifying components, in this format:

```
simple-name, Version=version, Culture=culture, PublicKeyToken=public-key
```

For example, the fully qualified name of *System.Xml.dll* is:

```
"System.Xml, Version=2.0.0.0, Culture=neutral,
PublicKeyToken=b77a5c561934e089"
```

If the assembly has no `AssemblyVersion` attribute, the version appears as "0.0.0.0". If it is unsigned, its public key token appears as "null".

An `Assembly` object's `FullName` property returns its fully qualified name. The compiler always uses fully qualified names when recording assembly references in the manifest.

 A fully qualified assembly name does not include a directory path to assist in locating it on disk. Locating an assembly residing in another directory is an entirely separate matter that we pick up in "Resolving and Loading Assemblies."

The AssemblyName Class

`AssemblyName` is a class with a typed property for each of the four components of a fully qualified assembly name. `AssemblyName` has two purposes:

- It parses or builds a fully qualified assembly name.
- It stores some extra data to assist in resolving (finding) the assembly.

You can obtain an `AssemblyName` object in any of the following ways:

- Instantiate an `AssemblyName`, providing a fully qualified name.
- Call `GetName` on an existing `Assembly`.
- Call `AssemblyName.GetAssemblyName`, providing the path to an assembly file on disk.

You can also instantiate an `AssemblyName` object without any arguments, and then set each of its properties to build a fully qualified name. An `AssemblyName` is mutable when constructed in this manner.

Here are its essential properties and methods:

```
string     FullName     { get; }         // Fully qualified name
string     Name         { get; set; }    // Simple name
```

```
Version     Version     { get; set; }       // Assembly version
CultureInfo CultureInfo { get; set; }       // For satellite assemblies
string      CodeBase    { get; set; }       // Location

byte[]      GetPublicKey( );                // 160 bytes
void        SetPublicKey (byte[] key);
byte[]      GetPublicKeyToken( );           // 8-byte version
void        SetPublicKeyToken (byte[] key;)
```

Version is itself a strongly typed representation, with properties for Major, Minor, Build, and Revision numbers. GetPublicKey returns the full cryptographic public key; GetPublicKeyToken returns the last eight bytes used in establishing identity.

To use AssemblyName to obtain the simple name of an assembly:

```
Console.WriteLine (typeof (string).Assembly.GetName( ).Name);  // mscorlib
```

To get an assembly version:

```
string v = myAssembly.GetName().Version.ToString( );
```

We'll examine the CodeBase property in the later section "Resolving and Loading Assemblies."

The Global Assembly Cache

As part of the .NET Framework installation, a central repository is created on the computer for storing .NET assemblies, called the *Global Assembly Cache*, or GAC. The GAC contains a centralized copy of the .NET Framework itself, and it can also be used to centralize your own assemblies.

The main factor in choosing whether to load your assemblies into the GAC relates to versioning. For assemblies in the GAC, versioning is centralized at the machine level and controlled by the computer's administrator. For assemblies outside the GAC, versioning is handled on an application basis, so each application looks after its own dependency and update issues (typically by maintaining its own copy of each assembly that it references).

The GAC is useful in the minority of cases where machine-centralized versioning is genuinely advantageous. For example, consider a suite of interdependent plug-ins, each referencing some shared assemblies. We'll assume each plug-in is in its own directory, and for this reason, there's a possibility of there being multiple copies of a shared assembly (maybe some later than others). Further, we'll assume the hosting application will want to load each shared assembly just once for the sake of efficiency and type compatibility. The task of assembly resolution is now difficult for the hosting application, requiring careful planning and an understanding of the subtleties of assembly loading contexts. The simple solution here is to put the shared assemblies into the GAC. This ensures that the CLR always makes straightforward and consistent assembly resolution choices.

In more typical scenarios, however, the GAC is best avoided because it adds the following complications:

- XCOPY or ClickOnce deployment is no longer possible; an administrative setup is required to install your application.
- Updating assemblies in the GAC also requires administrative privileges.

- Use of the GAC can complicate development and testing, because *fusion*, the CLR's assembly resolution mechanism, always favors GAC assemblies over local copies.

- Versioning and *side-by-side* execution require some planning, and a mistake may break other applications.

On the positive side, the GAC can improve startup time for very large assemblies, because the CLR verifies the signatures of assemblies in the GAC only once upon installation, rather than every time the assembly loads. In percentage terms, this is relevant if you've generated native images for your assemblies with the *ngen.exe* tool, choosing nonoverlapping base addresses. A good article describing these issues is available online at *http://msdn.microsoft.com/msdnmag/* and is titled "The Performance Benefits of NGen."

How to Install Assemblies to the GAC

To install assemblies to the GAC, the first step is to give your assembly a strong name. Then you can install it using the .NET command-line tool, gacutil:

```
gacutil /i MyAssembly.dll
```

If the assembly already exists in the GAC with the *same public key and version*, it's updated. You don't have to uninstall the old one first.

To uninstall an assembly (note the lack of a file extension):

```
gacutil /u MyAssembly
```

You can also specify that assemblies be installed to the GAC as part of a setup project in Visual Studio.

Calling gacutil with the /l switch lists all assemblies in the GAC. You can do the same with the *mscorcfg* MMC snap-in (from Window → Administrative Tools → Framework Configuration).

Once an assembly is loaded into the GAC, applications can reference it without needing a local copy of that assembly.

 If a local copy *is* present, it's *ignored in favor of the GAC image*. This means there's no way to reference or test a recompiled version of your library—until you update the GAC. This holds true as long as you preserve the assembly's version and identity.

GAC and Versioning

Changing an assembly's AssemblyVersion gives it a brand-new identity. To illustrate, let's say you write a *utils* assembly, version it "1.0.0.0", sign it, and then install it in the GAC. Then suppose later you add some new features, change the version to "1.0.0.1", recompile it, and reinstall it into the GAC. Instead of overwriting the original assembly, the GAC now holds *both* versions. This means:

- You can choose which version to reference when compiling another application that uses *utils*.

- Any application previously compiled to reference *utils* 1.0.0.0 will *continue to do so*.

Assemblies

This is called *side-by-side* execution. Side-by-side execution prevents the "DLL hell" that can otherwise occur when a shared assembly is unilaterally updated: applications designed for the older version might unexpectedly break.

A complication arises, though, when you want to apply bug fixes or minor updates to existing assemblies. You have two options:

- Reinstall the fixed assembly to the GAC with the same version number.
- Compile the fixed assembly with a new version number and install that to the GAC.

The difficulty with the first option is that there's no way to apply the update *selectively* to certain applications. It's all or nothing. The difficulty with the second option is that applications will not normally use the newer assembly version without being recompiled. There is a workaround—you can create a *publisher policy* allowing assembly version redirection—at the cost of increasing deployment complexity.

Side-by-side execution is good for mitigating some of the problems of shared assemblies. If you avoid the GAC altogether—instead allowing each application to maintain its own private copy of *utils*—you eliminate *all* of the problems of shared assemblies!

Resources and Satellite Assemblies

An application typically contains not only executable code, but also content such as text, images, or XML files. Such content can be represented in an assembly through a *resource*. There are two overlapping use cases for resources:

- Incorporating data that cannot go into source code, such as images
- Storing data that might need translation in a multilingual application

An assembly resource is ultimately a byte stream with a name. You can think of an assembly as containing a dictionary of byte arrays keyed by string. This can be seen in *ildasm* if we disassemble an assembly that contains a resource called *banner.jpg* and a resource called *data.xml*:

```
.mresource public banner.jpg
{
  // Offset: 0x00000F58 Length: 0x000004F6
}
.mresource public data.xml
{
  // Offset: 0x00001458 Length: 0x0000027E
}
```

In this case, *banner.jpg* and *data.xml* were included directly in the assembly—each as its own embedded resource. This is the simplest way to work.

The Framework also lets you add content through intermediate *.resources* containers. There are designed for holding content that may require translation into different languages. Localized *.resources* can be packaged as individual satellite assemblies that are automatically picked up at runtime, based on the user's operating system language.

Figure 16-3 illustrates an assembly that contains two directly embedded resources, plus a *.resources* container called *welcome.resources*, for which we've created two localized satellites.

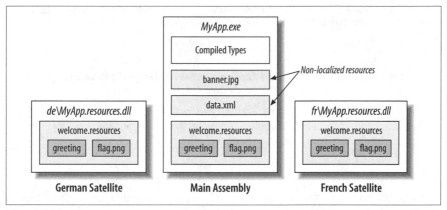

Figure 16-3. Resources

Directly Embedding Resources

To directly embed a resource at the command line, use the /resource switch when compiling:

```
csc /resource:banner.jpg /resource:data.xml MyApp.cs
```

You can optionally specify that the resource be given a different name in the assembly as follows:

```
csc /resource:<file-name>,<resource-name>
```

To directly embed a resource using Visual Studio:

- Add the file to your project.
- Set its build action to "Embedded Resource".

Visual Studio always prefixes resource names with the project's default namespace, plus the names of any subfolders in which the file is contained. So, if your project's default namespace was Westwind.Reports and your file was called *banner.jpg* in the folder *pictures*, the resource name would be *Westwind.Reports. pictures.banner.jpg*.

 Resource names are case-sensitive. This makes project subfolder names in Visual Studio that contain resources effectively case-sensitive.

To retrieve a resource, you call GetManifestResourceStream on the assembly containing the resource. This returns a stream, which you can then read as any other:

```
Assembly a = Assembly.GetEntryAssembly ();

using (Stream s = a.GetManifestResourceStream ("TestProject.data.xml"))
```

```
using (XmlReader r = XmlReader.Create (s))
  ...

System.Drawing.Image image;
using (Stream s = a.GetManifestResourceStream ("TestProject.banner.jpg"))
  image = System.Drawing.Image.FromStream (s);
```

The stream returned is seekable, so you can also do this:

```
byte[] data;
using (Stream s = a.GetManifestResourceStream ("TestProject.banner.jpg"))
  data = new BinaryReader (s).ReadBytes ((int) s.Length);
```

If you've used Visual Studio to embed the resource, you must remember to include the namespace-based prefix. To help avoid error, you can specify the prefix in a separate argument, using a *type*. The type's namespace is used as the prefix:

```
using (Stream s = a.GetManifestResourceStream (typeof (X), "XmlData.xml"))
```

X can be any type with the desired namespace of your resource (typically, a type in the same project folder).

 Setting a project item's build action in Visual Studio to "Resource" within a WPF application is *not* the same as setting its build action to "Embedded Resource". The former actually adds the item to a *.resources* file called *<AssemblyName>.g.resources*, whose content you access through WPF's Application class, using a URI as a key.

To add to the confusion, WPF further overloads the term "resource." *Static resources* and *dynamic resources* are both unrelated to assembly resources!

GetManifestResourceNames returns the names of all resources in the assembly.

.resources Files

.resources files are containers for potentially localizable content. A *.resources* file ends up as an embedded resource within an assembly—just like any other kind of file. The difference is that you must:

* Package your content into the *.resources* file to begin with.
* Access its content through a ResourceManager or *pack URI*, rather than a GetManifestResourceStream.

.resources files are structured in binary and so are not human-editable; therefore, you must rely on tools provided by the Framework and Visual Studio to work with them. The standard approach with strings or simple data types is to use the *.resx* format, which can be converted to a *.resources* file either by Visual Studio or the resgen tool. The *.resx* format is also suitable for images intended for a Windows Forms or ASP.NET application.

In a WPF application, you must use Visual Studio's "Resource" build action for images or similar content needing to be referenced by URI. This applies whether localization is needed or not.

We describe how to do each of these in the following sections.

.resx Files

A *.resx* file is a design-time format for producing *.resources* files. A *.resx* file uses XML and is structured with name/value pairs as follows:

```
<root>

  <!-- A special (not so friendly!) header is required here -->

  <data name="Greeting">
    <value>hello</value>
  </data>
  <data name="DefaultFontSize" type="System.Int32, mscorlib">
    <value>10</value>
  </data>
</root>
```

To create a *.resx* file in Visual Studio, add a project item of type "Resources File". The rest of the work is done automatically:

- The correct header is created.
- A designer is provided for adding strings, images, files, and other kinds of data.
- The *.resx* file is automatically converted to the *.resources* format and embedded into the assembly upon compilation.
- A class is written to help you access the data later on.

 The resource designer adds images as typed Image objects (*System. Drawing.dll*), rather than as byte arrays, making them unsuitable for WPF applications.

Creating a .resx file at the command line

If you're working at the command line, you must start with a *.resx* file that has a valid header. The easiest way to accomplish this is to create a simple *.resx* file programmatically. The ResXResourceWriter class (namespace = System.Resources; assembly = *System.Windows.Forms.dll*) does exactly this job:

```
using (ResXResourceWriter w = new ResXResourceWriter ("welcome.resx")) { }
```

From here, you can either continue to use the ResXResourceWriter to add resources (by calling AddResource) or manually edit the *.resx* file that it wrote.

The easiest way to deal with images is to treat the files as binary data and convert them to an image upon retrieval. This is also more versatile than encoding them as a typed Image object. You can include binary data within a *.resx* file in base 64 format as follows:

```
<data name="flag.png" type="System.Byte[], mscorlib">
  <value>Qk32BAAAAAAAAHYAAAAoAAAAMAMDAwACAgIAAAAD/AA....</value>
</data>
```

or as a reference to another file that is then read by resgen:

```
<data name="flag.png"
  type="System.Resources.ResXFileRef, System.Windows.Forms">
  <value>flag.png;System.Byte[], mscorlib</value>
</data>
```

When you're done, you must convert the *.resx* file by calling resgen. The following converts *welcome.resx* into *welcome.resources*:

```
resgen welcome.resx
```

The final step is to include the *.resources* file when compiling, as follows:

```
csc /resources:welcome.resources MyApp.cs
```

Reading .resources files

 If you create a *.resx* file in Visual Studio, a class of the same name is generated automatically with properties to retrieve each of its items.

The ResourceManager class reads *.resources* files embedded within an assembly:

```
ResourceManager r = new ResourceManager ("welcome",
                                  Assembly.GetExecutingAssembly( ));
```

(The first argument must be namespace-prefixed if the resource was compiled in Visual Studio.)

You can then access what's inside by calling GetString or GetObject with a cast:

```
string greeting = r.GetString ("Greeting");
int fontSize = (int) r.GetObject ("DefaultFontSize");
Image image = (Image) r.GetObject ("flag.png");      // (Visual Studio)
byte[] imgData = (byte[]) r.GetObject ("flag.png");   // (Command line)
```

To enumerate the contents of a *.resources* file:

```
ResourceManager r = new ResourceManager (...)
ResourceSet set = r.GetResourceSet (CultureInfo.CurrentUICulture,
                                  true, true);
foreach (System.Collections.DictionaryEntry entry in set)
  Console.WriteLine (entry.Key);
```

Creating a pack URI resource in Visual Studio

In a WPF application, XAML files need to be able to access resources by URI. For instance:

```
<Button>
  <Image Height="50" Source="flag.png"/>
</Button>
```

Or, if the resource is in another assembly:

```
<Button>
  <Image Height="50" Source="UtilsAssembly;Component/flag.png"/>
</Button>
```

(Component is a literal keyword.)

To create resources that can be loaded in this manner, you cannot use *.resx* files. Instead, you must add the files to your project and set their build action to "Resource" (not "Embedded Resource"). Visual Studio then compiles them into a *.resources* file called *<AssemblyName>.g.resources*—also the home of compiled XAML (*.baml*) files.

To load a URI-keyed resource programmatically, call Application.GetResource-Stream:

```
Uri u = new Uri ("flag.png", UriKind.Relative);
using (Stream s = Application.GetResourceStream (u).Stream)
```

Notice we used a relative URI. You can also use an absolute URI in exactly the following format (the three commas are not a typo):

```
Uri u = new Uri ("pack://application:,,,/flag.png");
```

If you'd rather specify an Assembly object, you can retrieve content instead with a ResourceManager:

```
Assembly a = Assembly.GetExecutingAssembly();
ResourceManager r = new ResourceManager (a.GetName().Name + ".g", a);
using (Stream s = r.GetStream ("flag.png"))
  ...
```

A ResourceManager also lets you enumerate the content of a *.g.resources* container within a given assembly.

Satellite Assemblies

Data embedded in *.resources* is localizable.

Resource localization is relevant when your application runs on a version of Windows built to display everything in a different language. For consistency, your application should use that same language too.

A typical setup is as follows:

- The main assembly contains *.resources* for the default or *fallback* language.
- Separate *satellite assemblies* contain localized *.resources* translated to different languages.

When your application runs, the Framework examines the language of the current operating system (from CultureInfo.CurrentUICulture). Whenever you request a resource using ResourceManager, the Framework looks for a localized satellite assembly. If one's available—and it contains the resource key you requested—it's used in place of the main assembly's version.

This means you can enhance language support simply by adding new satellites—without changing the main assembly.

 A satellite assembly cannot contain executable code; only resources.

Satellite assemblies are deployed in subdirectories of the assembly's folder as follows:

```
programBaseFolder\MyProgram.exe
              \MyLibrary.exe
              \XX\MyProgram.resources.dll
              \XX\MyLibrary.resources.dll
```

XX refers to the two-letter language code (such as "de" for German) or a language and region code (such as "en-GB" for English in Great Britain). This naming system allows the CLR to find and load the correct satellite assembly automatically.

Building satellite assemblies

Recall our previous *.resx* example, which included the following:

```
<root>
  ...
  <data name="Greeting"
    <value>hello</value>
  </data>
</root>
```

We then retrieved the greeting at runtime as follows:

```
ResourceManager r = new ResourceManager ("welcome",
                             Assembly.GetExecutingAssembly( ));
Console.Write (r.GetString ("Greeting"));
```

Suppose we want this to instead write "Hallo" if running on the German version of Windows. The first step is to add another *.resx* file named *welcome.de.resx* that substitutes *hello* for *hallo*:

```
<root>
  <data name="Greeting">
    <value>hallo<value>
  </data>
</root>
```

In Visual Studio, this is all you need to do—when you rebuild, a satellite assembly called *MyApp.resources.dll* is automatically created in a subdirectory called *de*.

If you're using the command line, you call resgen to turn the *.resx* file into a *.resources* file:

```
resgen MyApp.de.resx
```

and then call al to build the satellite assembly:

```
al /culture:de /out:MyApp.resources.dll /embed:MyApp.de.resources /t:lib
```

You can specify /template:MyApp.exe to import the main assembly's strong name.

Testing satellite assemblies

To simulate running on an operating system with a different language, you must change the CurrentUICulture using the Thread class:

```
System.Threading.Thread.CurrentThread.CurrentUICulture
    = new System.Globalization.CultureInfo ("de");
```

Note that CultureInfo.CurrentUICulture is a read-only version of the same property.

Visual Studio designer support

The designers in Visual Studio provide extended support for localizing components and visual elements. The WPF designer has its own workflow for localization; other Component-based designers use a design-time-only property to make it appear that a component or Windows Forms control has a Language property. To customize for another language, simply change the Language property and then start modifying the component. All properties of controls that are attributed as Localizable will be persisted to a *.resx* file for that language. You can switch between languages at any time just by changing the Language property.

Cultures and Subcultures

Cultures are split into cultures and subcultures. A culture represents a particular language; a subculture represents a regional variation of that language. The Framework follows the RFC1766 standard, which represents cultures and subcultures with two-letter codes. Here are the codes for English and German cultures:

```
en
de
```

Here are the codes for the Australian English and Austrian German subcultures:

```
en-AU
de-AT
```

A culture is represented in .NET with the System.Globalization.CultureInfo class. You can examine the current culture of your application as follows:

```
Console.WriteLine (System.Threading.Thread.CurrentThread.CurrentCulture);
Console.WriteLine (System.Threading.Thread.CurrentThread.CurrentUICulture);
```

Running this in Australia illustrates the difference between the two:

```
EN-AU
EN-US
```

CurrentCulture reflects the regional settings of the Windows control panel, whereas CurrentUICulture reflects the language of the operating system.

Regional settings include such things as time zone and the formatting of currency and dates. `CurrentCulture` determines the default behavior of such functions as `DateTime.Parse`. Regional settings can be customized to the point where they no longer resemble any particular culture.

`CurrentUICulture` determines the language in which the computer communicates with the user. Australia doesn't need a separate version of English for this purpose, so it just uses the U.S. one. If I spent a couple of months working in Austria, I would go to the control panel and change my `CurrentCulture` to Austrian-German. However, since I can't speak German, my `CurrentUICulture` would remain U.S. English.

`ResourceManager`, by default, uses the current thread's `CurrentUICulture` property to determine the correct satellite assembly to load. `ResourceManager` uses a fall-back mechanism when loading resources. If a subculture assembly is defined, that one is used; otherwise, it falls back to the generic culture. If the generic culture is not present, it falls back to the default culture in the main assembly.

Resolving and Loading Assemblies

A typical application comprises a main executable assembly plus a set of referenced library assemblies. For example:

```
AdventureGame.exe
Terrain.dll
UIEngine.dll
```

Assembly resolution refers to the process of locating referenced assemblies. Assembly resolution happens both at compile time and at runtime. The compile-time system is simple: the compiler knows where to find referenced assemblies because it's told where to look. You (or Visual Studio) provide the full path to referenced assemblies that are not in the current directory.

Runtime resolution is more complicated. The compiler writes to the manifest, the strong names of referenced assemblies—but not any hints as to where to find them. In the simple case where you put all referenced assemblies in the same folder as the main executable, there's no issue because that's (close to) the first place the CLR looks. The complexities arise:

- When you deploy referenced assemblies in other places
- When you dynamically load assemblies

Assembly and Type Resolution Rules

All types are scoped to an assembly. An assembly is like an address for a type. To give an analogy, we can refer to a person as "Joe" (type name without namespace) or "Joe Bloggs" (full type name), or "Joe Bloggs of 100 Barker Ave, WA" (assembly-qualified type name).

During compilation, we don't need to go further than a full type name for unique-ness, because you can't reference two assemblies that define the same full type name (at least not without special tricks). At runtime, though, it's possible to have many identically named types in memory. This happens within the Visual Studio designer, for instance, whenever you *rebuild* the components you're designing. The only way to distinguish such types is by their assembly; therefore, an assembly forms an essential part of a type's runtime identity. An assembly is also a type's handle to its code and metadata.

The CLR loads assemblies at the point in execution when they're first needed. This happens when you refer to one of the assembly's types. For example, suppose that *AdventureGame.exe* instantiates a type called `TerrainModel.Map`. Assuming no additional configuration files, the CLR answers the following questions:

- What's the fully qualified name of the assembly that contained `TerrainModel.Map` when *AdventureGame.exe* was compiled?
- Have I already loaded into memory an assembly with this fully qualified name, in the same (resolution) context?

If the answer to the second question is yes, it uses the existing copy in memory; otherwise, it goes looking for the assembly. The CLR first checks the GAC, then the *probing* paths (generally the application base directory), and as a final resort, fires the `AppDomain.AssemblyResolve` event. If none returns a match, the CLR throws an exception.

AssemblyResolve

The `AssemblyResolve` event allows you to intervene and manually load an assembly that the CLR can't find. If you handle this event, you can scatter referenced assemblies in a variety of locations and still have them load.

Within the `AssemblyResolve` event handler, locate the assembly and load it by calling one of three static methods in the `Assembly` class: `Load`, `LoadFrom`, or `LoadFile`. These methods return a reference to the newly loaded assembly, which you then return to the caller:

```
static void Main()
{
  AppDomain.CurrentDomain.AssemblyResolve += FindAssem;
  ...
}

static Assembly FindAssem (object sender, ResolveEventArgs args)
{
  string fullyQualifiedName = args.Name;
  Assembly a = Assembly.LoadFrom (...);
  return a;
}
```

The `ResolveEventArgs` event is unusual in that it has a return type. If there are multiple handlers, the first one to return a nonnull `Assembly` wins.

Loading Assemblies

The `Load` methods in `Assembly` are useful both inside and outside an `AssemblyResolve` handler. Outside the event handler, they can load and execute assemblies not referenced at compilation. An example of when you might do this is to execute a plug-in.

 Think carefully before calling Load, LoadFrom, or LoadFile: these methods permanently load an assembly into the current application domain—even if you do nothing with the resultant Assembly object. Loading an assembly has side effects: it locks the assembly files as well as affecting subsequent type resolution.

The only way to unload an assembly is to unload the whole application domain.

If you just want to examine an assembly without executing any of its code, you can instead use the reflection-only context (see Chapter 17).

To load an assembly from a fully qualified name (without a location), call Assembly.Load. This instructs the CLR to find the assembly using its normal automatic resolution system. The CLR itself uses Load to find referenced assemblies.

To load an assembly from a filename, call LoadFrom or LoadFile.

To load an assembly from a URI, call LoadFrom.

To load an assembly from a byte array, call Load.

 You can see what assemblies are currently loaded in memory by calling AppDomain's GetAssemblies method:

```
foreach (Assembly a in
AppDomain.CurrentDomain.GetAssemblies())
{
  Console.WriteLine (a.Location);        // file path
  Console.WriteLine (a.GetName().Name);  // simple name
}
```

Loading from a filename

LoadFrom and LoadFile can both load an assembly from a filename. They differ in two ways. First, if an assembly with the same identity has already been loaded into memory from another location, LoadFrom gives you the previous copy:

```
Assembly a1 = Assembly.LoadFrom (@"c:\temp1\lib.dll");
Assembly a2 = Assembly.LoadFrom (@"c:\temp2\lib.dll");
Console.WriteLine (a1 == a2);                        // true
```

LoadFile gives you a fresh copy:

```
Assembly a1 = Assembly.LoadFile (@"c:\temp1\lib.dll");
Assembly a2 = Assembly.LoadFile (@"c:\temp2\lib.dll");
Console.WriteLine (a1 == a2);                        // false
```

If you load twice from an *identical* location, however, both methods give you the previously cached copy. (In contrast, loading an assembly twice from an identical byte array gives you two distinct Assembly objects.)

Types from two identical assemblies in memory are incompatible. This is the primary reason to avoid loading duplicate assemblies, and hence a reason to favor `LoadFrom` over `LoadFile`.

Whether you use `LoadFrom` or `LoadFile`, the CLR always looks first for the requested assembly in the GAC, and then the *probing path* (normally the application base directory). If you *really* want to load an assembly from a particular path, the only way to do it is with `ReflectionOnlyLoadFrom` (which loads the assembly into a reflection-only context). Even loading from a byte array doesn't bypass the GAC, although it does bypass the probing path:

```
byte[] image = File.ReadAllBytes (assemblyPath);
Assembly a = Assembly.Load (image);
```

Loading from a byte array also gets around the problem of locking assembly files! The drawback is that you must handle the `AppDomain`'s `AssemblyResolve` event in order to resolve any assemblies that the loaded assembly itself references.

The second difference between `LoadFrom` and `LoadFile` is that `LoadFrom` hints the CLR as to the location of onward references, whereas `LoadFile` does not. To illustrate, suppose your application in *folder1* loads an assembly in *folder2* called *TestLib.dll*, which references *folder2\Another.dll*:

```
\folder1\MyApplication.exe

\folder2\TestLib.dll
\folder2\Another.dll
```

If you load *TestLib* with `LoadFrom`, the CLR will find and load *Another.dll*.

If you load *TestLib* with `LoadFile`, the CLR will be unable to find *Another.dll* and will throw an exception—unless you also handle the `AssemblyResolve` event.

In the following sections, we demonstrate these methods in the context of some practical applications.

Deploying Assemblies Outside the Base Folder

Sometimes you might choose to deploy assemblies to locations other than the application base directory, for instance:

```
..\MyProgram\Main.exe
..\MyProgram\Libs\V1.23\GameLogic.dll
..\MyProgram\Libs\V1.23\3DEngine.dll
..\MyProgram\Terrain\Map.dll
..\Common\TimingController.dll
```

To make this work, you must assist the CLR in finding the assemblies outside the base folder. The easiest solution is to handle the `AssemblyResolve` event.

In the following example, we assume all additional assemblies are located in *c:\ExtraAssemblies*:

```
using System;
using System.IO;
```

```
using System.Reflection;

public class Loader
{
  static void Main( )
  {
    AppDomain.CurrentDomain.AssemblyResolve += FindAssem;

    // We must switch to another class before attempting to use
    // any of the types in c:\ExtraAssemblies:
    Program.Go( );
  }

  static Assembly FindAssem (object sender, ResolveEventArgs args)
  {
    string simpleName = new AssemblyName (args.Name).Name;
    string path = @"c:\ExtraAssemblies\" + simpleName + ".dll";

    if (!File.Exists (path)) return null;    // Sanity check
    return Assembly.LoadFrom (path);         // Load it up!
  }
}

public class Program
{
  public static void Go( )
  {
    // Now we can reference types defined in c:\ExtraAssemblies
  }
}
```

 It's vitally important in this example not to reference types in *c:\ ExtraAssemblies* directly from the Loader class (e.g., as fields), because the CLR would then attempt to resolve the type before hitting Main( ).

In this example, we could use either LoadFrom or LoadFile. In either case, the CLR verifies that the assembly that we hand it has the exact identity it requested. This maintains the integrity of strongly named references.

In Chapter 21, we describe another approach that can be used when creating new application domains. This involves setting the application domain's Private-BinPath to include the directories containing the additional assemblies—extending the standard assembly probing locations. A limitation of this is that the additional directories must all be *below* the application base directory.

Packing a Single-File Executable

Suppose you've written an application comprising 10 assemblies: 1 main executable file, plus 9 DLLs. Although such granularity can be great for design and debugging, it's also good to be able to pack the whole thing into a single "click and run" executable—without demanding the user perform some setup or file extraction ritual. You can accomplish this by including the compiled assembly DLLs in the main executable project as embedded resources, and then writing an `AssemblyResolve` event handler to load their binary images on demand. Here's how it's done:

```
using System;
using System.IO;
using System.Reflection;
using System.Collections.Generic;

public class Loader
{
  static Dictionary <string, Assembly> libs
   = new Dictionary <string, Assembly> ();

  static void Main( )
  {
    AppDomain.CurrentDomain.AssemblyResolve += FindAssem;
    Program.Go( );
  }

  static Assembly FindAssem (object sender, ResolveEventArgs args)
  {
    string shortName = new AssemblyName (args.Name).Name;
    if (libs.ContainsKey (shortName)) return libs [shortName];

    using (Stream s = Assembly.GetExecutingAssembly( ).
          GetManifestResourceStream ("Libs." + shortName + ".dll"))
    {
       byte[] data = new BinaryReader (s).ReadBytes ((int) s.Length);
       Assembly a = Assembly.Load (data);
       libs [shortName] = a;
       return a;
    }
  }
}

public class Program
{
  public static void Go( )
  {
    // Run main program...
  }
}
```

Because the `Loader` class is defined in the main executable, the call to `Assembly.GetExecutingAssembly` will always return the main executable assembly, where we've included the compiled DLLs as embedded resources. In this example, we prefix the name of each embedded resource assembly with `"Libs."`. If the Visual Studio IDE was used, you would change `"Libs."` to the project's default namespace (go to Project Properties → Application). You would also need to ensure that the "Build Action" IDE property on each of the DLL files included in the main project was set to "Embedded Resource".

The reason for caching requested assemblies in a dictionary is to ensure that if the CLR requests the same assembly again, we return exactly the same object. Otherwise, an assembly's types will be incompatible with those loaded previously (despite their binary images being identical).

A variation of this would be to compress the referenced assemblies at compilation, then decompress them in `FindAssem` using a `DeflateStream`.

Selective Patching

Suppose in this example that we want the executable to be able to autonomously update itself—perhaps from a network server or web site. Directly patching the executable not only would be awkward and dangerous, but also the required file I/O permissions may not be forthcoming (if installed in *Program Files*, for instance). An excellent workaround is to download any updated libraries to isolated storage (each as a separate DLL) and then modify the `FindAssem` method such that it first checks for the presence of a library in its isolated storage area before loading it from a resource in the executable. This leaves the original executable untouched and avoids leaving any unpleasant residue on the user's computer. Security is not compromised if your assemblies are strongly named (assuming they were referenced in compilation), and if something goes wrong, the application can always revert to its original state—simply by deleting all files in its isolated storage.

Working with Unreferenced Assemblies

Sometimes it's useful to explicitly load assemblies that may not have been referenced in compilation.

If the assembly in question is an executable and you simply want to run it, calling `ExecuteAssembly` on the current application domain does the job. `ExecuteAssembly` loads the executable using `LoadFrom` semantics, and then calls its entry method with optional command-line arguments. For instance:

```
string dir = AppDomain.CurrentDomain.BaseDirectory;
AppDomain.CurrentDomain.ExecuteAssembly (Path.Combine (dir, "test.exe"));
```

`ExecuteAssembly` works synchronously, meaning the calling method is blocked until the called assembly exits. To work asynchronously, you must call `Execute-Assembly` on another thread (see Chapter 19).

In most cases, though, the assembly you'll want to load is a library. The approach then is to call `LoadFrom`, and then use reflection to work with the assembly's types. For example:

```
string ourDir = AppDomain.CurrentDomain.BaseDirectory;
string plugInDir = Path.Combine (ourDir, "plugins");
Assembly a = Assembly.LoadFrom (Path.Combine (plugInDir, "widget.dll"));
Type t = a.GetType ("Namespace.TypeName");
object widget = Activator.CreateInstance (t);    // (See Chapter 17)
...
```

We used `LoadFrom` rather than `LoadFile` to ensure that any private assemblies *widget.dll* referenced in the same folder were also loaded. We then retrieved a type from the assembly by name and instantiated it.

The next step could be to use reflection to dynamically call methods and properties on widget; we describe how to do this in the following chapter. An easier— and faster—approach is to cast the object to a type that both assemblies understand. This is often an interface defined in a common assembly:

```
public interface IPluggable
{
  void ShowAboutBox( );
  ...
}
```

This allows us to do this:

```
Type t = a.GetType ("Namespace.TypeName");
IPluggable widget = (IPluggable) Activator.CreateInstance (t);
widget.ShowAboutBox( );
```

You can use a similar system for dynamically publishing services in a WCF or Remoting Server. The following assumes the libraries we want to expose end in "server":

```
using System.IO;
using System.Reflection;
...
string dir = AppDomain.CurrentDomain.BaseDirectory;
foreach (string assFile in Directory.GetFiles (dir, "*Server.dll"))
{
  Assembly a = Assembly.LoadFrom (assFile);
  foreach (Type t in a.GetTypes( ))
    if (typeof (MyBaseServerType).IsAssignableFrom (t))
    {
      // Expose type t
    }
}
```

This does make it very easy, though, for someone to add rogue assemblies, maybe even accidentally! Assuming no compile-time references, the CLR has nothing against which to check an assembly's identity. If everything that you load is signed with a known public key, the solution is to check that key explicitly. In the following example, we assume that all libraries are signed with the same key pair as the executing assembly:

```
byte[] ourPK = Assembly.GetExecutingAssembly().GetName().GetPublicKey( );

foreach (string assFile in Directory.GetFiles (dir, "*Server.dll"))
{
  byte[] targetPK = AssemblyName.GetAssemblyName (assFile).GetPublicKey( );
  if (Enumerable.SequenceEqual (ourPK, targetPK))
  {
    Assembly a = Assembly.LoadFrom (assFile);
    ...
```

Notice how AssemblyName allows you to check the public key *before* loading the assembly. To compare the byte arrays, we used LINQ's SequenceEqual method (System.Linq).

17

Reflection and Metadata

As we saw in Chapter 16, a C# program compiles into an assembly that includes metadata, compiled code, and resources. Inspecting the metadata and compiled code at runtime is called *reflection*.

The compiled code in an assembly contains almost all of the content of the original source code. Some information is lost, such as local variable names, comments, and preprocessor statements. However, reflection can access pretty much everything else, even making it possible to write a decompiler.

Many of the services available in .NET and exposed via C# (such as dynamic binding, serialization, data binding, and Remoting) depend on the presence of metadata. Your own programs can also take advantage of this metadata, and even extend it with new information using custom attributes. The System.Reflection namespace houses the reflection API. It is also possible at runtime to dynamically create new metadata and executable instructions in IL (Intermediate Language) via the classes in the System.Reflection.Emit namespace.

The examples in this chapter assume that you import the System and System.Reflection, as well as System.Reflection.Emit namespaces.

Reflecting and Activating Types

In this section, we examine how to obtain a Type, inspect its metadata, and use it to dynamically instantiate an object.

Obtaining a Type

An instance of System.Type represents the metadata for a type. Since Type is widely used, it lives in the System namespace rather than the System.Reflection namespace.

You can get an instance of a System.Type by calling GetType on any object or with C#'s typeof operator:

```
Type t1 = DateTime.Now.GetType( );      // Type obtained at runtime
Type t2 = typeof (DateTime);            // Type obtained at compile time
```

You can use typeof to obtain array types and generic types as follows:

```
Type t3 = typeof (DateTime[]);          // 1-d Array type
Type t4 = typeof (DateTime[,]);         // 2-d Array type
Type t5 = typeof (Dictionary<int,int>); // Closed generic type
Type t6 = typeof (Dictionary<,>);       // Open generic type
```

You can also retrieve a Type by name. If you have a reference to its Assembly, call Assembly.GetType (we describe this further in the section "Reflecting Assemblies" later in this chapter):

```
Type t = Assembly.GetExecutingAssembly( ).GetType ("Demos.TestProgram");
```

If you don't have an Assembly object, you can obtain a type through its *assembly qualified name* (the type's full name followed by the assembly's fully qualified name). The assembly implicitly loads as if you called Assembly.Load(string):

```
Type t = Type.GetType ("System.Int32, mscorlib, Version=2.0.0.0, " +
                       "Culture=neutral, PublicKeyToken=b77a5c561934e089");
```

Once you have a System.Type object, you can use its properties to access the type's name, assembly, base type, visibility, and so on. For example:

```
Type stringType = typeof (String);
string name     = stringType.Name;        // String
Type baseType   = stringType.BaseType;     // typeof(Object)
Assembly assem  = stringType.Assembly;     // mscorlib.dll
bool isPublic   = stringType.IsPublic;     // true
```

A System.Type instance is a window into the entire metadata for the type—and the assembly in which it's defined.

 System.Type is abstract, so the typeof operator must actually give you a subclass of Type. The subclass that the CLR uses is internal to *mscorlib* and is called RuntimeType.

Obtaining array types

As we just saw, typeof and GetType work with array types. You can also obtain an array type by calling MakeArrayType on the *element* type:

```
Type tSimpleArray = typeof (int).MakeArrayType( );
Console.WriteLine (tSimpleArray == typeof (int[]));    // True
```

MakeArray can be passed an integer argument to make multidimensional rectangular arrays:

```
Type tCube = typeof (int).MakeArrayType (3);      // cube shaped
Console.WriteLine (tCube == typeof (int[,,]));    // True
```

GetElementType does the reverse: it dynamically retrieves an array type's element type:

```
Type e = typeof (int[]).GetElementType( );      // e == typeof (int)
```

GetArrayRank returns the number of dimensions of a rectangular array:

```
int rank = typeof (int[,,]).GetArrayRank( );   // 3
```

Obtaining nested types

To retrieve nested types, call GetNestedTypes on the containing type. For example:

```
foreach (Type t in typeof (System.Environment).GetNestedTypes( ))
  Console.WriteLine (t);
```

```
OUTPUT: System.Environment+SpecialFolder
```

The one caveat with nested types is that the CLR treats a nested type as having special "nested" accessibility levels. For example:

```
Type t = typeof (System.Environment.SpecialFolder);
Console.WriteLine (t.IsPublic);                    // False
Console.WriteLine (t.IsNestedPublic);              // True
```

Type Names

A type has Namespace, Name, and FullName properties. In most cases, FullName is a composition of the former two:

```
Type t = typeof (System.Text.StringBuilder);

Console.WriteLine (t.Namespace);      // System.Text
Console.WriteLine (t.Name);           // StringBuilder
Console.WriteLine (t.FullName);       // System.Text.StringBuilder
```

There are two exceptions to this rule: nested types and closed generic types.

 Type also has a property called AssemblyQualifiedName, which returns FullName followed by a comma and then the full name of its assembly. This is the same string that you can pass to Type.GetType, and it uniquely identifies a type within the default loading context.

Nested type names

With nested types, the containing type appears only in FullName:

```
Type t = typeof (System.Environment.SpecialFolder);

Console.WriteLine (t.Namespace);      // System
Console.WriteLine (t.Name);           // SpecialFolder
Console.WriteLine (t.FullName);       // System.Environment+StringBuilder
```

The + symbol differentiates the containing type from a nested namespace.

Generic type names

Generic type names are suffixed with the ` symbol, followed by the number of type parameters. If the generic type is open, this rule applies to both `Name` and `FullName`:

```
Type t = typeof (Dictionary<,>);
Console.WriteLine (t.Name);      // Dictionary`2
Console.WriteLine (t.FullName);  // System.Collections.Generic.Dictionary`2
```

If the generic type is closed, however, `FullName` (only) acquires a substantial extra appendage. Each type parameter's full *assembly qualified name* is enumerated:

```
Console.WriteLine (typeof (Dictionary<string,int>).FullName);
```

```
// OUTPUT:
System.Collections.Generic.Dictionary`2[[System.Int32, mscorlib,
Version=2.0.0.0, Culture=neutral, PublicKeyToken=b77a5c561934e089],
[System.String, mscorlib, Version=2.0.0.0, Culture=neutral,
PublicKeyToken=b77a5c561934e089]]
```

This ensures that `AssemblyQualifiedName` (a combination of the type's full name and assembly name) contains enough information to fully identify both the generic type and its type parameters.

Array and pointer type names

Arrays present with the same suffix that you use in a typeof expression:

```
Console.WriteLine (typeof ( int[]  ).Name);      // Int32[]
Console.WriteLine (typeof ( int[,] ).Name);      // Int32[,]
Console.WriteLine (typeof ( int[,] ).FullName);  // System.Int32[,]
```

Pointer types are similar:

```
Console.WriteLine (typeof (byte*).Name);      // Byte*
```

ref and out parameter type names

A `Type` describing a ref or out parameter has an `&` suffix:

```
Type t = typeof (bool).GetMethod ("TryParse").GetParameters( )[1]
                                          .ParameterType;
Console.WriteLine (t.Name);      // Boolean&
```

More on this in the later section "Reflecting and Invoking Members."

Base Types and Interfaces

`Type` exposes a `BaseType` property:

```
Type base1 = typeof (System.String).BaseType;
Type base2 = typeof (System.IO.FileStream).BaseType;

Console.WriteLine (base1.Name);      // Object
Console.WriteLine (base2.Name);      // Stream
```

The `GetInterfaces` method returns the interfaces that a type implements:

```
foreach (Type iType in typeof (Guid).GetInterfaces())
  Console.WriteLine (iType.Name);

IFormattable
IComparable
IComparable`1
IEquatable`1
```

Reflection provides two dynamic equivalents to C#'s static is operator:

IsInstanceOfType
: Accepts a type and instance

IsAssignableFrom
: Accepts two types

Here's an example of the first:

```
object obj  = Guid.NewGuid();
Type target = typeof (IFormattable);

bool isTrue  = obj is IFormattable;          // Static C# operator
bool alsoTrue = target.IsInstanceOfType (obj);   // Dynamic equivalent
```

IsAssignableFrom is more versatile:

```
Type target = typeof (IComparable), source = typeof (string);
Console.WriteLine (target.IsAssignableFrom (source));          // True
```

The IsSubclassOf method works on the same principle as IsAssignableFrom, but excludes interfaces.

Instantiating Types

The static Activator.CreateInstance method dynamically instantiates an object from its Type. CreateInstance accepts a Type and optional arguments that get passed to the constructor:

```
int i = (int) Activator.CreateInstance (typeof (int));

DateTime dt = (DateTime) Activator.CreateInstance (typeof (DateTime),
                                                   2000, 1, 1);
```

A MissingMethodException is thrown if the runtime can't find a suitable constructor.

Dynamic instantiation adds a few microseconds onto the time taken to construct the object. This is quite a lot in relative terms because the CLR is ordinarily very fast in instantiating objects (a simple new on a small class takes in the region of tens of nanoseconds).

CreateInstance lets you specify many other options, such as the assembly from which to load the type, the target application domain, and whether to bind to a nonpublic constructor.

To dynamically instantiate arrays based on just element type, first call MakeArrayType. You can also instantiate generic types: we describe this in the following section.

To dynamically instantiate a delegate, call Delegate.CreateDelegate. The following example demonstrates instantiating both an instance delegate and a static delegate:

```
class Program
{
  delegate int IntFunc (int x);

  static int Square (int x) { return x * x; }       // Static method
  int        Cube   (int x) { return x * x * x; }   // Instance method

  static void Main()
  {
    Delegate staticD = Delegate.CreateDelegate
      (typeof (IntFunc), typeof (Program), "Square");

    Delegate instanceD = Delegate.CreateDelegate
      (typeof (IntFunc), new Program(), "Cube");

    Console.WriteLine (staticD.DynamicInvoke (3));     // 9
    Console.WriteLine (instanceD.DynamicInvoke (3));   // 27
  }
}
```

You can invoke the Delegate object that's returned by calling DynamicInvoke, as we did in this example, or by casting to the typed delegate:

```
IntFunc f = (IntFunc) staticD;
Console.WriteLine (f(3));        // 9 (but much faster!)
```

You can pass a MethodInfo into CreateDelegate instead of a method name. We describe MethodInfo shortly, in the section "Reflecting and Invoking Members," along with the rationale for casting a dynamically created delegate back to the static delegate type.

Generic Types

A Type can represent a closed or open generic type. Just as at compile time, a closed generic type can be instantiated whereas an open type cannot:

```
Type closed = typeof (List<int>);
List<int> list = (List<int>) Activator.CreateInstance (closed);  // OK

Type open   = typeof (List<>);
object anError = Activator.CreateInstance (open);     // Runtime error
```

The MakeGenericType method converts an open into a closed generic type. Simply pass in the desired type arguments:

```
Type open   = typeof (List<>);
Type closed = open.MakeGenericType (typeof (int));
```

The `GetGenericTypeDefinition` method does the opposite:

```
Type open2 = closed.GetGenericTypeDefinition( );     // open == open2
```

The `IsGenericType` property returns true if a `Type` is generic, and the `IsGenericTypeDefinition` property returns true if the generic type is open. The following tests whether a type is a nullable value type:

```
Type nullable = typeof (bool?);
Console.WriteLine (
  nullable.IsGenericType &&
  nullable.GetGenericTypeDefinition( ) == typeof (Nullable<>));    // True
```

`GetGenericArguments` returns the type arguments for closed generic types:

```
Console.WriteLine (closed.GetGenericArguments( )[0]);     // System.Int32
Console.WriteLine (nullable.GetGenericArguments( )[0]);   // System.Boolean
```

For open generic types, `GetGenericArguments` returns pseudotypes that represent the placeholder types specified in the generic type definition:

```
Console.WriteLine (open.GetGenericArguments( )[0]);     // T
```

Reflecting and Invoking Members

The `GetMembers` method returns the members of a type. Consider the following class:

```
class Walnut
{
  private bool cracked;
  public void Crack( ) { cracked = true; }
}
```

We can reflect on its public members as follows:

```
MemberInfo[] members = typeof (Walnut).GetMembers( );
foreach (MemberInfo m in members)
  Console.WriteLine (m);
```

This is the result:

```
Void Crack( )
System.Type GetType( )
System.String ToString( )
Boolean Equals(System.Object)
Int32 GetHashCode( )
Void .ctor( )
```

When called with no arguments, `GetMembers` returns all the public members for a type (and its base types). `GetMember` retrieves a specific member by name—though it still returns an array because members can be overloaded:

```
MemberInfo[] m = typeof (Walnut).GetMember ("Crack");
Console.WriteLine (m[0]);                              // Void Crack( )
```

`MemberInfo` also has a property called `MemberType` of type `MemberTypes`. This is a flags enum with these values:

| All | Custom | Field | NestedType | TypeInfo |
| Constructor | Event | Method | Property | |

When calling GetMembers, you can pass in a MemberTypes instance to restrict the kinds of members that it returns. Alternatively, you can restrict the result set by calling GetMethods, GetFields, GetProperties, GetEvents, GetConstructors, or Get-NestedTypes. There are also singular versions of each of these to hone in on a specific member.

 It pays to be as specific as possible when retrieving a type member, so your code doesn't break if additional members are added later. If retrieving a method by name, specifying all parameter types ensures your code will still work if the method is later overloaded (we provide examples shortly, in the section "Method Parameters).

A MemberInfo object has a Name property and two Type properties:

DeclaringType
Returns the Type that defines the membe

ReflectedType
Returns the Type upon which GetMembers was called

The two differ with inherited members: DeclaringType returns the base type whereas RefectedType returns the subtype. The following example highlights this:

```
class Program
{
  static void Main( )
  {
    // MethodInfo is a subclass of MemberInfo; see Figure 17-1.

    MethodInfo test = typeof (Program).GetMethod ("ToString");
    MethodInfo obj  = typeof (object) .GetMethod ("ToString");

    Console.WriteLine (test.DeclaringType);    // System.Object
    Console.WriteLine (obj.DeclaringType);     // System.Object

    Console.WriteLine (test.ReflectedType);    // Program
    Console.WriteLine (obj.ReflectedType);     // System.Object

    Console.WriteLine (test == obj);           // False
  }
}
```

Because they have different ReflectedTypes, the test and obj objects are not equal. Their difference, however, is purely a fabrication of the reflection API; our Program type has no distinct ToString method in the underlying type system. We can verify that the two MethodInfo objects refer to the same method in either of two ways:

```
Console.WriteLine (test.MethodHandle == obj.MethodHandle);    // True

Console.WriteLine (test.MetadataToken == obj.MetadataToken    // True
               && test.Module == obj.Module);
```

A `MethodHandle` is unique to each (genuinely distinct) method within an application domain; a `MetadataToken` is unique across all types and members within an assembly module.

`MemberInfo` also defines methods to return custom attributes (see the section "Retrieving Attributes at Runtime" later in this chapter).

 You can obtain the `MethodBase` of the currently executing method by calling `MethodBase.GetCurrentMethod`.

Member Types

`MemberInfo` itself is light on members because it's an abstract base for the types shown in Figure 17-1.

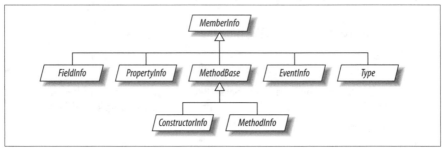

Figure 17-1. Member types

You can cast a `MemberInfo` to its subtype—based on its `MemberType` property. If you obtained a member via `GetMethod`, `GetField`, `GetProperty`, `GetEvent`, `GetConstructor`, or `GetNestedType` (or their plural versions), a cast isn't necessary. Table 17-1 summarizes what methods to use for each kind of C# construct.

Table 17-1. Retrieving member metadata

C# construct	Method to use	Name to use	Result
Method	GetMethod	Method name	MethodInfo
Property	GetProperty	Property name	PropertyInfo
Indexer	GetDefaultMembers		MemberInfo[] (containing PropertyInfo objects if compiled in C#)
Field	GetField	Field name	FieldInfo
Enum member	GetField	Member name	FieldInfo
Event	GetEvent	Event name	EventInfo
Constructor	GetConstructor		ConstructorInfo
Finalizer	GetMethod	"Finalize"	MethodInfo
Operator	GetMethod	"op_" + operator name	MethodInfo
Nested type	GetNestedType	Type name	Type

Each `MemberInfo` subclass has a wealth of properties and methods, exposing all aspects of the member's metadata. This includes such things as visibility, modifiers, generic type arguments, parameters, return type, and custom attributes.

Here is an example of using `GetMethod`:

```
MethodInfo m = typeof (Walnut).GetMethod ("Crack");
Console.WriteLine (m);                      // Void Crack()
Console.WriteLine (m.ReturnType);           // System.Void
```

All *Info instances are cached by the reflection API on first use:

```
MethodInfo method = typeof (Walnut).GetMethod ("Crack");
MemberInfo member = typeof (Walnut).GetMember ("Crack") [0];

Console.Write (method == member);       // True
```

As well as preserving object identity, caching improves the performance of what is otherwise a fairly slow API.

C# Members Versus CLR Members

The preceding table illustrates that some of C#'s functional constructs don't have a 1:1 mapping with CLR constructs. This makes sense because the CLR and reflection API were designed with all .NET languages in mind—you can use reflection even from Visual Basic.

Some C# constructs—namely indexers, enums, operators, and finalizers—are contrivances as far as the CLR is concerned. Specifically:

- A C# indexer translates to a property accepting one or more arguments, marked as the type's [DefaultMember].
- A C# enum translates to a subtype of System.Enum with a static field for each member.
- A C# operator translates to a specially named static method, starting in "op_"; for example, "op_Addition".
- A C# finalizer translates to a method that overrides Finalize.

Another complication is that properties and events actually comprise two things:

- Metadata describing the property or event (encapsulated by PropertyInfo or EventInfo)
- One or two backing methods

In a C# program, the backing methods are encapsulated within the property or event definition. But when compiled to IL, the backing methods present as ordinary methods that you can call like any other. This means GetMethods returns property and event backing methods alongside ordinary methods. To illustrate:

```
class Test { public int X { get { return 0; } set {} } }

void Demo()
{
  foreach (MethodInfo mi in typeof (Test).GetMethods())
    Console.Write (mi.Name + "   ");
```

```
}

// OUTPUT:
get_X  set_X  GetType  ToString  Equals  GetHashCode
```

You can identify these methods through the IsSpecialName property in
MethodInfo. IsSpecialName returns true for property, indexer, and event accessors—as well as operators. It returns false only for conventional C# methods—
and the Finalize method if a finalizer is defined.

Here are the backing methods that C# generates:

C# construct	Member type	Methods in IL
Property	Property	get_*XXX* and set_*XXX*
Indexer	Property	get_Item and set_Item
Event	Event	add_*XXX* and remove_*XXX*

Each backing method has its own associated MethodInfo object. You can access
these as follows:

```
PropertyInfo pi = typeof (Console).GetProperty ("Title");
MethodInfo getter = pi.GetGetMethod( );               // get_Title
MethodInfo setter = pi.GetSetMethod( );               // set_Title
MethodInfo[] both = pi.GetAccessors( );               // Length==2
```

GetAddMethod and GetRemoveMethod perform a similar job for EventInfo.

To go in the reverse direction—from a MethodInfo to its associated PropertyInfo
or EventInfo—you need to perform a query. LINQ is ideal for this job:

```
PropertyInfo p = mi.DeclaringType.GetProperties( )
                   .First (x => x.GetAccessors (true).Contains (mi));
```

Generic Type Members

You can obtain member metadata for both open and closed generic types:

```
PropertyInfo open   = typeof (IEnumerator<>)   .GetProperty ("Current");
PropertyInfo closed = typeof (IEnumerator<int>).GetProperty ("Current");

Console.WriteLine (open);     // T Current
Console.WriteLine (closed);   // Int32 Current

Console.WriteLine (open .PropertyType.IsGenericParameter);   // True
Console.WriteLine (closed.PropertyType.IsGenericParameter);  // False
```

The MemberInfo objects returned from open and closed generic types are always
distinct—even for members whose signatures don't feature generic type
parameters:

```
PropertyInfo open   = typeof (List<>)   .GetProperty ("Count");
PropertyInfo closed = typeof (List<int>).GetProperty ("Count");

Console.WriteLine (open);     // Int32 Count
Console.WriteLine (closed);   // Int32 Count
```

```
Console.WriteLine (open == closed);    // False

Console.WriteLine (open  .DeclaringType.IsGenericTypeDefinition); // True
Console.WriteLine (closed.DeclaringType.IsGenericTypeDefinition); // False
```

Members of open generic types cannot be *dynamically invoked*.

Dynamically Invoking a Member

Once you have a `MemberInfo` object, you can dynamically call it or get/set its value. This is called *dynamic binding* or *late binding*, because you choose which member to invoke at runtime rather than compile time.

To illustrate, the following uses ordinary *static binding*:

```
string s = "Hello";
int length = s.Length;
```

Here's the same thing performed dynamically with reflection:

```
object s = "Hello";
PropertyInfo prop = s.GetType( ).GetProperty ("Length");
int length = (int) prop.GetValue (s, null);              // 5
```

`GetValue` and `SetValue` get and set the value of a `PropertyInfo` or `FieldInfo`. The first argument is the instance, which can be `null` for a static member. Accessing an indexer is just like accessing a property called "Item," except that you provide indexer values as the second argument when calling `GetValue` or `SetValue`.

To dynamically call a method, call `Invoke` on a `MethodInfo`, providing an array of arguments to pass to that method. If you get any of the argument types wrong, an exception is thrown at runtime. With dynamic binding, you lose compile-time type safety, but still have runtime type safety.

Method Parameters

Suppose we want to dynamically call `string`'s `Substring` method. Statically, this would be done as follows:

```
Console.WriteLine ("stamp".Substring(2));                    // "amp"
```

Here's the dynamic equivalent:

```
Type type = typeof (string);
Type[] parameterTypes = { typeof (int) };
MethodInfo method = type.GetMethod ("Substring", parameterTypes);

object[] arguments = { 2 };
object returnValue = method.Invoke ("stamp", arguments);
Console.WriteLine (returnValue);                             // "amp"
```

Because the `Substring` method is overloaded, we had to pass an array of parameter types to `GetMethod` to indicate which version we wanted. Without the parameter types, `GetMethod` would throw an `AmbiguousMatchException`.

The GetParameters method, defined on MethodBase (the base class for MethodInfo and ConstructorInfo), returns parameter metadata. We can continue our previous example as follows:

```
ParameterInfo[] paramList = method.GetParameters();
foreach (ParameterInfo x in paramList)
{
  Console.WriteLine (x.Name);              // startIndex
  Console.WriteLine (x.ParameterType);     // System.Int32
}
```

To pass ref or out parameters, call MakeByRefType on the type before obtaining the method. For instance, this code:

```
int x;
bool successfulParse = int.TryParse ("23", out x);
```

can be dynamically executed as follows:

```
object[] args = { "23", 0 };
Type[] argTypes = { typeof (string), typeof (int).MakeByRefType() };
MethodInfo tryParse = typeof (int).GetMethod ("TryParse", argTypes);
bool successfulParse = (bool) tryParse.Invoke (null, args);

Console.WriteLine (successfulParse + " " + args[1]);       // True 23
```

This same approach works for both ref and out parameter types.

Using Delegates for Performance

Dynamic invocations are relatively inefficient, with an overhead typically in the few-microseconds region. If you're calling a method repeatedly in a loop, you can shift the per-call overhead into the nanoseconds region by instead calling a dynamically instantiated delegate that targets your dynamic method. In the following example, we dynamically call string's Trim method a million times without significant overhead:

```
delegate string StringToString (string s);

static void Main()
{
  MethodInfo trimMethod = typeof (string).GetMethod ("Trim", new Type[0]);
  var trim = (StringToString) Delegate.CreateDelegate
                              (typeof (StringToString), trimMethod);
  for (int i = 0; i < 1000000; i++)
    trim ("test");
}
```

This is faster because the costly dynamic binding (shown in bold) happens just once.

Accessing Nonpublic Members

All of the methods on types used to probe metadata (e.g., GetProperty, GetField, etc.) have overloads that take a BindingFlags enum. This enum serves as a meta-data filter and allows you to change the default selection criteria. The most common use for this is to retrieve nonpublic members.

For instance, consider the following class:

```
class Walnut
{
  private bool cracked;
  public void Crack() { cracked = true; }

  public override string ToString() { return cracked.ToString( ); }
}
```

We can *uncrack* the walnut as follows:

```
Type t = typeof (Walnut);
Walnut w = new Walnut( );
w.Crack( );
FieldInfo f = t.GetField ("cracked", BindingFlags.NonPublic |
                                      BindingFlags.Instance);
f.SetValue (w, false);
Console.WriteLine (w);         // False
```

Using reflection to access nonpublic members is powerful, but it is also dangerous, since you can bypass encapsulation, creating an unmanageable dependency on the internal implementation of a type.

The BindingFlags enum

BindingFlags is intended to be bitwise-combined. In order to get any matches at all, you need to start with one of the following four combinations:

```
BindingFlags.Public    | BindingFlags.Instance
BindingFlags.Public    | BindingFlags.Static
BindingFlags.NonPublic | BindingFlags.Instance
BindingFlags.NonPublic | BindingFlags.Static
```

NonPublic includes internal, protected, protected internal, and private.

The following example retrieves all the public static members of type object:

```
BindingFlags publicStatic = BindingFlags.Public | BindingFlags.Static;
MemberInfo[] members = typeof (object).GetMembers (publicStatic);
```

The following example retrieves all the nonpublic members of type object, both static and instance:

```
BindingFlags nonPublicBinding =
    BindingFlags.NonPublic | BindingFlags.Static | BindingFlags.Instance;

MemberInfo[] members = typeof (object).GetMembers (nonPublicBinding);
```

The DeclaredOnly flag excludes functions inherited from base types, unless they are overridden.

 The DeclaredOnly flag is somewhat confusing in that it *restricts* the result set (whereas all the other binding flags *expand* the result set).

Generic Methods

Generic methods cannot be invoked directly; the following throws an exception:

```
class Program
{
  public static T Echo<T> (T x) { return x; }

  static void Main()
  {
    MethodInfo echo = typeof (Program).GetMethod ("Echo");
    Console.WriteLine (echo.IsGenericMethodDefinition);    // True
    echo.Invoke (null, new object[] { 123 } );             // Exception
  }
}
```

An extra step is required, which is to call MakeGenericMethod on the MethodInfo, specifying concrete generic type arguments. This returns another MethodInfo, which you can then invoke as follows:

```
MethodInfo echo = typeof (Program).GetMethod ("Echo");
MethodInfo intEcho = echo.MakeGenericMethod (typeof (int));
Console.WriteLine (intEcho.IsGenericMethodDefinition);        // False
Console.WriteLine (intEcho.Invoke (null, new object[] { 3 } ));  // 3
```

Anonymously Calling Members of a Generic Type

Dynamic binding is useful when you need to invoke a member of a generic type and you don't know the type parameters until runtime. In theory, the need for this arises rarely if types are perfectly designed; of course, types are not always perfectly designed.

For instance, suppose we want to write a more powerful version of ToString that could expand the result of LINQ queries. We could start out as follows:

```
public static string ToStringEx <T> (IEnumerable<T> sequence)
{
  ...
}
```

This is already quite limiting. What if sequence contained *nested* collections that we also want to enumerate? We'd have to overload the method to cope:

```
public static string ToStringEx <T> (IEnumerable<IEnumerable<T>> sequence)
```

And then what if sequence contained groupings, or *projections* of nested sequences? The static solution of method overloading becomes impractical. What's needed is an approach that can scale to handle an arbitrary object graph:

```
public static string ToStringEx (object value)
{
  if (value == null) return "<null>";
  StringBuilder sb = new StringBuilder();

  if (value is List<>)                                        // Error
    sb.Append ("List of " + ((List<>) value).Count + " items");  // Error
```

```
    if (value is IGrouping<,>)                                      // Error
      sb.Append ("Group with key=" + ((IGrouping<,>) value).Key);   // Error

    // Enumerate collection elements if this is a collection,
    // recursively calling ToStringEx( )
    // ...

    return sb.ToString( );
}
```

Unfortunately, this won't compile: you cannot invoke members of an *open* generic type such as List<> or IGrouping<>. In the case of List<>, we can solve the problem by using the nongeneric IList interface instead:

```
    if (value is IList)
      sb.AppendLine ("A list with " + ((IList) value).Count + " items");
```

 We can do this because the designers of List<> had the foresight to implement IList classic (as well as IList *generic*). The same principle is worthy of consideration when writing your own generic types: having a nongeneric interface or base class upon which consumers can fall back can be extremely valuable.

The solution is not as simple for IGrouping<,>. Here's how the interface is defined:

```
    public interface IGrouping <TKey,TElement> : IEnumerable <TElement>,
                                                 IEnumerable
    {
      TKey Key { get; }
    }
```

There's no nongeneric type we can use to access the Key property, so here we must use reflection. The solution is not to invoke members of an open generic type (which is impossible), but to invoke members of a *closed* generic type, whose type arguments we establish at runtime.

The first step is to determine whether value implements IGrouping<,>, and if so, obtain its closed generic interface. We can do this most easily with a LINQ query. Then we retrieve and invoke the Key property:

```
    public static string ToStringEx (object value)
    {
      if (value == null) return "<null>";
      if (value.GetType().IsPrimitive) return value.ToString( );

      StringBuilder sb = new StringBuilder( );

      if (value is IList)
        sb.Append ("List of " + ((IList)value).Count + " items: ");

      Type closedIGrouping = value.GetType().GetInterfaces( )
        .Where (t => t.IsGenericType &&
                     t.GetGenericTypeDefinition( ) == typeof (IGrouping<,>))
        .FirstOrDefault( );
```

```
    if (closedIGrouping != null)    // Call the Key property on IGrouping<,>
    {
      PropertyInfo pi = closedIGrouping.GetProperty ("Key");
      object key = pi.GetValue (value, null);
      sb.Append ("Group with key=" + key + ": ");
    }

    if (value is IEnumerable)
      foreach (object element in ((IEnumerable)value))
        sb.Append (ToStringEx (element) + " ");

    if (sb.Length == 0) sb.Append (value.ToString());

    return "\r\n" + sb.ToString();
  }
```

The following demonstrates this method:

```
Console.WriteLine (ToStringEx (new List<int> { 5, 6, 7 } ));
Console.WriteLine (ToStringEx ("xyyzzz".GroupBy (c => c) ));

List of 3 items: 5 6 7

Group with key=x: x
Group with key=y: y y
Group with key=z: z z z
```

Reflecting Assemblies

You can dynamically reflect an assembly by calling GetType or GetTypes on an Assembly object. The following retrieves from the current assembly, the type called TestProgram in the Demos namespace:

```
Type t = Assembly.GetExecutingAssembly().GetType ("Demos.TestProgram");
```

The next example lists all the types in the assembly *mylib.dll* in *e:\demo*:

```
Assembly a = Assembly.LoadFrom (@"e:\demo\mylib.dll");

foreach (Type t in a.GetTypes())
  Console.WriteLine (t);
```

GetTypes returns only top-level and not nested types.

Loading an Assembly into a Reflection-Only Context

In the preceding example, we loaded an assembly into the current application domain in order to list its types. This can have undesirable side effects, such as executing static constructors or upsetting subsequent type resolution. The solution, if you just need to inspect type information (and not instantiate or invoke types), is to load the assembly into a *reflection-only* context:

```
Assembly a = Assembly.ReflectionOnlyLoadFrom (@"e:\demo\mylib.dll");
Console.WriteLine (a.ReflectionOnly);    // True

foreach (Type t in a.GetTypes())
  Console.WriteLine (t);
```

This is the starting point for writing a class browser.

There are three methods for loading an assembly into the reflection-only context:

- `ReflectionOnlyLoad (byte[])`
- `ReflectionOnlyLoad (string)`
- `ReflectionOnlyLoadFrom (string)`

 Even in a reflection-only context, it is not possible to load multiple versions of *mscorlib.dll*. For this reason, class browsers such as Lutz Roeder's .NET Reflector are written with custom classes and structs that map to the unmanaged metadata interfaces.

Modules

Calling `GetTypes` on a multimodule assembly returns all types in all modules. As a result, you can ignore the existence of modules and treat an assembly as a type's container. There is one case, though, where modules are relevant—and that's when dealing with metadata tokens.

A metadata token is an integer that uniquely refers to a type, member, string, or resource within the scope of a module. IL uses metadata tokens, so if you're parsing IL, you'll need to be able to resolve them. The methods for doing this are defined in the `Module` type and are called `ResolveType`, `ResolveMember`, `ResolveString`, and `ResolveSignature`. We revisit this in the final section of this chapter, in writing a disassembler.

You can obtain a list of all the modules in an assembly by calling `GetModules`. You can also access an assembly's main module directly—via its `ManifestModule` property.

Working with Attributes

The CLR allows additional metadata to be attached to types, members, and assemblies through attributes. This is the mechanism by which many CLR functions such as serialization and security are directed, making attributes an indivisible part of an application.

A key characteristic of attributes is that you can write your own, and then use them just as you would any other attribute to "decorate" a code element with additional information. This additional information is compiled into the underlying assembly and can be retrieved at runtime using reflection to build services that work declaratively, such as automated unit testing.

Attribute Basics

There are three kinds of attributes:

- Bit-mapped attributes
- Custom attributes
- Pseudocustom attributes

Of these, only *custom attributes* are extensible.

The term "attribute" by itself can refer to any of the three, although in the C# world, it most often refers to custom attributes or pseudocustom attributes.

Bit-mapped attributes (our terminology) map to dedicated bits in a type's metadata. Most of C#'s modifier keywords, such as public, abstract, and sealed, compile to bit-mapped attributes. These attributes are very efficient because they consume minimal space in the metadata (usually just one bit), and the CLR can locate them with little or no indirection. The reflection API exposes them via dedicated properties on Type (and other MemberInfo subclasses), such as IsPublic, IsAbstract, and IsSealed. The Attributes property returns a flags enum that describes most of them in one hit:

```
static void Main( )
{
  TypeAttributes ta = typeof (Console).Attributes;
  MethodAttributes ma = MethodInfo.GetCurrentMethod( ).Attributes;
  Console.WriteLine (ta + "\r\n" + ma);
}
```

Here's the result:

```
AutoLayout, AnsiClass, Class, Public, Abstract, Sealed, BeforeFieldInit
PrivateScope, Private, Static, HideBySig
```

In contrast, *custom attributes* compile to a blob that hangs off the type's main metadata table. All custom attributes are represented by a subclass of System. Attribute and, unlike bit-mapped attributes, are extensible. The blob in the metadata identifies the attribute class, and also stores the values of any positional or named argument that was specified when the attribute was applied. Custom attributes that you define yourself are architecturally identical to those defined in the .NET Framework.

Chapter 4 describes how to attach custom attributes to a type or member in C#. Here, we attach the predefined Obsolete attribute to the Foo class:

```
[Obsolete] public class Foo {...}
```

This instructs the compiler to incorporate an instance of ObsoleteAttribute into the metadata for Foo, which can then be reflected at runtime by calling GetCustomAttributes on a Type or MemberInfo object.

Pseudocustom attributes look and feel just like standard custom attributes. They are represented by a subclass of System.Attribute and are attached in the standard manner:

```
[Serializable] public class Foo {...}
```

The difference is that the compiler or CLR internally optimizes pseudocustom attributes by converting them to bit-mapped attributes. Examples include [Serializable] (Chapter 15), StructLayout, In, and Out (Chapter 22). Reflection exposes psuedocustom attributes through dedicated properties such as IsSerializable, and in many cases they are also returned as System.Attribute objects when you call GetCustomAttributes (SerializableAttribute included). This means you can (almost) ignore the difference between pseudo- and non-pseudocustom attributes (a notable exception is when using Reflection.Emit to generate types dynamically at runtime; see "Emitting Assemblies and Types" later in this chapter).

The AttributeUsage Attribute

AttributeUsage is an attribute applied to attribute classes. It tells the compiler how the target attribute should be used:

```
public sealed class AttributeUsageAttribute : Attribute
{
  public AttributeUsageAttribute (AttributeTargets validOn);

  public bool AllowMultiple     { get; set; }
  public bool Inherited         { get; set; }
  public AttributeTargets ValidOn { get; }
}
```

AllowMultiple controls whether the attribute being defined can be applied more than once to the same target; Inherited controls whether the attribute can be subtyped. ValidOn determines the set of targets (classes, interfaces, properties, methods, parameters, etc.) to which the attribute can be attached. It accepts any combination of values from the AttributeTargets enum, which has the following members:

All	Delegate	GenericParameter	Parameter
Assembly	Enum	Interface	Property
Class	Event	Method	ReturnValue
Constructor	Field	Module	Struct

To illustrate, here's how the authors of the .NET Framework have applied AttributeUsage to the Serializable attribute:

```
[AttributeUsage (AttributeTargets.Delegate |
                 AttributeTargets.Enum     |
                 AttributeTargets.Struct   |
                 AttributeTargets.Class,     Inherited = false)
]
public sealed class SerializableAttribute : Attribute
{
}
```

This is, in fact, almost the complete definition of the Serializable attribute. Writing an attribute class that has no properties or special constructors is this simple.

Defining Your Own Attribute

Here's how you write your own attribute:

1. Derive a class from System.Attribute or a descendent of System.Attribute. By convention, the class name should end with the word "Attribute," although this isn't required.

2. Apply the AttributeUsage attribute, described in the preceding section.

   If the attribute requires no properties or arguments in its constructor, the job is done.

3. Write one or more public constructors. The parameters to the constructor define the positional parameters of the attribute and will become mandatory when using the attribute.

4. Declare a public field or property for each named parameter you wish to support. Named parameters are optional when using the attribute.

> Attribute properties and constructor parameters must be of the following types:
> - A sealed primitive type; in other words, bool, byte, char, double, float, int, long, short, or string
> - The Type type
> - An enum type
> - A one-dimensional array of any of these
>
> When an attribute is applied, it must also be possible for the compiler to statically evaluate each of the properties or constructor arguments.

The following class defines an attribute for assisting an automated unit-testing system. It indicates that a method should be tested, the number of test repetitions, and a message in case of failure:

```
[AttributeUsage (AttributeTargets.Method)]
public sealed class TestAttribute : Attribute
{
  public int     Repetitions;
  public string  FailureMessage;

  public TestAttribute () : this (1)     {}
  public TestAttribute (int repetitions) { Repetitions = repetitions; }
}
```

Here's a Foo class with methods decorated in various ways with the Test attribute:

```
class Foo
{
  [Test]
  public void Method1() { ... }

  [Test(20)]
  public void Method2() { ... }

  [Test(20, FailureMessage="Debugging Time!")]
  public void Method3() { ... }
}
```

Retrieving Attributes at Runtime

There are two standard ways to retrieve attributes at runtime:

- Call GetCustomAttributes on any Type or MemberInfo object.
- Call Attribute.GetCustomAttribute or Attribute.GetCustomAttributes.

These latter two methods are overloaded to accept any reflection object that corresponds to a valid attribute target (Type, Assembly, Module, MemberInfo, or ParameterInfo).

Here's how we can enumerate each method in the preceding Foo class that has a TestAttribute:

```
foreach (MethodInfo mi in typeof (Foo).GetMethods())
{
  TestAttribute att = (TestAttribute) Attribute.GetCustomAttribute
    (mi, typeof (TestAttribute));

  if (att != null)
    Console.WriteLine ("Method {0} will be tested; reps={1}; msg={2}",
                       mi.Name, att.Repetitions, att.FailureMessage);
}
```

Here's the output:

```
Method Method1 will be tested; reps=1; msg=
Method Method2 will be tested; reps=20; msg=
Method Method3 will be tested; reps=20; msg=Debugging Time!
```

To complete the illustration on how we could use this to write a unit-testing system, here's the same example expanded so that it actually calls the methods decorated with the Test attribute:

```
foreach (MethodInfo mi in typeof (Foo).GetMethods())
{
  TestAttribute att = (TestAttribute) Attribute.GetCustomAttribute
    (mi, typeof (TestAttribute));

  if (att != null)
    for (int i = 0; i < att.Repetitions; i++)
      try
      {
        mi.Invoke (new Foo(), null);    // Call method with no arguments
      }
      catch (Exception ex)         // Wrap exception in att.FailureMessage
      {
        throw new Exception ("Error: " + att.FailureMessage, ex);
      }
}
```

Returning to attribute reflection, here's an example that lists the attributes present on a specific type:

```
[Serializable, Obsolete]
class Test
{
  static void Main()
  {
    object[] atts = Attribute.GetCustomAttributes (typeof (Test));
    foreach (object att in atts) Console.WriteLine (att);
  }
}
```

Output:

```
System.ObsoleteAttribute
System.SerializableAttribute
```

Retrieving Attributes in the Reflection-Only Context

Calling GetCustomAttributes on a member loaded in the reflection-only context is prohibited because it would require instantiating arbitrarily typed attributes (remember that object instantiation isn't allowed in the reflection-only context). To work around this, there's a special type called CustomAttributeData for reflecting over such attributes. Here's an example of how it's used:

```
IList<CustomAttributeData> atts = CustomAttributeData.GetCustomAttributes
                                  (myReflectionOnlyType);
foreach (CustomAttributeData att in atts)
{
  Console.Write (att.GetType());                  // Attribute type

  Console.WriteLine (" " + att.Constructor);    // ConstructorInfo object

  foreach (CustomAttributeTypedArgument arg in att.ConstructorArguments)
    Console.WriteLine ("  " +arg.ArgumentType + "=" + arg.Value);

  foreach (CustomAttributeNamedArgument arg in att.NamedArguments)
    Console.WriteLine ("  " + arg.MemberInfo.Name + "=" + arg.TypedValue);
}
```

In many cases, the attribute types will be in a different assembly to the one you're reflecting. One way to cope with this is to handle the ReflectionOnly-AssemblyResolve event on the current application domain:

```
ResolveEventHandler handler = (object sender, ResolveEventArgs args)
                              => Assembly.ReflectionOnlyLoad (args.Name);

AppDomain.CurrentDomain.ReflectionOnlyAssemblyResolve += handler;

// Reflect over attributes...

AppDomain.CurrentDomain.ReflectionOnlyAssemblyResolve -= handler;
```

Dynamic Code Generation

The System.Reflection.Emit namespace contains classes for creating metadata and IL at runtime. Generating code dynamically is useful for certain kinds of programming tasks. An example is the regular expressions API, which emits performant types tuned to specific regular expressions. Other uses of Reflection. Emit in the Framework include dynamically generating transparent proxies for Remoting and generating types that perform specific XSLT transforms with minimum runtime overhead.

Generating IL with DynamicMethod

The DynamicMethod class is a lightweight tool in the System.Reflection.Emit namespace for generating a method on the fly. Unlike TypeBuilder, it doesn't require that you first set up a dynamic assembly, module, and type in which to contain the method. This makes it suitable for simple tasks—as well as serving as a good introduction to Reflection.Emit.

> A DynamicMethod and the associated IL are garbage-collected when no longer referenced. This means you can repeatedly generate dynamic methods without filling up memory. In contrast, dynamic *assemblies* cannot be unloaded from memory unless the containing application domain is torn down.

Here is a simple use of DynamicMethod to create a method that writes Hello world to the console:

```
public class Test
{
  static void Main( )
  {
    var dynMeth = new DynamicMethod ("Foo", null, null, typeof (Test));
    ILGenerator gen = dynMeth.GetILGenerator( );
    gen.EmitWriteLine ("Hello world");
    gen.Emit (OpCodes.Ret);
    dynMeth.Invoke (null, null);                 // Hello world
  }
}
```

OpCodes has a static read-only field for every IL opcode. Most of the functionality is exposed through various opcodes, although ILGenerator also has specialized methods for generating labels and local variables and for exception handling. A method always ends in Opcodes.Ret, which means "return." The EmitWriteLine method on ILGenerator is a shortcut for Emitting a number of lower-level opcodes. We could have replaced the call to EmitWriteLine with this, and we would have gotten the same result:

```
MethodInfo writeLineStr = typeof (Console).GetMethod ("WriteLine",
                          new Type[] { typeof (string) });
```

```
gen.Emit (OpCodes.Ldstr, "Hello world");     // Load a string
gen.Emit (OpCodes.Call, writeLineStr);       // Call a method
```

Note that we passed typeof(Test) into DynamicMethod's constructor. This gives the dynamic method access to the nonpublic methods of that type, allowing us to do this:

```
public class Test
{
  static void Main( )
  {
    var dynMeth = new DynamicMethod ("Foo", null, null, typeof (Test));
    ILGenerator gen = dynMeth.GetILGenerator( );

    MethodInfo privateMethod = typeof(Test).GetMethod ("HelloWorld",
      BindingFlags.Static | BindingFlags.NonPublic);

    gen.Emit (OpCodes.Call, privateMethod);     // Call HelloWorld
    gen.Emit (OpCodes.Ret);

    dynMeth.Invoke (null, null);                // Hello world
  }

  static void HelloWorld( )      // private method, yet we can call it
  {
    Console.WriteLine ("Hello world");
  }
}
```

Understanding IL requires a considerable investment of time. Rather than understand all the opcodes, it's much easier to compile a C# program then to examine, copy, and tweak the IL. An assembly viewing tool such as *ildasm* or Lutz Roeder's Reflector is perfect for the job.

The Evaluation Stack

Central to IL is the concept of the *evaluation stack*. The evaluation stack is distinct from the stack used to store local variables and method parameters.

To call a method with arguments, you first push ("load") the arguments onto the evaluation stack, and then call the method. The method then pops the arguments it needs from the evaluation stack. We demonstrated this previously, in calling Console.WriteLine. Here's a similar example with an integer:

```
var dynMeth = new DynamicMethod ("Foo", null, null, typeof(void));
ILGenerator gen = dynMeth.GetILGenerator( );
MethodInfo writeLineInt = typeof (Console).GetMethod ("WriteLine",
                                new Type[] { typeof (int) });

// The Ldc* op-codes load numeric literals of various types and sizes.

gen.Emit (OpCodes.Ldc_I4, 123);        // Push a 4-byte integer onto stack
gen.Emit (OpCodes.Call, writeLineInt);

gen.Emit (OpCodes.Ret);
dynMeth.Invoke (null, null);           // 123
```

To add two numbers together, you first load each number onto the evaluation stack, and then call Add. The Add opcode pops two values from the evaluation stack and pushes the result back on. The following adds 2 and 2, and then writes the result using the writeLine method obtained previously:

```
gen.Emit (OpCodes.Ldc_I4, 2);          // Push a 4-byte integer, value=2
gen.Emit (OpCodes.Ldc_I4, 2);          // Push a 4-byte integer, value=2
gen.Emit (OpCodes.Add);                // Add the result together
gen.Emit (OpCodes.Call, writeLineInt);
```

To calculate 10 / 2 + 1, you can do either this:

```
gen.Emit (OpCodes.Ldc_I4, 10);
gen.Emit (OpCodes.Ldc_I4, 2);
gen.Emit (OpCodes.Div);
gen.Emit (OpCodes.Ldc_I4, 1);
gen.Emit (OpCodes.Add);
gen.Emit (OpCodes.Call, writeLineInt);
```

or this:

```
gen.Emit (OpCodes.Ldc_I4, 1);
gen.Emit (OpCodes.Ldc_I4, 10);
gen.Emit (OpCodes.Ldc_I4, 2);
gen.Emit (OpCodes.Div);
gen.Emit (OpCodes.Add);
gen.Emit (OpCodes.Call, writeLineInt);
```

Passing Arguments to a Dynamic Method

You can load an argument passed into a dynamic method onto the stack with the Ldarg and Ldarg_*XXX* opcodes. To return a value, leave exactly one value on the stack upon finishing. For this to work, you must specify the return type and argument types when calling DefineMethod. The following creates a dynamic method that returns the sum of two integers:

```
DynamicMethod dynMeth = new DynamicMethod ("Foo",
   typeof (int),                            // Return type = int
   new[] { typeof (int), typeof (int) },    // Parameter types = int, int
   typeof (void));

ILGenerator gen = dynMeth.GetILGenerator( );

gen.Emit (OpCodes.Ldarg_0);     // Push first arg onto eval stack
gen.Emit (OpCodes.Ldarg_1);     // Push second arg onto eval stack
gen.Emit (OpCodes.Add);         // Add them together (result on stack)
gen.Emit (OpCodes.Ret);         // Return with stack having 1 value

int result = (int) dynMeth.Invoke (null, new object[] { 3, 4 } );   // 7
```

> When you exit, the evaluation stack must have exactly 0 or 1 item (depending on whether your method returns a value). If you violate this, the CLR will refuse to execute your method. You can remove an item from the stack without processing it with OpCodes.Pop.

Rather than calling Invoke, it can be more convenient to work with a dynamic method as a typed delegate. The CreateDelegate method achieves just this. To illustrate, suppose we define a delegate called BinaryFunction:

```
delegate int BinaryFunction (int n1, int n2);
```

We could then replace the last line of our preceding example with this:

```
BinaryFunction f = (BinaryFunction) dynMeth.CreateDelegate
                                     (typeof (BinaryFunction));
int result = f (3, 4);      // 7
```

 A delegate also eliminates the overhead of dynamic method invocation—saving a few microseconds per call.

We demonstrate how to pass by reference later in the section "Emitting Type Members."

Generating Local Variables

You can declare a local variable by calling DeclareLocal on an ILGenerator. This returns a LocalBuilder object, which can be used in conjunction with opcodes such as Ldloc (load a local variable) or Stloc (store a local variable). Ldloc pushes the evaluation stack; Stloc pops it. For example, consider the following C# code:

```
int x = 6;
int y = 7;
x *= y;
Console.WriteLine (x);
```

The following generates the preceding code dynamically:

```
var dynMeth = new DynamicMethod ("Test", null, null, typeof (void));
ILGenerator gen = dynMeth.GetILGenerator( );

LocalBuilder localX = gen.DeclareLocal (typeof (int));    // Declare x
LocalBuilder localY = gen.DeclareLocal (typeof (int));    // Declare y

gen.Emit (OpCodes.Ldc_I4, 6);        // Push literal 6 onto eval stack
gen.Emit (OpCodes.Stloc, localX);    // Store in localX
gen.Emit (OpCodes.Ldc_I4, 7);        // Push literal 7 onto eval stack
gen.Emit (OpCodes.Stloc, localY);    // Store in localY

gen.Emit (OpCodes.Ldloc, localX);    // Push localX onto eval stack
gen.Emit (OpCodes.Ldloc, localY);    // Push localY onto eval stack
gen.Emit (OpCodes.Mul);              // Multiply values together
gen.Emit (OpCodes.Stloc, localX);    // Store the result to localX

gen.EmitWriteLine (localX);          // Write the value of localX
gen.Emit (OpCodes.Ret);

dynMeth.Invoke (null, null);         // 42
```

Lutz Roeder's Reflector is also great for examining dynamic methods for errors. If you decompile to C#, it's usually quite obvious where you've gone wrong! We explain how to save dynamic emissions to disk in the section "Emitting Assemblies and Types."

Branching

In IL, there are no while, do, and for loops; it's all done with labels and the equivalent of goto and conditional goto statements. These are the branching opcodes, such as Br (branch unconditionally), Brtrue (branch if the value on the evaluation stack is true), and Blt (branch if the first value is less than the second value).

To set a branch target, first call DefineLabel (this returns a Label object), and then call MarkLabel at the place where you want to anchor the label. For example, consider the following C# code:

```
int x = 5;
while (x <= 10) Console.WriteLine (x++);
```

We can emit this as follows:

```
ILGenerator gen = ...

Label startLoop = gen.DefineLabel( );              // Declare labels
Label endLoop = gen.DefineLabel( );

LocalBuilder x = gen.DeclareLocal (typeof (int));  // int x
gen.Emit (OpCodes.Ldc_I4, 5);                      //
gen.Emit (OpCodes.Stloc, x);                       // x = 5

gen.MarkLabel (startLoop);
  gen.Emit (OpCodes.Ldc_I4, 10);                   // Load 10 onto eval stack
  gen.Emit (OpCodes.Ldloc, x);                     // Load x onto eval stack

  gen.Emit (OpCodes.Blt, endLoop);                 // if (x > 10) goto endLoop

  gen.EmitWriteLine (x);                           // Console.WriteLine (x)

  gen.Emit (OpCodes.Ldloc, x);                     // Load x onto eval stack
  gen.Emit (OpCodes.Ldc_I4, 1);                    // Load 1 onto the stack
  gen.Emit (OpCodes.Add);                          // Add them together
  gen.Emit (OpCodes.Stloc, x);                     // Save result back to x

  gen.Emit (OpCodes.Br, startLoop);                // return to start of loop
gen.MarkLabel (endLoop);

gen.Emit (OpCodes.Ret);
```

Instantiating Objects and Calling Instance Methods

The IL equivalent of new is the Newobj opcode. This takes a constructor and loads the constructed object onto the evaluation stack. For instance, the code shown next constructs a StringBuilder.

```
var dynMeth = new DynamicMethod ("Test", null, null, typeof (void));
ILGenerator gen = dynMeth.GetILGenerator( );

ConstructorInfo ci = typeof (StringBuilder).GetConstructor (new Type[0]);
gen.Emit (OpCodes.Newobj, ci);
```

Once an object is on the evaluation stack, you can call its instance methods using the Call or Callvirt opcode. Extending this example, we'll query the String-Builder's MaxCapacity property by calling the property's get accessor, and then write out the result:

```
gen.Emit (OpCodes.Callvirt, typeof (StringBuilder)
                          .GetProperty ("MaxCapacity").GetGetMethod( ));

gen.Emit (OpCodes.Call, typeof (Console).GetMethod ("WriteLine",
                                       new[] { typeof (int) } ));
gen.Emit (OpCodes.Ret);
dynMeth.Invoke (null, null);              // 2147483647
```

To emulate C# calling semantics:

- Use Call to invoke static methods and value type instance methods.
- Use Callvirt to invoke reference type instance methods (whether or not they're declared virtual).

In our example, we used Callvirt on the StringBuilder instance—even though MaxProperty is not virtual. This doesn't cause an error: it simply performs a nonvirtual call instead. Always invoking reference type instance methods with Callvirt avoids risking the opposite condition: invoking a virtual method with Call. (The risk is real. The author of the target method may later *change* its declaration.)

 Invoking a virtual method with Call bypasses virtual calling semantics, and calls that method directly. This is rarely desirable and, in effect, violates type safety.

In the following example, we construct a StringBuilder passing in two arguments, append ", world!" to the StringBuilder, and then call ToString on it:

```
// We will call:   new StringBuilder ("Hello", 1000)

ConstructorInfo ci = typeof (StringBuilder).GetConstructor (
                     new[] { typeof (string), typeof (int) } );

gen.Emit (OpCodes.Ldstr, "Hello");    // Load a string onto the eval stack
gen.Emit (OpCodes.Ldc_I4, 1000);      // Load an int onto the eval stack
gen.Emit (OpCodes.Newobj, ci);        // Construct the StringBuilder

Type[] strT = { typeof (string) };
gen.Emit (OpCodes.Ldstr, ", world!");
gen.Emit (OpCodes.Call, typeof (StringBuilder).GetMethod ("Append", strT));
gen.Emit (OpCodes.Callvirt, typeof (object).GetMethod ("ToString"));
gen.Emit (OpCodes.Call, typeof (Console).GetMethod ("WriteLine", strT));
gen.Emit (OpCodes.Ret);
dynMeth.Invoke (null, null);          // Hello, world!
```

For fun we called `GetMethod` on `typeof(object)`, and then used `Callvirt` to perform a virtual method call on `ToString`. We could have gotten the same result by calling `ToString` on the `StringBuilder` type itself:

```
gen.Emit (OpCodes.Callvirt, typeof (StringBuilder).GetMethod ("ToString",
                                                   new Type[0] ));
```

(The empty type array is required in calling `GetMethod` because `StringBuilder` overloads `ToString` with another signature.)

> Had we called `object`'s `ToString` method nonvirtually:
>
> ```
> gen.Emit (OpCodes.Call,
>           typeof (object).GetMethod ("ToString"));
> ```
>
> the result would have been "System.Text.StringBuilder". In other words, we would have circumvented `StringBuilder`'s `ToString` override and called `object`'s version directly.

Exception Handling

`ILGenerator` provides dedicated methods for exception handling. The translation for the following C# code:

```
try                                 { throw new NotSupportedException( ); }
catch (NotSupportedException ex)    { Console.WriteLine (ex.Message);     }
finally                             { Console.WriteLine ("Finally");      }
```

is this:

```
MethodInfo getMessageProp = typeof (NotSupportedException)
                         .GetProperty ("Message").GetGetMethod( );

MethodInfo writeLineString = typeof (Console).GetMethod ("WriteLine",
                                        new[] { typeof (object) } );
gen.BeginExceptionBlock( );
  ConstructorInfo ci = typeof (NotSupportedException).GetConstructor (
                                               new Type[0] );
  gen.Emit (OpCodes.Newobj, ci);
  gen.Emit (OpCodes.Throw);
gen.BeginCatchBlock (typeof (NotSupportedException));
  gen.Emit (OpCodes.Callvirt, getMessageProp);
  gen.Emit (OpCodes.Call, writeLineString);
gen.BeginFinallyBlock( );
  gen.EmitWriteLine ("Finally");
gen.EndExceptionBlock( );
```

Just as in C#, you can include multiple catch blocks. To rethrow the same exception, emit the `Rethrow` opcode.

> `ILGenerator` provides a helper method called `ThrowException`. This contains a bug, however, preventing it from being used with a `DynamicMethod`. It works only with a `MethodBuilder` (see the next section).

Reflection and
Metadata

Emitting Assemblies and Types

Although `DynamicMethod` is convenient, it can generate only methods. If you need to emit any other construct—or a complete type—you need to use the full "heavyweight" API. This means dynamically building an assembly and module. The assembly need not have a disk presence, however; it can live entirely in memory.

Let's assume we want to dynamically build a type. Since a type must live in a module within an assembly, we must first create the assembly and module before we can create the type. This is the job of the `AssemblyBuilder` and `ModuleBuilder` types:

```
AppDomain appDomain = AppDomain.CurrentDomain;

AssemblyName aname = new AssemblyName ("MyDynamicAssembly");

AssemblyBuilder assemBuilder =
  appDomain.DefineDynamicAssembly (aname, AssemblyBuilderAccess.Run);

ModuleBuilder modBuilder = assemBuilder.DefineDynamicModule ("DynModule");
```

 You can't add a type to an existing assembly, because an assembly is immutable once created.

Once we have a module where the type can live, we can use `TypeBuilder` to create the type. The following defines a class called `Widget`:

```
TypeBuilder tb = modBuilder.DefineType ("Widget", TypeAttributes.Public);
```

The `TypeAttributes` flags enum supports the CLR type modifiers you see when disassembling a type with *ildasm*. As well as member visibility flags, this includes type modifiers such as `Abstract` and `Sealed`—and `Interface` for defining a .NET interface. It also includes `Serializable`, which is equivalent to applying the `[Serializable]` attribute in C#, and `Explicit`, which is equivalent to applying `[StructLayout(LayoutKind.Explicit)]`. We describe how to apply other kinds of attributes later in this chapter, in the section "Attaching Attributes."

 The `DefineType` method also accepts an optional base type:

- To define a struct, specify a base type of `System.ValueType`.
- To define a delegate, specify a base type of `System.MulticastDelegate`.
- To implement an interface, use the constructor that accepts an array of interface types.
- To define an interface, specify `TypeAttributes.Interface | TypeAttributes.Abstract`.

Defining a delegate type requires a number of extra steps. In his weblog at *http://blogs.msdn.com/joelpob/*, Joel Pobar demonstrates how this is done in his article titled "Creating delegate types via Reflection.Emit."

We can now create members within the type:

```
MethodBuilder methBuilder = tb.DefineMethod ("SayHello",
                                             MethodAttributes.Public,
                                             null, null);
ILGenerator gen = methBuilder.GetILGenerator( );
gen.EmitWriteLine ("Hello world");
gen.Emit (OpCodes.Ret);
```

We're now ready to create the type, which finalizes its definition:

```
Type t = tb.CreateType( );
```

Once the type is created, we use ordinary reflection to inspect and perform dynamic binding:

```
object o = Activator.CreateInstance (t);
t.GetMethod ("SayHello").Invoke (o, null);        // Hello world
```

Saving Emitted Assemblies

The Save method on AssemblyBuilder writes a dynamically generated assembly to a specified filename. For this to work, though, you must do two things:

- Specify an AssemblyBuilderAccess of Save or RunAndSave when constructing the AssemblyBuilder.
- Specify a filename when constructing the ModuleBuilder (this should match the assembly filename unless you want to create a multimodule assembly).

You can also optionally set properties of the AssemblyName object, such as Version or KeyPair (for signing).

For example:

```
AppDomain domain = AppDomain.CurrentDomain;

AssemblyName aname = new AssemblyName ("MyEmissions");
aname.Version = new Version (2, 13, 0, 1);

AssemblyBuilder assemBuilder = domain.DefineDynamicAssembly (
  aname, AssemblyBuilderAccess.RunAndSave);

ModuleBuilder modBuilder = assemBuilder.DefineDynamicModule (
  "MainModule", "MyEmissions.dll");

// Create types as we did previously...
// ...

assemBuilder.Save ("MyEmissions.dll");
```

This writes the assembly to the application's base directory. To save to a different location, you must provide the alternative directory when constructing Assembly-Builder:

```
AssemblyBuilder assemBuilder = domain.DefineDynamicAssembly (
  aname, AssemblyBuilderAccess.RunAndSave, @"d:\assemblies" );
```

A dynamic assembly, once written to a file, becomes an ordinary assembly just like any other. A program could statically reference the assembly we just built and do this:

```
Widget w = new Widget( );
w.SayHello( );
```

The Reflection.Emit Object Model

Figure 17-2 illustrates the essential types in System.Reflection.Emit. Each type describes a CLR construct and is based on a counterpart in the System.Reflection namespace. This allows you to use emitted constructs in place of normal constructs when building a type. For example, we previously called Console.WriteLine as follows:

```
MethodInfo writeLine = typeof(Console).GetMethod ("WriteLine",
                                    new Type[] { typeof (string) });
gen.Emit (OpCodes.Call, writeLine);
```

We could just as easily call a dynamically generated method by calling gen.Emit with a MethodBuilder instead of a MethodInfo. This is essential—otherwise, you couldn't write one dynamic method that called another in the same type.

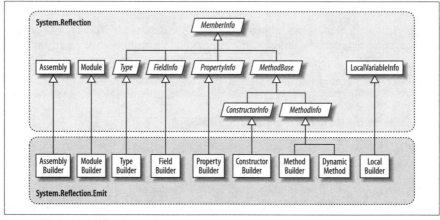

Figure 17-2. System.Reflection.Emit

Recall that you must call CreateType on a TypeBuilder when you've finished populating it. Calling CreateType seals the TypeBuilder and all its members—so nothing more can be added or changed—and gives you back a real Type that you can instantiate.

Before you call CreateType, the TypeBuilder and its members are in an "uncreated" state. There are significant restrictions on what you can do with uncreated constructs. In particular, you cannot call any of the members that return MemberInfo objects, such as GetMembers, GetMethod, or GetProperty—these all throw an exception. If you want to refer to members of an uncreated type, you must use the original emissions:

```
TypeBuilder tb = ...

MethodBuilder method1 = tb.DefineMethod ("Method1", ...);
MethodBuilder method2 = tb.DefineMethod ("Method2", ...);

ILGenerator gen1 = method1.GetILGenerator( );

// Suppose we want method1 to call method2:

gen1.Emit (OpCodes.Call, method2);                // Right
gen1.Emit (OpCodes.Call, tb.GetMethod ("Method2"));  // Wrong
```

After calling CreateType, you can reflect on and activate not only the Type returned, but also the original TypeBuilder object. The TypeBuilder, in fact, morphs into a proxy for the real Type. We'll see why this feature is important later in this chapter in the section "Awkward Emission Targets."

Emitting Type Members

All the examples in this section assume a TypeBuilder, tb, has been instantiated as follows:

```
AppDomain domain = AppDomain.CurrentDomain;
AssemblyName aname = new AssemblyName ("MyEmissions");

AssemblyBuilder assemBuilder = domain.DefineDynamicAssembly (
  aname, AssemblyBuilderAccess.RunAndSave);

ModuleBuilder modBuilder = assemBuilder.DefineDynamicModule (
  "MainModule", "MyEmissions.dll");

TypeBuilder tb = modBuilder.DefineType ("Widget", TypeAttributes.Public);
```

Emitting Methods

You can specify a return type and parameter types when calling DefineMethod, in the same manner as when instantiating a DynamicMethod. For instance, the following method:

```
public static double SquareRoot (double value)
{
  return Math.Sqrt (value);
}
```

can be generated like this:

```
MethodBuilder mb = tb.DefineMethod ("SquareRoot",
  MethodAttributes.Static | MethodAttributes.Public,
  CallingConventions.Standard,
  typeof (double),                    // Return type
  new[] { typeof (double) } );        // Parameter types

mb.DefineParameter (1, ParameterAttributes.None, "value");  // Assign name
```

```
ILGenerator gen = mb.GetILGenerator( );
gen.Emit (OpCodes.Ldarg_0);                                    // Load 1st arg
gen.Emit (OpCodes.Call, typeof(Math).GetMethod ("Sqrt"));
gen.Emit (OpCodes.Ret);

Type realType = tb.CreateType( );
double x = (double) tb.GetMethod ("SquareRoot").Invoke (null,
                                                new object[] { 10.0 });
Console.WriteLine (x);    // 3.16227766016838
```

Calling `DefineParameter` is optional and is typically done to assign the parameter a name. The number 1 refers to the first parameter (0 refers to the return value). If you call `DefineParameter`, the parameter is implicitly named `_ _p1`, `_ _p2`, and so on. Assigning names makes sense if you will write the assembly to disk; it makes your methods friendly to consumers.

> `DefineParameter` returns a `ParameterBuilder` object upon which you can call `SetCustomAttribute` to attach attributes (see "Attaching Attributes" later in this chapter).

To emit pass-by-reference parameters, such as in the following C# method:

```
public static void SquareRoot (ref double value)
{
  value = Math.Sqrt (value);
}
```

call `MakeByRefType` on the parameter type(s):

```
MethodBuilder mb = tb.DefineMethod ("SquareRoot",
  MethodAttributes.Static | MethodAttributes.Public,
  CallingConventions.Standard,
  null,
  new Type[] { typeof (double).MakeByRefType( ) } );

mb.DefineParameter (1, ParameterAttributes.None, "value");

ILGenerator gen = mb.GetILGenerator( );
gen.Emit (OpCodes.Ldarg_0);
gen.Emit (OpCodes.Ldarg_0);
gen.Emit (OpCodes.Ldind_R8);
gen.Emit (OpCodes.Call, typeof (Math).GetMethod ("Sqrt"));
gen.Emit (OpCodes.Stind_R8);
gen.Emit (OpCodes.Ret);

Type realType = tb.CreateType( );
object[] args = { 10.0 };
tb.GetMethod ("SquareRoot").Invoke (null, args);
Console.WriteLine (args[0]);                    // 3.16227766016838
```

The opcodes here were copied from a disassembled C# method. Notice the difference in semantics for accessing parameters passed by reference: `Ldind` and `Stind` mean "load indirectly" and "store indirectly," respectively. The R8 suffix means an 8-byte floating-point number.

The process for emitting out parameters is identical, except that you call DefineParameter as follows:

```
mb.DefineParameter (1, ParameterAttributes.Out, "value");
```

Generating instance methods

To generate an instance method, specify MethodAttributes.Instance when calling DefineMethod:

```
MethodBuilder mb = tb.DefineMethod ("SquareRoot",
  MethodAttributes.Instance | MethodAttributes.Public
  ...
```

With instance methods, argument zero is implicitly this; the remaining arguments start at 1. So, Ldarg_0 loads this onto the evaluation stack; Ldarg_1 loads the first real method argument.

HideBySig

If you're subclassing another type, it's nearly always worth specifying MethodAttributes.HideBySig when defining methods. HideBySig ensures that C#-style method hiding semantics are applied, which is that a base method is hidden only if a subtype defines a method with an identical *signature*. Without HideBySig, method hiding considers only the *name*, so Foo(string) in the subtype will hide Foo( ) in the base type, which is generally undesirable.

Emitting Fields and Properties

To create a field, you call DefineField on a TypeBuilder, telling it the desired field name, type, and visibility. The following creates a private integer field called "length":

```
FieldBuilder field = tb.DefineField ("length", typeof (int),
                            FieldAttributes.Private);
```

Creating a property or indexer requires a few more steps. First, call DefineProperty on a TypeBuilder, telling it the name and type of the property:

```
PropertyBuilder prop = tb.DefineProperty (
                    "Text",                    // Name of property
                    PropertyAttributes.None,
                    typeof (string),           // Property type
                    new Type[0]                // Indexer types
                );
```

(If you're writing an indexer, the final argument is an array of indexer types.) Note that we haven't specified the property visibility: this is done individually on the accessor methods.

The next step is to write the get and set methods. By convention, their names are prefixed with "get_" or "set_". You then attach them to the property by calling SetGetMethod and SetSetMethod on the PropertyBuilder.

To give a complete example, we'll take the following field and property declaration:

```
string _text;
public string Text
{
  get          { return _text; }
  internal set { _text = value; }
}
```

and generate it dynamically:

```
FieldBuilder field = tb.DefineField ("_text", typeof (string),
                              FieldAttributes.Private);
PropertyBuilder prop = tb.DefineProperty (
                    "Text",                       // Name of property
                    PropertyAttributes.None,
                    typeof (string),              // Property type
                    new Type[0]);                 // Indexer types

MethodBuilder getter = tb.DefineMethod (
  "get_Text",                                     // Method name
  MethodAttributes.Public | MethodAttributes.SpecialName,
  typeof (string),                                // Return type
  new Type[0]);                                   // Parameter types

ILGenerator getGen = getter.GetILGenerator();
getGen.Emit (OpCodes.Ldarg_0);      // Load "this" onto eval stack
getGen.Emit (OpCodes.Ldfld, field); // Load field value onto eval stack
getGen.Emit (OpCodes.Ret);          // Return

MethodBuilder setter = tb.DefineMethod (
  "set_Text",
  MethodAttributes.Assembly | MethodAttributes.SpecialName,
  null,                                           // Return type
  new Type[] { typeof (string) } );               // Parameter types

ILGenerator setGen = setter.GetILGenerator();
setGen.Emit (OpCodes.Ldarg_0);        // Load "this" onto eval stack
setGen.Emit (OpCodes.Ldarg_1);        // Load 2nd arg, i.e., value
setGen.Emit (OpCodes.Stfld, field);   // Store value into field
setGen.Emit (OpCodes.Ret);            // return

prop.SetGetMethod (getter);          // Link the get method and property
prop.SetSetMethod (setter);          // Link the set method and property
```

We can test the property as follows:

```
Type t = tb.CreateType();
object o = Activator.CreateInstance (t);
t.GetProperty ("Text").SetValue (o, "Good emissions!", new object[0]);
string text = (string) t.GetProperty ("Text").GetValue (o, null);

Console.WriteLine (text);            // Good emissions!
```

Notice that in defining the accessor `MethodAttributes`, we included `SpecialName`. This instructs compilers to disallow direct binding to these methods when statically referencing the assembly. It also ensures that the accessors are handled appropriately by reflection tools and Visual Studio's IntelliSense.

 You can emit events in a similar manner, by calling `DefineEvent` on a `TypeBuilder`. You then write explicit event accessor methods, and attach them to the `EventBuilder` by calling `SetAddOnMethod` and `SetRemoveOnMethod`.

Emitting Constructors

You can define your own constructors by calling `DefineConstructor` on a type builder. You're not obliged to do so—a default parameterless constructor is provided automatically if you don't. The default constructor calls the base class constructor if subtyping, just like in C#. Defining one or more constructors displaces this default constructor.

If you need to initialize fields, the constructor's a good spot. In fact, it's the only spot: C#'s field initializers don't have special CLR support—they are simply a syntactic shortcut for assigning values to fields in the constructor.

So, to reproduce this:

```
class Widget
{
  int _capacity = 4000;
}
```

you would define a constructor as follows:

```
FieldBuilder field = tb.DefineField ("_capacity", typeof (int),
                                     FieldAttributes.Private);
ConstructorBuilder c = tb.DefineConstructor (
  MethodAttributes.Public,
  CallingConventions.Standard,
  new Type[0]);                    // Constructor parameters

ILGenerator gen = c.GetILGenerator( );

gen.Emit (OpCodes.Ldarg_0);        // Load "this" onto eval stack
gen.Emit (OpCodes.Ldc_I4, 4000);   // Load 4000 onto eval stack
gen.Emit (OpCodes.Stfld, field);   // Store it to our field
gen.Emit (OpCodes.Ret);
```

Calling base constructors

If subclassing another type, the constructor we just wrote would *circumvent the base class constructor*. This is unlike C#, where the base class constructor is always called, whether directly or indirectly. For instance, given the following code:

```
class A    { public A() { Console.Write ("A"); } }
class B : A { public B() {} }
```

the compiler, in effect, will translate the second line into this:

```
class B : A { public B() : base() {} }
```

This is not the case when generating IL: you must explicitly call the base constructor if you want it to execute (which nearly always, you do). Assuming the base class is called B, here's how to do it:

```
gen.Emit (OpCodes.Ldarg_0);
ConstructorInfo baseConstr = typeof (B).GetConstructor (new Type[0]);
gen.Emit (OpCodes.Call, baseConstr);
```

Calling constructors with arguments is just the same as with methods.

Attaching Attributes

You can attach custom attributes to a dynamic construct by calling SetCustom-Attribute with a CustomAttributeBuilder. For example, suppose we want to attach the following attribute declaration to a field or property:

```
[XmlElement ("FirstName", Namespace="http://test/", Order=3)]
```

This relies on the XmlElementAttribute constructor that accepts a single string. To use CustomAttributeBuilder, we must retrieve this constructor, as well as the two additional properties we wish to set (Namespace and Order):

```
Type attType = typeof (XmlElementAttribute);

ConstructorInfo attConstructor = attType.GetConstructor (
  new Type[] { typeof (string) } );

var att = new CustomAttributeBuilder (
  attConstructor,                      // Constructor
  new object[] { "FirstName" },        // Constructor arguments
  new PropertyInfo[] {
    attType.GetProperty ("Namespace"),  // Properties
    attType.GetProperty ("Order")
  },
  new object[] { "FirstName", 3 }       // Property values
);

myFieldBuilder.SetCustomAttribute (att);
// or propBuilder.SetCustomAttribute (att);
// or typeBuilder.SetCustomAttribute (att);  etc
```

Emitting Generic Methods and Types

All the examples in this section assume that modBuilder has been instantiated as follows:

```
AppDomain domain = AppDomain.CurrentDomain;
AssemblyName aname = new AssemblyName ("MyEmissions");

AssemblyBuilder assemBuilder = domain.DefineDynamicAssembly (
  aname, AssemblyBuilderAccess.RunAndSave);
```

```
ModuleBuilder modBuilder = assemBuilder.DefineDynamicModule (
  "MainModule", "MyEmissions.dll");
```

Defining Generic Methods

To emit a generic method:

1. Call `DefineGenericParameters` on a `MethodBuilder` to obtain an array of `GenericTypeParameterBuilder` objects.
2. Call `SetSignature` on a `MethodBuilder` using these generic type parameters.
3. Optionally, name the parameters as you would otherwise.

For example, the following generic method:

```
public static T Echo<T> (T value)
{
  return value;
}
```

can be emitted like this:

```
TypeBuilder tb = modBuilder.DefineType ("Widget", TypeAttributes.Public);

MethodBuilder mb = tb.DefineMethod ("Echo", MethodAttributes.Public |
                                            MethodAttributes.Static);
GenericTypeParameterBuilder[] genericParams
  = mb.DefineGenericParameters ("T");

mb.SetSignature (genericParams[0],     // Return type
                 null, null,
                 genericParams,        // Parameter types
                 null, null);

mb.DefineParameter (1, ParameterAttributes.None, "value");   // Optional

ILGenerator gen = mb.GetILGenerator( );
gen.Emit (OpCodes.Ldarg_1);
gen.Emit (OpCodes.Ret);
```

The `DefineGenericParameters` method accepts any number of string arguments—these correspond to the desired generic type names. In this example, we needed just one generic type called T. `GenericTypeParameterBuilder` is based on `System. Type`, so it can be used in place of a `TypeBuilder` when emitting opcodes.

`GenericTypeParameterBuilder` also lets you specify a base type constraint:

```
genericParams[0].SetBaseTypeConstraint (typeof (Foo));
```

and interface constraints:

```
genericParams[0].SetInterfaceConstraints (typeof (IComparable));
```

To replicate this:

```
public static T Echo<T> (T value) where T : IComparable<T>
```

you would write:

```
genericParams[0].SetInterfaceConstraints (
  typeof (IComparable<>).MakeGenericType (genericParams[0]) );
```

For other kinds of constraints, call SetGenericParameterAttributes. This accepts a member of the GenericParameterAttributes enum, which includes the following values:

```
DefaultConstructorConstraint
NotNullableValueTypeConstraint
ReferenceTypeConstraint
```

Defining Generic Types

You can define generic types in a similar fashion. The difference is that you call DefineGenericParameters on the TypeBuilder rather than the MethodBuilder. So, to reproduce this:

```
public class Widget<T>
{
  public T Value;
}
```

you would do the following:

```
TypeBuilder tb = modBuilder.DefineType ("Widget", TypeAttributes.Public);

GenericTypeParameterBuilder[] genericParams
  = tb.DefineGenericParameters ("T");

tb.DefineField ("Value", genericParams[0], FieldAttributes.Public);
```

Generic constraints can be added just as with a method.

Awkward Emission Targets

All the examples in this section assume that a modBuilder has been instantiated as in previous sections.

Uncreated Closed Generics

Suppose you want to emit a method that uses a closed generic type:

```
public class Widget
{
  public static void Test() { var list = new List<int>(); }
}
```

The process is fairly straightforward:

```
TypeBuilder tb = modBuilder.DefineType ("Widget", TypeAttributes.Public);

MethodBuilder mb = tb.DefineMethod ("Test", MethodAttributes.Public |
                                            MethodAttributes.Static);
ILGenerator gen = mb.GetILGenerator();

Type variableType = typeof (List<int>);

ConstructorInfo ci = variableType.GetConstructor (new Type[0]);
```

```
LocalBuilder listVar = gen.DeclareLocal (variableType);
gen.Emit (OpCodes.Newobj, ci);
gen.Emit (OpCodes.Stloc, listVar);
gen.Emit (OpCodes.Ret);
```

Now suppose that instead of a list of integers, we want a list of widgets:

```
public class Widget
{
  public static void Test() { var list = new List<Widget>(); }
}
```

In theory, this is a simple modification: all we do is replace this line:

```
Type variableType = typeof (List<int>);
```

with this:

```
Type variableType = typeof (List<>).MakeGenericType (tb);
```

Unfortunately, this causes a NotSupportedException to be thrown when we then call GetConstructor. The problem is that you cannot call GetConstructor on a generic type closed with an uncreated type builder. The same goes for GetField and GetMethod.

The solution is unintuitive. TypeBuilder provides three static methods as follows:

```
public static ConstructorInfo GetConstructor (Type, ConstructorInfo);
public static FieldInfo       GetField       (Type, FieldInfo);
public static MethodInfo      GetMethod      (Type, MethodInfo);
```

Although it doesn't appear so, these methods exist specifically to obtain members of generic types closed with uncreated type builders! The first parameter is the closed generic type; the second parameter is the member you want on the *open* generic type. Here's the corrected version of our example:

```
MethodBuilder mb = tb.DefineMethod ("Test", MethodAttributes.Public |
                                            MethodAttributes.Static);
ILGenerator gen = mb.GetILGenerator();

Type variableType = typeof (List<>).MakeGenericType (tb);

ConstructorInfo open = typeof (List<>).GetConstructor (new Type[0]);
ConstructorInfo ci   = TypeBuilder.GetConstructor (variableType, open);

LocalBuilder listVar = gen.DeclareLocal (variableType);
gen.Emit (OpCodes.Newobj, ci);
gen.Emit (OpCodes.Stloc, listVar);
gen.Emit (OpCodes.Ret);
```

Circular Dependencies

Suppose you want to build two types that reference each other. For instance:

```
class A { public B Bee; }
class B { public A Aye; }
```

You can generate this dynamically as follows:

```
var publicAtt = FieldAttributes.Public;

TypeBuilder aBuilder = modBuilder.DefineType ("A");
TypeBuilder bBuilder = modBuilder.DefineType ("B");

FieldBuilder bee = aBuilder.DefineField ("Bee", bBuilder, publicAtt);
FieldBuilder aye = bBuilder.DefineField ("Aye", aBuilder, publicAtt);

Type realA = aBuilder.CreateType( );
Type realB = bBuilder.CreateType( );
```

Notice that we didn't call CreateType on aBuilder or bBuilder until we populated both objects. The principle is: first hook everything up, and then call CreateType on each type builder.

Interestingly, the realA type is valid but *dysfunctional* until you call CreateType on bBuilder. (If you started using aBuilder prior to this, an exception would be thrown when you tried to access field Bee.)

You might wonder how bBuilder knows to "fix up" realA after creating realB. The answer is that it doesn't: realA can fix *itself* the next time it's used. This is possible because after calling CreateType, a TypeBuilder morphs into a proxy for the real runtime type. So, realA, with its references to bBuilder, can easily obtain the metadata it needs for the upgrade.

This system works when the type builder demands simple information of the unconstructed type—information that can be *predetermined*—such as type, member, and object references. In creating realA, the type builder doesn't need to know, for instance, how many bytes realB will eventually occupy in memory. This is just as well, because realB has not yet been created! But now imagine that realB was a struct. The final size of realB is now critical information in creating realA.

If the relationship is noncyclical—for instance:

```
struct A { public B Bee; }
struct B {              }
```

you can solve this by first creating struct B, and then struct A. But consider this:

```
struct A { public B Bee; }
struct B { public A Aye; }
```

We won't try to emit this because it's nonsensical to have two structs contain each other (C# generates a compile-time error if you try). But the following variation is both legal and useful:

```
public struct S<T> { ... }    // S can be empty and this demo will work.

class A { S<B> Bee; }
class B { S<A> Aye; }
```

In creating A, a TypeBuilder now needs to know the memory footprint of B, and vice versa. To illustrate, we'll assume that struct S is defined statically. Here's the code to emit classes A and B:

```
var pub = FieldAttributes.Public;
```

```
TypeBuilder aBuilder = modBuilder.DefineType ("A");
TypeBuilder bBuilder = modBuilder.DefineType ("B");

aBuilder.DefineField ("Bee", typeof(S<>).MakeGenericType (bBuilder), pub);
bBuilder.DefineField ("Aye", typeof(S<>).MakeGenericType (aBuilder), pub);

Type realA = aBuilder.CreateType( );    // Error: cannot load type B
Type realB = bBuilder.CreateType( );
```

CreateType now throws a TypeLoadException no matter in which order you go:

- Call aBuilder.CreateType first and it says "cannot load type B".
- Call bBuilder.CreateType first and it says "cannot load type A"!

 You'll run into this problem if you emit typed LINQ to SQL DataContexts dynamically. The generic EntityRef type is a struct, equivalent to S in our examples. The circular reference happens when two tables in the database link to each other through reciprocal parent/child relationships.

To solve this, you must allow the type builder to create realB partway through creating realA. This is done by handling the TypeResolve event on the current application domain just before calling CreateType. So, in our example, we replace the last two lines with this:

```
TypeBuilder[] uncreatedTypes = { aBuilder, bBuilder };

ResolveEventHandler handler = delegate (object o, ResolveEventArgs args)
{
  var type = uncreatedTypes.FirstOrDefault (t => t.FullName == args.Name);
  return type == null ? null : type.CreateType( ).Assembly;
};

AppDomain.CurrentDomain.TypeResolve += handler;

Type realA = aBuilder.CreateType( );
Type realB = bBuilder.CreateType( );

AppDomain.CurrentDomain.TypeResolve -= handler;
```

The TypeResolve event fires during the call to aBuilder.CreateType, at the point when it needs you to call CreateType on bBuilder.

 Handling the TypeResolve event as in this example is also necessary when defining a nested type, when the nested and parent types refer to each other.

Parsing IL

You can obtain information about the content of an existing method by calling GetMethodBody on a MethodBase object. This returns a MethodBody object that has properties for inspecting a method's local variables, exception handling clauses, stack size—as well as the raw IL. Rather like the reverse of Reflection.Emit!

Inspecting a method's raw IL can be useful in profiling code. A simple use would be to determine which methods in an assembly have changed, when an assembly is updated.

To illustrate parsing IL, we'll write an application that disassembles IL in the style of *ildasm*. This could be used as the starting point for a code analysis tool or a higher-level language disassembler.

> Remember that in the reflection API, all of C#'s functional constructs are either represented by a MethodBase subtype, or (in the case of properties, events, and indexers) have MethodBase objects attached to them.

Writing a Disassembler

> You can download the source code for this at *http://www.albahari.com/nutshell/*.

Here is a sample of the output our disassembler will produce:

```
IL_00EB:  ldfld      Disassembler._pos
IL_00F0:  ldloc.2
IL_00F1:  add
IL_00F2:  ldelema    System.Byte
IL_00F7:  ldstr      "Hello world"
IL_00FC:  call       System.Byte.ToString
IL_0101:  ldstr      " "
IL_0106:  call       System.String.Concat
```

To obtain this output, we must parse the binary tokens that make up the IL. The first step is to call the GetILAsByteArray method on MethodBody to obtain the IL as a byte array. In order to make the rest of the job easier, we will write this into a class as follows:

```
public class Disassembler
{
  public static string Disassemble (MethodBase method)
  {
    return new Disassembler (method).Dis();
  }

  StringBuilder _output;    // The result to which we'll keep appending
  Module _module;           // This will come in handy later
  byte[] _il;               // The raw byte code
  int _pos;                 // The position we're up to in the byte code

  Disassembler (MethodBase method)
  {
    _module = method.DeclaringType.Module;
```

```
    _il = method.GetMethodBody().GetILAsByteArray();
  }

  string Dis()
  {
    _output = new StringBuilder();
    while (_pos < _il.Length) DisassembleNextInstruction();
    return _output.ToString();
  }
}
```

The static Disassemble method will be the only public member of this class. All other members will be private to the disassembly process. The Dis method contains the "main" loop where we process each instruction.

With this skeleton in place, all that remains is to write Disassemble-NextInstruction. But before doing so, it will help to load all the opcodes into a static dictionary, so we can access them by their 8- or 16-bit value. The easiest way to accomplish this is to use reflection to retrieve all the static fields whose type is OpCode in the OpCodes class:

```
static Dictionary<short,OpCode> _opcodes = new Dictionary<short,OpCode>();

static Disassembler()
{
  Dictionary<short, OpCode> opcodes = new Dictionary<short, OpCode>();
    foreach (FieldInfo fi in typeof (OpCodes).GetFields
                            (BindingFlags.Public | BindingFlags.Static))
      if (typeof (OpCode).IsAssignableFrom (fi.FieldType))
      {
        OpCode code = (OpCode) fi.GetValue (null);   // Get field's value
        if (code.OpCodeType != OpCodeType.Nternal)
            _opcodes.Add (code.Value, code);
      }
}
```

We've written it in a static constructor so that it executes just once.

Now we can write DisassembleNextInstruction. Each IL instruction consists of a 1- or 2-byte opcode, followed by an operand of zero, one, two, four, or eight bytes. (An exception is inline switch opcodes, which are followed by a variable number of operands). So, we read the opcode, then the operand, and then write out the result:

```
void DisassembleNextInstruction()
{
  int opStart = _pos;

  OpCode code = ReadOpCode();
  string operand = ReadOperand (code);

  _output.AppendFormat ("IL_{0:X4}:  {1,-12} {2}",
                        opStart, code.Name, operand);
  _output.AppendLine();
}
```

To read an opcode, we advance one byte and see whether we have a valid instruction. If not, we advance another byte and look for a 2-byte instruction:

```
OpCode ReadOpCode()
{
  byte byteCode = _il [_pos++];
  if (_opcodes.ContainsKey (byteCode)) return _opcodes [byteCode];

  if (_pos == _il.Length)  throw new Exception ("Unexpected end of IL");

  short shortCode = (short) (byteCode * 256 + _il [_pos++]);

  if (!_opcodes.ContainsKey (shortCode))
    throw new Exception ("Cannot find opcode " + shortCode);

  return _opcodes [shortCode];
}
```

To read an operand, we first must establish its length. We can do this based on the operand type. Because most are four bytes long, we can filter out the exceptions fairly easily in a conditional clause.

The next step is to call FormatOperand, which will attempt to format the operand:

```
string ReadOperand (OpCode c)
{
  int operandLength =
    c.OperandType == OperandType.InlineNone
      ? 0 :
    c.OperandType == OperandType.ShortInlineBrTarget ||
    c.OperandType == OperandType.ShortInlineI ||
    c.OperandType == OperandType.ShortInlineVar
      ? 1 :
    c.OperandType == OperandType.InlineVar
      ? 2 :
    c.OperandType == OperandType.InlineI8 ||
    c.OperandType == OperandType.InlineR
      ? 8 :
     c.OperandType == OperandType.InlineSwitch
      ? 4 * (BitConverter.ToInt32 (_il, _pos) + 1) :
      4;  // All others are 4 bytes

  if (_pos + operandLength > _il.Length)
    throw new Exception ("Unexpected end of IL");

  string result = FormatOperand (c, operandLength);
  if (result == null)
  {                          // Write out operand bytes in hex
    result = "";
    for (int i = 0; i < operandLength; i++)
      result += _il [_pos + i].ToString ("X2") + " ";
  }
  _pos += operandLength;
  return result;
}
```

If the result of calling FormatOperand is null, it means the operand needs no special formatting, so we simply write it out in hexadecimal. We could test the disassembler at this point by writing a FormatOperand method that always returns null. Here's what the output would look like:

```
IL_00A8:   ldfld        98 00 00 04
IL_00AD:   ldloc.2
IL_00AE:   add
IL_00AF:   ldelema      64 00 00 01
IL_00B4:   ldstr        26 04 00 70
IL_00B9:   call         B6 00 00 0A
IL_00BE:   ldstr        11 01 00 70
IL_00C3:   call         91 00 00 0A
...
```

Although the opcodes are correct, the operands are not much use. Instead of hexadecimal numbers, we want member names and strings. The FormatOperand method, once written, will address this—identifying the special cases that benefit from such formatting. These comprise most 4-byte operands and the short branch instructions:

```
string FormatOperand (OpCode c, int operandLength)
{
  if (operandLength == 0) return "";

  if (operandLength == 4)
    return Get4ByteOperand (c);
  else if (c.OperandType == OperandType.ShortInlineBrTarget)
    return GetShortRelativeTarget ();
  else if (c.OperandType == OperandType.InlineSwitch)
    return GetSwitchTarget (operandLength);
  else
    return null;
}
```

There are three kinds of 4-byte operands that we treat specially. The first is references to members or types—with these, we extract the member or type name by calling the defining module's ResolveMember method. The second case is strings—these are stored in the assembly module's metadata and can be retrieved by calling ResolveString. The final case is branch targets, where the operand refers to a byte offset in the IL. We format these by working out the absolute address *after* the current instruction (+ 4 bytes):

```
string Get4ByteOperand (OpCode c)
{
  int intOp = BitConverter.ToInt32 (_il, _pos);

  switch (c.OperandType)
  {
    case OperandType.InlineTok:
    case OperandType.InlineMethod:
    case OperandType.InlineField:
    case OperandType.InlineType:
      MemberInfo mi;
      try   { mi = _module.ResolveMember (intOp); }
```

```
      catch { return null; }
      if (mi == null) return null;

      if (mi.ReflectedType != null)
        return mi.ReflectedType.FullName + "." + mi.Name;
      else if (mi is Type)
        return ((Type)mi).FullName;
      else
        return mi.Name;

  case OperandType.InlineString:
    string s = _module.ResolveString (intOp);
    if (s != null) s = "'" + s + "'";
    return s;

  case OperandType.InlineBrTarget:
    return "IL_" + (_pos + intOp + 4).ToString ("X4");

  default:
    return null;
  }
}
```

 The point where we call ResolveMember is a good window for a code
analysis tool that reports on method dependencies.

For any other 4-byte opcode, we return null (this will cause ReadOperand to format
the operand as hex digits).

The final kinds of operand that need special attention are short branch targets and
inline switches. A short branch target describes the destination offset as a single
signed byte, as at the end of the current instruction (i.e., + 1 byte). A switch target
is followed by a variable number of 4-byte branch destinations:

```
string GetShortRelativeTarget()
{
  int absoluteTarget = _pos + (sbyte) _il [_pos] + 1;
  return "IL_" + absoluteTarget.ToString ("X4");
}

string GetSwitchTarget (int operandLength)
{
  int targetCount = BitConverter.ToInt32 (_il, _pos);
  string [] targets = new string [targetCount];
  for (int i = 0; i < targetCount; i++)
  {
    int ilTarget = BitConverter.ToInt32 (_il, _pos + (i + 1) * 4);
    targets [i] = "IL_" + (_pos + ilTarget + operandLength).ToString ("X4");
  }
  return "(" + string.Join (", ", targets) + ")";
}
```

This completes the disassembler. We can test it by disassembling one of its own methods:

```
MethodInfo mi = typeof (Disassembler).GetMethod (
  "ReadOperand", BindingFlags.Instance | BindingFlags.NonPublic);

Console.WriteLine (Disassembler.Disassemble (mi));
```

18

Security

In this chapter, we discuss the two main components of .NET security:

- Permissions
- Cryptography

Permissions, in .NET, provide a layer of security independent of that imposed by the operating system. Their job is twofold:

Sandboxing
Limiting the kinds of operations that untrusted or partially trusted .NET assemblies can perform

Authorization
Limiting *who* can do what

The cryptography support in .NET allows you to store or exchange high-value secrets, prevent eavesdropping, detect message tampering, generate one-way hashes for storing passwords, and create digital signatures.

The types covered in this chapter are defined in the following namespaces:

```
System.Security;
System.Security.Permissions;
System.Security.Principal;
System.Security.Cryptography;
```

In Chapter 13, we covered *isolated storage*, which serves another useful role in a secure environment.

Permissions

The Framework uses permissions for both sandboxing and authorization. A *permission* acts as a gate that conditionally prevents code from executing. Sandboxing uses *code access* permissions; authorization uses *identity* and *role* permissions.

Although both follow a similar model, they feel quite different to use. Part of the reason for this is that they typically put you on a different side of the fence: with code access security, you're usually the *untrusted* party; with identity and role security, you're usually the *untrusting* party. Code access security is most often forced upon you by the CLR (for the benefit of the end user) whereas authorization is usually something you implement to prevent unprivileged callers from accessing your program.

As an application developer, you'll need to understand code access security to deal elegantly with execution restrictions. The CLR, by default, places execution restrictions on assemblies that run directly from a network path or web site. The solution—in one sentence—is to determine your assembly's security requirements and then declare them *upfront* with assembly attributes. Another use for code access security is to sandbox a less trusted assembly.

The main scenario for identity and role security is when writing middle tier or web application servers. You typically decide on a set of roles, and then for each method that you expose, you demand that callers are members of a particular role.

CodeAccessPermission and PrincipalPermission

There are two types of permissions:

CodeAccessPermission
> The abstract base class for all code access permissions, such as FileIO-Permission, ReflectionPermission, or PrintingPermission

PrincipalPermission
> Describes an identity and/or role (e.g., "Mary" or "Human Resources")

The term *permission* is somewhat misleading in the case of CodeAccessPermission, because it suggests something has been granted. This is not the case. A CodeAccessPermission object describes a *privileged operation*.

For instance, a FileIOPermission object describes the privilege of being able to Read, Write, or Append to a particular set of files or directories. Such an object can be used in a variety of ways:

- To verify that you and all your callers have the rights to perform these actions (Demand)
- To verify that your immediate caller has the rights to perform these actions (LinkDemand)
- To declare your assembly's need to perform these actions (RequestMinimum)
- To request that your assembly be refused permission to perform these actions (RequestRefuse)
- To Assert your assembly-given rights to perform these actions, regardless of callers' privileges
- To Deny rights to perform these actions to code that you call

PrincipalPermission is much simpler. Its only security method is Demand, which checks that the specified user or role is valid given the current execution thread.

IPermission

Both `CodeAccessPermission` and `PrincipalPermission` implement the `IPermission` interface:

```
public interface IPermission
{
  void Demand( );
  IPermission Intersect (IPermission target);
  IPermission Union (IPermission target);
  bool IsSubsetOf (IPermission target);
  IPermission Copy( );
}
```

The crucial method here is `Demand`. It performs a spot-check to see whether the permission or privileged operation is currently permitted, and it throws a `SecurityException` if not. If you're the *untrusting* party, *you* will be Demanding. If you're the *untrusted* party, code that you *call* will be Demanding.

For example, to ensure that only Mary can run management reports, you could write this:

```
new PrincipalPermission ("Mary", null).Demand( );
// ... run management reports
```

In contrast, suppose your assembly was sandboxed such that file I/O was prohibited, so the following line threw a `SecurityException`:

```
using (FileStream fs = new FileStream ("test.txt", FileMode.Create))
  ...
```

The `Demand`, in this case, is made by code that you call—in other words, `FileStream`'s constructor. Decompiling `FileStream` reveals this:

```
...
new FileIOPermission (...).Demand( );
```

 A code access security `Demand` checks right up the call stack, in order to ensure that the requested operation is allowed for every party in the calling chain. You can prevent this by calling `Assert` on a `CodeAccessPermission` object. After calling `Assert`, only *your* permissions are considered—not those of your callers. An `Assert` ends either when the current method finishes or when you call `CodeAccessPermission.RevertAssert`.

The `Intersect` and `Union` methods combine two same-typed permission objects into one. The result of `Intersect` is *more* restrictive when Demanded, requiring *both* permissions to be met. The result of `Union` is *less* restrictive when Demanded, requiring *either* permission to be met.

`IsSubsetOf` returns true if the given target is at least as permissive:

```
PrincipalPermission jay = new PrincipalPermission ("Jay", null);
PrincipalPermission sue = new PrincipalPermission ("Sue", null);

PrincipalPermission jayOrSue = (PrincipalPermission) jay.Union (sue);
Console.WriteLine (jay.IsSubsetOf (jayOrSue));  // True
```

In this example, calling `Intersect` on `jay` and `sue` would generate an empty permission, because they don't overlap.

PermissionSet

A `PermissionSet` represents a collection of differently typed `IPermission` objects. The following creates a permission set with three code access permissions, and then `Demands` all of them in one hit:

```
PermissionSet ps = new PermissionSet (PermissionState.None);

ps.AddPermission (new UIPermission (PermissionState.Unrestricted));
ps.AddPermission (new SecurityPermission (
                        SecurityPermissionFlag.UnmanagedCode));
ps.AddPermission (new FileIOPermission (
                        FileIOPermissionAccess.Read, @"c:\docs"));
ps.Demand( );
```

`PermissionSet`'s constructor accepts a `PermissionState` enum, which indicates whether the set should be considered "unrestricted." An unrestricted permission set is treated as though it contained every possible permission (even though its collection is empty).

When you call `AddPermission`, the permission set looks to see whether a same-typed permission is already present. If so, it `Unions` the new and existing permissions; otherwise, it adds the new permission to its collection. Calling `AddPermission` on an unrestricted permission set has no effect.

You can `Union` and `Intersect` permission sets just as you can with `IPermission` objects.

> You can test whether you have unrestricted permissions with the following:
> ```
> new PermissionSet (PermissionState.Unrestricted).Demand( );
> ```

Declarative Versus Imperative Security

So far, we manually instantiated permission objects and called `Demand` on them. This is *imperative security*. You can achieve the same result by adding attributes to a method, constructor, class, struct, or assembly—this is *declarative security*. Although imperative security is more flexible, declarative security has a couple of advantages:

- It can mean less coding.
- It allows the CLR to determine in advance what permissions your assembly requires.

Here's an example:

```
[PrincipalPermission (SecurityAction.Demand, Name="Mary")]
public void GetReports( )
{
  ...
}
```

This works because every permission type has a sister attribute type in the .NET Framework. `PrincipalPermission` has a `PrincipalPermissionAttribute` sister. The first argument of the attribute's constructor is always a `SecurityAction`, which indicates what security method to call once the permission object is constructed (usually `Demand`). The remaining named parameters mirror the properties on the corresponding permission object.

Code Access Security

The `CodeAccessPermission` types that are enforced throughout the (entire) .NET Framework are listed by category in Tables 18-1 through 18-5. Collectively, these are intended to cover all the means by which a program can do mischief!

Table 18-1. Core permissions

Type	Enables	Intranet?	Internet?
SecurityPermission	Advanced operations, such as calling unmanaged code	Execute, assert	Execute only
ReflectionPermission	Use of reflection	Emit only	-
EnvironmentPermission	Reading/writing command-line environment settings	Read username	-
RegistryPermission	Reading or writing to the Windows Registry	-	-
UIPermission	Creating windows and inter-acting with the clipboard	Unrestricted	Safe windows; own clipboard
PrintingPermission	Accessing a printer	Default printing	Safe printing

SecurityPermission accepts a SecurityPermissionFlag argument. This is an enum that allows any combination of the following:

```
AllFlags                ControlThread
Assertion               Execution
BindingRedirects        Infrastructure
ControlAppDomain        NoFlags
ControlDomainPolicy     RemotingConfiguration
ControlEvidence         SerializationFormatter
ControlPolicy           SkipVerification
ControlPrincipal        UnmanagedCode
```

The significant members of this enum are Execution, without which code will not run at all; ControlAppDomain, which allows the creation of new application domains (see Chapter 21); and UnmanagedCode, which allows you to call native methods (see Chapter 22).

Table 18-2. I/O and data permissions

Type	Enables	Intranet?	Internet?
FileIOPermission	Reading/writing files and directories	-	-
FileDialogPermission	Reading/writing to a file chosen through an Open or Save dialog	Unrestricted	Open only

Table 18-2. I/O and data permissions (continued)

Type	Enables	Intranet?	Internet?
IsolatedStorageFilePermission	Reading/writing to own isolated storage	Unrestricted	Limited to 512 KB
ConfigurationPermission	Reading of application configuration files	-	-
SqlClientPermission, OleDb-Permission, OdbcPermission	Communicating with a data-base server using the SqlClient, OleDb, or Odbc classes	-	-
DistributedTransaction-Permission	Participation in distributed transactions	-	-

FileDialogPermission controls access to the OpenFileDialog and SaveFileDialog classes. These classes are defined in Microsoft.Win32 (for use in WPF applications) and in System.Windows.Forms (for use in Windows Forms applications). For this to work, UIPermission is also required. FileIOPermission is not also required, however, if you access the chosen file by calling OpenFile on the OpenFileDialog or SaveFileDialog object.

Table 18-3. Networking permissions

Type	Enables	Intranet?	Internet?
DnsPermission	DNS lookup	Unrestricted	-
WebPermission	WebRequest-based network access	-	-
SocketPermission	Socket-based network access	-	-
SmtpPermission	Sending mail through the SMTP libraries	-	-
NetworkInformationPermission	Use of Ping	-	-
AspNetHostingPermission	Allows custom ASP.NET hosting	-	-

Table 18-4. Encryption permissions

Type	Enables	Intranet?	Internet?
DataProtectionPermission	Use of the Windows data protection methods	-	-
KeyContainerPermission	Public key encryption and signing	-	-
StorePermission	Access to X.509 certificates	-	-

Table 18-5. Diagnostics permissions

Type	Enables	Intranet?	Internet?
EventLogPermission	Reading or writing to the Windows event log	-	-
PerformanceCounterPermission	Use of Windows performance counters	-	-

Security

How the CLR Allocates Permissions

The CLR grants permissions to .NET assemblies based on a complex set of rules and mappings, defined by the computer's .NET Framework configuration. You can imagine there's an engine on the computer that accepts assembly *evidence* as input and emits a *permission set* as output. Assembly evidence is a collection of information describing the properties of an assembly relevant to security, such as where it came from and its strong name.

By default, assemblies on your local hard drive execute with the "FullTrust" permission set. This has no code access security restrictions, so all Demands on CodeAccessPermission types succeed. Assemblies that run from a network drive or UNC path, however, execute with the limited "LocalIntranet" permission set, and assemblies that run from a URI execute with the even more limited "Internet" permission set.

"FullTrust," "LocalIntranet," and "Internet" are *named permission sets* defined in the computer's Runtime Security Policy. The default allocation of permission for "LocalIntranet" and "Internet" are shown in the two righthand columns in Tables 18-1 through 18-5.

The decision as to what named permission set to award a given assembly is determined by a code group (also in the computer's Runtime Security Policy). A code group maps a membership condition (e.g., "Zone = Local Intranet") to a named permission set (e.g., "LocalIntranet").

Code groups themselves can exist at three levels: Enterprise, Machine, and User. During .NET Framework installation, the three default code groups are created at the Machine level. These can be overridden, however, by the user—or by Enterprise-level settings imposed by a network domain administrator. An example of this might be to change the "LocalIntranet" set to create a brand-new code group, or to add certain trusted sites to an existing code group.

 You can view and adjust security policy with either the *mscorcfg. msc* MMC plug-in (Control Panel → Administrative Tools → Microsoft .NET Framework Configuration) or the *caspol.exe* command-line tool. The MMC plug-in no longer ships as standard with the .NET Framework: you must install either the .NET Framework SDK or Visual Studio.

The security configuration is ultimately stored in an XML file called *security.config*, in the Framework's configuration folder. You can obtain this as follows:

```
string dir = Path.Combine
  (System.Runtime.InteropServices.RuntimeEnvironment
            .GetRuntimeDirectory( ), "config");

string configFile = Path.Combine (dir, "security.config");
```

From a programmer's perspective, the upshot of all this is that a .NET application may end up running under an arbitrary set of restricted permissions with which you need to deal. This can be particularly so in a locked-down corporate environment.

Running in a Sandbox

You can make assemblies robust in the face of restricted privileges by stating declaratively the minimum permissions they require. If the permissions are not met, an exception is thrown upon startup, which is generally less frustrating to the user than if it happens partway through execution. More significantly, an administrator can reliably determine the complete set of permissions that your application requires before deploying it across an organization or network.

To declaratively state an assembly's minimum permissions:

1. Determine what permissions your program requires, using Tables 18-1 through 18-5.

2. For each required permission add a declarative security attribute to the assembly, specifying a SecurityAction of RequestMinimum.

For example, the following requests permission to write to the local Windows Event Log, along with unlimited reflection and UI permissions:

```
using System;
using System.Diagnostics;
using System.Security.Permissions;

[assembly: EventLogPermission
  (SecurityAction.RequestMinimum, MachineName = ".",
   PermissionAccess = EventLogPermissionAccess.Write)]

[assembly: ReflectionPermission
  (SecurityAction.RequestMinimum, Unrestricted = true)]

[assembly: UIPermission
  (SecurityAction.RequestMinimum, Unrestricted = true)]
```

If you know your application will *not* need certain permissions, you can ask explicitly to be denied them, using SecurityAction.RequestRefuse. This prevents you from being Trojaned by other, less privileged applications on the computer. The effort is worthwhile if your application's surface area makes it vulnerable to this kind of attack—an example would be if you expose an automation interface.

The following prohibits all file I/O:

```
[assembly: FileIOPermission
  (SecurityAction.RequestRefuse, Unrestricted = true)]
```

"Unrestricted," in this context, means you're refusing unrestricted access—in other words, all access.

Assembly-attributed permissions are not enforced if you perform a Demand directly in an entry method of an assembly! Rarely is this a problem, though, because real-world Demands will nearly always be made within methods that you call.

Optional Permissions

In profiling your application, you might find that certain permissions are required only for optional features of your program. For example, you might need IsolatedStorageFilePermission only when saving a user's preferences—a feature your program can function without. In such situations, a RequestMinimum assembly permission attribute is unsuitable—you need a more dynamic approach. There are a couple of ways to proceed. One is to explicitly check that you have appropriate permission before trying to access a resource, either by calling Demand around a try/catch block or by calling SecurityManager.IsGranted:

```
IsolatedStorageFilePermission p = new IsolatedStorageFilePermission
                                 (PermissionState.None);
p.UsageAllowed = IsolatedStorageContainment.DomainIsolationByRoamingUser;

if (SecurityManager.IsGranted (p))
    // Save user settings ...
```

A better approach, though, is to omit this step and just try and perform the action (within a try/catch block). The advantage of doing so is that you can also catch an UnauthorizedAccessException arising from operating system security restrictions (see the section "Operating System Security" later in this chapter).

SecurityAction.RequestOptional

In addition to writing try/catch blocks, you can take the extra step of declaring optional permissions as assembly attributes with a SecurityAction of Request-Optional. This has no effect on the permission itself; although it affects every other permission! Precisely, it implicitly adds a RequestRefuse on every permission that's gone unmentioned in your assembly. So, if you use RequestOptional at all, you must use it thoroughly.

Hence, there are two approaches in using assembly-based security attributes:

1. Specify MinimumRequests + RequestRefuses.
2. Specify MinimumRequests + RequestOptionals.

The second approach is easier if you really want to lock down an assembly, because you don't have to RequestRefuse dozens of permissions. If you forget any permissions, though, your application will fall over—even if run in full trust mode.

Sandboxing Another Assembly

Suppose you write an application that allows consumers to install third-party plug-ins. Most likely you'd want to prevent plug-ins from leveraging your privileges as a trusted application, so as not to destabilize your application—or the end user's computer. The best way to achieve this is to run each plug-in in its own sandboxed application domain.

For this example, we'll assume a plug-in is packaged as a .NET assembly called *plugin.exe* and that activating it is simply a matter of starting the executable. (In

---

Chapter 21, we describe how to load a library into an application domain and interact with it in a more sophisticated way.)

Here's the complete code:

```
using System;
using System.IO;
using System.Net;
using System.Reflection;
using System.Security;
using System.Security.Policy;
using System.Security.Permissions;

class Program
{
  static void Main( )
  {
    string pluginFolder = AppDomain.CurrentDomain.BaseDirectory;
    string plugInPath = Path.Combine (pluginFolder, "plugin.exe");

    PermissionSet ps = new PermissionSet (PermissionState.None);

    ps.AddPermission
      (new SecurityPermission (SecurityPermissionFlag.Execution));

    ps.AddPermission
      (new FileIOPermission (FileIOPermissionAccess.PathDiscovery |
                             FileIOPermissionAccess.Read, plugInPath));

    ps.AddPermission (new UIPermission (PermissionState.Unrestricted));

    AppDomainSetup setup = AppDomain.CurrentDomain.SetupInformation;
    AppDomain sandbox = AppDomain.CreateDomain ("sbox", null, setup, ps);
    sandbox.ExecuteAssembly (plugInPath);
    AppDomain.Unload (sandbox);
  }
}
```

First, we create a limited permission set to describe the privileges we want to give to the sandbox. This must include at least execution rights and permission for the plug-in to read its own assembly; otherwise, it won't start. In this case, we also give unrestricted UI permissions. Then we construct a new application domain, specifying our custom permission set, which will be awarded to all assemblies loaded into that domain. We then execute the plug-in assembly in the new domain, and unload the domain when the plug-in finishes executing.

Link Demands and Partially Trusted Callers

By default, a partially trusted assembly cannot call a fully trusted assembly. This is because the CLR implicitly enforces a *link demand* on every method of the target assembly. A link demand checks the permissions of the immediate caller—in this case, demanding that it be fully trusted.

You circumvent implicit link demands by adding the following attribute to the target assembly:

```
[assembly: AllowPartiallyTrustedCallers]
```

All the .NET Framework assemblies have this attribute—if they didn't, partially trusted assemblies couldn't use the Framework! Adding this attribute to your own assemblies means you should consider the security consequences of being called by a partially trusted assembly. For example, suppose your assembly exposed the following method:

```
public static byte[] GetUserPasswordHash (string username)
{
  ...
}
```

The result of an untrusted assembly calling this method would depend on how the method was written. If it performed a database query, a SecurityException would be thrown because the untrusted caller would lack SqlClientPermission. (Remember that Demand checks right up the call stack.) But now imagine that for performance reasons, the method cached the database table containing user information in a Dictionary. GetUserPasswordHash might now succeed with a permissionless caller!

A simple way to minimize such risk is to isolate the functionality you need to expose to partially trusted callers in a separate assembly.

You can also reinstate link demands on individual methods as follows:

```
[PermissionSet (SecurityAction.LinkDemand, Unrestricted = true)]
public static byte[] GetUserPasswordHash (string username)
{
  ...
```

Making Assertions

Assertions are useful when writing methods that can be called from a less trusted assembly.

Recall that we previously wrote an application that ran third-party plug-ins in a restricted permission set. Suppose we want to extend this by providing a library of safe methods for plug-ins to call. For instance, we might prohibit plug-ins from accessing a database directly, and yet still allow them to perform certain queries through methods in a library that we provide. Or we might want to expose a method for writing to a logfile—without giving them any file-based permission.

The first step in doing this is to create a separate assembly for this (e.g., *utilities*) and add the AllowPartiallyTrustedCallers attribute. Then we can expose a method as follows:

```
public static void WriteLog (string msg)
{
  // Write to log
  ...
}
```

The difficulty here is that writing to a file query requires `FileIOPermission`. Even though our *utilities* assembly will be fully trusted, the caller won't be, and so any file-based `Demand`s will fail. The solution is to first `Assert` the permission:

```
public class Utils
{
  public static void WriteLog (string msg)
  {
    FileIOPermission f = new FileIOPermission (PermissionState.None);
    f.AllLocalFiles = FileIOPermissionAccess.AllAccess;
    f.Assert( );

    // Write to log
    ...
  }
}
```

Remember that `Demand` performs a spot-check and throws an exception if the permission is not satisfied. An assertion starts by doing the same, but then makes a mark on the stack, indicating that from now on, the caller's rights should be ignored and only the current assembly's rights should be considered. An `Assert` ends when the method finishes or when you call `CodeAccessPermission.RevertAssert`.

To complete our example, the remaining step is to create a sandboxed application domain that fully trusts the *utilities* assembly. Then we can instantiate a `StrongName` object that describes the assembly, and pass it into `AppDomain`'s `CreateDomain` method:

```
static void Main( )
{
  string pluginFolder = AppDomain.CurrentDomain.BaseDirectory;
  string pluginPath = Path.Combine (pluginFolder, "plugin.exe");

  PermissionSet ps = new PermissionSet (PermissionState.None);

  // Add desired permissions to ps as we did before
  // ...

  AssemblyName utilAssembly = typeof (Utils).Assembly.GetName( );

  StrongName utils = new StrongName (
    new StrongNamePublicKeyBlob (utilAssembly.GetPublicKey( )),
    utilAssembly.Name,
    utilAssembly.Version);

  AppDomainSetup setup = AppDomain.CurrentDomain.SetupInformation;
  AppDomain sandbox = AppDomain.CreateDomain ("sbox", null, setup, ps,
                                              utils);
  sandbox.ExecuteAssembly (pluginPath);
  AppDomain.Unload (sandbox);
}
```

For this to work, the *utilities* assembly must be signed with a strong name.

Operating System Security

The operating system can further restrict what an application can do, based on the user's login privileges. In Windows, there are two types of accounts:

- An administrative account that imposes no restrictions in accessing the local computer
- A limited permissions account that restricts administrative functions and visibility of other users' data

A feature called User Access Control (UAC) introduced in Windows Vista means that administrators receive two tokens or "hats" when logging in: an administrative hat and an ordinary user hat. By default, programs run wearing the ordinary user hat—with restricted permissions—unless the program requests *administrative elevation*. The user must then approve the request via a dialog that's presented.

For application developers, UAC means that *by default*, your application will run with restricted user privileges. This means you must either:

- Write your application such that it can run without administrative privileges.
- Demand administrative elevation in the application manifest.

The first option is safer and more convenient to the user. Designing your program to run without administrative privileges is easy in most cases: the restrictions are much less draconian than those of a typical *code access security* sandbox.

 You can find out whether you're running under an administrative account with the following method:

```
[DllImport ("shell32.dll", EntryPoint = "#680")]
static extern bool IsUserAnAdmin( );
```

With UAC enabled, this returns true only if the current process has administrative elevation.

Running in a Standard User Account

Here are the key things that you *cannot* do in a standard Windows user account:

- Write to the following directories:
  - The operating system folder (typically *Windows*) and subdirectories
  - The program files folder (*Program Files*) and subdirectories
  - The root of the operating system drive (e.g., *C:*)
- Write to the HKEY_LOCAL_MACHINE branch of the Registry.
- Read performance monitoring (WMI) data.

Additionally, as an ordinary user you may be refused access to files or resources that belong to other users. Windows uses a system of Access Control Lists (ACLs) to protect such resources—you can query and assert your own rights in the ACLs via types in System.Security.AccessControl. ACLs can also be applied to cross-process wait handles, described in Chapter 19.

If you're refused access to anything as a result of operating system security, an `UnauthorizedAccessException` is thrown. This is different from the `Security-Exception` thrown when a .NET permission demand fails.

 The .NET code access permission classes are independent of ACLs. This means you can successfully `Demand` a `FileIOPermission`—but still get an `UnauthorizedAccessException` due to ACL restrictions when trying to access the file.

In most cases, you can deal with standard user restrictions as follows:

- Write files to their recommended locations.
- Avoid using the Registry for information that can be stored in files.
- Register ActiveX or COM components during setup.

The recommended location for user documents is `SpecialFolder.MyDocuments`:

```
string docsFolder = Environment.GetFolderPath
                    (Environment.SpecialFolder.MyDocuments);

string path = Path.Combine (docsFolder, "test.txt");
```

The recommended location for configuration files that a user might need to modify outside of your application is `SpecialFolder.ApplicationData` (current user only) or `SpecialFolder.CommonApplicationData` (all users). You typically create subdirectories within these folders, based on your organization and product name.

The best place to put data that need only be accessed within your application is isolated storage.

Perhaps the most inconvenient aspect of running in a standard user account is that a program doesn't have write access to its files, making it difficult to implement an automatic update system. One option is to deploy with ClickOnce: this allows updates to be applied without administrative elevation, but places significant restrictions on the setup procedure (e.g., you cannot register ActiveX controls). Applications deployed with ClickOnce may also be sandboxed with code access security, depending on their mode of delivery. We described another, more sophisticated solution in Chapter 16, in the section "Packing a Single-File Executable."

Administrative Elevation and Virtualization

In Chapter 16, we described how to deploy an application manifest. With an application manifest, you can request that Windows prompt the user for administrative elevation whenever running your program:

```
<?xml version="1.0" encoding="utf-8"?>
<assembly manifestVersion="1.0" xmlns="urn:schemas-microsoft-com:asm.v1">
  <trustInfo xmlns="urn:schemas-microsoft-com:asm.v2">
    <security>
      <requestedPrivileges>
        <requestedExecutionLevel level="requireAdministrator" />
```

Security

```
    </requestedPrivileges>
  </security>
 </trustInfo>
</assembly>
```

If you replace requireAdministrator with asInvoker, it instructs Windows that administrative elevation is *not* required. The effect is almost the same as not having an application manifest at all—except that *virtualization* is disabled. Virtualization is a temporary measure introduced with Windows Vista to help old applications run correctly without administrative privileges. The absence of an application manifest with a requestedExecutionLevel element activates this backward-compatibility feature.

Virtualization comes into play when an application writes to the *Program Files* or *Windows* directory, or the HKEY_LOCAL_MACHINE area of the Registry. Instead of throwing an exception, changes are redirected to a separate location on the hard disk where they can't impact the original data. This prevents the application from interfering with the operating system—or other well-behaved applications.

Identity and Role Security

Identity and role-based security is useful when writing a middle tier server or an ASP.NET application. It allows you to restrict functionality according to the authenticated user's name or role. An *identity* describes a username; a *role* describes a group. A *principal* is an object that describes an identity and/or a role. Hence, a PrincipalPermission class enforces identity and/or role security.

In a typical application server, you demand a PrincipalPermission on all methods exposed to the client. For example, the following requires that the caller be a member of the "finance" role:

```
[PrincipalPermission (SecurityAction.Demand, Role = "finance")]
public decimal GetGrossTurnover (int year)
{
  ...
}
```

To enforce that only a particular user can call a method, you can specify a Name instead:

```
[PrincipalPermission (SecurityAction.Demand, Name = "sally")]
```

To allow a combination of identities or roles, you have to use imperative security instead. This means instantiating PrincipalPermission objects, calling Union to combine them, and then calling Demand on the end result.

Assigning Users and Roles

Before a PrincipalPermission demand can succeed, you must attach an IPrincipal object to the current thread.

You can instruct that the current Windows user be used as an identity in either of two ways, depending on whether you want to impact the whole application domain or just the current thread:

```
AppDomain.CurrentDomain.SetPrincipalPolicy (PrincipalPolicy.
                                            WindowsPrincipal);
// or:
Thread.CurrentPrincipal = new WindowsPrincipal (WindowsIdentity.
                                                GetCurrent( ));
```

If you're using WCF or ASP.NET, their infrastructures can help with impersonating the client's identity. You can also do this yourself with the GenericPrincipal and GenericIdentity classes. The following creates a user called "Jack" and assigns him three roles:

```
GenericIdentity id = new GenericIdentity ("Jack");
GenericPrincipal p = new GenericPrincipal
   (id, new string[] { "accounts", "finance", "management" } );
```

For this to take effect, you'd assign it to the current thread as follows:

```
Thread.CurrentPrincipal = p;
```

A principal is thread-based because an application server typically processes many client requests concurrently—each on its own thread. As each request may come from a different client, it needs a different principal.

You can subclass GenericIdentity and GenericPrincipal—or implement the IIdentity and IPrincipal interfaces directly in your own types. Here's how the interfaces are defined:

```
public interface IIdentity
{
  string Name { get; }
  string AuthenticationType { get; }
  bool IsAuthenticated { get; }
}

public interface IPrincipal
{
  IIdentity Identity { get; }
  bool IsInRole (string role);
}
```

The key method is IsInRole. Notice that there's no method returning a list of roles, so you're obliged only to rule on whether a particular role is valid for that principal. This can be the basis for more elaborate authorization systems.

Cryptography Overview

Table 18-6 summarizes the cryptography options in .NET. In the remaining sections, we explore each of these.

Table 18-6. Encryption and hashing options in .NET

Option	Keys to manage	Speed	Strength	Notes
File.Encrypt	0	Fast	Moderate	Protects files transparently with filesystem support. A key is derived implicitly from the logged-in user's credentials.
Windows Data Protection	0	Fast	Moderate	Encrypts and decrypts byte arrays using an implicitly derived key.
Hashing	0	Fast	High	One-way (irreversible) transformation. Used for storing passwords, comparing files, and checking for data corruption.
Symmetric Encryption	1	Fast	High	For general-purpose encryption/decryption. The same key encrypts and decrypts. Can be used to secure messages in transit.
Public Key Encryption	2	Slow	High	Encryption and decryption use different keys. Used for exchanging a symmetric key in message transmission and for digitally signing files.

The Framework also provides more specialized support for creating and validating XML-based signatures in System.Security.Cryptography.Xml and types for working with digital certificates in System.Security.Cryptography.X509Certificates.

Windows Data Protection

In the section "File and Directory Operations" in Chapter 13, we described how you could use File.Encrypt to request that the operating system transparently encrypt a file:

```
File.WriteAllText ("myfile.txt", "");
File.Encrypt ("myfile.txt");
File.AppendAllText ("myfile.txt", "sensitive data");
```

The encryption in this case uses a key derived from the logged-in user's password. You can use this same implicitly derived key to encrypt a byte array with the Windows Data Protection API. The Data Protection API is exposed through the ProtectedData class—a simple type with two static methods:

```
public static byte[] Protect (byte[] userData, byte[] optionalEntropy,
                        DataProtectionScope scope);

public static byte[] Unprotect (byte[] encryptedData, byte[]
optionalEntropy,
                        DataProtectionScope scope);
```

 Most types in System.Security.Cryptography live in *mscorlib.dll*. ProtectedData is an exception: it lives in *System.Security.dll*.

Whatever you include in optionalEntropy is added to the key, thereby increasing its security. The DataProtectionScope enum argument allows two options: CurrentUser or LocalMachine. With CurrentUser, a key is derived from the logged-in user's credentials; with LocalMachine, a machine-wide key is used, common to all users. A LocalMachine key provides less protection, but works under a Windows Service or a program needing to operate under a variety of accounts.

Here's a simple encryption and decryption demo:

```
byte[] original = {1, 2, 3, 4, 5};
DataProtectionScope scope = DataProtectionScope.CurrentUser;

byte[] encrypted = ProtectedData.Protect (original, null, scope);
byte[] decrypted = ProtectedData.Unprotect (encrypted, null, scope);
// decrypted is now {1, 2, 3, 4, 5}
```

Windows Data Protection provides moderate security against an attacker with full access to the computer, depending on the strength of the user's password. With LocalMachine scope, it's effective only against those with restricted physical and electronic access.

Hashing

Hashing provides one-way encryption. This is ideal for storing passwords in a database, as you might never need (or want) to see a decrypted version. To authenticate, simply hash what the user types in and compare it to what's stored in the database.

A hash code is always a small fixed size regardless of the source data length. This makes it good for comparing files or detecting errors in a data stream (rather like a checksum). A single-bit change anywhere in the source data results in a significantly different hash code.

To hash, you call ComputeHash on one of the HashAlgorithm subclasses such as SHA256 or MD5:

```
byte[] hash;
using (Stream fs = File.OpenRead ("checkme.doc"))
  hash = MD5.Create().ComputeHash (fs);          // hash is 16 bytes long
```

The ComputeHash method also accepts a byte array, which is convenient for hashing passwords:

```
byte[] data = System.Text.Encoding.UTF8.GetBytes ("stRhong%pword");
byte[] hash = SHA256.Create().ComputeHash (data);
```

 The GetBytes method on an Encoding object converts a string to a byte array; the GetString method converts it back. An Encoding object cannot, however, convert an encrypted or hashed byte array to a string, because scrambled data usually violates text encoding rules. Instead, use Convert.ToBase64String and Convert.FromBase64String: these convert between any byte array and a legal (and XML-friendly) string.

MD5 and SHA256 are two of the HashAlgorithm subtypes provided by the .NET Framework. Here are all the major algorithms, in ascending order of security (and hash length, in bytes):

MD5(16) → SHA1(20) → SHA256(32) → SHA384(48) → SHA512(64)

The shorter the algorithm, the faster it executes. MD5 is more than 20 times faster than SHA512 and is well suited to calculating file checksums. You can hash hundreds of megabytes per second with MD5, and then store its result in a Guid. (A Guid happens to be exactly 16 bytes long, and as a value type it is more tractable than a byte array; you can meaningfully compare Guids with the simple equality operator, for instance.)

 Use *at least* SHA1 when hashing passwords; MD5 is considered insecure for this purpose.

The SHA algorithms are suitable for password hashing, but they require that you enforce a strong password policy to mitigate a *dictionary attack*—a strategy whereby an attacker builds a password lookup table by hashing every word in a dictionary. You can provide additional protection against this by "stretching" your password hashes—repeatedly rehashing to obtain more computationally intensive byte sequences. If you rehash 100 times, a dictionary attack that might otherwise take 1 month would take 8 years.

The Framework also provides a 160-bit RIPEMD hashing algorithm, slightly above SHA1 in security. It suffers an inefficient .NET implementation, though, making it slower to execute than even SHA512.

Symmetric Encryption

Symmetric encryption uses the same key for encryption as for decryption. The Framework provides four symmetric algorithms, of which Rijndael is the premium (pronounced "Rhine Dahl" or "Rain Doll"). Also called AES (Advanced Encryption Standard), Rijndael is both fast and secure.

Rijndael allows symmetric keys of length 16, 24, or 32 bytes. Here's how to encrypt a series of bytes as they're written to a file, using a 16-byte key:

```
byte[] key = {145,12,32,245,98,132,98,214,6,77,131,44,221,3,9,50};
byte[] iv  = {15,122,132,5,93,198,44,31,9,39,241,49,250,188,80,7};

byte[] data = { 1, 2, 3, 4, 5 };   // This is what we're encrypting.

using (SymmetricAlgorithm algorithm = Rijndael.Create())
using (ICryptoTransform encryptor = algorithm.CreateEncryptor (key, iv))
using (Stream f = File.Create ("encrypted.bin"))
using (Stream c = new CryptoStream (f, encryptor, CryptoStreamMode.Write))
  c.Write (data, 0, data.Length);
```

From Framework 3.5, you can choose between calling `Rijndael.Create` or `AesCryptoServiceProvider.Create`. The latter returns an encryptor that's functionally identical—except that it doesn't allow you to change the block size from the default value of 128 bits. This is to comply with FIPS certification rules.

The following code decrypts the file:

```
byte[] key = {145,12,32,245,98,132,98,214,6,77,131,44,221,3,9,50};
byte[] iv  = {15,122,132,5,93,198,44,31,9,39,241,49,250,188,80,7};

byte[] decrypted = new byte[5];

using (SymmetricAlgorithm algorithm = Rijndael.Create())
using (ICryptoTransform decryptor = algorithm.CreateDecryptor (key, iv))
using (Stream f = File.OpenRead ("encrypted.bin"))
using (Stream c = new CryptoStream (f, decryptor, CryptoStreamMode.Read))
  for (int b; (b = c.ReadByte()) > -1;)
    Console.Write (b + " ");                    // 1 2 3 4 5
```

In this example, we made up a key of 16 randomly chosen bytes. If the wrong key was used in decryption, `CryptoStream` would throw a `CryptographicException`. Catching this exception is the only way to test whether a key is correct.

As well as a key, we made up an IV, or *Initialization Vector*. This 16-byte sequence forms part of the cipher—much like the key—but is not considered *secret*. If transmitting an encrypted message, you would send the IV in plain text (perhaps in a message header) and then *change it with every message*. This would render each encrypted message unrecognizable from any previous one—even if their unencrypted versions were similar or identical.

If you don't need—or want—the protection of an IV, you can defeat it by using the same 16-byte value for both the key and the IV.

The cryptography work is divided among the classes. `Rijndael` is the mathematician; it applies the cipher algorithm, along with its encryptor and decryptor transforms. `CryptoStream` is the plumber; it takes care of stream plumbing. You can replace `Rijndael` with a different symmetric algorithm, yet still use `CryptoStream`.

`CryptoStream` is *bidirectional*, meaning you can either read or write to the stream depending on whether you choose `CryptoStreamMode.Read` or `CryptoStreamMode.Write`. Both encryptors and decryptors are read- *and* write-savvy, yielding four combinations—the choice can have you staring at a blank screen for a while! It can be helpful to model reading as "pulling" and writing as "pushing." If in doubt, start with `Write` for encryption and `Read` for decryption; this is often the most natural.

To generate a random key or IV, use `RandomNumberGenerator` in `System.Cryptography`. The numbers it produces are genuinely unpredictable, or *cryptographically strong* (the `System.Random` class does not offer the same guarantee). Here's an example:

```
byte[] key = new byte [16];
byte[] iv  = new byte [16];
RandomNumberGenerator rand = RandomNumberGenerator.Create( );
rand.GetBytes (key);
rand.GetBytes (iv);
```

If you don't specify a key and IV, cryptographically strong random values are generated automatically. You can query these through the `Rijndael` object's `Key` and `IV` properties.

Encrypting in Memory

With a `MemoryStream`, you can encrypt and decrypt entirely in memory. Here are helper methods that do just this, with byte arrays:

```
public static byte[] Encrypt (byte[] data, byte[] key, byte[] iv)
{
  using (Rijndael algorithm = Rijndael.Create( ))
  using (ICryptoTransform encryptor = algorithm.CreateEncryptor (key, iv))
    return Crypt (data, key, iv, encryptor);
}

public static byte[] Decrypt (byte[] data, byte[] key, byte[] iv)
{
  using (Rijndael algorithm = Rijndael.Create( ))
  using (ICryptoTransform decryptor = algorithm.CreateDecryptor (key, iv))
    return Crypt (data, key, iv, decryptor);
}

static byte[] Crypt (byte[] data, byte[] key, byte[] iv,
                     ICryptoTransform cryptor)
{
  MemoryStream m = new MemoryStream( );
  using (Stream c = new CryptoStream (m, cryptor, CryptoStreamMode.Write))
    c.Write (data, 0, data.Length);
  return m.ToArray( );
}
```

Here, `CryptoStreamMode.Write` works best for both encryption and decryption, since in both cases we're "pushing" into a fresh memory stream.

Here are overloads that accept and return strings:

```
public static string Encrypt (string data, byte[] key, byte[] iv)
{
  return Convert.ToBase64String (
    Encrypt (Encoding.UTF8.GetBytes (data), key, iv));
}
```

```
public static string Decrypt (string data, byte[] key, byte[] iv)
{
  return Encoding.UTF8.GetString (
    Decrypt (Convert.FromBase64String (data), key, iv));
}
```

The following demonstrates their use:

```
byte[] kiv = new byte[16];
RandomNumberGenerator.Create( ).GetBytes (kiv);

string encrypted = Encrypt ("Yeah!", kiv, kiv);
Console.WriteLine (encrypted);              // R1/5gYvcxyR2vzPjnT7yaQ==

string decrypted = Decrypt (encrypted, kiv, kiv);
Console.WriteLine (decrypted);              // Yeah!
```

Chaining Encryption Streams

CryptoStream is a decorator, meaning it can be chained with other streams. In the following example, we write compressed encrypted text to a file, and then read it back:

```
// Use default key/iv for demo.
using (Rijndael algorithm = Rijndael.Create( ))
{
  using (ICryptoTransform encryptor = algorithm.CreateEncryptor( ))
  using (Stream f = File.Create ("serious.bin"))
  using (Stream c = new CryptoStream (f,encryptor,CryptoStreamMode.Write))
  using (Stream d = new DeflateStream (c, CompressionMode.Compress))
  using (StreamWriter w = new StreamWriter (d))
    w.WriteLine ("Small and secure!");

  using (ICryptoTransform decryptor = algorithm.CreateDecryptor( ))
  using (Stream f = File.OpenRead ("serious.bin"))
  using (Stream c = new CryptoStream (f, decryptor, CryptoStreamMode.Read))
  using (Stream d = new DeflateStream (c, CompressionMode.Decompress))
  using (StreamReader r = new StreamReader (d))
    Console.WriteLine (r.ReadLine( ));          // Small and secure!
}
```

In this example, all one-letter variables form part of a chain. The mathematicians—algorithm, encryptor, and decryptor—are there to assist CryptoStream in the cipher work. Figure 18-1 shows this diagrammatically.

Chaining streams in this manner demands little memory, regardless of the ultimate stream sizes.

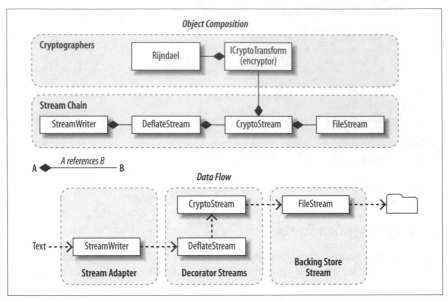

Figure 18-1. Chaining encryption and compression streams

 As an alternative to nesting multiple using statements, you can construct a chain as follows:

```
using (ICryptoTransform encryptor = algorithm.
CreateEncryptor())
using
  (StreamWriter w = new StreamWriter (
    new DeflateStream (
      new CryptoStream (
        File.Create ("serious.bin"),
        encryptor,
        CryptoStreamMode.Write
      ),
      CompressionMode.Compress)
  )
)
```

This is less robust than the previous approach, however, because should an exception be thrown in an object's constructor (e.g., DeflateStream), any objects already instantiated (e.g., FileStream) would not be disposed.

Disposing Encryption Objects

Disposing a CryptoStream ensures that its internal cache of data is flushed to the underlying stream. Internal caching is necessary for encryption algorithms because they process data in blocks, rather than one byte at a time.

`CryptoStream` is unusual in that its `Flush` method does nothing. To flush a stream (without disposing it) you must call `FlushFinalBlock`. In contrast to `Flush`, `FlushFinalBlock` can be called only once, and then no further data can be written.

In our examples, we also disposed the mathematicians—the `Rijndael` algorithm and `ICryptoTransform` objects (encryptor and decryptor). Disposal is actually optional with the Rijndael transforms, because their implementations are purely managed. Disposal still serves a useful role, however: it wipes the symmetric key and related data from memory, preventing subsequent discovery by other software running on the computer (we're talking malware). You can't rely on the garbage collector for this job because it merely flags sections of memory as available; it doesn't write zeros over every byte.

The easiest way to dispose a `Rijndael` object outside of a `using` statement is to call `Clear`. Its `Dispose` method is hidden via explicit implementation (to signal its unusual disposal semantics).

Key Management

It is inadvisable to hardcode encryption keys because popular tools exist to decompile assemblies with little expertise. A better option is to manufacture a random key for each installation, storing it securely with Windows Data Protection. If you're encrypting a message stream, public key encryption provides the best option still.

Public Key Encryption and Signing

Public key cryptography is *asymmetric*, meaning that encryption and decryption use different keys.

Unlike symmetric encryption, where any arbitrary series of bytes of appropriate length can serve as a key, asymmetric cryptography requires specially crafted key pairs. A key pair contains a *public key* and *private key* component that work together as follows:

- The public key encrypts messages.
- The private key decrypts messages.

The party "crafting" a key pair keeps the private key secret while distributing the public key freely. A special feature of this type of cryptography is that you cannot calculate a private key from a public key. So, if the private key is lost, encrypted data cannot be recovered; conversely, if a private key is leaked, the encryption system becomes useless.

A public key handshake allows two computers to communicate securely over a public network, with no prior contact and no existing shared secret. To see how this works, suppose computer *Origin* wants to send a confidential message to computer *Target*:

1. *Target* generates a public/private key pair, and then sends its public key to *Origin*.
2. *Origin* encrypts the confidential message using *Target*'s public key, then sends it to *Target*.
3. *Target* decrypts the confidential message using its private key.

An eavesdropper will see the following:

- *Target*'s public key
- The secret message, encrypted with *Target*'s public key

But without *Target*'s private key, the message cannot be decrypted.

The secret message sent from *Origin* to *Target* typically contains a fresh key for subsequent *symmetric* encryption. This allows public key encryption to be abandoned for the remainder of the session, in favor of a faster symmetric algorithm. This protocol is particularly secure if a fresh public/private key pair is generated for each session, as no keys then need to be stored on either computer.

 Public key encryption is slow. It's designed for encrypting only small amounts of data, such as a key for subsequent symmetric encryption.

The RSA Class

The .NET Framework provides two asymmetric algorithms: DSA and RSA; RSA being more secure. Here's how to encrypt and decrypt with RSA:

```
byte[] data = { 1, 2, 3, 4, 5 };   // This is what we're encrypting.

using (RSACryptoServiceProvider rsa = new RSACryptoServiceProvider())
{
  byte[] encrypted = rsa.Encrypt (data, true);
  byte[] decrypted = rsa.Decrypt (encrypted, true);
}
```

Because we didn't specify a public or private key, the cryptographic provider automatically generated a key pair, using the default length of 1,024 bits. This length is considered secure for most purposes; you can request longer keys in increments of eight bytes, through the constructor:

```
RSACryptoServiceProvider rsa = new RSACryptoServiceProvider (2048);
```

Generating a key pair is computationally intensive—taking perhaps 100 ms. For this reason, the RSA implementation delays this until a key is actually needed, such as when calling Encrypt. This gives you the chance to load in an existing key—or key pair, should it exist.

The methods ImportCspBlob and ExportCspBlob load and save keys in byte array format. FromXmlString and ToXmlString do the same job in a string format, the string containing an XML fragment. A boolean flag lets you indicate whether to include the private key when saving. Here's how to manufacture a key pair and save it to disk:

```
using (RSACryptoServiceProvider rsa = new RSACryptoServiceProvider())
{
  File.WriteAllText ("PublicKeyOnly.xml", rsa.ToXmlString (false));
  File.WriteAllText ("PublicPrivate.xml", rsa.ToXmlString (true));
}
```

Since we didn't provide existing keys, ToXmlString forced the manufacture of a fresh key pair. In the next example, we read back these keys and use them to encrypt and decrypt a message:

```
byte[] data = Encoding.UTF8.GetBytes ("Message to encrypt");

string publicKeyOnly = File.ReadAllText ("PublicKeyOnly.xml");
string publicPrivate = File.ReadAllText ("PublicPrivate.xml");

byte[] encrypted, decrypted;

using (var rsaPublicOnly = new RSACryptoServiceProvider())
{
  rsaPublicOnly.FromXmlString (publicKeyOnly);
  encrypted = rsaPublicOnly.Encrypt (data, true);

  // The next line would throw an exception because you need the private
  // key in order to decrypt:
  // decrypted = rsaPublicOnly.Decrypt (encrypted, true);
}

using (var rsaPublicPrivate = new RSACryptoServiceProvider())
{
  // With the private key we can successfully decrypt:
  rsaPublicPrivate.FromXmlString (publicPrivate);
  decrypted = rsaPublicPrivate.Decrypt (encrypted, true);
}
```

Digital Signing

Public key algorithms can also be used to digitally sign messages or documents. A signature is like a hash, except that its production requires a private key and so cannot be forged. The public key is used to verify the signature. Here's an example:

```
byte[] data = Encoding.UTF8.GetBytes ("Message to sign");
byte[] publicKey;
byte[] signature;
object hasher = SHA1.Create();        // Our chosen hashing algorithm.

// Generate a new key pair, then sign the data with it:
using (var publicPrivate = new RSACryptoServiceProvider())
{
  signature = publicPrivate.SignData (data, hasher);
  publicKey = publicPrivate.ExportCspBlob (false);    // get public key
}

// Create a fresh RSA using just the public key, then test the signature.
using (var publicOnly = new RSACryptoServiceProvider())
{
  publicOnly.ImportCspBlob (publicKey);
  Console.Write (publicOnly.VerifyData (data, hasher, signature)); // True

  // Let's now tamper with the data, and recheck the signature:
```

```
data[0] = 0;
Console.Write (publicOnly.VerifyData (data, hasher, signature)); // False

// The following throws an exception as we're lacking a private key:
signature = publicOnly.SignData (data, hasher);
}
```

Signing works by first hashing the data, and then applying the asymmetric algorithm to the resultant hash. Because hashes are of a small fixed size, large documents can be signed quickly. If you want, you can do the hashing yourself, and then call SignHash instead of SignData:

```
using (var rsa = new RSACryptoServiceProvider( ))
{
  byte[] hash = SHA1.Create( ).ComputeHash (data);
  signature = rsa.SignHash (hash, CryptoConfig.MapNameToOID ("SHA1"));
  ...
}
```

SignHash still needs to know what hash algorithm you used; CryptoConfig. MapNameToOID provides this information in the correct format from a friendly name such as "SHA1".

RSACryptoServiceProvider produces 128-bit signatures—equivalent in size to a Guid. Currently, no mainstream algorithm produces significantly smaller secure signatures (suitable for product activation codes, for instance).

 For signing to be effective, the recipient must know, and trust, the sender's public key. This can happen via prior communication, pre-configuration, or a site certificate. A site certificate is an electronic record of the originator's public key and name—itself signed by an independent trusted authority. The namespace System.Security. Cryptography.X509Certificates defines the types for working with certificates.

19

Threading

C# allows you to execute code in parallel through multithreading.

A thread is analogous to the operating system process in which your application runs. Just as processes run in parallel on a computer, threads run in parallel *within a single process*. Processes are fully isolated from each other; threads have just a limited degree of isolation. In particular, threads share (heap) memory with other threads running in the same application domain. This, in part, is why threading is useful: one thread can fetch data in the background while another thread displays the data as it arrives.

This chapter describes the language and Framework features for creating, configuring, and communicating with threads, and how to coordinate their actions through locking and signaling. It also covers the predefined types that assist threading: `BackgroundWorker`, `ReaderWriterLock`, and the `Timer` classes.

Threading's Uses and Misuses

A common use for multithreading is to maintain a responsive user interface while a time-consuming task executes. If the time-consuming task runs on a parallel "worker" thread, the main thread is free to continue processing keyboard and mouse events.

Whether or not a user interface is involved, multithreading can be useful when awaiting a response from another computer or piece of hardware. If a worker thread performs the task, the instigator is immediately free to do other things, taking advantage of the otherwise unburdened computer.

Another use for multithreading is in writing methods that perform intensive calculations. Such methods can execute faster on a multiprocessor or multicore computer if the workload is shared among two or more threads. Asynchronous delegates are particularly well suited to this. (You can test for the number of processors via the `Environment.ProcessorCount` property.)

Some features of the .NET Framework implicitly create threads. If you use ASP. NET, WCF, Web Services, or Remoting, incoming client requests can arrive concurrently on the server. You may be unaware that multithreading is taking place; unless, perhaps, you use static fields to cache data without appropriate locking, running afoul of thread safety.

Threads also come with strings attached. The biggest is that multithreading can increase complexity. Having lots of threads does not in itself create complexity; it's the interaction between threads (typically via shared data) that does. This applies whether or not the interaction is intentional, and can cause long development cycles and an ongoing susceptibility to intermittent and nonreproducible bugs. For this reason, it pays to keep interaction to a minimum, and to stick to simple and proven designs wherever possible. This chapter is largely on dealing with just these complexities; remove the interaction and there's relatively little to say!

Threading also comes with a resource and CPU cost in allocating and switching threads. Multithreading will not always speed up your application—it can even slow it down if used excessively or inappropriately. For example, when heavy disk I/O is involved, it can be faster to have a couple of worker threads run tasks in sequence than to have 10 threads executing at once. (In the later section "Signaling with Wait and Pulse," we describe how to implement a producer/ consumer queue, which provides just this functionality.)

Getting Started

A C# program starts in a single thread that's created automatically by the CLR and operating system (the "main" thread). Here it lives out its life as a single-threaded application, unless you do otherwise, by creating more threads (directly or indirectly).

The simplest way to create a thread is to instantiate a Thread object and to call its Start method. The constructor for Thread takes a ThreadStart delegate: a parameterless method indicating where execution should begin. Here's an example:

```
class ThreadTest
{
  static void Main()
  {
    Thread t = new Thread (WriteY);      // Kick off a new thread
    t.Start();                            // running WriteY()

    // Simultaneously, do something on the main thread.
    for (int i = 0; i < 1000; i++) Console.Write ("x");
  }

  static void WriteY()
  {
    for (int i = 0; i < 1000; i++) Console.Write ("y");
  }
}
```

```
// Output:
xxxxxxxxxxxxxxxxxxxyyyyyyyyyyyyyyyyyyyyyyyyyyyyyyyyyyyyy
xxxxxxxxxxxxxxxxxxxxxxxxxxxxxxxxxxxxxxxxyyyyyyyyyyyyyyy
yyyyyyyyyyyyyyyyyyyyyyyyyyyyyyyyyyyxxxxxxxxxxxxxxxxxxxx
xxxxxxxxxxxxxxxxxxxxxxxxxyyyyyyyyyyyyyyyyyyyyyyyyyyyyyy
yyyyyyyyyyyyyxxxxxxxxxxxxxxxxxxxxxxxxxxxxxxxxxxxxxxxxxx
...
```

 All examples assume the following namespaces are imported, unless otherwise specified:

```
using System;
using System.Threading;
```

The main thread creates a new thread t on which it runs a method that repeatedly prints the character "y". Simultaneously, the main thread repeatedly prints the character "x", as shown in Figure 19-1. On a single-processor computer, the operating system must allocate "slices" of time to each thread (typically 20 ms in Windows) to simulate concurrency, resulting in repeated blocks of "x" and "y". On a multiprocessor or multicore machine, the two threads can genuinely execute in parallel, although you still get repeated blocks of "x" and "y" because of subtleties in the mechanism by which Console handles concurrent requests.

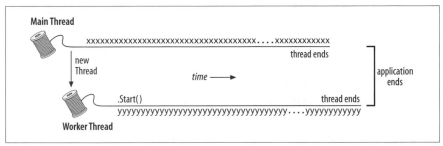

Figure 19-1. Starting a new thread

 A thread is said to be *preempted* at the points where its execution is interspersed with the execution of code on another thread. The term often crops up in explaining why something has gone wrong!

Once started, a thread's IsAlive property returns true, until the point where the thread ends. A thread ends when the method referenced in the Thread's constructor finishes—in this case, WriteY. Once ended, a thread cannot restart.

You can wait for another thread to end by calling its Join method. Here's an example:

```
static void Main()
{
  Thread t = new Thread (Go);
  t.Start();
  t.Join();
```

```
    Console.WriteLine ("Thread t has ended!");
  }

  static void Go( ) { for (int i = 0; i < 1000; i++) Console.Write ("y"); }
```

This prints "y" 1,000 times, followed by "Thread t has ended!" straight afterward. You can include a timeout when calling Join, either in milliseconds or as a TimeSpan. It then returns true if the thread ended or false if it timed out.

Thread.Sleep pauses the current thread for a specified period:

```
    Thread.Sleep (TimeSpan.FromHours (1));  // sleep for 1 hour
    Thread.Sleep (500);                     // sleep for 500 milliseconds
    Thread.Sleep (0);                       // relinquish CPU time-slice
```

Thread.Sleep(0) relinquishes the processor just long enough to allow any other active threads present in a time-slicing queue (should there be one) to be executed.

> Thread.Sleep(0) is occasionally useful in production code for advanced performance tweaks. It's also an excellent diagnostic tool for helping to uncover thread safety issues: if inserting Thread.Sleep(0) anywhere in your code makes or breaks the program, you almost certainly have a bug.

Each thread has a Name property that you can set for the benefit of debugging. This is particularly useful in Microsoft Visual Studio, since the thread's name is displayed in the Debug Location toolbar. You can set a thread's name just once; attempts to change it later will throw an exception.

The static Thread.CurrentThread property allows you to refer to the currently executing thread:

```
    Console.WriteLine (Thread.CurrentThread.Name);
```

Passing Data to a Thread

Let's say we want to pass an argument to the method on which a thread starts. Here's how it's done:

```
    static void Main( )
    {
      Thread t = new Thread (Print);
      t.Start ("Hello from t!");
      Print ("Hello from the main thread!");
    }

    static void Print (object messageObj)
    {
      string message = (string) messageObj;
      Console.WriteLine (message);
    }
```

```
// Output:
Hello from t!
Hello from the main thread!
```

To make this possible, Thread's constructor is overloaded to accept either of two delegates:

```
public delegate void ThreadStart();
public delegate void ParameterizedThreadStart (object obj);
```

The limitation of ParameterizedThreadStart is that it accepts only one argument. And because it's of type object, it usually needs to be cast. An alternative is to use the parameterless ThreadStart in conjunction with an anonymous method as follows:

```
static void Main()
{
  Thread t = new Thread (delegate() { Print ("Hello from t!"); });
  t.Start();
}
static void Print (string message) { Console.WriteLine (message); }
```

The advantage is that the target method (in this case, Print) can accept any number of arguments, and no casting is required. The flip side, though, is that you must keep outer-variable semantics in mind, as the following example demonstrates:

```
static void Main()
{
  string text = "t1";
  Thread t1 = new Thread (delegate() { Print (text); });

  text = "t2";
  Thread t2 = new Thread (delegate() { Print (text); });

  t1.Start();
  t2.Start();
}
static void Print (string message) { Console.WriteLine (message); }

// Output:
t2
t2
```

Sharing Data Between Threads

The preceding example demonstrated that local variables captured in an anonymous method are shared between threads. This, however, is an unusual (and generally undesirable) scenario. Let's examine what normally happens with local variables on a thread. Consider this program:

```
static void Main()
{
  new Thread (Go).Start();    // Call Go() on a new thread
  Go();                       // Call Go() on the main thread
}
```

```
static void Go( )
{
  // Declare and use a local variable - 'cycles'
  for (int cycles = 0; cycles < 5; cycles++) Console.Write (cycles);
}
```

```
// OUTPUT:   0123401234
```

Each thread as it enters the Go method gets a separate copy of the cycles variable and so is unable to interfere with another concurrent thread. The CLR and operating system achieve this by assigning each thread its own private memory stack for local variables.

If threads do want to share data, they usually do so via a common reference. Here's an example:

```
class ThreadTest
{
  static void Main( )
  {
    Introducer intro = new Introducer( );
    intro.Message = "Hello";

    new Thread (intro.Run).Start( );

    Console.ReadLine( );
    Console.WriteLine (intro.Reply);
  }
}

class Introducer
{
  public string Message;
  public string Reply;

  public void Run( )
  {
    Console.WriteLine (Message);
    Reply = "Hi right back!";
  }
}
```

```
// Output:
Hello
Hi right back!    (after pressing Enter)
```

This system allows both for passing data to a new thread and for receiving data back from it later on. Moreover, it's the means by which threads can communicate with each other as they're running.

> Shared data is the primary cause of complexity and obscure errors in multithreading. Although often essential, it pays to keep it as simple as possible.

Fields declared as static are also shared between threads. Static fields, in fact, offer the simplest approach to sharing data, where application-wide scope is appropriate.

Thread Pooling

Whenever you start a thread, a few hundred microseconds are spent organizing such things as a fresh private local variable stack. Each thread also consumes around 1 MB of memory. The *thread pool* cuts these overheads by sharing and recycling threads, allowing multithreading to be applied at a more granular level without performance penalty.

The easiest way into the thread pool is by calling `ThreadPool.QueueUserWorkItem` instead of instantiating and starting a `Thread` object. Here's an example:

```
static void Main( )
{
  ThreadPool.QueueUserWorkItem (Go);
  ThreadPool.QueueUserWorkItem (Go, 123);
  Console.ReadLine( );
}

static void Go (object data)
{
  Console.WriteLine ("Hello from the thread pool! " + data);
}

// Output:
Hello from the thread pool!
Hello from the thread pool! 123
```

Our target method, `Go`, must accept a single object argument (to satisfy the `WaitCallback` delegate). This provides a convenient way of passing data to the method, just like with `ParameterizedThreadStart`.

The thread pool also keeps a lid on the total number of worker threads it will run simultaneously. Too many threads throttle the operating system with administrative burden. You can set the upper limit by calling `ThreadPool.SetMaxThreads`; the default is 50 (this may vary according to the hardware and operating system). Once exceeded, jobs queue up and start only when another finishes.

The thread pool makes arbitrarily concurrent applications possible, such as a web server. If you start a new thread on the server for every client request, a heavy spurt of concurrent client activity could choke the server. The thread pool addresses this problem by limiting the number of active threads. (The *asynchronous method* pattern takes this further by making highly efficient use of the pooled threads; see Chapter 20.)

You get just one thread pool per application. You can query if you're currently executing on a pooled thread via the property `Thread.CurrentThread.IsThread-PoolThread`.

The following automatically use the thread pool:

- Asynchronous delegates
- The BackgroundWorker helper class
- System.Timers.Timer and System.Threading.Timer
- WCF, Remoting, ASP.NET, and Web Services application servers

Optimizing the pool

The pool manager creates threads only as they're needed; this ensures that a "Hello, world" program doesn't allocate 50 threads and consume 50 MB of memory. But suppose a program rapidly enqueues 50 tasks to the pool as follows:

```
static void Main( )
{
  for (int i = 0; i < 50; i++) ThreadPool.QueueUserWorkItem (Go);
}

static void Go (object notUsed)
{
  // Compute a hash on a 100,000 byte random byte sequence:
  byte[] data = new byte [100000];
  new Random( ).NextBytes (data);
  System.Security.Cryptography.SHA1.Create( ).ComputeHash (data);
}
```

The pool manager stops short of creating 50 threads. In fact, to begin with, it stops right at the number of processors or CPU cores; on a dual-core computer, the pool manager will create just two threads and queue the remaining 48 jobs to these two threads. Matching the thread count to the core count allows a program to retain a small memory footprint without hurting performance—as long as the threads are efficiently used (which in this case they are). But now suppose we insert a Thread.Sleep statement before computing the hash, idling the CPU for a while (or run a time-consuming database query). The pool manager's thread-economy strategy breaks down; it would now do better to create 50 threads, so all the jobs could sleep (or wait for the database server) simultaneously.

Fortunately, the pool manager has a backup plan. If its queue remains stationary for more than half a second, it responds by creating more threads—one every half-second—up to the capacity of the thread pool. Once created, a thread's in the pool for life, so it will always be available immediately to service new requests.

The half-second delay is a two-edged sword. On the one hand, it means that a one-off burst of brief activity (such as in our example, without the sleep) doesn't make a program suddenly consume an extra unnecessary 50 MB of memory. On the other hand, it can needlessly delay things when a pooled thread blocks, such as when querying a database or calling WebClient.DownloadFile. For this reason, you can tell the pool manager not to delay in the allocation of the first x threads, as follows:

```
ThreadPool.SetMinThreads (50, 50);
```

This makes sense on client applications that use the thread pool; if you're writing an application server using a technology such as WCF or ASP.NET, the infrastructure does this automatically.

Foreground and Background Threads

By default, threads you create explicitly are foreground threads; pooled threads are background threads. The difference is that foreground threads keep the application alive for as long as any one of them is running; background threads do not. Once all foreground threads finish, the application ends, and any background threads still running abruptly terminate.

 A thread's foreground/background status has no relation to its priority or allocation of execution time.

You can query or change a thread's background status using its IsBackground property. Here's an example:

```
class PriorityTest
{
  static void Main (string[] args)
  {
    Thread worker = new Thread (delegate() { Console.ReadLine(); });
    if (args.Length > 0) worker.IsBackground = true;
    worker.Start();
  }
}
```

If this program is called with no arguments, the worker thread assumes foreground status and will wait on the ReadLine statement for the user to press Enter. Meanwhile, the main thread exits, but the application keeps running because a foreground thread is still alive.

On the other hand, if an argument is passed to Main(), the worker is assigned background status, and the program exits almost immediately as the main thread ends (terminating the ReadLine).

When a background thread terminates in this manner, any finally blocks are circumvented. This is a problem if your program employs finally blocks (or the using keyword) to perform cleanup work such as releasing resources or deleting temporary files. To avoid this, you can explicitly wait out such background threads upon exiting an application. There are two ways to accomplish this:

- If you've created the thread yourself, call Join on the thread.
- If you're using the thread pool, use an event wait handle (discussed later in this chapter in the section "Signaling with Event Wait Handles").

In either case, you should specify a timeout, so you can abandon a renegade thread should it refuse to finish for some reason. This is your backup exit strategy: in the end, you want your application to close—without the user having to enlist help from the Task Manager!

If a user uses the Task Manager to forcibly end a .NET process, all threads "drop dead" as though they were background threads. This is observed rather than documented behavior, and it could vary depending on the CLR and operating system version.

Foreground threads don't require this treatment, but you must take care to avoid bugs that could cause the thread not to end. A common cause for applications failing to exit properly is the presence of active foregrounds threads.

Thread Priority

A thread's `Priority` property determines how much execution time it gets relative to other active threads in the same process, on the following scale:

```
enum ThreadPriority { Lowest, BelowNormal, Normal, AboveNormal, Highest }
```

This becomes relevant only when multiple threads are simultaneously active.

Elevating a thread's priority doesn't make it capable of performing real-time work, because it's still limited by the application's process priority. To perform real-time work, you must also elevate the process priority using the `Process` class in `System.Diagnostics` (we didn't tell you how to do this):

```
Process.GetCurrentProcess().PriorityClass = ProcessPriorityClass.High;
```

`ProcessPriorityClass.High` is actually one notch short of the highest priority: `Realtime`. Setting a process priority to `Realtime` instructs the OS that you never want the process to yield CPU time to another process. If your program enters an accidental infinite loop, you might find even the operating system locked out, with nothing short of the power button left to rescue you! For this reason, `High` is usually the best choice for real-time applications.

If your real-time application has a user interface, elevating the process priority gives screen updates excessive CPU time, slowing down the entire computer (particularly if the UI is complex). Lowering the main thread's priority in conjunction with raising the process's priority ensures that the real-time thread doesn't get preempted by screen redraws, but doesn't solve the problem of starving other applications of CPU time, because the operating system will still allocate disproportionate resources to the process as a whole. An ideal solution is to have the real-time worker and user interface run as separate applications with different process priorities, communicating via Remoting or memory-mapped files. Memory-mapped files are ideally suited to this task; we explain how they work in "Shared Memory" in Chapter 22.

Even with an elevated process priority, there's a limit to the suitability of the managed environment in handling hard real-time requirements. In Chapter 12, we described the issues of garbage collection and the workarounds. Further, the operating system may present additional challenges—even for unmanaged applications—that are best solved with dedicated hardware or a specialized real-time platform.

Exception Handling

Any try/catch/finally blocks in scope when a thread is created are of no relevance to the thread when it starts executing. Consider the following program:

```
public static void Main( )
{
  try
  {
    new Thread (Go).Start( );
  }
  catch (Exception ex)
  {
    // We'll never get here!
    Console.WriteLine ("Exception!");
  }
}

static void Go( ) { throw null; }
```

The try/catch statement in this example is useless, and the newly created thread will be encumbered with an unhandled NullReferenceException. This behavior makes sense when you consider that each thread has an independent execution path.

The remedy is to move the exception handler into the Go method:

```
public static void Main( )
{
  new Thread (Go).Start( );
}

static void Go( )
{
  try
  {
    ...
    throw null;      // this exception will get caught below
    ...
  }
  catch (Exception ex)
  {
    Typically log the exception, and/or signal another thread
    that we've come unstuck
    ...
  }
}
```

You need an exception handler on all thread entry methods in production applications—just as you do (usually at a higher level, in the execution stack) on your main thread. An unhandled exception causes the whole application to shut down. With an ugly dialog!

The "global" exception-handling event for Windows Forms applications, `Application.ThreadException`, works only for exceptions thrown on the main UI thread. You still must handle exceptions on worker threads manually.

`AppDomain.CurrentDomain.UnhandledException` fires on any unhandled exception, but provides no means of preventing the application from shutting down afterward.

There are, however, two cases where you don't need to handle exceptions on a worker thread, because the .NET Framework does it for you. These are:

- Asynchronous delegates
- `BackgroundWorker`

Asynchronous Delegates

In the preceding section, we described how to pass data to a thread, using `ParameterizedThreadStart` and `ThreadPool.QueueWorkerItem`. Sometimes you need to go the other way and get return values back from a thread when it finishes executing. Asynchronous delegates offer a convenient mechanism for this, allowing any number of typed arguments to be passed in both directions. Furthermore, unhandled exceptions on asynchronous delegates are conveniently rethrown on the original thread (or more accurately, the thread that calls `EndInvoke`), and so they don't need explicit handling.

Asynchronous delegates always use the thread pool.

Don't confuse asynchronous delegates with asynchronous methods (methods starting with "Begin" or "End", such as `File.BeginRead`/`File.EndRead`). Asynchronous methods follow a similar protocol outwardly, but they exist to solve a much harder problem, which we describe in Chapter 20.

Here's how you start a worker task via an asynchronous delegate:

1. Declare a delegate whose signature matches the method you want to run in parallel.
2. Instantiate the delegate.
3. Call `BeginInvoke` on the delegate, saving its `IAsyncResult` return value.

   `BeginInvoke` returns immediately to the caller. You can then perform other activities while the pooled thread is working. When you need its results, go to step 4.
4. Call `EndInvoke` on the delegate, passing in the saved `IAsyncResult` object.

In the following example, we use an asynchronous delegate to execute concurrently with the main thread, a simple method that returns a string's length:

```
delegate int WorkInvoker (string text);

static void Main()
```

```
{
  WorkInvoker method = Work;
  IAsyncResult cookie = method.BeginInvoke ("test", null, null);
  //
  // ... here's where we can do other work in parallel...
  //
  int result = method.EndInvoke (cookie);
  Console.WriteLine ("String length is: " + result);
}

static int Work (string s) { return s.Length; }
```

EndInvoke does three things. First, it waits for the asynchronous delegate to finish executing, if it hasn't already. Second, it receives the return value (as well as any ref or out parameters). Third, it throws any unhandled worker exception back to the calling thread.

If the method you're calling with an asynchronous delegate has no return value, you are still (technically) obliged to call EndInvoke. In practice, this is open to debate; there are no EndInvoke police to administer punishment to noncompliers! If you choose not to call EndInvoke, however, you'll need to consider exception handling on the worker method to avoid silent failures.

You can also specify a callback delegate when calling BeginInvoke—a method accepting an IAsyncResult object that's automatically called upon completion. This allows the instigating thread to "forget" about the asynchronous delegate, but it requires a bit of extra work at the callback end:

```
static void Main( )
{
  WorkInvoker method = Work;
  method.BeginInvoke ("test", Done, method);
  // ...
  //
}

delegate int WorkInvoker (string text);

static int Work (string s) { return s.Length; }

static void Done (IAsyncResult cookie)
{
  WorkInvoker method = (WorkInvoker) cookie.AsyncState;
  int result = method.EndInvoke (cookie);
  Console.WriteLine ("String length is: " + result);
}
```

The final argument to BeginInvoke is a user state object that populates the AsyncResult property of IAsyncResult. It can contain anything you like; in this case, we're using it to pass the method delegate to the completion callback, so we can call EndInvoke on it.

`ThreadPool.QueueUserWorkItem` can provide a good alternative to asynchronous delegates used in this fashion. Asynchronous delegates have the advantage of typed method arguments; `QueueUserWorkItem` has the advantage of needing less plumbing code.

Synchronization

So far, we've described how to start a task on a thread, how to configure a thread, and how to pass data in both directions. We've also described how local variables are private to a thread and how references can be shared among threads allowing them to communicate via common fields.

The next step is *synchronization*: coordinating the actions of threads for a predictable outcome. Synchronization is particularly important when threads access the same data; it's surprisingly easy to run aground in this area.

Synchronization constructs can be divided into four categories:

Simple blocking methods
> These wait for another thread to finish or for a period of time to elapse. `Sleep`, `Join`, and `EndInvoke` are simple blocking methods.

Locking constructs
> These enforce exclusive access to a resource, such as a field or section of code, ensuring that only one thread can enter at a time. Locking is the primary thread-safety mechanism, allowing threads to access common data without interfering with each other. The locking constructs are `lock` and `Mutex` (and a variation called `Semaphore`).

Signaling constructs
> These allow a thread to pause until receiving a notification from another, avoiding the need for inefficient polling. There are two signaling devices: event wait handles and `Monitor`'s `Wait`/`Pulse` methods.

Nonblocking synchronization constructs
> These protect access to a common field by calling upon processor primitives. The `Interlocked` class and the `volatile` keyword are the two constructs in this category.

Blocking is essential to all but the last category. Let's briefly examine this concept.

Blocking

A thread is deemed *blocked* when its execution is paused for some reason, such as when waiting for another to end via `Join` or `EndInvoke`. A blocked thread consumes almost no processor time; the CLR and operating system know about blocked threads, and provide appropriate support to keep them in a dormant state, waking them up when their blocking conditions are satisfied. You can test for a thread being blocked via its `ThreadState` property:

```
bool blocked = (someThread.ThreadState & ThreadState.WaitSleepJoin) != 0;
```

ThreadState is a flags enum, combining three "layers" of data in a bitwise fashion. Most values, however, are redundant, unused, or deprecated. The following code strips a ThreadState to one of four useful values: Unstarted, Running, WaitSleepJoin, and Stopped:

```
public static ThreadState SimpleThreadState (ThreadState ts)
{
  return ts & (ThreadState.Unstarted |
               ThreadState.WaitSleepJoin |
               ThreadState.Stopped);
}
```

The ThreadState property is useful for diagnostic purposes, but unsuitable for synchronization, because a thread's state may change in between testing ThreadState and acting upon that information.

Blocking Versus Spinning

Sometimes a thread must pause until a certain condition is met. Signaling constructs achieve this efficiently by blocking while their condition is unsatisfied. However, there is a grotesque alternative: a thread can await a condition by *spinning* in a polling loop. For example:

```
while (!proceed);
```

or:

```
while (DateTime.Now < nextStartTime);
```

This is very wasteful on processor time: as far as the CLR and operating system are concerned, the thread is performing an important calculation, and so gets allocated resources accordingly!

Sometimes a hybrid between blocking and spinning is used as a variation:

```
while (!proceed) Thread.Sleep (10);    // "Spin-Sleeping!"
```

Although inelegant, this is far more efficient than outright spinning. Problems can arise, though, due to concurrency issues on the proceed flag. Proper use of locking and signaling avoids this.

SpinWait

Amazingly, the Thread class provides a method that does nothing other than spin! SpinWait, unlike Sleep, doesn't block or relinquish the CPU. Instead, it loops endlessly, keeping the processor "uselessly busy" for the given number of iterations. Fifty iterations might equate to a pause of around a microsecond, although this could vary depending on CPU speed and load. SpinWait is rarely used; its primary purpose is to wait on a resource or field that's expected to change *extremely* soon (well, inside a microsecond) without relinquishing the processor time slice. This technique is rarely used outside of the CLR and operating system.

Locking

Exclusive locking is used to ensure that only one thread can enter particular sections of code at a time. The .NET Framework provides two exclusive locking constructs: lock and Mutex. Of the two, the lock construct is faster and more convenient. Mutex, though, has a niche in that its lock can span applications in different processes on the computer.

This section focuses on the lock construct; later we show how Mutex can be used for cross-process locking. Finally, we introduce Semaphore, .NET's nonexclusive locking construct.

Let's start with the following class:

```
class ThreadUnsafe
{
  static int val1, val2;

  static void Go()
  {
    if (val2 != 0) Console.WriteLine (val1 / val2);
    val2 = 0;
  }
}
```

This class is not thread-safe: if Go was called by two threads simultaneously, it would be possible to get a division-by-zero error, because val2 could be set to zero in one thread right as the other thread was in between executing the if statement and Console.WriteLine.

Here's how lock can fix the problem:

```
class ThreadSafe
{
  static object locker = new object();
  static int val1, val2;

  static void Go()
  {
    lock (locker)
    {
      if (val2 != 0) Console.WriteLine (val1 / val2);
      val2 = 0;
    }
  }
}
```

Only one thread can lock the synchronizing object (in this case, locker) at a time, and any contending threads are blocked until the lock is released. If more than one thread contends the lock, they are queued on a "ready queue" and granted the lock on a first-come, first-served basis. Exclusive locks are sometimes said to enforce *serialized* access to whatever's protected by the lock, because one thread's access cannot overlap with that of another. In this case, we're protecting the logic inside the Go method, as well as the fields val1 and val2.

A thread blocked while awaiting a contended lock has a ThreadState of WaitSleepJoin. In the section "Interrupt and Abort," later in this chapter, we describe how a blocked thread can be forcibly released via another thread. This is a fairly heavy-duty technique that might be used in ending a thread.

C#'s lock statement is in fact a syntactic shortcut for a call to the methods Monitor.Enter and Monitor.Exit, with a try-finally block. Here's what's actually happening within the Go method of the preceding example:

```
Monitor.Enter (locker);
try
{
  if (val2 != 0) Console.WriteLine (val1 / val2);
  val2 = 0;
}
finally { Monitor.Exit (locker); }
```

Calling Monitor.Exit without first calling Monitor.Enter on the same object throws an exception.

Monitor also provides a TryEnter method that allows a timeout to be specified, either in milliseconds or as a TimeSpan. The method then returns true if a lock was obtained, or false if no lock was obtained because the method timed out. TryEnter can also be called with no argument, which "tests" the lock, timing out immediately if the lock can't be obtained right away.

Choosing the Synchronization Object

Any object visible to each of the partaking threads can be used as a synchronizing object, subject to one hard rule: it must be a reference type. It's also highly recommended that the synchronizing object be privately scoped to the class (i.e., a private instance field) to prevent unintentional interaction from external code locking the same object. Subject to these rules, the synchronizing object can double as the object it's protecting, such as with the list field in the following example:

```
class ThreadSafe
{
  List <string> list = new List <string>();

  void Test()
  {
    lock (list)
    {
      list.Add ("Item 1");
      ...
```

A dedicated field (such as locker, in the example prior) allows precise control over the scope and granularity of the lock. The containing object (this)—or even its type—can also be used as a synchronization object:

```
lock (this) { ... }
```

or:

```
lock (typeof (Widget)) { ... }    // For protecting access to statics
```

Both are discouraged, however, because they offer excessive scope to the synchronization object. Code in other places may lock on that same instance (or type) with an unpredictable outcome. A lock on a type may even seep through application domain boundaries!

 Locking doesn't restrict access to the synchronizing object itself in any way. In other words, x.ToString( ) will not block because another thread has called lock(x); both threads must call lock(x) in order for blocking to occur.

Nested Locking

A thread can repeatedly lock the same object, via multiple calls to Monitor.Enter, or nested lock statements. The object is subsequently unlocked when a corresponding number of Monitor.Exit statements have executed or when the outermost lock statement has exited. This allows for the most natural semantics when one method calls another as follows:

```
static object x = new object( );

static void Main( )
{
  lock (x)
  {
      Console.WriteLine ("I have the lock");
      Nest( );
      Console.WriteLine ("I still have the lock");
  }
  // Now the lock is released.
}

static void Nest( )
{
  lock (x) { }
  // We still have the lock on x!
}
```

A thread can block on only the first, or outermost, lock.

When to Lock

As a basic rule, you should lock before accessing *any field comprising writable shared state*. Even in the simplest case—an assignment operation on a single field—you must consider synchronization. In the following class, neither the Increment nor the Assign method is thread-safe:

```
class ThreadUnsafe
{
  static int x;
  static void Increment() { x++; }
  static void Assign()    { x = 123; }
}
```

Here are thread-safe versions of Increment and Assign:

```
class ThreadSafe
{
  static object locker = new object( );
  static int x;

  static void Increment( ) { lock (locker) x++; }
  static void Assign( )    { lock (locker) x = 123; }
}
```

In the section "Nonblocking Synchronization," later in this chapter, we explain how this need arises, and how the volatile and Interlocked constructs can provide an alternative to locking in these simple situations.

Locking and Atomicity

If a group of variables are always read and written within the same lock, you can say the variables are read and written *atomically*. Let's suppose fields x and y are always read and assigned within a lock on object locker:

```
lock (locker) { if (x != 0) y /= x; }
```

One can say x and y are accessed atomically, because the code block cannot be divided or preempted by the actions of another thread in such a way that will change x or y and *invalidate its outcome*. You'll never get a division-by-zero error, providing x and y are always accessed within this same exclusive lock.

Instruction atomicity is a different, although analogous concept: an instruction is atomic if it executes indivisibly on the underlying processor (see the later section "Nonblocking Synchronization").

Performance, Races, and Deadlocks

Locking is fast: you can expect to acquire and release a lock in less than 100 nano-seconds on a 3 GHz computer if the lock is uncontended. If it is contended, the consequential blocking and task-switching move the overhead closer to the micro-second region, although it may be longer before the thread is actually rescheduled. This, in turn, is dwarfed by the hours of overhead—or overtime—that can result from not locking when you should have!

If used improperly, locking can have adverse effects: impoverished concurrency, deadlocks, and lock races. Impoverished concurrency occurs when too much code is placed in a lock statement, causing other threads to block unnecessarily. A deadlock is when two threads each wait for a lock held by the other, so neither can proceed. A lock race happens when it's possible for either of two threads to obtain a lock first; the program breaks if the "wrong" thread wins.

Deadlocks are most commonly a syndrome of too many synchronizing objects. A good rule is to start on the side of having fewer synchronizing objects, increasing the locking granularity only when a plausible need arises. Locking objects in a consistent order, where possible, also alleviates deadlocking.

The CLR, in a standard hosting environment, is not like SQL Server and does not automatically detect and resolve deadlocks by terminating one of the offenders. A threading deadlock causes participating threads to block indefinitely, unless you've specified a locking timeout. (Under the SQL CLR integration host, however, deadlocks *are* automatically detected and a [catchable] exception is thrown on one of the threads).

An excellent article describing the intricacies of deadlocking is available at *http://research.microsoft.com/~birrell/papers/ThreadsCSharp.pdf.*

Mutex

A Mutex is like a C# lock, but it can work across multiple processes. In other words, Mutex can be *computer-wide* as well as *application-wide.*

Acquiring and releasing an uncontended Mutex takes a few microseconds; about 50 times slower than a lock.

With a Mutex class, you call the WaitOne method to lock and ReleaseMutex to unlock. Just as with the lock statement, a Mutex can be released only from the same thread that obtained it.

A common use for a cross-process Mutex is to ensure that only one instance of a program can run at a time. Here's how it's done:

```
class OneAtATimePlease
{
  // Naming a Mutex makes it available computer-wide. Use a name that's
  // unique to your company and application (e.g., include your URL).

  static Mutex mutex = new Mutex (false, "oreilly.com OneAtATimeDemo");

  static void Main( )
  {
    // Wait a few seconds if contended, in case another instance
    // of the program is still in the process of shutting down.

    if (!mutex.WaitOne (TimeSpan.FromSeconds (3), false))
    {
      Console.WriteLine ("Another instance of the app is running. Bye!");
      return;
    }
    try
    {
      Console.WriteLine ("Running. Press Enter to exit");
      Console.ReadLine( );
    }
    finally { mutex.ReleaseMutex( ); }
  }
}
```

A good feature of Mutex is that if the application terminates without ReleaseMutex being called, the CLR releases the Mutex automatically.

Semaphore

A Semaphore is like a nightclub: it has a certain capacity, enforced by a bouncer. Once it's full, no more people can enter and a queue builds up outside. Then, for each person that leaves, one person enters from the head of the queue. The constructor requires a minimum of two arguments: the number of places currently available in the nightclub and the club's total capacity.

A Semaphore with a capacity of one is similar to a Mutex or lock, except that the Semaphore has no "owner"—it's *thread-agnostic*. Any thread can call Release on a Semaphore, whereas with Mutex and lock, only the thread that obtained the lock can release it.

Semaphores can be useful in limiting concurrency—preventing too many threads from executing a particular piece of code at once. In the following example, five threads try to enter a nightclub that allows only three threads in at once:

```
class TheClub      // No door lists!
{
  static Semaphore s = new Semaphore (3, 3);   // Available=3; Capacity=3

  static void Main( )
  {
    for (int i = 1; i <= 5; i++) new Thread (Enter).Start (i);
  }

  static void Enter (object id)
  {
    Console.WriteLine (id + " wants to enter");
    s.WaitOne( );
    Console.WriteLine (id + " is in!");         // Only three threads
    Thread.Sleep (1000 * (int) id);             // can be here at
    Console.WriteLine (id + " is leaving");     // a time.
    s.Release( );
  }
}

1 wants to enter
1 is in!
2 wants to enter
2 is in!
3 wants to enter
3 is in!
4 wants to enter
5 wants to enter
1 is leaving
4 is in!
2 is leaving
5 is in!
```

If the Sleep statement was instead performing intensive disk I/O, the Semaphore would improve overall performance by limiting excessive concurrent hard-drive activity.

A Semaphore, if named, can span processes in the same way as a Mutex.

Thread Safety

A program or method is thread-safe if it has no indeterminacy in the face of any multithreading scenario. Thread safety is achieved primarily with locking and by reducing the possibilities for thread interaction.

General-purpose types are rarely thread-safe in their entirety, for the following reasons:

- The development burden in full thread safety can be significant, particularly if a type has many fields (each field is a potential for interaction in an arbitrarily multithreaded context).

- Thread safety can entail a performance cost (payable, in part, whether or not the type is actually used by multiple threads).

- A thread-safe type does not necessarily make the program using it thread-safe, and sometimes the work involved in the latter can make the former redundant.

Thread safety is hence usually implemented just where it needs to be, in order to handle a specific multithreading scenario.

There are, however, a few ways to "cheat" and have large and complex classes run safely in a multithreaded environment. One is to sacrifice granularity by wrapping large sections of code—even access to an entire object—around a single exclusive lock, enforcing serialized access at a high level. This tactic is, in fact, essential if you want to use thread-unsafe third-party code (or most Framework types, for that matter) in a multithreaded context. The trick is simply to use the same exclusive lock to protect access to all properties, methods, and fields on the thread-unsafe object. The solution works well if the object's methods all execute quickly (otherwise, there will be a lot of blocking).

 Primitive types aside, few .NET Framework types, when instantiated, are thread-safe for anything more than concurrent read-only access. The onus is on the developer to superimpose thread safety, typically with exclusive locks.

Another way to cheat is to minimize thread interaction by minimizing shared data. This is an excellent approach and is used implicitly in "stateless" middle-tier application and web page servers. Since multiple client requests can arrive simultaneously, the server methods they call must be thread-safe. A stateless design (popular for reasons of scalability) intrinsically limits the possibility of interaction, since classes do not persist data between requests. Thread interaction is then limited just to static fields one may choose to create, for such purposes as caching commonly used data in memory and in providing infrastructure services such as authentication and auditing.

The final approach in implementing thread safety is to use an automatic locking regime. The .NET Framework does exactly this, if you subclass Context-BoundObject and apply the Synchronization attribute to the class. Whenever a method or property on such an object is then called, an object-wide lock is automatically taken for the whole execution of the method or property. Although this reduces the thread-safety burden, it creates problems of its own: deadlocks that would not otherwise occur, impoverished concurrency, and unintended reentrancy. For these reasons, manual locking is generally a better option—at least until a less simplistic automatic locking regime becomes available.

Thread Safety and .NET Framework Types

Locking can be used to convert thread-unsafe code into thread-safe code. A good application of this is the .NET Framework: nearly all of its nonprimitive types are not thread-safe when instantiated, and yet they can be used in multithreaded code if all access to any given object is protected via a lock. Here's an example, where two threads simultaneously add items to the same List collection, then enumerate the list:

```
class ThreadSafe
{
  static List <string> list = new List <string>( );

  static void Main( )
  {
    new Thread (AddItems).Start( );
    new Thread (AddItems).Start( );
  }

  static void AddItems( )
  {
    for (int i = 0; i < 100; i++)
      lock (list)
        list.Add ("Item " + list.Count);

    string[] items;
    lock (list) items = list.ToArray( );
    foreach (string s in items) Console.WriteLine (s);
  }
}
```

In this case, we're locking on the list object itself. If we had two interrelated lists, we would have to choose a common object upon which to lock (we could nominate one of the lists, or use an independent field).

Enumerating .NET collections is also thread-unsafe in the sense that an exception is thrown if another thread alters the list during enumeration. Rather than locking for the duration of enumeration, in this example, we first copy the items to an array. This avoids holding the lock excessively if what we're doing during enumeration is potentially time-consuming. (Another solution is to use a reader/writer lock; see the section "ReaderWriterLockSlim" later in this chapter.)

Locking around thread-safe objects

Sometimes you also need to lock around accessing thread-safe objects. To illustrate, imagine that the Framework's List class was, indeed, thread-safe, and we want to add an item to a list:

```
if (!myList.Contains (newItem)) myList.Add (newItem);
```

Whether or not the list was thread-safe, this statement is certainly not! The whole if statement would have to be wrapped in a lock in order to prevent preemption in between testing for containership and adding the new item. This same lock would then need to be used everywhere we modified that list. For instance, the following statement would also need to be wrapped, in the identical lock:

```
myList.Clear( );
```

to ensure that it did not preempt the former statement. In other words, we would have to lock exactly as with our thread-unsafe collection classes (making the List class's hypothetical thread safety redundant).

Static methods

Wrapping access to an object around a custom lock works only if all concurrent threads are aware of—and use—the lock. This may not be the case if the object is widely scoped. The worst case is with static members in a public type. For instance, imagine if the static property on the DateTime struct, DateTime.Now, was not thread-safe, and that two concurrent calls could result in garbled output or an exception. The only way to remedy this with external locking might be to lock the type itself—lock(typeof(DateTime))—before calling DateTime.Now. This would work only if all programmers agreed to do this (which is unlikely). Furthermore, locking a type creates problems of its own.

For this reason, static members on the DateTime struct are guaranteed to be thread-safe. This is a common pattern throughout the .NET Framework: *static members are thread-safe; instance members are not.* Following this pattern also makes sense when writing custom types, so as not to create impossible thread-safety conundrums.

 When writing components for public consumption, a good policy is to program at least such as not to preclude thread safety. This means being particularly careful with static members, whether used internally or exposed publicly, and considering more granular thread safety if you have long-running methods.

Thread Safety in Application Servers

Application servers need to be multithreaded to handle simultaneous client requests. WCF, ASP.NET, and Web Services applications are implicitly multithreaded; the same holds true for Remoting server applications that use a network channel such as TCP or HTTP. This means that when writing code on the server side, you must consider thread safety if there's any possibility of interaction among the threads processing client requests. Fortunately, such a possibility is rare; a typical server class either is stateless (no fields) or has an activation model that creates a separate object instance for each client or each request. Interaction only usually arises through static fields, sometimes used for caching in memory parts of a database to improve performance.

For example, suppose you have a RetrieveUser method that queries a database:

```
// User is a custom class with fields for user data
internal User RetrieveUser (int id) { ... }
```

If this method was called frequently, you could improve performance by caching the results in a static Dictionary. Here's a solution that takes thread safety into account:

```
static class UserCache
{
  static Dictionary <int, User> _users = new Dictionary <int, User>( );

  internal static User GetUser (int id)
  {
    User u = null;

    lock (_users)
      if (_users.TryGetValue (id, out u))
        return u;

    u = RetrieveUser (id);          // Method to retrieve from database;
    lock (_users) _users [id] = u;
    return u;
  }
}
```

We must, at a minimum, lock around reading and updating the dictionary to ensure thread safety. In this example, we choose a practical compromise between simplicity and performance in locking. Our design actually creates a very small potential for inefficiency: if two threads simultaneously called this method with the same previously unretrieved id, the RetrieveUser method would be called twice—and the dictionary would be updated unnecessarily. Locking once across the whole method would prevent this, but would create a worse inefficiency: the entire cache would be locked up for the duration of calling RetrieveUser, during which time other threads would be blocked in retrieving *any* user.

Thread Safety in Rich Client Applications

Both the Windows Forms and Windows Presentation Foundation (WPF) libraries have special threading models. Although each has a separate implementation, they are both very similar in how they function.

The objects that make up a rich client are primarily based on Control in the case of Windows Forms or DependencyObject in the case of WPF. None of these objects is thread-safe, and so cannot be safely accessed from two threads at once. To ensure that you obey this, WPF and Windows Forms have models whereby *only the thread that instantiates a UI object can call any of its members*. Violate this and an exception is thrown.

On the positive side, this means you don't need to lock around accessing a UI object. On the negative side, if you want to call a member on object X created on another thread Y, you must marshal the request to thread Y. You can do this explicitly as follows:

- In Windows Forms, call `Invoke` or `BeginInvoke` on the control.
- In WPF, call `Invoke` or `BeginInvoke` on the element's `Dispatcher` object.

`Invoke` and `BeginInvoke` both accept a delegate, which references the method on the target control that you want to run. `Invoke` works *synchronously*: the caller blocks until the marshal is complete. `BeginInvoke` works asynchronously: the caller returns immediately and the marshaled request is queued up (using the same message queue that handles keyboard, mouse, and timer events).

 `BackgroundWorker` allows you to avoid explicitly marshaling with `Invoke` and `BeginInvoke`. We describe this later in this chapter, in the section "BackgroundWorker."

It's helpful to think of a rich client application as having two distinct categories of threads: UI threads and worker threads. UI threads instantiate (and subsequently "own") UI elements; worker threads do not. Worker threads typically execute long-running tasks such as fetching data.

Most rich client applications have a single UI thread (which is also the main application thread) and periodically spawn worker threads—either directly or using `BackgroundWorker`. These workers then marshal back to the main UI thread in order to update controls or report on progress.

So, when would an application have multiple UI threads? The main scenario is when you have an application with multiple top-level windows, often called a *Single Document Interface* (SDI) application, such as Microsoft Word. Each SDI window typically shows itself as a separate "application" on the taskbar and is mostly isolated, functionally, from other SDI windows. By giving each such window its own UI thread, the application can be made more responsive.

Nonblocking Synchronization

Earlier, we said that the need for synchronization arises even in the simple case of assigning or incrementing a field. Although locking can always satisfy this need, a contended lock means that a thread must block, suffering the overhead and latency of being temporarily descheduled. The .NET Framework's *nonblocking* synchronization constructs can perform simple operations without ever blocking, pausing, or waiting. These involve using instructions that are strictly atomic or instructing the compiler to use "volatile" read and write semantics.

The nonblocking constructs are also simpler to use—in some situations—than locks.

Atomicity and Interlocked

A statement is intrinsically *atomic* if it executes as a single indivisible instruction on the underlying processor. Strict atomicity precludes any possibility of preemption. In C#, a simple read or assignment on a field of 32 bits or less is atomic on a 32-bit processor. (An Intel Core 2 or Pentium D processor with 64-bit addressing extensions is still essentially 32-bit.) Operations on fields larger than the width of the processor are nonatomic, as are statements that combine more than one read/write operation:

```
class Atomicity          // This assumes we're running on a 32-bit CPU.
{
  static int x, y;
  static long z;

  static void Test( )
  {
    long myLocal;
    x = 3;              // Atomic
    z = 3;              // Nonatomic (z is 64 bits)
    myLocal = z;        // Nonatomic (z is 64 bits)
    y += x;             // Nonatomic (read AND write operation)
    x++;                // Nonatomic (read AND write operation)
  }
}
```

Reading and writing 64-bit fields is nonatomic on 32-bit CPUs because it requires two separate instructions; one for each 32-bit memory location. So, if thread A reads a 64-bit value while thread B is updating it, thread A may end up with a bitwise combination of the old and new values.

Unary operators of the kind x++ are implemented by reading a variable, processing it, and then writing it back. Consider the following class:

```
class ThreadUnsafe
{
  static int x = 1000;
  static void Go( ) { for (int i = 0; i < 100; i++) x--; }
}
```

You might expect that if 10 threads concurrently run Go, x would end up as 0. However, this is not guaranteed, because it's possible for one thread to preempt another in between retrieving x's current value, decrementing it, and writing it back (resulting in an out-of-date value being written).

One way to address these issues is to wrap the nonatomic operations in a lock statement. Locking, in fact, simulates atomicity if consistently applied. The Interlocked class, however, provides an easier and faster solution for such simple operations:

```
class Program
{
  static long sum;

  static void Main( )                                          // sum
  {
    // Simple increment/decrement operations:
    Interlocked.Increment (ref sum);                           // 1
    Interlocked.Decrement (ref sum);                           // 0
```

```
        // Add/subtract a value:
        Interlocked.Add (ref sum, 3);                                // 3

        // Read a 64-bit field:
        Console.WriteLine (Interlocked.Read (ref sum));              // 3

        // Write a 64-bit field while reading previous value:
        // (This prints "3" while updating sum to 10)
        Console.WriteLine (Interlocked.Exchange (ref sum, 10));      // 10

        // Update a field only if it matches a certain value (10):
        Interlocked.CompareExchange (ref sum, 123, 10);             // 123
    }
}
```

Interlocked works by making its need for atomicity known to the operating system and virtual machine. Using Interlocked is generally more efficient than obtaining a lock, because it can never block and suffer the overhead of its thread being temporarily descheduled.

Interlocked is also valid across multiple processes, in contrast to the lock statement, which is effective only across threads in the current process. An example of where this might be useful is in reading and writing process-shared memory.

Memory Barriers and Volatility

Consider this class:

```
class Unsafe
{
    static bool endIsNigh, repented;

    static void Main()
    {
        new Thread (Wait).Start();       // Start up the spinning waiter
        Thread.Sleep (1000);             // Give it a second to warm up!

        repented = true;
        endIsNigh = true;
    }

    static void Wait()
    {
        while (!endIsNigh);              // Spin until endIsNigh
        Console.Write (repented);
    }
}
```

Is it possible for the Wait method to write "False"?

The answer is yes, on a multicore or multiprocessor machine. The repented and endIsNigh fields can be cached in CPU registers to improve performance, meaning a delay before their updated values are written back to memory. And when the CPU registers are written back to memory, it's not necessarily in the order they were originally updated.

The static methods `Thread.VolatileRead` and `Thread.VolatileWrite` circumvent this caching. `VolatileRead` means "read the latest value"; `VolatileWrite` means "write immediately to memory." You can achieve the same thing more elegantly by declaring the field with the `volatile` modifier:

```
class ThreadSafe
{
  // Always use volatile read/write semantics:
  volatile static bool endIsNigh, repented;
  ...
```

> If the volatile keyword is used in preference to the `VolatileRead` and `VolatileWrite` methods, one can think in the simplest terms— that is, "never thread-cache this field!"

If access to `repented` and `endIsNigh` is wrapped in a `lock` statement, volatile read and write semantics are applied automatically, and the `volatile` keyword is unnecessary. This is because an (intended) side effect of locking is to create a *memory barrier*: a guarantee that the volatility of fields used within the lock statement will not extend outside the `lock` statement's scope. In other words, the fields will be fresh on entering the lock (*volatile read*) and be written to memory before exiting the lock (*volatile write*). Locking makes `volatile` redundant.

A `lock` statement has further advantages. In this case, it would allow us to access the fields `repented` and `endIsNigh` as a single atomic unit so that we could safely run something like this:

```
object locker = new object();
...
lock (locker) { if (endIsNigh) repented = true; }
```

A `lock` is also preferable when a field is used many times in a loop (assuming the lock is held for the duration of the loop). Although a volatile read or write beats a lock in performance, a thousand volatile read/writes are unlikely to beat one lock!

Volatility applies to reference types, primitive integral types, and unsafe pointer types. Other value types such as `DateTime` cannot be cached in CPU registers and so need not (and cannot) be declared with the `volatile` keyword. Volatile read and write semantics are also unnecessary when fields are accessed via the `Interlocked` class.

Signaling with Event Wait Handles

Event wait handles are used for *signaling*. Signaling is when one thread waits until it receives notification from another. Event wait handles are the simplest of the signaling constructs, and they are unrelated to C# events. They come in two flavors, `AutoResetEvent` and `ManualResetEvent`. Both are based on the common `EventWaitHandle` class, where they derive all their functionality.

An `AutoResetEvent` is much like a ticket turnstile: inserting a ticket lets exactly one person through. The "auto" in the class's name refers to the fact that an open turnstile automatically closes or "resets" after someone steps through. A thread waits, or blocks, at the turnstile by calling WaitOne (wait at this "one" turnstile until it opens), and a ticket is inserted by calling the Set method. If a number of threads call WaitOne, a queue builds up behind the turnstile. A ticket can come from any thread; in other words, any (unblocked) thread with access to the AutoResetEvent object can call Set on it to release one blocked thread.

In the following example, a thread is started whose job is simply to wait until signaled by another thread (see Figure 19-2):

```
class BasicWaitHandle
{
    static EventWaitHandle wh = new AutoResetEvent (false);

    static void Main()
    {
        new Thread (Waiter).Start();
        Thread.Sleep (1000);                // Pause for a second...
        wh.Set();                           // Wake up the Waiter.
    }

    static void Waiter()
    {
        Console.WriteLine ("Waiting...");
        wh.WaitOne();                       // Wait for notification
        Console.WriteLine ("Notified");
    }
}

// Output:
Waiting... (pause) Notified.
```

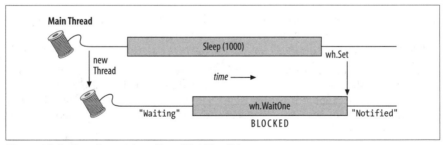

Figure 19-2. Signaling with an EventWaitHandle

If Set is called when no thread is waiting, the handle stays open for as long as it takes until some thread calls WaitOne. This behavior helps avoid a race between a thread heading for the turnstile, and a thread inserting a ticket ("Oops, inserted the ticket a microsecond too soon, bad luck, now you'll have to wait indefinitely!"). However, calling Set repeatedly on a turnstile at which no one is waiting doesn't allow a whole party through when they arrive: only the next single person is let through and the extra tickets are "wasted."

A ManualResetEvent functions like an ordinary gate. Calling Set opens the gate, allowing any number of threads calling WaitOne to be let through. Calling Reset closes the gate. Threads that call WaitOne on a closed gate will block; when the gate is next opened, they will be released all at once.

The Reset method also works on an AutoResetEvent. Its effect is then to close the turnstile (should it be open) without waiting or blocking.

WaitOne accepts an optional timeout parameter, returning false if the wait ended because of a timeout rather than obtaining the signal. WaitOne can also be instructed to exit the current synchronization context for the duration of the wait (if an automatic locking regime is in use) in order to prevent excessive blocking.

> Calling WaitOne with a timeout of zero tests whether a wait handle is "open," without blocking the caller.

Creating and Disposing Wait Handles

Event wait handles can be created in one of two ways. The first is via their constructors:

```
EventWaitHandle auto = new AutoResetEvent (false);
EventWaitHandle manual = new ManualResetEvent (false);
```

If the boolean argument is true, the handle's Set method is called automatically, immediately after construction. The other method of instantiation is via the base class, EventWaitHandle:

```
var auto = new EventWaitHandle (false, EventResetMode.AutoReset);
var manual = new EventWaitHandle (false, EventResetMode.ManualReset);
```

Once you've finished with a wait handle, you can call its Close method to release the operating system resource. Alternatively, you can simply drop all references to the wait handle and allow the garbage collector to do the job for you sometime later (wait handles implement the disposal pattern whereby the finalizer calls Close). This practice is (arguably) acceptable with wait handles because they have a light OS burden (asynchronous delegates rely on exactly this mechanism to release their IAsyncResult's wait handle).

Wait handles are released automatically when an application domain unloads.

Two-Way Signaling

Let's say we want the main thread to signal a worker thread three times in a row. If the main thread simply calls Set on a wait handle several times in rapid succession, the second or third signal may get lost, since the worker may take time to process each signal.

The solution is for the main thread to wait until the worker's ready before signaling it. This can be done with another AutoResetEvent, as follows:

```
class TwoWaySignaling
{
  static EventWaitHandle ready = new AutoResetEvent (false);
  static EventWaitHandle go = new AutoResetEvent (false);
```

```csharp
  static volatile string message;        // We must either use volatile
                                          // or lock around this field
  static void Main()
  {
    new Thread (Work).Start();

    ready.WaitOne();              // First wait until worker is ready
    message = "ooo";
    go.Set();                     // Tell worker to go!

    ready.WaitOne();
    message = "ahhh";             // Give the worker another message
    go.Set();

    ready.WaitOne();
    message = null;               // Signal the worker to exit
    go.Set();
  }

  static void Work()
  {
    while (true)
    {
      ready.Set();                        // Indicate that we're ready
      go.WaitOne();                       // Wait to be kicked off...
      if (message == null) return;        // Gracefully exit
      Console.WriteLine (message);
    }
  }
}

// Output:
ooo
ahhh
```

Figure 19-3 shows this process visually.

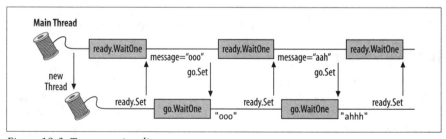

Figure 19-3. Two-way signaling

Here, we're using a null message to indicate that the worker should end. With threads that run indefinitely, it's important to have an exit strategy!

Creating a Cross-Process EventWaitHandle

EventWaitHandle's constructor allows a "named" EventWaitHandle to be created, capable of operating across multiple processes. The name is simply a string, and it can be any value that doesn't unintentionally conflict with someone else's name! If the name is already in use on the computer, you get a reference to the same underlying EventWaitHandle; otherwise, the operating system creates a new one. Here's an example:

```
EventWaitHandle wh = new EventWaitHandle (false, EventResetMode.AutoReset,
                                          "MyCompany.MyApp.SomeName");
```

If two applications each ran this code, they would be able to signal each other: the wait handle would work across all threads in both processes.

Pooling Wait Handles

If your application has lots of threads that spend most of their time blocked on a wait handle, you can reduce the resource burden via the *thread pool*. The thread pool economizes by coalescing many wait handles onto a few threads.

To use the thread pool, register your wait handle along with a delegate to be executed when the wait handle is signaled. Do this by calling ThreadPool. RegisterWaitForSingleObject, as in this example:

```
class Test
{
  static ManualResetEvent starter = new ManualResetEvent (false);

  public static void Main()
  {
    ThreadPool.RegisterWaitForSingleObject (starter, Go, "hello", -1, true);
    Thread.Sleep (5000);
    Console.WriteLine ("Signaling worker...");
    starter.Set();
    Console.ReadLine();
  }

  public static void Go (object data, bool timedOut)
  {
    Console.WriteLine ("Started " + data);
    // Perform task...
  }
}

// Output:
(5 second delay)
Signaling worker...
Started hello
```

In addition to the wait handle and delegate, RegisterWaitForSingleObject accepts a "black box" object that it passes to your delegate method (rather like ParameterizedThreadStart), as well as a timeout in milliseconds (–1 meaning no timeout) and a boolean flag indicating whether the request is one-off rather than recurring.

`RegisterWaitForSingleObject` is particularly valuable in an application server that must handle many concurrent requests. Suppose you need to block on a `ManualResetEvent` and simply call `WaitOne`:

```
void AppServerMethod( )
{
  wh.WaitOne( );
  // ... continue execution
}
```

If 100 clients called this method, 100 server threads would be tied up for the duration of the blockage. Replacing `wh.WaitOne` with `RegisterWaitForSingleObject` allows the method to return immediately, wasting no threads:

```
void AppServerMethod
{
  ThreadPool.RegisterWaitForSingleObject (wh, Resume, null, -1, true);
}

static void Resume (object data, bool timedOut)
{
  // ... continue execution
}
```

The data object passed to `Resume` allows continuance of any transient data.

WaitAny, WaitAll, and SignalAndWait

In addition to the `Set`, `WaitOne`, and `Reset` methods, there are static methods on the `WaitHandle` class to crack more complex synchronization nuts. The `WaitAny`, `WaitAll`, and `SignalAndWait` methods wait across multiple handles. The wait handles can be of differing types, and they include `Mutex` and `Semphore` objects, since these also derive from the abstract `WaitHandle` class.

`SignalAndWait` is perhaps the most useful: it calls `WaitOne` on one `WaitHandle`, while calling `Set` on another `WaitHandle`, in an atomic operation. You can use this method on a pair of `EventWaitHandles` to set up two threads to rendezvous or "meet" at the same point in time, in a textbook fashion. Either `AutoResetEvent` or `ManualResetEvent` will do the trick. The first thread does the following:

```
WaitHandle.SignalAndWait (wh1, wh2);
```

whereas the second thread does the opposite:

```
WaitHandle.SignalAndWait (wh2, wh1);
```

`WaitHandle.WaitAny` waits for any one of an array of wait handles; `WaitHandle.WaitAll` waits on all of the given handles. `WaitAll` is of dubious value because of a weird connection to apartment threading—a throwback to the legacy COM architecture. `WaitAll` requires that the caller be in a multithreaded apartment, the model least suitable for interoperability. The main thread of a Windows application, for example, is unable to interact with the clipboard in this mode. Fortunately, the .NET Framework provides another signaling mechanism that one can use when wait handles are awkward or unsuitable: `Wait` and `Pulse`.

Signaling with Wait and Pulse

The `Monitor` class provides another signaling construct, via two static methods: `Wait` and `Pulse`. The principle is that you write the signaling logic yourself using custom flags and fields (enclosed in `lock` statements), and then introduce `Wait` and `Pulse` commands to mitigate CPU spinning. The advantage of this low-level approach is that with just `Wait`, `Pulse`, and the `lock` statement, you can achieve the functionality of `AutoResetEvent`, `ManualResetEvent`, and `Semaphore`, as well as `WaitHandle`'s static methods `WaitAll` and `WaitAny`. Furthermore, `Wait` and `Pulse` can be amenable in situations where all of the wait handles are parsimoniously challenged.

`Wait` and `Pulse` signaling, however, has a number of disadvantages over event wait handles:

- `Wait`/`Pulse` cannot span application domains or processes on a computer.
- `Wait`/`Pulse` cannot be used in the asynchronous method pattern (see Chapter 20) because the thread pool offers `Monitor.Wait` no equivalent of `RegisterWaitForSingleObject`, so a blocked `Wait` cannot avoid monopolizing a thread.
- You must remember to protect all variables related to the signaling logic with locks.
- `Wait`/`Pulse` programs may confuse developers relying on the MSDN for documentation.

The documentation problem arises because it's not obvious how `Wait` and `Pulse` are supposed to be used, even when you've read up on how they work. `Wait` and `Pulse` also have a peculiar aversion to dabblers: they will seek out any holes in your understanding and then delight in tormenting you! Fortunately, there is a simple pattern of use that tames `Wait` and `Pulse`.

In terms of performance, `Wait` and `Pulse` are faster than an event wait handle if you expect the waiter *not* to block. Otherwise, they are similar, each with an over-head in the few-microseconds region.

How to Use Wait and Pulse

Here's how you use `Wait` and `Pulse`:

1. Define a single field for use as the synchronization object, such as:

   ```
   object locker = new object( );
   ```

2. Define field(s) for use in your custom blocking condition(s). For example:

   ```
   bool go; or int semaphoreCount;
   ```

3. Whenever you want to block, include the following code:

   ```
   lock (locker)
     while ( <blocking-condition> )
       Monitor.Wait (locker);
   ```

4. Whenever you change (or potentially change) a blocking condition, include this code:

```
    lock (locker)
    {
      < alter the field(s) or data that might
        impact the blocking condition(s) >
      Monitor.PulseAll (locker);
    }
```

(If you change a blocking condition *and* want to block, you can incorporate steps 3 and 4 in a single lock statement.)

This pattern allows any thread to wait at any time for any condition. Here's a simple example, where a worker thread waits until the go field is set to true:

```
class SimpleWaitPulse
{
  static object locker = new object();
  static bool go;

  static void Main()
  {                                 // The new thread will block
    new Thread (Work).Start();      // because go==false.

    Console.ReadLine();             // Wait for user to hit Enter

    lock (locker)                   // Let's now wake up the thread by
    {                               // setting go=true and pulsing.
      go = true;
      Monitor.PulseAll (locker);
    }
  }

  static void Work()
  {
    lock (locker)
      while (!go)
        Monitor.Wait (locker);

    Console.WriteLine ("Woken!!!");
  }
}

// Output
Woken!!!    (after pressing Enter)
```

For thread safety, we ensure that all shared fields are accessed within a lock. Hence, we add lock statements around both reading and updating the go flag. This is essential.

The Work method is where we block, waiting for the go flag to become true. The Monitor.Wait method does the following, in order:

1. Releases the lock on locker
2. Blocks until locker is "pulsed"
3. Reacquires the lock on locker

Execution then continues at the next statement. Monitor.Wait is designed for use within a lock statement; it throws an exception if called otherwise. The same goes for Monitor.Pulse.

In the Main method, we signal the worker by setting the go flag (within a lock) and calling PulseAll. As soon as we *release the lock*, the worker resumes execution, reiterating its while loop.

The Pulse and PulseAll methods release threads blocked on a Wait statement. Pulse releases a maximum of one thread; PulseAll releases them all. In our example, just one thread is blocked, so their effects are identical. With our suggested pattern, call PulseAll if in doubt.

 In order for Wait to communicate with Pulse or PulseAll, the synchronizing object (locker, in our case) must be the same.

In our pattern, pulsing indicates that *something might have changed*, and that waiting threads should recheck their blocking conditions. In the Work method, this check is accomplished via the while loop. The *waiter* then decides whether to continue, *not the notifier*. If pulsing by itself is taken as instruction to continue, the Wait construct is stripped of any real value; you end up with an inferior version of an AutoResetEvent.

If we abandon our pattern, removing the while loop, the go flag, and the ReadLine, we get a bare-bones Wait/Pulse example:

```
static void Main( )
{
  new Thread (Work).Start( );
  lock (locker) Monitor.Pulse (locker);
}

static void Work( )
{
  lock (locker) Monitor.Wait (locker);
  Console.WriteLine ("Woken!!!");
}
```

It's not possible to display the output, because it's nondeterministic! A race ensues between the main thread and the worker. If Wait executes first, the signal works. If Pulse executes first, the *pulse is lost* and the worker remains forever stuck. This differs from the behavior of an AutoResetEvent, where its Set method has a memory or "latching" effect, so it is still effective if called before WaitOne.

The reason Pulse has no latching effect is that you're expected to write the latch yourself, using a "go" flag as we did before. This is what makes Wait and Pulse versatile: with a boolean flag, we can make it function as an AutoResetEvent; with an integer field, we can imitate a Semaphore. With more complex data structures, we can go further and write such constructs as a producer/consumer queue.

Producer/Consumer Queue

A producer/consumer queue is a common requirement in threading. Here's how it works:

- A queue is set up to describe tasks.
- When a task needs executing, it's enqueued, allowing the caller to get on with other things.
- One or more worker threads plug away in the background, picking off and executing queued tasks.

The advantage of this model is that you have precise control over how many worker threads execute at once. This can allow you to limit not only consumption of CPU time, but other resources as well. If the tasks perform intensive disk I/O, for instance, you might have just one worker thread to avoid starving the operating system and other applications. Another type of application may have 20. You can also dynamically add and remove workers throughout the queue's life.

 A producer/consume queue is rather like an independent thread pool.

Here's a producer/consumer queue that uses a string (for simplicity) to represent a task:

```
using System;
using System.Threading;
using System.Collections.Generic;

public class TaskQueue : IDisposable
{
  object locker = new object();
  Thread[] workers;
  Queue<string> taskQ = new Queue<string>();

  public TaskQueue (int workerCount)
  {
    workers = new Thread [workerCount];

    // Create and start a separate thread for each worker
    for (int i = 0; i < workerCount; i++)
      (workers [i] = new Thread (Consume)).Start();
  }

  public void Dispose()
  {
    // Enqueue one null task per worker to make each exit.
    foreach (Thread worker in workers) EnqueueTask (null);
  }

  public void EnqueueTask (string task)
  {
```

```
   lock (locker)
   {
     taskQ.Enqueue (task);        // We must pulse because we're
     Monitor.Pulse (locker);      // changing a blocking condition.
   }
 }

 void Consume( )
 {
   while (true)                   // Keep consuming until
   {                              // told otherwise
     string task;
     lock (locker)
     {
       while (taskQ.Count == 0) Monitor.Wait (locker);
       task = taskQ.Dequeue( );
     }
     if (task == null) return;    // This signals our exit
     Console.Write (task);        // Perform task.
     Thread.Sleep (1000);         // Simulate time-consuming task
   }
 }
}
```

Again we have an exit strategy: enqueuing a null task signals a consumer to finish after completing any outstanding tasks (if we want it to quit sooner, we could use an independent "exit" flag). Because we're supporting multiple consumers, we must enqueue one null task per consumer to completely shut down the queue.

Here's a Main method that starts a task queue, specifying two concurrent consumer threads, and then enqueues 10 tasks to be shared among the two consumers:

```
static void Main( )
{
  using (TaskQueue q = new TaskQueue (2))
  {
    for (int i = 0; i < 10; i++)
    q.EnqueueTask (" Task" + i);

    Console.WriteLine ("Enqueued 10 tasks");
    Console.WriteLine ("Waiting for tasks to complete...");
  }

  // Exiting the using statement runs TaskQueue's Dispose method, which
  // shuts down the consumers, after all outstanding tasks are completed.

  Console.WriteLine ("\r\nAll tasks done!");
}

// Output:
Enqueued 10 tasks
Waiting for tasks to complete...
 Task1 Task0 (pause...) Task2 Task3 (pause...) Task4 Task5 (pause...)
 Task6 Task7 (pause...) Task8 Task9 (pause...)
All tasks done!
```

Let's revisit `TaskQueue` and examine the `Consume` method, where a worker picks off and executes a task from the queue. We want the worker to block while there's nothing to do; in other words, when there are no items on the queue. Hence, our blocking condition is `taskQ.Count==0`:

```
string task;
lock (locker)
{
  while (taskQ.Count == 0) Monitor.Wait (locker);
  task = taskQ.Dequeue();
}
if (task == null) return;        // This signals our exit
Console.Write (task);
Thread.Sleep (1000);             // Simulate time-consuming task
```

The `while` loop exits when `taskQ.Count` is nonzero, meaning that (at least) one task is outstanding. We must dequeue the task *before* releasing the lock—otherwise, the task may not be there for us to dequeue; the presence of other threads means things can change while you blink. In particular, another consumer just finishing a previous job could sneak in and dequeue our task if we weren't meticulous with locking.

After the task is dequeued, we release the lock immediately. If we held on to it while performing the task, we would unnecessarily block other consumers and producers. We don't pulse after dequeuing, as no other consumer can ever unblock by there being fewer items on the queue.

 Aim to lock briefly, when using `Wait` and `Pulse`, to avoid unnecessarily blocking other threads. Locking across many lines of code is fine—providing they all execute quickly. Remember that you're helped by `Monitor.Wait`'s releasing the underlying lock while awaiting a pulse!

For the sake of efficiency, we call `Pulse` instead of `PulseAll` when enqueuing a task. This is because (at most) one consumer need be woken per task. If you had just one ice cream, you wouldn't wake a class of 30 sleeping children to queue for it; similarly, with 30 consumers, there's no benefit in waking them all—only to have 29 spin a useless iteration on their `while` loop before going back to sleep. We wouldn't break anything functionally, however, by replacing `Pulse` with `PulseAll`.

Wait Timeouts

You can specify a timeout when calling `Wait`, either in milliseconds or as a `TimeSpan`. The `Wait` method then returns `false` if it gave up because of a timeout. The timeout applies only to the *waiting phase*. Hence, a `Wait` with a timeout does the following:

1. Releases the underlying lock
2. Blocks until pulsed, *or the timeout elapses*
3. Reacquires the underlying lock

Specifying a timeout is like asking the CLR to give you a "virtual pulse" after the timeout interval. A timed-out `Wait` will still perform step 3 and reacquire the lock—just as if pulsed.

 Should `Wait` block in step 3 (while reacquiring the lock), any timeout is ignored. This is rarely an issue, though, because other threads will lock only briefly in a well-designed `Wait/Pulse` application. So, reacquiring the lock should be a near-instant operation.

`Wait` timeouts have a useful application. Sometimes it may be unreasonable or impossible to `Pulse` whenever an unblocking condition arises. An example might be if a blocking condition involves calling a method that derives information from periodically querying a database. If latency is not an issue, the solution is simple—one can specify a timeout when calling `Wait`, as follows:

```
lock (locker)
  while ( <blocking-condition> )
    Monitor.Wait (locker, <timeout> );
```

This forces the blocking condition to be rechecked at the interval specified by the timeout, as well as when pulsed. The simpler the blocking condition, the smaller the timeout can be without creating inefficiency. In this case, we don't care whether the `Wait` was pulsed or timed out, so we ignore its return value.

The same system works equally well if the pulse is absent due to a bug in the program. It can be worth adding a timeout to all `Wait` commands in programs where synchronization is particularly complex, as an ultimate backup for obscure pulsing errors. It also provides a degree of bug immunity if the program is modified later by someone not on the `Pulse`!

Two-Way Signaling

Let's say we want to signal a thread five times in a row:

```
class Race
{
  static object locker = new object( );
  static bool go;

  static void Main( )
  {
    new Thread (SaySomething).Start( );

    for (int i = 0; i < 5; i++)
      lock (locker) { go = true; Monitor.PulseAll (locker); }
  }

  static void SaySomething( )
  {
    for (int i = 0; i < 5; i++)
      lock (locker)
      {
        while (!go) Monitor.Wait (locker);
```

```
              go = false;
              Console.WriteLine ("Wassup?");
          }
      }
  }

  // Expected Output:
  Wassup?
  Wassup?
  Wassup?
  Wassup?
  Wassup?

  //Actual Output:
  Wassup? (hangs)
```

This program is flawed: the for loop in the main thread can freewheel right through its five iterations anytime the worker doesn't hold the lock, and possibly before the worker even starts! The producer/consumer example didn't suffer from this problem because if the main thread got ahead of the worker, each request would queue up. But in this case, we need the main thread to block at each iteration if the worker's still busy with a previous task.

We can solve this by adding a ready flag to the class, controlled by the worker. The main thread then waits until the worker's ready before setting the go flag.

 This is analogous to the two-way signaling example in the section "Signaling with Event Wait Handles" earlier in this chapter.

Here it is:

```
class Solved
{
  static object locker = new object( );
  static bool ready, go;

  static void Main( )
  {
    new Thread (SaySomething).Start( );

    for (int i = 0; i < 5; i++)
      lock (locker)
      {
        while (!ready) Monitor.Wait (locker);
        ready = false;
        go = true;
        Monitor.PulseAll (locker);
      }
  }
```

```
static void SaySomething()
{
  for (int i = 0; i < 5; i++)
    lock (locker)
    {
      ready = true;
      Monitor.PulseAll (locker);        // Remember that calling
      while (!go) Monitor.Wait (locker);  // Monitor.Wait releases
      go = false;                        // and reacquires the lock.
      Console.WriteLine ("Wassup?");
    }
}
}

// Output:
Wassup? (repeated five times)
```

In the Main method, we clear the ready flag, set the go flag, and pulse, all in the same lock statement. The benefit of doing this is that it offers robustness if we later introduce a third thread into the equation. Imagine another thread trying to signal the worker at the same time. Our logic is watertight in this scenario; in effect, we're clearing ready and setting go, *atomically*.

Simulating Wait Handles

You might have noticed a pattern in the preceding example: both waiting loops have the following structure:

```
lock (locker)
{
  while (!flag) Monitor.Wait (locker);
  flag = false;
  ...
}
```

where flag is set to true in another thread. This is, in effect, mimicking an AutoResetEvent. If we omitted flag=false, we'd have a ManualResetEvent; if we replaced the flag with an integer field, we'd have a Semaphore.

Simulating the static methods that work across a set of wait handles is, in most cases, easy. The equivalent of calling WaitAll across event wait handles is nothing more than a blocking condition that incorporates all the flags used in place of the wait handles:

```
lock (locker)
  while (!flag1 && !flag2 && !flag3...)
    Monitor.Wait (locker);
```

This can be particularly useful given that WaitAll is often unusable due to COM legacy issues. Simulating WaitAny is simply a matter of replacing the && operator with the || operator.

SignalAndWait is trickier. Recall that this method signals one handle while waiting on another in an atomic operation. We have a situation analogous to a distributed database transaction: we need a two-phase commit! Assuming we wanted to signal flagA while waiting on flagB, we'd have to divide each flag into two, resulting in code that might look like this:

```
lock (locker)
{
  flagAphase1 = true;
  Monitor.Pulse (locker);
  while (!flagBphase1) Monitor.Wait (locker);

  flagAphase2 = true;
  Monitor.Pulse (locker);
  while (!flagBphase2) Monitor.Wait (locker);
}
```

with additional "rollback" logic to retract flagAphase1 if the first Wait statement threw an exception as a result of being interrupted or aborted. This is a situation where wait handles are easier. True atomic signaling and waiting, however, is actually an unusual requirement.

Interrupt and Abort

All blocking methods—Sleep, Join, EndInvoke, WaitOne, and Wait—block forever if the unblocking condition is never met and no timeout is specified. Occasionally, it can be useful to release a blocked thread prematurely; for instance, when ending an application. Two methods accomplish this:

- Thread.Interrupt
- Thread.Abort

The Abort method is also capable of ending a nonblocked thread—stuck, perhaps, in an infinite loop.

Interrupt

Calling Interrupt on a blocked thread forcibly releases it, throwing a Thread-InterruptedException, as follows:

```
static void Main( )
{
  Thread t = new Thread (delegate( )
  {
    try
    {
      Thread.Sleep (Timeout.Infinite);
    }
    catch (ThreadInterruptedException)
    {
      Console.Write ("Forcibly ");
    }
    Console.WriteLine ("Woken!");
  });
```

```
    t.Start();
    t.Interrupt();
}

// Output:
Forcibly Woken!
```

Interrupting a thread does not cause the thread to end, unless the ThreadInterruptedException is unhandled.

If Interrupt is called on a thread that's not blocked, the thread continues executing until it next blocks, at which point a ThreadInterruptedException is thrown. This avoids the need for the following test:

```
if ((worker.ThreadState & ThreadState.WaitSleepJoin) > 0)
    worker.Interrupt();
```

which is not thread-safe because of the possibility of preemption between the if statement and worker.Interrupt.

Interrupting a thread arbitrarily is dangerous, however, because any framework or third-party methods in the calling stack could unexpectedly receive the interrupt rather than your intended code. All it would take is for the thread to block briefly on a simple lock or synchronization resource, and any pending interruption would kick in. If the method isn't designed to be interrupted (with appropriate cleanup code in finally blocks), objects could be left in an unusable state or resources incompletely released.

Interrupting a thread is safe when you are sure exactly where the thread is; for instance, through a signaling construct that you monopolize.

Abort

A blocked thread can also be forcibly released via its Abort method. This has an effect similar to calling Interrupt, except that a ThreadAbortException is thrown instead of a ThreadInterruptedException. Furthermore, the exception will be rethrown at the end of the catch block (in an attempt to terminate the thread for good) unless Thread.ResetAbort is called within the catch block. In the interim, the thread has a ThreadState of AbortRequested.

> An unhandled ThreadAbortException does not cause application shutdown, unlike all other types of Exception.

The big difference between Interrupt and Abort is what happens when it's called on a thread that is not blocked. Whereas Interrupt waits until the thread next blocks before doing anything, Abort throws an exception on the thread right where it's executing (unmanaged code excepted). This is a problem because .NET Framework code might be aborted; code that is not abort-safe. This rules out using Abort in almost any nontrivial context.

There are two cases, though, where you can safely use Abort. One is if you are willing to tear down a thread's application domain after it's aborted. A good example of when you might do this is in writing a unit-testing framework. (We discuss application domains fully in Chapter 21.) Another case where you can call Abort safely is on your own thread. We describe this in the following section.

Safe Cancellation

An alternative to aborting another thread is to implement a pattern whereby the worker periodically checks a cancel flag, exiting if the flag is true. To abort, the instigator simply sets the flag, and then waits for the worker to comply:

```
class ProLife
{
  public static void Main()
  {
    RulyWorker w = new RulyWorker();
    Thread t = new Thread (w.Work);
    t.Start();
    Thread.Sleep (1000);

    Console.WriteLine ("aborting");
    w.Abort();                        // Safely abort the worker.
    Console.WriteLine ("aborted");
  }

  public class RulyWorker
  {
    volatile bool abort;
    public void Abort() { abort = true; }

    public void Work()
    {
      while (true)
      {
        CheckAbort();
        // Do stuff...
        try      { OtherMethod(); }
        finally  { /* any required cleanup */ }
      }
    }

    void OtherMethod()
    {
      // Do stuff...
      CheckAbort();
    }

    void CheckAbort() { if (abort) Thread.CurrentThread.Abort(); }
  }
}
```

The disadvantage is that the worker method must be written explicitly to support cancellation. Nonetheless, this is one of the few safe cancellation patterns.

In our example, the worker calls `Abort` on its own thread upon noticing that the abort field is true. This is safe because we're aborting from a known place, and it results in a graceful exit up the execution stack (without circumventing code in `finally` blocks). Throwing a custom exception works equally well, although you must then catch the exception at the top level in your thread entry method to avoid application shutdown (a good idea, anyway, with any type of exception).

The `BackgroundWorker` helper class supports a similar flag-based cancellation pattern.

Local Storage

Much of this chapter has focused on synchronization constructs and the issues arising from having threads concurrently access the same data. Sometimes, however, you want to keep data isolated, ensuring that each thread has a separate copy. Local variables achieve exactly this, but they are useful only with transient data.

The `Thread` class provides `GetData` and `SetData` methods for storing nontransient isolated data in "slots" whose values persist between method calls. You might be hard-pressed to think of a requirement: data you'd want to keep isolated to a thread tends to be transient by nature. Its main application is for storing "out-of-band" data—that which supports the execution path's infrastructure, such as messaging, transaction, and security tokens. Passing such data around in method parameters is extremely clumsy and alienates all but your own methods; storing such information in static fields means sharing it between all threads.

`Thread.GetData` reads from a thread's isolated data store; `Thread.SetData` writes to it. Both methods require a `LocalDataStoreSlot` object to identify the slot. This is just a wrapper for a string that names the slot; the same slot can be used across all threads and they'll still get separate values. Here's an example:

```
class Test
{
  // The same LocalDataStoreSlot object can be used across all threads.
  LocalDataStoreSlot secSlot = Thread.GetNamedDataSlot ("securityLevel");

  // This property has a separate value on each thread.
  int SecurityLevel
  {
    get
    {
      object data = Thread.GetData (secSlot);
      return data == null ? 0 : (int) data;    // null == uninitialized
    }
    set { Thread.SetData (secSlot, value); }
  }
  ...
```

`Thread.FreeNamedDataSlot` will release a given data slot across all threads, but only once all `LocalDataStoreSlot` objects of the same name have dropped out of scope and been garbage-collected. This ensures that threads don't get data slots pulled out from under their feet, as long as they keep a reference to the appropriate LocalDataStoreSlot object while the slot is needed.

BackgroundWorker

BackgroundWorker is a helper class in the System.ComponentModel namespace for managing a worker thread. It provides the following features:

- A cancel flag for signaling a worker to end without using Abort
- A standard protocol for reporting progress, completion, and cancellation
- An implementation of IComponent allowing it be sited in Visual Studio's designer
- Exception handling on the worker thread
- The ability to update Windows Forms or WPF controls in response to worker progress or completion

The last two features are particularly useful. You don't have to include a try/catch block in your worker method, and you can safely update Windows Forms controls or WPF elements without needing to call Control.Invoke or Dispatcher. Invoke.

BackgroundWorker uses the thread pool, which means you should never call Abort on a BackgroundWorker thread.

Here are the minimum steps in using BackgroundWorker:

1. Instantiate BackgroundWorker and handle the DoWork event.
2. Call RunWorkerAsync, optionally with an object argument.

This then sets it in motion. Any argument passed to RunWorkerAsync will be forwarded to DoWork's event handler, via the event argument's Argument property. Here's an example:

```
class Program
{
  static BackgroundWorker bw = new BackgroundWorker( );

  static void Main( )
  {
    bw.DoWork += bw_DoWork;
    bw.RunWorkerAsync ("Message to worker");
    Console.ReadLine( );
  }

  static void bw_DoWork (object sender, DoWorkEventArgs e)
  {
    // This is called on the worker thread
    Console.WriteLine (e.Argument);        // writes "Message to worker"
    // Perform time-consuming task...
  }
}
```

BackgroundWorker also provides a RunWorkerCompleted event that fires after the DoWork event handler has done its job. Handling RunWorkerCompleted is not mandatory, but one usually does so in order to query any exception that was thrown in DoWork. Furthermore, code within a RunWorkerCompleted event handler is able to update user interface controls without explicit marshaling; code within the DoWork event handler cannot.

To add support for progress reporting:

1. Set the WorkerReportsProgress property to true.

2. Periodically call ReportProgress from within the DoWork event handler with a "percentage complete" value, and optionally, a user-state object.

3. Handle the ProgressChanged event, querying its event argument's Progress-Percentage property.

4. Code in the ProgressChanged event handler is free to interact with UI controls just as with RunWorkerCompleted. This is typically where you will update a progress bar.

To add support for cancellation:

1. Set the WorkerSupportsCancellation property to true.

2. Periodically check the CancellationPending property from within the DoWork event handler. If it's true, set the event argument's Cancel property to true, and return. (The worker can also set Cancel and exit without Cancellation-Pending being true if it decides that the job is too difficult and it can't go on.)

3. Call CancelAsync to request cancellation.

Here's an example that implements all the preceding features:

```
using System;
using System.Threading;
using System.ComponentModel;

class Program
{
  static BackgroundWorker bw;

  static void Main( )
  {
    bw = new BackgroundWorker( );
    bw.WorkerReportsProgress = true;
    bw.WorkerSupportsCancellation = true;
    bw.DoWork += bw_DoWork;
    bw.ProgressChanged += bw_ProgressChanged;
    bw.RunWorkerCompleted += bw_RunWorkerCompleted;

    bw.RunWorkerAsync ("Hello to worker");

    Console.WriteLine ("Press Enter in the next 5 seconds to cancel");
    Console.ReadLine( );
    if (bw.IsBusy) bw.CancelAsync( );
    Console.ReadLine( );
  }
```

```
static void bw_DoWork (object sender, DoWorkEventArgs e)
{
  for (int i = 0; i <= 100; i += 20)
  {
    if (bw.CancellationPending) { e.Cancel = true; return; }
    bw.ReportProgress (i);
    Thread.Sleep (1000);      // Just for the demo... don't go sleeping
  }                           // for real in pooled threads!

  e.Result = 123;     // This gets passed to RunWorkerCompleted
}

static void bw_RunWorkerCompleted (object sender,
                                   RunWorkerCompletedEventArgs e)
{
  if (e.Cancelled)
    Console.WriteLine ("You cancelled!");
  else if (e.Error != null)
    Console.WriteLine ("Worker exception: " + e.Error.ToString());
  else
    Console.WriteLine ("Complete: " + e.Result);     // from DoWork
}

static void bw_ProgressChanged (object sender,
                                ProgressChangedEventArgs e)
{
  Console.WriteLine ("Reached " + e.ProgressPercentage + "%");
}
}

// Output:
Press Enter in the next 5 seconds to cancel
Reached 0%
Reached 20%
Reached 40%
Reached 60%
Reached 80%
Reached 100%
Complete: 123

Press Enter in the next 5 seconds to cancel
Reached 0%
Reached 20%
Reached 40%

You cancelled!
```

Subclassing BackgroundWorker

BackgroundWorker is not sealed and provides a virtual OnDoWork method, suggesting
another pattern for its use. In writing a potentially long-running method, you
could write an additional version returning a subclassed BackgroundWorker,
preconfigured to perform the job concurrently. The consumer then needs to

handle only the RunWorkerCompleted and ProgressChanged events. For instance, suppose we wrote a time-consuming method called GetFinancialTotals:

```
public class Client
{
  Dictionary <string,int> GetFinancialTotals (int foo, int bar) { ... }
  ...
}
```

We could refactor it as follows:

```
public class Client
{
  public FinancialWorker GetFinancialTotalsBackground (int foo, int bar)
  {
    return new FinancialWorker (foo, bar);
  }
}

public class FinancialWorker : BackgroundWorker
{
  public Dictionary <string,int> Result;    // You can add typed fields.
  public volatile int Foo, Bar;             // Exposing them via properties
                                            // protected with locks would
  public FinancialWorker()                  // also work well.
  {
    WorkerReportsProgress = true;
    WorkerSupportsCancellation = true;
  }

  public FinancialWorker (int foo, int bar) : this()
  {
    this.Foo = foo; this.Bar = bar;
  }

  protected override void OnDoWork (DoWorkEventArgs e)
  {
    ReportProgress (0, "Working hard on this report...");

    // Initialize financial report data
    // ...

    while (!<finished report>)
    {
      if (CancellationPending) { e.Cancel = true; return; }
      // Perform another calculation step ...
      // ...
      ReportProgress (percentCompleteCalc, "Getting there...");
    }
    ReportProgress (100, "Done!");
    e.Result = Result = <completed report data>;
  }
}
```

Whoever calls `GetFinancialTotalsBackground` then gets a `FinancialWorker`: a wrapper to manage the background operation with real-world usability. It can report progress, can be canceled, and is friendly with WPF and Windows Forms applications. It's also exception-handled, and it uses a standard protocol (in common with that of anyone else using `BackgroundWorker`!).

Subclassing `BackgroundWorker` in this manner yields the benefits of implementing the event-based asynchronous pattern, but in a tidier fashion and with less effort.

ReaderWriterLockSlim

Quite often, instances of a type are thread-safe for concurrent read operations, but not for concurrent updates (nor for a concurrent read and update). This can also be true with resources such as a file. Although protecting instances of such types with a simple exclusive lock for all modes of access usually does the trick, it can unreasonably restrict concurrency if there are many readers and just occasional updates. An example of where this could occur is in a business application server, where commonly used data is cached for fast retrieval in static fields. The `ReaderWriterLockSlim` class is designed to provide maximum-availability locking in just this scenario.

 `ReaderWriterLockSlim` is new to Framework 3.5 and is a replacement for the older "fat" `ReaderWriterLock` class. The latter is similar in functionality, but it is several times slower and has an inherent design fault in its mechanism for handling lock upgrades.

With both classes, there are two basic kinds of lock—a read lock and a write lock:

- A write lock is universally exclusive.
- A read lock is compatible with other read locks.

So, a thread holding a write lock blocks all other threads trying to obtain a read *or* write lock (and vice versa). But if no thread holds a write lock, any number of threads may concurrently obtain a read lock.

`ReaderWriterLockSlim` defines the following methods for obtaining and releasing read/write locks:

```
public void EnterReadLock( );
public void ExitReadLock( );
public void EnterWriteLock( );
public void ExitWriteLock( );
```

Additionally, there are "Try" versions of all `EnterXXX` methods that accept timeout arguments in the style of `Monitor.TryEnter` (timeouts can occur quite easily if the resource is heavily contended). `ReaderWriterLock` provides similar methods, named `AcquireXXX` and `ReleaseXXX`. These throw an `ApplicationException` if a timeout occurs rather than returning `false`.

The following program demonstrates `ReaderWriterLockSlim`. Three threads continually enumerate a list, while two further threads append a random number to the list every second. A read lock protects the list readers, and a write lock protects the list writers:

```
class SlimDemo
{
  static ReaderWriterLockSlim rw = new ReaderWriterLockSlim( );
  static List<int> items = new List<int>( );
  static Random rand = new Random( );

  static void Main( )
  {
    new Thread (Read).Start( );
    new Thread (Read).Start( );
    new Thread (Read).Start( );

    new Thread (Write).Start ("A");
    new Thread (Write).Start ("B");
  }

  static void Read( )
  {
    while (true)
    {
      rw.EnterReadLock( );
      foreach (int i in items) Thread.Sleep (10);
      rw.ExitReadLock( );
    }
  }

  static void Write (object threadID)
  {
    while (true)
    {
      int newNumber = GetRandNum (100);
      rw.EnterWriteLock( );
      items.Add (newNumber);
      rw.ExitWriteLock( );
      Console.WriteLine ("Thread " + threadID + " added " + newNumber);
      Thread.Sleep (100);
    }
  }

  static int GetRandNum (int max) { lock (rand) return rand.Next (max); }
}
```

 In production code, you'd typically add try/finally blocks to ensure that locks were released if an exception was thrown.

Here's the result:

```
Thread B added 61
Thread A added 83
Thread B added 55
Thread A added 33
...
```

`ReaderWriterLockSlim` allows more concurrent Read activity than would a simple lock. We can illustrate this by inserting the following line to the `Write` method, at the start of the while loop:

```
Console.WriteLine (rw.CurrentReadCount + " concurrent readers");
```

This nearly always prints "3 concurrent readers" (the Read methods spend most of their time inside the foreach loops). As well as `CurrentReadCount`, `ReaderWriterLockSlim` provides the following properties for monitoring locks:

```
public bool IsReadLockHeld            { get; }
public bool IsUpgradeableReadLockHeld { get; }
public bool IsWriteLockHeld           { get; }

public int  WaitingReadCount          { get; }
public int  WaitingUpgradeCount       { get; }
public int  WaitingWriteCount         { get; }

public int  RecursiveReadCount        { get; }
public int  RecursiveUpgradeCount     { get; }
public int  RecursiveWriteCount       { get; }
```

Upgradeable Locks and Recursion

Sometimes it's useful to swap a read lock for a write lock in a single atomic operation. For instance, suppose you want to add an item to a list only if the item wasn't already present. Ideally, you'd want to minimize the time spent holding the (exclusive) write lock, so you might proceed as follows:

1. Obtain a read lock.
2. Test if the item is already present in the list, and if so, release the lock and return.
3. Release the read lock.
4. Obtain a write lock.
5. Add the item.

The problem is that another thread could sneak in and modify the list (adding the same item, for instance) between steps 3 and 4. `ReaderWriterLockSlim` addresses this through a third kind of lock called an *upgradeable lock*. An upgradeable lock is like a read lock except that it can later be promoted to a write lock in an atomic operation. Here's how you use it:

1. Call `EnterUpgradeableReadLock`.
2. Perform read-based activities (e.g., test whether the item is already present in the list).
3. Call `EnterWriteLock` (this converts the upgradeable lock to a write lock).
4. Perform write-based activities (e.g., add the item to the list).
5. Call `ExitWriteLock` (this converts the write lock back to an upgradeable lock).
6. Perform any other read-based activities.
7. Call `ExitUpgradeableReadLock`.

From the caller's perspective, it's rather like nested or recursive locking. Functionally, though, in step 3, ReaderWriterLockSlim releases your read lock and obtains a fresh write lock, atomically.

There's another important difference between upgradeable locks and read locks. While an upgradeable lock can coexist with any number of *read* locks, only one upgradeable lock can itself be taken out at a time. This prevents conversion deadlocks by *serializing* competing conversions—just as update locks do in SQL Server:

SQL Server	ReaderWriterLockSlim
Share lock	Read lock
Exclusive lock	Write lock
Update lock	Upgradeable lock

We can demonstrate an upgradeable lock by changing the Write method in the preceding example such that it adds a number to list only if not already present:

```
while (true)
{
  int newNumber = GetRandNum (100);
  rw.EnterUpgradeableReadLock();
  if (!items.Contains (newNumber))
  {
    rw.EnterWriteLock();
    items.Add (newNumber);
    rw.ExitWriteLock();
    Console.WriteLine ("Thread " + threadID + " added " + newNumber);
  }
  rw.ExitUpgradeableReadLock();
  Thread.Sleep (100);
}
```

> ReaderWriterLock can also do lock conversions—but unreliably because it doesn't support the concept of upgradeable locks. This is why the designers of ReaderWriterLockSlim had to start fresh with a new class.

Lock recursion

Ordinarily, nested or recursive locking is prohibited with ReaderWriterLockSlim. Hence, the following throws an exception:

```
var rw = new ReaderWriterLockSlim();
rw.EnterReadLock();
rw.EnterReadLock();
rw.ExitReadLock();
rw.ExitReadLock();
```

It runs without error, however, if you construct ReaderWriterLockSlim as follows:

```
var rw = new ReaderWriterLockSlim (LockRecursionPolicy.SupportsRecursion);
```

This ensures that recursive locking can happen only if you plan for it. Recursive locking can bring undesired complexity because it's possible to acquire more than one kind of lock:

```
rw.EnterWriteLock( );
rw.EnterReadLock( );
Console.WriteLine (rw.IsReadLockHeld);    // True
Console.WriteLine (rw.IsWriteLockHeld);   // True
rw.ExitReadLock( );
rw.ExitWriteLock( );
```

The basic rule is that once you've acquired a lock, subsequent recursive locks can be less, but not greater, on the following scale:

Read Lock → Upgradeable Lock → Write Lock

A request to promote an upgradeable lock to a write lock, however, is always legal.

Timers

If you need to execute some method repeatedly at regular intervals, the easiest way is with a *timer*. Timers are convenient, and they are efficient in their use of memory and resources—compared with techniques such as the following:

```
new Thread (delegate( ) {
                        while (enabled)
                        {
                          DoSomeAction( );
                          Thread.Sleep (TimeSpan.FromHours (24));
                        }
                      }).Start( );
```

Not only does this permanently tie up a thread resource, but without additional coding, DoSomeAction will happen at a later time each day. Timers solve these problems.

The .NET Framework provides four timers. Two of these are general-purpose multithreaded timers:

- System.Threading.Timer
- System.Timers.Timer

The other two are special-purpose single-threaded timers:

- System.Windows.Forms.Timer (Windows Forms timer)
- System.Windows.Threading.DispatcherTimer (WPF timer)

The multithreaded timers are more powerful, accurate, and flexible; the single-threaded timers are safer and more convenient for running simple tasks that update Windows Forms controls or WPF elements.

Multithreaded Timers

System.Threading.Timer is the simplest multithreaded timer: it has just a constructor and two methods (a delight for minimalists, as well as book authors!). In the following example, a timer calls the Tick method, which writes "tick..." after five seconds have elapsed, and then every second after that, until the user presses Enter:

```
using System;
using System.Threading;

class Program
{
  static void Main( )
  {
    // First interval = 5000ms; subsequent intervals = 1000ms
    Timer tmr = new Timer (Tick, "tick...", 5000, 1000);
    Console.ReadLine( );
    tmr.Dispose( );                    // Ends the timer
  }

  static void Tick (object data)
  {
    // This runs on a pooled thread
    Console.WriteLine (data);          // Writes "tick..."
  }
}
```

You can change a timer's interval later by calling its Change method. If you want a timer to fire just once, specify Timeout.Infinite in the constructor's last argument.

The .NET Framework provides another timer class of the same name in the System. Timers namespace. This simply wraps the System.Threading.Timer, providing additional convenience while using the identical underlying engine. Here's a summary of its added features:

- A Component implementation, allowing it to be sited in Visual Studio's designer
- An Interval property instead of a Change method
- An Elapsed *event* instead of a callback delegate
- An Enabled property to start and stop the timer (its default value being false)
- Start and Stop methods in case you're confused by Enabled
- An AutoReset flag for indicating a recurring event (default value is true)

Here's an example:

```
using System;
using System.Timers;   // Timers namespace rather than Threading

class SystemTimer
{
  static void Main( )
```

```
    {
        Timer tmr = new Timer( );          // Doesn't require any args
        tmr.Interval = 500;
        tmr.Elapsed += tmr_Elapsed;        // Uses an event instead of a delegate
        tmr.Start( );                      // Start the timer
        Console.ReadLine( );
        tmr.Stop( );                       // Stop the timer
        Console.ReadLine( );
        tmr.Start( );                      // Restart the timer
        Console.ReadLine( );
        tmr.Dispose( );                    // Permanently stop the timer
    }

    static void tmr_Elapsed (object sender, EventArgs e)
    {
        Console.WriteLine ("Tick");
    }
}
```

Multithreaded timers use the thread pool to allow a few threads to serve many timers. This means that the callback method or Tick event may fire on a different thread each time it is called. Furthermore, a Tick always fires on time—regardless of whether the previous Tick has finished executing. Hence, callbacks or event handlers must be thread-safe.

The precision of multithreaded timers depends on the operating system, and is typically in the 10–20 milliseconds region. If you need greater precision, you can use P/Invoke interop and call the Windows multimedia timer. This has precision down to 1 ms and it is defined in *winmm.dll*. First call timeBeginPeriod to inform the operating system that you need high timing precision, and then call timeSetEvent to start a multimedia timer. When you're done, call timeKillEvent to stop the timer and timeEndPeriod to inform the OS that you no longer need high timing precision. Chapter 22 demonstrates calling external methods with P/Invoke. You can find complete examples on the Internet that use the multimedia timer by searching for the keywords *dllimport winmm.dll timesetevent*.

Single-Threaded Timers

The .NET Framework provides timers designed to eliminate thread-safety issues for Windows Forms and WPF applications:

- System.Windows.Forms.Timer (Windows Forms)
- System.Windows.Threading.DispatcherTimer (WPF)

 The single-threaded timers are not designed to work outside their respective environments. If you use a Windows Forms timer in a Windows Service application, for instance, the Timer event won't fire!

Both are like System.Timers.Timer in the members that they expose (Interval, Tick, Start, and Stop) and are used in a similar manner. However, they differ in how they work internally. Instead of using the thread pool to generate timer events, the Windows Forms and WPF timers rely on the message pumping mechanism of their underlying user interface model. This means that the Tick event always fires on the same thread that originally created the timer—which, in a normal application, is the same thread used to manage all user interface elements and controls. This has a number of benefits:

- You can forget about thread safety.
- A fresh Tick will never fire until the previous Tick has finished processing.
- You can update user interface elements and controls directly from Tick event handling code, without calling Control.Invoke or Dispatcher.Invoke.

It sounds too good to be true, until you realize that a program employing these timers is not really multithreaded—*there is no parallel execution*. One thread serves all timers—as well as the processing UI events. This brings us to the disadvantage of single-threaded timers:

- Unless the Tick event handler executes quickly, the user interface becomes unresponsive.

This makes the Windows Forms and WPF timers suitable for only small jobs, typically those that involve updating some aspect of the user interface (e.g., a clock or countdown display). Otherwise, you need a multithreaded timer.

In terms of precision, the single-threaded timers are similar to the multithreaded timers (tens of milliseconds), although they are typically less *accurate*, because they can be delayed while other user interface requests (or other timer events) are processed.

20

Asynchronous Methods

In Chapter 19, we saw how a thread provides a parallel execution path. We took for granted that whenever you needed to run something in parallel, you could assign a new or pooled thread to the job. Although this usually holds true, there are exceptions. Suppose you were writing a TCP sockets or web server application that needed to process 1,000 concurrent requests. If you dedicated a thread to each incoming request, you would consume a gigabyte of memory purely on thread overhead.

Asynchronous methods address this problem through a pattern by which many concurrent activities are handled by a few pooled threads. This makes it possible to write highly concurrent applications—as well as highly *thread-efficient* applications.

To avoid getting lost, you'll need to be familiar with threading (Chapter 19) and streams (Chapter 13).

Why Asynchronous Methods Exist

The problem just described might be insoluble if every thread needed to be busy all of the time. But this is not the case: fetching a web page, for instance, might take up to several seconds from start to end (because of a potentially slow connection) and yet consume only a fraction of a millisecond of CPU time in total. Processing an HTTP request is not computationally intensive.

This means that a thread dedicated to processing a single web request might spend 99 percent of its time blocked—representing huge economy potential. The *asynchronous method* pattern exploits just this potential, allowing a handful of fully utilized threads to take on thousands of concurrent jobs.

If you don't need high concurrency, avoid asynchronous methods; they will unnecessarily complicate your program. Further, they are not guaranteed to execute in parallel with the caller. If you need parallel execution, consider using asynchronous delegates or BackgroundWorker—or simply starting a new thread.

An asynchronous method aims never to block *any thread*, instead using a pattern of returning with a callback. Blocking means entering a WaitSleepJoin state (or causing another thread to do the same), "wasting" a precious thread resource. To achieve this, an asynchronous method must abstain from calling any blocking method.

A method that takes awhile to execute because it performs computationally intensive work does not violate the system. The purpose of asynchronous methods isn't to provide a convenient mechanism for executing a method in parallel with the caller; it's to *optimize thread resources*. Here's the golden rule that asynchronous methods follow:

Make good use of the CPU, or exit with a callback!

This means an asynchronous method such as BeginRead may not return immediately to the caller. It can make the caller wait as long as it likes—while making good use of the processor or another constrained resource. It can even finish the entire task synchronously—providing it never blocked and never caused another thread to do the same.

There is an exception to the nonblocking rule. It's generally okay to block while calling a database server—if other threads are competing for the *same* server. This is because in a highly concurrent system, the database must be designed such that the majority of queries execute extremely quickly. If you end up with thousands of concurrent queries, it means that requests are hitting the database server *faster than it can process them*. The thread pool is then the least of your worries!

The primary use for asynchronous methods is in dealing with potentially slow network connections.

Asynchronous Method Signatures

Asynchronous methods, by convention, all start with "Begin", have a pairing method starting with "End", and have signatures like those of asynchronous delegates:

```
IAsyncResult BeginXXX (in/ref-args, AsyncCallback callback, object state);

return-type EndXXX (out/ref-args, IAsyncResult asyncResult);
```

Here's an example from NetworkStream:

```
public IAsyncResult BeginRead (byte[] buffer, int offset, int size,
                               AsyncCallback callback, object state);

public int EndRead (IAsyncResult asyncResult);
```

The Begin method returns an IAsyncResult object:

```
public interface IAsyncResult
{
  object AsyncState { get; }             // "state" object passed to Begin.
  WaitHandle AsyncWaitHandle { get; }    // Allows caller to wait it out.
  bool CompletedSynchronously { get; }   // Did it complete on BeginX?
  bool IsCompleted { get; }              // Has it completed yet?
}
```

This same IAsyncResult object is passed to the completion callback. Here's its delegate:

```
public delegate void AsyncCallback (IAsyncResult ar);
```

As with asynchronous delegates, the End*XXX* method allows the return value to be retrieved, as well as any out/ref arguments. This is also where exceptions are rethrown.

 If you fail to call the End*XXX* method, exceptions won't get rethrown, meaning silent failure.

To avoid blocking, you will nearly always call the End*XXX* method from inside the callback method. Callbacks always run on pooled threads.

Asynchronous Methods Versus Asynchronous Delegates

Asynchronous method signatures look exactly like those of asynchronous delegates. Their behavior, however, is very different:

Asynchronous methods	Asynchronous delegates
Rarely or never blocks any thread.	May block for any length of time.
Begin method may not return immediately to the caller.	BeginInvoke returns immediately to the caller.
An agreed protocol with no C# language support.	Built-in compiler support

The purpose of asynchronous methods is to allow many tasks to run on few threads; the purpose of asynchronous delegates is to execute a task in parallel with the caller.

You can use an asynchronous delegate to call an asynchronous method—so that execution is guaranteed to return immediately to the caller, while still following the nonblocking asynchronous method model. If you use an asynchronous delegate to call a blocking method, however, you're back to square one: the server will either suffer limited concurrency or need thousands of threads to do its job.

Using Asynchronous Methods

Let's write a simple TCP sockets server that behaves as follows:

1. It waits for a client request.

2. It reads a 5,000-byte fixed-length message.

3. It reverses the bytes in the message, and then returns them to the client.

Let's first write this using a standard multithreaded *blocking* pattern. Here is the code, exception handling aside:

```
using System;
using System.Threading;
using System.Net;
using System.Net.Sockets;

public class Server
{
  public void Serve (IPAddress address, int port)
  {
    ThreadPool.SetMinThreads (50, 50);     // Refer to Chapter 19
    TcpListener listener = new TcpListener (address, port);
    listener.Start();
    while (true)
    {
      TcpClient c = listener.AcceptTcpClient();
      ThreadPool.QueueUserWorkItem (Accept, c);
    }
  }

  void Accept (object clientObject)
  {
    using (TcpClient client = (TcpClient) clientObject)
    using (NetworkStream n = client.GetStream())
    {
      byte[] data = new byte [5000];

      int bytesRead = 0; int chunkSize = 1;
      while (bytesRead < data.Length && chunkSize > 0)
        bytesRead +=
          chunkSize = n.Read
            (data, bytesRead, data.Length - bytesRead);     // BLOCKS

      Array.Reverse (data);
      n.Write (data, 0, data.Length);                       // BLOCKS
    }
  }
}
```

 You can download a Visual Studio project containing all the code in this chapter—along with a client test harness—at *http://www.albahari.com/nutshell/async.zip*.

Our use of the thread pool prevents an arbitrarily large number of threads from being created (possibly taking down the server) and eliminates the time wasted in creating a new thread per request. Our program is simple and fast, but it is limited to 50 concurrent requests.

In order to scale to 1,000 concurrent requests—without increasing the thread count—we must employ the asynchronous method pattern. This means avoiding the blocking I/O methods altogether and instead calling their asynchronous counterparts. Here's how to do it:

```
class Server
{
  public void Serve (IPAddress address, int port)
  {
    ThreadPool.SetMinThreads (50, 50);
    TcpListener listener = new TcpListener (address, port);
    listener.Start();
    while (true)
    {
      TcpClient c = listener.AcceptTcpClient();
      ThreadPool.QueueUserWorkItem (ReverseEcho, c);
    }
  }

  void ReverseEcho (object client)
  {
    new ReverseEcho().Begin ((TcpClient)client);
  }
}

class ReverseEcho
{
  volatile TcpClient      _client;
  volatile NetworkStream _stream;
  byte[]                 _data = new byte [5000];
  volatile int           _bytesRead = 0;

  internal void Begin (TcpClient c)
  {
    try
    {
      _client = c;
      _stream = c.GetStream();
      Read();
    }
    catch (Exception ex) { ProcessException (ex); }
  }

  void Read()              // Read in a nonblocking fashion.
  {
    _stream.BeginRead (_data, _bytesRead, _data.Length - _bytesRead,
                   ReadCallback, null);
  }

  void ReadCallback (IAsyncResult r)
  {
    try
    {
      int chunkSize = _stream.EndRead (r);
```

```
      _bytesRead += chunkSize;
      if (chunkSize > 0 && _bytesRead < _data.Length)
      {
        Read( );        // More data to read!
        return;
      }
      Array.Reverse (_data);
      _stream.BeginWrite (_data, 0, _data.Length, WriteCallback, null);
    }
    catch (Exception ex) { ProcessException (ex); }
  }

  void WriteCallback (IAsyncResult r)
  {
    try { _stream.EndWrite (r); }
    catch (Exception ex) { ProcessException (ex); }
    Cleanup( );
  }

  void ProcessException (Exception ex)
  {
    Cleanup( );
    Console.WriteLine ("Error: " + ex.Message);
  }

  void Cleanup( )
  {
    if (_stream != null) _stream.Close( );
    if (_client != null) _client.Close( );
  }
}
```

On a 3 GHz processor, this program handles 1,000 concurrent requests on fewer than 10 pooled threads (and in less than one second).

Each client request is processed without calling any blocking methods. The one exception is in the Serve method: listener.AcceptTcpClient blocks while there are no pending client requests. One blocked thread doesn't hurt performance and is also unavoidable (if we instead called BeginAcceptTcpClient the while loop would spin, rapidly enqueuing millions of tasks).

The ReverseEcho class encapsulates a request's state for its lifetime. We can no longer use local variables for this job, because the execution stack disappears each time we exit (after each call to an asynchronous method). This also complicates cleanup and means that a simple using statement is no longer suitable for closing our TcpClient and stream.

Another complicating factor is that we can't use types such as BinaryReader and BinaryWriter, because they don't offer asynchronous versions of their methods. The asynchronous pattern often forces you to work at a lower level than you might otherwise.

Writing Asynchronous Methods

Returning to our previous example, suppose that the 5,000-byte exchange was just a small part of a more sophisticated communication protocol. It would be nice to turn what we've already written into a method like this:

```
public byte[] ReverseEcho (TcpClient client);
```

The problem, of course, is that this method signature is synchronous; we need to offer an asynchronous version—in other words, BeginReverseEcho. Further, if an exception is encountered, it's no good writing it to the Console; we need to throw it back to the consumer at some point. So, to usefully partake in the pattern, we must also offer EndReverseEcho and write a class that implements IAsyncResult.

Our ReverseEcho class is an excellent candidate for IAsyncResult, since it already encapsulates the operation's state. All we really need to add is some plumbing code to rethrow any exception upon calling EndReverseEcho, and a wait handle to signal at completion.

 There's no significantly shorter way to achieve this, other than cutting out the whitespace. Asynchronous methods are hard work!

Here's a real-world example, complete with exception handling and thread safety:

```
// This sample can be downloaded at http://www.albahari.com/nutshell/

public class MessagingServices
{
  public static IAsyncResult BeginReverseEcho (TcpClient client,
                                               AsyncCallback callback,
                                               object userState)
  {
    var re = new ReverseEcho();
    re.Begin (client, callback, userState);
    return re;
  }

  public static byte[] EndReverseEcho (IAsyncResult r)
  {
    return ((ReverseEcho)r).End();
  }
}

class ReverseEcho : IAsyncResult
{
  volatile TcpClient      _client;
  volatile NetworkStream  _stream;
  volatile object         _userState;
  volatile AsyncCallback  _callback;
  ManualResetEvent        _waitHandle = new ManualResetEvent (false);
  volatile int            _bytesRead = 0;
  byte[]                  _data = new byte [5000];
```

```csharp
volatile Exception      _exception;

internal ReverseEcho() { }

// IAsyncResult members:

public object AsyncState          { get { return _userState;   } }
public WaitHandle AsyncWaitHandle { get { return _waitHandle; } }
public bool CompletedSynchronously { get { return false;      } }
public bool IsCompleted
{
  get { return _waitHandle.WaitOne (0, false); }
}

internal void Begin (TcpClient c, AsyncCallback callback, object state)
{
  _client = c;
  _callback = callback;
  _userState = state;
  try
  {
    _stream = _client.GetStream();
    Read();
  }
  catch (Exception ex) { ProcessException (ex); }
}

internal byte[] End()    // Wait for completion + rethrow any error.
{
  AsyncWaitHandle.WaitOne();
  AsyncWaitHandle.Close();
  if (_exception != null) throw _exception;
  return _data;
}

void Read()    // This is always called from an exception-handled method
{
  _stream.BeginRead (_data, _bytesRead, _data.Length - _bytesRead,
                     ReadCallback, null);
}

void ReadCallback (IAsyncResult r)
{
  try
  {
    int chunkSize = _stream.EndRead (r);
    _bytesRead += chunkSize;
    if (chunkSize > 0 && _bytesRead < _data.Length)
    {
      Read();         // More data to read!
      return;
    }
    Array.Reverse (_data);
    _stream.BeginWrite (_data, 0, _data.Length, WriteCallback, null);
```

```
    }
    catch (Exception ex) { ProcessException (ex); }
  }

  void WriteCallback (IAsyncResult r)
  {
    try { _stream.EndWrite (r); }
    catch (Exception ex) { ProcessException (ex); return; }
    Cleanup( );
  }

  void ProcessException (Exception ex)
  {
    _exception = ex;    // This exception will get rethrown when
    Cleanup();          // the consumer calls the End( ) method.
  }

  void Cleanup( )
  {
    try
    {
      if (_stream != null) _stream.Close( );
    }
    catch (Exception ex)
    {
      if (_exception != null) _exception = ex;
    }
    // Signal that we're done and fire the callback.
    _waitHandle.Set( );
    if (_callback != null) _callback (this);
  }
}
```

In `Cleanup`, we closed _stream but not _client, because the caller may want to continue using _client after performing the reverse echo.

 When writing asynchronous methods, you must meticulously catch all exceptions, saving the exception object so that it can be rethrown when the consumer calls the End*XXX* method.

Fake Asynchronous Methods

In general, any Framework method that starts in "Begin" and that returns an `IASyncResult` follows the asynchronous pattern. There are, however, some exceptions, based on the `Stream` class:

```
BufferedStream
CryptoStream
DeflateStream
MemoryStream
```

These types rely on fallback asynchronous implementations in the base `Stream` class, which offer no nonblocking guarantees. Instead, they use an asynchronous delegate to call a *blocking* method such as `Read` or `Write`. Although this approach is perfectly valid in the case of MemoryStream (it never blocks in the first place, so it is excused), it creates a problem with BufferedStream and CryptoStream—if wrapping anything other than a MemoryStream. In other words, if you call BeginRead or BeginWrite on a CryptoStream that wraps a NetworkStream, some thread is going to block at some point, violating the scalability of the asynchronous method pattern. This is a shame, because the CryptoStream's decorator architecture is otherwise efficient.

A workaround with CryptoStream is to first read the underlying stream asynchronously into a MemoryStream, and then have the CryptoStream wrap the MemoryStream. This means reading the whole stream into memory, though, which on a highly concurrent server is not great for scalability, either. If you really need an asynchronous encryption, a solution is to work at a lower level than CryptoStream—that is, ICryptoTransform. You can see exactly how CryptoStream uses ICryptoTransform to do its work with a disassembly tool such as Lutz Roeder's Reflector.

DeflateStream does actually follow the asynchronous pattern—or at least tries to. The problem is that it doesn't properly handle exceptions. If the underlying stream is corrupt, for instance, BeginRead throws an exception on a pooled thread rather than marshaling it back to EndRead. This is an uncatchable exception that takes down your whole application.

The FileStream class is another violator—it touts *fake* asynchronous methods (i.e., it relies on Stream's default implementation). However, it does make an attempt at true asynchronous behavior if constructed as follows:

```
Stream s = new FileStream ("large.bin", FileMode.Create, FileAccess.Write,
                          FileShare.None, 0x1000, true);
```

The boolean argument at the end instructs FileStream not to use asynchronous delegates—and instead (to attempt) a nonblocking approach. The problem is that asynchronous file I/O requires operating system support, which may not be forthcoming. If the OS fails to oblige, BeginRead blocks the calling thread in a WaitSleepJoin state.

Lack of asynchronous file I/O is rarely a problem, though, assuming you're accessing a local filesystem (in fact, it can be a good idea not to use asynchronous file I/O at all). Small file requests are likely to be served from an operating system or hard drive cache and so be brief and CPU-bound; large file I/O requests are going to seriously limit concurrency if not broken up or throttled in some way, no matter what the threading model. A more insidious blocking issue arises if you're using a FileStream on a UNC network path: the solution is instead to use lower-level networking classes (such as those described) for communicating between computers.

Alternatives to Asynchronous Methods

Chapter 19 described three analogous techniques—all of which coalesce many tasks onto a few threads:

- ThreadPool.RegisterWaitForSingleObject
- The producer/consumer queue
- The threading and system timers

ThreadPool.RegisterWaitForSingleObject can be helpful in implementing the asynchronous method pattern. A custom producer/consumer queue can provide a complete alternative—with your own pool of workers—but is of no help if you want to interoperate with the .NET Framework (e.g., to read from a NetworkStream). The threading and system timers are excellent if your work is executed in a periodic fashion, rather than in response to requests.

Asynchronous Events

The asynchronous event pattern is quite separate from both asynchronous methods and delegates and was introduced in .NET 2.0, possibly as an attempt to simplify, or "dumb down," asynchronous methods. Unfortunately, it suffers an unclear design purpose, vacillating on whether to follow the semantics of asynchronous methods (nonblocking) or asynchronous delegates (parallel execution).

Asynchronous events offer automatic context marshaling for Windows Forms and other context-dependent applications, and a protocol for cancellation and progress reporting. They are used in just a few places in the .NET Framework; one example is the WebClient façade class (look for the method names ending in "Async"). Calling DownloadFileAsync to download a small web page over a slow connection blocks the caller for around two seconds—most of the duration of the retrieval. Given that it doesn't take two seconds of CPU time to retrieve a small web page, this behavior is incompatible with both nonblocking and parallel execution semantics, making it useless in practice as well as theory!

An excellent replacement for simple parallel execution is the BackgroundWorker class, described in Chapter 19. This offers the same set of features as the asynchronous event model, but with a clear purpose (parallel execution). It can be instantiated directly (equivalent, perhaps, to consuming asynchronous events) or subclassed (equivalent to implementing the asynchronous event pattern).

21

Application Domains

An *application domain* is the runtime unit of isolation in which a .NET program runs. It provides a managed memory boundary, a container for loaded assemblies and application configuration settings—as well as delineating a communication boundary for distributed applications.

Each .NET process usually hosts just one application domain: the default domain, created automatically by the CLR when the process starts. It's also possible—and sometimes useful—to create additional application domains within the same process. This provides isolation while avoiding the overhead and communication complications that arise with having separate processes. It's useful in scenarios such as load testing and application patching, and in implementing robust error recovery mechanisms.

Application Domain Architecture

Figure 21-1 illustrates the application domain architectures for single-domain, multidomain, and typical distributed client/server applications. In most cases, the processes housing the application domains are created implicitly by the operating system—when the user double-clicks your .NET executable file or starts a Windows service. However, an application domain can also be hosted in other processes such as IIS or in SQL Server through CLR integration.

In the case of a simple executable, the process ends when the default application domain finishes executing. With hosts such as IIS or SQL Server, however, the process controls the lifetime, creating and destroying .NET application domains as it sees fit.

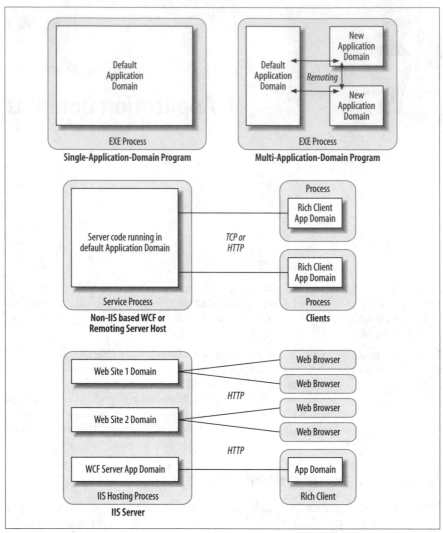

Figure 21-1. Application domain architecture

Creating and Destroying Application Domains

You can create and destroy additional application domains in a process by calling the static methods AppDomain.CreateDomain and AppDomain.UnloadDomain. In the following example, *test.exe* is executed in an isolated application domain, which is then unloaded:

```
static void Main( )
{
  AppDomain newDomain = AppDomain.CreateDomain ("New Domain");
  newDomain.ExecuteAssembly ("test.exe");
  AppDomain.Unload (newDomain);
}
```

Note that when the default application domain (the one created by the CLR at startup) is unloaded, all other application domains automatically unload, and the application closes. A domain can "know" whether it's the default domain via the AppDomain property IsDefaultDomain.

The AppDomainSetup class allows options to be specified for a new domain. The following properties are the most useful:

```
public string ApplicationName { get; set; }      // "Friendly" name
public string ApplicationBase { get; set; }       // Base folder

public string ConfigurationFile { get; set; }
public string LicenseFile       { get; set; }

// To assist with automatic assembly resolution:
public string PrivateBinPath      { get; set; }
public string PrivateBinPathProbe { get; set; }
```

The ApplicationBase property controls the application domain base directory, used as the root for automatic assembly probing. In the default application domain, this is the main executable's folder. In a new domain that you create, it can be anywhere you like:

```
AppDomainSetup setup = new AppDomainSetup( );
setup.ApplicationBase = @"c:\MyBaseFolder";
AppDomain newDomain = AppDomain.CreateDomain ("New Domain", null, setup);
```

It's also possible to subscribe a new domain to assembly resolution events defined in the instigator's domain:

```
static void Main( )
{
  AppDomain newDomain = AppDomain.CreateDomain ("test");
  newDomain.AssemblyResolve += new ResolveEventHandler (FindAssem);
  ...
}
static Assembly FindAssem (object sender, ResolveEventArgs args)
{
  ...
}
```

This is acceptable providing the event handler is a static method defined a type available to both domains. The CLR is then able to execute the event handler in the correct domain. In this example, FindAssem would execute from within newDomain, even though it was subscribed from the default domain.

The PrivateBinPath property is a semicolon-separated list of subdirectories below the base directory that the CLR should automatically search for assemblies. (As with the application base folder, this can only be set prior to the application domain starting.) Take, for example, a directory structure where a program has in its base folder a single executable (and perhaps a configuration file) and all the referenced assemblies in subfolders as follows:

```
c:\MyBaseFolder\              -- Startup executable
        \bin
        \bin\v1.23            -- Latest assembly DLLs
        \bin\plugins          -- More DLLs
```

Here's how an application domain would be set up to use this folder structure:

```
AppDomainSetup setup = new AppDomainSetup( );
setup.ApplicationBase = @"c:\MyBaseFolder";
setup.PrivateBinPath = @"bin\v1.23;bin\plugins";
AppDomain d = AppDomain.CreateDomain ("New Domain", null, setup);
d.ExecuteAssembly (@"c:\MyBaseFolder\Startup.exe");
```

Note that PrivateBinPath is always relative to, and below, the application base folder. Specifying absolute paths is illegal. AppDomain also provides a PrivateBin-PathProbe property, which, if set to anything other than a blank string, excludes the base directory itself from being part of the assembly search path. (The reason PrivateBinPathProbe is a string rather than a bool type relates to COM compatibility.)

Just before any nondefault application domain unloads, the DomainUnload event fires. You can use this event for tear-down logic: the unloading of the domain (and the application as a whole, if necessary) is delayed until the execution of all DomainUnload event handlers completes.

Just before the application itself closes, the ProcessExit event fires on all loaded application domains (including the default domain). Unlike with the DomainUnload event, ProcessExit event handlers are timed: the default CLR host gives event handlers two seconds per domain, and three seconds in total, before terminating their threads.

Using Multiple Application Domains

Multiple application domains have the following key uses:

- Providing process-like isolation with minimum overhead
- Allowing assembly files to be unloaded without restarting the process

When additional application domains are created within the same process, the CLR provides each with a level of isolation akin to that of running in separate processes. This means that each domain has separate memory, and objects in one domain cannot interfere with those in another. Furthermore, static members of the same class have independent values in each domain. ASP.NET uses exactly this approach to allow many sites to run in a shared process without affecting each other.

With ASP.NET, the application domains are created by the infrastructure—without your intervention. There are times, however, when you can benefit from explicitly creating multiple domains inside a single process. Suppose you've written a custom authentication system, and as part of unit testing, you want to stress-test the server code by simulating 20 clients logging in at once. You have three options in simulating 20 concurrent logins:

- Start 20 separate processes by calling Process.Start 20 times.
- Start 20 threads in the same process and domain.
- Start 20 threads in the same process—each in its own application domain.

The first option is clumsy and resource-intensive. It's also hard to communicate with each of the separate processes, should you want to give them more specific instructions on what to do.

The second option relies on the client-side code being thread-safe, which is unlikely—especially if static variables are used to store the current authentication state. And adding a lock around the client-side code would prevent the parallel execution that we need to stress-test the server.

The third option is ideal. It keeps each thread isolated—with independent state—and yet within easy reach of the hosting program.

Another reason to create a separate application domain is to allow assemblies to be unloaded without ending the process. This stems from the fact that there's no way to unload an assembly other than closing the application domain that loaded it. This is a problem if it was loaded in the default domain, because closing this domain means closing the application. An assembly's file is locked while loaded and so cannot be patched or replaced. Loading assemblies in a separate application domain that can be torn down gets around this problem—as well as helping to reduce the memory footprint of an application that occasionally needs to load large assemblies.

By default, assemblies that load into an explicitly created application domain are reprocessed by the JIT compiler. This includes:

- Assemblies that have already been JIT-compiled in the caller's domain
- Assemblies for which a native image has been generated with the *ngen.exe* tool
- All of the .NET Framework assemblies (except for *mscorlib*)

This can be a major performance hit, particularly if you repeatedly create and unload application domains that reference large .NET Framework assemblies. A workaround is to attach the following attribute to your program's main entry method:

```
[LoaderOptimization (LoaderOptimization.MultiDomainHost)]
```

This instructs the CLR to load GAC assemblies *domain-neutral*, so native images are honored and JIT images shared across application domains. This is usually ideal, because the GAC includes all .NET Framework assemblies (and possibly some invariant parts of your application).

You can go a stage further by specifying `LoaderOptimization.MultiDomain`: this instructs *all* assemblies to be loaded domain-neutral (excluding those loaded outside the normal assembly resolution mechanism). This is undesirable, however, if you want assemblies to unload with their domain. A domain-neutral assembly is shared between all domains and so does not unload until the parent process ends.

Using DoCallBack

Let's revisit the most basic multidomain scenario:

```
static void Main( )
{
  AppDomain newDomain = AppDomain.CreateDomain ("New Domain");
  newDomain.ExecuteAssembly ("test.exe");
  AppDomain.Unload (newDomain);
}
```

Calling ExecuteAssembly on a separate domain is convenient but offers little opportunity to interact with the domain. It also requires that the target assembly is an executable, and it commits the caller to a single entry point. The only way to incorporate flexibility is to resort to an approach such as passing a string of arguments to the executable.

A more powerful approach is to use AppDomain's DoCallBack method. This executes on another application domain, a method on a given type. The type's assembly is automatically loaded into the domain (the CLR will know where it lives if the current domain can reference it). In the following example, a method in the currently executing class is run in a new domain:

```
class Program
{
  static void Main ()
  {
    AppDomain newDomain = AppDomain.CreateDomain ("New Domain");
    newDomain.DoCallBack (new CrossAppDomainDelegate (SayHello));
    AppDomain.Unload (newDomain);
  }

  static void SayHello( )
  {
    Console.WriteLine ("Hi from " + AppDomain.CurrentDomain.FriendlyName);
  }
}
```

The example works because the delegate is referencing a static method, meaning it points to a type rather than an instance. This makes the delegate "domain-agnostic" or agile. It can run in any domain, and in the same way, as there's nothing tying it to the original domain. It's also possible to use DoCallBack with a delegate referencing an instance method. However, the CLR will attempt to apply Remoting semantics (described later), which in this case happens to be the opposite of what we want.

Domains and Threads

When you call a method in another application domain, execution blocks until the method finishes executing—just as though you called a method in your own domain. Although this behavior is usually desirable, there are times when you need to run a method concurrently. You can do that with multithreading.

We talked previously about using multiple application domains to simulate 20 concurrent client logins in order to test an authentication system. By having each client log in on a separate application domain, each would be isolated and unable to interfere with another client via static class members. To implement this example, we need to call a "Login" method on 20 concurrent threads, each in its own application domain:

```
class Program
{
  static void Main( )
  {
    // Create 20 domains and 20 threads.
    AppDomain[] domains = new AppDomain [20];
    Thread[] threads = new Thread [20];

    for (int i = 0; i < 20; i++)
    {
      domains [i] = AppDomain.CreateDomain ("Client Login " + i);
      threads [i] = new Thread (LoginOtherDomain);
    }

    // Start all the threads, passing to each thread its app domain.
    for (int i = 0; i < 20; i++) threads [i].Start (domains [i]);

    // Wait for the threads to finish
    for (int i = 0; i < 20; i++) threads [i].Join ( );

    // Unload the app domains
    for (int i = 0; i < 20; i++) AppDomain.Unload (domains [i]);
    Console.ReadLine ( );
  }

  // Parameterized thread start - taking the domain on which to run.
  static void LoginOtherDomain (object domain)
  {
    ((AppDomain) domain).DoCallBack (Login);
  }

  static void Login( )
  {
    Client.Login ("Joe", "");
    Console.WriteLine ("Logged in as: " + Client.CurrentUser + " on " +
      AppDomain.CurrentDomain.FriendlyName);
  }
}

class Client
{
  // Here's a static field that would interfere with other client logins
  // if running in the same app domain.
  public static string CurrentUser = "";

  public static void Login (string name, string password)
  {
```

```
      if (CurrentUser.Length == 0)     // If we're not already logged in...
      {
        // Sleep to simulate authentication...
        Thread.Sleep (500);
        CurrentUser = name;              // Record that we're authenticated.
      }
    }
  }
}

// Output:
Logged in as: Joe on Client Login 0
Logged in as: Joe on Client Login 1
Logged in as: Joe on Client Login 4
Logged in as: Joe on Client Login 2
Logged in as: Joe on Client Login 3
Logged in as: Joe on Client Login 5
Logged in as: Joe on Client Login 6
...
```

Chapter 19 provides detailed information on multithreading.

Sharing Data Between Domains

Sharing Data Via Slots

Application domains can use named slots to share data, as in the following
example:

```
class Program
{
  static void Main()
  {
    AppDomain newDomain = AppDomain.CreateDomain ("New Domain");

    // Write to a named slot called "Message" - any string key will do.
    newDomain.SetData ("Message", "guess what...");

    newDomain.DoCallBack (SayMessage);
    AppDomain.Unload (newDomain);
  }

  static void SayMessage()
  {
    // Read from the "Message" data slot
    Console.WriteLine (AppDomain.CurrentDomain.GetData ("Message"));
  }
}

// Output:
guess what...
```

A slot is created automatically the first time it's used. The data being communi-
cated (in this example, "guess what . . . ") must either be *serializable* (see Chapter 15),

or be based on `MarshalByRefObject`. If the data is serializable (such as the string in our example), it's copied to the other application domain. If it implements `MarshalByRefObject`, Remoting semantics are applied.

Intra-Process Remoting

The most flexible way to communicate with another application domain is to instantiate objects *in the other domain* via a proxy. This is called *Remoting*.

The class being "Remoted" must inherit from `MarshalByRefObject`. The client then calls a `CreateInstanceXXX` method on the remote domain's `AppDomain` class to remotely instantiate the object.

The following instantiates the type `Foo` in another application domain, and then calls its `SayHello` method:

```
class Program
{
  static void Main( )
  {
    AppDomain newDomain = AppDomain.CreateDomain ("New Domain");

    Foo foo = (Foo) newDomain.CreateInstanceAndUnwrap (
                    typeof (Foo).Assembly.FullName,
                    typeof (Foo).FullName);

    Console.WriteLine (foo.SayHello( ));
    AppDomain.Unload (newDomain);
    Console.ReadLine( );
  }
}

public class Foo : MarshalByRefObject
{
  public string SayHello( )
  {
    return "Hello from " + AppDomain.CurrentDomain.FriendlyName;
  }

  public override object InitializeLifetimeService( )
  {
    // This ensures the object lasts for as long as the client wants it
    return null;
  }
}
```

When the `foo` object is created on the other application domain (called the "remote" domain), we don't get back a direct reference to the object, because the application domains are isolated. Instead, we get back a transparent proxy; transparent because it *appears* as though it was a direct reference to the remote object. When we subsequently call the `SayHello` method on `foo`, a message is constructed behind the scenes, which is forwarded to the "remote" application domain where it is then executed on the "real" `foo`. Any return value is turned into a message and sent back to the caller.

Before Windows Communication Foundation was released in .NET Framework 3.0, Remoting was one of the two principal technologies for writing distributed applications (Web Services being the other). In a distributed Remoting application, you explicitly set up an HTTP or TCP/IP communication channel at each end, allowing communication to cross process and network boundaries.

Although WCF is superior to Remoting for distributed applications, Remoting still has a niche in inter-domain communication within a process. Its advantage in this scenario is that it requires no configuration—the communication channel is automatically created (a fast in-memory channel), and no type registration is required. You simply start using it.

The methods on `Foo` can return more `MarshalByRefObject` instances, in which case more transparent proxies are generated when those methods are called. Methods on `Foo` can also accept `MarshalByRefObject` instances as arguments—in which Remoting happens in reverse. The caller will hold the "remote" object, while the callee will have a proxy.

As well as marshaling objects by reference, application domains can exchange scalar values, or any *serializable* object. A type is serializable if it either has the `Serializable` attribute or implements `ISerializable`. Then, when crossing the application domain boundary, a complete copy of the object is returned, rather than a proxy. In other words, the object is marshaled by *value* rather than reference.

Remoting within the same process is client-activated, meaning that the CLR doesn't attempt to share or reuse remotely created objects with the same or other clients. In other words, if the client creates two `Foo` objects, two objects will be created in the remote domain, and two proxies in the client domain. This provides the most natural object semantics; however, it means that the remote domain is dependent on the client's garbage collector: the foo object in the remote domain is released from memory only when the client's garbage collector decides that the foo (proxy) is no longer in use. If the client domain crashes, it may never get released. To protect against this scenario, the CLR provides a lease-based mechanism for managing the lifetime of remotely created objects. The default behavior is for remotely created objects to self-destruct after five minutes of nonuse.

Because in this example the client runs in the default application domain, the client doesn't have the luxury of crashing. Once it ends, so does the whole process! Hence, it makes sense to disable the five-minute lifetime lease. This is the purpose of overriding `InitializeLifetimeService`—by returning a null lease, remotely created objects are destroyed only when garbage-collected by the client.

Isolating Types and Assemblies

In the preceding example, we remotely instantiated an object of type `Foo` as follows:

```
Foo foo = (Foo) newDomain.CreateInstanceAndUnwrap (
            typeof (Foo).Assembly.FullName,
            typeof (Foo).FullName);
```

Here's the method's signature:

```
public object CreateInstanceFromAndUnwrap (string assemblyName,
                                           string typeName)
```

Because this method accepts an assembly and type *name* rather than a Type object, you can remotely instantiate an object without loading its type locally. This is useful when you want to avoid loading the type's assembly into the caller's application domain.

 AppDomain also provides a method called CreateInstance**From**-AndUnwrap. The difference is:

- CreateInstanceAndUnwrap accepts a *fully qualified assembly name* (see Chapter 16).
- CreateInstance**From**AndUnwrap accepts a *path or filename*.

To illustrate, suppose we were writing a text editor that allows the user to load and unload third-party plug-ins. We demonstrated this in Chapter 18 in the section "Sandboxing Another Assembly," from the perspective of security. When it came to actually executing the plug-in, however, all we did was call ExecuteAssembly. With Remoting, we can interact with plug-ins in a richer fashion.

The first step is to write a common library that both the host and the plug-ins will reference. This library will define an interface describing what plug-ins can do. Here's a simple example:

```
namespace Plugin.Common
{
  public interface ITextPlugin
  {
    string TransformText (string input);
  }
}
```

Next, we need to write a simple plug-in. We'll assume the following is compiled to *AllCapitals.dll*:

```
namespace Plugin.Extensions
{
  public class AllCapitals : MarshalByRefObject, Plugin.Common.ITextPlugin
  {
    public string TransformText (string input) { return input.ToUpper( ); }
  }
}
```

Here's how to write a host that loads *AllCapitals.dll* into a separate application domain, calls TransformText using Remoting, and then unloads the application domain:

```
using System;
using System.Reflection;
using Plugin.Common;

class Program
```

```
  {
    static void Main( )
    {
      AppDomain domain = AppDomain.CreateDomain ("Plugin Domain");

      ITextPlugin plugin = (ITextPlugin) domain.CreateInstanceFromAndUnwrap
        ("AllCapitals.dll", "Plugin.Extensions.AllCapitals");

      // Call the TransformText method using Remoting:
      Console.WriteLine (plugin.TransformText ("hello"));    // "HELLO"

      AppDomain.Unload (domain);

      // The AllCapitals.dll file is now completely unloaded and could
      // be moved or deleted.
    }
  }
```

Because this program interacts with the plug-in solely through the common interface, ITextPlugin, the types in AllCapitals are never loaded into the caller's application domain. This maintains the integrity of the caller's domain and ensures that no locks are held on the plug-in assembly files after their domain is unloaded.

Type discovery

In our preceding example, a real application would need some means of discovering plug-in type names, such as Plugin.Extensions.AllCapitals.

You can achieve this by writing a discovery class in the *common* assembly that uses reflection as follows:

```
public class Discoverer : MarshalByRefObject
{
  public string[] GetPluginTypeNames (string assemblyPath)
  {
    List<string> typeNames = new List<string> ();
    Assembly a = Assembly.LoadFrom (assemblyPath);
    foreach (Type t in a.GetTypes ())
      if (t.IsPublic
          && t.IsMarshalByRef
          && typeof (ITextPlugin).IsAssignableFrom (t))
      {
        typeNames.Add (t.FullName);
      }
    return typeNames.ToArray ();
  }
}
```

The catch is that `Assembly.LoadFrom` loads the assembly into the current application domain. Therefore, you must call this method *in the plug-in domain*:

```
class Program
{
  static void Main( )
  {
    AppDomain domain = AppDomain.CreateDomain ("Plugin Domain");

    Discoverer d = (Discoverer) domain.CreateInstanceAndUnwrap (
      typeof (Discoverer).Assembly.FullName,
      typeof (Discoverer).FullName);

    string[] plugInTypeNames = d.GetPluginTypeNames ("AllCapitals.dll");

    foreach (string s in plugInTypeNames)
      Console.WriteLine (s);                    // Plugin.Extensions.AllCapitals

    ...
```

> In the *System.AddIn.Contract* assembly is an API new to Framework 3.5 that develops these concepts into a complete framework for program extensibility. It addresses such issues as isolation, versioning, discovery, activation, and so on. For a good source of online information, search for "CLR Add-In Team Blog" on *http://blogs.msdn.com*.

22

Integrating with Native DLLs

This chapter describes how to integrate with unmanaged code in native DLLs. Unless otherwise stated, the types mentioned in this chapter exist in either the System or the System.Runtime.InteropServices namespace.

Calling into DLLs

P/Invoke, short for *Platform Invocation Services*, allows you to access functions, structs, and callbacks in unmanaged DLLs. For example, consider the MessageBox function, defined in the Windows DLL *user32.dll* as follows:

```
int MessageBox (HWND hWnd, LPCTSTR lpText, LPCTSTR lpCation, UINT uType);
```

You can call this function directly by declaring a static method of the same name, applying the extern keyword, and adding the DllImport attribute:

```
using System;
using System.Runtime.InteropServices;

class MsgBoxTest
{
  [DllImport("user32.dll")]
  static extern int MessageBox (IntPtr hWnd, string text, string caption,
                                int type);
  public static void Main()
  {
    MessageBox (IntPtr.Zero,
                "Please do not press this again.", "Attention", 0);
  }
}
```

The MessageBox classes in the System.Windows and System.Windows.Forms namespaces themselves call similar unmanaged methods.

The CLR includes a marshaler that knows how to convert parameters and return values between .NET types and unmanaged types. In this example, the int parameters translate directly to 4-byte integers that the function expects, and the string parameters are converted into null-terminated arrays of 2-byte Unicode characters. IntPtr is a struct designed to encapsulate an unmanaged handle, and is 32 bits wide on 32-bit platforms and 64 bits wide on 64-bit platforms.

Marshaling Common Types

On the unmanaged side, there can be more than one way to represent a given data type. A string, for instance, can contain single-byte ANSI characters or double-byte Unicode characters, and can be length-prefixed, null-terminated, or of fixed length. With the MarshalAs attribute, you can tell the CLR marshaler the variation in use, so it can provide the correct translation. Here's an example:

```
[DllImport("...")]
static extern int Foo ( [MarshalAs (UnmanagedType.LPWStr)] string s );
```

The UnmanagedType enumeration includes all the Win32 and COM types that the marshaler understands. In this case, the marshaler was told to translate to LPStr, which is a null-terminated single-byte ANSI string. (All UnmanagedType members are listed at the end of this chapter.)

On the .NET side, you also have some choice as to what data type to use. Unmanaged handles, for instance, can map to IntPtr, int, uint, long, or ulong.

Most unmanaged handles encapsulate an address or pointer, and so must be mapped to IntPtr for compatibility with both 32- and 64-bit operating systems. A typical example is HWND.

Quite often with Win32 functions, you come across an integer parameter that accepts a set of constants, defined in a C++ header file such as *WinUser.h*. Rather than defining these as simple C# constants, you can define them within an enum instead. Using an enum can make for tidier code as well as increase static type safety. We provide an example in the later section "Shared Memory."

When installing Microsoft Visual Studio, be sure to install the C++ header files—even if you choose nothing else in the C++ category. This is where all the native Win32 constants are defined. You can then locate all header files by searching for *.h* in the Visual Studio program directory.

Receiving strings from unmanaged code back to .NET requires that some memory management take place. The marshaler performs this work automatically if you declare the external method with a StringBuilder rather than a string, as follows:

```
using System;
using System.Text;
using System.Runtime.InteropServices;

class Test
{
```

```
[DllImport("kernel32.dll")]
static extern int GetWindowsDirectory (StringBuilder sb, int maxChars);

static void Main( )
{
  StringBuilder s = new StringBuilder (256);
  GetWindowsDirectory (s, 256);
  Console.WriteLine (s);
}
}
```

 If you are unsure how to call a particular Win32 method, you will usually find an example on the Internet if you search for the method name and *DllImport*. The site *http://www.pinvoke.net* is a wiki that aims to document all Win32 signatures.

Marshaling Classes and Structs

Sometimes you need to pass a struct to an unmanaged method. For example, GetSystemTime in the Win32 API is defined as follows:

```
void GetSystemTime (LPSYSTEMTIME lpSystemTime);
```

LPSYSTEMTIME conforms to this C struct:

```
typedef struct _SYSTEMTIME {
  WORD wYear;
  WORD wMonth;
  WORD wDayOfWeek;
  WORD wDay;
  WORD wHour;
  WORD wMinute;
  WORD wSecond;
  WORD wMilliseconds;
} SYSTEMTIME, *PSYSTEMTIME;
```

In order to call GetSystemTime, we must define a .NET class or struct that matches this C struct:

```
using System;
using System.Runtime.InteropServices;

[StructLayout(LayoutKind.Sequential)]
class SystemTime
{
  public ushort Year;
  public ushort Month;
  public ushort DayOfWeek;
  public ushort Day;
  public ushort Hour;
  public ushort Minute;
  public ushort Second;
  public ushort Milliseconds;
}
```

The StructLayout attribute instructs the marshaler how to map each field to its unmanaged counterpart. LayoutKind.Sequential means that we want the fields aligned sequentially on *pack-size* boundaries (we'll see what this means shortly), just as they would be in a C struct. The field names here are irrelevant; it's the ordering of fields that's important.

Now we can call GetSystemTime:

```
[DllImport("kernel32.dll")]
static extern void GetSystemTime (SystemTime t);

static void Main()
{
  SystemTime t = new SystemTime();
  GetSystemTime (t);
  Console.WriteLine (t.Year);
}
```

In both C and C#, fields in an object are located at *n* number of bytes from the address of that object. The difference is that in a C# program, the CLR finds this offset by looking it up using the field name; C field names are compiled directly into offsets. For instance, in C, wDay is just a token to represent whatever is at the address of a SystemTime instance plus 24 bytes.

For access speed and to allow future widening of a data type, these offsets are usually in multiples of a minimum width, called the *pack size*. For .NET types, the pack size is usually set at the discretion of the runtime, but by using the StructLayout attribute, field offsets can be controlled. When using this attribute, the default pack size is 4 bytes, but it can be set to 1, 2, 4, 8, or 16 bytes (pass Pack=*packsize* to the StructLayout constructor). There are also explicit options to control individual field offsets (see the section "Simulating a C Union" later in this chapter).

In and Out Marshaling

In the previous example, we implemented SystemTime as a class. We could have instead chosen a struct—providing GetSystemTime was declared with a ref or out parameter:

```
static extern void GetSystemTime (out SystemTime t);
```

In most cases, C#'s directional parameter semantics work the same with external methods. Pass-by-value parameters are copied in, C# ref parameters are copied in/out, and C# out parameters are copied out. However, there are some exceptions for types that have special conversions. For instance, array classes and the StringBuilder class require copying when coming out of a function, so they are in/out. It is occasionally useful to override this behavior, with the In and Out attributes. For example, if an array should be read-only, the in modifier indicates to only copy the array going into the function and not coming out of it:

```
static extern void Foo ( [In] int[] array);
```

Callbacks from Unmanaged Code

The P/Invoke layer does its best to present a natural programming model on both sides of the boundary, mapping between relevant constructs where possible. Since C# not only can call out to C functions but also can be called back from the C functions (via function pointers), the P/Invoke layer needs to map unmanaged function pointers onto something natural for the managed world. The managed equivalent of a function pointer is a delegate, so the P/Invoke layer automatically maps between delegates (in C#) and function pointers (in C).

As an example, you can enumerate all top-level window handles with this method in *User32.dll*:

```
BOOL EnumWindows (WNDENUMPROC lpEnumFunc, LPARAM lParam);
```

WNDENUMPROC is a callback that gets fired with the handle of each window in sequence (or until the callback returns false). Here is its definition:

```
BOOL CALLBACK EnumWindowsProc (HWND hwnd, LPARAM lParam);
```

To use this, we declare a delegate with a matching signature, and then pass a delegate instance to the external method:

```
using System;
using System.Runtime.InteropServices;

class CallbackFun
{
  delegate bool EnumWindowsCallback (IntPtr hWnd, IntPtr lParam);

  [DllImport("user32.dll")]
  static extern int EnumWindows (EnumWindowsCallback hWnd, IntPtr lParam);

  static bool PrintWindow (IntPtr hWnd, IntPtr lParam)
  {
    Console.WriteLine (hWnd.ToInt64());
    return true;
  }

  static void Main()
  {
  EnumWindows (PrintWindow, IntPtr.Zero);
  }
}
```

Simulating a C Union

Each field in a struct is given enough room to store its data. Consider a struct containing one int and one char. The int is likely to start at an offset of 0 and is guaranteed at least four bytes. So, the char would start at an offset of at least 4. If, for some reason, the char started at an offset of 2, you'd change the value of the int if you assigned a value to the char. Sounds like mayhem, doesn't it? Strangely enough, the C language supports a variation on a struct called a *union* that does exactly this. You can simulate this in C# using `LayoutKind.Explicit` and the `FieldOffset` attribute.

It might be hard to think of a case in which this would be useful. However, suppose you want to play a note on an external synthesizer. The Windows Multimedia API provides a function for doing just this via the MIDI protocol:

```
[DllImport ("winmm.dll")]
public static extern int midiOutShortMsg (int handle, int message);
```

The second argument, `message`, describes what note to play. The problem is in constructing this 32-bit integer: it's divided internally into bytes, representing a MIDI channel, note, and velocity at which to strike. One solution is to shift and mask via the bitwise `<<`, `>>`, `&`, and `|` operators to convert these bytes to and from the 32-bit "packed" message. Far simpler, though, is to define a struct with explicit layout:

```
[StructLayout (LayoutKind.Explicit)]
public struct NoteMessage
{
  [FieldOffset(0)] public int PackedMsg;    // 4 bytes long

  [FieldOffset(0)] public byte Channel;     // FieldOffset also at 0
  [FieldOffset(1)] public byte Note;
  [FieldOffset(2)] public byte Velocity;
}
```

The `Channel`, `Note`, and `Velocity` fields deliberately overlap with the 32-bit packed message. This allows you to read and write using either. No calculations are required to keep other fields in sync:

```
NoteMessage n = new NoteMessage( );
Console.WriteLine (n.PackedMsg);     // 0

n.Channel = 10;
n.Note = 100;
n.Velocity = 50;
Console.WriteLine (n.PackedMsg);     // 3302410

n.PackedMsg = 3328010;
Console.WriteLine (n.Note);          // 200
```

Shared Memory

Memory-mapped files, or *shared memory*, is a feature in Windows that allows multiple processes on the same computer to share data, without the overhead of Remoting or WCF. Shared memory is extremely fast and, unlike pipes, offers *random* access to the shared data. In summary, an excellent use case for P/Invoke!

The Win32 `CreateFileMapping` function allocates shared memory. You tell it how many bytes you need and the name with which to identify the share. Another application can then subscribe to this memory by calling `OpenFileMapping` with same name. Both methods return a *handle*, which you can convert to a pointer by calling `MapViewOfFile`.

Here's a class that encapsulates access to shared memory:

```
using System;
using System.Runtime.InteropServices;

public class SharedMem : IDisposable
{
  // Here we're using enums because they're safer than constants

  enum FileProtection : uint      // constants from winnt.h
  {
    ReadOnly = 2,
    ReadWrite = 4
  }

  enum FileRights : uint          // constants from WinBASE.h
  {
    Read = 4,
    Write = 2,
    ReadWrite = Read + Write
  }

  static readonly IntPtr NoFileHandle = new IntPtr (-1);

  [DllImport ("kernel32.dll", SetLastError = true)]
  static extern IntPtr CreateFileMapping (IntPtr hFile,
                                          int lpAttributes,
                                          FileProtection flProtect,
                                          uint dwMaximumSizeHigh,
                                          uint dwMaximumSizeLow,
                                          string lpName);

  [DllImport ("kernel32.dll", SetLastError=true)]
  static extern IntPtr OpenFileMapping (FileRights dwDesiredAccess,
                                        bool bInheritHandle,
                                        string lpName);

  [DllImport ("kernel32.dll", SetLastError = true)]
  static extern IntPtr MapViewOfFile (IntPtr hFileMappingObject,
                                      FileRights dwDesiredAccess,
                                      uint dwFileOffsetHigh,
                                      uint dwFileOffsetLow,
                                      uint dwNumberOfBytesToMap);
  [DllImport ("Kernel32.dll")]
  static extern bool UnmapViewOfFile (IntPtr map);

  [DllImport ("kernel32.dll")]
  static extern int CloseHandle (IntPtr hObject);

  IntPtr fileHandle, fileMap;

  public IntPtr Root { get { return fileMap; } }

  public SharedMem (string name, bool existing, uint sizeInBytes)
```

```
{
  if (existing)
    fileHandle = OpenFileMapping (FileRights.ReadWrite, false, name);
  else
    fileHandle = CreateFileMapping (NoFileHandle, 0,
                             FileProtection.ReadWrite,
                             0, sizeInBytes, name);
  if (fileHandle == IntPtr.Zero)
    throw new Exception
      ("Open/create error: " + Marshal.GetLastWin32Error( ));

  // Obtain a read/write map for the entire file
  fileMap = MapViewOfFile (fileHandle, FileRights.ReadWrite, 0, 0, 0);

  if (fileMap == IntPtr.Zero)
    throw new Exception
      ("MapViewOfFile error: " + Marshal.GetLastWin32Error( ));
}

public void Dispose( )
{
  if (fileMap != IntPtr.Zero) UnmapViewOfFile (fileMap);
  if (fileHandle != IntPtr.Zero) CloseHandle (fileHandle);
  fileMap = fileHandle = IntPtr.Zero;
}
}
```

In this example, we set SetLastError=true on the DllImport methods that use the SetLastError protocol for emitting error codes. This allows us to later query an error by calling Marshal.GetLastWin32Error. Without this, it can be difficult to find the cause when a null handle is returned.

In order to demonstrate this class, we need to run two applications. The first one creates the shared memory, as follows:

```
using (SharedMem sm = new SharedMem ("MyShare", false, 1000))
{
  IntPtr root = sm.Root;
  // I have shared memory!

  Console.ReadLine( );        // Here's where we start a second app...
}
```

The second application subscribes to the shared memory by constructing a SharedMem object of the same name, with the existing argument true:

```
using (SharedMem sm = new SharedMem ("MyShare", true, 1000))
{
  IntPtr root = sm.Root;
  // I have the same shared memory!
  // ...
}
```

The net result is that each program has an IntPtr—a pointer to (the same) unmanaged memory. The two applications now need somehow to read and write to memory via this common pointer. One approach is to write a serializable class that encapsulates all the shared data, then serialize (and deserialize) the data to the unmanaged memory using an `UnmanagedMemoryStream`. This is inefficient, however, if there's a lot of data. Imagine if the shared memory class had a megabyte worth of data, and just one integer needed to be updated. A better approach is to define the shared data construct as a struct, and then map it directly into shared memory. We discuss this in the following section.

Mapping a Struct to Unmanaged Memory

A struct with a `StructLayout` of `Sequential` or `Explicit` can be mapped directly into unmanaged memory. Consider the following struct:

```
[StructLayout (LayoutKind.Sequential)]
unsafe struct MySharedData
{
  public int Value;
  public char Letter;
  public fixed float Numbers [50];
}
```

The `fixed` directive allows us to define fixed-length value-type arrays, and it is what takes us into the `unsafe` realm. Space in this struct is allocated inline for 50 floating-point numbers, right after `Letter`. Unlike with standard C# arrays, `NumberArray` is not a *reference* to an array—it *is* the array. If we run the following:

```
static unsafe void Main( )
{
  Console.WriteLine (sizeof (MySharedData));
}
```

the result is 208: 50 4-byte floats, plus the 4 bytes for the `Value` integer, plus 2 bytes for the `Letter` character. (The total, 206, is rounded to 208 due to the default struct packing size of 4 bytes.)

We can demonstrate `MySharedData` in an `unsafe` context, most simply, with stack-allocated memory:

```
MySharedData d;
MySharedData* data = &d;        // Get the address of d

data->Value = 123;
data->Letter = 'X';
data->Numbers[10] = 1.45f;
```

or:

```
MySharedData* data = stackalloc MySharedData[1];

data->Value = 123;
data->Letter = 'X';
data->Numbers[10] = 1.45f;
```

Of course, we're not demonstrating anything that couldn't otherwise be achieved in a managed context. Suppose, however, that we want to store an instance of

MySharedData on the *unmanaged heap*, outside the realm of the CLR's garbage collector. This is where pointers become really useful:

```
MySharedData* data = (MySharedData*)
  Marshal.AllocHGlobal (sizeof (MySharedData)).ToPointer( );

data->Value = 123;
data->Letter = 'X';
data->Numbers[10] = 1.45f;
```

Marshal.AllocHGlobal allocates memory on the unmanaged heap. Here's how to later free the same memory:

```
Marshal.FreeHGlobal (new IntPtr (data));
```

(The result of forgetting to free the memory is a good old-fashioned memory leak.)

In keeping with its name, we'll now use MySharedData in conjunction with the SharedMem class we wrote in the preceding section. The following program allocates a block of shared memory, and then maps the MySharedData struct into that memory:

```
static unsafe void Main( )
{
  using (SharedMem sm = new SharedMem ("MyShare", false, 1000))
  {
    void* root = sm.Root.ToPointer( );
    MySharedData* data = (MySharedData*) root;

    data->Value = 123;
    data->Letter = 'X';
    data->Numbers[10] = 1.45f;
    Console.WriteLine ("Written to shared memory");

    Console.ReadLine( );

    Console.WriteLine ("Value is " + data->Value);
    Console.WriteLine ("Letter is " + data->Letter);
    Console.WriteLine ("11th Number is " + data->Numbers[10]);
    Console.ReadLine( );
  }
}
```

Here's a second program that attaches to the same shared memory, reading the values written by the first program. (It must be run while the first program is waiting on the ReadLine statement, since the shared memory object is disposed upon leaving its using statement.)

```
static unsafe void Main( )
{
  using (SharedMem sm = new SharedMem ("MyShare", true, 1000))
  {
    void* root = sm.Root.ToPointer ( );
    MySharedData* data = (MySharedData*) root;

    Console.WriteLine ("Value is " + data->Value);
```

```
        Console.WriteLine ("Letter is " + data->Letter);
        Console.WriteLine ("11th Number is " + data->Numbers[10]);

        // Our turn to update values in shared memory!
        data->Value++;
        data->Letter = '!';
        data->Numbers[10] = 987.5f;
        Console.WriteLine ("Updated shared memory");
        Console.ReadLine( );
    }
}
```

The output from each of these programs is as follows:

```
// First program:

Written to shared memory
Value is 124
Letter is !
11th Number is 987.5

// Second program:

Value is 123
Letter is X
11th Number is 1.45
Updated shared memory
```

Don't be put off by the pointer semantics: C++ programmers use pointers throughout whole applications and are still able to get everything working. At least most of the time! This sort of usage is fairly simple by comparison.

As it happens, our example is unsafe—quite literally—for another reason. We've not considered the thread-safety (or more precisely, process-safety) issues that arise with two programs accessing the same memory at once. To use this in a production application, we'd need to add the volatile keyword to the Value and Letter fields in the MySharedData struct to prevent fields from being cached in CPU registers. Furthermore, as our interaction with the fields grew beyond the trivial, we would most likely need to protect their access via a cross-process Mutex, just as we would use lock statements to protect access to fields in a multithreaded program. We discussed thread safety in detail in Chapter 19.

fixed and fixed {...}

One limitation of mapping structs directly into memory is that the struct can contain only unmanaged types. If you need to share string data, for instance, you must use a fixed character array instead. This means manual conversion to and from the string type. Here's how to do it:

```
[StructLayout (LayoutKind.Sequential)]
unsafe struct MySharedData
{
  ...
```

```
// Allocate space for 200 chars (i.e., 400 bytes).
fixed char message [200];

// One would most likely put this code into a helper class:
public string Message
{
  get { fixed (char* cp = message) return new string (cp); }
  set
  {
    fixed (char* cp = message)
    {
      int i = 0;
      for (; i < value.Length && i < 199; i++)
        cp [i] = value [i];

      // Add the null terminator
      cp [i] = '\0';
    }
  }
}
}
```

 There's no such thing as a reference to a fixed array; instead, you get a pointer. When you index into a fixed array, you're actually performing pointer arithmetic!

With the first use of the fixed keyword, we allocate space, inline, for 200 characters in the struct. The same keyword when used later, in the property definition, has a different meaning. It tells the CLR that should it decide to perform a garbage collection inside the fixed block, not to move the underlying struct about on the memory heap, since its contents are being iterated via direct memory pointers. Looking at our program, you might wonder how MySharedData could ever shift in memory, given that it lives not on the heap, but in the unmanaged world, where the garbage collector has no jurisdiction. The compiler doesn't know this, however, and is concerned that we *might* use MySharedData in a managed context, so it insists that we add the fixed keyword, to make our unsafe code safe in managed contexts. And the compiler does have a point—here's all it would take to put MySharedData on the heap:

```
object obj = new MySharedData( );
```

This results in a boxed MySharedData—on the heap and eligible for transit during garbage collection.

This example illustrates how a string can be represented in a struct mapped to unmanaged memory. For more complex types, you also have the option of using existing serialization code. The one proviso is that the serialized data must never exceed, in length, its allocation of space in the struct; otherwise, the result is an unintended union with subsequent fields.

Interop Attribute Reference

This section describes in more detail the attributes used in this chapter. All exist in the System.Runtime.InteropServices namespace.

The DllImport Attribute

The DllImport attribute annotates an external function that defines a DLL entry point. For example:

```
[DllImport ("winmm.dll", EntryPoint="midiOutShortMsg")]
public static extern int MidiOutMessage (int handle, int message);
```

[DllImport] supports the following parameters, all of which are optional:

EntryPoint (string)
> A string specifying the function name inside the DLL. If you include this, the name of your C# function need not match the name of the DLL function.

CharSet (CharSet)
> A CharSet enum, specifying the character encoding to use by default when marshaling string-typed parameters. The options are Ansi (one byte per character), Unicode (two bytes per character), and Auto. The default is Auto, which translates to Unicode (except on Windows 9x and Windows ME).

SetLastError (bool)
> If true, the marshaler preserves the Win32 error information, which can later be queried by calling Marshal.GetLastWin32Error. This works only if the unmanaged code sets the Win32 error, by calling SetLastError. Some functions do not and instead use an ordinary return value to indicate success or failure. The default is false.

ExactSpelling (bool)
> If true, the EntryPoint must exactly match the function. If false, name-matching heuristics are used. The default is false.

PreserveSig (bool)
> If true, the method signature is preserved exactly as it was defined. If false, an HRESULT transformation is performed. The default is true.

CallingConvention (CallingConvention)
> A CallingConvention enum, which defines the "plumbing" protocol for communicating parameters and return values. StdCall is the default and is used for calling into _stdcall-declared functions, encompassing most of the Win32 API. Cdecl is used for calling functions declared directly from C or C++, such as printf.

The StructLayout Attribute

The StructLayout attribute specifies how the data members of a class or struct should be laid out in memory. For example:

```
[StructLayout (LayoutKind.Explicit)]
struct NoteMessage
{
  ...
}
```

This attribute lets you ensure that types passed to or returned from native DLLs have a predicable internal structure. In conjunction with `LayoutKind.Explicit`, it also allows you to define highly efficient data structures suited to file and network I/O.

`LayoutKind` can be `Sequential` (which lays out fields one after the next with a minimum pack size), `Explicit` (where each field has a custom offset), or `Auto` (decided by the CLR). If no `StructLayout` attribute is applied, the default is `Auto` for reference types and `Sequential` for value types. `Auto` precludes unmanaged interop.

The other parameters for this attribute are as follows:

Size (int)
> Specifies the size of the struct or class. This has to be at least as large as the sum of all the members.

Pack (int)
> An integer specifying the field alignment boundaries. This must be 0, 1, 2, 4, 8, 16, 32, 64, or 128 bytes. Zero means the CLR's default value is applied.

CharSet (CharSet)
> A `CharSet` enum, specifying the character encoding to use when marshaling string-type fields within the type. The options are `Ansi` (one byte per character), `Unicode` (two bytes per character), and `Auto`. The default is `Auto`, which translates to `Unicode` (except on Windows 9x and Windows ME).

Native DLLs

The FieldOffset Attribute

The `FieldOffset` attribute is used on every field in a class or struct that has a `StructLayoutKind` of `Explicit`. It specifies the field's offset in bytes from the start of the type. Field offsets need not be in increasing order, since fields are allowed to overlap, creating a union data structure.

For an example, see the section "Simulating a C Union," earlier in this chapter.

The MarshalAs Attribute

The `MarshalAs` attribute overrides the default marshaling behavior for a field, method, parameter, or return value. For example:

```
[DllImport("...")]
static extern int Foo ( [MarshalAs (UnmanagedType.LPStr)] string s );
```

`UnmanagedType` is an enum that describes the unmanaged type to which the CLR should marshal.

The `MarshalAs` attribute also defines as number of additional properties, most of which are relevant only for specific `UnmanagedType` values. In particular:

SizeConst (int)
> Indicates the number of elements in a fixed-length string or array. This applies to `UnmanagedType.ByValArray` and `UnmanagedType.ByValTStr`.

ArraySubType (UnmanagedType)

Indicates the unmanaged type of each element in a fixed-length array. This applies to UnmanagedType.ByValArray.

SafeArraySubType (VarEnum)

Indicates the default unmanaged type of elements in an UnmanagedType. SafeArray.

UnmanagedType members

For marshaling strings:

UnmanagedType	Length protocol	Bytes per character
AnsiBStr	Length-prefixed	1
BStr	Length-prefixed	2
	Length-prefixed	2 from Windows 2000 1 on Windows 98
LPStr	Null-terminated	1
LPTStr	Null-terminated	2 from Windows 2000 1 on Windows 98
LPWStr	Null-terminated	2
ByValTStr	Fixed length; SizeConst indicates actual length	According to the CharSet specified in StructLayout

For marshaling signed integrals:

UnmanagedType	C# equivalent
I1	sbyte
I2	short
I4	int
I8	long
SysInt	int on 32-bit operating systems; long on 64-bit operating systems (or IntPtr on either)

For marshaling unsigned integrals:

UnmanagedType	C# equivalent
U1	byte
U2	ushort
U4	uint
U8	ulong
SysUInt	uint on 32-bit operating systems; ulong on 64-bit operating systems (or UIntPtr on either)

For marshaling floating-point numbers:

UnmanagedType	C# equivalent
R4	float
F8	double
Currency	decimal (marshals the COM currency type to decimal)

For marshaling bool types:

UnmanagedType	Length
Bool	4 bytes (equivalent to the Win32 BOOL type)
VariantBool	2 bytes (equivalent to the OLE VARIANT_BOOL type)

For marshaling arrays:

UnmanagedType	Meaning
ByValArray	Fixed-length array (must specify SizeConst and ArraySubType)
LPArray	Fixed-length array (must specify SizeConst and SizeParamIndex)
SafeArray	Self-describing variable-length array

For marshaling other types:

UnmanagedType	Meaning
AsAny	Marshals according to the type as determined at runtime
CustomMarshaler	Custom marshaling for advanced scenarios; used in conjunction with MarshalType, MarshalTypeRef, and MarshalCookie
Error	Four-byte integer corresponding to an HRESULT value
FunctionPtr	Callback (i.e., Delegate)
IDispatch	IDispatch pointer for COM
Interface	COM interface
IUnknown	IUnknown pointer for COM
Struct	A VARIANT

23

Diagnostics

When things go wrong, it's important that information is available to aid in diagnosing the problem. An IDE or debugger can assist greatly to this effect—but it is usually available only during development. Once an application ships, the application itself must gather and record diagnostic information. To meet this requirement, the .NET Framework provides a set of facilities to log diagnostic information, monitor application behavior, detect runtime errors, and integrate with debugging tools if available.

The types in this chapter are defined primarily in the System.Diagnostics namespace.

Conditional Compilation

You can conditionally compile any section of code in C# with *preprocessor directives*. Preprocessor directives are special instructions to the compiler that begin with the # symbol (and, unlike other C# constructs, must appear on a line of their own). The preprocessor directives for conditional compilation are #if, #else, #endif, and #elif.

The #if directive instructs the compiler to ignore a section of code unless a specified *symbol* has been defined. You can define a symbol with either the #define directive or a compilation switch. #define applies to a particular *file*; a compilation switch applies to a whole *assembly*:

```
#define TESTMODE        // #define directives must be at top of file
                        // Symbol names are uppercase by convention.
using System;

class Program
{
  static void Main()
  {
```

```
    #if TESTMODE
    Console.WriteLine ("in test mode!");      // OUTPUT: in test mode!
    #endif
  }
}
```

If we deleted the first line, the program would compile with the `Console.WriteLine` statement completely eliminated from the executable.

The #else statement is analogous to C#'s else statement, and #elif is equivalent to #else followed by #if. The ||, &&, and ! operators can be used to perform *or*, *and*, and *not* operations:

```
#if TESTMODE && !PLAYMODE       // if TESTMODE and not PLAYMODE
  ...
```

Bear in mind, however, that you're not building an ordinary C# expression, and the symbols upon which you operate have absolutely no connection to *variables*—static or otherwise.

To define a symbol assembly-wide, specify the /define switch when compiling:

```
csc Program.cs /define:TESTMODE,PLAYMODE
```

Visual Studio provides an option to enter conditional compilation symbols under Project Properties.

If you've defined a symbol at the assembly level and then want to "undefine" it for a particular file, you can do so with the #undef directive.

Conditional Compilation Versus Static Variable Flags

The preceding example could instead be implemented with a simple static field:

```
static internal bool TestMode = true;

static void Main( )
{
  if (TestMode) Console.WriteLine ("in test mode!");
}
```

This has the advantage of allowing runtime configuration. So, why choose conditional compilation? The reason is that conditional compilation can take you places variable flags cannot, such as:

- Conditionally including an attribute
- Changing the declared type of variable
- Switching between different namespaces or type aliases in a using directive—for example:

```
using TestType =
  #if V2
      MyCompany.Widgets.GadgetV2;
  #else
      MyCompany.Widgets.Gadget;
  #endif
```

You can even perform major refactoring under a conditional compilation directive, so you can instantly switch between old and new versions.

Another advantage of conditional compilation is that debugging code can refer to types in assemblies that are not included in deployment.

The Conditional Attribute

The Conditional attribute instructs the compiler to ignore any calls to a particular class or method, if the specified symbol has not been defined.

To see how this is useful, suppose you write a method for logging status information as follows:

```
static void LogStatus (string msg)
{
  string logFilePath = ...
  System.IO.File.AppendAllText (logFilePath, msg + "\r\n");
}
```

Now imagine you wanted this to execute only if the LOGGINGMODE symbol is defined. The first solution is to wrap all calls to LogStatus around an #if directive:

```
#if LOGGINGMODE
LogStatus ("Message Headers: " + GetMsgHeaders( ));
#endif
```

This gives an ideal result, but it is tedious. The second solution is to put the #if directive inside the LogStatus method. This, however, is problematic should LogStatus be called as follows:

```
LogStatus ("Message Headers: " + GetComplexMessageHeaders( ));
```

GetComplexMessageHeaders would always get called—which might incur a performance hit.

We can combine the functionality of the first solution with the convenience of the second by attaching the Conditional attribute (defined in System.Diagnostics) to the LogStatus method:

```
[Conditional ("LOGGINGMODE")]
static void LogStatus (string msg)
{
  ...
}
```

This instructs the compiler to implicitly wrap any calls to LogStatus in an #if LOGGINGMODE directive. If the symbol is not defined, any calls to LogStatus get eliminated entirely in compilation—including their argument evaluation expressions. This works even if LogStatus and the caller are in different assemblies.

 The Conditional attribute is ignored at runtime—it's purely an instruction to the compiler.

Alternatives to the Conditional attribute

The `Conditional` attribute is useless if you need to dynamically enable or disable functionality at runtime: instead, you must use a variable-based approach. This leaves the question of how to elegantly circumvent the evaluation of arguments when calling conditional logging methods. A functional approach solves this:

```
using System;
using System.Linq;

class Program
{
  public static bool EnableLogging;

  static void LogStatus (Func<string> message)
  {
    string logFilePath = ...
    if (EnableLogging)
      System.IO.File.AppendAllText (logFilePath, message() + "\r\n");
  }
}
```

A lambda expression lets you call this method without syntax bloat:

```
LogStatus ( () => "Message Headers: " + GetComplexMessageHeaders() );
```

If `EnableLogging` is false, `GetComplexMessageHeaders` is never evaluated.

Debug and Trace Classes

`Debug` and `Trace` are static classes that provide basic logging and assertion capabilities. The two classes are very similar; the main differentiator is their intended use. The `Debug` class is intended for debug builds; the `Trace` class is intended for both debug and release builds. To this effect:

> All methods of the `Debug` class are defined with `[Conditional("DEBUG")]`.
> All methods of the `Trace` class are defined with `[Conditional("TRACE")]`.

This means that all calls that you make to `Debug` or `Trace` are eliminated by the compiler unless you define `DEBUG` or `TRACE` symbols. By default, Visual Studio defines both `DEBUG` and `TRACE` symbols in a project's *debug* configuration—and just the `TRACE` symbol in the *release* configuration.

Both the `Debug` and `Trace` classes provide `Write`, `WriteLine`, and `WriteIf` methods. By default, these send messages to the debugger's output window:

```
Debug.Write     ("Data");
Debug.WriteLine (23 * 34);
int x = 5, y = 3;
Debug.WriteIf   (x > y, "x is greater than y");
```

`Debug` and `Trace` also provide `Fail` and `Assert` methods. By default, `Fail` displays the message in dialog as well as sending it to the debug output:

```
Debug.Fail ("File data.txt already exists");
```

Assert simply calls Fail if the bool argument is false, and it is useful for verifying *code invariants* (conditions that should always evaluate to true if your code is bug-free). Specifying a message is optional:

```
Debug.Assert (!File.Exists ("data.txt"), "File data.txt already exists");
var result = ...
Debug.Assert (result != null);
```

The Write, Fail, and Assert methods are also overloaded to accept a string category in addition to the message, which can be useful in processing the output.

In the Trace class, there are the additional methods TraceInformation, TraceWarning, and TraceError. The difference in behavior between these and the Write methods depends on the active TraceListeners.

TraceListener

The Debug and Trace classes each have a Listeners property, comprising a static collection of TraceListener instances. These are responsible for processing the content emitted by the Write, Fail, and Trace methods.

By default, the Listeners collection of each includes a single listener (DefaultTraceListener). The default listener has two key features:

- When connected to a debugger such as Visual Studio, messages are written to the debug output window; otherwise, message content is ignored.
- When the Fail method is called (or an assertion fails), a dialog appears asking the user whether to continue or abort—regardless of whether a debugger is attached.

You can change this behavior by removing the default listener, and then adding one or more of your own. You can write trace listeners from scratch (by subclassing TraceListener) or use one of the predefined types:

- TextWriterTraceListener writes to a Stream or TextWriter or appends to a file.
- EventLogTraceListener writes to the Windows event log.
- EventProviderTraceListener writes to the Event Tracing for Windows (ETW) subsystem in Windows Vista.
- WebPageTraceListener writes to an ASP.NET web page.

TextWriterTraceListener is further subclassed to ConsoleTraceListener, DelimitedListTraceListener, XmlWriterTraceListener, and EventSchemaTraceListener.

 None of these listeners displays a dialog when Fail is called—only DefaultTraceListener has this behavior.

The following example clears Trace's default listener, then adds three listeners— one that appends to a file, one that writes to the console, and one that writes to the Windows event log:

```
// Clear the default listener:
Trace.Listeners.Clear( );

// Add a writer that appends to the trace.txt file:
Trace.Listeners.Add (new TextWriterTraceListener ("trace.txt"));

// Obtain the Console's output stream, then add that as a listener:
System.IO.TextWriter tw = Console.Out;
Trace.Listeners.Add (new TextWriterTraceListener (tw));

// Set up a Windows Event log source and then create/add listener:
if (!EventLog.SourceExists ("DemoApp"))
  EventLog.CreateEventSource ("DemoApp", "Application");

Trace.Listeners.Add (new EventLogTraceListener ("DemoApp"));
```

In the case of the Windows event log, messages that you write with the Write, Fail, or Assert methods always display as "Information" messages in the Windows event viewer. Messages that you write via the TraceWarning and TraceError methods, however, show up as warnings or errors.

TraceListener also has a Filter of type TraceFilter that you can set to control whether a given message gets written to that listener. To do this, either instantiate one of the predefined subclasses (EventTypeFilter or SourceFilter) or subclass TraceFilter and override the ShouldTrace method. You could use this to filter by category, for instance.

TraceListener also defines IndentLevel and IndentSize properties for controlling indentation, and the TraceOutputOptions property for writing extra data:

```
TextWriterTraceListener tl = new TextWriterTraceListener (Console.Out);
tl.TraceOutputOptions = TraceOptions.DateTime | TraceOptions.Callstack;
```

TraceOutputOptions are applied when using the Trace methods:

```
Trace.TraceWarning ("Orange alert");

DiagTest.vshost.exe Warning: 0 : Orange alert
    DateTime=2007-03-08T05:57:13.6250000Z
    Callstack=   at System.Environment.GetStackTrace(Exception e, Boolean
needFileInfo)
    at System.Environment.get_StackTrace( )
    at ...
```

Flushing and Closing Listeners

Some listeners, such as TextWriterTraceListener, ultimately write to a stream that is subject to caching. This has two implications:

- A message may not appear in the output stream or file immediately.
- You must close—or at least flush—the listener before your application ends; otherwise, you lose what's in the cache (4 KB if you're writing to a file).

The Trace and Debug classes provide static Close and Flush methods that call Close or Flush on all listeners (which in turn calls Close or Flush on any underlying writers and streams). Close implicitly calls Flush, closes file handles, and prevents further data from being written.

As a general rule, call Close before an application ends and call Flush anytime you want to ensure that current message data is written. This applies if you're using stream- or file-based listeners.

Trace and Debug also provide an AutoFlush property, which, if true, forces a Flush after every message.

 It's a good policy to set AutoFlush to true on Debug and Trace if you're using any file- or stream-based listeners. Otherwise, if an unhandled exception or critical error occurs, the last 4 KB of diagnostic information may be lost.

Debugger Integration

Sometimes it is useful for an application to interact with a debugger if one is available. During development, the debugger is usually your IDE (e.g., Visual Studio); in deployment, the debugger is more likely to be:

- DbgCLR
- One of the lower-level debugging tools, such as WinDbg, Cordbg, or Mdgb

DbgCLR is Visual Studio stripped of everything but the debugger, and it is a free download with the .NET Framework SDK. It's the easiest debugging option when an IDE is not available, although it requires that you download the whole SDK.

Attaching and Breaking

The static Debugger class in System.Diagnostics provides basic functions for interacting with a debugger—namely Break, Launch, Log, and IsAttached.

A debugger must first attach to an application in order to debug it. If you start an application from within an IDE, this happens automatically, unless you request otherwise (by choosing "Start without debugging"). Sometimes, though, it's inconvenient or impossible to start an application in debug mode within the IDE. An example is a Windows Service application or (ironically) a Visual Studio designer. One solution is to start the application normally, and then choose Debug Process in your IDE. This doesn't allow you to set breakpoints early in the program's execution, however.

The workaround is to call Debugger.Break from within your application. This method launches a debugger, attaches to it, and suspends execution at that point. (Launch does the same, but without suspending execution.) Once attached, you can log messages directly to the debugger's output window with the Log method. You can tell whether you're attached to a debugger with the IsAttached property.

Debugger Attributes

The DebuggerStepThrough and DebuggerHidden attributes provide suggestions to the debugger on how to handle single-stepping for a particular method, constructor, or class.

DebuggerStepThrough requests that the debugger step through a function without any user interaction. This attribute is useful in automatically generated methods and in proxy methods that forward the real work to a method somewhere else. In the latter case, the debugger will still show the proxy method in the call stack if a breakpoint is set within the "real" method—unless you also add the Debugger-Hidden attribute. These two attributes can be combined on proxies to help the user focus on debugging the application logic rather than the plumbing:

```
[DebuggerStepThrough, DebuggerHidden]
void DoWorkProxy()
{
  // setup...
  DoWork();
  // teardown...
}

void DoWork() {...}   // Real method...
```

Processes and Process Threads

We described in the last section of Chapter 6 how to launch a new process with Process.Start. The Process class also allows you to query and interact with other processes running on the same, or another, computer.

Examining Running Processes

The Process.GetProcess*XXX* methods retrieve a specific process by name or process ID, or all processes running on the current or nominated computer. This includes both managed and unmanaged processes. Each Process instance has a wealth of properties mapping statistics such as name, ID, priority, memory and processor utilization, window handles, and so on. The following sample enumerates all the running processes on the current computer:

```
foreach (Process p in Process.GetProcesses())
{
  Console.WriteLine (p.ProcessName);
  Console.WriteLine ("  PID:      " + p.Id);
  Console.WriteLine ("  Started:  " + p.StartTime);
  Console.WriteLine ("  Memory:   " + p.WorkingSet64);
  Console.WriteLine ("  CPU time: " + p.TotalProcessorTime);
  Console.WriteLine ("  Threads:  " + p.Threads.Count);
}
```

Process.GetCurrentProcess returns the current process. If you've created additional application domains, all will share the same process.

You can terminate a process by calling its Kill method.

Examining Threads in a Process

You can also enumerate over the threads of other processes, with the Process. Threads property. The objects that you get, however, are not System.Threading. Thread objects, but rather ProcessThread objects, and are intended for administrative rather than synchronization tasks. A `ProcessThread` object provides diagnostic information about the underlying thread and allows you to control some aspects of it such as its priority and processor affinity:

```
public void EnumerateThreads (Process p)
{
  foreach (ProcessThread pt in p.Threads)
  {
    Console.WriteLine (pt.Id);
    Console.WriteLine ("   State:    " + pt.ThreadState);
    Console.WriteLine ("   Priority: " + pt.PriorityLevel);
    Console.WriteLine ("   Started:  " + pt.StartTime);
    Console.WriteLine ("   CPU time: " + pt.TotalProcessorTime);
  }
}
```

StackTrace and StackFrame

The `StackTrace` and `StackFrame` classes provide a read-only view of an execution call stack. You can obtain stack traces for the current thread, another thread in the same process, or an `Exception` object. Such information is useful mostly for diagnostic purposes, though it can also be used in programming (hacks). `StackTrace` represents a complete call stack; `StackFrame` represents a single method call within that stack.

If you instantiate a `StackTrace` object with no arguments—or with a `bool` argument—you get a snapshot of the current thread's call stack. The `bool` argument, if true, instructs `StackTrace` to read the assembly *.pdb* (project debug) files if they are present, giving you access to filename, line number, and column offset data.

 Project debug files are generated when you compile with the /debug switch. Visual Studio compiles with this switch unless you request otherwise via *Advanced Build Settings*.

Once you've obtained a `StackTrace`, you can examine a particular frame by calling `GetFrame`—or obtain the whole lot with `GetFrames`:

```
static void Main() { A (); }
static void A()    { B (); }
static void B()    { C (); }
static void C()
{
  StackTrace s = new StackTrace (true);

  Console.WriteLine ("Total frames:   " + s.FrameCount);
  Console.WriteLine ("Current method: " + s.GetFrame(0).GetMethod( ).Name);
  Console.WriteLine ("Calling method: " + s.GetFrame(1).GetMethod( ).Name);
  Console.WriteLine ("Entry method:   " + s.GetFrame
                                          (s.FrameCount-1).GetMethod( ).Name);
  Console.WriteLine ("Call Stack:");
  foreach (StackFrame f in s.GetFrames())
    Console.WriteLine (
```

```
              "  File: "    + f.GetFileName() +
              "  Line: "    + f.GetFileLineNumber() +
              "  Col: "     + f.GetFileColumnNumber() +
              "  Offset: "  + f.GetILOffset() +
              "  Method: "  + f.GetMethod().Name);
    }
```

Here's the output:

```
    Total frames:   4
    Current method: C
    Calling method: B
    Entry method: Main
    Call stack:
      File: C:\Test\Program.cs  Line: 15  Col: 4  Offset: 7  Method: C
      File: C:\Test\Program.cs  Line: 12  Col: 22  Offset: 6  Method: B
      File: C:\Test\Program.cs  Line: 11  Col: 22  Offset: 6  Method: A
      File: C:\Test\Program.cs  Line: 10  Col: 25  Offset: 6  Method: Main
```

A shortcut to obtaining the essential information for an entire StackTrace is to call ToString on it. Here's what the result looks like:

```
    at DebugTest.Program.C() in C:\Test\Program.cs:line 16
    at DebugTest.Program.B() in C:\Test\Program.cs:line 12
    at DebugTest.Program.A() in C:\Test\Program.cs:line 11
    at DebugTest.Program.Main() in C:\Test\Program.cs:line 10
```

To obtain the stack trace for another thread, pass the other Thread into StackTrace's constructor. This can be a useful strategy for profiling a program. The one proviso is that you suspend the thread first, by calling its Suspend method (and Resume when you're done). This is the one valid use for Thread's deprecated Suspend and Resume methods!

You can also obtain the stack trace for an Exception object (showing what led up to the exception being thrown) by passing the Exception into StackTrace's constructor.

> Exception already has a StackTrace property; however, this property returns a simple string—not a StackTrace object. A StackTrace object is far more useful in logging exceptions that occur after deployment—where no *.pdb* files are available—because you can log the *IL offset* in lieu of line and column numbers. With an IL offset and *ildasm*, you can pinpoint where within a method an error occurred.

Windows Event Logs

The Win32 platform provides a centralized logging mechanism, in the form of the Windows event logs.

The Debug and Trace classes we used earlier write to a Windows event log if you register an EventLogTraceListener. With the EventLog class, however, you can write directly to a Windows event log without using Trace or Debug. You can also use this class to read and monitor event data.

Writing to the Windows event log makes sense in a Windows Service application, because if something goes wrong, you can't pop up a user interface directing the user to some special file where diagnostic information has been written. Also, because it's common practice for services to write to the Windows event log, this is the first place an administrator is likely to look if your service falls over.

There are three standard Windows event logs, identified by these names:

- Application
- System
- Security

The *Application* log is where most applications normally write.

Writing to the Event Log

To write to a Windows event log:

1. Choose one of the three event logs (usually *Application*).
2. Decide on a *source name* and create it if necessary.
3. Call EventLog.WriteEntry with the log name, source name, and message data.

The *source name* is an easily identifiable name for your application. You must register a source name before you use it—the CreateEventSource method performs this function. You can then call WriteEntry:

```
const string SourceName = "MyCompany.WidgetServer";

if (!EventLog.SourceExists (SourceName))
  EventLog.CreateEventSource (SourceName, "Application");

EventLog.WriteEntry (SourceName,
  "Service started; using configuration file=...",
  EventLogEntryType.Information);
```

EventLogEntryType can be Information, Warning, Error, SuccessAudit, or Failure-Audit. Each displays with a different icon in the Windows event viewer. You can also optionally specify a category and event ID (each is a number of your own choosing) and provide optional binary data.

CreateEventSource also allows you to specify a machine name: this is to write to another computer's event log, if you have sufficient permissions.

Reading the Event Log

To read an event log, instantiate the EventLog class with the name of the log you wish to access and optionally the name of another computer on which the log resides. Each log entry can then be read via the Entries collection property:

```
EventLog log = new EventLog ("Application");

Console.WriteLine ("Total entries: " + log.Entries.Count);

EventLogEntry last = log.Entries [log.Entries.Count - 1];
Console.WriteLine ("Index:   " + last.Index);
Console.WriteLine ("Source:  " + last.Source);
Console.WriteLine ("Type:    " + last.EntryType);
Console.WriteLine ("Time:    " + last.TimeWritten);
Console.WriteLine ("Message: " + last.Message);
```

You can enumerate over all logs for the current (or another) computer with the static method EventLog.GetEventLogs (this requires administrative privileges):

```
foreach (EventLog log in EventLog.GetEventLogs())
  Console.WriteLine (log.LogDisplayName);
```

This normally prints *Application*, *Security*, and *System*.

Monitoring the Event Log

You can be alerted whenever an entry is written to a Windows event log, via the EntryWritten event. This works for event logs on the local computer, and it fires regardless of what application logged the event.

To enable log monitoring:

1. Instantiate an EventLog and set its EnableRaisingEvents property to true.
2. Handle the EntryWritten event.

For example:

```
static void Main()
{
  EventLog log = new EventLog ("Application");
  log.EnableRaisingEvents = true;
  log.EntryWritten += DisplayEntry;
  Console.ReadLine();
}

static void DisplayEntry (object sender, EntryWrittenEventArgs e)
{
  EventLogEntry entry = e.Entry;
  Console.WriteLine (entry.Message);
}
```

Performance Counters

The logging mechanisms we've discussed to date are useful for capturing information for future analysis. However, to gain insight into the current state of an application (or the system as a whole), a more real-time approach is needed. The Win32 solution to this need is the performance-monitoring infrastructure, which consists of a set of performance counters that the system and applications expose, and the Microsoft Management Console (MMC) snap-ins used to monitor these counters in real time.

Performance counters are grouped into categories such as "System," "Processor," ".NET CLR Memory," and so on. These categories are sometimes also referred to as "performance objects" by the GUI tools. Each category groups a related set of performance counters that monitor one aspect of the system or application. Examples of performance counters in the ".NET CLR Memory" category include "% Time in GC," "# Bytes in All Heaps," and "Allocated bytes/sec."

Each category may optionally have one or more instances that can be monitored independently. For example, this is useful in the "% Processor Time" performance counter in the "Processor" category, which allows one to monitor CPU utilization. On a multiprocessor machine, this counter supports an instance for each CPU, allowing one to monitor the utilization of each CPU independently.

The following sections illustrate how to perform commonly needed tasks, such as determining which counters are exposed, monitoring a counter, and creating your own counters to expose application status information.

 Reading performance counters or categories requires administrator privileges on the local or target computer.

Enumerating the Available Counters

The following example enumerates over all of the available performance counters on the computer. For those that have instances, it enumerates the counters for each instance:

```
PerformanceCounterCategory[] cats =
  PerformanceCounterCategory.GetCategories();

foreach (PerformanceCounterCategory cat in cats)
{
  Console.WriteLine ("Category: " + cat.CategoryName);

  string[] instances = cat.GetInstanceNames();
  if (instances.Length == 0)
  {
    foreach (PerformanceCounter ctr in cat.GetCounters())
      Console.WriteLine ("  Counter: " + ctr.CounterName);
  }
  else    // Dump counters with instances
  {
    foreach (string instance in instances)
    {
      Console.WriteLine ("  Instance: " + instance);
      if (cat.InstanceExists (instance))
        foreach (PerformanceCounter ctr in cat.GetCounters (instance))
          Console.WriteLine ("    Counter: " + ctr.CounterName);
    }
  }
}
```

The result is more than 10,000 lines long! It also takes awhile to execute because PerformanceCounterCategory.InstanceExists has an inefficient implementation. In a real system, you'd want to retrieve the more detailed information only on demand.

The next example uses a LINQ query to retrieve just .NET performance counters, writing the result to an XML file:

```
var x =
  new XElement ("counters",
    from PerformanceCounterCategory cat in
        PerformanceCounterCategory.GetCategories()
    where cat.CategoryName.StartsWith (".NET")
    let instances = cat.GetInstanceNames()
    select new XElement ("category",
      new XAttribute ("name", cat.CategoryName),
      instances.Length == 0
      ?
        from c in cat.GetCounters ()
        select new XElement ("counter",
          new XAttribute ("name", c.CounterName))
      :
        from i in instances
        select new XElement ("instance", new XAttribute ("name", i),
          !cat.InstanceExists (i)
          ?
            null
          :
            from c in cat.GetCounters (i)
            select new XElement ("counter",
              new XAttribute ("name", c.CounterName))
        )
    )
  );
x.Save ("counters.xml");
```

Reading Performance Counter Data

To retrieve the value of a performance counter, instantiate a PerformanceCounter object and then call the NextValue or NextSample method. NextValue returns a simple float value; NextSample returns a CounterSample object that exposes a more advanced set of properties, such as CounterFrequency, TimeStamp, BaseValue, and RawValue.

PerformanceCounter's constructor takes a category name, counter name, and optional instance. So, to display the current processor utilization for all CPUs, you would do the following:

```
using (PerformanceCounter pc = new PerformanceCounter ("Processor",
                                            "% Processor Time",
                                            "_Total"))

  Console.WriteLine (pc.NextValue());
```

Diagnostics

Or to display the "real" (i.e., private) memory consumption of the current process:

```
string procName = Process.GetCurrentProcess().ProcessName;
using (PerformanceCounter pc = new PerformanceCounter ("Process",
                                                       "Private Bytes",
                                                       procName))
    Console.WriteLine (pc.NextValue());
```

PerformanceCounter doesn't expose a ValueChanged event, so if you want to monitor for changes, you must poll. In the next example, we poll every 200 ms—until signaled to quit by an EventWaitHandle:

```
// need to import System.Threading as well as System.Diagnostics

static void Monitor (string category, string counter, string instance,
                     EventWaitHandle stopper)
{
  if (!PerformanceCounterCategory.Exists (category))
    throw new InvalidOperationException ("Category does not exist");

  if (!PerformanceCounterCategory.CounterExists (counter, category))
    throw new InvalidOperationException ("Counter does not exist");

  if (instance == null) instance = "";   // "" == no instance (not null!)
  if (instance != "" &&
      !PerformanceCounterCategory.InstanceExists (instance, category))
    throw new InvalidOperationException ("Instance does not exist");

  float lastValue = 0f;
  using (PerformanceCounter pc = new PerformanceCounter (category,
                                                  counter, instance))
    while (!stopper.WaitOne (200, false))
    {
      float value = pc.NextValue();
      if (value != lastValue)          // Only write out the value
      {                                // if it has changed.
        Console.WriteLine (value);
        lastValue = value;
      }
    }
}
```

Here's how we can use this method to simultaneously monitor processor and hard-disk activity:

```
static void Main()
{
  EventWaitHandle stopper = new ManualResetEvent (false);
  new Thread (delegate()
    { Monitor ("Processor", "% Processor Time", "_Total", stopper); }
  ).Start();
  new Thread (delegate()
    { Monitor ("LogicalDisk", "% Idle Time", "C:", stopper); }
  ).Start();
  Console.WriteLine ("Monitoring - press any key to quit");
```

```
    Console.ReadKey();
    stopper.Set();
}
```

Creating Counters and Writing Performance Data

Before writing performance counter data, you need to create a performance category and counter. You must create the performance category along with all the counters that belong to it in one step, as follows:

```
string category = "Nutshell Monitoring";

// We'll create two counters in this category:
string eatenPerMin = "Macadamias eaten so far";
string tooHard = "Macadamias deemed too hard";

if (!PerformanceCounterCategory.Exists (category))
{
  CounterCreationDataCollection cd = new CounterCreationDataCollection();

  cd.Add (new CounterCreationData (eatenPerMin,
          "Number of macadamias consumed, including shelling time",
          PerformanceCounterType.NumberOfItems32));

  cd.Add (new CounterCreationData (tooHard,
          "Number of macadamias that will not crack, despite much effort",
          PerformanceCounterType.NumberOfItems32));

  PerformanceCounterCategory.Create (category, "Test Category",
    PerformanceCounterCategoryType.SingleInstance, cd);
}
```

The new counters then show up in the Windows performance-monitoring tool when you choose Add Counters, as shown in Figure 23-1.

If you later want to define more counters in the same category, you must first delete the old category by calling PerformanceCounterCategory.Delete.

 Creating and deleting performance counters requires administrative privileges. For this reason, it's usually done as part of the application setup.

Once a counter is created, you can update its value by instantiating a PerformanceCounter, setting ReadOnly to false, and setting RawValue. You can also use the Increment and IncrementBy methods to update the existing value:

```
string category = "Nutshell Monitoring";
string eatenPerMin = "Macadamias eaten so far";

using (PerformanceCounter pc = new PerformanceCounter (category,
                                                eatenPerMin, ""))
{
  pc.ReadOnly = false;
  pc.RawValue = 1000;
```

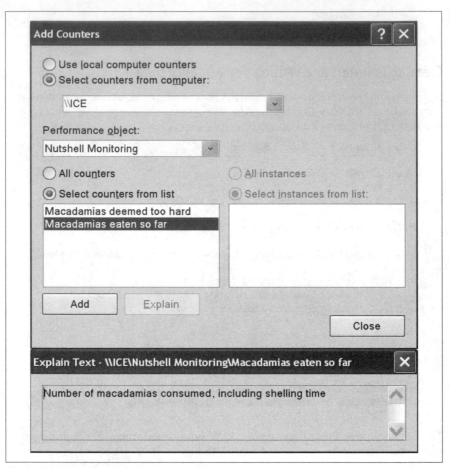

Figure 23-1. Custom performance counter

```
    pc.Increment( );
    pc.IncrementBy (10);
    Console.WriteLine (pc.NextValue( ));    // 1011
}
```

The Stopwatch Class

The Stopwatch class provides a convenient mechanism for measuring execution times. Stopwatch uses the highest-resolution mechanism that the operating system and hardware provide, which is typically 1–2 ms on a computer without a special high-resolution clock.

To use Stopwatch, call StartNew—this instantiates a Stopwatch and starts it ticking. (Alternatively, you can instantiate it manually and then call Start.) The Elapsed property returns the elapsed interval as a TimeSpan:

```
Stopwatch s = Stopwatch.StartNew( );
System.IO.File.WriteAllText ("test.txt", new string ('*', 30000000));
Console.WriteLine (s.Elapsed);        // 00:00:01.4322661
```

Stopwatch also exposes an ElapsedTicks property, which returns the number of elapsed "ticks" as a long integer. To convert from ticks to seconds, divide by StopWatch.Frequency.

Calling Stop freezes Elapsed and ElapsedTicks. There's no background activity incurred by a "running" Stopwatch, so calling Stop is optional.

24

Regular Expressions

The regular expressions language identifies character patterns. The .NET types supporting regular expressions are based on Perl 5 regular expressions and support both search and search/replace functionality.

Regular expressions are used for tasks such as:

- Validating text input such as passwords and phone numbers (ASP.NET provides the RegularExpressionValidator control just for this purpose)
- Parsing textual data into more structured forms (e.g., extracting data from an HTML page for storage in a database)
- Replacing patterns of text in a document (e.g., whole words only)

This chapter is split into both conceptual sections teaching the basics of regular expressions in .NET and reference sections describing the regular expressions language.

All regular expression types are defined in System.Text.RegularExpressions.

 For more on regular expressions, *http://regular-expressions.info* is a good online reference with lots of examples, and *Mastering Regular Expressions* by Jeffrey E. F. Friedl (O'Reilly), is invaluable for the serious.

Regular Expression Basics

One of the most common regular expression operators is a *quantifier*. ? is a quantifier that matches the preceding item 0 or 1 time. In other words, ? means *optional*. An item is either a single character or a complex structure of characters in square brackets. For example, the regular expression "colou?r" matches color and colour, but not colouur:

```
Console.WriteLine (Regex.Match ("color",   @"colou?r").Success);  // True
Console.WriteLine (Regex.Match ("colour",  @"colou?r").Success);  // True
Console.WriteLine (Regex.Match ("colouur", @"colou?r").Success);  // False
```

Regex.Match searches within a larger string. The object that it returns has properties for the Index and Length of the match, as well as the actual Value matched:

```
Match m = Regex.Match ("any colour you like", @"colou?r");

Console.WriteLine (m.Success);      // True
Console.WriteLine (m.Index);        // 4
Console.WriteLine (m.Length);       // 6
Console.WriteLine (m.Value);        // colour
Console.WriteLine (m.ToString( ));  // colour
```

You can think of Regex.Match as a more powerful version of the string's IndexOf method. The difference is that it searches for a *pattern* rather than a literal string.

The IsMatch method is a shortcut for calling Match and then testing the Success property.

The regular expressions engine works from left to right by default, so only the left-most match is returned. You can use the NextMatch method to return more matches:

```
Match m1 = Regex.Match ("One color? There are two colours in my head!",
                        @"colou?rs?");
Match m2 = m1.NextMatch( );
Console.WriteLine (m1);      // color
Console.WriteLine (m2);      // colours
```

The Matches method returns all matches in an array. We can rewrite the preceding example as follows:

```
foreach (Match m in Regex.Matches
    ("One color? There are two colours in my head!", @"colou?rs?"))
  Console.WriteLine (m);
```

Another common regular expressions operator is the *alternator*, expressed with a vertical bar, |. An alternator expresses alternatives. The following matches "Jen", "Jenny", and "Jennifer":

```
Console.WriteLine (Regex.IsMatch ("Jenny", "Jen(ny|nifer)?"));  // True
```

The brackets around an alternator separate the alternatives from the rest of the expression.

Compiled Regular Expressions

In some of the preceding examples, we called a static RegEx method repeatedly with the same pattern. An alternative approach in these cases is to instantiate a Regex object with the pattern and then call instance methods:

```
Regex r = new Regex (@"sausages?");
Console.WriteLine (r.Match ("sausage"));   // sausage
Console.WriteLine (r.Match ("sausages"));  // sausages
```

This is not just a syntactic convenience: under the covers, a RegEx instance uses lightweight code generation (DynamicMethod in Reflection.Emit) to dynamically build and compile code tailored to that particular regular expression. This results in (up to 10 times) faster matching, at the expense of a small initial compilation cost (a few tens of microseconds).

A Regex instance is immutable.

> The regular expressions engine is fast. Even without compilation, a simple match typically takes less than a microsecond.

RegexOptions

The RegexOptions flags enum lets you tweak matching behavior. A common use for RegexOptions is to perform a case-insensitive search:

```
Console.WriteLine (Regex.Match ("a", "A", RegexOptions.IgnoreCase)); // a
```

Most of the RegexOptions flags can also be activated within a regular expression itself, using a single-letter code as follows:

```
Console.WriteLine (Regex.Match ("a", @"(?i)A"));                    // a
```

You can turn options on and off throughout an expression as follows:

```
Console.WriteLine (Regex.Match ("AAAa", @"(?i)a(?-i)a"));          // Aa
```

Another useful option is IgnorePatternWhitespace or **(?x)**. This allows you to insert whitespace to make a regular expression more readable—without the whitespace being taken literally.

Table 24-1 lists all RegExOptions values along with their single-letter codes.

Table 24-1. Regular expression options

Enum value	Regular expressions code	Description
None		
IgnoreCase	i	Ignores case (by default, regular expressions are case-sensitive).
Multiline	m	Changes ^ and $ so that they match the start/end of a line instead of start/end of the string.
ExplicitCapture	n	Captures only explicitly named or explicitly numbered groups.
Compiled	c	Forces compilation of regular expression to IL.
Singleline	s	Makes . match every character (instead of matching every character except \n).
IgnorePattern-Whitespace	x	Eliminates unescaped whitespace from the pattern.
RightToLeft	r	Searches from right to left; can't be specified midstream.
ECMAScript		Forces ECMA compliance (by default, the implementation is not ECMA-compliant).
CultureInvariant		Turns off culture-specific behavior (by default, CultureInfo.CurrentCulture influences string comparison rules).

Character Escapes

Regular expressions have the following metacharacters, which have a special rather than literal meaning:

    \ * + ? | { [( ) ^ $. #

To refer to a metacharacter literally, you must prefix the character with a backslash. In the following example, we escape the ? character to match the string "what?":

```
Console.WriteLine (Regex.Match ("what?", @"what\?")); // what? (correct)
Console.WriteLine (Regex.Match ("what?", @"what?"));  // what  (incorrect)
```

 If the character is inside a *set* (square brackets), this rule does not apply, and the metacharacters are interpreted literally. We discuss sets in the following section.

The Regex's Escape and Unescape methods convert a string containing regular expression metacharacters by replacing them with escaped equivalents, and vice versa. For example:

```
Console.WriteLine (Regex.Escape   (@"?"));   // \?
Console.WriteLine (Regex.Unescape (@"\?"));   // ?
```

All the regular expression strings in this chapter we express with the C# @ literal. This is to bypass C#'s escape mechanism, which also uses the backslash. Without the @, a literal backslash would require four backslashes:

```
Console.WriteLine (Regex.Match ("\\", "\\\\"));   // \
```

Unless you include the **(?x)** option, spaces are treated literally in regular expressions:

```
Console.Write (Regex.IsMatch ("hello world", @"hello world"));  // True
```

Character Sets

Character sets act as wildcards for a particular set of characters.

Expression	Meaning	Inverse ("not")
[abcdef]	Matches a single character in the list	[^abcdef]
[a-f]	Matches a single character in a *range*	[^a-f]
\d	Matches a decimal digit Same as [0-9]	\D
\w	Matches a *word* character (by default, varies according to CultureInfo.CurrentCulture; for example, in English, same as [a-zA-Z_0-9])	\W
\s	Matches a whitespace character Same as [\n\r\t\f]	\S
\p{*category*}	Matches a character in a specified *category*	\P
.	(Default mode) Matches any character except \n	\n
.	(SingleLine mode) Matches any character	\n

To match exactly one of a set of characters, put the character set in square brackets:

```
Console.Write (Regex.Matches ("That is that.", "[Tt]hat").Count);   // 2
```

To match any character *except* those in a set, put the set in square brackets with a ^ symbol before the first character:

```
Console.Write (Regex.Match ("quiz qwerty", "q[^aeiou]").Index);    // 5
```

You can specify a range of characters with a hyphen. The following regular expression captures a chess move:

```
Console.Write (Regex.Match ("b1-c4", @"[a-h]\d-[a-h]\d").Success);  // True
```

\d indicates a digit character, so **\d** will match any digit. **\D** matches any nondigit character.

\w indicates a word character, which includes letters, numbers, and the underscore. **\W** matches any nonword character. These work as expected for non-English letters too, such as Cyrillic.

. matches any character except \n (but allows \r).

\p matches a character in a specified category, such as **{Lu}** for uppercase letter or **{P}** for punctuation (we list the categories in the reference section later in the chapter):

```
Console.Write (Regex.IsMatch ("Yes, please", @"\p{P}"));   // True
```

We will find more uses for **\d**, **\w**, and . when we combine them with *quantifiers*.

Quantifiers

Quantifiers match an item a specified number of times.

Quantifier	Meaning
*	Zero or more matches
+	One or more matches
?	Zero or one match
{*n*}	Exactly *n* matches
{*n*,}	At least *n* matches
{*n*,*m*}	Between *n* and *m* matches

The * quantifier matches the preceding character or group zero or more times. The following matches *cv.doc*, along with any numbered versions of the same file (e.g., *cv2.doc*, *cv15.doc*):

```
Console.Write (Regex.Match ("cv15.doc", @"cv\d*\.doc").Success);  // True
```

Notice that we have to escape out the period in the file extension with a backslash.

The following allows anything between *cv* and *.doc* and is equivalent to `dir cv*.doc`:

```
Console.Write (Regex.Match ("cvjoint.doc", @"cv.*\.doc").Success);  // True
```

The + quantifier matches the preceding character or group one or more times. For example:

```
Console.Write (Regex.Matches ("slow! yeah slooow!", "slo+w").Count);  // 2
```

The {} quantifier matches a specified number (or range) of repetitions. The following matches a blood pressure reading:

```
Regex bp = new Regex (@"\d{2,3}/\d{2,3}");
Console.WriteLine (bp.Match ("It used to be 160/110"));  // 160/110
Console.WriteLine (bp.Match ("Now it's only 115/75"));   // 115/75
```

Greedy Versus Lazy Quantifiers

By default, quantifiers are *greedy*, as opposed to *lazy*. A greedy quantifier repeats as *many* times as it can before proceeding. A lazy quantifier repeats as *few* times as it can before proceeding. You can make any quantifier lazy by suffixing it with the ? symbol. To illustrate the difference, consider the following HTML fragment:

```
string html = "<i>By default</i> quantifiers are <i>greedy</i> creatures";
```

Suppose we want to extract the two phrases in italics. If we execute the following:

```
foreach (Match m in Regex.Matches (html, @"<i>.*</i>"))
    Console.WriteLine (m);
```

the result is not two matches, but a *single* match, as follows:

```
<i>By default</i> quantifiers are <i>greedy</i>
```

The problem is that our * quantifier greedily repeats as many times as it can before matching </i>. So, it chomps right through the first </i>, stopping only at the final </i> (the *last point* at which the rest of the expression can still match).

If we make the quantifier lazy:

```
foreach (Match m in Regex.Matches (html, @"<i>.*?</i>"))
    Console.WriteLine (m);
```

the * bails out at the *first* point at which the rest of the expression can match. Here's the result:

```
<i>By default</i>
<i>greedy</i>
```

Zero-Width Assertions

The regular expressions language lets you place conditions on what should occur *before* or *after* a match, through lookbehind, lookahead, anchors, and word boundaries. These are called *zero-width* assertions, because they don't increase the width (or length) of the match itself.

Lookahead and Lookbehind

The **(?=**_expr_**)** construct checks whether the text that follows matches _expr_, without including expr in the result. This is called _positive lookahead_. In the following example, we look for a number followed by the word "miles":

```
Console.WriteLine (Regex.Match ("say 25 miles more", @"\d+\s(?=miles)"));
```

OUTPUT: 25

Notice the word "miles" was not returned in the result, even though it was required to _satisfy_ the match.

After a successful lookahead, matching continues as though the sneak preview never took place. So, if we append `.*` to our expression as follows:

```
Console.WriteLine (Regex.Match ("say 25 miles more", @"\d+\s(?=miles).*"));
```

the result is 25 miles more.

Lookahead can be useful in validating a strong password. Suppose a password has to be at least six characters and contain at least one digit. With a lookup, we could achieve this as follows:

```
string password = "...";
bool ok = Regex.IsMatch (password, @"(?=.*\d).{6,}");
```

This first performs a lookahead to ensure that a digit occurs somewhere in the string. If satisfied, it returns to its position before the sneak preview began and matches six or more characters. (In the section "Cookbook Regular Expressions," later in this chapter, we include a more substantial password validation example.)

The opposite is the _negative lookahead_ construct, **(?!**_expr_**)**. This requires that the match _not_ be followed by _expr_. The following expression matches "good"—unless "however" or "but" appears later in the string:

```
string regex = "(?i)good(?!.*(however|but))";
Console.WriteLine (Regex.IsMatch ("Good work! But...", regex)); // False
Console.WriteLine (Regex.IsMatch ("Good work! Thanks!", regex)); // True
```

The **(?<=**_expr_**)** construct denotes _positive lookbehind_ and requires that a match be _preceded_ by a specified expression. The opposite construct, **(?<!**_expr_**)**, denotes _negative lookbehind_ and requires that a match _not be preceded_ by a specified expression. For example, the following matches "good"—unless "however" appears _earlier_ in the string:

```
string regex = "(?i)(?<!however.*)good";
Console.WriteLine (Regex.IsMatch ("However good, we...", regex)); // False
Console.WriteLine (Regex.IsMatch ("Very good, thanks!" , regex)); // True
```

We could improve these examples by adding _word boundary assertions_, which we will introduce shortly.

Anchors

The anchors ^ and $ match a particular _position_. By default:

^   Matches the _start_ of the string.

$ Matches the _end_ of the string.

^ has two context-dependent meanings: an *anchor* and a *character class negator*.

$ has two context-dependent meanings: an *anchor* and a *replacement group denoter*.

For example:

```
Console.WriteLine (Regex.Match ("Not now", "^[Nn]o"));    // No
Console.WriteLine (Regex.Match ("f = 0.2F", "[Ff]$"));    // F
```

If you specify RegexOptions.Multiline or include **(?m)** in the expression:

- ^ matches the start of the string or *line* (directly after a \n).
- $ matches the end of the string or *line* (directly before an \n).

There's a catch to using $ in multiline mode: a new line in Windows is nearly always denoted with \r\n rather than just \n. This means that for $ to be useful, you must usually match the \r as well, with a *positive lookahead*:

(?=\r?$)

The positive lookahead ensures that \r doesn't become part of the result. The following matches lines that end in ".txt":

```
string fileNames = "a.txt" + "\r\n" + "b.doc" + "\r\n" + "c.txt";
string r = @".+\.txt(?=\r?$)";
foreach (Match m in Regex.Matches (fileNames, r, RegexOptions.Multiline))
  Console.Write (m + " ");

OUTPUT: a.txt c.txt
```

The following matches all empty lines in string s:

```
MatchCollection emptyLines = Regex.Matches (s, "^(?=\r?$)",
                                            RegexOptions.Multiline);
```

The following matches all lines that are either empty or contain only whitespace:

```
MatchCollection blankLines = Regex.Matches (s, "^[ \t]*(?=\r?$)",
                                            RegexOptions.Multiline);
```

 Since an anchor matches a position rather than a character, specifying an anchor on its own matches an empty string:

```
Console.WriteLine (Regex.Match ("x", "$").Length);    // 0
```

Word Boundaries

The word boundary assertion \b matches where word characters (/w) adjoin either:

- Nonword characters (/W)
- The beginning/end of the string (^ and $)

/b is often used to match whole words. For example:

```
foreach (Match m in Regex.Matches ("Wedding in Sarajevo", @"\b\w+\b"))
  Console.WriteLine (m);

Wedding
In
Sarajevo
```

The following statements highlight the effect of a word boundary:

```
int one = Regex.Matches ("Wedding in Sarajevo", @"\bin\b").Count; // 1
int two = Regex.Matches ("Wedding in Sarajevo", @"in").Count;     // 2
```

The next query uses positive lookahead to return words followed by "(sic)":

```
string text = "Don't loose (sic) your cool";
Console.Write (Regex.Match (text, @"\b\w+\b\s(?=\(sic\))"));  // loose
```

Groups

Often a match is composed of *groups*. Consider the following regular expression that represents a U.S. phone number:

\d{3}-\d{3}-\d{4}

This really comprises two distinct groups—an area code and the local code. We can use parentheses to *capture* groups. For example:

(\d{3})-(\d{3}-\d{4})

We can retrieve the groups programmatically as follows:

```
Match m = Regex.Match ("206-465-1918", @"(\d{3})-(\d{3}-\d{4})");

Console.WriteLine (m.Groups[1]);   // 206
Console.WriteLine (m.Groups[2]);   // 465-1918
```

The zeroeth group represents the entire match. In other words, it has the same value as the match's Value:

```
Console.WriteLine (m.Groups[0]);   // 206-465-1918
Console.WriteLine (m);             // 206-465-1918
```

Groups are part of the regular expressions language itself. This means you can refer to a group within a regular expression. The \n syntax lets you index the group by group number n within the expression. For example, the expression (\w)ee\1 matches deed and peep. In the following example, we find all words in a string starting and ending in the same letter:

```
foreach (Match m in Regex.Matches ("pop pope peep", @"\b(\w)\w+\1\b"))
  Console.Write (m + " ");  // pop peep
```

The brackets around the \w instruct the regular expressions engine to store the submatch in a group (in this case, a single letter), so it can be used later. We refer to that group later using \1, meaning the first group in the expression.

Named Groups

In a long or complex expression, it can be easier to work with groups by *name* rather than index. Here's a rewrite of the previous example, using a group that we name 'letter':

```
string regEx =
  @"\b"              + // word boundary
  @"(?'letter'\w)"   + // match first letter, and name it 'letter'
  @"\w+"             + // match middle letters
  @"\k'letter'"      + // match last letter, denoted by 'letter'
  @"\b";               // word boundary

foreach (Match m in Regex.Matches ("bob pope peep", regEx))
  Console.Write (m + " ");  // bob peep
```

To name a captured group:

```
(?'group-name'group-expr)  or  (?<group-name>group-expr)
```

To refer to a group:

```
\k'group-name'  or  \k<group-name>
```

The following example matches a simple (nonnested) XML element, by looking for start and end nodes with a matching name:

```
string regFind =
  @"<(?'tag'\w+?).*>" + // match first tag, and name it 'tag'
  @"(?'text'.*?)"     + // match text content, name it 'text'
  @"</\k'tag'>";        // match last tag, denoted by 'tag'

Match m = Regex.Match ("<h1>hello</h1>", regFind);
Console.WriteLine (m.Groups ["tag"]);     // h1
Console.WriteLine (m.Groups ["text"]);    // hello
```

Allowing for all possible variations in XML structure, such as nested elements, is more complex. The .NET regular expressions engine has a sophisticated extension called "matched balanced constructs" that can assist with nested tags—information on this is available on the Internet and in *Mastering Regular Expressions*, by Jeffrey E. F. Friedl (O'Reilly).

Replacing and Splitting Text

The RegEx.Replace method works like string.Replace, except that it uses a regular expression.

The following replaces "cat" with "dog". Unlike with string.Replace, "catapult" won't change into "dogapult", because we match on word boundaries:

```
string find = @"\bcat\b";
string replace = "dog";
Console.WriteLine (Regex.Replace ("catapult the cat", find, replace));

OUTPUT: catapult the dog
```

The replacement string can reference the original match with the **$0** substitution construct. The following example wraps numbers within a string in angle brackets:

```
string text = "10 plus 20 makes 30";
Console.WriteLine (Regex.Replace (text, @"\d+", @"<$0>"));
```

OUTPUT: <10> plus <20> makes <30>

You can access any captured groups with **$1**, **$2**, **$3**, and so on, or **${**name**}** for a named group. To illustrate how this can be useful, consider the regular expression in the previous section that matched a simple XML element. By rearranging the groups, we can form a replacement expression that moves the element's content into an XML attribute:

```
string regFind =
  @"<(?'tag'\w+?).*>" +   // match first tag, and name it 'tag'
  @"(?'text'.*?)"    +   // match text content, name it 'text'
  @"</\k'tag'>";         // match last tag, denoted by 'tag'

string regReplace =
  @"<${tag}"    +    // <tag
  @" value="""  +    // value="
  @"${text}"    +    // text
  @"""/>";           // "/>

Console.Write (Regex.Replace ("<msg>hello</msg>", regFind, regReplace));
```

Here's the result:

```
<msg value="hello"/>
```

MatchEvaluator Delegate

Replace has an overload that takes a MatchEvaluator delegate, which is invoked per match. This allows you to delegate the content of the replacement string to C# code when the regular expressions language isn't expressive enough. For example:

```
Console.WriteLine (Regex.Replace ("5 is less than 10", @"\d+",
                    m => (int.Parse (m.Value) * 10).ToString()) );
```

OUTPUT: 50 is less than 100

In the cookbook, we show how to use a MatchEvaluator to escape Unicode characters appropriately for HTML.

Splitting Text

The static Regex.Split method is a more powerful version of the string.Split method, with a regular expression denoting the separator pattern. In this example, we split a string, where any digit counts as a separator:

```
foreach (string s in Regex.Split ("a5b7c", @"\d"))
  Console.Write (s + " ");      // a b c
```

The result, here, doesn't include the separators themselves. You can include the separators, however, by wrapping the expression in a positive lookahead. The following splits a camel-case string into separate words:

```
foreach (string s in Regex.Split ("oneTwoThree", @"(?=[A-Z])"))
  Console.Write (s + " ");   // one Two Three
```

Cookbook Regular Expressions

Recipes

Matching U.S. Social Security number/phone number

```
string ssNum = @"\d{3}-\d{2}-\d{4}";

Console.WriteLine (Regex.IsMatch ("123-45-6789", ssNum));      // True

string phone = @"(?x)
  ( \d{3}[-\s] | \(\d{3}\)\s? )
    \d{3}[-\s]?
    \d{4}";

Console.WriteLine (Regex.IsMatch ("123-456-7890",   phone));   // True
Console.WriteLine (Regex.IsMatch ("(123) 456-7890", phone));   // True
```

Extracting "name = value" pairs (one per line)

Note that this starts with the *multiline* directive (?m):

```
string r = @"(?m)^\s*(?'name'\w+)\s*=\s*(?'value'.*)\s*(?=\r?$)";

string text =
  @"id = 3
    secure = true
    timeout = 30";

foreach (Match m in Regex.Matches (text, r))
  Console.WriteLine (m.Groups["name"] + " is " + m.Groups["value"]);

id is 3
secure is true
timeout is 30
```

Strong password validation

The following checks whether a password has at least six characters, and whether it contains a digit, symbol, or punctuation mark:

```
string r = @"(?x)^(?=.* ( \d | \p{P} | \p{S} )).{6,}";

Console.WriteLine (Regex.IsMatch ("abc12", r));    // False
Console.WriteLine (Regex.IsMatch ("abcdef", r));   // False
Console.WriteLine (Regex.IsMatch ("ab88yz", r));   // True
```

Lines of at least 80 characters

```
string r = @"(?m)^.{80,}(?=\r?$)";

string fifty = new string ('x', 50);
string eighty = new string ('x', 80);

string text = eighty + "\r\n" + fifty + "\r\n" + eighty;

Console.WriteLine (Regex.Matches (text, r).Count);   // 2
```

Parsing dates/times (N/N/N H:M:S AM/PM)

This expression handles a variety of numeric date formats—and works whether the year comes first or last. The **(?x)** directive improves readability by allowing whitespace; the **(?i)** switches off case sensitivity (for the optional AM/PM designator). You can then access each component of the match through the Groups collection:

```
string r = @"(?x)(?i)
  (\d{1,4}) [./-]
  (\d{1,2}) [./-]
  (\d{1,4}) [\sT]  (\d+):(\d+):(\d+) \s? (A\.?M\.?|P\.?M\.?)?";

string text = "01/02/2008 5:20:50 PM";

foreach (Group g in Regex.Match (text, r).Groups)
  Console.WriteLine (g.Value + " ");
```

```
01/02/2008 5:20:50 PM
01
02
2008
5
20
50
PM
```

Matching Roman numerals

```
string r =
  @"(?i)\bm*"          +
  @"(d?c{0,3}|c[dm])" +
  @"(l?x{0,3}|x[lc])" +
  @"(v?i{0,3}|i[vx])" +
  @"\b";

Console.WriteLine (Regex.IsMatch ("MCMLXXXIV", r));   // True
```

Removing repeated words

Here, we capture a named grouped called dupe:

```
string r = @"(?'dupe'\w+)\W\k'dupe'";

string text = "In the the beginning...";
```

```
Console.WriteLine (Regex.Replace (text, r, "${dupe}"));

In the beginning
```

Word count

```
string r = @"\b(\w|[-'])+\b";

string text = "It's all mumbo-jumbo to me";
Console.WriteLine (Regex.Matches (text, r).Count);   // 5
```

Matching a Guid

```
string r =
  @"(?i)\b"              +
  @"[0-9a-fA-F]{8}\-" +
  @"[0-9a-fA-F]{4}\-" +
  @"[0-9a-fA-F]{4}\-" +
  @"[0-9a-fA-F]{4}\-" +
  @"[0-9a-fA-F]{12}"  +
  @"\b";

string text = "Its key is {3F2504E0-4F89-11D3-9A0C-0305E82C3301}.";
Console.WriteLine (Regex.Match (text, r).Index);                // 12
```

Parsing an XML tag

```
string r =
  @"<(?'tag'\w+?).*>"  +  // match first tag, and name it 'tag'
  @"(?'text'.*?)"      +  // match text content, name it 'text'
  @"</\k'tag'>";          // match last tag, denoted by 'tag'

string text = "<h1>hello</h1>";

Match m = Regex.Match (text, r);

Console.WriteLine (m.Groups ["tag"]);        // h1
Console.WriteLine (m.Groups ["text"]);       // hello
```

Splitting a camel-cased word

This requires a positive lookahead to include the uppercase separators:

```
string r = @"(?=[A-Z])";

foreach (string s in Regex.Split ("oneTwoThree", r))
  Console.Write (s + " ");     // one Two Three
```

Obtaining a legal filename

```
string input = "My \"good\" <recipes>.txt";

char[] invalidChars = System.IO.Path.GetInvalidPathChars();
string invalidString = Regex.Escape (new string (invalidChars));

string valid = Regex.Replace (input, "[" + invalidString + "]", "");
```

```
Console.WriteLine (valid);

My good recipes.txt
```

Escaping Unicode characters for HTML

```
string htmlFragment = "© 2007";

string result = Regex.Replace (htmlFragment, @"[\u0080-\uFFFF]",
        m => @"&#" + ((int)m.Value[0]).ToString() + ";");

Console.WriteLine (result);        // &#169; 2007
```

Regular Expressions Language Reference

Tables 24-2 through 24-12 summarize the regular expressions grammar and syntax supported in the .NET implementation. For further information on regular expressions, we recommend the definitive *Mastering Regular Expressions* by Jeffrey E. F. Friedl (O'Reilly).

All the syntax described in the tables should match the Perl5 syntax, with specific exceptions noted.

Table 24-2. Character escapes

Escape code sequence	Meaning	Hexadecimal equivalent
\a	Bell	\u0007
\b	Backspace	\u0008
\t	Tab	\u0009
\r	Carriage return	\u000A
\v	Vertical tab	\u000B
\f	Form feed	\u000C
\n	Newline	\u000D
\e	Escape	\u001B
\nnn	ASCII character nnn as octal (e.g., \n052)	
\xnn	ASCII character nn as hex (e.g., \x3F)	
\cl	ASCII control character l (e.g., \cG for control-G)	
\unnnn	Unicode character nnnn as hex (e.g., \u07DE)	
\symbol	A nonescaped symbol	

Special case: within a regular expression, \b means word boundary, except in a [ ] set, in which \b means the backspace character.

Table 24-3. Character sets

Expression	Meaning	Inverse ("not")
[abcdef]	Matches a single character in the list	[^abcdef]
[a-f]	Matches a single character in a *range*	[^a-f]

Table 24-3. Character sets (continued)

Expression	Meaning	Inverse ("not")
\d	Matches a decimal digit Same as [0-9]	\D
\w	Matches a *word* character (by default, varies according to CultureInfo.CurrentCulture; for example, in English, same as [a-zA-Z_0-9])	\W
\s	Matches a whitespace character Same as [\n\r\t\f]	\S
\p{*category*}	Matches a character in a specified *category* (see Table 24-6)	\P
.	(Default mode) Matches any character except \n	\n
.	(SingleLine mode) Matches any character	\n

Table 24-4. Character categories

Quantifier	Meaning
\p{L}	Letters
\p{Lu}	Uppercase letters
\p{Ll}	Lowercase letters
\p{N}	Numbers
\p{P}	Punctuation
\p{M}	Diacritic marks
\p{S}	Symbols
\p{Z}	Separators
\p{C}	Control characters

Table 24-5. Quantifiers

Quantifier	Meaning
*	Zero or more matches
+	One or more matches
?	Zero or one match
{*n*}	Exactly *n* matches
{*n*,}	At least *n* matches
{*n*,*m*}	Between *n* and *m* matches

The ? suffix can be applied to any of the quantifiers to make them *lazy* rather than *greedy*.

Table 24-6. Substitutions

Expression	Meaning
$0	Substitutes the matched text
$*group-number*	Substitutes an indexed *group-number* within the matched text
${*group-name*}	Substitutes a text *group-name* within the matched text

Substitutions are specified only within a replacement pattern.

Table 24-7. Zero-width assertions

Expression	Meaning
^	Start of string (or line in *multiline* mode)
$	End of string (or line in *multiline* mode)
\A	Start of string (ignores *multiline* mode)
\z	End of string (ignores *multiline* mode)
\Z	End of line or string
\G	Where search started
\b	On a word boundary
\B	Not on a word boundary
(?=*expr*)	Continue matching only if expression *expr* matches on right (positive lookahead)
(?!*expr*)	Continue matching only if expression *expr* doesn't match on right (negative lookahead)
(?<=*expr*)	Continue matching only if expression *expr* matches on left (positive lookbehind)
(?<!*expr*)	Continue matching only if expression *expr* doesn't match on left (negative lookbehind)
(?>*expr*)	Subexpression *expr* is matched once and not backtracked

Table 24-8. Grouping constructs

Syntax	Meaning
(*expr*)	Capture matched expression *expr* into indexed group
(?*number*)	Capture matched substring into a specified group *number*
(?'*name*')	Capture matched substring into group *name*
(?'*name1-name2*')	Undefine *name2*, and store interval and current group into *name1*; if *name2* is undefined, matching backtracks; *name1* is optional
(?:*expr*)	Noncapturing group

Table 24-9. Back references

Parameter syntax	Meaning
index	Reference a previously captured group by *index*
\k<*name*>	Reference a previously captured group by *name*

Table 24-10. Alternation

Expression syntax	Meaning
|	Logical OR
(?(*expr*)*yes*|*no*)	Matches *yes* if expression matches; otherwise, matches *no* (*no* is optional)
(?(*name*)*yes*|*no*)	Matches *yes* if named group has a match; otherwise, matches *no* (*no* is optional)

Table 24-11. Miscellaneous constructs

Expression syntax	Meaning
`(?#comment)`	Inline comment
`#comment`	Comment to end of line (works only in `IgnorePatternWhitespace` mode)

Table 24-12. Regular expression options

Option	Meaning
`(?i)`	Case-insensitive match ("ignore" case)
`(?m)`	Multiline mode; changes ^ and $ so that they match beginning and end of any line
`(?n)`	Captures only explicitly named or numbered groups
`(?c)`	Compiles to IL
`(?s)`	Single-line mode; changes meaning of "." so that it matches every character
`(?x)`	Eliminates unescaped whitespace from the pattern
`(?r)`	Searches from right to left; can't be specified midstream

A

C# Keywords

abstract
: A class modifier that specifies a class cannot be instantiated and the full implementation will be provided by a subclass.

: A method modifier that specifies a method is implicitly virtual and without an implementation.

alias
: Suffixes an extern directive.

as
: A binary operator that casts the left operand to the type specified by the right operand and returns null rather than throwing an exception if the cast fails.

ascending
: A query comprehension operator used in conjunction with orderby.

base
: A variable with the same meaning as this, except that it accesses a base-class implementation of a member.

bool
: A logical datatype that can be true or false.

break
: A jump statement that exits a loop or switch statement block.

by
: A query comprehension operator used in conjunction with group.

byte
: A one-byte, unsigned integral data type.

case
: A selection statement that defines a particular choice in a switch statement.

catch
> A keyword for the clause in a try statement to catch exceptions of a specific type.

char
> A two-byte, Unicode character data type.

checked
> A statement or operator that enforces arithmetic bounds checking on an expression or statement block.

class
> A type declaration keyword for a custom reference type; typically used as a blueprint for creating objects.
>
> A generic type constraint, indicating the generic type must be a reference type.

const
> A modifier for a local variable or field declaration that indicates that the value is statically evaluated and immutable.

continue
> A jump statement that skips the remaining statements in a statement block and continues to the next iteration in a loop.

decimal
> A 16-byte precise decimal datatype.

default
> A special label in a switch statement specifying the action to take when no case statements match the switch expression.
>
> An operator that returns the default value for a type.

delegate
> A type declaration keyword for a type that defines a protocol for a method.

descending
> A query comprehension operator used in conjunction with orderby.

do
> A loop statement to iterate a statement block until an expression at the end of the loop evaluates to false.

double
> An eight-byte, floating-point data type.

else
> A conditional statement that defines the action to take when a preceding if expression evaluates to false.

enum
> A type declaration keyword that defines a value type representing a group of named numeric constants.

equals
> A query comprehension operator that performs an equijoin, used in conjunction with join.

event
> A member modifier for a field or property of a delegate type that indicates that only the += and -= methods of the delegate can be accessed.

explicit
> An operator that defines an explicit conversion.

extern
> A method modifier that indicates that the method is implemented with unmanaged code.
>
> A directive that declares a reference to an external namespace, which must correspond to an argument passed to the C# compiler.

false
> A literal of the bool type.

finally
> The keyword in the clause of a try statement that executes whenever control leaves the scope of the try block.

fixed
> A statement to pin down a reference type so the garbage collector won't move it during pointer arithmetic operations.
>
> A field modifier within an unsafe struct to declare a fixed length array.

float
> A four-byte, floating-point data type.

for
> A loop statement that combines an initialization statement, continuation condition, and iterative statement into one statement.

foreach
> A loop statement that iterates over collections that implement IEnumerable.

from
> A query comprehension operator that specifies the sequence from which to query.

get
> The name of the accessor that returns the value of a property.

global
> A keyword placed in front of an identifier to indicate the identifier is qualified with the global namespace.

goto
> A jump statement that jumps to a label within the same method and same scope as the jump point.

group
> A query comprehension operator that splits a sequence into a group given a key value to group by.

if
> A conditional statement that executes its statement block if its expression evaluates to true.

implicit
> An operator that defines an implicit conversion.

in
> The operator between a type and an IEnumerable in a foreach statement.
>
> A query comprehension operator used in conjunction with from.

int
> A 4-byte, signed integral data type.

into
> A query comprehension operator that specifies a name for an output sequence.

interface
> A type declaration keyword for a custom reference type that defines a contract for a type comprising a set of implicitly abstract members.

internal
> An access modifier that indicates that a type or type member is accessible only to other types in the same assembly.

is
> A relational operator that evaluates to true if the left operand's type matches, is derived from, or implements the type specified by the right operand.

let
> A query comprehension operator that introduces a new variable into each element in a sequence.

lock
> A statement that acquires a lock on a reference-type object to help multiple threads cooperate.

long
> An 8-byte, signed integral data type.

namespace
> A keyword for defining a name that encloses a set of types in a hierarchical name.

new
> An operator that calls a constructor on a type, allocating a new object on the heap if the type is a reference type or initializing the object if the type is a value type.
>
> A type member modifier that hides an inherited member with a new member with the same signature.

> A reference-type literal meaning no object is referenced.

object
> A predefined type that is the ultimate base class for all types.

on
> A query comprehension operator used in conjunction with join or group.

operator
> A method modifier that overloads operators.

orderby
> A query comprehension operator that sorts a sequence.

out
> A parameter and argument modifier that specifies that the variable is passed by reference and must be assigned by the method being called.

override
> A method modifier that indicates that a method of a class overrides a virtual method defined by a base class.

params
> A parameter modifier that specifies that the last parameter of a method may accept multiple parameters of the same type.

partial
> A class or method modifier that indicates the definition of the class or method is split (typically across files).

private
> An access modifier that indicates that only the containing type can access the member.

protected
> An access modifier that indicates that only the containing type or derived types can access the member.

public
> An access modifier that indicates that a type or type member is accessible to all other types.

readonly
> A field modifier specifying that a field can be assigned only once, either in its declaration or in its containing type's constructor.

ref
> A parameter and argument modifier that specifies that the variable is passed by reference and is assigned before being passed to the method.

return
> A jump statement that that exits a method, specifying a return value when the method is not void.

sbyte
> A 1-byte, signed integral data type.

sealed
> A class modifier that indicates a class cannot be derived from.

set
> The name of the accessor that sets the value of a property.

short
> A 2-byte, signed integral data type.

sizeof
> An operator that returns the size in bytes of a struct.

stackalloc
> An operator that returns a pointer to a specified number of value types allocated on the stack.

static
> A type member modifier that indicates that the member applies to the type rather than to an instance of the type.
>
> A class modifier indicating the class is comprised of only static members and cannot be instantiated.

string
> A predefined reference type that represents an immutable sequence of Unicode characters.

struct
> A type declaration keyword for a custom value type; typically used as a blueprint for creating light-weight instances.
>
> A generic type constraint, indicating the generic type must be a value type.

switch
> A selection statement that allows a selection of choices to be made based on the value of a predefined type.

this
> A variable that references the current instance of a class or struct.
>
> A parameter modifier for the first parameter in a static method, making the method an extension method.

throw
> A jump statement that throws an exception when an abnormal condition has occurred.

true
> A literal of the bool type.

try
> A statement that defines a statement block where errors can be caught and handled.

typeof
> An operator that returns the type of an object as a System.Type object.

uint
: A 4-byte, unsigned integral data type.

ulong
: An 8-byte, unsigned integral data type.

unchecked
: A statement or operator that prevents arithmetic bounds checking on an expression.

unsafe
: A type modifier, member modifier, or statement that permits executing code that is not type-safe (notably, that uses pointer arithmetic).

ushort
: A 2-byte, unsigned integral data type.

using
: A directive that specifies that types in a particular namespace can be referred to without requiring their fully qualified type names.

: A statement that allows an object implementing IDisposable to be disposed of at the end of the statement's scope.

value
: A name used for the implicit variable set by the set accessor of a property.

virtual
: A class method modifier that indicates that a method can be overridden by a derived class.

void
: A keyword used in place of a type for methods that don't have a return value.

volatile
: A field modifier indicating that a field's value may be modified in a multi-threaded scenario; neither the compiler nor runtime should perform optimizations with that field.

while
: A loop statement to iterate a statement block while an expression at the start of each iteration evaluates to false.

yield
: A statement that yields the next element from an iterator block.

B

Namespace-to-Assembly Reference

Table B-1 is an alphabetical summary of namespaces and the list of assemblies in which each namespace is located.

Table B-1. Namespace-to-assembly reference

Namespace	Assemblies
Microsoft.Win32	*mscorlib*
	PresentationFramework
	System
Microsoft.Win32.SafeHandles	*mscorlib*
	System.Core
Microsoft.Windows.Themes	*PresentationFramework.Aero*
	PresentationFramework.Classic
	PresentationFramework.Luna
	PresentationFramework.Royale
System	*mscorlib*
	System
	System.Core
System.AddIn	*System.AddIn*
	System.Core
System.AddIn.Contract	*System.AddIn.Contract*
System.AddIn.Contract.Automation	*System.AddIn.Contract*
System.AddIn.Contract.Collections	*System.AddIn.Contract*
System.AddIn.Hosting	*System.Core*
System.AddIn.Pipeline	*System.Core*
System.CodeDom	*System*
System.CodeDom.Compiler	*System*
System.Collections	*mscorlib*

Namespace	Assemblies
System.Collections.Generic	*mscorlib*
	System
	System.Core
	System.ServiceModel
System.Collections.ObjectModel	*mscorlib*
	WindowsBase
System.Collections.Specialized	*System*
	WindowsBase
System.ComponentModel	*PresentationFramework*
	System
	WindowsBase
System.ComponentModel.Design	*System*
	System.Design
System.ComponentModel.Design.Data	*System.Design*
System.ComponentModel.Design.Serialization	*System*
	System.Design
System.Configuration	*System*
	System.Configuration
System.Configuration.Assemblies	*mscorlib*
System.Configuration.Install	*System.Configuration.Install*
System.Configuration.Provider	*System.Configuration*
System.Data	*System.Data*
	System.Data.Entity
System.Data.Common	*System.Data*
	System.Data.Entity
System.Data.Common.CommandTrees	*System.Data.Entity*
System.Data.Design	*System.Design*
System.Data.EntityClient	*System.Data.Entity*
System.Data.EntityModel	*System.Data.Entity*
System.Data.Mapping	*System.Data.Entity*
System.Data.Metadata.Edm	*System.Data.Entity*
System.Data.Objects	*System.Data.Entity*
System.Data.Objects.DataClasses	*System.Data.Entity*
System.Data.Odbc	*System.Data*
System.Data.OleDb	*System.Data*
System.Data.OracleClient	*System.Data.OracleClient*
System.Data.Sql	*System.Data*
System.Data.SqlClient	*System.Data*
System.Data.SqlServerCe	*System.Data.SqlServerCe*
System.Data.SqlTypes	*System.Data*

Namespace	Assemblies
System.Diagnostics	*mscorlib*
	System
	System.Configuration.Install
	System.Core
	WindowsBase
System.Diagnostics.CodeAnalysis	*mscorlib*
System.Diagnostics.Design	*System.Design*
System.Diagnostics.Eventing	*System.Core*
System.Diagnostics.PerformanceData	*System.Core*
System.Diagnostics.SymbolStore	*ISymWrapper*
	mscorlib
System.DirectoryServices	*System.DirectoryServices*
System.DirectoryServices.ActiveDirectory	*System.DirectoryServices*
System.DirectoryServices.Protocols	*System.DirectoryServices.Protocols*
System.Drawing	*System.Drawing*
System.Drawing.Design	*System.Drawing*
	System.Drawing.Design
System.Drawing.Drawing2D	*System.Drawing*
System.Drawing.Imaging	*System.Drawing*
System.Drawing.Printing	*System.Drawing*
System.Drawing.Text	*System.Drawing*
System.EnterpriseServices	*System.EnterpriseServices*
System.EnterpriseServices.CompensatingResourceManager	*System.EnterpriseServices*
System.Globalization	*mscorlib*
	sysglobl
System.IdentityModel.Claims	*System.IdentityModel*
System.IdentityModel.Policy	*System.IdentityModel*
System.IdentityModel.Selectors	*System.IdentityModel*
	System.IdentityModel.Selectors
System.IdentityModel.Tokens	*System.IdentityModel*
System.IO	*mscorlib*
	System
	System.Core
	System.ServiceModel
	WindowsBase
System.IO.Compression	*System*
System.IO.IsolatedStorage	*mscorlib*
System.IO.Log	*System.IO.Log*
System.IO.Packaging	*PresentationCore*
	WindowsBase
System.IO.Pipes	*System.Core*
System.IO.Ports	*System*
System.Linq	*System.Core*

Namespace	Assemblies
System.Linq.Expressions	*System.Core*
System.Management	*System.Management*
System.Management.Instrumentation	*System.Management*
System.Media	*System*
System.Messaging	*System.Messaging*
System.Messaging.Design	*System.Design*
	System.Messaging
System.Net	*System*
System.Net.Cache	*System*
System.Net.Configuration	*System*
System.Net.Mail	*System*
System.Net.Mime	*System*
System.Net.NetworkInformation	*System*
System.Net.Security	*System*
System.Net.Sockets	*System*
System.Numeric	*System.Core*
System.Printing	*ReachFramework*
	System.Printing
System.Printing.IndexedProperties	*System.Printing*
System.Printing.Interop	*ReachFramework*
System.Reflection	*mscorlib*
System.Reflection.Emit	*mscorlib*
System.Resources	*mscorlib*
	System.Windows.Forms
System.Resources.Tools	*System.Design*
System.Runtime	*mscorlib*
System.Runtime.CompilerServices	*mscorlib*
	System.Core
System.Runtime.Hosting	*mscorlib*
System.Runtime.InteropServices	*mscorlib*
	System
System.Runtime.InteropServices.ComTypes	*mscorlib*
	System
System.Runtime.InteropServices.CustomMarshalers	*CustomMarshalers*
System.Runtime.InteropServices.Expando	*mscorlib*
System.Runtime.Remoting	*mscorlib*
System.Runtime.Remoting.Activation	*mscorlib*
System.Runtime.Remoting.Channels	*mscorlib*
	System.Runtime.Remoting
System.Runtime.Remoting.Channels.Http	*System.Runtime.Remoting*
System.Runtime.Remoting.Channels.Ipc	*System.Runtime.Remoting*
System.Runtime.Remoting.Channels.Tcp	*System.Runtime.Remoting*

Table B-1. Namespace-to-assembly reference (continued)

Namespace	Assemblies
System.Runtime.Remoting.Contexts	*mscorlib*
System.Runtime.Remoting.Lifetime	*mscorlib*
System.Runtime.Remoting.Messaging	*mscorlib*
System.Runtime.Remoting.Metadata	*mscorlib*
System.Runtime.Remoting.Metadata.W3cXsd2001	*mscorlib*
System.Runtime.Remoting.MetadataServices	*System.Runtime.Remoting*
System.Runtime.Remoting.Proxies	*mscorlib*
System.Runtime.Remoting.Services	*mscorlib* *System.Runtime.Remoting*
System.Runtime.Serialization	*mscorlib* *System.Runtime.Serialization*
System.Runtime.Serialization.Configuration	*System.Runtime.Serialization*
System.Runtime.Serialization.Formatters	*mscorlib*
System.Runtime.Serialization.Formatters.Binary	*mscorlib*
System.Runtime.Serialization.Formatters.Soap	*System.Runtime.Serialization.* *Formatters.Soap*
System.Runtime.Versioning	*mscorlib*
System.Security	*mscorlib* *System.Core*
System.Security.AccessControl	*mscorlib* *System* *System.Core*
System.Security.Authentication	*System*
System.Security.Cryptography	*mscorlib* *System* *System.Core* *System.Security*
System.Security.Cryptography.Pkcs	*System.Security*
System.Security.Cryptography.X509Certificates	*mscorlib* *System* *System.Core* *System.Security*
System.Security.Cryptography.Xml	*System.Security*
System.Security.Permissions	*mscorlib* *System* *System.Security* *WindowsBase*
System.Security.Policy	*mscorlib*
System.Security.Principal	*mscorlib*
System.Security.RightsManagement	*WindowsBase*
System.ServiceModel	*System.ServiceModel*
System.ServiceModel.Activation	*System.ServiceModel*
System.ServiceModel.Activation.Configuration	*System.ServiceModel*

Namespace	Assemblies
System.ServiceModel.Channels	*System.ServiceModel*
System.ServiceModel.ComIntegration	*System.ServiceModel*
System.ServiceModel.Configuration	*System.ServiceModel*
System.ServiceModel.Description	*System.ServiceModel*
System.ServiceModel.Diagnostics	*System.ServiceModel*
System.ServiceModel.Dispatcher	*System.ServiceModel*
System.ServiceModel.Install.Configuration	*System.ServiceModel.Install*
System.ServiceModel.MsmqIntegration	*System.ServiceModel*
System.ServiceModel.PeerResolvers	*System.ServiceModel*
System.ServiceModel.Security	*System.ServiceModel*
System.ServiceModel.Security.Tokens	*System.ServiceModel*
System.ServiceProcess	*System.ServiceProcess*
System.ServiceProcess.Design	*System.Design*
	System.ServiceProcess
System.Speech.AudioFormat	*System.Speech*
System.Speech.Recognition	*System.Speech*
System.Speech.Recognition.SrgsGrammar	*System.Speech*
System.Speech.Synthesis	*System.Speech*
System.Speech.Synthesis.TtsEngine	*System.Speech*
System.Text	*mscorlib*
System.Text.RegularExpressions	*System*
System.Threading	*mscorlib*
	System
	System.Core
System.Timers	*System*
System.Transactions	*System.Transactions*
System.Transactions.Configuration	*System.Transactions*
System.Web	*System*
	System.Web
System.Web.Caching	*System.Web*
System.Web.Compilation	*System.Web*
System.Web.Configuration	*System.Web*
System.Web.Handlers	*System.Web*
System.Web.Hosting	*System.Web*
System.Web.Mail	*System.Web*
System.Web.Management	*System.Web*
	System.Web.Extensions
System.Web.Mobile	*System.Web.Mobile*
System.Web.Profile	*System.Web*
System.Web.RegularExpressions	*System.Web.RegularExpressions*

Namespace	Assemblies
System.Web.Security	*System.Web*
	System.Web.Extensions
System.Web.Services	*System.Web.Services*
System.Web.Services.Configuration	*System.Web.Services*
System.Web.Services.Description	*System.Web.Services*
System.Web.Services.Discovery	*System.Web.Services*
System.Web.Services.Protocols	*System.Web.Services*
System.Web.SessionState	*System.Web*
System.Web.UI	*System.Web*
System.Web.UI.Adapters	*System.Web*
System.Web.UI.Design	*System.Design*
System.Web.UI.Design.MobileControls	*System.Web.Mobile*
System.Web.UI.Design.MobileControls.Converters	*System.Web.Mobile*
System.Web.UI.Design.WebControls	*System.Design*
	System.Web.Extensions
System.Web.UI.Design.WebControls.WebParts	*System.Design*
System.Web.UI.HtmlControls	*System.Web*
System.Web.UI.MobileControls	*System.Web.Mobile*
System.Web.UI.MobileControls.Adapters	*System.Web.Mobile*
System.Web.UI.MobileControls.Adapters.XhtmlAdapters	*System.Web.Mobile*
System.Web.UI.WebControls	*System.Web*
	System.Web.Extensions
System.Web.UI.WebControls.Adapters	*System.Web*
System.Web.UI.WebControls.WebParts	*System.Web*
System.Web.Util	*System.Web*
System.Windows	*PresentationCore*
	PresentationFramework
	WindowsBase
System.Windows.Annotations	*PresentationFramework*
System.Windows.Annotations.Storage	*PresentationFramework*
System.Windows.Automation	*PresentationCore*
	UIAutomationClient
	UIAutomationTypes
System.Windows.Automation.Peers	*PresentationCore*
	PresentationFramework
	WindowsFormsIntegration
System.Windows.Automation.Provider	*UIAutomationProvider*
System.Windows.Automation.Text	*UIAutomationClient*
	UIAutomationTypes
System.Windows.Controls	*PresentationFramework*
System.Windows.Controls.Primitives	*PresentationFramework*
System.Windows.Converters	*WindowsBase*

Namespace	Assemblies
System.Windows.Data	*PresentationFramework* *WindowsBase*
System.Windows.Documents	*PresentationCore* *PresentationFramework* *PresentationUI*
System.Windows.Documents.DocumentStructures	*PresentationFramework*
System.Windows.Documents.Serialization	*PresentationFramework*
System.Windows.Forms	*System.Windows.Forms*
System.Windows.Forms.ComponentModel.Com2Interop	*System.Windows.Forms*
System.Windows.Forms.Design	*System.Design* *System.Windows.Forms*
System.Windows.Forms.Design.Behavior	*System.Design*
System.Windows.Forms.Integration	*WindowsFormsIntegration*
System.Windows.Forms.Layout	*System.Windows.Forms*
System.Windows.Forms.VisualStyles	*System.Windows.Forms*
System.Windows.Ink	*PresentationCore*
System.Windows.Input	*PresentationCore* *PresentationFramework* *WindowsBase*
System.Windows.Input.StylusPlugIns	*PresentationCore*
System.Windows.Interop	*PresentationCore* *PresentationFramework* *WindowsBase*
System.Windows.Markup	*PresentationBuildTasks* *PresentationCore* *PresentationFramework* *WindowsBase*
System.Windows.Markup.Localizer	*PresentationFramework*
System.Windows.Markup.Primitives	*PresentationFramework* *WindowsBase*
System.Windows.Media	*PresentationCore* *PresentationFramework* *WindowsBase*
System.Windows.Media.Animation	*PresentationCore* *PresentationFramework*
System.Windows.Media.Converters	*PresentationCore* *WindowsBase*
System.Windows.Media.Effects	*PresentationCore*
System.Windows.Media.Imaging	*PresentationCore*
System.Windows.Media.Media3D	*PresentationCore*
System.Windows.Media.Media3D.Converters	*PresentationCore*
System.Windows.Media.TextFormatting	*PresentationCore*

Namespace-to-Assembly

Table B-1. Namespace-to-assembly reference (continued)

Namespace	Assemblies
System.Windows.Navigation	*PresentationCore* *PresentationFramework*
System.Windows.Resources	*PresentationCore* *PresentationFramework*
System.Windows.Shapes	*PresentationFramework*
System.Windows.Threading	*WindowsBase*
System.Windows.Xps	*ReachFramework* *System.Printing*
System.Windows.Xps.Packaging	*ReachFramework*
System.Windows.Xps.Serialization	*ReachFramework*
System.Workflow.Activities	*System.Workflow.Activities*
System.Workflow.Activities.Configuration	*System.Workflow.Activities*
System.Workflow.Activities.Rules	*System.Workflow.Activities*
System.Workflow.Activities.Rules.Design	*System.Workflow.Activities*
System.Workflow.ComponentModel	*System.Workflow.ComponentModel*
System.Workflow.ComponentModel.Compiler	*System.Workflow.ComponentModel*
System.Workflow.ComponentModel.Design	*System.Workflow.ComponentModel*
System.Workflow.ComponentModel.Serialization	*System.Workflow.ComponentModel*
System.Workflow.Runtime	*System.Workflow.Runtime*
System.Workflow.Runtime.Configuration	*System.Workflow.Runtime*
System.Workflow.Runtime.DebugEngine	*System.Workflow.Runtime*
System.Workflow.Runtime.Hosting	*System.Workflow.Runtime*
System.Workflow.Runtime.Tracking	*System.Workflow.Runtime*
System.Xml	*System.Data* *System.Runtime.Serialization* *System.Xml*
System.Xml.Linq	*System.Xml.Linq*
System.Xml.Schema	*System.Xml* *System.Xml.Linq*
System.Xml.Serialization	*System.Xml*
System.Xml.Serialization.Advanced	*System.Xml*
System.Xml.Serialization.Configuration	*System.Xml*
System.Xml.XPath	*System.Xml* *System.Xml.Linq*
System.Xml.Xsl	*System.Xml*
System.Xml.Xsl.Runtime	*System.Data.SqlXml*

Index

We'd like to hear your suggestions for improving our indexes. Send email to *index@oreilly.com*.

?? (null coalescing) operator, 138, 377
|= (Or self by) operator, 45
.. (parent node) operator, 415
% (percent sign), remainder
        operator, 23, 45
  use with nullable types, 137
. (period)
  member access operator, 44
  regular expression
        metacharacter, 759
+ (plus sign)
  addition operator, 23, 45
    use with enums, 94
    use with nullable types, 137
    using with time spans, 182
  positive value of operator, 44, 137
  regular expression
        metacharacter, 759
  regular expression quantifier, 761
  string concatenation operator, 30
-> (pointer-to-member) operator, 150
-> (printer to struct) operator
        (unsafe), 44
? (question mark)
  in nullable types, 135
  regular expression
        metacharacter, 759
  regular expression quantifier, 756
<< (shift left) operator, 45
  use with nullable types, 137
>> (shift right) operator, 45
  use with nullable types, 137
<<= (shift self left by) operator, 45
>>= (shift self right by) operator, 45
/ (slash)
  division operator, 23, 45
    use with nullable types, 137
  XPath, child operator, 415
-= (subtract from self) operator, 45
  event accessor implementation, 116
  use with enums, 94
  using with delegate operands, 107
~ (tilde)
  bitwise complement operator, 25, 44
    use with enums, 94
  logical complement operator, use
      with nullable types, 137
  prefixing finalizers, 71
:: token for namespace alias
      qualification, 59

| (vertical bar)
  bitwise Or operator, 25
    operating on combined enum
      values, 93
    use with nullable types, 137
  logical Or operator, 45
    use with bool? type
      operands, 137
    use with nullable types, 137
  regular expression
        metacharacter, 759
  regular expressions, alternation, 757
// XPath operator, querying all child
      nodes, 415

Numbers

\0 (nulls, escape sequence), 29
8- and 16-bit integral types, 25

A

\a (alert) escape sequence, 29
Abort method, Thread class, 683
  Interrrupt method vs., 683
  safe cancellation, 684
absolute filenames, 438
absolute URIs, 551
abstract classes and abstract
      members, 76
  interface members, 87
abstract modifier, 775
  events, 117
access modifiers, 85
  examples of use, 86
  restrictions on, 86
accessibility
  capping, 86
  virtual and overridden methods, 76
accessors, event, 116
ACLs (Access Control Lists), 624
acronyms, networking, 470
Action delegates, 242
Action delegates, 119
Activator class, CreateInstance
      method, 566
add and remove keywords, 117
AddAfterSelf (LINQ to XML), 375
AddBeforeSelf method (LINQ to
      XML), 375

B

\b (backspace), 29
\b (word boundary) regular expressions, assertion, 763
backend technologies, 167
background threads, 647
BackgroundWorker class, 686–690
  cancellation support, adding, 687
  disposal of, 425
  minimum steps in using, 686
  progress reporting support, adding, 687
  RunWorkerCompleted event, 687
  subclassing, 688
backing store streams, 433, 437
  chaining
    compression example, 462
  closing, 436
backing stores, 432
base 64 encoding, converting, 208
base class generic constraint, 101
base classes
  constructors, order of execution, 79
  inheritance from, 74
  specifying for partial classes, 72
base keyword, 79, 775
base types, 206
Basic Multilingual Plane (BMP), Unicode, 181
BeginInvoke and EndInvoke methods, 650
BeginInvoke and Invoke methods, 664
BeginReverseEcho and EndReverseEcho methods (example), 704–706
big-endian or little-endian order, 450
binary formatters
  BinaryFormatter class, 518
  two-way versioning robustness, 521
  using with data contract serializers, 505
  XML formatters vs., 501
binary search methods, arrays, 244
binary serialization, 519–525
  with ISerializable, 522–525
    subclassing serializable classes, 524
  [NonSerialized] attribute, 519
  [OnDeserializing] and [OnDeserialized] attributes, 519

[OnSerializing] and [OnSerialized] attributes, 520
[OptionalField] attribute and versioning, 521
binary serializer, 498, 500, 517–518
  adding [Serializable] attribute to a type, 517
  formatters, 517
  shaping of output by formatters, 501
binary stream adapters, 450
BinaryReader and BinaryWriter classes, 450
  encoding text messages between TCP client/server, 495
binding, dynamic, 573
  reducing with use of delegates, 574
BindingFlags enum, 574
  retrieving nonpublic members with, 575
BitArray class, 253
BitConverter class, 209, 445
bit-mapped attributes, 580
bitwise operators, 25
  working with combined enum values, 93
blocked threads
  forcibly releasing with Abort method, 683
  forcibly releasing with Interrupt method, 682
blocking threads, 652
  asynchronous methods and, 698
  spinning vs., 653
BMP (Basic Multilingual Plane), Unicode, 181
bool? type operands, use with & and | operators, 137
bool types, 14, 27
  conversions, 28
  equality and comparison operators, 28
bounds-checking array indexing, 34
boxing and unboxing, 82
  boxing forced by object.Equals method on value types, 218
  copying semantics of, 82
  interfaces and boxing, 91
  nullable values, 136
branching execution
  bool type, 14
  in IL, 589

break statements, 51
broadcasters, 112
BufferedStream class, 445
    asynchronous method pattern
        and, 707
buffers
    fixed size, 150
    size for a FileStream, 440
built-in types, 14
byte type, 25

C

C#
    compiler, xiv
    new features in Version 3.0, 4–7
    platform support, 3
    relationship with CLR, 3
<c> tag, XML, 156
C++ templates, C# generics vs., 103
Calendar object, use with
        DateTime, 185
callbacks, P/Invoke layer and, 726
cancellation (threads), 684
    BackgroundWorker class, 687
capping accessibility, 86
capturing, outer variables, 120
CardSpace, 169
case-insensitive comparisons,
        strings, 176
cast operator, 44
Cast query operator, 353
casting, 74
    as operator, using, 75
    boxing and unboxing, 82
    downcasting, 75
    enums to and from underlying
        integral type, 94
    in explicit type conversions, 16
    explicit cast of nullable types, 136
    to nullable types, use with Element
        and Attribute methods, 377
    between numeric types, 207
    object to any interface it
        implements, 87
    struct to an interface, 91
    upcasting, 75
    value types, to and from object, 81
catch clause (try statements), 122
    multiple catch clauses to specify
        specific exception types, 124

preventing program termination, 123
    specifying type of exception to
        catch, 123
CDATA (XML file), 398
certificates, SSL, 486
Char class, 170
char keyword, 776
char literal escape sequences, use in
        strings, 30
char type, 29, 170
    static methods for categorizing
        characters, 170
character encodings, 449
character sets, 179
    in regular expressions, 759
characters, escape sequence, 29
/checked+ command-line switch, 25
checked keyword, 776
checked operator, 24, 44
child nodes
    navigation in X-DOM, 369–372
    updating, 374
circular dependencies, 603
class keyword, 776
classes, 1, 60
    abstract, and abstract members, 76
    attribute, 147
    constants, 69
    declaring, 60
    defined, 10
    equality comparisons, GetHashCode
        method, 221
    equality customization and, 219
    fields, 60
    finalizers, 71
    implementing interfaces, 87
    indexers, 67
    inheritance (see inheritance)
    instance constructors, 62
    interfaces vs., when to use, 91
    marshaling, 724
    methods, 61
    object initializers, 64
    partial classes and methods, 72
    properties, 65
    sealing, 78
    static, 15, 71
    static constructors, 70
    this reference, 64
ClickOnce, applications deployed
        with, 625

Close method, 424
    stream adapters, 451
    Stream class, 436
closed generic types, 97
    static data, uniqueness of, 103
    typeof operator, using, 100
CLR (Common Language Runtime), 3
    place in .NET Framework, 159
    (see also garbage collection)
code
    examples from this book, using, xvi
    generating dynamically, 585–591
    unsafe, 148
code access security, 618
code invariants, 742
code point (Unicode), 179
<code> tag, XML, 156
CodeAccessPermission class, 613
    RevertAssert method, 623
    subclasses, 616
CollectionDataContract attribute, 512
collections, 229–273
    Array class, 239–247
        construction and
            indexing, 241–242
        enumeration, 242
        length and rank, finding, 243
        reversing elements, 246
        searching, 243
        sorting, 245
    BitArray class, 253
    customizable and proxies, 262–268
        CollectionBase class, 264
        Collection<T> class, 262–264
        DictionaryBase class, 267
        KeyedCollection<TKey,TItem>,
            265–267
        ReadOnlyCollection<T>, 267
    dictionaries, 256–262
        dictionary classes, listed, 256
        IDictionary and
            IDictionary<TKey,-
            TValue>, 257
        sorted dictionaries, 260
    enumeration, 230–236
        IDictionaryEnumerator
            interface, 236
        IEnumerable and
            IEnumerator, 230
        implementing
            interfaces, 232–235
        thread safety and, 661

equality comparisons, 219
HashSet<T>, 254
ICollection and IList
        interfaces, 236–238
    IList and IList<T>, 238
lists, 247–252
    LinkedList<T> class, 250
    List<T> and ArrayList, 248–250
namespaces, 229
plug-in equality and order, 268–273
    IComparer and Comparer, 270
    IEqualityComparer and
        EqualityComparer, 268
    StringComparer, 272
queues, 252
serialization with data contract
        serializers, 511–513
    customizing collection and
        element names, 512
    subclassed collection
        elements, 512
serialization with
        XmlSerializer, 530–532
stacks, 253
[Column] attribute, 307
COM+ and MSMQ, 168
COM interoperability, online material
        covering, 164
combinable enums, 93
comments, 8, 13
    XML, 398
    XML documentation
        comments, 153–158
        predefined XML tags, 155–157
        type or member cross-
            references, 157
        user-defined XML tags, 157
CommonApplicationData folder, 459
    isolated storage vs., 463
Comparer<T> class, 271
CompareTo method
    IComparable interfaces, 224
    String class, 175, 177, 224
    strings, 31
comparison operators, 28
    strings and, 31
    using with enums, 94
Comparison<T> delegate, 245
compilation, 10
    conditional (see conditional
        compilation)
compile time, type safety enforced at, 2

numeric, summary of, 209
query operators, 353–355
type converters, 208
XmlConvert class, 208
(see also Convert class; formatting and parsing)
Convert class, 206
base 64 conversions, 208
converting base types to every other base type, 206
dynamic conversions with ChangeType method, 207
parsing numbers in base 2, 8, and 16, 207
rounding real to integral conversions, 207
cookies, 484
forms authentication and, 485
Count query operator, 357
covariance, 111
generic types and, 102
CredentialCache object, 479
DefaultNetworkCredentials property, 479
Credentials property, WebClient or WebRequest class, 478
cross-platform code, writing in C#, 3
cross-references
<see> tag, XML, 156
<seealso> tag, XML, 156
XML type or member cross-references, 157
cryptographically strong random values, 632
cryptography, 627–638
encryption permissions, 617
hashing, 629
public key, encryption and signing, 635–638
digital signing, 637
RSA class, 636
summary of options in .NET, 627
support in .NET, 612
symmetric encryption, 630–635
chaining encryption streams, 633
encrypting in memory, 632
Windows Data Protection, 628
CryptoStream class, 631
asynchronous method pattern and, 707

chaining with other streams, 633
disposal of, 426, 634
CryptoStreamMode enum, 631
.cs files (source code), 10
csc.exe (see compiler)
culture codes, 553
culture-dependent comparison, strings, 224
CultureInfo class, 196, 553
format providers and, 196
cultures, 553
AssemblyCulture attribute, 543
culture-sensitive comparisons, strings
case-sensitive order comparison, 177
ordinal comparison vs., 176
CurrentCulture property, 553
CurrentUICulture property, 553
custom attributes, 580
attaching to dynamic constructs, 600
retrieving at runtime, 583
custom format strings, 199
numeric, 201
CustomAttributeData class, 584

D

data contract name, 504
data contract namespace, 504
data contract serializers, 498, 502–511
attaching attributes to make types serializable, 503
binary formatter, using, 505
DataContractSerializer, 502
extending, 513–517
binary interoperability, 515
interoperating with IXmlSerializable, 516
serialization and deserialization hooks, 514
instantiating and calling WriteObject or ReadObject, 503
NetDataContractSerializer, 502
null or empty values for data members, 510
object references, 507
preserving, 508
ordering of data members, 510
overriding names for data members, 504
overview, 500
purpose of, 499

interface generic constraint, 101
interfaces, 1, 87–92
  boxing and, 91
  classes vs., when to use, 91
  collections, 236
  delegates vs., 109
  explicit implementation, 88
  extending, 88
  extension methods, 145
  getting interface implemented by a
    type, 565
  IList, 238
  implementing, 87
  implementing members virtually, 89
  reimplementing in a subclass, 89
    alternatives to, 90
Interlocked class, 665
Intermediate Language (see IL)
internal (access modifier), 85
internal type with public members, 86
Internet addressing systems, 471
Interop attribute reference, 734–737
interpreted queries (LINQ), 300–306
  AsEnumerable operator, 305
  combining with local queries, 304
  expression trees, 315
  how they work, 302–304
    execution, 302
  querying SQL table, 301
interprocess communication (IPC), 441
Interrupt method, Thread class, 682
  Abort method vs., 683
Intersect and Union methods
    (Permissions)
  combining IPermission objects of
    same type, 614
  combining permission sets, 615
Intersect query operator, 352
into keyword, 296, 299
  scoping rules for query
    variables, 297
InvalidOperationException, 128, 482
invariant culture, 196
Invoke and BeginInvoke methods, 664
IP addresses, converting to domain
    names, 491
IP (Internet Protocol), 471
IPAddress class, 471
IPEndPoint class, 472

IPermission interface, 614
  Demand method, 614
  Intersect and Union methods, 614
IPrincipal interface, 626, 627
IPv4, 471
IPv6, 471
IQueryable<> interface, 300
is operator, 45, 75
IsAssignableFrom method, 566
ISerializable interface
  binary serialization with, 522–525
    interface definition, 522
    subclassing serializable
      classes, 524
  data contract serializers and, 516
IsInstanceOfType method, 566
isolated storage, 463–468
  assembly and domain isolation, 464
  enumerating
    IsolatedStorageScope enum, 468
  enumerating with
    IsolatedStorageFile, 467
  isolated storage compartments,
    listed, 464
  IsolatedStorageStream class, 463
  isolation types, 463
  locations of files, 466
  reading and writing, 465
    IsolatedStorageFileStream, 465
isolated thread data (nontransient),
    storing, 685
IsolatedStorageFilePermission class, 620
IsolatedStorageFileStream object, 464
IsolatedStorageScope enum, 465
IsSubclassOf method, 566
iteration, collections and, 230
iteration statements, 50–51
  for loops, 50
  while and do-while loops, 50
iteration variables, 283, 284
iterators, 131
  composing sequences, 133
  implementation of IEnumerable and
    IEnumerator, 232
  iterator semantics, 132
IV (Initialization Vector), 631
IXmlSerializable interface, 499, 501,
    533
  data contract serializers and, 516
  rules for implementing, 533

J

jagged arrays, 33
JIT (Just-In-Time) compiler, 3
  inlining property accessors, 67
joining (query operators), 339–346
jump statements, 51
  break, 51
  continue, 52
  goto, 52
  return, 52
  throw, 53

K

KeyedCollection<TKey,TItem>
      class, 265–267
  ChangeItemForKey method, 265
  GetItemForKey method, 265
  implementation (example), 265
KeyValuePair structs, 258
keywords, 11
  conflict with identifiers, avoiding, 12
  contextual, 12
  listing of C# keywords, 11
  reference, 775–781

L

label statements, 52
labels
  defining for branch target in IL, 589
lambda expressions, 118–121
  as argument for query operators, 276
  BNF form, 118
  building, 317–319
  code rewritten as statement
      block, 119
  converting to method and calling the
      method through a
      delegate, 118
  explicitly specifying parameter
      types, 119
  generic, func delegates and, 119
  outer variables, 120
lambda operator (=>), 45
lambda queries, 276–282
  chaining query operators, 276–279
    extension methods, 278
  composing lambda
      expressions, 279–281
    element typing, 280
    Func signatures, 280

comprehension syntax vs., 285
ordering of input sequences, 281
LambdaExpression class, 317
Language Integrated Query (see LINQ)
languages
  cultures and subcultures, 553
  resource localization, 551
Last query operator, 356
LastNode property (LINQ to
      XML), 370
LastOrDefault query operator, 356
late binding, 573
lazy quantifiers, Regex, 761
left-associative operators, 43
length of arrays, 243
Length property of an array, 31
let keyword, 299
link demands (security), 621
LINQ (Language Integrated Query), 4,
      274–319
  building query expressions, 315–319
    delegates vs. expression
        trees, 315–317
    lambda expressions, 317–319
  composing, 295–298
    progressive query
        construction, 295
    using into keyword, 296
    wrapping queries, 297
  comprehension queries, 282–286
    iteration variables, 284
    lambda syntax vs. comprehension
        syntax, 285
    mixed syntax queries, 285
    SQL syntax vs., 284
  deferred execution queries, 286–292
    chaining decorators, 290
    how deferred execution
        works, 288
    how they're executed, 291
    outer variables, 287
    reevaluation, 287
  interpreted queries, 300–306
    AsEnumerable operator, 305
    combining with local queries, 304
    how they work, 302–304
  lambda queries, 276–282
    chaining query
        operators, 276–279
    composing lambda
        expressions, 279–281

Nodes method (LINQ to XML), 370
nonblocking synchronization, 664–667
    atomicity and Interlocked class, 664
    memory barriers and volatility, 666
nonpublic members, accessing, 574
[NonSerialized] attribute, 519
nonzero-based arrays, 241
NotImplementedException class, 128
NotSupportedException class, 128
null keyword, 779
null values
    data members, 510
    in equality comparisons for objects
        with Equals method, 217
    references, 19
    strings, 172
nullable types, 135
    alternatives to, 139
    bool? operands, use with & and |
        operators, 137
    boxing and unboxing nullable
        values, 136
    casting to, using with Element and
        Attribute methods, 377
    implicit and explicit nullable
        conversions, 135
    lifted operators, 136
        all other operators, 137
        equality operators, 137
        mixing nullable and nonnullable
            types, 137
        relational operators, 137
    null coalescing operator (??), 138
    Nullable<T> struct, 135
    scenarios for use, 138
    using with DateTime and
        DateTimeOffset, 188
NullReferenceException, 217
NumberFormatInfo class, 196
    using, 197
numbers
    conversions, 22, 209
    Math class, 210
    Random class, 210
NumberStyles enum, 197, 202
numeric format strings, 199
    custom, 201
numeric literals, type inference, 21
numeric suffixes, 22
numeric types, 20–27
    8- and 16-bit integral types, 25
    arithmetic operators, 23

    comparison operators, using, 28
    conversions, summary of, 209
    double vs. decimal, 27
    floating-point types, special
        values, 26
    increment and decrement
        operators, 24
    numeric literals, 21
    predefined in C#, listed, 20
    real number rounding errors, 27
    special float and double values, 26
    specialized integral operations, 24

O

Object class, 81–84
    Equals and GetHashCode methods,
        overriding, 141
    Equals method, 26, 216
    Finalize method, 71
    GetHashCode method,
        overriding, 220
    GetType method and typeof
        operator, 83
    members, listed, 84
    ReferenceEquals method, 218
    static and dynamic type checking, 82
    ToString method, 83
    using reflection to load all methods
        into sorted list, 261
    value types, casting to and from
        object, 81
object graphs, 498
    data contract serializer and, 500
    XmlSerializer and, 500
object initializers, 64
    projection strategy in LINQ
        queries, 298
    use in anonymous type creation, 146
object references (see references)
object type, 779
    boxing and unboxing, 82
    retreiving all nonpublic
        members, 575
ObjectDisposedException class, 128
object-orientation, key features of C#, 1
objects
    reference types, 18
    storage in the heap, 35
    storage overhead, 19
    tracking (DataContext), 308
OfType method, 250

overloading
    constructors, 63
    methods, 62
overridden function members, accessing
    from subclass, 79
overridden modifier, events, 117
override keyword, 76, 779
overriding explicitly implemented
    interface members, 89
    alternatives to reimplementation, 90

P

pack size, 725
<para> tag, XML, 157
parallel execution, 479
    replacement with
        BackgroundWorker class, 708
<param> tag, XML, 155
ParameterizedThreadStart delegate, 643
parameterless base class constructor,
    implicit calling of, 80
parameterless constructor
    constraint, 101
parameters, 37–41
    attribute, 147
    delegate, compatibility of, 111
    generic, 97
        constraints on, 100
        declared for a generic method, 98
        declaring, 99
        delegate types, 108
    indexers, 69
    lambda expression, 317
        explicitly specifying types, 119
    method, 9
        retrieving metadata for, 573
    modifiers, 37
    out modifier, 40
    params modifier, 41
    pass-by-value vs. pass-by-
        reference, 62
    passing arguments by value, 38
    passing by reference, ref modifier, 39
    storage in the heap, 35
    variables as, 35
<paramref> tag, XML, 156
params keyword, 41, 779
parent navigation (X-DOM), 372
parent node, updating children
    through, 375

Parse method, 195
    numeric types, NumberStyles
        argument, 202
parsing
    DateTimeStyles flags enum, 205
    and misparsing DateTime format
        strings, 204
    numbers in base 2, 8, and 16 with
        Convert class methods, 207
    (see also formatting and parsing)
partial classes and methods, 72, 309
    partial keyword, 779
partially trusted callers, 621
passing by reference
    emitting pass-by-reference
        parameters, 596
    implications of, 40
    out parameters, 40
    ref parameters, 39
passing by value, 38
password changes, 454
password hashing, 630
paths
    Path class, 457
    URI, 472
        construction of, 473
peer node navigation (X-DOM), 373
performance
    array element type and, 32
    locking and, 657
performance counters, 749–754
    categories, 750
    creating counters and writing
        performance data, 753
    enumerating, 750
    reading data, 751
<permission> tag, XML, 155
permissions, 612–627
    authorization, 612
    code access, 616–618
        CLR allocation of
            permissions, 618
        diagnostics, 617
        encryption permissions, 617
        I/O and data, 616
        networking permissions, 617
    CodeAccessPermission class, 613
    declarative vs. imperative
        security, 615
    file, 455
    identity and role-based, 626
        assigning users and roles, 626

ReadOnlyCollection<T> class, 267
real literals, 21
real number types, 21
real numbers
    rounding errors, 27
    rounding in real to integral
        conversions, 207
Realtime process priority, 648
rectangular arrays, 32
recursive functions returning child
        elements or nodes, 371
recursive locking, 693
red/black tree data structure, 260
reevaluation, deferred execution
        queries, 287
ref and out parameters
    external methods and, 725
    passing to methods in dynamic
        invocation, 574
    type names, 565
ref modifier, 39, 779
reference types, 17, 18
    array elements, 32, 242
    arrays, 32
    assigning a reference type
        variable, 18
    default value, 100
    equality comparisons, 28
    instance methods, calling in IL, 590
    instances, storage in memory, 35
    null coalescing operator (??), using
        with, 138
    null values, 19
    object, 81
    passing object by value, 38
    pointers to value typed declared
        within, 149
    predefined in C#, 20
    representing null reference, 135
ReferenceEquals method, Object
        class, 218
references, 18
    casting, 74
    polymorphic, 74
    serialization with data contract
        serializers, 507
    storage overhead, 20
referential equality, 215
    objects, comparing with ==
        operator, 216

reflection
    defined, 562
    loading all methods in System.Object
        into sorted list, 261
reflection and metadata
    attributes, 579–584
        attribute basics, 579
        AttributeUsage attribute, 581
        defining your own, 581
        retrieving at runtime, 583
        retrieving in reflection-only
            context, 584
    awkward emission targets, 602–605
        circular dependencies, 603
        uncreated closed generics, 602
    dynamic code generation, 585–591
        generating IL with
            DynamicMethod, 585
        local variables, 588
    emitting assemblies and
        types, 592–595
        Reflection.Emit object
            model, 594
        saving emitted assemblies, 593
    emitting generic methods and
        types, 600–602
    emitting type members, 595–600
        attaching attributes, 600
        emitting constructors, 599
        emitting fields and
            properties, 597
        emitting methods, 595–597
    parsing IL, 605–611
        writing a disassembler, 606–611
    reflecting and activating
        types, 562–568
        base types and interfaces, 565
        generic types, 567
        instantiating types, 566
        obtaining a type, 562–564
        type names, 564
    reflecting and invoking
        members, 568–578
        accessing nonpublic
            members, 574
        C# vs. CLR members, 571
        dynamically invoking a
            member, 573
        generic methods, 576
        generic type members, 572

emitting, 592
generic delegate, 108
generic types names, standard LINQ query operators, 280
identifiers, 11
isolating, 718–721
nested, 95
nullable, 135
numeric types, 20
obtaining array types, 563
predefined, 20
predefined and custom, symmetry of, 15
predefined (examples), 13
resolution rules for, 554
string types, 30
thread safety and, 660, 661
unififed type system, 1
upcasting to object, 81
value vs. reference types, 17
XML type ID prefixes in comments, 157
(see also reflection and metadata)

U

\u (or \x) escape sequence, specifying any Unicode character, 29
UAC (User Access Control), 624
standard user account, 624
UDP (Universal Datagram Protocol), 471, 493
addresses and ports, 472
unary operators, 44
right-associativity, 44
UnauthorizedAccessException, 620, 625
unboxing and boxing, 82
UNC (Universal Naming Convention), 471
paths, conversion to URIs, 473
unchecked operator, 25, 44
uncreated constructs
restrictions on, 594
uncreated closed generics, 602
#undef directive, 739
Unicode, 179
\u or \x escape sequence, 29
UTF-16 encoding, 181
surrogates (two-word characters), 181
UnicodeCategory enumeration, 171

unified type system, 1
Union method
combining permission sets, 615
combining same-typed permission objects, 614
Union query operator, 282, 352
unions (C language), 726
unmanaged code
pointers to, 151
(see also integrating with native DLLs)
unmanaged memory, obtaining, 431
UnmanagedCode permission, 616
UnmanagedType enumeration, 723
members, 736
unreferenced assemblies, 560
unsafe code, pointers and, 148–151
unsafe keyword, 148, 781
upcasting, 74, 75
any type to object, 81
updates
elements and attributes in X-DOM, 373–376
child nodes and attributes, 374
sequence of nodes or attributes, 375
through the parent, 375
value updates, 374
LINQ to SQL entities, 313
to shared assemblies, 546
single-file executable application, 560
upgradeable locks, 692
URIs (Uniform Resource Identifiers), 471, 472
converting strings to URLs, 474
relative, 473
resource files for applications, 550
Uri class, 472
constructing Uri objects, 473
UriBuilder object, 473
URLs (Uniform Resource Locators), 471
User Access Control (UAC), 624
user interface technologies, 165
user-defined tags, XML, 157
ushort type, 25
using directive, 10
importing a namespace, 54
nested within a namespace, 57
using keyword, 781

W

XText class
    automatic concatenation, 378
    values and, 378

Y

yield break statement in an iterator
        block, 133
yield return statement, 232

Z

zero-width assertions, 761–764
    anchors, 762
    lookahead and lookbehind, 762
    word boundaries, 763

About the Authors

Joseph Albahari is a core C# design architect at Egton Software Services in Australia, which supplies the largest primary healthcare software vendor in the UK. He has been developing large-scale enterprise applications on .NET and other platforms for more than 15 years, working in medical, telecommunication, and education industries. Joseph specializes in designing custom components and has written application frameworks for three companies.

Ben Albahari is a former Program Manager at Microsoft, where he worked on several projects, including the .NET Compact Framework and ADO.NET. He was the cofounder of Genamics, a provider of tools for C# and J++ programmers, as well as software for DNA and protein sequence analysis. He is a coauthor of *C# Essentials*, the first C# book from O'Reilly, and of previous editions of *C# in a Nutshell*.

Colophon

The animal on the cover of *C# 3.0 in a Nutshell* is a numidian crane. The numidian crane (*Antropoides virgo*) is also called the demoiselle crane because of its grace and symmetry. This species of crane is native to Europe and Asia and migrates to India, Pakistan, and northeast Africa in the winter.

Though numidian cranes are the smallest cranes, they defend their territories as aggressively as other crane species, using their loud voices to warn others of trespassing. If necessary, they will fight. Numidian cranes nest in uplands rather than wetlands and will even live in the desert if there is water within 200 to 500 meters. They sometimes make nests out of pebbles in which to lay their eggs, though more often they will lay eggs directly on the ground, protected only by spotty vegetation.

Numidian cranes are considered a symbol of good luck in some countries and are sometimes even protected by law.

The cover image is an original engraving from the 19th century. The cover font is Adobe ITC Garamond. The text font is Linotype Birka; the heading font is Adobe Myriad Condensed; and the code font is LucasFont's TheSans Mono Condensed.

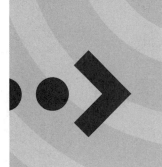

Related Titles from O'Reilly

.NET

ADO.NET Cookbook

ASP.NET 2.0 Cookbook, *2nd Edition*

ASP.NET 2.0: A Developer's Notebook

C# Cookbook, *2nd Edition*

C# in a Nutshell, *2nd Edition*

C# Language Pocket Reference

Learning C# 2005, *2nd Edition*

Learning WCF

MCSE Core Elective Exams in a Nutshell

.NET and XML

.NET Gotchas

Programming .NET Components, *2nd Edition*

Programming .NET Security

Programming .NET Web Services

Programming ASP.NET, *3rd Edition*

Programming Atlas

Programming C#, *4th Edition*

Programming MapPoint in .NET

Programming Visual Basic 2005

Programming WCF Services

Programming Windows Presentation Foundation

Visual Basic 2005: A Developer's Notebook

Visual Basic 2005 Cookbook

Visual Basic 2005 in a Nutshell, *3rd Edition*

Visual Basic 2005 Jumpstart

Visual C# 2005: A Developer's Notebook

Visual Studio Hacks

Windows Developer Power Tools

XAML in a Nutshell

Our books are available at most retail and online bookstores.

To order direct: 1-800-998-9938 • *order@oreilly.com* • *www.oreilly.com*

Online editions of most O'Reilly titles are available by subscription at *safari.oreilly.com*